T0305160

THE TRANSPORT SYSTEM AND TRANSPORT POLICY

THE TRANSPORT SYSTEM AND TRANSPORT POLICY

AN INTRODUCTION

SECOND EDITION

EDITED BY

BERT VAN WEE

Professor of Transport Policy, Delft University of Technology, the Netherlands

JAN ANNE ANNEMA

Associate Professor of Transport Policy, Delft University of Technology, the Netherlands

DAVID BANISTER

Emeritus Professor of Transport Studies, School of Geography and the Environment and Senior Research Fellow, St Anne's College, University of Oxford, UK

BAIBA PUDĀNE

Assistant Professor, Delft University of Technology, the Netherlands

Cheltenham, UK • Northampton, MA, USA

Published by
Edward Elgar Publishing Limited
The Lypiatts
15 Lansdown Road
Cheltenham
Glos GL50 2JA
UK

Edward Elgar Publishing, Inc.
William Pratt House
9 Dewey Court
Northampton
Massachusetts 01060
USA

A catalogue record for this book
is available from the British Library

Library of Congress Control Number:
2023939456

ISBN 978 1 80220 675 3 (cased)
ISBN 978 1 80220 677 7 (eBook)
ISBN 978 1 80220 676 0 (paperback)

Printed and bound by CPI Group (UK) Ltd, Croydon, CR0 4YY

CONTENTS IN BRIEF

FULL CONTENTS

ABBREVIATIONS

ABS	antilock braking systems
ACC	adaptive cruise control
ADAS	advanced driver assistance systems
ANPR	automatic number plate recognition
BAC	blood alcohol content
BPR	bypass ratio
CA	capability approach
CAFE	corporate average fuel economy
CBA	cost–benefit analysis
CO	carbon monoxide
CO_2	carbon dioxide
CS	consumer surplus
DALY	disability adjusted life years
DAP	dynamic adaptive policies
dB	decibel
DSRC	dedicated short range communication
EEVC	European Enhanced Vehicle-Safety Committee
EGR	exhaust gas recirculation
EMA	exploratory modelling and analysis
EU	European Union
EV	electric vehicle
FCV	fuel cell vehicle
GDP	gross domestic product
GHG	greenhouse gas
GIS	geographic information systems
GNP	gross national product
GNSS	global navigations satellite system
GPRS	general packet radio system
GTC	generalized transport costs
H_2	hydrogen
ICAO	International Civil Aviation Organization
ICE	internal combustion engine
IEA	International Energy Agency
IMO	International Maritime Organization

IPCC	Intergovernmental Panel on Climate Change
ISA	intelligent speed adaptation
ITS	intelligent transport systems
LCA	life cycle assessment
LMS	Landelijk Model Systeem [National Model System]
LUTI	land-use transportation interaction
MASTIC	model of action spaces in time intervals and clusters
MCA	multi-criteria analysis
MNL	multinomial logit
MPG	miles per gallon
NAM	norm activation model
NCAP	new car assessment programme
NFD	network fundamental diagram
MNVOC	non-methane volatile organic compounds
NO	nitrogen oxide
NOA (model)	needs, opportunities, abilities
NO_x	nitrogen oxides
NST/R	Nomenclature uniforme des marchandises pour les Statistiques de Transports, Revisée
OBD	onboard diagnostic systems
OBU	onboard unit
O–D	origin–destination
OECD	Organisation for Economic Co-operation and Development
PBC	perceived behaviour control
PCV	positive crankcase ventilation
PEM	proton exchange membrane
PESASP	programme evaluating the set of alternative sample path
PM	particulate matter. PM2.5: very small particulates, PM10: small particulates
PPP	public–private partnership
PT	public transport
QALY	quality adjusted life years
RDM	robust decision making
RFID	radio-frequency identification
RP	revealed preference
SCBA	social cost–benefit analysis
SCR	selective catalytic reduction

SEM	structural equation model
SO2	sulphur dioxide
SP	stated preference
SPITS	sources, production, inventories, transport and sales
TPB	theory of planned behaviour
TTB	travel time budgets
UFOV	useful field of view
UK	United Kingdom
UMTS	universal mobile telecommunications system
US	United States
VOC	volatile organic compounds
VOR	value of reliability
VOSL	value of statistical life
VOT	value of time
VTTS	value of travel time savings
WHO	World Health Organization
WTA	willingness to accept
WTP	willingness to pay
ZEV	zero-emission vehicles

CONTRIBUTORS

Jan Anne Annema, Associate Professor of Transport Policy, Delft University of Technology, the Netherlands

David Banister, Emeritus Professor of Transport Studies, University of Oxford, UK

Natalia Barbour, Assistant Professor, Delft University of Technology, the Netherlands

Gonçalo Homem de Almeida Correia, Associate Professor of Multimodal Urban Transport And Smart Mobility, Delft University of Technology, the Netherlands

Martin Dijst, Director Urban Development and Mobility, LISER, Luxembourg and Affiliated Professor of Urban Development and Mobility, University of Luxembourg

Dick Ettema, Professor of Urban Accessibility and Social Inclusion, Utrecht University, the Netherlands

Karst Geurs, Professor of Transport Planning, University of Twente, the Netherlands

Serge Hoogendoorn, Professor of Traffic Operations and Management, Delft University of Technology, the Netherlands

Victor L. Knoop, Associate Professor of Traffic Flow Modelling, Delft University of Technology, the Netherlands

Vincent Marchau, Professor of Uncertainty and Adaptivity of Societal Systems, Radboud University, the Netherlands

Niek Mouter, Associate Professor of Infrastructure Policy Appraisal, Delft University of Technology, the Netherlands

Baiba Pudāne, Assistant Professor, Delft University of Technology, the Netherlands

Piet Rietveld[†], Professor of Transport Economics, Vrije Universiteit Amsterdam, the Netherlands

Kees Ruijgrok, Emeritus Professor of Transport and Logistics Management, TiasNimbas Business School of Tilburg University, the Netherlands

Paul Schepers, Senior Road Safety Advisor, Ministry of Infrastructure and the Environment, Rijkswaterstaat/Utrecht University, the Netherlands

Linda Steg, Professor of Environmental Psychology, University of Groningen, the Netherlands

Lóránt Tavasszy, Professor of Freight and Logistics, Delft University of Technology, the Netherlands

Janet Veldstra, Assistant Professor Traffic Psychology, University of Groningen, the Netherlands

Erik Verhoef, Professor of Spatial Economics, Vrije Universiteit Amsterdam, the Netherlands

Warren Walker, Emeritus Professor of Policy Analysis, Delft University of Technology, the Netherlands

Bert van Wee, Professor of Transport Policy, Delft University of Technology, the Netherlands

Fred Wegman, Emeritus Professor of Traffic Safety, Delft University of Technology, the Netherlands

ACKNOWLEDGMENTS

We thank TRAIL Research School, the Netherlands, for its financial support and Blandine de Pindray d'Ambelle (in 2022: student at TUDelft, the Netherlands) for her support with respect to layout and checking references.

PREFACE

Bert van Wee, Jan Anne Annema, David Banister, and Baiba Pudāne

To the best of our knowledge, a multidisciplinary book that introduces the reader to the transport system, its effects on accessibility, the environment and safety, while linking these effects with transport policy and drawing from broad related research, did not exist prior to the publication of the first edition of this book in 2013. Other books generally discuss transport from the viewpoint of one discipline, for example economics, or focus on one policy-relevant effect, for example the environment. This book aims to fill this gap, and it provides a revised and updated version of the first edition.

The book is written primarily for educational purposes, for use either in courses at universities or in other education programmes or for self-study. We realize that we do not, and cannot, cover all of the expectations that readers may have from a book like this. However, we consider that this book provides an appropriate general introduction to the transport system, and its effects on society and policy.

This book is based on a Dutch language book (Verkeer en Vervoer in Hoofdlijnen) that was published in 2002 and updated in 2009 and 2014. The book in its multiple versions has been used at several universities and in several professional education programmes. We did not just translate the book, but we replaced most Dutch cases with examples from other countries, added international literature and a new chapter on traffic flow theory and modelling. In this second edition we added another chapter on transport impacts on health and well-being, because of the increasing attention that this topic receives both in research and policy making.

In addition to the paper version, this book can be downloaded from the website of TRAIL Research School (www.rstrail.nl/books). Additional material to support teachers, such as slides, can be found at www.tudelft.nl/tbm/onderzoek/publicaties/transport-systems-and -transport-policy.

We hope that this will stimulate courses to use the book and that we are thereby making a small contribution to reducing the costs of education. We are very glad that Edward Elgar has again had the courage to publish the printed version of this book. We especially thank Alex Pettifer for the pleasant collaboration. We hope that at least staff members and libraries, in addition to many students, will buy the printed version of this book.

This book is made possible thanks to the Dutch transport research school TRAIL (www .rstrail.nl), which supported us financially and by doing a lot of work related to layout, editing, indexing, and the like. We especially thank Conchita van der Stelt (TRAIL) for her support and encouragement.

If you have any suggestions or questions related to this book in general or parts of it, please contact us. We wish that you enjoy this book and find it a useful source in your study of the transport system and policy!

1
Introduction to *The Transport System and Transport Policy*

Bert van Wee, Jan Anne Annema, David Banister and Baiba Pudāne

This book aims to give a general introduction to the transport system, the factors that drive it and its impact on accessibility, safety, the environment, health and well-being. It also covers aspects related to transport policy making and evaluation.

The target group of this book are students at universities and colleges (bachelor's and master's level), as well as professionals who already have a degree in another area and need an introduction to the transport field. In addition, we address Ph.D. students who may have started research in transport while having a background in a different field. In fact, we consider such a migration to the transport field as beneficial. We think that the transport system and its impacts on society can best be understood by combining the insights from multiple disciplines, including civil engineering, economics, psychology and geography. As a result, this book is multi-disciplinary. The background of the authors contributing to this book reflects this basic principle.

Here's a short explanation of the way we have organised this book. After this introductory chapter, Chapter 2 summarises the structure of the book via a conceptual framework. This framework shows how transport system components shape travel behaviour and how the resulting transport flows impact the environment, accessibility, safety, health and well-being. It explains, for instance, how factors like the wants and needs of people and companies, the land-use system and the overall resistance to travel (in terms of travel cost, time and effort) interact, and jointly with technology and the driving behaviour determine the characteristics of transport flows.

Part I (Chapters 3–8) introduces the core components of the transport system. Chapter 3 explains how the wants and needs of people drive passenger transport. It explains that most people's trips result from them wanting to participate in activities located in different places. Activity and travel patterns result from the wishes, possibilities and constraints of people. Chapter 4 is the counterpart of Chapter 3 for goods transport. It describes the needs of companies to transport goods. It concludes that goods transport is very diverse: all kinds of goods, ranging from computer chips to raw materials, have to be transported for all kinds of markets using modes such as lorries, vans, barges, pipelines, aircraft and sea-going ships. Those goods are produced by all kinds of producers, and bought by a wide range of clients, ranging from other producers to customers. The huge heterogeneities result in complex relationships between the economy, society and logistics. Chapter 5 focuses on the impact of the land-use system on transport. It explains how transport is shaped by dominant land-use factors, such as densities, the level of mixed use, neighbourhood design and distances between origins and destinations, and the distribution of public transport nodal points such as railway stations. Chapter 6 introduces the reader to how transport resistance (time, costs and effort) influences transport. It explains how changes in infrastructure, prices and other resistance components steer passenger and goods transport. Chapter 7 then focuses on traffic flows, and it explains how traffic flows, the capacities of networks, demand and congestion levels are all interrelated. Finally, Chapter 8 discusses transport technologies as they have substantial impacts on accessibility, the environment, safety and health.

Part II, Chapters 9–12, discusses the impacts of the transport system on accessibility, the environment, safety and health respectively. Chapter 9 presents a definition of accessibility and several accessibility concepts, including their pros and cons, which depend on the purpose of use. Chapter 10 gives an overview of all important environmental impacts of the transport system, with a focus on climate change. Chapter 11 discusses transport safety as well as factors that have an impact on safety, of which the most important are infrastructure, the users of infrastructure and vehicles. Chapter 12 explains the multiple ways in which the transport system has an impact on the health of people, ranging from travel as a form of exercise, to exposure to pollutants, noise, and risks, and finally the complex relationships between travel and well-being.

Part III, Chapters 13–16, gives an introduction to transport policy and related research. Chapter 13 introduces the reader to the reasons why governments develop transport policies, and how policy tasks range from local to (inter)national governmental bodies. Chapter 14 gives an overview of methods to explore the future, including the area of developing scenarios via forecasting and backcasting, and exploratory modelling. Chapter 15 discusses evaluation methods, including cost–benefit analysis (CBA) and multi-criteria analysis (MCA), the two most important methods to evaluate candidate policy options ex ante. To conclude, Chapter 16 discusses transport models and their applications, models that are widely used ex ante to evaluate changes in travel demand and travel times that result from policy options such as changes in infrastructure, land use and pricing. Such changes in travel demand and travel times are input for the evaluation methods, such as CBAs and MCAs, discussed in Chapter 15.

In summary, the parts and chapters of this book proceed in a logical order: firstly the transport system is described, next the societal effects of the system, and finally, the research on transport policy that aims to maximise the positive and minimise the negative societal impacts of transport. Readers can read the chapters independently and not no necessarily have to read all preceding chapters. To avoid overlap we cross-refer between chapters.

2
The transport system and its effects on accessibility, the environment, safety, health and well-being: an introduction

Bert van Wee

People travel because they want to carry out activities such as living, working, shopping and visiting friends and relatives at different locations. Goods are transported because several stages of production are spatially separated. For example, components for cars may be produced at different locations, whereas the assembly is in the main factory. Cars finally have to be transported to distribution centres in several countries, and to dealers where people can buy them.

Developments in transport are relevant for several reasons. Firstly, without transport modern societies would not be able to function. Because no reasonable person would question the absolute relevance of transport, what matters more is the impact of changes in the transport system on changes in the economy or the wider society. Secondly, transport causes negative impacts: environmental pressure (such as noise, and polluting and greenhouse gas emissions), safety impacts and congestion being the three most important negative impacts. It also influences health and well-being, both positively and negatively. For example, walking and cycling are a form of exercise and thus healthy, and some forms of transport positively influence well-being. Negative health impacts can result from traffic accidents, the intake of pollutants and stress. Thirdly, developments in transport trigger policies in several areas, including infrastructure planning, land-use planning, pricing policies and subsidies, and regulations with respect to safety (such as maximum speeds or the crash-worthiness of vehicles) or the environment (such as emissions standards for pollutants, CO_2 and noise). Therefore, many questions are relevant for both researchers and policy makers, such as: what determines the transport flows? How do the components of the transport system affect the environment, accessibility and safety? This chapter deals with such questions. Its goal is to provide an overview of the subjects that are dealt with in the next chapters and of the relationships between these subjects.[1] In this chapter, we firstly give a general overview of factors having an impact on transport as well as of factors having an impact on the environment, accessibility, safety, health and well-being. We then elaborate on these factors.

Given the population size and its decomposition by household class and age, transport volumes and their decomposition by modes and vehicle types result from:

1. the wants, needs, preferences and choice options of people and firms;
2. the locations of activities such as living, working and shopping;
3. transport resistance, often expressed in time, money, costs and other factors, which we refer to as 'effort' and which include, among others, risks, reliability of the transport system and comfort.

Individual wants and needs, locations and resistance shape the individual travel behaviour, which in turn determines the aggregate transport and traffic flows. The three factors also have an impact on accessibility. In this book we define accessibility as:

> The extent to which land-use and transport systems enable (groups of) individuals to reach activities or destinations by means of a (combination of) transport mode(s) at various times of the day (*perspective of persons*), and the extent to which land-use and transport systems enable companies, facilities and other activity places to receive people, goods and information at various times of the day (*perspective of locations of activities*). (See Chapter 9)

For some societally relevant impacts, at least well-being, transport (expressed in terms of passenger or tonne kilometres) matters, for environmental impacts traffic (expressed in vehicle kilometres) is way more important than transport, and for safety both are relevant.

Technology and people's driving behaviour (as expressed by speed and acceleration/deceleration behaviour) have an impact on travel times and travel comfort (components of transport resistance) and therefore on accessibility, and they also have an impact on safety, the environment, health and well-being. Technology can also influence the value people attach to travel times, an extreme example being the anticipated introduction of self-driving cars, leading to lower values of time (Milakis et al., 2020).

Driving behaviour is influenced by people's preferences. Not only does driving fast reduce travel times but people may actually like it. Also, resistance influences driving behaviour, in particular through its 'effort' component. If, enabled by the design of infrastructure and speed limits as well as the driving behaviour of other traffic participants, the traveller perceives the trip to be effortless, then the driver may pay less attention to the driving task, which would influence his or her driving behaviour.

The division of traffic and transport over space and time also has an impact on safety, the environment and accessibility. The division over space includes the breakdown between traffic within and outside the built-up area and by road class. For example, traffic on a road where hardly any houses are sited causes less noise nuisance compared to traffic on a road along which many houses are located close together. Concentrations of pollutants on pavements are higher if the pavement is located near a (busy) road. For the division over time, the breakdown by hour of the day is very relevant for the impact of traffic on noise nuisance, since night traffic causes much more noise nuisance than daytime traffic. On the other hand, night traffic causes hardly any congestion. Health of travellers is influenced by safety levels, exposure to pollutants and night-time noise, travel behaviour (because exercise in the form of walking and cycling is healthy), the driving behaviour (more specifically: the speed of cycling and walking) and well-being. Figure 2.1 visualizes these factors and their mutual relationships. Only dominant relationships are included.

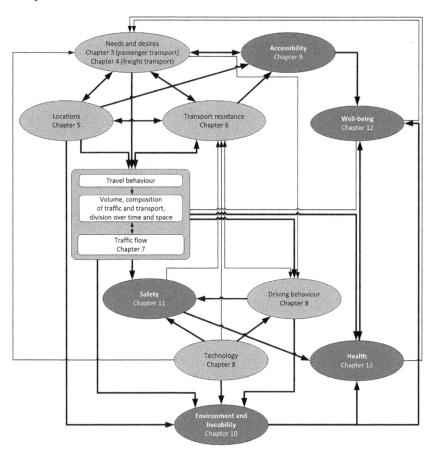

Figure 2.1   A conceptual framework for the book: How the transport system shapes travel behaviour and impacts accessibility, the environment, safety, health and well-being

We will now elaborate on the factors and relationships presented in Figure 2.1. We will first focus on passenger transport and then briefly reflect on the transport of goods.

THE NEEDS, DESIRES, WANTS, PREFERENCES AND CAPABILITIES OF PEOPLE

People have wants, needs and preferences, both with respect to which activities to carry out at which locations, and with respect to travel. Preferences here only relate to activities (what to do at which location) and travel, not to having, for example, a higher income. Of course, wants, needs and preferences vary strongly between people (see Chapter 3). For example, young people may prefer to go to pubs more than older people. Economists often relate this factor to income: if someone's income rises, s/he may fulfil more needs, especially those that have a higher price. People with high incomes have more money to spend on holidays or visiting the theatre. Note that not all needs have a price. For example, a walking trip is free. Apart from generally recognized factors such as income, age, sex and household structure, lifestyle factors and related preferences and attitudes have an impact on travel behaviour (Kitamura et al., 1997; Kroesen et al., 2017).

In line with this notion, not only economists pay attention to this subject; psychologists do too. They conclude that, by buying a car, people can fulfil their needs with respect to status, power and territory drifts (the desire to 'cover' a certain space). Although status might be less important now than a few decades ago, it still has an impact on vehicle choice. A new Mercedes or Tesla gives more status than an old Toyota Aygo. By pushing the throttle, a car driver controls power, which might result in a good feeling. If people park their car in front of their house, they have the feeling of expanding their territory (for the impact of symbolic and affective factors, see, for example, Steg, 2005; Jansen et al., 2021).

But not all people's wants can be realized. First, money poses constraints on people's choice options, as does time. Of course, all people have 24 hours a day to spend, but the time people need for different activities varies greatly between individuals and depends, among other things, on work- and family-related constraints. People working full time have less free time to spend than those working part time. People raising children may need more time when they are young. Finally, it should be noted that the capabilities that people have vary between individuals. Not all adults have a driving licence or the physical ability to walk over longer distances. Some people have time constraints because they have to combine tasks, reducing their choice options for activities.

Mainly, economists and geographers pay attention to the impact of time on activity patterns and travel behaviour.

The role the transport system plays in fulfilling people's needs depends on time and space. To illustrate the impact of time: at the turn of the twentieth century, when in some countries a man with a red flag walked in front of a car, the car was a first-class status object. Now many people really need a car. To illustrate the impact of space: the aeroplane is a rather common means of transport in the US, especially for long distances, but in developing countries it is an option for only a very small fraction of the population.

WHERE ACTIVITIES TAKE PLACE – LOCATION

Another category of factors affecting transport is the location of activities (see Chapter 5). As we have explained above, transport is needed to allow people to fulfil activities at different places or to transport goods between different locations. Therefore, transport volumes depend on the 'locations of these activities'. In this context only location-related activities are relevant. Some activities such using a mobile phone, brushing one's hair or thinking about the next holiday destination are not location-related and therefore not relevant for transport. It is not only the division of activities over space that is relevant, but also the division of people over houses, workplaces and other destinations. If people living in London work in Cambridge or vice versa, much more transport results than if people who live in London or Cambridge also work in the same location. Therefore, what can be seen on the map matters (land-use patterns), as well as the functional relationships between the locations of living, working, services and so on. Spatial scientists such as geographers and planners look at transport from this viewpoint.

TRANSPORT RESISTANCE

A third category of factors relevant for developments in transport is the resistance needed to travel between locations, including travel time, monetary costs and other aspects such as comfort and safety (see Chapter 6). The sum of these costs is often referred to as generalized transport costs (GTC). Lower GTC results in more transport. First, GTC depends on the quality and quantity of infrastructures of all types (roads, rail, rivers and canals, airline and port connections). Second, traffic volumes at a certain infrastructure section related to its capacity are relevant: if demand exceeds capacity, congestion occurs, and this results in longer travel times. Third, infrastructure related regulations have an impact on GTC, especially maximum speeds. Fourth, the characteristics of vehicles matter, especially the comfort levels and costs. Fifth, safety levels matter, and they depend on the infrastructure and vehicle characteristics and the way people use vehicles (driving style). Finally, monetary costs of private and public transport have an impact on GTC. We will now briefly review the time, cost and effort components of transport resistance.

If we look at the time component, we see that, owing to significant motorway expansion over the last few decades, travel times between cities and towns have strongly decreased. Due to the increase in the number of airline connections, travel times by plane between many destinations are now much shorter compared to a few years ago.

For monetary costs, many people have the perception that fuel costs are dominant. These depend not only on fuel prices but also on the fuel efficiency of vehicles and on the fuel types (for cars: petrol, diesel, electricity, and in the future maybe hydrogen). Fuel efficiency expresses how far one can drive with a certain volume of fuel (often expressed as miles per gallon, kilometres per litre or litres/100 km) or battery capacity (expressed in kilowatt hours) in the case of an electric vehicle. Other variable costs are maintenance and repair costs. Variable costs are related to the amount of kilometres or miles travelled. Fixed costs are independent of the amount travelled and include the purchase price of cars combined with average age at the time of scrapping, and insurance costs and taxes. The average age of cars has increased significantly during the last few decades. Whereas in many Western countries in the 1970s a large majority of scrapped cars were less than ten years old, now in the same countries cars generally last on average at least 15 years. If cars last longer, their (yearly) fixed costs decrease. In the last few decades prices of airline tickets have decreased strongly, allowing an increasing number of people to fly and allowing the same people to travel more.

Although time and costs have an important impact on transport resistance, these are not the only factors. Travel resistance also depends on factors such as comfort, reliability of travel times, safety, crowdedness in public transport as well as the perceived positive or negative aspects of walking and cycling. Cars are now much more comfortable than those in the past owing to better noise insulation, seats, handling, reliability and design. The chance of getting killed in an accident has greatly decreased in the last few decades. Between 2011 and 2018 in the EU, the number of people killed in road accidents decreased from 54,900 to 25,150, despite the increase in road traffic (EC, n.d.). Flying also is much safer now than in the past. Between 2006 and 2019 the yearly number of fatalities worldwide decreased from 905 to 289 (Statista, 2021). In 2020 this number further decreased to 137, at least partly because of COVID-19 and the related decrease in flying.

A final resistance factor that has become increasingly important is Information and Communication Technology (ICT). Finding information before a trip (options and their characteristics) and while travelling (such as route guidance based on real time information), booking (such as airline tickets) and making reservations (such as for shared vehicles) and access to other services, all have improved tremendously thanks to ICT, reducing GTC.

Several disciplines study transport resistance. Economists mainly consider time and monetary costs. In addition, many transport economists study travel behaviour using the notion of utility, which, similarly to the GTC, is a comprehensive measure of transport resistance. Civil engineers focus on infrastructure and its impact on travel times and therefore transport volumes. Geographers study the impact of time- and space-related constraints and the impact transport resistance has on these constraints. On average people seem to have a constant travel time budget (see Chapter 6). Therefore, if average travel speeds double, for example because of better infrastructure, distances travelled will also double. Social scientists consider psychological, sociological and cultural factors in relation to transport.

TRAVEL BEHAVIOUR AND AGGREGATE TRANSPORT FLOWS

All three types of factors described earlier (needs and desires; locations; and transport resistance) have an impact on travel behaviour of people, expressed in terms of trip frequency and kilometres travelled, mode, route and departure time choices. Mode choice is mainly determined by the transport system in terms of mode-specific generalized transport costs (see Chapter 6). Route choice depends on generalized transport costs of route options available for each mode. Departure time choices mainly depend on characteristics of activity locations, but also on variations of generalized transport costs over a day (e.g., due to congestion levels, and timetables of public transport). The individual travel behaviour choices determine four characteristics of aggregate transport flows (see the Travel Behaviour Box in Figure 2.1): transport volume, composition of traffic and transport, division over time and over space, and finally traffic flows, which are briefly discussed next. As a reminder, transport is expressed in terms of passenger or tonne kilometres, whereas traffic is expressed in vehicle kilometres.

First, income levels and travel times (or more general: resistance) probably have the largest impact on trip frequency and kilometres travelled (transport volume). Mode choice also plays a key role in determining the traffic volume (sometimes denoted as VKT – vehicle kilometres travelled), which is closely related to congestion and environmental impacts of transport), because modes have different (average) travel speeds.

Second, composition of traffic and transport refers mainly to the modal split (the distribution of all trips and kilometres travelled over transport modes, mainly car, public transport (train, bus, tram, metro), bicycle, walking), but it can also refer to the distribution over vehicle types. The distribution over vehicle types (for example, electric cars versus diesel or petrol cars, car size) can influence emissions and safety levels.

Third, given a certain traffic volume, the spatial division (equivalently: division over space in Figure 2.1) of traffic has an impact on congestion, safety, the environment and health. The spatial division includes the breakdown of road class, for example into motorways, other rural roads and urban roads. Cars and lorries driving on urban roads cause more noise nuisance and health impacts related to emissions than vehicles driving in non-urban areas. And, if vehicles are travelling on urban roads, the negative impacts are related to the number of dwellings close to the roads. Therefore, it is not only the spatial division of traffic that is of importance but also the spatial division of the activities of people, and how they are located in relation to the roads.

Fourth, the temporal division (equivalently: division over time in Figure 2.1) of traffic is relevant. Night traffic causes more noise nuisance than daytime traffic. Combining the division over time and space, a more balanced division of traffic over time causes less congestion (and this is a reason why economists often favour time (and space) dependent road user charges).

Fifth, location, time and space of traffic and the capacity of road networks are seen to influence traffic flows, and these flows in turn influence the speed specific capacity of roads (see Chapter 7).

INTERACTIONS BETWEEN CATEGORIES OF FACTORS

Needs and desires, locations and transport resistance have an impact on each other, in all directions (see Figure 2.1). The transport system (the main determinant for resistance) influences the wants and needs of people. For example, a lower transport resistance may fuel the wish to participate in more remote activities. High risk factors may reduce the wish to travel. The option to buy fancy cars may fuel people's wishes to own one for status reasons. And the wants and needs of people influence the transport system via their travel behaviour, and therefore congestion levels, and high congestion levels may lead to building more roads.

Also land-use and the transport system mutually interact. In the past decades, in many countries, offices have relocated from central locations to the edge of town, often close to motorways. This means that accessibility by public transport has decreased whereas accessibility by car has increased. In other words: changes in location have an impact on transport resistance of travelling by car and public transport, and this may result in an increased desire to own a (second) car. The transport system also influences land-use. We give two examples. Firstly, as a result of more and more frequent flight connections to several destinations and cheaper flights, tourist facilities were developed at many locations that probably would not have been developed assuming no improvements in the airline network and no price decreases. Secondly, as the road network has strongly improved in many countries, firms have moved to more locations at the edge of cities, close to the motorways. In more general terms: more roads may fuel urban sprawl (dwellings, workplaces …), and urban sprawl increases the need for roads and reduces the potential for public transport. To summarize: a lower transport resistance results in new locations for activities and increases in distances travelled.

Land-use also influences peoples wants and needs. For example, people may develop the wish to visit recreation parks or shopping malls once they are built. And peoples wants and needs influence the land-use system. For example, if more people visit restaurants, this may increase the number of restaurants.

Because all three categories of factors change continuously, a stable equilibrium does not exist. The relationships between factors also imply that a policy focusing on one of the factors may have several indirect effects. For example, the direct and short-term effect of higher fuel prices is that people will reduce car use, for example by changing to other modes or choosing closer destinations. An indirect effect that occurs in the longer term is that people might move to a house closer to their job.

DEMOGRAPHY

So far we have assumed a constant population size and composition. Of course, demographic changes also have an impact on aggregate transport volumes, shares of different modes, the aggregate use of specific services (such as shared vehicles) and driving behaviour. By composition we refer to factors such as age and household classes (for example, single-person households, a couple without children, families with children). Different needs of population groups also influence the needs and desires for transport services and for locations of destination types (shops, health care, recreation, etc.),

TRAVEL FOR THE FUN OF IT

We also assumed that people travel to fulfil activities at several places. From this viewpoint travel is derived demand. But some people also travel for the fun of it (see, for example, Mokhtarian and Salomon, 2001). For some people travel is a form of recreation, examples being recreational car trips for tourists or cycling for recreation. In this book we do not pay any further attention to this type of travel.

GOODS TRANSPORT

So far we have mainly paid attention to passenger transport. For goods transport, the same categories of factors are relevant: volumes of goods transport, expressed in tonne kilometres per mode, and traffic volumes, expressed in kilometres per vehicle type, result from the locations of activities that generate goods transport, the wants and needs of producers and consumers and transport resistance. The relationships between these factors are also relevant (see Chapter 4). For example, in many Western countries the improvements in the road network have resulted in a decrease in transport costs and other location choices of firms, other spatial patterns of origins and destinations of goods transport. Transport costs are also relevant for the emergence of logistical concepts (such as the 'just-in-time' concept). Logistical choices include, amongst others, the trade-off between supplies and transport and the number and location of distribution centres for a certain firm. Spatial effects include, for example, the location of the production of car components and the assembly of the cars.

TECHNOLOGY

The technologies applied in transport include both those for vehicles and those for infrastructure. They may have an impact on transport volumes. For example, more fuel-efficient cars result in lower fuel costs and may therefore lead to an increase in car use (Goodwin et al., 2004; Bastian et al., 2016). Technology also has an impact on the environment, safety and accessibility. For example, despite the growth in transport volumes, between 1990 and 2017 in the EU the emissions of CO, NO_x, PM2.5, NMVOC and SO_2 all decreased by 40–95% (EEA, 2019). During the last few decades, the active and passive safety of cars has improved significantly, contributing to the decrease in people killed in road accidents in many countries, as mentioned above. Active safety relates to the possibilities of avoiding crashes, passive safety to the possibilities of reducing the impact of crashes once they take place. For active safety the quality of brakes and tyres is relevant; for passive safety factors such as airbags and crash performance are relevant. Technology can also have an impact on accessibility. For example, owing to traffic lights regulating the volumes and timing of cars entering the motorway network, congestion levels on motorways have decreased. Technologies also influence driving behaviour. Modern cars are technically well capable of driving 150 km/h and more, whereas most cars in the 1950s had a top speed that was way below that level. In the future, technologies such as self-driving vehicles, intelligent speed adaptation (ISA), lane departure warning systems and technologies that allow cars to drive at high speeds at close distances may be introduced (see also Chapter 8). These technologies may increase the capacity of the motorway network and reduce congestion levels on these roads significantly, and they may make the road system safer. Another example: porous asphalts increase visibility during rain or when surfaces are wet and thereby increase safety, while at the same time reducing noise emissions.

Not only technologies for cars matter, so do those for other modes, such as aeroplanes, sea-going ships and lorries. If, for example, in the future aircraft would fly on synthetic fuels produced using sustainably produced electricity, that would dramatically reduce the climate change impact of flying (Åkerman et al., 2021).

DRIVING BEHAVIOUR

Not only are the technologies used relevant, but it is also the way people use them. Firstly, driving behaviour is relevant for environmental impacts. Emissions per kilometre of carbon dioxide (CO_2, which causes climate change), nitrogen oxides (NO_x, which causes acidification and poor air quality) and noise, and fuel consumption of an average passenger car are much higher at 140 km/h than at 80 km/h. Driving during congestion, including frequent acceleration and braking, results in higher levels of polluting emissions (Choudhary and Gokhale, 2016). Secondly, travel times and transport resistance are related to speed. Road capacity is higher if cars drive at 90 km/h than if they drive at 140 km/h (see Chapter 7). As long as intensities on roads are well below the capacities of these roads (there is no congestion), travel times, and thereby travel resistance, decrease if speeds are higher. Thirdly, safety is related to driving behaviour. The main effect is that accident risks increase with speed. In summary, driving behaviour is related to environmental and safety impacts and to transport resistance.

THE EVALUATION OF POLICY OPTIONS

National, regional and local authorities make transport policy, as do unions of countries, such as the European Union (EU). Many policy options are available to change the transport system, varying from building new infrastructure to changing public transport subsidies (see Chapter 13). This raises the question of how to assess these options. Because many impacts of transport are related to the location of activities, and thus land-use, the assessment of transport policy options can often best include policies addressing both the transport as well as the land-use system. Ex ante evaluations should include, as much as possible, all relevant positive and negative impacts, and should compare outcomes to goals and government targets (see Chapter 15). Positive impacts (benefits) include accessibility and travel time benefits, and in some cases health benefits. Negative impacts (costs) include both financial and non-financial costs and external effects (effects the user does not include in his or her decision), such as environmental, congestion and safety impacts. Apart from these more general costs and benefits, governments may have equity or fairness objectives; for example, they may strive for more equal accessibility levels among people or regions or set a minimum standard of accessibility to key destinations (e.g., Pereira et al., 2017).

ACCESSIBILITY

In many countries, regions, cities and towns, improving accessibility is an important government goal. Many definitions of accessibility exist. As explained above, in this book we define accessibility as 'the extent to which land-use and transport systems enable (groups of) individuals to reach activities or destinations by means of a (combination of) transport mode(s) at various times of the day' (perspective of persons), and 'the extent to which land-use and transport systems enable companies, facilities and other activity places to receive people, goods and information at various times of the day' (perspective of locations of activities) (see Chapter 9). According to this definition, the level of accessibility depends on the location of activities, quality and quantity of infrastructures and needs of people and companies. The level of accessibility has an impact on the economy, because a well-functioning transport system in combination with the land-use system is a condition sine qua non for economic development. Accessibility is not only relevant for the economy but also fulfils a social role. People appreciate the ability to visit relatives and friends within certain time budgets. Even though these trips do not or hardly affect GDP or unemployment levels, people value these trips positively. Welfare economics include such wider (non-GDP-related) benefits.

THE ENVIRONMENT

In many countries, including the wider EU, reducing the environmental impacts of transport is an important policy goal. Transport is a major contributor to environmental problems. In many Western countries the share in CO_2 emissions is around 20–25%, and the share in other pollutants such as NO_x, CO, volatile organic compounds (VOC) and PM varies between 30 and 75% (see statistics of the European Environment Agency for European data – see https://www.eea.europa .eu/en, or Davis & Boundy, 2021, for US data). Other environmental impacts include negative visual effects, the barrier effects of infrastructure for humans and animals, noise nuisance and local environmental (liveability) impacts resulting from moving and parked vehicles. An example of the latter is the fact that in many places children cannot play on the streets anymore.

SAFETY

In almost all countries, the safety impacts of transport are considered to be a major problem. One can distinguish between internal and external safety. Internal safety is related to the risks of being mobile. It includes the risk of being mobile for oneself as well as the risk imposed on other road users. External safety refers to the risks for the non-traveller of being the victim of a transport-related risk, such as an aeroplane crash, explosions due to the transport of hazardous substances, or air quality problems due to accidents with vehicles transporting hazardous gases or liquids. As explained above, in most Western countries accident risks have decreased sharply (see Chapter 11), more than compensating for the increased levels of mobility or vehicle kilometres. Despite the positive trends in the EU, there were still over 22,800 people killed in road accidents in 2019 (Eurostat, 2021).

HEALTH

Transport, especially travel behaviour, influences the health of people in multiple ways (see Chapter 12). Firstly, walking and cycling are ways of exercising, and exercise is healthy. Secondly, risk factors vary by mode (see Chapter 11), so travel mode choices influence health via safety impacts of using modes. Thirdly, the exposure to pollutants influences health, and this exposure depends on mode choice, travel times and places where people travel. Fourth, travel behaviour and health mutually influence each other. In addition to travel behaviour related health effects, the transport system also influences health of non-travellers, because non-travellers are exposed to noise and pollution levels and third-party risks, such as risks of aeroplane crashes.

Table 2.1   The chapters in this book related to Figure 2.1

Oval in Figure 2.1	Chapter
Needs and desires of people (passenger transport)	3
Needs and desires of companies (goods transport)	4
Locations	5
Transport resistance	6
Traffic flow theory	7
Technology	8
Way of using vehicles	8
Accessibility	9
Environment	10
Safety	11
Health	12

WELL-BEING

Increasingly researchers acknowledge that there is an overarching concept to which all these effects contribute, which is captured by the terms well-being, the quality of life, or happiness (e.g., Delbosc, 2012, Li et al., 2022). The well-being effects of the transport system depend at least on the levels of accessibility, safety and health impacts. Environmental impacts influence well-being indirectly via health but also directly, for example via the attractiveness of the environment, liveability and noise levels: apart from the heath impact of noise, it is a form of nuisance. Travel behaviour also influences well-being. For example, using active travel modes can not only improve one's health, but also overall happiness and well-being (see Chapter 12).

Because well-being and health effects are strongly related, we discuss both in Chapter 12, which discusses the dominant factors influencing health, including the impact of well-being on health.

TO SUM UP

In this chapter we have presented a conceptual model of the core elements in the transport system, discussed how these elements shape travel behaviour, which further impacts accessibility, the environment, safety, health and well-being. In the following chapters we will describe this model in more detail. The model forms the basis of the structure of Parts I and II of this book. Table 2.1 explains the links between the model and the book chapters.

As explained in Chapter 1, Part III of the book discusses transport policy and related research, and it considers all aspects of the system as conceptualized in Figure 2.1.

NOTE

1. In this chapter we have limited the number of references. For more references relevant to the contents of this chapter we refer to the following chapters.

REFERENCES

Åkerman, J., A. Kamb, J. Larsson and J. Nässén (2021), 'Low-carbon scenarios for long-distance travel 2060'. *Transportation Research Part D*, 99, 103010.

Bastian, A., M. Börjesson and J. Eliasson (2016), 'Explaining "peak car" with economic variables'. *Transportation Research Part A: Policy and Practice*, 88, 236–50.

Choudhary, A. and S. Gokhale (2016), 'Urban real-world driving traffic emissions during interruption and congestion', *Transportation Research Part D*, 43, 59–70.

Davis, S.C., and R.G. Boundy (2021), *Transportation Energy Data Book: edition 39*, Oak Ridge, TN: Oak Ridge National Laboratory.

Delbosc, A. (2012), 'The role of well-being in transport police', *Transport Policy*, 23, 25–33.

EC (n.d.), 'Road Safety 2018. how is your country doing?' accessed 1 July 2021 at https://op.europa.eu/en/publication-detail/-/publication/f483a9a9–0b50–11ea-8c1f-01aa75ed71a1.

EEA (European Environment Agency) (2019), 'Trends in emissions of air pollutants from transport', accessed 1 July 2021 at www.eea.europa.eu/data-and-maps/daviz/trend-in-emissions-of-air-pollutants-6#tab-chart_3.

Eurostat (2021), 'Road accident fatalities – statistics by type of vehicle', accessed 1 July 2021 at https://ec.europa.eu/eurostat/statistics-explained/index.php?title=Road_accident_fatalities_-_statistics_by_type_of_vehicle.

Goodwin, P., J. Dargay and M. Hanly (2004), 'Elasticities of road traffic and fuel consumption with respect to price and income: a review', Transport Reviews, 24(3), 275–92.

Jansen, P., F.A. Schroter, P. Hofmann and R. Rundberg (2021), 'The Individual Green-Washing Effect in E-Mobility: Emotional Evaluations of Electric and Gasoline Cars', *Frontiers in Psychology*, 12, 594844.

Kitamura, R., P.L. Mokhtarian and L. Laidet (1997), 'A micro-analysis of land use and travel in five neighbourhoods in the San Francisco Bay Area', Transportation, 24(2), 125–58.

Kroesen, M., S. Handy and C. Chorus (2017), 'Do attitudes cause behavior or vice versa? An alternative conceptualization of the attitude-behavior relationship in travel behavior modeling', *Transportation Research Part A*, 101, 190–202.

Li, S.A., X. Guan and D. Wang (2022), 'How do constrained car ownership and car use influence travel and life satisfaction?', *Transportation Research Part A: Policy and Practice*, 155, 202–18.

Milakis, D., N. Thomopoulos and B. van Wee (eds.) (2020). *Policy Implications of Autonomous Vehicles*. Cambridge/San Diego/Oxford/London: Elsevier.

Mokhtarian, P.L. and I. Salomon (2001), 'How derived is the demand for travel? Some conceptual and measurement considerations', Transportation Research Part A, 35(8), 695–719.

Pereira, R.H.M, T. Schwanen and D. Banister (2017), 'Distributive justice and equity in transportation', *Transport Reviews*, 37(2), 170–91.

Statista (2021), 'Number of worldwide air traffic fatalities from 2006 to 2020', accessed 1 July 2021 at www.statista.com/statistics/263443/worldwide-air-traffic-fatalities/.

Steg, L. (2005), 'Car use: lust and must. Instrumental, symbolic and affective motives for car use', *Transportation Research Part A: Policy and Practice*, 39(2–3), 147–62.

PART I
THE TRANSPORT SYSTEM

3

Individual needs, opportunities and travel behaviour: a multidisciplinary perspective based on psychology, economics and geography

Martin Dijst, Piet Rietveld, Linda Steg, Janet Veldstra and Erik Verhoef

3.1   INTRODUCTION

Reducing the use of the private car and stimulating the patronage of public transport, use of active and shared transport modes to combat congestion, climate change and improve public health and well-being are objectives that have prominent positions on the policy agendas of Western countries. Despite the efforts of scientists, policy makers and public and private investors, many transport problems seem hard to solve. This might be due to the following factors. Firstly, economic growth and the increase in population size (largely caused by net migration) and expansion of the number of households are relatively autonomous processes which are largely outside the control of at least transport policy makers. These could have an impact on the volume of traffic. Secondly, many interventions in transport are not sufficiently focused on all relevant determinants and not coordinated and as a consequence, suffer in their effectiveness. For example, investments in public transport are often not accompanied by pricing measures on car use. Yet, congestion charging in London, Stockholm and Singapore (Metz, 2018) show the effectiveness of a combination of policies. The emerging concept of MaaS (Mobility-as-a-Service) has the objective to integrate transport modes and mobility services into one mobility service accessible on demand, but it is unclear how to stimulate adoption of these services and whether and under which conditions the public will adopt these (Butler et al., 2021; Arias-Molinares and García-Palomares, 2020). The final reason for difficulties in solving the above-mentioned transport problems is that car use is highly habitual (Ramos et al., 2020), which could be modified when choice situations change substantially. For example, a change in work and/or residential location might trigger a change in modal split too.

To increase the effectiveness of policies a thorough understanding of the factors influencing travel behaviour of people is needed. For example, to increase the use of MaaS, we need to know what motivates and enables people to use MaaS, and which strategies can be effective to promote MaaS (Butler et al., 2021; Arias-Molinares and García-Palomares, 2020). Often knowledge on travel behaviour has a monodisciplinary character and is not based on the complementary value of the perspectives of behavioural disciplines, such as psychology, economics and geography. An integrated approach to understanding the needs and preferences of people and their willingness and opportunities to change behaviour would lead to the development of more effective integral transport policies. It is the aim of this chapter to discuss the three disciplinary perspectives and to show their connections from a cross-disciplinary perspective. We will ask questions like: Why do we travel? What are the drivers and constraints for travel behaviour? What is the relationship between travel behaviour and other choices, such as the choice of housing, work and ownership of transport modes? Which factors influence these choices?

Based on the contributions from psychology, economics and geography, Section 3.2 will provide a conceptual framework for understanding travel behaviour. Successively, in Sections 3.3, 3.4 and 3.5 we will discuss the perspectives of each of these scientific disciplines on travel behaviour. In Section 3.6 the major conclusions of this chapter will be presented.

3.2   CONCEPTUAL MODEL OF TRAVEL BEHAVIOUR

In national statistics, travel behaviour of people is usually represented by some key indicators differentiated by socio-demographics. In Annex 1 for the United Kingdom and the Netherlands, Table A3.1 shows data on the possession of driving licences and car ownership and Table A3.2 presents averages for the number of trips and kilometres per day. Both tables are differentiated by gender, age and income level. Although differences between the two countries exist, Table A3.1 makes clear that car-driving license holding and car ownership are higher for men, middle aged persons, and higher income households. Similar differences are shown in Table A3.2, for trips and kilometres per day. The only exception seems to be the number of trips which is higher for women than for men.

Although this information on travel behaviour of people is informative, these national statistics hardly give an in-depth understanding of the drivers and constraints of behavioural choices which are behind these socio-demographic differences in travel behaviour. In essence, social disciplines explain behavioural choices by needs, motivations, abilities and contextual factors of people for certain travel choices. The differences between psychology, economics and geography are in their conceptualizations, and emphasis put on different determinants and behavioural mechanisms. The aim of this section is to present a general conceptual framework to understand travel behavioural choices.

Travel is typically not an aim in itself but a means to reach activities and locations, which is whe transport demand is frequently refered to as a 'derived' demand. Pas (1980: 3–4) said: 'if all the activities in which an individual wished to participate were located at the same place, that individual would be expected to undertake little or no travel at all.' This could imply that, if an individual can choose between an attractive destination at a distance of 1 kilometre and in all respects equally attractive destination at 10 kilometres she will definitely opt for the first alternative. Banister (2008) states that this traditional and predominant view on transport should be rethought. Many scholars have argued that travel is not only a derived demand but also has an intrinsic value (see also Chapters 2 and 6). That intrinsic value is expressed in its symbolic and affective factors (Steg, 2003), productivity (e.g. with activities during travel), health and well-being evoked by travelling, or the desire to spend some time between being at two locations such as home and work (Cornet et al., 2021; De Vos et al., 2015; Mokhtarian et al., 2015).

To explain travel behaviour it is important to understand first why people participate in activities at their destination(s) or while travelling (e.g. making a phone call or reading a book) and the options they have to fulfil these needs. Figure 3.1 describes the NOA model from psychology which could serve as a general conceptual framework to explain travel behaviour. As will be shown in Sections 3.3–3.5, the social disciplines put central in this chapter differ in the interpretation of these concepts and the behavioural mechanisms they consider. This model distinguishes three general factors that influence (travel) behaviour: needs, opportunities and abilities. The motivation for behaviour arises from needs (N) (e.g. to travel safely, to buy food) and the presence of opportunities (O) in an individual's context to fulfil these needs, like the supply of transport alternatives and distance to destinations. Individual abilities (A) refer to the available time, money, skills and capacity for certain travel choices. These abilities, in combination with the contextual opportunities, determine the choice set of an individual – the feasibility of different travel and activity options. This figure makes clear that travel behaviour can change in response to changes in needs, opportunities and individual abilities.

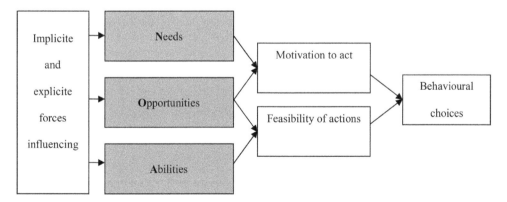

Figure 3.1   Individual factors influencing travel behaviour: the NOA model

Source: Steg et al. (1998)

Notably, it is important to not only consider the observed or 'objective' feasibility of options, but also or even more so the perceived feasibility of options that affects choices people actually make. Notably, perceptions may diverge from reality. For example, people often systematically overestimate the advantages of their own behaviour (like time to drive to work), while systematically underestimating the disadvantages of this behaviour (e.g. costs of driving). And the reverse: people tend to overestimate the negative aspects of alternative behavioural options (like the time needed to commute by public transport) and underestimate the positive aspects of it (Golob et al., 1979). This may be partly due because people often lack information and knowledge on behavioural alternatives.

Feasibility and motivation for behaviour are not independent of each other. A lack of motivation to engage in a behaviour might lead to a denial of opportunities or abilities to use it. On the other hand, if specific behaviour options are difficult or even not feasible, we may trivialize or deny the negative consequences caused by our behaviour. This mechanism is called 'cognitive dissonance reduction' (Festinger, 1957): a person may experience cognitive dissonance when his or her behaviour (e.g. 'I travel by car') does not match with his or her attitudes (e.g. 'Car use causes environmental problems'). This causes negative feelings, which can be solved by adjusting the behaviour (reduce car use) or the cognition ('Car use does not have a big negative impact on the environment'). In general, it will be easier to change one's attitudes than one's behaviour (Steg and Tertoolen, 1999).

The needs, opportunities and abilities of an individual are related to developments in society. Economic growth, changes in the demographic composition of population and households, changes in the values and norms of different groups in society are examples of developments that may affect individual needs, opportunities and abilities. These changes between two moments in time (T0 and T1) are taking place at the macro-level (Figure 3.2). At the same time, individual behaviour changes may aggregate to macro-level changes. For example, when more people travel with a private car, congestion levels in a city may increase, and CO_2 emissions can increase. Next, travel behaviour in the short term depends on other choices of people in the mid-term, like the purchase of a private car, choice of a dwelling and lifestyle choices in the long-term for work, household and leisure. Cullen (1978) was one of the first studying in particular the integrative character of time (see also van Acker et al., 2016; Gerhrke et al., 2019; Salomon and Ben-Akiva, 1983). Figure 3.3 makes clear that all these decisions are related to each other. As an analogue to the choices for travel behaviour, mid- and long-term choices are influenced by the variables included in the NOA model in Figure 3.2.

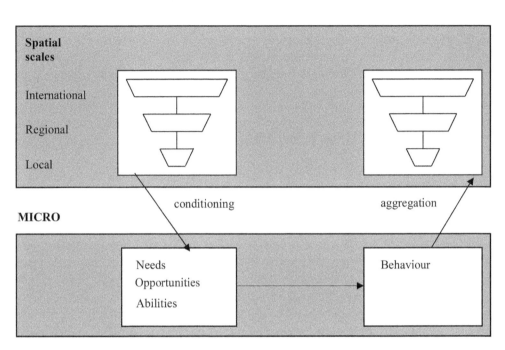

Figure 3.2   Relation between macro- and micro-developments for behavioural choices in time

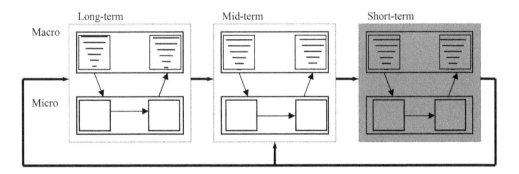

Figure 3.3   Continuum of related choices at various temporal scales

As shown in Figures 3.2 and 3.3, the macro-level at which changes take place can be disaggregated into various spatial scales like the neighbourhood, a city, a region, country or continent. At these spatial scales, economic, demographic and cultural changes can manifest differently. In geographic research, a multilevel perspective including attributes of structures at various spatial scales is often used to explain transitions in society (Geels, 2020; Kleider and Toubeau, 2022; Moradi and Vagnoni, 2018). In various scientific disciplines, theories and models have been developed which explain the travel choices of people and the factors which influence their choice options. Psychology, economics and geography are by far the most dominant disciplines studying travel behaviour. In the next three sections these disciplinary perspectives will be discussed. Although these disciplinary perspectives show differences in describing and conceptualizing different determinants and behavioural mechanisms, they cannot be discussed in isolation from each other. Implicitly, they often take into account the ideas from other disciplines.

3.3   BEHAVIOURAL CHOICES FROM A PSYCHOLOGICAL PERSPECTIVE

In psychology, different theoretical perspectives have been put forward to study behaviour and, more particularly, travel behaviour. Below, we describe three lines of research that focus on different types of individual motivation that affect travel behaviour: perceived cost and benefits, moral and normative concerns, and affect, respectively. We also indicate how these different perspectives may be integrated into an all-encompassing framework. Next, we identify two shortcomings of these theoretical perspectives. First, they do not pay explicit attention to the effects of contextual factors (as reflected in opportunities; see Figure 3.1) on travel behaviour. We propose ways to study individual and contextual factors simultaneously. Second, they implicitly assume that people make reasoned choices. However, in many cases people act habitually, which we discuss at the end of this section.

3.3.1   Motivational Factors: Three Lines of Research

Weighing various individual costs and benefits

Various studies on travel behaviour started from the assumption that individuals make reasoned choices and choose alternatives with the highest benefits against the lowest costs, thereby not only considering financial cost and benefits, but also social costs and benefits, effort, time and convenience, among others. One influential framework is the theory of planned behaviour (TPB) (e.g. Ajzen, 1991), which assumes that behaviour results from an intention to engage in the relevant behaviour. Intention is assumed to depend on three factors: attitudes, subjective norms and perceived behavioural control (PBC). Attitudes reflect how positively or negatively people evaluate a particular action. They depend on beliefs that a behaviour will result in particular outcomes and thus will yield different costs and benefits (e.g. driving a car is expensive, saves time, provides freedom or enhances one's status) and on how important these outcomes (i.e. costs and benefits) are for an individual. Social norms reflect the extent to which one believes that important others (e.g. friends, family members, colleagues) approve or disapprove of the behaviour, and the motivation to comply with these expectations, and thus reflects social costs and benefits of actions. PBC reflects the extent to which people think they are capable of engaging in the relevant behaviour (see Figure 3.4), which reflects the perceived feasibility of a behaviour. PBC can influence behaviour indirectly, via intentions, but also directly. For example, people can have the intention to travel by bus and feel capable of doing so (for example, because they know the timetable and can afford to buy a ticket), but, if they then learn that the bus drivers are on strike, PBC will affect behaviour directly.

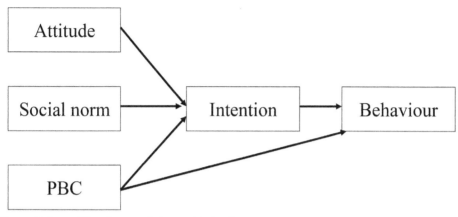

Figure 3.4   The theory of planned behaviour

The TPB assumes that other factors, such as demographics and personal values, affect behaviour indirectly, via attitudes, subjective norms and PBC. For example, men may travel more by car because they like driving (a positive attitude), low-income groups may drive less because they have a lower PBC (e.g. they cannot afford to drive more) and people with strong environmental values may drive less because they are concerned about the negative environmental consequences of driving, resulting in less positive attitudes towards driving. However, as of yet, studies have hardly tested explicitly whether demographics and values indeed affect travel behaviour indirectly, via attitudes, subjective norms and PBC. The extent to which attitudes, subjective norms and perceived behaviour influence intentions and behaviour differs across different types of behaviour. For example, subjective norms are likely to be less influential when the particular behaviour is private and hardly visible to others (e.g. your friends are unlikely to observe which route you take to your holiday in France). In such cases, attitudes and PBC are likely to exert a stronger influence on behaviour than subjective norms.

The TPB has proven to be successful in explaining travel mode choice (Verplanken et al., 1998; Harland et al., 1999; Heath and Gifford, 2002; Bamberg and Rölle, 2003; Donald et al., 2014; Zhang and Li, 2020).

Various scholars have added further factors to the TPB, such as habits (Verplanken et al., 1997; see below). Others have added positive and negative affect as predictors to the TPB. This reflects the extent to which individuals anticipate that behaviour will result in positive or negative affect (we elaborate on the role of affect below). For example, some people may anticipate positive feelings when cycling in sunny weather or when driving during rain, which may motivate them to cycle and drive, respectively. Most studies testing the TPB rely on correlational evidence, so the causality of the relationship between predictors and travel behaviour remains unclear. Yet, some studies suggest that people may adapt their attitudes to their behaviour (Kroesen et al., 2017).

Moral and normative concerns

Many people evaluate car use much more favourably than using public transport (Steg, 2003). This implies that reductions in car use are not very likely when people base their decisions mainly on weighing the various individual costs and benefits of different travel modes or when travel behaviour became habitual. They will probably only reduce their car use when they value the environment and when they are concerned about the problems caused by car use. This implies that morality may play a key role in motivating people to reduce car use: people need to forgo individual benefits to safeguard collective benefits like environmental quality.

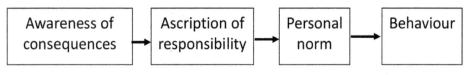

Figure 3.5   The norm activation theory

Various studies have examined the role of moral and normative considerations underlying travel behaviour, in particular to reduce car use, from different theoretical perspectives. First, scholars have tested the Norm Activation Model(NAM) to understand the role of moral considerations (see Figure 3.5; Schwartz, 1977; Schwartz and Howard, 1981). The NAM posits that people will engage in certain behaviours when they feel morally obliged to do so, which is reflected in personal norms. For example, when one holds strong personal norms to reduce CO_2 emissions, one would be more likely to engage in sustainable mobility behaviour. According to the NAM, personal norms are activated when people are aware of the consequences of their behaviour, such as the air pollution or CO_2 emissions caused by their car use. In other words, they need to have some level of problem awareness. Additionally, they need to feel responsible for these problems and think their actions can be effective in reducing these problems (outcome efficacy, e.g. 'When I drive less, local air pollution will reduce'). People can be highly aware of the problems of climate change but if they believe their actions do not matter or that they are not able to change, they may feel less morally obliged to do so (Bamberg and Rölle, 2003; de Groot and Steg, 2009; Steg and de Groot, 2010; Jakovcevic and Steg, 2013; Hiratsuka et al., 2018; Ünal et al., 2018; Ünal, Steg and Granskaya, 2019).

The NAM appeared to be successful in explaining travel behaviour, and particularly willingness to reduce car use (e.g. Nordlund and Garvill, 2003; Eriksson et al., 2006; de Groot and Steg, 2009; Steg and de Groot, 2010). However, the TPB appears to predict car use better than the NAM (Bamberg and Rölle, 2003; Matthies and Blöbaum, 2007). Other studies also suggest that the NAM is particularly successful in explaining low-cost behaviour changes and good intentions, while the predictive power is less in situations characterized by high behavioural costs or strong constraints on behaviour, such as reducing car use (e.g. Hunecke et al., 2001; Bamberg and Rölle, 2003; Keizer et al., 2019).

The value-belief-norm (VBN) theory builds on the NAM model and proposes that problem awareness is rooted in personal values. Values are defined as general goals that transcend time and situations and that act as guiding principles in people's life (Schwartz, 1992). In general, a distinction is made between self-enhancement values, in which individuals are particularly concerned about their own interests, and self-transcendence values, in which individuals are particularly concerned with the interests of others and society (i.e. altruistic values), and nature and the environment (i.e. biospheric values). Studies have revealed that the more strongly individuals subscribe to values beyond their immediate own interests, that is, the more strongly they endorse self-transcendent, and specifically altruistic and biospheric values, the more favourably they evaluate reductions in car use and the more they are willing to do so (Nordlund and Garvill, 2003; Jakovcevic and Steg 2013; Ünal et al., 2019).

Strong biospheric and/or altruistic values are found to trigger a process of norm activation by strenghtening problem awareness (Jakovcevic and Steg, 2013; Nordlund and Garvill, 2003; Ünal et al., 2018, 2019), which in turn was found to be related to recognizing one's own contribution to these problems (i.e. outcome efficacy) and feeling a moral obligation to act sustainably (i.e. personal norms). On the other hand, strong hedonic and egoistic values (i.e. striving for pleasure and enhancing one's reserouces, respectively) were found to be either not related to problem awareness or negatively related to it (De Groot and Steg, 2007; Jakovcevic and Steg, 2013; Ünal et al., 2018, 2019). These findings indicate that values can act as a motivational source for sustainable mobility decisions and behaviours.

Affect and symbolic factors

Various studies have explicitly examined the role of affect in explaining travel behaviour, mostly in relation to car use (see Gatersleben, 2007, for a review). These studies assume that travel behaviours are motivated not only by the (anticipated) instrumental outcomes of this behaviour (e.g. 'If I drive to takes less time than taking the train'), but also the symbolic outcomes (e.g. 'If I take the bus to work my colleagues will think I am a loser') and the affective outcomes (e.g. 'Driving to work is more fun than taking the bus'). So it is assumed that three types of motives may underlie travel behaviour: instrumental, symbolic and affective motives.

A study by Steg (2003) revealed that commuter car use was most strongly related to symbolic and affective motives, while instrumental motives (such as costs) appeared less important. This suggests that, even for highly functional trips such as commuting, affective and symbolic motives play an important role; this may be even more so for leisure trips (Anable and Gatersleben, 2005). Also, most group differences were found in the evaluation of the symbolic and affective functions of car use, while people tended to agree more on the relative importance of instrumental functions of car use. More specifically, young people and low-income groups generally valued the affective function of the car more than older respondents and higher-income groups, while male drivers valued the symbolic (and some affective) functions more strongly than female drivers did (Steg et al., 2001; Steg, 2003). Also, the car is evaluated much more favourably on these aspects than public transport (e.g. Steg, 2003).

People might choose a certain transport mode or type of car to signal the uniqueness of one's own identity and status. For example, intentions to purchase an electric vehicle were better predicted by the evaluation of the symbolic and environmental aspects of the electric vehicle than by its instrumental aspects, although participants indicated that instrumental aspects were more important to them in their decision to buy an electric vehicle (Noppers et al., 2014). These findings suggest that the intention to purchase an electric vehicle is associated with the motive to enhance one's status. More generally, adoption of innovations is associated with high-status amongst early adopters (Egbue and Long, 2012).

An integrative perspective on motivations to engage in travel behaviour

The three general lines of research just described involve rather different antecedents of travel behaviour, with all three perspectives being predictive of at least some types of travel behaviour. The three theoretical perspectives are not mutually exclusive, as behaviour is likely to result from multiple motivations. Goal-framing theory (Lindenberg and Steg, 2007) postulates that goals govern or 'frame' the way people process information and act upon it. Three general goal-frames are distinguished: a hedonic goal-frame 'to feel better right now', a gain goal-frame 'to guard and improve one's resources (such as money, social recognition)' and a normative goal-frame 'to act appropriately'. When a goal is focal (that is, when it is the 'goal-frame'), it influences how people perceive and evaluate different aspects of a situation and act upon it. Goal-framing theory proposes that, typically, multiple goals are active at a given time: one goal is focal and influences information processing the most (that is, it is a goal-frame), while other goals are in the background and increase or decrease the strength of the focal goal. The three goal-frames remarkably coincide with the three theoretical frameworks described above. That is, theories and models on affect focus on hedonic goals, the TPB focuses on gain goals, while the NAM and theories on values focus on normative goals. Thus, goal-framing theory provides an integrative framework for understanding motivations underlying travel behaviour.

3.3.2   Contextual Factors

The theories discussed above focus on individual motivations influencing travel behaviour, and do not explicitly include the role of contextual factors, although the TPB considers individuals' perceptions of contextual factors, as expressed in PBC. Obviously, travel behaviour does not depend on motivation alone. Many contextual factors may facilitate or constrain travel behaviour by influencing the opportunities people face. For example, the quality of public transport or petrol price regimes can strongly affect travel behaviour (e.g. Santos, 2008; see also Sections 3.4 and 3.5). In some cases, constraints may even be so strong that motivation hardly influences travel behaviour. Therefore, it is important to consider individual motivation vis-à-vis contextual factors (as reflected in the NOA model; see Figure 3.1). The mutual influence of motivation and contextual factors can be conceptualized in four different ways. First, contextual factors may directly affect travel behaviour. For example, one cannot travel by bus when no bus service is available, while a free bus ticket may result in an increase in bus ridership (e.g. Bamberg and Rölle, 2003; Fujii and Kitamura, 2004). Second, contextual factors may affect behaviour indirectly, via motivational factors such as attitudes, affect or personal norms. For example, the introduction of a cycle path may result in more positive attitudes towards cycling (e.g. because it is safer) and positive attitudes may in turn promote cycling. Third, contextual factors may moderate the relationship between motivational factors and behaviour. For example, environmental values may only result in reductions in car use when feasible alternatives are available and cycling facilities may promote cycling only among those with strong environmental values. Fourth, related to the third point, following goal-framing theory, contextual factors may determine which type of motivation (and thus which goal) most strongly affects behaviour. For example, normative goals may be strongly related to frequency of cycling when good cycling facilities are available, while gain or hedonic goals may be prominent if cycling facilities are poor.

3.3.3   Habitual Behaviour

The theoretical frameworks discussed in Section 3.3.1 largely imply that individuals make reasoned choices, that is, they assume that choices are based on a careful deliberation of the pros and cons of different behavioural alternatives. However, in many cases, behaviour is habitual and guided by automated cognitive processes, rather than being preceded by elaborate reasoning, particularly if people face the same choice situation frequently. After all, we cannot possibly consider all the pros and cons of all choices that we face during a day. We simply do not have the cognitive capacity and time to do so. We just repeat the same action over and over again when we face similar choice situations. Habits are formed when behaviour results in the anticipated positive consequences over and over again. In that case, behaviour is automatically elicited by contextual cues.

Habits have three important characteristics (Aarts et al., 1998). First, habits require a goal to be achieved. Second, the same course of action is likely to be repeated when outcomes are generally satisfactory. Third, habitual responses are mediated by mental processes. When people frequently act in the same way in a particular situation, that situation will be mentally associated with the relevant goal-directed behaviour. The more frequently this occurs, the stronger and more accessible the association becomes, and the more likely it is that an individual acts accordingly. Thus, habitual behaviour is triggered by a cognitive structure that is learned and stored in and retrieved from memory when individuals perceive a particular situation.

Habits refer to the way behavioural choices are made, and not merely to the frequency of behaviour. The so-called response-frequency measure aims to measure habit strength by asking people to indicate which travel mode they will use in different situations, relying on the assumption that goals automatically activate mental representations of habitual choices. This measure is far more accurate than simply asking people how frequently they engage in a particular behaviour, as it focuses on how choices are made. The measure has been successfully employed in various studies on travel behaviour (e.g. Aarts et al., 1998; Aarts and Dijksterhuis, 2000; Klockner et al., 2003; Friedrichsmeier et al., 2013).

Habitual behaviour may involve misperceptions and selective attention: people tend to focus on information that confirms their choices, and neglect information that is not in line with their habitual behaviour. It is also possible that people change their beliefs in line with their habitual behaviour; for example, habitual car users may evaluate driving a car even more positively and travelling by public transport more negatively to rationalize their behavioural choices (i.e. cognitive dissonance reduction; Festinger, 1957), or because they adjust their beliefs based on their observed behaviour (Bem, 1972).

In many cases, habits are highly functional because they enable us to cope efficiently with limited cognitive resources and time. However, when choice circumstances have changed, people may no longer make optimal decisions when they have strong habits. In general, habits are reconsidered only when the context changes significantly. For example, temporarily forcing car drivers to use alternative travel modes induced long-term reductions in car use (Fujii et al., 2001; Fujii and Gärling, 2003). The impacts of such temporary changes were particularly strong for habitual car drivers. Lifestyle changes may also result in reconsidering habitual behaviour, for example moving to a new house, changing jobs, having children or the COVID-19 pandemic (Verplanken and Wood, 2006; Walker et al., 2014; Fujii and Gärling, 2003; Corker et al., 2022).

3.4   BEHAVIOURAL CHOICE FROM AN ECONOMIC PERSPECTIVE

In the economic discipline, models of individuals' travel behaviour share important features with models of other types of consumption behaviour. Standard economic analysis departs from the assumption that consumers base their choice on rational considerations. This means that they will make the choice from which they expect it will give them greatest overall satisfaction. The word 'expect' signals that not everything needs to be known beforehand to be able to act rationally in the economic sense, so that the *ex post* actually experienced satisfaction may deviate from the a priori expected value; and 'overall' reflects that satisfaction may very well be codetermined by personal tastes and emotions, and may thus include aspects that in daily speech may be deemed 'irrational'. Preferences of consumers are then the starting point of many analyses. These preferences mean that consumers – when they have the choice between options A, B and C – can compare these in terms of desirability; for example, B may be preferred above A, and A may be preferred above C. The classical assumption is that consumers are able to arrive at a complete and consistent ranking; in the foregoing example meaning that we can infer that B is also preferred over C (consistency), and that all pairs of alternatives can be compared (completeness); see, for example, Varian (1992). At the individual level, this is often a relatively mild assumption: most readers will find it hard to think of a counter example for their own preferences, e.g. when looking at a restaurant menu a vegetarian dish would be preferred over fish, and a fish dish over a meat meal, but the meat meal in turn looks more attractive than the vegetarian dish. Or, indeed, when a bike trip would be preferred over walking and walking over tram, but tram over cycling. Still, for social choice situations such paradoxes may more easily occur, e.g. when there is majority preferring A over B, a majority that prefers B over C, but also a majority that prefers C over A (Atkinson and Stiglitz, 2015). And, when attributes of transportation systems depend on the choices of others, as we see with frequency benefits or crowding disutility in public transport, or congestion in car traffic, individual rankings may also become dependent on other individuals' choices so that the rankings become endogenous when considering and modelling the full transportation system.

The classical economic model of consumer choice can in more advanced specifications allow for aspects such as imperfect information, endogenous habitual behaviour when the (perceived) cost and effort of information acquisition and processing make it irrational to do so at high frequency, or taste variations that may in daily speech be considered irrational. Economic science keeps exploring ways to further improve the understanding and modelling of human behaviour, often integrating elements that stem from other behavioural sciences including psychology such as discussed above. This is in particular characteristic for the – multiple Nobel Prize winning – field of 'behavioural economics'. This literature has for example given rise to concepts such as bounded rationality (Simon, 1955); underlines the importance of habitual behaviour (see Section 3.3.3 above); develops models that explain seemingly irrational behaviour from economic modelling of behaviour (e.g. Becker and Murphy, 1988); assesses how nudges in choice architecture steers behaviour (Thaler and Sunstein, 2021); and emphasizes that there may be an asymmetry in the valuation of gains and losses as in the 'prospect theory' proposed by Kahneman and Tversky (1979). For an explorative assessment on the potential applicability of behavioural economics to the study of transport behaviour, we refer to Garcia-Sierra et al. (2015).

When we apply the preference-based approach to the domain of transport, the choice alternatives, may for example, be various transport modes with different scores on attributes such as price, speed and comfort. Transport behaviour entails many behavioural 'margins' than just modes. Other choices of interest include route, time of day, vehicle technology, origin, destination, speed, and driving style. Economic research often focuses on such functional and observable properties of transport modes (see also Section 3.2), for one because these form important aspects that government can affect in policies. Still, also non-observable preferences play an important role in economic modelling. These are, for instance, in discrete-choice models captured in 'alternative-specific constants', which represent the average value that travellers attach to a certain option on top of what can be explained from observed features such as the ones just mentioned; and the so-called 'idiosyncratic preferences', which capture additional preferences that are individual or even choice specific (e.g. Small et al., 2023).

In empirical work, both types of unobservable preferences can, despite their unobservability, to a meaningful extent be identified in the estimation of choice models. A relevant alternative-specific constant would show up if a constant term added to the utility function for an alternative, on top of components that capture the impact of observable attributes such as time and costs, is statistically and economically (in terms of relative size) significant (see also Chapter 16). Even though the researcher then does not yet know what it is that makes the traveller, for example, more inclined to take the car than public transport if all observable attributes were equal, it is clear that there is 'something else', on top of what can be explained for instance by travel times and monetary cost. Likewise, the importance of idiosyncratic preferences can be inferred from the relative importance of the so-called systematic part of utility, expressed in observed variables and possibly alternative-specific constants as discussed above, compared to the importance of some random term in the utility function.

The latter is, not coincidentally, also reflected in the name that has been used to indicate this type of model: random utility theory. In many statistical applications the random term is interpreted as some sort of 'error'. In contrast, in random utility models it is not an error at all, but instead reflects the specific preference that an individual has for a certain alternative and takes into consideration in her choices, but that is not directly measurable for the researcher.

Consequently, when estimating measures of benefits that travellers attach to alternatives, this random term is included as well. For the workhorse random utility model that has become known as the 'logit model', these benefits are captured in the so-called 'log-sum' measure of benefits. The interested reader will soon encounter this term when further exploring this literature (see for example, among many others, Train, 2003; and Haghani et al., 2021).

In economics, the standard way to represent the preferences of consumers is to use utility functions. The utility functions give the summary score for the alternatives, where the various attributes are weighted according to their importance. This approach is similar to computing the attitude component in the model of planned behaviour (see Section 3.3). Since people are different, it may well be that each consumer bases her choice on an individual-specific utility function. Now, a reasonably well-performing billiard player's behaviour can be described by using a model that assumes she solves the interdependent set of complex dynamic equations that describe the courses of the balls on the table, even if in reality no such mathematical operations are executed in the billiard player's mind. In the same way, utility functions are best thought of as the mathematical constructs that describe the consumer's behaviour as accurately as possible, even though in reality the consumer does not know or would not even recognize these mathematical functions. Nevertheless, the consumer's behaviour can be characterized as if she maximized that function, and for that reason it gives a natural representation of what aspects matter to which extent the consumer. Utility functions, once empirically estimated, are therefore also at the basis of much of the applied welfare analysis that underlies economic policy analysis in the field of transport. This reflects the principle of 'consumer sovereignty': the individual is the best judge of her own preferences and welfare; rather than, for example, politicians or civil servants.

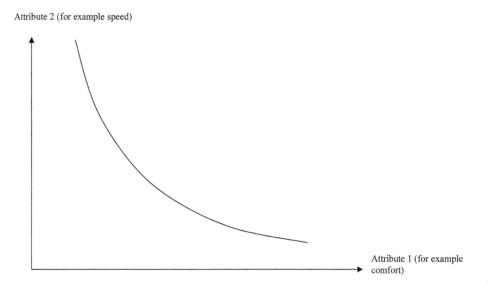

Figure 3.6   Illustration of a utility function with two attributes

Figure 3.6 shows how utility functions are typically used in graphical and analytical expositions of consumer behaviour. The figure shows the so-called indifference curve implied by the utility function: the curve that contains the set of all combinations of attributes (for example, speed and comfort) that is being valued equally by the consumer, implying that she is indifferent to these alternatives and assigns the same utility to them. The curve contains rather different combinations of attributes, some with high speed and low comfort, and other alternatives with the opposite attribute combination, but all of them are valued equally by this consumer. Of course, there will be additional relevant attributes, but for the ease of presentation we focus on these two attributes here. In graphical representations, it is common to restrict the choice set to two goods only just to keep the diagram legible, but in analytical treatments the notion is easily generalized to arbitrarily large numbers of goods.

Preferences are defined here in a way that is different from the NOA model (Figure 3.1). The NOA model focuses on fundamental needs such as safety and health, while economic models deal with 'wants'. Wants relate to preferences for ways to satisfy needs. Economic models are usually based on the assumption that wants are not fully satisfied in the ranges where the model is applied: more consumption of a good is better, and so is less consumption of a bad. In other words, economic models typically consider goods or bads for which a change in the quantity or quality matters to the individual. This has much to do with the nature of economic science: to study individual and collective decisions under conditions of scarcity. If, in the observed situation, wants are exhausted, there is no more scarcity for that feature and the choice problem in that dimension is no longer economic in nature. Still, sometimes economic research addresses satiation phenomena. For example, people value an extra hour of sleep positively, but this value decreases as people sleep longer, and the valuation of an extra hour of sleep may even become negative if waking up is not under direct control.

An important observation is that wants, in an economic sense, cannot always be fulfilled, since the consumer lacks the financial means or the required time. Many people in the world would like to travel by car, but a considerable number do not have the money to purchase one. In a free market, only the wants that are accompanied by sufficient purchasing power determine which transport services will be supplied, not the needs of the consumer. If so desired, governments can help to satisfy fundamental needs, for example, by subsidies for public transport in order to guarantee that long-distance trips can also be made by people with a low income.

A central theme in the economic study of consumer and traveller behaviour concerns the allocation of monetary and time budgets over alternative possible uses. In classic economic modelling of a consumer this involves the analysis of how a consumer creates a bundle of consumption items that maximize her utility, given her income level and the prices of these various consumption items; and, given her preferences as represented by the utility function. In mobility research, analysts pay attention not only to income constraints but also to time constraints. This means that consumers consider not only the price of goods, but also the time needed for consumption. For travel behaviour this means that consumers consider not only the price per kilometre, but also speed (see, for example, Becker, 1965; Golob et al., 1981; Small et al., 2023). The trade-offs that individuals then make between time and money reflect their so-called value of time, to which we will turn in more detail below. In brief, it reflects the ratio of marginal utilities of time and money, and thus implies which simultaneous compensating changes in travel time and monetary travel cost would leave the traveller exactly equally well off as she is initially.

The optimization of utility by the consumer, as a function of attributes of trips, implies a so-called demand function for kilometres travelled: the function that shows how the size of travel demand depends on the price per kilometre and the time needed to travel a kilometre, taking as given factors such as income and prices of other goods. Knowing the demand function is of great use when one wants to predict what will happen when the price per kilometre or income changes. Often, the researcher observes combinations of quantities demanded and these determining factors. Then, the same relation between utility and demand functions is established but then in the reverse direction. The utility function is then derived from the observed demand function, as that utility function for which it is true that its maximization leads to the observed demand function.

There are various ways to express the results of economic analysis for practical purposes. We will now turn to the ones that we believe the analyst is most likely to encounter in practice: valuation of travel time, price elasticity, time elasticity and income elasticity.

3.4.1   Value of Travel Time

An often-used indicator of consumer preferences in travel is the so-called value of time (VOT) or value of travel time savings (VTTS). In the present chapter, we confine ourselves to a short introduction. The value of time is the core of the trade-off consumers make between price and speed when they compare various travel alternatives (Small et al., 2023). Estimations of the value of travel time for the Netherlands usually range from 5 to 25 euros per hour. A valuation of travel time of 25 euros per hour means that, when a consumer compares a railway trip that takes 6 hours with a flight that takes only 3 hours, she will prefer the train as long as it is 75 euros cheaper than the flight and the two alternatives are considered equally attractive in all other relevant aspects. Note, however, that other attributes such as comfort, access and egress times, or perceived sustainability – think of 'flight shame' – will for most travellers also play a role in this trade-off. Knowledge of the value of travel time is an important tool when one wants to predict travel choices.

Different travellers will have different values of time; and the same traveller will have different values of time at different moments and in different circumstances. The value of time will obviously depend on what people would do with their time when they save travel time. If they would use this time to work more hours, that would of course lead to higher income. People with a higher wage rate per hour will therefore have a higher value of time, all else being equal. The VOT also depends on the trip purpose. Business trips have the highest values of time, followed by commuting and finally other trip purposes. Situational conditions also play a role here. Someone who has an important appointment and who faces the risk of being late because of a delay will have a high value of time under those circumstances.

In more sophisticated economic models of travel time valuation, values of travel time are separated from values of schedule delays (meaning, the value attached to arriving too early or too late), and also from values of travel time uncertainty, to better represent such situations (see for example Kouwenhoven et al., 2014). In the given example, the individual's value of leaving another 5 minutes earlier will be lower than the valuation of arriving 5 minutes too late, even though in both cases the travel time becomes 5 minutes longer. The values of schedule delay represent this. Note also that the VOT will depend on the time that is already used for travel. Someone who already travels a lot for his work will probably have less time for other activities, so that she will be prepared to pay higher amounts for trip alternatives that will save time. The value of time may also depend on the duration of the trip: travellers may be inclined to judge an extra 30 minutes travelling differently when it is in a relative sense a smaller or bigger part of the total travel time – imagine a trip that is expected to take 10 minutes versus one that is expected to take 6 hours – and may also have prepared to undertake different activities during a longer trip which makes extension less of nuisance – think of working on a presentation or report.

Another important concept in transport economics is that of generalized costs of a trip (see Chapter 6). The generalized costs are the sum of the monetary costs and the time-related costs (see, for example, Bruinsma et al., 2000). As people become richer, they will be prepared to pay more to save travel time. Hence, one may expect a tendency for the share of time costs in generalized transport costs to show an increasing trend. This also means that the behavioural relevance of financial attributes such as fares or tolls of a given size may be expected to gradually decrease as people get richer (see also Chapter 6), and consumers will increasingly pay attention to attributes like quality, speed, reliability and comfort. At the same, the increase in the value of time will also make congestion costs more important, so that the optimal levels of financial incentives such as tolls also increase. In the end, financial incentives may then very well become even more relevant than in a world with very low incomes.

3.4.2   Price Elasticity

The price elasticity of demand for kilometres is the usual way to express the sensitivity of demand with respect to prices, and has the great advantage of being expressed in a unit-free way, namely as the percentage change in demand (q) when the price per kilometre (p) increases by 1%:

Price elasticity of demand = $[Dq/q]/[Dp/p]$

For example, when the fuel price elasticity of demand for car kilometres is −0.2, this means that when the fuel price increases by 10%, the number of kilometres driven will decrease by 2%. The price elasticity of demand for public transport is usually considerably closer to −1. This means that the demand for public transport is much more sensitive to price changes than is car transport to fuel price changes. One of the explanations for this is that the fuel costs have a rather limited share in total costs.

The elasticity as defined above is often called the 'own' price elasticity, since it gives the sensitivity to the price of the good or service itself. A related elasticity concept is the cross-price elasticity, implying the percentage change in the demand for the one good after a change in the price of another good. Often the cross-price elasticity is positive. For example, a higher ticket price for rail would mean that the demand for car use will increase. This is an example of substitution between travel modes. However, negative cross-price elasticities cannot be ruled out. For example, when the price of railway tickets decreases this may mean that more people will travel by train and hence also more people will travel by bus to go to the railway station. This would be an example of complementarity, a result one may expect in the case of multimodal transport chains.

3.4.3   Travel Time Elasticity

The demand function for transport reflects that travel behaviour depends on the duration – and hence the speed – of trips. This can be expressed by the travel time elasticity. It appears that the speed does indeed have a strong influence on the demand for transport. The long-term travel time elasticity of the demand for transport is close to −1. This means that a decrease in the average travel time per unit of distance by a certain percentage will lead to a similar percentage increase in the total distance travelled. This elasticity of −1 would thus imply that the total time that is used for travelling is about constant over the course of time (Zahavi, 1979) (see also Chapter 6). Van Wee et al. (2006) even find indications that there is a gradual increase in the total time spent travelling.

An aggregate elasticity of −1 for an individual, meaning that she has a constant daily amount of travelling, does not mean she has that same elasticity for every individual travel option. The improvement of a certain option does not mean she will use that option more frequently to keep the total time spent in it constant, but may instead well mean that she starts making trips to other (further) destinations. In the context of time elasticities, cross-travel time elasticities may also be relevant. Consider for example a multimodal trip chain with train as the main transport mode. Access modes bringing passengers to the railway station are often slow, hence the demand for rail transport may well be rather sensitive to the speed of access modes.

3.4.4   Income Elasticity

The last factor we discuss here in the context of the demand function is the impact of income on the demand for transport. This can be expressed by the income elasticity. Consumer goods are defined as luxury goods when the income elasticity is higher than 1. In that case, consumers spend an increasing part of their income on these particular goods when income rises. Another category of goods has an income elasticity of between 0 and 1: consumption of these goods increases with income, but at a decreasing rate. A last category of goods has a negative income elasticity: as people get richer they will consume it less and less (so-called inferior goods).

Aviation has a high-income elasticity, clearly higher than 1. This is one of the reasons why aviation has grown so rapidly over the last few decades, at least up until the COVID-19 crisis. The immediate consequence is that aviation is also a sector that will be hurt particularly strongly in the case of an economic recession, also when excluding business travel. Cycling and walking are transport modes with a very low-income elasticity (close to zero). At the same time there is also a relationship between people's income and the trip purposes for which they would use certain transport modes. For example, people with high incomes may use

Table 3.1 Relationship between annual income and distance travelled per person per day, the Netherlands, 2019

Annual income (standardized)	Distance travelled per person per day, as car driver (km and % of all modes)	Distance travelled per person per day, all modes (km)
First 20%-group	7.96 (32%)	25.09
Second 20%-group	11.34 (42%)	26.71
Third 20%-group	17.32 (48%)	35.74
Fourth 20%-group	20.85 (53%)	39.61
Fifth 20%-group	28.14 (59%)	47.61

Source: CBS (2022); www.cbs.nl/nl-nl/cijfers/detail/84709NED

the bicycle mainly for recreational activities when the weather is good, instead of using it as a transport mode for daily purposes (Rietveld, 2001).

As people have higher incomes they tend to travel more kilometres. For example, in the Netherlands, people in the lower income brackets travel about 25 kilometres daily. People in the high-income brackets travel nearly 50 kilometres per day (see Table 3.1). Furthermore, people with higher incomes choose transport modes that are relatively expensive and fast, and within a given transport mode they choose the more expensive versions (for example, first-versus second-class seats on the train).

When we consider household expenditure, the 30% of the population with the lowest incomes spend about 7.3% of their income on travel. For the next 30% this is about 11.1% (CBS, 2015). This jump can mainly be explained by the difference in car ownership between these two income groups. A remarkable relationship is found between income and the use of public transport. The use of bus, tram and metro decreases (or stabilizes) when income increases. According to the definition given above, so in terms of income elasticity, these are thus inferior goods. For the train a different pattern is found. It is high for low-income groups (in particular students, who enjoy free public transport in the Netherlands), then for median incomes it is much lower and finally it clearly increases again for higher incomes. Thus, railway trips tend to be considered luxury goods in the higher part of the income distribution.

3.5   BEHAVIOURAL CHOICES FROM A GEOGRAPHICAL PERSPECTIVE

Geographers study behavioural choices from three perspectives: behavioural geography, utility theory and time geography. Behavioural geography focuses on the cognitive processes underlying decision-making. As such it relies heavily on psychological concepts and mechanisms (see Sections 3.2 and 3.3). Utility theories are based on the economic discipline (see Section 3.4). In this section we focus on time geography, since it is the theory which is most unique to the geographical perspective. This theory and perspective also explain the links between needs and desires, location choices and accessibility in Figure 2.1. First, in Sections 3.5.1–3.5.4

classical time geography as developed in the former century will be presented and thereafter in Section 3.5.5 methodological and theoretical innovations of the last 20 years will be discussed.

3.5.1   Classical Time Geography

Until the 1960s transport problems were studied using a trip-based approach (see also Chapter 16). This means that the basis of the analysis is the trips, which are studied independently of each other. Connections with activities and with the behaviour of other people were rarely the subject of study in this approach (Jones, 1979; Delhoum et al., 2020). Time geographer Hägerstrand (1970: 9), in his legendary paper 'What about people in regional science?', wrote the following words on these selective approaches in social sciences:

> It is common to study all sorts of segments in the population mass, such as labour force, commuters, migrants, shoppers, tourists, viewers of television, members of organizations, etc., each segment being analysed very much in isolation from the others ... we regard the population as made up of 'dividuals' instead of individuals.

In the 1970s, as a reaction to the shortcomings of the trip-based approach, the activity-based approach was developed. 'Activity-based approach' is a collective term for a range of studies on the trips people (want to) make. Goodwin (1983) describes this approach as a way in which observed behaviour depends on the activity patterns of people and households within their constraints in time and place. In this integral approach emphasis is put on people's needs or preferences as well as on constraints for individual choices (see also Miller, 2021, and Chapter 16 for activity-based models).

Time geography was originally developed by Hägerstrand (1970). This theory is based on the idea that the life of an individual, but also of other organisms and material objects, describes an uninterrupted 'path' through time and across space. The timescale of these paths can vary from a day to the whole lifespan. Every organism or thing is constantly in movement, even when it is itself at rest. In this manner one can see a society as being built up from a large number of webs or networks composed of uninterrupted paths that have been drawn by people, other organisms and non-living elements through time and space (Dijst, 2020). In this theory, participation in activities is not a matter of choice, but subject to three types of constraints:

1. **Capability constraints**: biological, mental and instrumental limitations. For example, people sleep on average seven to eight hours a night at home, need to eat at regular moments, have a certain level of skills to carry out activities, and have transport modes at their disposal which enable them to travel through time and across space at various speeds.
2. **Coupling constraints**: people need to meet or access equipment and other materials at certain times and locations, in order to carry out joint activities like attending a lecture at a university or doing the groceries in a supermarket. Different time schedules and the different locations of people can complicate this coupling of individual paths.
3. **Authority constraints**: these regulate the access of individuals to activity places through social rules, laws, financial barriers and power relationships. Business hours, the price of admission and the timetable of public transport are some examples of these regulatory constraints.

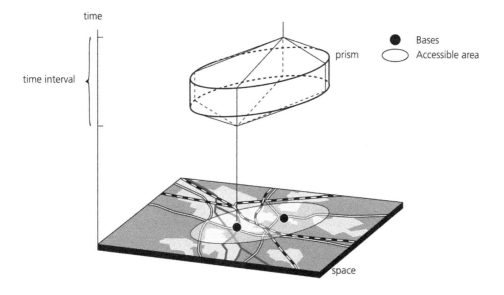

Figure 3.7   Prism and potential action space

In time geography, it is assumed that some activities such as work and home activities are fixed in time and in locations called 'bases'. These base locations, like fixed work and home locations, determine the opportunities to conduct more flexible activities such as buying the groceries and attending the theatre. These flexible activities can be pursued in 'time intervals', also called 'time windows', which represent blocks of time in which travel and relatively flexible activities can be carried out.

The capability, coupling and authority constraints define, for a certain time interval, a three-dimensional 'prism', which embraces the set of opportunities for travelling to activity places and to participate in activities (Figure 3.7). The projection of a prism in a three-dimensional space designates the 'potential action space'. This area contains all the activity places that can be visited within a certain time window: in other words, it represents the accessible area (Dijst, 2020).

Within this theoretical approach two behavioural rules can be distinguished which influence travel behaviour: fixation in time and space, and travel time ratio.

3.5.2   Fixation in Time and Space

As mentioned before, it is assumed that some activities are fixed in time and base locations. In Section 3.2, we called choices for these base locations mid-term choices. Why are these base locations so important? According to Cullen and Godson (1975: 9), 'Activities to which the individual is strongly committed and which are both space and time fixed tend to act as pegs around which the ordering of other activities are arranged and shuffled according to their flexibility ratings.' As explained above, these flexible activities, like daily shopping, can be pursued in 'time intervals', also called 'time windows', which represent blocks of time in which travel and relatively flexible activities can be carried out. In general, people have shorter than longer intervals. In a working day, typical time intervals are: before the commuting trip at home, while commuting to work, during the lunch break at work, while commuting to home, after dinner. On non-working days people may use fewer but larger time intervals.

Fixations in time have meaning for the type of activity places people attend. Empirical research (e.g. Kitamura and Kermanshah, 1983; Dijst and Vidakovic, 2000; Hafezi et al., 2019) has shown that similar activities take place in the same time intervals. Mandatory activities, like daily shopping and taking children to school or day care centres, usually take place in relatively short intervals of a maximum of 1.5 hours. However, for leisure activities like social visits and attending performances in theatres or exhibitions in museums people usually need large time intervals. One of the arguments for this temporal sorting of activities is that people want to secure scarce intervals for compulsory activities as much as possible. Dual-income households, especially, apply this strategy to avoid fragmentation of their leisure time.

Although time regimes show increasing levels of flexibility these can also lead to a temporal sorting of activities. For example, parents usually have to chauffeur their children two to four times a day to or from school. Often theatres cannot be visited during the daytime, and shops also have limited business hours. The duration of films, plays and sports matches are also often prescribed. Finally, the length of a time interval offers the option to take a longer time to travel to visit activity places that are at a relatively greater distance geographically.

3.5.3   Travel Time Ratio

The prism concept (Figure 3.7) makes it clear that individuals are constrained in their trade-offs between travel time and activity duration. Capability, coupling and authority constraints restrict the set of opportunities individuals have for travelling to activity places and to participate in activities. An individual has, in principle, three temporal choices without violating the constraints:

1. to spend the entire available time budget on travel without spending any time in an activity place;
2. to stay in a base location without travelling outside; or
3. to spend time on travel as well as on activities in one or more activity places.

To study the relationship between travel time and activity duration empirically Dijst and Vidakovic (2000) proposed the travel time ratio concept, which is defined as the ratio obtained by dividing the travel time to a particular activity place by the sum of travel time and activity duration for the same activity location. Schwanen and Dijst (2002) have shown that Dutch workers spend on average 10.5% of their time available for work and travel on commuting. This corresponds to 28 minutes for an eight-hour work day. The travel time ratio for work varies systematically with socio-demographics. For example, a household type defined by the presence of a partner and children and employment status accounts for almost one-tenth of the variation. On average, daily shopping has a ratio of 0.40 and for social leisure activities 0.25 (Susilo and Dijst, 2010). The concept is used in various studies, like on spatial planning (He et al., 2020), transportation networks (Irshaid et al., 2021), daily mobility patterns (Su et al., 2021) and health studies (Tan and Arcaya, 2020).

3.5.4   Model Applications of Classical Time Geography

Based on the time geographical perspective for planning purposes, simulation models have been developed to assess the effects of planning measures on the choice opportunities that individuals of various types have. PESASP (programme evaluating the set of alternative sample path) and its improved version MASTIC (model of action spaces in time intervals and clusters) are good representatives of this type of model. These models facilitate the assessment of the potential impact of time policies (for example, the business hours of shops, flexible working hours and adjusted public transport schedules), transport policies (for example, new road construction and new bus stops) and spatial policies (for example, changes in the density or mixture of activity places) on the opportunities offered to people to participate in their desired activities (Dijst et al., 2002).

3.5.5   Beyond Classical Time Geography

Due to theoretical, methodological and technological developments, classical time geography as framed by Hägerstrand has been enriched and transformed into a more comprehensive theory. The supply and use of Information and Communication Technologies (ICTs) in daily life offer tremendous new opportunities to (re)organize activities, which are less bounded in time and space. The widespread use of smartphones and the internet stimulate online shopping, teleworking, digital learning, navigation, on-demand transport services and other e-activities. These opportunities became even more important during the COVID-19 pandemic.

At the same time, these new technologies produce large volumes of real-time and high-resolution georeferenced Big Data (Kitchin and McArdle, 2016). The availability of these data in combination with an increase in the power of personal computers stimulated the development of geocomputation in Geographical Information Systems (GIS). Geocomputation refers to a set of computer-based techniques, such as data mining, genetic algorithms, cellular automata, fractal modelling and visualization. Algorithms have been developed to refine the analysis of the spatio-temporal opportunities available for individuals and their behaviours in time and across space. Miller and Goodchild (2015) are convinced that data and methodological developments could lead to significant discoveries in geography on the meaning of geographical contexts and spatial modelling.

Based on geocomputation techniques, Kwan (2000, 2004) has developed several algorithms to visualize concepts from time geography. Her three-dimensional figures offer realistic representations of urban environments, showing individual time–space paths and the location of activity places (see: http://meipokwan.org/Gallery/STPaths.htm). Navigation tools such as fly-through, zooming, panning and dynamic rotation, together with multimedia capabilities, allow the users of this visualization to create their own virtual images of the urban world.

Kwan (2008) was also one of the first geographers to visualize in GIS the emotional experiences along time–space paths (see also Huang et al., 2020). In recent years, GIS-based geocomputation is increasingly used to measure and visualize exposures to air pollution along mobility routes which are important for health (Richardson et al., 2013; Wang et al., 2021).

The conceptual and geometric time geographic framework is supplemented by Harvey Miller's measurement theory (Miller, 2005a). This theory consists of a series of analytical formulations for basic concepts and relationships of time geography. With this analytical framework, it is possible to infer time geographic entities and relationships from high-resolution measurement of mobile objects in space and time. As such it meets the analytical demands of location-aware technologies (LATs), like GPS tracking, and location-based services (LBS), such as navigation and social network services. Miller's theory has been extended to virtual interactions and velocity fields. To include virtual interaction he introduced two concepts. First, the concept of the (wired or wireless) 'portal', which is a station where actors can have access to appropriate communication services. Second, the 'message window' that defines the time interval when actors interact with portals (Miller, 2005b). Measurement theory has been supplemented with a field-based theory which addresses continuous changing travel velocities across space. In contrast, classical time geography is based on an uniform velocity assumption (Miller and Bridwell, 2009).

In time geography the prism represents the space–time volume of potential paths or opportunities actors have to participate in joint activities. For some social problems in time and space, it is important to know what the chances are of finding a person in a particular area or to determine the likelihood that two persons meet each other. To that purpose, a probabilistic approach to time geography is developed (Winter and Yin, 2011). This approach relies on knowledge about the behaviours of people in time and space, which are dependent on the variety of behaviours leading to different probability distributions.

By embracing and integrating other theoretical perspectives, for example, theories from social psychology, sociology and philosophy, it is possible to include concepts like emotions, perceptions and attitudes in time geography. Unlike in classical time geography, in a relational interpretation of time geography space and time are constructed within relational networks of humans and non-humans and not as pre-given dimensions of a container as in classical time geography. It also emphasizes the relevance of embodied experiences, intentions and meanings. This relational perspective allows studying existential feelings and relational needs of people in daily interactions in geographical environments (Dijst, 2018). This can increase the understanding of health and health-related behaviours and social issues, such as social integration and cohesion. This perspective leads for example to a reinterpretation of the concept 'authority constraint'. Not only an external authority but also the individual herself can act as an authority who can impose constraints on contact with others. Based on perceived or presumed negative appreciation and acceptance of another's biological and cultural appearance and behaviour a person could avoid specific places and disapproving gazes (McQuoid and Dijst, 2012).

3.6   CONCLUSIONS AND SYNTHESIS

Below we summarize the most important conclusions of this chapter and give a synthesis of the links between the discussed disciplines. Before presenting this synthesis it might be good to mention that in this chapter we have put a strong emphasis on three individual behavioural perspectives. However, research and policy making is often particularly interested in patterns at the aggregate levels rather than the choices or behaviours of individuals (see also Figure 3.2). Various multivariate models, some of them have been briefly mentioned in this chapter, are used to identify these patterns. There are also models available, such as micro-simulation or agent-based models, which makes use of behavioural rules to make predictions about future aggregate behaviours.

1. The three disciplines discussed in this chapter differ in the concepts they use, the identification of relevant determinants and behavioural mechanisms. However, each discipline focuses on and explains only a part of the reality of behavioural choices. The combination of these disciplinary perspectives can therefore lead to a more comprehensive understanding of travel behaviour and there is no 'competition' between disciplines as to which offers the 'best' way to study behaviour. The best strategy is to benefit from the insights that each discipline has to offer, and to combine these as well as possible in the integrative conceptual framework on this chapter.

2. A comparison of economics and psychology shows that psychology explicitly describes a wider range of behavioural aspects than economics. Economic studies typically assume that people make rational choices in the economic sense. This means that people do not systematically choose options for which they know or expect that alternatives are available that would provide higher satisfaction against the same cost, or the same satisfaction against lower cost. Determinants of that satisfaction include, also in economic models, many hard-to-observe features of individuals, including tastes and preferences that in daily speech could be called 'irrational' (but are not seen as such in the economic perspective), as well as unobserved characteristics of choice alternatives.

3. Psychology explicitly analyses a wider range of factors, including emotions, morality and habits than the economic approach. Psychologists also analyse the impact of other people on behavioural choices in different ways than economists do, who tend to focus on market failures such as the reciprocal impacts of congestion, crowding, traffic safety, pollution, noise or consumer externalities. Finally, economists put more emphasis on financial and temporal opportunities and constraints. They treat some of the aspects that psychologists focus on such as abilities and skills as exogenous in the short run, while longer-run models in, for example, labour and spatial economics explicitly consider choices on education, learning and knowledge spillovers. Likewise, what psychologists call perceived opportunities is in economics often reflected in choice set generation, in the degree of completeness of information, and becomes endogenous when information acquisition is modelled explicitly.

4. In comparison with psychology and geography, economics has a stronger focus on quantitative analyses that offer opportunities to predict the impact of economic, technological and other societal trends on travel choices from the long-run equilibrium perspective, taking into account the effects of feedbacks and interactions in travel and spatial behaviour. The effectiveness of economic policy measures can also be assessed in such modelling

frameworks. Examples are changes in prices, impacts of investments in new infrastructure, or the planning of new residential areas. However, owing to the previously discussed limitations, these predictions are never certain, and sensitivity analyses are an important tool to deal with this.

5. The geographical approach is largely comparable with economics utility maximization theory. However, in this chapter we have focused on the spatio-temporal constraints people experience in daily life. This geographical approach is complementary to a psychological and economic approach. Geographers also study short-term daily activity and travel behaviour in conjunction with the mid-term (e.g. choices of work and residential location and transport and communication modes) and long-term decisions (e.g. lifestyle choices) in the life course of individuals. In addition, a relational approach of time geography is increasingly integrating perspectives from psychology.

6. The different disciplines study the same phenomena from different angles and with different emphases. Terminology and jargon may differ as we have seen above, but this is bridgeable. More intrinsically, where emphases that disciplines place diverge, it is usually the case that the one discipline studies what the other – often implicitly – takes as given. An important synergy from interdisciplinary behavioural study in transport sciences is that it helps identifying such implicit assumptions, and brings on board the expertise that is needed to oversee and understand the potential implications of this, as well as knowledge of and experience with the theories and tools needed to remedy the associated shortcomings whenever deemed desirable.

REFERENCES

Aarts, H. and A.P. Dijksterhuis (2000), 'The automatic activation of goal-directed behaviour: the case of travel habit', *Journal of Environmental Psychology*, 20, 75–82.

Aarts, H., B. Verplanken and A. Van Knippenberg (1998), 'Predicting behaviour from actions in the past: Repeated decision making or a matter of habit?', *Journal of Applied Social Psychology*, 28, 1355–74.

Acker, V. van, P. Goodwin and F. Witlox (2016), 'Key research themes on travel behavior, lifestyle, and sustainable urban mobility', *International Journal of Sustainable Transportation*, 10(1), 25–32. http://dx.doi.org/10.1080/15568318.2013.821003.

Ajzen, I. (1991), 'The theory of planned behavior', *Organizational Behavior and Human Decision Processes*, 50, 179–211.

Anable, J. and B. Gatersleben (2005), 'All work and no play? The role of instrumental and affective factors in work and leisure journeys by different travel modes', *Transportation Research A: Policy and Practice*, 39, 163–81.

Arias-Molinares, D. and J.C. García-Palomares (2020), 'The Ws of MaaS: Understanding mobility as a service from a literature review', *IATSS Research*, 44, 253–63. https://doi.org/10.1016/j.iatssr.2020.02.001.

Atkinson, A.B. and J.E. Stiglitz (2015), *Lectures on Public Economics* (second edition), Princeton: Princeton University Press.

Bamberg, S. and D. Rölle (2003), 'Determinants of people's acceptability of pricing measures: replication and extension of a causal model', in J. Schade and B. Schlag (eds), *Acceptability of Transport Pricing Strategies*, Oxford: Elsevier Science, pp. 235–48.

Banister, D. (2008), 'The sustainable mobility paradigm', *Transport Policy*, 15, 73–80.

Becker, G.S. (1965), 'A theory of the allocation of time', *Economic Journal*, 75, 493–517.

Becker, G.S. and K.M. Murphy (1988) 'A theory of rational addiction', *Journal of Political Economy*, 96 (4), 675–700.

Bem, D.J. (1972), 'Self-perception theory', in L. Berkowitz (ed.), *Advances in Experimental Social Psychology*, New York: Academic Press, pp. 1–62.

Bruinsma, F.R., P. Rietveld and M. Brons (2000), 'Comparative study of hub airports in Europe: ticket prices, travel time and rescheduling costs', *TESG*, 91 (3), 278–92.

Butler, L., T. Yigitcanlar and A. Paz (2021), 'Barriers and risks of Mobility-as-a-Service (MaaS) adoption in cities: A systematic review of the literature', *Cities*, 109. https://doi.org/10.1016/j.cities.2020.103036.

CBS (2015), *Bestedingen huishoudens*, www.cbs.nl/nl-nl/cijfers/detail/83679NED.

CBS (2022), *Mobiliteit; per persoon, persoonskenmerken, vervoerwijzen en regio's*, www.cbs.nl/nl-nl/cijfers/detail/84709NED.

CBS Statline (2019), https://opendata.cbs.nl/statline/#/CBS/en/

Corker, E., K. Mitev, A.N. Lewis, M. Tamis, T. Bouman, S. Homlid, F. Lambe, S. Michie, M. Osborne, R.J. Renes, L. Steg and L. Whitmarsh (2022), 'The impact of COVID-19 related regulations and restrictions on mobility and potential for sustained climate mitigation across the Netherlands, Sweden and the UK: A data-based commentary', *UCL Open Environment*, 4, doi: 10.14324/111.444/ucloe.000032.

Cornet, Y., G. Lugano, C. Georgouli, and D. Milakis (2021), 'Worthwhile travel time: a conceptual framework of the perceived value of enjoyment, productivity and fitness while travelling', *Transport reviews*. DOI: 10.1080/01441647.2021.1983067.

Cullen, I.G. (1978), 'The treatment of time in the explanation of spatial behaviour', in T. Carlstein, D. Parkes and N. Thrift (eds), *Human Activity and Time Geography*, London: Edward Arnold, pp. 27–38.

Cullen, I. and V. Godson (1975), 'Urban networks: the structure of activity patterns', *Progress in Planning*, 4 (1), 1–96.

De Groot J. and E.M. Steg (2007), 'General beliefs and the theory of planned behaviour - The role of environmental concerns and the TPB', *Journal of Applied Psychology*, 37, 1817–36.

De Groot, J.I.M. and L. Steg (2009), 'Morality and prosocial behavior: the role of awareness, responsibility and norms in the norm activation model', *Journal of Social Psychology*, 149 (4), 425–49.

De Vos, J., T. Schwanen, V. Van Acker and F. Witlox,(2015), 'How satisfying is the Scale for Travel Satisfaction?', *Transportation Research Part F*, 29, 121–30.

Delhoum, Y., R. Belaroussi, F. Dupin and M. Zargayouna (2020), 'Activity-Based Demand Modeling for a Future Urban District', *Sustainability*, 12 (14), 5821, https://doi.org/10.3390/su1214582.

Donald, I.J., S.R. Cooper and S.M. Conchie (2014), 'An extended theory of planned behaviour model of the psychological factors affecting commuters' transport mode use', *Journal of Environmental Psychology*, 40, 39–48.

Dijst, M., (2018), 'A relational interpretation of time geography', in K. Ellegård (ed.), *Time-Geography in the Global Context: An Anthology*, London: Routledge, pp. 113–34.

Dijst, M. (2020), 'Time Geographic Analysis', in A. Kobayashi (ed.), *International Encyclopedia of Human Geography*, 2nd edition, vol. 13, Elsevier, pp. 271–82. https://dx.doi.org/10.1016/B978-0-08-102295-5.10326-9.

Dijst, M., T. de Jong and J. Ritsema van Eck (2002), 'Opportunities for transport mode change: an exploration of a disaggregated approach', *Environment and Planning B*, 29, 413–30.

Dijst, M. and V. Vidakovic (2000), 'Travel time ratio: the key factor of spatial reach', *Transportation*, 27, 179–199.

Egbue, O. and S. Long (2012), 'Barriers to widespread adoption of electric vehicles: An analysis of consumer attitudes and perceptions', *Energy Policy*, 48, 717–29. doi.org/10.1016/j.enpol.2012.06.009.

Eriksson, L., J. Garvill and A. Nordlund (2006), 'Acceptability of travel demand management measures: the importance of problem awareness, personal norm, freedom, and fairness', *Journal of Environmental Psychology*, 26, 15–26.

Festinger, L. (1957), *A Theory of Cognitive Dissonance*, Stanford, CA: Stanford University Press.

Friedrichsmeier, T., E. Matthies and C.A. Klöckner (2013), 'Explaining stability in travel mode choice: An empirical comparison of two concepts of habit', *Transportation Research F*, 16, 1–13.

Fujii, S. and T. Gärling (2003), 'Development of script-based travel mode choice after forced change', *Transportation Research Part F*, 6 (2), 117–24.

Fujii, S., T. Gärling and R. Kitamura (2001), 'Changes in drivers' perceptions and use of public transport during a freeway closure: effects of temporary structural change on cooperation in a real-life social dilemma', *Environment and Behavior*, 33, 796–808.

Fujii, S. and R. Kitamura (2004), 'What does a one-month free bus ticket do to habitual drivers? An experimental analysis of habit and attitude change', *Transportation*, 30, 81–95.

Garcia-Sierra, M., J. van den Bergh and C. Miralles-Guasch (2015), 'Behavioural economics, travel behaviour and environmental-transport policy', *Transportation Research Part D Transport and Environment*, 41, 288–305. 10.1016/j.trd.2015.09.023.

Gatersleben, B. (2007), 'Affective and symbolic aspects of car use', in T. Gärling and L. Steg (eds), *Threats to the Quality of Urban Life from Car Traffic: Problems, Causes, and Solutions*, Amsterdam: Elsevier, pp. 219–33.

Geels, F.W. (2020), 'Micro-foundations of the multi-level perspective on socio-technical transitions: Developing a multi-dimensional model of agency through crossovers between social constructivism, evolutionary economics and neo-institutional theory', *Technological Forecasting and Social Change*, 152, 119894.

Gerhrke, S.R., P.A. Singleton and K.J. Clifton (2019), 'Understanding stated neighborhood preferences: The roles of lifecycle stage, mobility style, and lifestyle aspirations', *Travel Behaviour and Society*, 17, 62–71. https://doi.org/10.1016/j.tbs.2019.07.001.

Golob, T.F., M.J. Beckmann and Y. Zahavi (1981), 'A utility-theory travel demand model incorporating travel budgets', *Transportation Research B*, 15B, 375–89.

Golob, T.F., A.D. Horowitz and M. Wachs (1979), 'Attitude–behaviour relationships in travel-demand modelling', in D.A. Hensher and P.R. Stopher (eds), *Behavioural Travel Modelling*, London: Croom Helm, pp. 739–57.

Goodwin, P. (1983), 'Some problems in activity approaches to travel demand', in S.M. Carpenter and P.M. Jones (eds), *Recent Advances in Travel Demand Analysis*, Aldershot: Gower, pp. 470–74.

Hafezi, M.H., L. Liu and H. Millward (2019), 'A time-use activity-pattern recognition model for activity-based travel demand modeling', *Transportation*, 46 (4), pp. 1369–94.

Hägerstrand, T. (1970), 'What about people in regional science?' *Papers of the Regional Science Association*, 24, 7–21.

Haghani, M., M.C.J. Bliemer and D.A. Hensher (2021), 'The landscape of econometric discrete choice modelling research', *Journal of Choice Modelling*, 40, 100303.

Harland, P., H. Staats and H. Wilke (1999), 'Explaining proenvironmental behavior by personal norms and the theory of planned behavior', *Journal of Applied Social Psychology*, 29, 2505–28.

He, S.Y., S. Tao, M.K. Ng and H. Tieben (2020), 'Evaluating Hong Kong's spatial planning in new towns from the perspectives of job accessibility, travel mobility, and work–life balance', *Journal of the American Planning Association*, 86 (3), 324–38.

Heath, Y. and R. Gifford (2002), 'Extending the theory of planned behaviour: predicting the use of public transportation', *Journal of Applied Social Psychology*, 32, 2154–85.

Hiratsuka, J., G. Perlaviciute and L. Steg (2018), 'Testing VBN theory in Japan: Relationships between values, beliefs, norms, and acceptability and expected effects of a car pricing policy', *Transportation Research F*, 53, 74–83. doi: 10.1016/j.trf.2017.12.015.

Huang, Y., T. Fei, M-P. Kwan, Y. Kang, J. Li, Y. Li, X. Li, and M. Bian (2020), 'GIS-based emotional computing: a review of quantitative approaches to measure the emotion', *ISPRS International Journal of Geo-Information*, 9, 551. doi:10.3390/ijgi9090551.

Hunecke, M., A. Blöbaum, E. Matthies and R. Höger (2001), 'Responsibility and environment: ecological norm orientation and external factors in the domain of travel mode choice behav ior', *Environment and Behavior*, 33, 830–52.

Irshaid, H., M.M. Hasan, R. Hasan and J.S. Oh (2021), 'User activity and trip recognition using spatial positioning system data by integrating the geohash and GIS approaches', *Transportation Research Record*, 2675 (4), 391–405.

Jakovcevic, A. and L. Steg (2013), 'Sustainable transportation in Argentina: Values, beliefs, norms and car use reduction', *Transportation Research-F*, 20, 70–79.

Jones, P.M. (1979), 'New approaches to understanding travel behavior: the human activity approach', in D.A. Hensher and P.R. Stopher (eds), *Behavioral Travel Modelling*, London: Croom Helm, pp. 55–80.

Kahneman, D. and A. Tversky (1979), 'Prospect Theory: An analysis of decision under risk', *Econometrica*, 47, 263–91.

Keizer, M., R. Sargission, M. Van Zomeren and L. Steg (2019), 'When personal norms predict the acceptability of push and pull car-reduction policies: Testing the ABC model and low-cost hypothesis', *Transportation Research F*, 64, 413–23. doi: 10.1016/j.trf.2019.06.005.

Kitamura, R. and M. Kermanshah (1983), 'Identifying time and history dependencies of activity choice', *Transportation Research Record*, 944, 22–30.

Kitchin, R. and G. McArdle (2016), 'What makes Big data, Big data? Exploring the ontological characteristics of 26 datasets', *Big Data Soc*, 1–10.

Kleider, H. and S. Toubeau (2022), 'Public policy in multi-level systems: A new research agenda for the study of regional-level policy', *Regional and Federal Studies*, 32 (3), 277–305.

Klockner, C.A., E. Matthies and M. Hunecke (2003), 'Problems of operationalising habits and integrating habits in normative decision-making models', *Journal of Applied Social Psychology*, 33, 396–417.

Kouwenhoven, M., G. Jong, P. Koster, V. van den Berg, E. Verhoef, J. Bates and P. Warffemius (2014), 'New values of time and reliability in passenger transport in The Netherlands', *Research in Transportation Economics*, 47, 37–49.

Kroesen, M., S. Handy and C. Chorus (2017), 'Do attitudes cause behavior or vice versa? An alternative conceptualization of the attitude-behavior relationship in travel behavior modeling', *Transportation Research Part A: Policy and Practice*, 101, 190–202.

Kwan, M.-P. (2000), 'Interactive geovisualization of activity-travel patterns using three-dimensional geographical information systems: a methodological exploration with a large data set', *Transportation Research C*, 8, 185–203.

Kwan, M.-P. (2004), 'GIS methods in time-geographic research: geocomputation and geovisualization of human activity patterns', *Geographical Analysis*, 86B, 267–80.

Kwan, M.-P. (2008), 'From oral histories to visual narratives: re-presenting the post-September 11 experiences of the Muslim women in the USA', *Social and Cultural Geography*, 9, 653–69.

Lindenberg, S. and L. Steg (2007), 'Normative, gain and hedonic goal-frames guiding environ-mental behavior', *Journal of Social Issues*, 63 (1), 117–37.

Matthies, E. and A. Blöbaum (2007), 'Ecological norm orientation and private car use', in T. Gärling and L. Steg (eds), *Threats to the Quality of Urban Life from Car Traffic: Problems, Causes, and Solutions*, Amsterdam: Elsevier, pp. 251–71.

McQuoid, J. and M.J. Dijst (2012), 'Bringing emotions to time geography: the case of mobilities of poverty', *Journal of Transport Geography*, 23, 26–34.

Metz, D. (2018), 'Tackling urban traffic congestion: The experience of London, Stockholm and Singapore', *Transport Policy*, 6 (4), 494–98. https://doi.org/10.1016/j.cstp.2018.06.002.

Miller, H.J. (2005a), 'A measurement theory for time geography', *Geographical Analysis*, 37, 17–45.

Miller, H.J. (2005b), 'Necessary space-time conditions for human interaction', *Environment and Planning B*, 32, 381–401.

Miller, H.J. (2021), 'Activity-Based Analysis', in M.M. Fischer and P. Nijkamp (eds), *Handbook of Regional Science*, Berlin, Heidelberg: Springer. https://doi.org/10.1007/978-3-662-60723-7_106.

Miller, H.J. and S.A. Bridwell (2009), 'A field-based theory for time geography', *Annals of the Association of American Geographers*, 99, 49–75.

Miller, H.J. and M.F. Goodchild (2015), 'Data-driven geography', *GeoJournal*, 80, 449–61.

Mokhtarian, P.L., F. Papon, M. Goulard and M. Diana (2015), 'What makes travel pleasant and/or tiring? An investigation based on the French National Travel Survey', *Transportation*, 42, 1103–128. DOI 10.1007/s11116-014-9557-y.

Moradi, A. and E. Vagnoni (2018), 'A multi-level perspective analysis of urban mobility system dynamics: what are the future transition pathways?', *Technological Forecasting and Social Change*, 126, 231–43.

NL–ODiN (2019), https://www.cbs.nl/nl-nl/onze-diensten/methoden/onderzoeksomschrijvingen/aanvullende-onderzoeksomschrijvingen/onderweg-in-nederland--odin---onderzoeksbeschrijving-2019.

Noppers, E.H., K. Keizer, J.W. Bolderdijk and L. Steg (2014), 'The adoption of sustainable innovations: Driven by symbolic and environmental motives', *Global Environmental Change*, 25, 52–62.

Nordlund, A.M. and J. Garvill (2003), 'Effects of values, problem awareness, and personal norm on willingness to reduce personal car use', *Journal of Environmental Psychology*, 23, 339–47.

Pas, E.I. (1980), *Toward the Understanding of Urban Travel Behavior through the Classification of Daily Urban Travel/Activity Patterns*, Ph.D. thesis, Evanston, IL: Northwestern University.

Ramos, E.M.S., C.J. Bergstad and J. Nässén (2020), 'Understanding daily car use: Driving habits, motives, attitudes, and norms across trip purposes', *Transportation Research Part F*, 68, 306–15. https://doi.org/10.1016/j.trf.2019.11.013.

Richardson, D.B., N.D. Volkow, M.-P. Kwan, R.M. Kaplan, M.F. Goodchild and R.T. Croyle (2013), 'Spatial turn in health research', *Science*, 339, 1390–92.

Rietveld, P. (2001), 'Biking and walking: the position of non-motorized transport modes in transport systems', in K.J. Button and D.A. Hensher (eds), *Handbook of Transport Systems and Traffic Control*, Handbooks in Transport, vol. 3, Oxford: Elsevier Science, pp. 299–320.

Salomon, I. and M. Ben-Akiva (1983), The use of the life-style concept in travel demand models, *Environment and Planning A*, 15, 623–38.

Santos, G. (2008), 'The London experience', in E. Verhoef, M. Bliemer, L. Steg and B. van Wee (eds), *Pricing in Road Transport: A Multi-Disciplinary Perspective*, Cheltenham, UK and Northampton, MA, USA: Edgar Elgar, pp. 273–92.

Schwanen, T. and M. Dijst (2002), 'Travel-time ratios for visits to the workplace: the relationship between commuting time and work duration', *Transportation Research A*, 36, 573–92.

Schwartz, S.H. (1977), 'Normative influences on altruism', in L. Berkowitz (ed.), *Advances in Experimental Social Psychology*, 10, New York: Academic Press, pp. 221–79.

Schwartz, S. H. (1992), 'Universals in the content and structure of values: Theoretical advances and empirical tests in 20 countries', *Advances in Experimental Social Psychology*, 25, 1–65.

Schwartz, S.H. and J.A. Howard (1981), 'A normative decision-making model of altruism', in J.P. Rushton (ed), *Altruism and Helping Behaviour: Social, Personality and Developmental Perspectives*, Hillsdale, NJ: Erlbaum, pp. 189–211.

Simon, H.A. (1955), 'A Behavioral Model of Rational Choice', *The Quarterly Journal of Economics*, 69 (1), 99–118.

Small, K.A., E.T. Verhoef and R. Lindsey (2023), *The Economics of Urban Transportation (3rd edition)*, London: Routledge.

Steg, L. (2003), 'Can public transport compete with the private car?', *IATSS Research*, 27 (2), 27–35.

Steg, L. and J.I.M. de Groot (2010), 'Explaining prosocial intentions: testing causal relationships in the norm activation model', *British Journal of Social Psychology*, 49, 725–43.

Steg, L., W. Jager and C. Vlek (1998). Gedrag, gedragsverandering en beleid toegespitst op het autogebruik (Behaviour, behaviour change, and policy in relation to car use), in G. Bartels, W. Nelissen and H. Ruelle (eds), *De transactionele overheid; communicatie als instrument, zes thema's in de overheidsvoorlichting (The transactional government: communication as instrument)*. Deventer: Kluwer Bedrijfsinformatie, 290–307.

Steg, L. and G. Tertoolen (1999), 'Sustainable transport policy: contribution of behavioural scientists', *Public Money and Management*, 19, 63–69.

Steg, L., C. Vlek and G. Slotegraaf (2001), 'Instrumental-reasoned and symbolic-affective motives for using a motor car', *Transportation Research Part F*, 4, 151–69.

Su, R., E.C. McBride and K.G. Goulias (2021), 'Unveiling daily activity pattern differences between telecommuters and commuters using human mobility motifs and sequence analysis', *Transportation Research Part A: Policy and Practice*, 147, pp.106–32.

Susilo, Y.S. and M.J. Dijst (2010), 'Behavioural decisions of travel-time ratios for work, maintenance and leisure activities in the Netherlands', *Transportation Planning and Technology*, 33, 19–34.

Tan, S.B. and M. Arcaya (2020), 'Where we eat is who we are: a survey of food-related travel patterns to Singapore's hawker centers, food courts and coffee shops', *International Journal of Behavioral Nutrition and Physical Activity*, 17 (1), 1–14.

Thaler, R. H. and C.R. Sunstein (2021), *Nudge: the Final Edition – Improving Decisions About Money, Health, And The Environment*, London: Penguin.

Train, K. (2003), *Discrete Choice Methods with Simulation*, Cambridge: Cambridge University Press.

UK–NTS (2009), http://www2.dft.gov.uk/pgr/statistics/datatablespublications/nts/.

Ünal, A.B., L. Steg and M. Gorsira (2018), 'Values versus environmental knowledge as triggers of a process of activation of personal norms for eco-driving', *Environment and Behavior*, 50, 1092–118.

Ünal, A.B., L. Steg and J. Granskaya (2019), 'To support or not to support, that is the question: Testing the VBN theory in predicting support for car use reduction policies in Russia', *Transportation Research Part A: Policy and Practice*, 119, 73–81.

van Wee, B., P. Rietveld and H. Meurs (2006), 'Is average daily travel time expenditure constant? In search of explanations for an increase in average travel time', *Journal of Transport Geography*, 14, 109–22.

Varian, H.R. (1992), *Microeconomic Analysis*, New York: Norton.

Verplanken, B., H. Aarts and A. van Knippenberg (1997), 'Habit, information acquisition, and the process of making travel mode choices', *European Journal of Social Psychology*, 27, 539–60.

Verplanken, B., H. Aarts, A. van Knippenberg and A. Moonen (1998), 'Habit versus planned behaviour: a field experiment', *British Journal of Social Psychology*, 37, 111–28.

Verplanken, B. and W. Wood (2006), 'Interventions to break and create consumer habits', *Journal of Public Policy and Marketing*, 25, 90–103.

Walker, I., G.O. Thomas and B. Verplanken (2014), 'Old habits die hard: Travel habit formation and decay during an office relocation', *Environment and Behaviour*, 47, 1089–106.

Wang, J., L. Kou, M-P. Kwan, R.M. Shakespeare, K. Lee and Y.M. Park (2021), 'An Integrated Individual Environmental Exposure Assessment System for Real-Time Mobile Sensing in Environmental Health Studies', *Sensors 2021*, 21, 4039. https://doi.org/10.3390/s21124039.

Winter, S. and Z-C. Yin (2011), 'The elements of probabilistic time geography', *GeoInformatica*, 15, 417–34.

Zahavi, Y. (1979), *The UMOT Project*, Report DOT-RSPA-DPB-2-79-3, Washington, DC: US Department of Transportation.

Zhang, Y. and L. Li (2020), 'Intention of Chinese college students to use carsharing: An application of the theory of planned behavior', *Transportation Research F*, 75, 106–19.

ANNEX 1   SOME KEY INDICATORS OF TRAVEL BEHAVIOUR FOR THE UNITED KINGDOM AND THE NETHERLANDS

The data in both tables are taken from the National Travel Surveys of the United Kingdom (NTS) and the Netherlands (ODiN). Comparing both countries should be done with caution. The travel surveys differ in sample size and composition, survey methods and operationalization of variables. The data refer to the year 2019, which is the most recent year not influenced by the changes in travel behaviour caused by the COVID-19 pandemic.

Table A3.1 Holders of car-driving licences and car ownership in the United Kingdom and the Netherlands by socio-demographics in 2019

Socio-demographics		United Kingdom (%)	The Netherlands (%)
Car-driving licence holders:			
Gender			
Men		80.0	84.6
Women		71.0	75.3
Age UK in years	Age Netherlands in years		
17–20	18–19	35.0	43.7
	20–24		70.7
21–29	25–29	62.0	77.8
30–39	30–39	79.0	81.4
40–49	40–49	86.0	86.9
50–59	50–59	86.0	88.3
	60–64		87.7
60–69	65–69	85.0	85.1
≥70	≥70	67.0	68.4
Car ownership:			
Gender			
Men		64.0[a]	82.1[b]
Women		54.0[a]	79.0[b]
Household income: Netherlands	Household income: UK		
First 20%	Lowest level	55.0	73.6
Second 20%	Second level	72.0	78.6
Third 20%	Third level	82.0	81.2
Fourth 20%	Fourth level	85.0	82.4
Fifth 20%	Highest level	87.0	82.7

Notes:

[a] For main driver

[b] Member of household with ≥ 1 car

Source: UK–NTS (2019); NL–ODiN (2019).

Table A3.2 Travel attributes in the United Kingdom and the Netherlands by socio-demographics in 2019

Socio-demographics		No. of trips per day		Kilometres per day	
		United Kingdom	The Netherlands	United Kingdom	The Netherlands
Gender					
Men		2.5	2.6	30.7	40.7
Women		2.7	2.8	26.3	31.3
Age UK in years	Age Netherlands in years				
17–20	18–24	2.3	2.6	23.0	41.6
21–29	25–34	2.4	2.8	27.8	45.5
30–39	35–49	2.9	3.2	35.0	44.1
40–49	50–64	3.1	2.8	36.5	40.5
50–59	65–74	2.8	2.3	36.6	29.7
60–69	≥75	2.7	1.6	32.0	18.2
≥70		2.2		20.7	
Household income:	Household income:				
UK	Netherlands				
Lowest level	First 20%	2.4	2.3	18.1	25.1
Second level	Second 20%	2.5	2.4	22.3	26.7
Third level	Third 20%	2.7	2.8	26.4	35.7
Fourth level	Fourth 20%	2.8	3.0	35.1	39.6
Highest level	Fifth 20%	2.7	3.0	40.5	47.6
Car ownership[a]					
No	No	2.0	2.8	12.5	34.6
1	Yes	2.6	2.9	25.7	43.5
≥2		2.9		37.3	

Note: [a] UK including vans; NL only for driving licence holders
Source: UK–NTS (2019); CBS Statline (2019).

4
Freight transport: indicators, determinants and drivers of change

Lóránt Tavasszy and Kees Ruijgrok

4.1   INTRODUCTION

Freight transport flows are a result of the interplay between economic activities such as production and consumption on the one side, and the supply of logistics and transport services on the other. This chapter discusses how freight transport flows result from this interplay. We examine freight transport from three angles:

1. **Indicators** for the description of freight transport flows: measures related to the weight of the goods moved and to the resulting transport and traffic performance as well as the impact on the environment from these activities.
2. **Determinants** of freight transport: the primary decisions of the actors within the logistics system that create the need for freight movements.
3. **Drivers of change** in freight transport, i.e. external forces that influence demand: economic growth, globalization, technology, consumer preferences and pressures to keep the system sustainable.

The chapter is organized as follows (see Figure 4.1). The indicators for freight transport and their interrelations are treated in Section 4.2, while Section 4.3 describes the determinants of freight transport. Section 4.4 takes an exploratory perspective, discussing future trends or trend breaks and their influence on freight transport, including the (un)sustainability of freight transport. We summarize and conclude the chapter in Section 4.5.

We use mostly data material from Europe to illustrate the characteristics of the freight transport system, also pointing out differences between Europe and other continents in the world, where the available data allows to.

Figure 4.1   Structure of this chapter, arrows indicating how change occurs in the freight system

4.2   INDICATORS OF FREIGHT TRANSPORT

There are various ways to describe the volumes and patterns of freight transport and the developments in the different modes of transport. We elaborate on four key indicators:

- Volume of transport, measured by the **weight lifted** of the goods. This is measured by the mass of the goods expressed in metric tonnes.
- **Transport performance**, which includes the distance the freight moved (ton kilometres). This integrative indicator is a measure of the need for movement and is used most often to characterize freight transport.
- **Traffic performance**, measured in distance moved by the transport means in question (e.g. vehicle kilometres).
- The **environmental emissions** of harmful gases and particulates that this creates.

We also discuss the interrelationships between the four and conclude the section with a discussion of the economic importance of freight transport.

4.2.1   Weight Lifted

Volumes of freight transport are generally expressed in transport statistics by means of the weight of the shipments moved. Note that this requires a translation from statistics of international trade, which are part of the standard registration system of the economic households of countries and noted in monetary terms (for example, US dollars). Figure 4.2 shows the main volumes of trade within and to or from the European Union in 2020, including their modal split, measured by the weight of the shipments moved (tonnes).

The balance of transport modes used depends strongly on whether one looks at intra- or intercontinental flows. Within the EU, road transport dominates, and alternative modes such as rail and inland waterways carry far less freight, with volumes sometimes around a tenth in size of those of road freight. Due to the relatively short transport distances and the fragmented national systems for rail transport, this mode has a considerably lower share than in other regions of the world, where the rail shares lie in the range between 10% for the USA (FHWA,

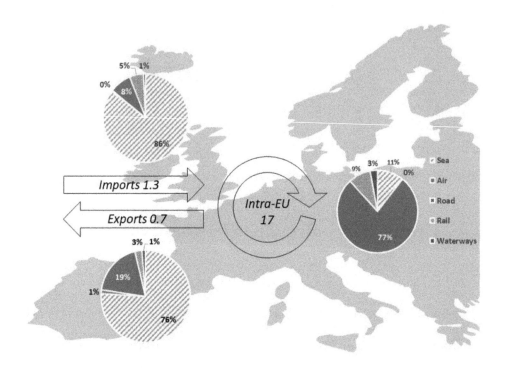

Note: Flows totals in arrows in billion tonnes
Source: Eurostat (2022).

Figure 4.2   Freight transport flows by mode within and to/from Europe (2020)

2010) and 40% in Russia (Rosstat, 2010). Sea transport dominates intercontinental flows, but it also has an important role for intra-European international traffic: deep sea and short sea together carry as many tonnes of freight between countries as the railways. This important role for sea for continental transport is also found in Asia, but much less so in other continents. Geographical differences such as availability of infrastructure and their consequences for cost per mode of transport explain these variations.

A second important characteristic of freight transport demand is its heterogeneity. There are many types of commodities associated with various sectors, with each sector organizing its movements differently. This heterogeneity is nicely illustrated by the use of modes of transport by the different commodity groups. Figure 4.3 shows the distribution of goods types across the different inland modes of transport; this tends to change little over time. We see that almost half of the weight of road transport is occupied by building materials. This is due to the short distances that these materials move; here, road transport offers the most flexibility in building projects. As we will see later, this does not translate into a high transport performance (in ton kilometres) because of the short distances. The weight share of the other two modes is dominated by bulk products such as solid and liquid fuels, ores and building materials (e.g. sand).

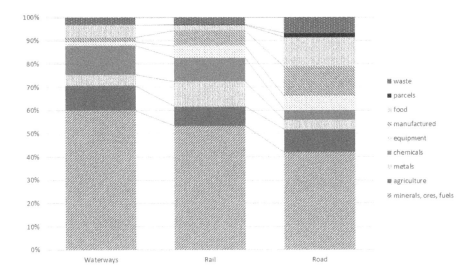

Source: Eurostat (2022).

Figure 4.3   Share of commodities for three modes of transport in the EU (2020)

4.2.2   Transport Performance

When measuring freight transport in terms of weight lifted (tonnes) we need to interpret statistics with care, as tonnes lifted is not necessarily the same as tonnes produced or consumed. As individual transport movements are often part of a larger transport chain, the same unit of freight may appear more than once in the statistics, if the chain has several transport modes. Every time goods are unloaded and loaded onto a next mode of transport, they will be counted again as registration occurs on a transport mode basis. One tonne of goods produced may thus appear as two tonnes or more in transport statistics. This implies that the number of tonnes will depend on the structure of the transport chain and the transport technology used (intermodal or door-to-door unimodal transport). When we measure freight demand in tonne kilometres, this risk is absent, as tonnes will only be counted for the distance moved.

Another drawback of tonnes lifted as a measure of freight demand is that it does not reveal much about the economic importance or societal impacts of transport. Concerning the economic impacts, the value density of goods (this is the value per m^2) may vary with several orders of magnitude, from 10 USD/tonne for raw minerals such as sand and gravel, to over 10,000 USD/tonne for manufactured products. Secondly, indicators such as costs, energy use and emissions of transport are all distance related. Hence, an indicator that includes distance will be a more accurate basis for examining the social costs and benefits of transport, its energy use and the environmental effects. We measure transport performance in tonne kilometres, the weight moved multiplied by the distance that it is moved.

It is useful to address the differences between the tonnes lifted and transport performance, especially when we speak of the modal split in freight transport. Figure 4.4 shows the differences in the share of modes measured in tonnes lifted and ton kilometres. Road transport is carried out more frequently on shorter distances than rail or inland navigation, therefore transport performance of these modes is comparatively higher than for road transport.

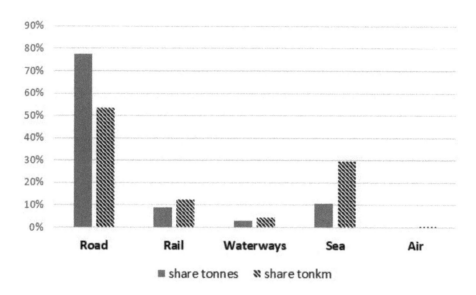

Source: Eurostat (2022).

Figure 4.4   Freight modal split in the EU27: measured by tonnes lifted and tonne kilometres, tonnes based modal split estimated based on time series (2006–19)

Although this measure for transport performance is easier to interpret from a policy perspective than the weight measure, we note also that the concept of tonne kilometres is not homogeneous and should be treated with care, as the shipment sizes vary widely between and within modes. Taking one ton of freight over 1000 kilometres will involve a different usage of resources than 1000 tonnes over 1 kilometre, because of economies of scale and density, or the technology available for that size of shipment and distance. Taking into account the number of vehicles needed to move freight eliminates part of the problem.

4.2.3   Traffic Performance

Once we can convert tonnes moved into the number of vehicles, and we can express freight demand in terms of traffic, this provides us with additional information for transport network design and the measurement of transport costs, energy use, etc. Many policy measures are related to the individual vehicles and, directly or indirectly, to the exact network distances driven (e.g. taxes, tolls, permits). Knowledge of vehicle kilometres driven makes assessment of these measures easier. Conversion from tonnes to vehicles is not straightforward, however. Average load factors vary by country and typically lie between 40% and 60%, when measured in weight. Empty running typically varies between 20% and 40%. Note that a load factor of 50% may seem low, until we consider that a full truck leaving for a return trip and arriving empty will be half full on average. The only option is to pick up freight on the way and to organize a round trip, which is not always possible. As these measures relate to the truck capacity in weight and not vehicle size, the real efficiency of the system is probably higher. This is the case, for example, if the maximum amount of goods that can be transported is not restricted by weight limitations but by volume, e.g. the transport of empty plastic bottles.

A distinction between types of vehicles used is also useful. Freight transport is carried out by many types of vehicles, from vans up to trucks and (sometimes double or even triple) trailers. Also for sea transport and inland navigation, a huge variation in transport means exists, each with its own characteristics.

4.2.4   Emissions from Freight Transport

As one can see in Chapter 8 of this book, all the activities that are performed in the Transport sector create emissions, not only by the transport activities themselves but also by the production of vehicles and infrastructure. These emissions involve noise and toxic gases such as NO_x, Particulate Matter and SO_2, but the most attention nowadays goes to Greenhouse gases (GHG), because of their effect on climate change. The freight transport sector is responsible for a large share of emissions, dependent on the size of the vehicles it uses and the type of fuel it consumes.

As shown in Figure 4.5 below, light-duty vehicles (passenger cars and vans) are the greatest contributor to EU transport GHG emissions, followed by heavy-duty vehicles (trucks and buses), marine navigation and aviation.

Figure 4.5 highlights the direct transport emissions: emissions from fuel production refining, and distribution are included in the other sectors' total. Carbon dioxide (CO_2) accounts for roughly 99% of these direct transport carbon dioxide equivalent (CO_{2e}) emissions, based on a 100-year global warming potential. For a more detailed description of this issue, we refer to Chapters 8 and 10 of this book. Approaches to improve the sustainability of freight transport are also briefly discussed in section 4.4.5.

4.2.5   Evolution of Different Indicators Through Time

With certain regularity, global supply chains have seen major economic and social disruptions throughout the decades, like the economic crisis of 2008 and the recent COVID-19 pandemic. In the past, the resilience of the total economic system has been such that old patterns have re-emerged quickly, as illustrated by Figure 4.6 (and later in this Chapter, Figure 4.11, which shows the initial COVID effects). Overall, the evolution of these indicators has shown to be quite robust over decades. Nevertheless, every new disruption brings new uncertainty about the spatial scale of its impacts and the time needed for the global economy to rebound to (or close to) earlier patterns of growth.

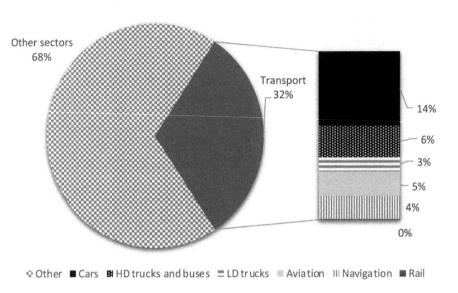

Source: EEA (2021).

Figure 4.5　　Shares of EU wide GHG emissions in 2018 by subsector (total 3.9 Gt CO$_2$e)

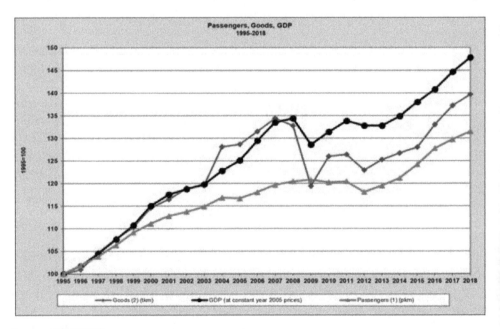

Source: EC (2020).

Figure 4.6　　Comparison of trends in passenger and goods transport in comparison with GDP development

Demand for freight transport is generated through decisions made by shippers and transport companies that operate on the freight transport market as representatives of the demand side and of the supply side respectively. In the next section we focus on the decision and the decision makers from the demand side.

4.3   DETERMINANTS OF FREIGHT TRANSPORT

Transport is said to be a derived demand, as it depends on the demands for goods and services originating from manufacturing sectors, consumers and governments. In this section, we characterize the supply chain system that determines the demand for transport as one consisting of five elements: Sources, Production, Inventories, Transport and Sales (SPITS). Figure 4.7 illustrates these elements and their relations.

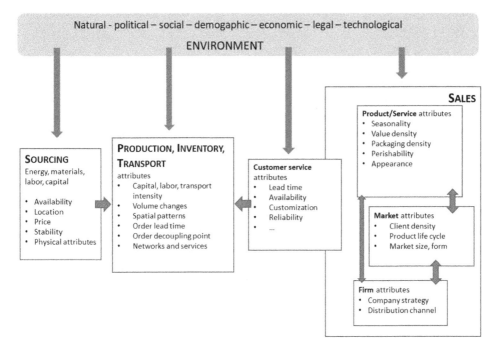

Source: Kuipers et al. (1995).

Figure 4.7   SPITS Model

The way the elements interact was described in the SPITS model in the Netherlands in the early 1990s (Kuipers et al., 1995). The elements of the system follow the supply chain from raw material (source) to the final demand by the customer (sales). The components P, I and T are central in this system and interact with each other to connect source and sales, by optimization of the supply chain, given the service requirements of the customers (Christopher, 2016). We summarize this objective into the following optimization function:

Min GLC | Service
GLC = T + I + H,

where GLC is the Generalized Logistics Cost (which is the sum of Transport (T), Inventory (I) and Handling (H)), to be minimized, given the service requirements (Service).

To the extent that service requirements do not act as a constraint to the design of logistics services, there is scope for further optimization. In most cases, however, there will be service requirements (e.g. pick-up and delivery times) that bound the solution space. The possibilities for minimizing the Generalized Logistics Costs rely on the opportunities to use economies of scale and scope as well as smart trade-offs between the three cost components of GLC. Supply chain management aims at exploiting these optimization possibilities. In many logistics processes, scale economies are essential to achieve a lower cost per item. Scale economies can be achieved by e.g.:

1. bundling of individual products into larger shipments;
2. using larger-scale modes of transport;
3. combining inventories upstream into central warehouses.

In this section, we describe in further detail these three main determinants of the logistic system: P(roduction), I(nventories) and T(ransport). We do this by highlighting the main trends of the last few decades in the development of these activities and the strategic decision factors that have governed the changes in their spatial and functional design.

4.3.1   Production

The number of production steps in a supply chain is increasing as companies continue to focus on their core business, trying to improve their competitive power by specializing and gaining scale advantages. This vertical disintegration of the supply chain applies to services as well as production steps and is also a response to a customer base that is increasing geographically. During the twentieth century, the world economy has emerged from a period with a high degree of economic protection and isolation into the present state that is characterized mainly by free trade and a high degree of specialization. One of the main drivers behind this growth of trade has been the differences in cost of producing the same type of product in different places around the world, which are due to differences in factor costs (especially labour costs but sometimes also cost of capital) and the availability of natural resources. As a result of reduced trade barriers, production moved from the West towards Eastern Europe, Eurasia and the Far East. Together with the cost of overcoming the distance, one can determine whether it is more attractive to import the products from elsewhere and to carry the burden of transporting goods over large distances or to avoid the costs involved in transporting these goods and producing them locally. Despite the general improvement of wage levels in Asia and Africa, there is no clear sign yet of massive re-shoring of business closer to consumer areas in Europe, the US or China (Delis et al., 2017). Possibly this may change after the strong perturbation of global supply chains during the COVID-19 pandemic era, or while trade barriers are increasing again due to a shifting global power balance from West to East.

Both the organization of production and transport economies of scale play an important role in the choice of production and physical distribution. An often-cited case is the production of automobiles. In general, the assembly of automobiles takes place not too far from the final customer but some of the parts are produced by factories that distribute their products to customers spread worldwide. The location of production plants is normally a long-term investment decision, and thus the geographic spread of production patterns used to be rather stable over time. Nowadays, the location of factories is re-evaluated more frequently and those that are not ideally located or have a lack of governmental support are under the threat of being closed down. Assembly plants, however, are more footloose and their location can change, influenced by regulatory measures (subsidies, regulation on the share of local content), the relative importance of transport costs in the cost of final products, congestion and other capacity restrictions (Dicken, 2003).

4.3.2   Inventories

Stocks or inventories of goods are inevitable where the processes of demand and supply do not handle the same amount of goods per unit of time, or if the batch sizes of these processes differ. Also, they have the benefit that they help to hedge against possible stock-outs if the demand or supply of products is uncertain. Inventories can build up in warehouses at the site of producers, at consumer households or at intermediate storage points in distribution centres. These centres can help to consolidate stocks at strategic and central locations, reducing the amount of inventory needed and allowing the storage of goods closer to consumers, thereby also reducing the distance for expensive movements and saving transport costs. Distribution centres are also used to sort goods from different manufacturers towards general retail outlets, a process called cross-docking. The spatial configuration of inventories, depots, cross-docking places for the distribution of goods is also called a distribution structure. Distribution structure designs are highly product and service specific (Fisher, 1997) and depend on many contextual factors (Onstein, 2021).

The advent of supply chain management, made possible by the mass introduction of personal computing and data processing facilities, was marked by a professionalization of firms' service quality improvement and cost control practices. Over the past decades, companies have become increasingly aware of the possibilities to optimize their inventories (Vermunt and Binnekade, 2000). Nowadays, supply chain management goes far beyond just-in-time deliveries. Supply chain management techniques developed in the last decade go under various names which we will not treat in detail here, such as quick response, lead-time management, lean logistics, agile logistics, efficient consumer response and process and pipeline mapping (see e.g. Christopher, 2016). These techniques have helped firms to drastically reduce their inventories while increasing service levels. Low volume but high-value segments have greatly expanded, benefiting from these new techniques and the opening up of new markets for customized and highly responsive services.

Distribution structures have been evolving throughout decades in waves (Tavasszy et al., 2012). The first wave of change took place in the '90s and involved the reduction of shipment sizes, an increase in frequencies and just-in-time transport as a first sign of mass individualization. This caused a fragmentation of goods flows into smaller streams. Driven by the need to keep costs under control, this was followed by a second wave of development (which reached a summit around 2000), which involved the internal rationalization of logistics processes within the company's own supply chain. In a recent third wave of change (2010's and onwards), firms are looking for economies of scale by means of external collaboration, across the company boundaries and their own supply chains. This so-called horizontal cooperation (as opposed to vertical cooperation, between vendor and supplier firms within the same supply chain) is seen as one of the major innovations which has transformed the logistics business landscape. We refer to Mason et al., 2007 for an early signalling of the phenomenon and Montreuil, 2011 for its framing in the Physical Internet system which is still a leading vision today for logistics professionals (ALICE, 2020). We return to this further in the chapter.

The increased transparency of the logistics process in supply chains and the technological means to plan and control logistics much better using advanced planning tools and IT systems have all increased. But it is also apparent that the practical application of these technologies is often hampered by a lack of cooperation and standardization. Real supply chain cooperation is then difficult to achieve because of transaction costs and countervailing powers between the supply chain partners. On the other hand, in order to achieve substantial cost efficiencies, this type of cooperation is essential to synchronize the activities in the supply chain and to take full benefit of potential scale economies.

4.3.3   Transport Logistics

Transport logistics concern the decision of the mode of transport to be used on a strategic level, i.e. which type of network to be built and given the available networks, at the tactical and operational level, the planning of movements and the routing of the freight, embodied by the design of the logistical organization and the planning of daily operations. We limit our discussion here to the strategic level decision of mode choice, i.e. the choice between different networks used by the modes of transport. As we have seen above, companies increasingly favour road, air and sea transport. Part of the explanation for this lies in external, socio-economic factors, like globalization and the individualization of society (see Section 4.4). In order to understand how such developments can translate into changes in mode usage we need to look into the mechanisms that govern these choices. Below, we discuss the influence of product and service characteristics on mode choice.

Jordans et al. (2006) found that 95% of the mode choices can be related to transport distances and basic product characteristics such as value density and packaging density. For many transport flows, transport distances and basic product characteristics are given and cannot be influenced. At the same time, mode choice is also governed by preferences of firms that are more difficult to observe and relate to the performance characteristics of transport modes such as transport time reliability, lead time and prices per shipment (see e.g. Vieira, 1992). We illustrate this relationship between supply chain characteristics and mode choice by means of the element of shipment size. The size of shipment, as one of the product characteristics, is an important decision variable in the minimization of GLC given required service levels. Figure 4.8 shows the average shipment sizes and related transport prices of some modes of transport. From this picture, it becomes clear that huge differences exist between the respective modes. Mode choice will be determined in part by the size of the shipment, as economies of scale in terms of shipment sizes can easily materialize by choosing a mode that allows lower unit costs. The figure clearly shows the pattern of costs across modes of transport.

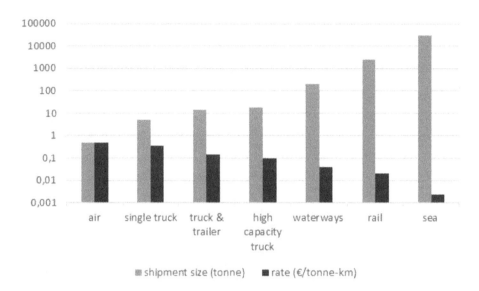

Source: Dutch cost survey after Panteia (2021).

Figure 4.8   Differences in shipment size and transport charges for different modes of transport

Generalizing this further, one can specify continuous cost functions with different influences. Figure 4.9 shows two examples of such cost functions, for long distance shipments and two modes of transport, also called a-modal or mode-abstract cost function: (a) the joint effect of average transport times and shipment sizes on unit costs (here: per kg) and (b) the influence of uncertainty and value density on costs per unit. Higher value densities will lead to higher capital costs of inventory-in-transport, as we will illustrate further on in some more detail.

Figure 4.9 (a) shows an example of how two long-distance overseas modes (air and sea transport, as well as combinations of sea and air) can both be optimal solutions, depending on the circumstances. By specifying the weight of the shipment and the required speed, the mode choice and the generalized transport cost per kg can be derived easily, if all modes are available. 100,000 tonnes of crude oil will be transported by ship, a box of diamonds by air. There will be no discussion on the mode choice decision in these circumstances, at least in densely populated developed economies, where all the above-mentioned modes of transport are present, and the speed requirements of the shipments do not restrict the choice options. Figure 4.9(b)

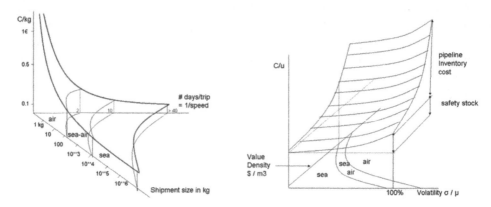

Figure 4.9   Unit generalized logistical costs as function of (a) speed and shipment size and (b) of value density and volatility

shows how lead time uncertainty (which is influenced both by demand uncertainty – here labelled 'volatility' – and the amount of safety stocks) affects transport costs, besides value density. When taking into account the value of the product and the volatility of demand (in the figure: demand variance σ divided by mean demand μ) we can also visualize the effect of inventory costs via increased safety stocks and the effect of pipeline inventory costs, adding to generalized transport costs/unit (C/u in the figure). When the value density is low, pipeline costs (the inventory costs during transport) will be negligible. When the value density becomes larger, the pipeline cost becomes significant. We provide an example of this trade-off below for the concrete case of laptop computers.

Example: laptops

In the case of a shipment of one container with 1000 laptops (20 pallets of 50 laptops) with a production value of $500 per laptop, each container will have a pipeline inventory cost of $5000 (500*1000*0.1*36/365) if the trip takes 36 days and the yearly interest rate is 10%. The average shipping rate of this container from Asia to Europe is $1500, so the pipeline cost for this shipment will exceed the sea transport cost by more than a factor of 3. The generalized logistics costs of $6500 would be roughly the same when these products would have used the air mode. At 3kg per laptop at $2 per kg, the transport charge would be $6000, whereas, with an assumed total travel time of half a week, the pipeline costs would not be more than $500.

The example shows that, although transport costs differ substantially by mode of transport, generalized costs show less variation, taking into account other logistic cost factors. When the volatility is high, retailers and distributors do need safety stocks in order to avoid empty shelves if the demand for a product is higher than the stock and the demand during the reorder period. Safety stocks can be avoided for a great deal if fast and reliable transport options exist that can guarantee the delivery of products within the customer service requirements. So, trade-offs exist between inventory costs and transport costs and the generalized cost concept should take these trade-offs into account.

4.4 DRIVERS OF CHANGE IN FREIGHT TRANSPORT

4.4.1 Introduction

Over the longer term, the continued growth of global freight flows is expected, given, of course, that there will be no big economic crises or disruptions such as the COVID pandemic. Although this growth will be most conspicuous in the emerging Asian economies (especially China and India), flows are expected to continue to grow. Some sources predict more than a doubling of present flows between 2015 and 2050 (OECD-ITF, 2021).

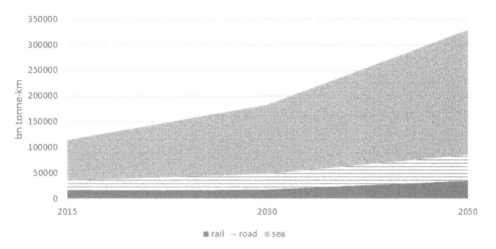

Source: OECD-ITF (2021).

Figure 4.10   Projection for international freight per mode of transport

Apart from a large increase in welfare levels of developing countries due to economic growth and technological development, the expectation of further growth in freight transport was fuelled by continued globalization, via a decrease of barriers to international trade and transport. These projections were made before COVID-19 and it has become more difficult than before to indicate which scenarios are likely and which are not. However, there are clear reasons to expect that trade growth will be less excessive in the future than we have seen before:

1. equalization of income of developing countries with those in developed countries, leading to equalization of production costs and prices;
2. transport costs increasing due to supply chain congestion and internalization of external costs;
3. geopolitical instabilities, leading to the wish to become less dependent on the availability of products from elsewhere.

Towards the future, then, one needs to look at the megatrends and stable relations shaping these developments. In the next sections, we discuss three drivers of change in freight transport that have influenced production and consumption, trade, logistics and transport decisions: (1) economic growth, (2) globalization and (3) (information) technology in combination with mass individualization.

We discuss these main drivers in three separate subsections and conclude the Section in 4.4.5.

4.4.2   Economic Growth and Globalization

GDP appears to have a strong overall explanatory power for freight transport growth: earlier World Bank research suggests that it explains over 89% of the variation in observed freight volumes (Bennathan et al., 1992). In this study of about 17 countries, a fairly reliable indication of this relationship was that every million US dollar in GDP would add 170,000 road ton kilometres in transport performance. In other words, economic performance seems to be a strong driver of transport performance and we can expect economic growth to explain changes in freight transport flows as well. Roughly, freight transport has grown one-on-one with the economy. Some studies indicate, however, that growth of GDP and transport has been decoupling, with the possible implication that GDP would be a less important driver in the future than it is now. Industrialization and servitization of economies appears to create significant decoupling (see McKinnon, 2007; Tapio, 2005; Verny, 2005; Kveiborg and Fosgerau, 2007; Alises et al., 2014; Zhu et al., 2020). Within the US, decoupling between GDP and freight activity had already taken place (Gilbert and Nadeau, 2002). Indeed, it seems that domestic transport growth is decoupling from national GDP, due to dematerialization of flows and changes in logistics. At the same time, the economic integration between countries results in a growth of international trade, with growth above that suggested by GDP. These can balance each other out in open economies.

As mentioned, trade is an intermediate variable that has a significant effect on transport flows. The growth of world trade is directly linked to the demand for international freight transport, maritime transport and air freight. Complex global trading networks have evolved to exploit labour cost differences, regional production specialization, global product differentiation opportunities and availability of raw materials in particular countries. Their development has been facilitated by major regulatory changes. Trade liberalization, particularly within trading blocs such as the EU and North American Free Trade Agreement (NAFTA), has removed constraints on cross-border movement and has reduced the related barrier costs. Along with the reduction in transport costs, the relaxation of trade barriers since World War II has given a great stimulus to the development of global trade (Hesse and Rodrigue 2004, Rodrigue, 2006a and b). Up to recent times, one can look beyond the short-term volatility of world trade to see a stable, though not constant, growth trend (Figure 4.11).

The net sum of the influences of GDP and trade growth on transportation depends on the relative share of domestic and international transport and the rates of growth in each segment. An illustrative example is the analysis of the relationship between GDP and transport for the Netherlands (KiM, 2006). Figure 4.12 nicely illustrates the counteracting forces typical for an

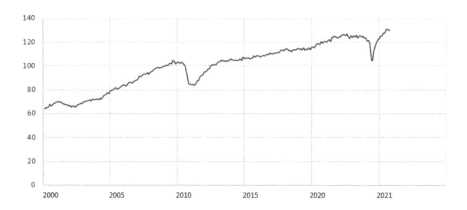

Source: CPB (2021).

Figure 4.11   World trade trend and volatility 2000–21 (index 2010=100)

international economy such as the Netherlands. The net increase in transport performance that occurred in these years can largely be explained by relatively strong growth in international flows on top of modest growth in the domestic economy. Although the numbers have changed since then, this pattern has remained largely the same for the Netherlands (KiM, 2019).

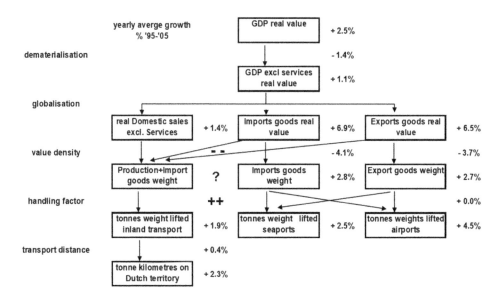

Source: KiM (2006).

Figure 4.12   Causal analysis of changes in yearly transport performance

In a more recent study by Knoope and Francke (2020) the development of freight transport in the Netherlands is explained by a time series analysis which assesses the relative importance of various explanatory variables mentioned in the literature, such as economic growth, globalization development of service industry, growth of population, dematerialization, transport costs and domestic consumption. They show that the development of domestic Dutch freight transport is largely explained by the development of the GDP of the Netherlands, the growth of the building sector, the service industry and the decline of the agricultural sector. The development of international freight transport to and from the Netherlands is largely explained by the growth of world trade.

A next dimension of change comes from the organization of supply chains, and in particular the increasing complexity of production and distribution processes, leading to more transportation steps and handling movements for products over longer distances. What is the implication of long-term changes in logistical structures upon transport flows at various spatial levels (local, regional, continental and global)?

4.4.3   Changes in Supply Chain Architectures

Since the middle of the previous century, there has been an increase in product variety, up to the level of single product or service units being individualized and unique. This is the result of the trend towards adjusting the supply of products to consumer preferences and using the principles of mass individualization, supported by the reduction of logistics costs and globalization. The developments in the field of information technology and the availability of internet connections have led to a worldwide visibility of supply chains that facilitated improved consumer services and the organization of efficient and effective supply chains. Here we distinguish between two types of change. Firstly, supply chains are being reorganized vertically to serve more diverse consumer needs, by increasing the degree of specialization of firms and the number of segments in the supply chain. Secondly, there is also a drive towards rationalization of logistics processes through horizontal collaboration between firms, by means of coordinated procurement, shared use of transport assets and bundled logistics operations. This helps to reduce the pressure on product costs caused by vertical disintegration. We discuss these two trends below.

Vertical reorganization

The vertical organization of supply chains is visible in the number of steps that it takes to produce and distribute products to final markets. As a symptom of the mass-individualization of products and services, intermediate production steps have been added and logistics services have become more specialized. Overall, this has led to an increase in the demand for freight transport. Mass-individualization can be observed in two main dimensions: product customization and increased responsiveness of services (see Vermunt and Binnekade, 2000). These are supported by different chain configurations to satisfy product and service demand (see the seminal papers by Fisher, 1997 and Lee, 2001), including different production systems (building to order, flexible production, smaller batches, 3D printing), distribution structures (widespread inventories, just-in-time replenishment) and different locations of production and stocks, both centrally and close to consumer regions.

Figure 4.13 shows examples of different supply chain configurations that result from the change from standard to customized products and conventional to responsive services. The figure shows four segments:

1. Top right: standard products with a long order lead time (e.g. smartphones, chips)
2. Top left: customized products with long order lead time (e.g. cars, machines)
3. Bottom right: standard products with a short lead time (e.g. spare parts, medicines)
4. Bottom left: customized products with a short lead time (e.g. fresh pizzas, flowers)

The figure also shows the geographical dimensions from the global scale (outer ring) towards the local market (noted as **M** in the centre of the figure), indicating how far production and inventories are located from markets.

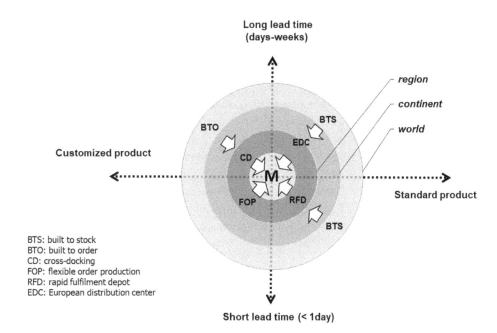

Source: adapted from Vermunt and Binnekade (2000).

Figure 4.13   Chain configurations in four demand segments

Typical changes in chain configuration concern the move from continental distribution centres, based on production to stock, towards production to order at a global scale, where delivery takes place directly or with an intermediate step of value-added logistics (e.g. packaging to prepare for the local market). Also, new concepts like *rapid fulfilment depots* (for low demand but urgent products like spare parts) and *flexible order production* (allowing fast switching in batch size and end-product specifications, close to the consumer market) are being introduced to allow for better responsiveness. The more individualized products are, the more these activities will be located closely to consumer markets. *Centralized international distribution*, introduced to reduce inventory and building on the decrease of trade barriers, is being supplemented by *regional distribution centres*. These systems will not operate exclusively, but simultaneously, to offer more choice in service levels. This development is also termed as *the omni-channel revolution* (see e.g. Galipoglu et al., 2018).

Horizontal rationalization

The move towards more customer-oriented logistics structures will inevitably increase logistics costs as shares of product costs. As also pictured in Figure 4.8, firms will only be able to control their logistics costs through a further rationalization of logistics processes. After some time, firms will have depleted the potential of improvements within the company and will try to make gains by cooperation with others. Horizontal collaboration, or consolidation and cooperation between firms at the same level of a chain, is a logical way to generate lower cost per unit of freight (Cruijssen, 2020). Through consolidation of flows, larger vehicles can be used so that the loading efficiency is optimized. Note that the high level of responsiveness that is required could possibly conflict with the above-mentioned need for smoother flows of goods. Avoiding this possible conflict is one of the biggest challenges in the design of logistic networks. The set-up of a hybrid supply chain, which allows different possibilities for flows to reach their destination, creates the flexibility required (Groothedde et al., 2005). This is supported by intermodal transport networks which combine slow and cheap modes with fast and flexible modes.

The volatile part of the demand is supplied by a fast (and more expensive) mode like road or air transport, while the stable part of demand is being delivered through the slow, large-scale modes via networks of consolidation hubs, which allows the exploitation of potential economies of scale. This intermodal logistics system has more recently been developed to allow flexible transport options in a network to be fully exploited, under the name of synchromodality (Tavasszy et al., 2018; Dong et al., 2018).

4.4.4   Innovations in Logistics Services: The Physical Internet

In the previous sections, we have elaborated on some important megatrends concerning trade and the design of supply chains. These create new and advanced demands for logistics service providers, of global reach and ultimate flexibility, at the lowest costs possible. There are many technological and organizational innovations in logistics services that can help to realize this new demand; these build on e.g.:

1. digitalization of information exchange;
2. automation of all processes, from transport and transhipment to decision making; and
3. new organizational approaches for the coordination of supply and service networks.

The Physical Internet (PI) is a strategic vision of logistics that binds these innovations together. Since the turn of the century, the logistics industry has been creating globally coordinated efforts to collaborate around this vision (Pan et al., 2011). The system is described in various publications (such as Mervis, 2014; Montreuil, 2017; and Pan, 2017). The vision includes a roadmap for the development of logistics innovations, which attempts to position several innovations in one consistent framework (ALICE, 2020):

1. A new standardized hierarchy of container sizes and shapes
2. Protocols for vertical and horizontal collaboration of multi-modal carriers
3. Routing algorithms and service protocols to connect shippers and carriers
4. Global network designs that allow system-optimal allocation of capacity
5. Information systems that allow nodes to help decide the routing of shipments
6. Specialized equipment to allow managing shipments below container level.

Besides aiming to create one coherent vision for innovations in freight transportation and logistics, the PI vision is also important as it addresses the soft side of innovation in terms of (1) human and business management factors influencing adoption and (2) the public/private governance aspects, including regulatory issues and corporate social responsibility. The ALICE roadmap shows that major steps are needed before the comprehensive PI vision becomes reality.

The expected added societal value of these logistics innovations is high. It is said to amount to 3.5 trillion USD (WEF, 2016), due to new business value created (1.3 tn. USD), a reduction of logistics costs (2 tn. USD) and increased sustainability (0.2 tn. USD). This is more than one-third of the 2020 business value of the global logistics industry.

4.4.5 Environmental Effects of Freight Transport, Decarbonization and Sustainability

In this section, we focus on the effects on nature via the emissions that freight transport activities create, CO_2 emissions in particular because of their importance for climate policies trying to reduce GHG emissions. Of course, the environmental problems are larger and also relate to other external effects such as health, safety and noise nuisance, but presently the dangers of all the potential negative effects of climate change gets the most attention because of its potential impact on extreme weather conditions, and the health impacts of direct and indirect effects, (IPCC, 2021). For further treatment of the environmental aspects of transport, we refer to Chapter 10 of this book.

McKinnon (2018) developed a useful framework for decarbonization in freight transport. The framework connects key indicators of the road freight transport system to opportunities for change in logistics organization, transport operations and technology. A comparable framework, adapted for a multimodal context, has been used by the ALICE alliance to formulate a roadmap for zero-emissions logistics in 2050, which includes in a list of potential GHG-reducing policies, including:

- managing freight demand volumes through e.g. restructuring of supply chains;
- shifting freight to low-emission modes;
- increasing freight asset utilization by e.g. consolidation of freight shipments and inventory;
- reducing energy use in transport by fuel-efficient driving and increased engine efficiency;
- change of drivetrains to more carbon-efficient sources of energy.

This provides a structure for a roadmap with policy options, each of which has to be justified by a careful calculation of return-on-investment not only to reduce GHG, but also to achieve efficiency and effectiveness. A qualitative assessment of the expected impact and feasibility of these options is given in ALICE (2019). Of course, the success of these policies relies on the willingness of companies, forwarders as well as transport companies, to invest in (planning) systems and technology and they will do that, in general, only if they are convinced of the benefits they create. The EU has set itself a long-term goal of limiting global warming to 1.5–2 degrees Celsius. The 2.0-degree target translates into reducing GHG emissions by 80–95% in 2050 compared with 1990 levels. To achieve this goal, emissions from transport must be reduced to over 60% below 1990 levels by 2050, all assuming a linear decline in emissions over time (CE Delft et al., 2020). Continuous economic growth is expected to increase the CO_2 reduction gap.

In 2021 the EU set an intermediate target of 55% emission reduction for transport between 1990 and 2030 in the 'Fit for 55' policy proposal (EC, 2021). To achieve this strong increase in carbon productivity requires an integrated approach that makes full use of the opportunities available to cost effectively increase energy efficiency, decarbonizing energy sources, and accelerating the development and deployment of new low-carbon technologies. For further reading on this subject we refer to Chapter 8 of this book. Furthermore, it should grasp opportunities for optimizing supply chains and logistics operations and changing business and consumer behaviour. CO_2 abatement options are needed at all system levels, i.e. energy carriers, powertrains, vehicles, fleets, logistics operations, behaviours and so on, and in all transport areas and for all transport modes (CE Delft et al., 2020).

As we have seen in subsection 4.4.2 the economy has quickly jumped back to old-growth levels after the COVID-19 pandemic. However, this crisis now also shows the risks of globalization and 'dragging around' people and goods. Combined with a shift in economic and political power, growth scenarios for production and trade may have to be redrawn completely. For instance, a return of production from the Far East to Europe is one of the potential developments that can apply to various segments. If so, supply chains will be redesigned accordingly. The main challenge for the logistics sector will remain the decarbonization task as required by the Paris Climate Agreement. As both size and character of international flows are uncertain, it is also hard to predict whether the freight transport sector will be capable of meeting the challenge of achieving zero-emission by 2050. Whereas the freight volume of perishables, non-perishables and industrial goods are expected to grow much faster than that of bulk and especially liquid bulk, the CO_2 reduction per volume needs to decline much more in these segments. The non-bulk segment relies more on the more carbon-intensive road transport, but at the time of writing this chapter (2022) the decarbonization strategies for road seem closer to implementation than those for inland waterway transport. The logistics chains will probably change due to the above-mentioned developments, but the need for transport, distribution and value-added services will remain – as will the negative impacts of road transport in terms of congestion, noise, safety and land use. The development of highly responsive logistics has led to the increased speed of delivery of individual consignments, which also asks for well-coordinated delivery networks, including automation of sorting and transhipment. It has also resulted in a big increase in activities from delivery vans and bicycle delivery services involved in City Logistics. Some of these services have increased the environmental burden of transport-related services; questions on the sustainable nature of these services could be raised.

These trends in logistics make the reduction target an ambitious one. The number of trucks and vans active in European freight transport has increased considerably over the last decades. Presently (2021) there are more than two million vans in Europe, and because of the COVID pandemic and the increased number of home deliveries, this number is expected to grow further. The number of trucks in Europe has stabilized at around 400,000, after a decline because of the economic crisis of 2008–10. It is not the volumes they transport that are declining, nor is it the decline of the fleet itself, it is the use of cleaner engines that has to achieve the target for GHG reductions (ICCT, 2020).

Efficiency improvements within the road transport sector can also lead towards a reverse modal shift, for instance when Super EcoCombis are competing with rail and barge transport. The reduction of transport emissions of bulk segments will rely particularly on zero-emission energy carriers, such as electricity and hydrogen, whereas the non-bulk segments will also be able to introduce more energy-efficient logistics concepts, mainly due to network optimization (see also Chapter 8 of this book). The supply chains of these segments are generally more complex, with larger numbers of links, logistics activities and actors. The contribution of sustainable, energy-efficient transhipment and storage is low in all segments except for perishables. The expected contribution of vehicle and vessel technologies, autonomous driving and Intelligent Transportation Systems (ITS) is applicable for all segments, while the impact of logistics measures, including modal shift, is far more important for the non-bulk segments. Consumer and investor pressure will push leading companies in markets close to consumers (B2C) towards the implementation of zero-emission technologies and more efficient logistics. Together with governments, these companies will act as front-runners and lead the followers in the market. This requires new and optimized business models using vertical integration, better utilization of equipment and investing in advanced-low/zero-emission technologies.

In the Netherlands, the logistics sector has stated that reaching a six-fold improvement in carbon productivity and, thus, the Paris goals seem possible *without* impacting the competitiveness of the logistics sector and the prices of products shipped (CE Delft et al., 2018, 2020). The transition will, however, require changes to the current structure of how logistics is organized, affecting individual interests and parties. The speed of the transition and its impact on CO_2 emissions will depend partly on how governments will implement policies such as standards and financial incentives to create the required level playing field for zero-emission technologies, while helping to accelerate large-scale implementation. Concluding, one can say that the freight transport sector has to explore all the options mentioned before, in order to be able to reach its CO_2 reduction targets.

4.5   SUMMARY AND CONCLUSIONS

In this chapter we have described a number of different dimensions of freight transport. We have discussed three basic indicators of freight transport activity: the total weight lifted (tonnes), transport performance (tonne kilometres) and traffic performance (vehicle kilometres). The relationships between these three depends on the structure of the supply chains, in terms of production, trade relations, inventories and transport modes used. These indicators should be used with caution, as an inappropriate choice of indicator can unnecessarily inflate or hide policy-relevant numbers.

We have looked at the most relevant causes for changes through time. In brief, transport is growing by all measures, and is increasing in efficiency. Freight transport growth is uneven across modes, however, with the environment-unfriendly modes taking the major share of increase in demand. Explaining these changes and their interrelations is not straightforward as demand for freight transport depends on many factors and many different users with dispersed needs. User needs depend on the type of products that are being transported and the logistics context of these products. An important constant is the fact that growth is still dominantly determined by GDP growth. This appears to be only weakly disturbed by dematerialization of economies and – over longer time periods – largely robust against world crises.

We have introduced generalized logistics costs as an important determinant in the process of logistics optimization, given demand requirements. We have seen that through combinations of smart planning and network design it is possible to minimize logistics cost and maximize customer service at the same time. The process of logistics cost minimization has run in parallel with deregulation, liberalization of trade and improvements in transport and information technologies. Lately, mass individualization has led to a strong fragmentation of supply chains. This places higher demand on the responsiveness of transport systems and increases its costs, internally and externally. An important solution lies in restructuring of flows to become consolidated wherever possible. For this, a coordinated effort within the logistics sector, across firms and between competitors, may be needed. Recent roadmaps for the decarbonization of logistics and the Physical Internet are instrumental to this effort.

The outlook for the transport sector is one of continued growth and difficulty to reduce its negative sustainability impacts. World trade is expected to continue to grow for decades ahead, even after occasional global economic recessions and pandemics. As a result, the growth of transport will also continue, spurring new demand for transport services and infrastructure. These developments will clash with the increased urgency to adapt to climate change and to internalize the external costs of transport.

REFERENCES

ALICE (2019), 'A framework and process for the development of a roadmap towards zero emissions logistics 2050', accessed 21 January 2022 at www.etp-logistics.eu.

ALICE (2020), 'Physical Internet roadmap', accessed 21 January 2022 at www.etp-logistics.eu.

Alises, A., J.M. Vassallo and A.F. Guzmán (2014), 'Road freight transport decoupling: A comparative analysis between the United Kingdom and Spain', *Transport Policy*, 32, 186–93.

Bennathan, E., J. Fraser and L.S. Thompson (1992), 'What determines demand for freight transport', Policy Research Working Papers, Washington, DC: Transport, Infrastructure and Urban Development Department, World Bank.

CE Delft, TNO and Connekt (2018), *Outlook Hinterland and Continental Freight 2018*, Delft: Connekt.

CE Delft, TNO and Connekt (2020), *Outlook Hinterland and Continental Freight 2020*, Delft: Connekt.

Christopher, M. (2016), *Logistics and Supply Chain Management*, 5th edition, Harlow: Pearson Education.

CPB (2021*), Word Trade Monitor*, CPB Wereldhandelsmonitor, accessed 21 January 2022 at www.cpb .nl.

Cruijssen, F. (2020), *Cross-chain Collaboration in Logistics*, Berlin: Springer International Publishing.

Delis, A., N. Driffield and Y. Temouri (2017), 'The global recession and the shift to re-shoring: Myth or reality?', *Journal of Business Research*, 103, 632–43.

Dicken, P. (2003), 'Global production networks in Europe and East Asia: the automobile components industries', GPN Working Paper 7, University of Manchester.

Dong, C., R. Boute, A. McKinnon and M. Verelst (2018), 'Investigating synchromodality from a supply chain perspective', *Transportation Research Part D: Transport and Environment*, 61, 42–57.

EC (2020), *European Transport in Figures*, Statistical Pocketbook, Brussels: European Commission.

EC (2021), *Communication on 'Fit for 55': delivering the EU's 2030 climate target on the way to climate neutrality*, COM(2021)550 final, Brussels: European Commission.

EEA (2021), Greenhouse gas emissions by source sector [ENV_AIR_GGE__custom_3787456], accessed 21 January 2021 at https://ec.europa.eu/eurostat/databrowser/product/page/ENV_AIR_GGE_ _custom_3787456.

Eurostat (2007), 'Average loads, distances and empty running in road freight transport: 2005', *Statistics in Focus*, 117/2007, Brussels: European Communities.

Eurostat (2020a), 'Energy, transport and environment statistics 2020 edition', Luxembourg: Publications Office of the European Union.

Eurostat (2020b), 'Freight transport statistics – modal split Statistics Explained', Luxembourg: Publications Office of the European Union.

Eurostat (2020c), 'International trade in goods for the EU, an Overview', Luxembourg: Publications Office of the European Union.

Eurostat (2022), 'Data explorer', accessed 17 April 2023 at https://ec.europa.eu/eurostat/data/database.

FHWA (2010), *Freight Analysis Framework*, Washington, DC: US Department of Transportation.

Fisher, M.L. (1997), 'What is the right supply chain for your product?', *Harvard Business Review*, 75, 105–17.

Galipoglu, E., H. Kotzab, C. Teller, I.Ö. Yumurtaci Hüseyinoglu and J. Pöppelbuß (2018), 'Omni-channel retailing research – state of the art and intellectual foundation', *International Journal of Physical Distribution and Logistics Management*, 48 (4), 365–90.

Gilbert, R. and Nadeau, K. (2002), 'Decoupling economic growth and transport: a requirement for sustainability', paper presented at Transportation and Economic Development conference in Portland organized by US Transportation Research Board, 5–7 May.

Groothedde, B., C. Ruijgrok and L. Tavasszy (2005), 'Towards collaborative, intermodal hub networks: a case study in the fast moving consumer goods market', *Transportation Research Part E*, 41 (6), 567–83.

Hesse, M. and J.-P. Rodrigue (2004), 'The transport geography of logistics and freight distribution', *Journal of Transport Geography*, 12 (3), 171–84.

ICCT (2020), 'European vehicle market statistics', *Pocketbook 2020/21*, Berlin: ICCT.

IPCC (2021), 'Sixth Assessment report', accessed 21 January 2022 at www.ipcc.ch.

Jordans, M., B. Lammers, C.J Ruijgrok, L.A. Tavasszy (2006), *Base potential of inland waterways, rail and short sea*, Delft: TNO (in Dutch).

KiM (2006), *Mobiliteitsbalans*, Netherlands Institute for Transport Policy Analysis, Ministry of Infrastructure & Environment, The Hague (in Dutch).

KiM (2019), *Mobiliteitsbeeld 2019*, Ministry of Infrastructure and Waterways, The Hague (in Dutch).

Knoope, M. and J. Francke (2020), 'Verklaring van de ontwikkeling van het goederenvervoer in Nederland' ('explanation of the development of freight transport in the Netherlands'), *Tijdschrift Vervoerwetenschap*, 56 (2), 1–26.

Kuipers, B., H. van Rooden, A.D.M. van de Ven and A.A.C.M. Wierikx (1995), 'De logistieke wereld bezien door de bril van de overheid', *Tijdschrift voor Vervoerwetenschap*, 1, 55–76.

Kveiborg, O. and M. Fosgerau (2007), 'Decomposing the decoupling of Danish road freight traffic growth and economic growth', *Transport Policy*, 14 (1), 39–48.

Lee, H.L. (2001), 'Aligning supply chain strategies with product uncertainties', *California Management Review*, 44 (3), 105–19.

Mason, R., C. Lalwani and R. Boughton (2007), 'Combining vertical and horizontal collaboration for transport optimization', *Supply Chain Management*, 12 (3), 187–99.

McKinnon, A. (2018), *Decarbonizing Logistics*, London: Kogan Page.

McKinnon, A.C. (2007), 'Decoupling of road freight transport and economic growth trends in the UK: an exploratory analysis', *Transport Reviews*, 27 (1), 37–64.

Mervis, J. (2014), 'The information highway gets physical', *Science*, 344 (6188), 1104–07.

Montreuil, B. (2011), 'Toward a Physical Internet: meeting the global logistics sustainability grand challenge', *Logistics Research*, 3 (2), 71–87.

OECD-ITF (2021), 'ITF Transport Outlook 2021', Paris: OECD Publishing.

Onstein, A.T.C. (2021), 'Factors determining distribution structure design', Ph.D. thesis, TU Delft, TRAIL Thesis Series no. T2021/28, TRAIL, Delft.

Pan, S., E. Ballot, G.Q. Huang and B. Montreuil (2017), 'Physical Internet and interconnected logistics services: research and applications', *International Journal of Production Research*, 55 (9), 2603–09.

Panteia (2021), *Cost Figures for Freight Transport*, Panteia: Zoetermeer.

Rodrigue, J-P. (2006a), 'Transportation and the geographical and functional integration of global production networks', *Growth and Change*, 37 (4), 510–25.

Rodrigue, J.-P. (2006b), 'Challenging the derived transport demand thesis: issues in freight distribution', *Environment and Planning A*, 38 (8), 1449–62.

Rosstat, *Russian Statistics* (2010), Moscow: Business Monitor International.

Tapio, P. (2005), 'Towards a theory of decoupling: degrees of decoupling in the EU and the case of road traffic in Finland between 1970 and 2001', *Transport Policy*, 12 (2), 137–51.

Tavasszy, L.A., K. Ruijgrok and I. Davydenko (2012), 'Incorporating logistics in freight trans port demand models: state-of-the-art and research opportunities', *Transport Reviews*, 32 (2), 203–19.

Tavasszy, L., Behdani, B., & Konings, R. (2018). 'Intermodality and synchromodality'. In Geerlings, H., B. Kuipers., R. Zuidwijk (eds.), *Ports and Networks*, Abingdon: Routledge, 251–66.

Vermunt, J. and F. Binnekade (2000), *European Logistics*, The Hague: Holland International Distribution Council.

Verny, J. (2005), 'The problem of decoupling between freight transport and economic growth', paper presented at the 8th NECTAR conference, Las Palmas, Gran Canaria, 2–4 June.

Vieira, L.F.M. (1992), 'The value of service in freight transportation', Ph.D. thesis, Massachusetts Institute of Technology, Boston, MA.

WEF (2016), *Digital Transformation of Industries Logistics Industry*, Geneva: World Economic Forum.

Zhu, F., X. Wu and Y. Gao (2020), 'Decomposition analysis of decoupling freight transport from economic growth in China', *Transportation Research. D: Transport and Environment*, 78, 102201.

5
Land use and transport

Bert van Wee

5.1   INTRODUCTION

As explained in Chapter 2 people travel because they want to carry out activities such as living, working, shopping and visiting friends and relatives at different locations. Land-use patterns therefore would seem to have a potentially large impact on transport. After decades of scientific and policy debate, there is still no consensus about the impact of land use on travel behaviour, but the meta-analyses of the quantitative impacts of land-use variables of Ewing and Cervero (2010) is generally accepted to summarize the state of knowledge. Still, important debates remain, a first topic being the role of residential self-selection, and another topic being the possible change in attitudes of people, due to the exposure to the built environment (see below).

Note that land use (and infrastructure) has a long-term impact on travel behaviour. Once a residential area is designed and built, it will be very hard to change, for example, densities (e.g. dwellings per square kilometre), or locations of shops and services. So, if 'wrong' choices are made, these will be difficult to 'repair', and the impacts on travel behaviour will be long-lasting. On the other hand, it will take several years before the impacts of land use on travel behaviour are fully materialized. A mismatch between preferences of households and the characteristics of their residential areas may be long-lasting, and may only disappear after households relocate.

The purpose of this chapter is:

1. to discuss the theory explaining the potential impacts of land use on travel behaviour;
2. to give an overview of research findings; and
3. to discuss the pros and cons of the effectiveness of land-use policies.

The chapter is limited to passenger transport, because much more is known about the impact of land use on passenger transport than on goods transport.

Section 5.2 examines the impact of land use on travel behaviour from the perspective of Chapter 2 (especially Figure 2.1). Section 5.3 explains from a theoretical perspective why land use, at least theoretically, affects travel behaviour. Section 5.4 gives examples of studies of land-use impacts on transport. Section 5.5 discusses reasons for the differences in conclusions between the studies. Section 5.6 discusses the evaluation of the impact of land use on travel behaviour in general, and is followed by section 5.7, which goes into the trade-off between environmental versus accessibility benefits of land-use concepts in more depth. Finally, section 5.8 summarizes the most important conclusions.[1]

5.2   A CONCEPTUAL MODEL FOR TRENDS IN PASSENGER TRANSPORT – THE LINK WITH CHAPTER 2

As expressed in Chapter 2, given the overall population size and demographic characteristics, the total volume of passenger transport and the split between transport modes depend on the locations of human activities, the needs, wants, desires and preferences of people and the transport resistance (generalized transport costs). Locations include activities such as living, working, shopping, recreation and education. The needs and desires of people are related to socio-economic, cultural and personal factors. Income, age, education level and household characteristics are important socio-economic variables (see Chapter 3). Cultural factors, for example, (partly) explain why in some cultures cycling is 'uncool', whereas in others it is very common. Personal factors relate to attitudes and people's preferences (regardless of variables such as age and income; see Chapter 3). Transport resistance depends on monetary factors, travel times, comfort and the reliability of all the options (see Chapter 6). The top of Figure 2.1 illustrates the relationships between these determinant categories. The current situation reflects a kind of continuously changing equilibrium (or maybe a better term is 'disequilibrium'). This is because new changes occur in advance of the long-term equilibrium actually coming about.

5.3   WHY SHOULD AND HOW CAN LAND USE AFFECT TRAVEL BEHAVIOUR?

This section explains why theoretically land-use related determinants can affect travel behaviour. The general theoretical underpinnings are discussed, and this is followed by a summary of the most often mentioned land-use determinants: density, mixed land use (also labelled as 'diversity'), neighbourhood design and distance of origins and destinations to public transport modes, such as railway stations. Subsection 5.3.3 explores the relationships between land-use variables, other variables and travel behaviour. An overview of the literature on empirical findings related to the theoretical underpinnings is given in section 5.4.

5.3.1   The Potential Impacts of Land Use on Travel Behaviour: The Theory of Utilitarian Travel Demand

The theoretical foundation for the impact of land use on travel behaviour can be found in the theory of utilitarian travel demand (see handbooks on transport economics, e.g., Button, 2010; see also Chapter 3). This theory postulates that the demand for travel does not derive its utility from the trip itself, but originates rather from the need to reach the locations where activities take place, such as the dwelling, the workplace, and services and facilities. So, from this perspective of utility, travel is seen as 'derived demand'.[2] The demand for travel depends, on the one hand, on the utility of the activity and, on the other, on the (aggregate) costs to reach that destination. These aggregate costs, often labelled as the generalized transport costs (GTC) (the individual's valuation of the time, money and effort needed to cover the distance; see Chapter 6), are determined by characteristics of the transport system and by the spatial structure, such as the distribution of activities over space (see Chapter 2). So according to this theory the locations of activity, in combination with the utility of the activities at those locations and the characteristics of the transport system, have a strong impact on people's travel behaviour. The importance of location of origins and potential destinations for travel behaviour is reflected in the so-called traditional four-step model (see Chapter 16) and was recognized more than half a century ago (Mitchell and Rapkin, 1954).

5.3.2 Key Land-Use Variables and Their Impact on Travel Behaviour

The key land-use variables influencing travel behaviour are often labelled by 5 Ds (Density, Diversity, Design, Destination accessibility, Distance to transit), as proposed by (amongst others) Cervero in many publications. Below I discuss these. One can debate if the best approach to discuss the impact of land use on travel behaviour is the common 5Ds approach. Handy (2018) argues that it is better to depart from accessibility and its impact on travel behaviour, for several reasons. Some important reasons are first that all Ds influence accessibility, that the terminology is confusing, and that several of the Ds mutually interact so that synergy effects can occur, and that the stand-alone impact of the Ds on travel behaviour becomes less relevant. We nevertheless depart from the 5 Ds firstly because this is common practice in almost all research in the area, and secondly because departing from accessibility would not allow us to disentangle the impact of the land-use system on travel behaviour from that of the transport system (and maybe even the needs and desires of people). Such an approach would conflict our conceptual model of Chapter 2.

Density

Densities refer to the number of opportunities per square kilometre (or acre or any other surface indicator), such as dwellings, households, people and jobs. Gross densities relate to overall available space, net densities to the space that is (or can be) developed (excluding roads, open space, water, etc.). A fundamental question here is: why should density influence travel behaviour? Let us assume two equal land-use scenarios, but with densities in scenario A higher than those in scenario B. Other factors such as average travel speeds for all modes and the type of dwellings, households, jobs, shops and so on are equal. Travel for almost all modes costs money. Other factors being equal, people will prefer to travel less to save money. And travel also costs time. Many studies have shown that people value travel time negatively (see, for example, Wardman, 1998; Gunn, 2001; see also Chapter 6). Other factors being constant, people in scenario A, where density is greater, will travel less than in scenario B: people can reach the same locations for their activities while travelling fewer kilometres and so save time and money. In addition, because of the shorter distances more destinations can be reached through active modes (walking, cycling), theoretically resulting in a shift from car to active modes of transport.

Of course, other factors do not remain constant. For example, owing to the higher densities people can get to more activities at the same time. At least part of the potentially saved travel time can be compensated if people choose a more remote destination: the additional utility for reaching a more remote destination may be greater than the disutility of additional travel (see also section 5.7). Nevertheless, higher densities offer the possibility of travelling less. In order to obtain the benefits from higher densities, housing, offices and other locations should be built in higher densities.

It is important to notice that the spatial scale at which densities occur matters. If, for example, a new residential area of 1000 inhabitants with high densities is built in a region with low densities outside the new residential area, travel behaviour will hardly be affected because almost all destinations will be outside the neighbourhood. And people in that residential area will still have only a few opportunities within reach for a given time (or GTC) budget.

Mixed land use

This factor focuses on the level of mixing of several categories of land use, such as dwellings, workplaces (firms), shops, schools and medical services.

Let us again assume two scenarios for a town. In scenario A all shops, schools and other services are located in the centre of town. In scenario B some of the shops, schools and other services are spread across town throughout all the neighbourhoods. The average distance from all dwellings to the nearest services is much smaller in scenario B than in scenario A. Keeping mode choice constant, the smaller distances will result in fewer passenger and vehicle kilometres. There is also an effect on modal choice, as active modes will be relatively more attractive because of the shorter distances.

Again, part of the initial effect might be lost. In the centre, for instance, there might be relatively fewer parking places, the distances from these parking places to the shops and services might be greater, and, unlike in the neighbourhoods, there might be paid parking. So, although distances from dwellings to the services are greater, the share of the car might be lower in scenario A than in scenario B. Nevertheless, potentially mixed land use can influence travel behaviour.

Neighbourhood design

Neighbourhood design is related to land use at the lowest scale, starting from the dwellings or buildings and linked to the direct vicinity of the dwellings. Design quality might be important for travel behaviour (Marshall and Banister, 2000; Boddy, 2007; Liu et al., 2021). For example, if at the dwelling the place where bicycles are stored is near the road, the bicycles' share might be larger compared to dwellings where the bicycle storage facilities are at the back. If the car can be parked near the dwelling, on one's own property or in a public parking place near the dwelling, car use will be more attractive than where there are central parking places further away from dwellings. An attractive environment might stimulate people to walk or cycle. This attractiveness relates to allocation of space for several land-use categories, the architecture of the built environment and the presence of features such as parks and trees. Road infrastructure design may also be of relevance. For example, if there are attractive pavements and cycle lanes the share of active modes may be larger than if there are no or less attractive facilities for active modes.

Distance to public transport connections

The distance to railway stations may have an impact on modal choice as (differences in) travel times by car and train are very important. For public transport, total travel time contains both the 'in vehicle' (in train) time and the access and egress time (e.g. from home to the station by bus or bike or walking, and from the station to the office by walking or taking local public transport). If more dwellings and opportunities (e.g. jobs) are located near railway stations, access and egress times are shorter for a larger number of trips, resulting in a higher share for the train as compared to the car. In this way, distance and connections to railway stations may result in a higher share for public transport.

Destination access

The variables discussed so far focus on the origin of the trips, more specifically on the residential area. But, of course also the destination matters. If the destination is close to a railway station, the likelihood that people travel by train is higher compared to if it is not. And if parking near the destination is not easy or even impossible, such as in many inner cities, people are less inclined to travel by car.

Interactions between determinants

The determinants (5 Ds) can interact. For example, the effect of building in higher densities may have an additional impact on mode choice if the areas are located near railway stations. Then there is an additional effect on modal choice which was not mentioned in the section above on densities. And if the area around a railway station is attractive it can encourage more people to take the train, increasing the modal shift potential of building in higher densities.

5.3.3 Relationships Between Land-Use Variables, Other Variables and Travel Behaviour

Very old studies sometimes directly investigated correlations between land-use variables and travel behaviour variables, ignoring other variables (see Figure 5.1). Since the late 1980s, studies into the impact of land use on travel behaviour have included socio-economic and demographic variables, as visualized in Figure 5.2 (see Chapter 3 for the general impact of socio-economic and demographic variables). Figure 5.2 shows that travel behaviour is influenced not only by land-use variables but also by socio-economic and demographic variables, such as income, age, education level and household variables. The studies find lower impacts of land-use variables on travel behaviour variables, as part of the impact is accounted for by the socio-economic and demographic variables. For example, people with higher incomes can afford to live in relatively expensive houses in lower-density residential areas. The impact of densities on travel behaviour would be overestimated if the difference in income levels was ignored.

Figure 5.1   Relationships between land-use variables and demographic variables and travel behaviour – the traditional approach

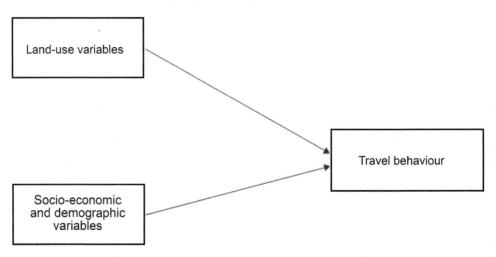

Figure 5.2   Relationships between land-use variables, socio-economic and demographic variables, and travel behaviour

Most recently, three more (often interrelated) changes have been made that are not included in Figure 5.2. Firstly, researchers have added more people and household variables not covered by socio-economic and demographic variables. These variables relate to attitudes, lifestyles and preferences for modes. Such variables express the possibility that people with the same socio-economic and demographic variables can still differ. Such attitudes, lifestyles and preferences relate to the needs of people, as explained in Chapter 3. For example, some people may have a more pro-environmental attitude and lifestyle, or a more culture-oriented lifestyle as opposed to a more material lifestyle, or people might simply prefer, more than others, to travel by car ('car lovers'), public transport ('public transport lovers') or in some countries by active modes. Studies that include such variables generally find a decrease in the impact of land-use variables compared to studies that do not include such variables. The second change is that researchers have recognized that people self-select themselves to locate in specific residential areas. Mokhtarian and Cao (2008: 205), based on Litman (2005), state that self-selection refers to 'the tendency of people to choose locations based on their travel abilities, needs and preferences'. Self-selection can then result from 'traditional' variables such as income but also from attitudes and lifestyles or preferences for modes. Thirdly, and partly related to the phenomenon of residential self-selection, researchers have changed the model structure of variable categories by explicitly adding that socio-economic and demographic variables, and variables related to attitudes, lifestyles and preferences for modes have an impact on residential choice. The more complex relationships between the categories of variables that result can be estimated by so-called structural equation models (SEM models). Figure 5.3 conceptualizes the three changes that result from including additional variables and the more complex model structure.

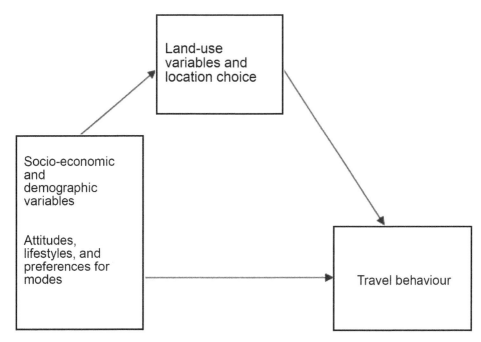

Figure 5.3   Relationships between land-use variables and location choice, socio-economic and demographic variables, attitude variables and travel behaviour – the current approach

The debates about the causal structure of (clusters of) variables still continues, and more advanced models are proposed (see, for example Cao et al., 2009 and Heinen et al., 2018). A topic that has been discussed frequently is the question about whether attitudes are stable or not *see* for example Kroesen et al. (2017), who show that the built environment can indeed change attitudes, or see van Wee et al. (2019) explaining the complex mechanisms via which attitudes can change in general. Another discussion relates to the question if the impact of land-use variables on travel behaviour is linear or not and if threshold values for such variables exist (e.g., Tu et al., 2021). At the time of writing this chapter, 2022, the debates were not at all finished.

5.4   THE IMPACT OF LAND USE ON TRANSPORT – A SHORT OVERVIEW OF THE LITERATURE

The aim of this section is not to give an extensive review but to summarize some empirical examples of the theory as discussed in section 5.3. I first give examples of studies into the impact of densities, mixed use, neighbourhood design and distance to public transport connections, followed by studies that add attitude, lifestyle and preference of modes variables and the use of SEM models.

5.4.1   Densities

One of the most frequently cited studies on the impact of densities are the study by Newman and Kenworthy (1988, 1999; see also Kenworthy and Laube, 1999), who concluded that energy use for travel per inhabitant is negatively related to urban density. Ewing and Cervero (2010) give an overview on the quantitative impacts of densities on vehicle miles travelled, concluding that the elasticity of local density for vehicle miles travelled and vehicle trips is around -0.05. In other words: a 1 per cent in increase of local densities results in a 0.05 per cent decrease in vehicle miles travelled and vehicle trips.

Most studies in the area of land use (or the built environment) on travel behaviour in general, and also with respect to the impact of densities, focus on OECD countries, but increasingly studies from other countries have been published. For example, Ahmadipour et al. (2021) present results from Tehran, Iran, confirming the impact of densities and mixed use on travel behaviour of earlier studies.

5.4.2   Mixed Use

The impact of mixed use on travel behaviour is often studied together with other land-use characteristics. Ewing and Cervero (2010) conclude that a 1 per cent increase in diversity (mixing uses) results in a decrease of -0.03 per cent in vehicle trips, and a 0.05 per cent decrease in vehicle miles travelled.

5.4.3   Neighbourhood Design

Manaugh and El-Geneidy (2011) show for Montreal that, if walkability of a neighbourhood is high, people make significantly more walking trips for most non-work purposes. Pan et al. (2009) found that, in the pedestrian- and cyclist-friendly neighbourhoods in Shanghai, residents travel shorter distances than in other neighbourhoods, and that pedestrian- and cyclist-friendly urban form makes the non-motorized modes feasible options. Recent studies sometimes also include bike sharing infrastructure. For example, Shaer et al. (2021) show that local bike sharing infrastructure influences cycling levels in Tehran.

5.4.4   Distance to Public Transport Connections, Destination Accessibility

Distances to public transport connections relate to both the origin and the destination of trips. An important category of destinations is work locations, including offices. Brons et al. (2009) show that access to railway stations contributes to travel by train. They conclude that expanding access services to the railway station can increase the mode share of rail. Cervero (2006: 53) emphasizes the importance of both ends of a trip: concentrating 'housing near rail stops will do little to lure commuters to trains and buses unless the other end of the trip – the workplace – is similarly convenient to and conducive to using transit'.

5.4.5   Attitudes, Lifestyles and Preferences for Modes, Residential Self-Selection and SEM Models

One of the first studies that included attitude variables was the study by Kitamura et al. (1997). They studied travel behaviour of people living in five neighbourhoods in the San Francisco Bay area, including socio-economic and demographic variables, land-use variables and 39 attitudinal variables. They found that attitudinal variables explained the highest proportion of the variation in the data *see* Cao et al. (2009) for an overview of empirical studies in the area of residential self-selection; see Mokhtarian and Cao (2008) for an overview of methodologies of studies in the area of residential self-selection, in both bases up to around 2007–08. Since then numerous studies have been published. For example, Faber et al. (2021) show that travel-related reasons (defined as 'the extent to which a travel preference actually affected the final decision to live in a certain neighbourhood', p.121), more than general travel mode attitudes, influence location choices of households. In addition, and in line with the study of Kroesen et al. (2017) referred to above, they conclude that attitudes and travel-related reasons influence residential choice and travel behaviour, but also vice versa.

   Note that self-selection is not limited to residential self-selection but may also occur with respect to work location choice or the choice of other destinations (van Wee, 2009). Studies that include land-use variables and socio-economic and demographic variables, together with variables related to attitudes, lifestyles and preferences for modes, residential self-selection and travel behaviour, generally use SEM models to disentangle the relationships between variables.

   An overall conclusion of such studies is that travel behaviour results from a complex interplay of all these variables, as conceptualized by Figure 5.3. The impact of land-use variables on travel behaviour can easily be overestimated if such complex relationships are overlooked. An important question then becomes what the impact of overestimation would be. Should the conclusion be that land-use policies that encourage people to travel by public transport or active modes or over shorter distances do not make sense, or at least make less sense than often assumed? Some people do not agree with this conclusion. For example, Næss (2014) even speaks about 'tempest in a teapot': he argues that, even if attitudes of people explain residential choice as well as travel preferences, people will only act according to their preferences if their residential area allows them to do so. Secondly, he argues that car ownership, and to some extent also transport attitudes, is influenced by the characteristics of the residential locations.

A third reason is provided by Schwanen and Mokhtarian (2005), namely that some people face a lack of congruence between physical neighbourhood structure and their preferences. One could argue that, for quality-of-life reasons, reducing such a lack of congruence matters.

5.5   WHY ARE THE CONCLUSIONS DIFFERENT?

Why do researchers find different results with respect to the possible impact of land use on transport? There are several reasons for this and some of them will be presented in this section.

5.5.1   The Research Method

A major source of differences as found between studies relates to research methods. Section 5.4 has already explained the importance of including other variables that have an impact on travel behaviour, including the importance of phenomena such as residential self-selection and ensuring an adequate structure between variables. Generally speaking, Handy (1996) concludes that more advanced research methods have generally found smaller and less significant effects of land use on travel behaviour.

Next, I discuss more reasons why study results differ, some of them also being methodological reasons.

5.5.2   The Level of Difference in Crucial Factors

One of the causes for different results from research is that the study areas sometimes do not really differ with respect to the most important land-use factors that influence transport, such as densities and the level of mixed land use. Small differences between areas with respect to important land-use factors of course result in small differences in travel behaviour.

5.5.3   The Geographical Scale

An often-neglected aspect in the discussion is the geographical scale. Firstly, the definitions or indicators for densities differ between studies (see subsection 5.3.2, the remark on gross versus net densities). Secondly, the size of the area at which forms of mixed use or densities occur matters (see subsection 5.3.2). Thirdly, several scales can be distinguished, including the direct surroundings of the dwellings, the neighbourhood, the town or city, the region, the part of a country, the whole country and even the international scale. The scale of research may affect the results. For example, Newman and Kenworthy (1988, 1999) focus on large cities. In several countries such as Denmark or Belgium, such cities do not exist. Therefore, it is not possible to conclude beforehand that building in high-density locations in such countries will result in lower energy use for transportation equivalent to the results found by Newman and Kenworthy.

5.5.4 The Time Horizon

Another reason may be the time horizon included. It is generally recognized in academic literature that, after changes in determinants for travel behaviour, people will not change their behaviour instantaneously. This comment relates not only to changes in land use but also to changes in infrastructure and prices. The relevance of how much time has passed since changes took place and when the empirical research is undertaken has implications for the findings. Suppose a new railway station is built in or near a residential area or office park. Many people might not immediately change their travel behaviour (in this example, their mode choice) but people might move from the residential area and new households that move to the dwellings that become available might be more inclined to travel by train. As explained above, people self-select themselves into residential areas based on their attitudes toward travel and preferences for modes. As a result, the impact of the new railway station will probably increase over time.

5.5.5 Differences Between Countries

Differences between countries (and even within countries, regions) complicate the transferability of results. Firstly, concepts play an important role in the discussion on the impact of land use on transport. Let us assume the compact city. What is considered to be a low-density residential area in many European regions and countries may be an example of compact building in the USA. In other words, what people consider as compact will differ between regions and countries.

There are other reasons that make the translation of land-use effects from one country to another risky. Examples relate to the role of different modes in the transport system but also to cultural differences. In Denmark and the Netherlands, and since recently also in several other cities and regions worldwide, the bicycle plays an important role in the transport system. For short distances, the bike may compete with the car or local public transport. But in many other countries, cities and regions the role of the bike is limited or absent. The role of the public transport system also varies from country to country. Such differences may result in other effects of the same land-use concepts. For example, as rail transport is a minor form of passenger travel in the US, results from empirical research there on the impacts of distances to and from stations would have little relevance to Europe, where levels of rail use are much higher, and vice versa.

Cultural differences may also be of importance, not only between, but even within, countries. As already explained in section 5.2, in some cultures cycling is not at all 'sexy', whereas in others such cultural barriers do not exist.

5.5.6 Indirect Effects

Figure 2.1 shows that land use may have a direct impact on passenger travel, but it also shows the existence of several indirect effects. These effects may be very complex – see all the arrows in Figure 2.1. It is very complicated to distinguish all the kinds of direct and indirect effects quantitatively.

5.5.7   The Impact of Policy

Policy can also affect land-use patterns. The travel behaviour of people living in a high-density, public-transport-oriented city such as Tokyo may differ strongly from the travel behaviour of people living in a low-density, car-oriented city such as Los Angeles. But this does not mean that it will be easy to implement Tokyo's urbanization patterns and infrastructure systems in the USA. So, even if land use has an impact on travel behaviour, it does not mean that it is easy to use land-use policy as an instrument to influence travel behaviour. The effect of land-use policies may therefore be limited compared to the effect of land use in general. Generally speaking, researchers who assume relatively strong impacts of policy on land use are more optimistic about possibilities to influence travel behaviour by land-use planning than those who have not made this assumption (Anderson et al., 1996).

To summarize, there are many reasons for different researchers and policy-makers to draw different conclusions with respect to the impact of land use on travel behaviour. Probably methodological reasons dominate. A systematic analysis of possible causes for differences will be needed to discover these reasons.

5.6   EVALUATING THE IMPACT OF LAND USE ON TRAVEL BEHAVIOUR: INDICATORS AND EVALUATION METHODS

Several of the more advanced studies have found significant impacts of land-use variables on travel behaviour, even though there is no consensus on this impact (Cao et al., 2009). Here, and in line with for example Ewing and Cervero (2010), it is assumed that there is enough empirical evidence to conclude that land-use characteristics as discussed above have an impact on travel behaviour. And several options for policy-making exist, such as building in higher densities, mixing land use, building in high densities near railway stations, and design options for walking- and cycling-friendly neighbourhoods. Would the conclusion then be that policy-makers should be advised to base land-use planning only on impacts on travel behaviour, or even only on impacts on car use? Probably not, as choices with respect to land-use policies should be made considering all relevant aspects, including travel behaviour but also impacts. This section will first discuss these impacts, followed by a discussion on how to evaluate land-use alternatives using these criteria.

5.6.1   Indicators

Most research (and policy documents) on the impact of land use on travel behaviour places the topic in an environmental context: land use could improve the environment by reducing car use and its negative impacts. Research generally uses the following indicators to express this impact: (1) kilometres (vehicles, passengers), mostly by mode, often by trip purpose; and (2) the number of trips, mostly by mode, often by trip purpose. Furthermore, some studies also focus on trip distances. Only a small minority of studies provide environmental indicators, such as CO_2 and NO_x emissions. These indicators are relevant but very often are not produced on a comprehensive scale. Additional (categories of) indicators are now discussed. It should be noted that some of the suggestions are related or even overlap. The first three suggestions are related to the positive aspects of travel, aspects that are very often neglected in transport discussions in general and in discussions on the impact of land use on transport.

Accessibility

Many studies do not use indicators that express the quality of the land-use and infrastructure system: to what extent does this system enable us to travel between locations we want to visit and thereby participate in the activities desired? Therefore additional accessibility indicators could be used, including those used in geography (potential accessibility, time–space related accessibility indicators), utility-based indicators (see Geurs and van Wee, 2004, for a literature review of accessibility indicators) and travel time indicators (e.g. Schwanen et al., 2002). So far the use of such indicators has been limited, but Handy (2020) hypothesises that this might change in the future *see* section 5.7 for further discussion.

The option value

Current evaluations focus on user benefits only, but if non-user benefits are relevant, then the option value may be important. The option value in the context of land use and transport can be described as an individual's valuation of the opportunity to be able to use a particular transport mode or piece of infrastructure in the future that is not being used in the present, or the option to have access to a specific destination that is currently not visited. For example, car owners may value the ability to use a public transport service when they cannot make use of the car, for example owing to unavailability or a breakdown, bad weather, increases in fuel prices or other car costs, or the loss of the ability to operate a car. Or a person may value having access to shops she does not currently visit (see Geurs et al., 2006 and Bondemark et al., 2021) for empirical studies of option values).

The consumer surplus

The consumer surplus plays an important role in evaluations (including cost–benefit analyses – CBAs) of infrastructure projects. The consumer surplus is the difference between the market price of a product or service and the value for a consumer. For example, if a consumer is willing to pay 50 euros for a book but the price is 20 euros, the consumer's surplus is 30 euros. Some trips probably have a very high consumer surplus. For example, if one wants to visit a relative in hospital, the visit may be worth much more than the costs of travel. Let us assume two scenarios: scenario A with the current pattern of hospitals and scenario B with many fewer hospitals (e.g. in order to profit from scale effects). In scenario A, visiting a relative in the hospital is possible after a ten-minute cycling trip, whereas in scenario B a car trip of half an hour is needed. Assuming the visiting frequency is the same in both scenarios, the consumer surplus of scenario A is much larger than that of scenario B. The difference is the GTC of the car trip in scenario B minus the GTC of the bicycle trip in scenario A (costs include both monetary and non-monetary costs such as travel time).

Safety

Safety impacts of land-use and transport alternatives may differ. If they do, such impacts should be included in the *ex ante* evaluation of these alternatives.

Health impacts due to exercise

If people travelled more by active modes, this would have not only environmental and safety advantages but also health advantages (see Chapter 12).

Environmental impacts

If environmental impacts are included, it is usually done by listing emissions levels. However, for local air pollution, exposure is very important. The same amount of kilograms of emissions may have different exposure impacts. It is highly relevant if pollutants are emitted on a road with many people (living, working, carrying out recreational activities) in its vicinity as opposed to a road in an agricultural area (see Chapter 10). Noise effects are also highly dependent on the direct vicinity of a road or railway. The literature hardly pays attention to wider liveability effects, such as the impacts resulting from moving and parked vehicles, regardless of their exhaust and noise emissions (such as the fact that in many places children cannot play on the streets anymore) (see Chapter 2), but such impacts are also relevant for the evaluation of land-use policies.

Valuation by the people

Much is known about residential choice preferences (see, for example, Huang et al., 2014). Many people prefer living in spacious homes on spacious plots. On the other hand, building in low densities results in less accessibility to opportunities and to the public transport system. Building in low densities also results in a larger space claim on residential areas and thus in less green space between cities and towns. How do people value such items? We hardly know. But people's opinions are relevant for an overall view of the pros and cons of land-use scenarios.

We probably know even less about what people think of the job location. What do people prefer – a job location on the edge of town, near a motorway or in the inner city near a railway station? Probably different groups of people have different preferences. Such valuations of people could be relevant for the *ex ante* evaluation of land-use concepts.

Financial aspects

The relevant factors here include the costs of construction, maintenance and exploitation of land-use and transport alternatives. We know more about the financial aspects of the transport system, in general, and more about infrastructure costs, in particular, than we know about costs of land-use alternatives. The impact on GDP (and unemployment) is also relevant. The (valuation of) indirect effects of land-use and transport alternatives (such as effects on the labour and housing market) are much more difficult to estimate than the direct effects (see SACTRA, 1999, or Banister and Berechman, 2000, for a discussion of the indirect effects of infrastructure). A distinction should be made between costs for society as a whole, for the government and for the users or consumers.

Robustness

Another issue is the robustness of the land-use and transport system. Here I use the term 'robustness'; other terms often being used for more or less the same concept are 'flexibility', 'reliability', 'resilience', 'vulnerability' (about the opposite of robustness) and 'substitutability': the last concept can be defined as 'the extent to which the preferred travel alternative can be substituted by other initially less preferred alternatives' (van Wee et al., 2019: 1). Robustness plays a role at several terms, ranging from the short term of being able to change routes while travelling, for example because of a road block, to long-term robustness playing a role over several decades. For the long term questions are raised about: how vulnerable are we to, for example, an expected or unexpected limitation on energy availability for transport? Energy limitations may be the result of political instability in oil-producing countries, much higher oil prices (for example, due to 'peak oil'; see Chapter 10) or stringent environmental (climate) policies. Preferences of consumers and firms might also differ in the future. In addition, what will happen if sustainably produced energy becomes available at reasonable prices? The question then will change from 'How can land use contribute to reducing transport problems?' to 'How can land use enable us to perform activities in different places under different conditions?' This changing role is important not only for land use but also for the role of public transport and active modes, and for information and communication technology (ICT). Probably land-use transport strategies that are positively valued with respect to travel behaviour impacts will be robust. Such strategies include compact building, mixed land use and availability of good-quality public transport.

Fairness

In addition to the scores of candidate policies on the criteria discussed above, fairness is an upcoming topic in both research and policy-making (see Chapter 15). Distribution effects play an important role in fairness discussions, dominant examples being distributions across population groups by income or region.

5.6.2   Evaluation Methods

The use of a multi-criteria analysis (MCA) or a CBA for land-use scenarios is generally recommended (see Chapter 15). A lot is known about the valuations of reductions in travel time and benefits of additional travel. Much is also known about people's willingness to pay for noise reductions or risk reductions. However, choosing price tags (CBA) or weight factors (MCA) for several other output indicators is partly a political choice. This includes aspects like the value of CO_2 emissions reduction, nature conservation and 'spatial quality'. Researchers can assist policy-makers who have to weight components, and they can advise on methods, carry out research and use the results of other studies. For this reason, combining a CBA and an MCA provides an interesting basis for policy-making. For a further discussion on evaluation methods, see Chapter 15.

5.7   EVALUATING THE IMPACT OF LAND USE ON TRAVEL BEHAVIOUR: THE ENVIRONMENT VERSUS ACCESSIBILITY

As explained above, research into the area of land use and transport has generally placed itself in the context of environmental gains: land use could contribute to lower levels of car use, and an increase in the use of active modes and public transport. However, as explained above, several researchers have found only limited impacts of land use on travel behaviour. Some of them have concluded that related policies therefore make no sense. In line with insights from economics, it can be argued that land use potentially could decrease motorized mobility (including car use), but in practice people may not travel less using motorized modes. Then there must be accessibility gains that at least equal the potential gains in savings of GTC. Therefore, the general way of evaluating land-use concepts on (only) travel behaviour and environmental gains is insufficient, and accessibility benefits should be added. Van Wee (2011: 1530) expands on this proposition: 'If the potential (theoretically possible) impact of land use on travel behaviour does not occur in practice, there must be accessibility benefits for travellers, that they value at least as highly as the benefits of the potential decreases in Generalized Transport Costs.'

I define accessibility benefits as all the benefits that provide utility to travellers, related to the activities they carry out at different locations (working, shopping, visiting friends, etc.). For the net benefits these benefits should be corrected for the disutility of travel (GTC; see section 5.3 and Chapter 6).

For economists and others with a background in utility-based discrete choice theory, the proposition is not at all surprising, as it formulates the economic approach to accessibility.

Below, the proposition is explained using a simple example. Suppose we could 'shrink' a certain region to 25 per cent of its original size. I assume a closed region (no external trips). In addition, I assume that all other determinants remain constant, in particular the locations of activities. In this case, trip distances would be reduced by 50 per cent (surface area expands quadratically with an increase in radius). I assume all trips are made by car. If there were no behavioural changes other than distance reductions, people could participate in the same activities by travelling only half of the kilometres and would need only half of the original travel time. More generally, GTC would be reduced by 50 per cent. But, according to the theory of constant travel time budgets (TTB) – see Chapter 5 – because people trade-off the benefits of activities and the disutility (GTC) of travel, it can be expected that people will choose more remote destinations. They could, for example, visit another, more remote supermarket because it is cheaper or offers more products. Or they could choose another job at a greater distance from their home because it pays better, is more challenging or offers more career prospects. Note that, according to the theory of constant TTB, not all people would change their behaviour, and certainly not everyone would travel as many kilometres as before the 'shrink'; the TTB is about averages over a large group. Some people might not change jobs at all, but others might choose a job at a distance four times the commuting distance after the shrink. Now let us assume that at the level of all people who travel in the region the potential decrease in travel times and distances completely disappears because of behavioural changes.

In that case no effects of land use would be found even though there must be accessibility benefits with a value that at least equals the potential savings of GTC. If not, people would take advantage of the decrease of GTC by 50 per cent. It is also likely that there will be greater benefits from choosing the more remote destinations. Again, please note that this insight is not new for economists; it applies to all goods and services with elastic demand.

Of course, reality is more complex than our example. People can adapt their behaviour in more respects, such as a mode change or a change in trip frequencies. A shrinkage, as in our example, might lead to a decrease in average travel speeds due to higher densities on the road network and parking capacity problems. These complexities change the potential reduction of GTC due to the 'shrink' but do not change the principle that the behavioural changes after the shrink, other than simply reducing travel distance and time, must have benefits that at least equal the value of the benefits of the potential reduction of GTC.

The same line of reasoning applies for mixed use or a reduction in distances to public transport nodal points: thanks to the land-use changes a potential reduction in GTC is possible owing to distance reduction and/or mode change, and that is valued positively. If, in practice, people did not travel less (but travelled to destinations further away) there must be accessibility benefits that the travellers value at least as much as the benefits that would be possible from the reduction of GTC.

To conclude, if research showed that land-use concepts that allow for a reduction in GTC would not result in people really reducing their GTC, it is not correct to reject such concepts because then significant accessibility effects occur.

5.8   CONCLUSIONS AND DISCUSSION

These are the most important conclusions of this chapter:

1. The theoretical foundation for the impact of land use on travel behaviour can be found in the theory of utilitarian travel demand. This theory postulates that the demand for travel does not derive its utility from the trip itself, but rather it originates from the need to reach the locations of activities.
2. The land-use related determinants that have an impact on travel behaviour that are most often mentioned in the literature are density, mixed land use, neighbourhood design, distance of origins and destinations to public transport nodes such as railway stations, and destination accessibility.
3. Travel behaviour results from a complex interplay of land-use variables, socio-economic and demographic variables, variables related to attitudes, lifestyles and preferences for modes, and residential self-selection. The impact of land-use variables on travel behaviour can easily be overestimated if such complex relationships are overlooked.
4. Empirical studies into the impact of land use on travel behaviour often find different and even contradicting results, methodological reasons probably being the most important cause of these differences.
5. Land-use concepts are often promoted because of policy reasons, environmental reasons being the most mentioned. However, most studies focus only on impacts of land use on travel behaviour. To make such studies more relevant for policy, additional output

variables are relevant. These include environmental impacts, accessibility impacts, the option value, the consumers' surplus, safety and health impacts, the valuation of land-use concepts by people, financial aspects, long-term robustness of the land-use and transport system, and fairness.

6. If most effects of land-use concepts can be quantified and expressed in monetary terms, a CBA could be an attractive method to evaluate such concepts *ex ante*. If important effects are difficult to quantify or express in monetary terms, combining a CBA and an MCA provides an interesting basis for such evaluation.

7. If the potential (theoretically possible) impact of land use on travel behaviour does not occur in practice, there must be accessibility benefits for travellers that they value at least as highly as those of potential decreases in GTC.

NOTES

1. Sections 5.3 to 5.6 are partly based on van Wee (2002). Section 5.7 is based on van Wee (2011).
2. Note that not all travel is derived (see Mokhtarian and Salomon, 2001, and Chapters 2 and 3 in this volume).

REFERENCES

Ahmadipour, F., A.R. Mamdoohi and A. Wulf-Holger (2021), 'Impact of built environment on walking in the case of Tehran, Iran', *Journal of Transport and Health*, 22, 101083.
Anderson, W.P., P.S. Kanaroglou and E.J. Miller (1996), 'Urban form, energy and the environment: a review of issues, evidence and policy', *Urban Studies*, 33 (1), 7–35.
Banister, D. and J. Berechman (2000), Transport Investment and Economic Development, London: University College London Press.
Boddy, M. (2007), 'Designer neighbourhoods: new-build residential development in nonmetropolitan UK cities – the case of Bristol', *Environment and Planning A*, 39 (1), 86–105.
Bondemark, A., E. Johansson and F. Kopsch (2021), 'Accessibility and uncertainty: An empirical analysis of option value in transport', *Journal of Transport and Land Use*, 14 (1), 463–77.
Brons, M., M. Givoni and P. Rietveld (2009), 'Access to railway stations and its potential in increasing rail use', *Transportation Research Part A*, 43 (2), 136–49.
Button, K.J. (2010), *Transport Economics*, 3rd edition, Cheltenham, UK and Northampton, MA, USA: Edward Elgar.
Cao, X., P.L. Mokhtarian and S. Handy (2009), 'Examining the impact of residential self-selection on travel behavior: a focus on empirical findings', *Transport Reviews*, 29 (3), 359–95.
Cervero, R. (2006), 'Office Development, Rail Transit, and Commuting Choices', *Journal of Public Transportation*, 9(5), 41–55.
Ewing, R. and R. Cervero (2010), Travel and the built environment. *Journal of the American Planning Association*, 76 (3), 265–94.
Faber, R., R. Merkies, W. Damen, L. Oirbans, D. Massa, M. Kroesen and E. Molin (2021), 'The role of travel-related reasons for location choice in residential self-selection', *Travel Behaviour and Society*, 25, 120–32.
Geurs, K., R. Haaijer and B. van Wee (2006), 'Option value of public transport: methodology for measurement and case study for regional rail links in the Netherlands', *Transport Reviews*, 26 (5), 613–43.
Geurs, K.T. and B. van Wee (2004), 'Accessibility evaluation of land-use and transport strategies: review and research directions', *Transport Geography*, 12 (2), 127–40.
Gunn, H. (2001), 'Spatial and temporal transferability of relationships between travel demand, trip cost and travel time', *Transportation Research E*, 37 (2–3), 163–89.

Handy, S. (1996), 'Methodologies for exploring the link between urban form and travel behaviour', *Transportation Research D*, 1 (2), 151–65.

Handy, S., (2018), 'Enough with the "D's" Already – Let's Get Back to "A"', *Transfers*, Spring, accessed 23 May 2023 at https://transfersmagazine.org/enough-with-the-ds-already-lets-get-back-to-a/.

Handy, S. (2020), 'Is accessibility an idea whose time has finally come?', *Transportation Research Part D*: 102319.

Heinen, E., B. van Wee, J. Panter, R. Mackett and D. Ogilvie (2018), 'Residential self-selection in quasi-experimental and natural experimental studies: An extended conceptualization of the relationship between the built environment and travel behaviour', *Journal of Transport and Land Use*, 11 (1), 939–59.

Huang, Q., D.C. Parker, T. Filatova and S. Sun (2014), 'A review of urban residential choice models using agent-based modeling', *Environment and Planning B*, 41 (4), 661–89.

Kenworthy, J. and F. Laube (1999), 'A global review of energy use in urban transport systems and its implications for urban transport and land-use policy', *Transportation Quarterly*, 53 (4), 23–48.

Kitamura, R., P.L. Mokhtarian and L. Laidet (1997), 'A micro-analysis of land use and travel in five neighbourhoods in the San Francisco Bay area', *Transportation*, 24 (2), 125–58.

Kroesen, M., S. Handy, and C. Chorus (2017), 'Do attitudes cause behavior or vice versa? An alternative conceptualization of the attitude-behavior relationship in travel behavior modeling', *Transportation Research Part*, 101, 190–202.

Litman, T.A. (2005), 'Land use impacts on transport: how land use factors affect travel behavior', accessed 1 January 2006 at www.vtpi.org/landtravel.pdf.

Liu, L., E.A. Silva and Z. Yang (2021), 'Similar outcomes, different paths: Tracing the relationship between neighborhood-scale built environment and travel behavior using activity-based modelling', *Cities*, 110, 10306.

Manaugh, K. and A. El-Geneidy (2011), 'Validating walkability indices: how do different households respond to the walkability of their neighbourhood?', *Transportation Research Part D*, 16, 309–15.

Marshall, S. and D. Banister (2000), 'Travel reduction strategies: intentions and outcomes', *Transportation Research Part A: Policy and Practice*, 34 (5), 321–38.

Mitchell, R.B. and C. Rapkin (1954), *Urban Traffic: A Function of Land Use*, New York: Columbia University Press.

Mokhtarian, P.L. and X. Cao (2008), 'Examining the impacts of residential self-selection on travel behavior: a focus on methodologies', *Transportation Research Part B*, 42 (3), 204–28.

Mokhtarian, P.L. and I. Salomon (2001), 'How derived is the demand for travel? Some conceptual and measurement considerations', *Transportation Research Part A*, 35 (8), 695–719.

Næss, P. (2014). 'Tempest in a teapot: The exaggerated problem of transport-related residential self-selection as a source of error in empirical studies', *Journal of Transport and Land Use* 7 (3), 57–79.

Newman, P.W.G. and J.R. Kenworthy (1988), 'The transport energy trade-off: fuel-efficient traffic versus fuel-efficient cities', *Transportation Research A*, 22A (3), 163–74.

Newman, P. and J. Kenworthy (1999), *Sustainability and Cities: Overcoming Automobile Dependence*, Washington, DC: Island Press.

Pan, H., Q. Shen and M. Zhang (2009), 'Influence of urban form on travel behaviour in four neighbourhoods of Shanghai', *Urban Studies*, 46 (2), 275–94.

SACTRA (Standing Advisory Committee on Trunk Road Assessment) (1999), *Transport and the Economy*, London: Department of the Environment, Transport and the Regions.

Schwanen, T., M. Dijst, F. Dieleman (2002), 'A microlevel analysis of residential context and travel time', *Environment and Planning A*, 34 (8), 1487–1507.

Schwanen, T. and P.L. Mokhtarian (2005), 'What if you live in the wrong neighborhood? The impact of residential neighborhood type dissonance on distance travelled', *Transportation Research Part D*, 10 (2), 127–51.

Shaer, A., M. Rezaei, B. Moghani Rahimi and F. Shaer (2021), 'Examining the associations between perceived built environment and active travel, before and after the COVID-19 outbreak in Shiraz city, Iran', *Cities*, 115, 103255.

Tu, M., W. Li, O. Orfila, Y. Li and D. Gruyer (2021), 'Exploring nonlinear effects of the built environment on ridesplitting: Evidence from Chengdu', *Transportation Research Part D*, 93, 102776.

van Wee, B. (2002), 'Land use and transport: research and policy challenges', *Transport Geography*, 10 (4), 259–71.

van Wee, B. (2009), 'Self-selection: a key to a better understanding of location choices, travel behaviour and transport externalities?' *Transport Reviews*, 29 (3), 279–92.

van Wee, B. (2011), 'Evaluating the impact of land use on travel behaviour: the environment versus accessibility', *Journal of Transport Geography*, 19 (6), 1530–33.

van Wee, B., J. De Vos and K. Maat (2019), 'Impacts of the built environment and travel behaviour on attitudes: Theories underpinning the reverse causality hypothesis', *Journal of Transport Geography*, 80, 102540.

Wardman, M. (1998), 'The value of travel time: a review of British evidence', *Journal of Transport Economics and Policy*, 32 (3), 285–316.

6

Transport resistance factors: time, money and effort

Jan Anne Annema

6.1   INTRODUCTION

As explained in Chapter 2, passenger and freight transport volume is determined by the locations of activities, needs and resistance factors. This chapter aims to describe the transport resistance factors and their impact on passenger and freight transport demand.

From a physical perspective, resistance is everything that stops or obstructs a force. In this image the locations of activities and the need for trips are 'forces', resulting in transport. Resistance factors such as travel time, money costs and effort obstruct these 'forces'. The lower the resistance factors, the higher the amount of transport. For, with low resistance factors even the less important trips will still be made. The opposite is true also: the higher the resistance factors, the lower the amount of transport.

Economists use other jargon but the same basic idea as used in the physical analogy to explain transport. In the economic utility theory, the idea is that a trip results in benefits (see also Chapter 2), for if there are no benefits the trip would not be made. At the same time, the trip comes with costs – the resistance factors. The trip takes time, perhaps a fare or petrol has to be paid and perhaps the trip has to be made in a highly busy and too warm train compartment. The utility theory (see also Chapter 3) states that only if the benefits outweigh the costs will the trip be made. Thus, in countries or regions with poor road infrastructure and, consequently, high costs, relatively few long-distance road trips – only the highly beneficial ones – will be made. Here, it is important to realize that resistance factors not only influence the amount of transport but also the modal choice. For example, if rail carriers succeed in improving rail freight services (e.g., lowering costs, increasing frequencies) some freight will probably be shifted from road to rail.

It is clear from the previous paragraphs that, in this chapter, we define transport resistance broadly. Resistance is not only related to travel time and monetary costs but also to the more vague but sometimes important concepts of 'effort' in passenger transport and 'transport services' in freight transport. Effort and transport services are terms for a broad class of factors influencing the decision to make a trip, such as discomfort, worries about reliability, et cetera.

Most of these 'effort' factors influence the decision to travel or to transport goods negatively. Perhaps the only exception is the effort-related factor 'health benefits' which people experience when travelling in an active mode which may influence the decisions to travel in a positive way (for more on health and transport, see Chapter 12). Economists sometimes use the term generalized travel or transport costs. With this term, they mean the whole of transport resistance factors. In most cases, they add up all the different transport resistance factors into one generalized travel cost unit, mostly a monetary unit, sometimes a time unit.

Transport experts often speak of demand and supply factors to explain transport volumes. In these terms, forces and resistance factors can also be recognized. For example, a demand factor for freight transport is the number of goods produced and consumed at different locations. A supply factor for freight transport is the infrastructure quality which determines freight transport transit times and tariffs. The final freight transport volume is a result of inter-action between demand and supply, or, in other words, between transport attraction forces and resistance.

The importance of resistance factors such as travel time and travel out-of-pocket money costs will be explained in this chapter using so-called elasticities, amongst others (see Chapter 3). In economics, elasticity is the ratio of the percentage change in one variable to the percent-age change in another variable. Elasticity in this chapter is a tool for explaining the responsive-ness of transport volumes to changes in resistance factors such as travel time and money. For example, the fuel price elasticity of car use explains the responsiveness of car use to changes in fuel price. If the fuel price elasticity is -0.2 it means that a fuel price increase of 1% results in a car use decrease of 0.2%, all other factors explaining car use being equal.

Sections 6.2 to 6.4 discuss the resistance factors time, money and effort for passenger trans-port respectively. The impact of resistance factors on freight transport is explained in section 6.5. Section 6.6 summarizes the main conclusions.

6.2   THE ROLE OF TRAVEL TIME IN PASSENGER TRANSPORT

6.2.1   Travel Time Components

The time required to make a trip is an important resistance factor. Table 6.1 shows that travel time can be unravelled in different components.

When comparing total travel time from origin to destination between different transport modes, it could be an idea to just add up all the different time components (Table 6.1). However, by doing so the comparer forgets that people value time components differently. For example, public transport waiting time can be perceived as especially burdensome when travellers have to wait in difficult environments, such as in cold, hot or rainy weather, or in a seemingly unsafe or insecure condition. In a large UK study, it was found that on average London bus travellers value changes in their waiting time two times more than changes in their in-vehicle time (Lu et al., 2018). Iseki et al. (2006) found that car time spent in congested traffic conditions is, on average, valued 34% more highly than time spent in free-flow traffic.

Table 6.1 Possible travel time components from origin to destination (from top to bottom) for four modes of transport

Time – passenger transport			
Car	Public transport	Bike	Walking
	Hidden waiting time[a]		
Walking time to the parking lot	Time to get to the bus stop, bus, train or metro station	Time to get to the bike storage location	
In-vehicle travel time: free-flow time congestion time	In-vehicle travel time	Biking time	Walking time
Time to find the parking lot	Walking time transfer	Time to store bike	
Walking time from parking lot to final destination	Waiting time transfer	Time to get from bike storage facility to final destination	
	Time to get from bus, train or metro station to final destination		

Note: [a] Public transport travellers are dependent on the departure schedule as decided by the transport companies. Therefore, travellers sometimes have to wait at their origin location before it makes sense for them to depart.

In other words, people are willing to pay more money to avoid congestion time than to have lower free-flow in-vehicle time. To state the obvious: people feel more resistance to congestion time than to free-flow time.

In some transport studies, researchers apply a weighted summation for the different time components (Table 6.1). In such summations, e.g., one-minute walk time in a public transport transfer weighs heavier than one-minute in-vehicle time.

6.2.2   Value of Time

As already remarked in the introduction to this chapter, the basic economic idea is that people and shippers choose transport modes with the lowest resistance. If only travel time determines resistance, people and shippers would choose the fastest transport mode. For, with faster modes people get more time to carry out their preferred activities such as shopping, visiting family and friends and doing fun activities on their holidays. Also, shippers tend to prefer low freight travel times because in that case, they can transport the same amount of goods with fewer vehicles and fewer personnel, and, thus, save money. Therefore, in transport economics, the concepts of Value of Travel Time (often abbreviated to VOTT) or Marginal Value of Travel Time Savings (MVTTS) play an important role (see also Chapters 3 and 13). MVTTS can be considered as the 'best' term from a theoretical perspective because MVTTS clearly expresses that people value the change in travel time. Marginal in economics relates to costs or benefits of the change (e.g., ten minutes extra or less travel time). For sake of simplicity, in this chapter, the term VOTT will be used from now on.

Table 6.2 gives, as an illustration, some VOTT estimates for short- and long-distance trips by car for different travel purposes (Van Essen et al., 2019). The table shows that per country VOTTs differ which can be explained by income differences between countries. High-income people are on average willing to pay more for travel time savings compared to people with lower incomes. In transport cost–benefit analyses (see also Chapter 15), many countries ignore this difference for ethical reasons, departing from the idea of 'Equity Value of Time'. We refer to Börjesson and Eliasson (2019) for a discussion on this concept. Also, the table shows that people value their travel time less when they travel to family/friends, go shopping or do something recreational ('personal' reasons to travel) compared to travel time for business and commuting trips.

Table 6.2 Value of travel time estimates for car trips for a selection of European countries by travel purpose, euro/hour

Country	Short distance (urban)		Long distance (inter-urban)	
	Commuting – business	Personal	Commuting – business	Personal
Austria	16.9	7.8	19.8	7.8
Belgium	15.6	7.2	21.2	7.2
Bulgaria	6.5	3.0	8.5	3.0
Cyprus	11.0	5.1	12.5	5.1
Croatia	8.0	3.7	9.6	3.7
Czech Republic	11.6	5.4	14.0	5.4
Denmark	16.4	7.6	20.7	7.6
Estonia	10.0	4.6	12.1	4.6
Finland	14.5	6.7	20.6	6.7
France	13.8	6.4	15.7	6.4
Germany	16.4	7.6	20.0	7.6

Source: Van Essen et al. (2019), in prices 2018.

The VOTT refers to the amount of money consumers or shippers are willing to pay to save a certain amount of travel time. In a cost–benefit analysis for new road infrastructure travel time savings (in money terms) are in most cases the most important societal benefit category.

Different cities and countries have estimated total annual congestion costs: for example, £4.9 billion for London in 2019 (Inrix, 2022) and €3.3 to €4.3 billion in 2018 for the Netherlands (KIM, 2019). In these studies using VOTT estimates, the direct travel time losses compared to the 'ideal' free-flow situations are valued in monetary terms. These direct travel time losses are the main cost item in these estimates. In these estimates also so-called indirect travel time costs are considered. The reason is that in often congested areas some people and haulers will involuntarily choose to avoid the traffic jams. For example, some people will choose to go by public transport and some haulers will decide to change their planning by transporting goods outside rush hour. In both cases these involuntary choices are considered to be benefit losses (or costs) because in the free-flow situation these people and haulers would choose differently.

There is some expectation that in the future so-called autonomous vehicles (AVs) will be used instead of conventional cars. Theoretically, this might lead for the driver to a lower VOTT if s/he travels with an AV compared with a conventional car because s/he can now spend his/her time more usefully. Correia et al. (2019) indeed found in a Stated Choice experiment that the average VOTT for an AV with an office interior (5.50 €/h) to be lower than the VOTT for a conventional car (7.47 €/h). Pudane and Correia (2020, p. 327) point out that 'AVs may "give back" the travel time to the travellers.' In a large survey in the Netherlands, Pudane et al. (2021) found that respondents expect that they will spend their on-board time in an AV on activities such as more frequent work and meals, longer work and leisure.

6.2.3 Constant Time Budgets

Consumers devote a limited amount of their time to travel. This is not extraordinary. However, the remarkable aspect is that this limited travel time budget has remained relatively constant on average on a country level over the past decennia. Szalai (1972) and others carried out travel time research at the beginning of the 1970s in Eastern Europe, Western Europe and the United States. They concluded that the average travel time per person is similar in all three regions despite the large differences in transport means and infrastructure. Schafer and Victor (2000) concluded that on average people spend 1.1 hours on travelling. They do that in the US, in Europe, in Africa, in South America and so forth. Of course, on an individual level large differences in travel time exist between, for example, a person living in a small African village and an inhabitant of Shanghai, but on the most aggregate level travel time budgets seem to be similar and fairly constant (Mokhtarian and Chen, 2004), although these authors conclude that for different regions and times of study results for the average hour on travelling per person can be highly diverging. Stopher et al. (2017) used data of GPS devices and found in their study that the average expenditure of travel time is around an hour per person per day. They found significant difference in travel time per person per day at a disaggregate level, although a majority (around 55%) average within ±15 minutes of the overall mean of 1 hour and 2 minutes.

The theory of constant travel time budgets on the most aggregate level has important implications, as illustrated by Figure 6.1 (Schafer, 2006). If people keep their time budgets constant, they will travel longer distances when the transport resistance factor 'time' decreases, all other things being equal. All over the World there was a tendency of increasing market share in person kilometres travelled of fast modes at the cost of the slower modes (Figure 6.1). Schafer (2006) expects this trend to continue; see the shaded surfaces in Figure 6.1. His expectation is based on two main assumptions. First, people or households will need a higher absolute transport money budget in the future in order to be able to afford the faster but more expensive travel modes. As the world has shown on average continuing economic growth (despite some occasional major dips), this first assumption of an increasing absolute household transport budget seems not to be too wild. Secondly, faster transport modes will have to be available in the future. Also, this assumption seems not to be too far off from reality as, for example, many governments at the time of writing this book chapter (June 2022) invest or have plans to invest in new airports capacity and high-speed rails.

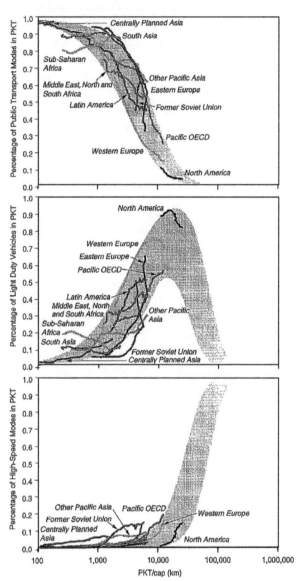

Source: Schafer (2006).

Figure 6.1   Three phases in worldwide persons mobility development (1950–2000): the decreasing share of the relatively slow public transport (top), the growth and decline of the passenger car (middle) and the start of the high-speed era (high-speed trains and aircraft)

If transport resistance factor time decreases and, consequently, people travel long distances, the question is: why? Faster transportation options could also result in smaller travel time budgets because, thanks to the speed increase, people could decide to travel the same distance in less travel time; in other words, they could trade-off their travel time for spending time on other things. Still, the constant Travel Time Budget (TTB) combined with faster transport modes seems to imply that people on average prefer to expand their distances. Marchetti (1994) thinks of an anthropologic explanation. According to him, history shows that humankind lives just like an animal defending and expanding its territory. Trying to find and explore new territories located farther away is a basic instinct, in his view. Thus, if travel time resistance is increasingly lower, people tend to expand their territory. Economists argue that the probability of finding a new partner, a new job or a new house that satisfies people's preferences is perhaps higher in a larger searching area compared to looking in one's own village or town. Thus, chances for higher benefits drive the need for travelling longer distances, according to them. Others point at novelty- or variety-seeking behaviour as explanations for a drive for travelling (for example, Lal, 2006 explains long-distance migration partly on genetic causes). An interesting question is if teleactivities will replace physical travel. In a large review study, Mouratidis et al. (2021) conclude that teleactivities may substitute some trips but generate others. They found that tel-ecommuting and teleconferencing may result in reductions in total travel distances. However, their study showed that online shopping, online education, teleleisure, telehealth and online social networking do not seem to reduce overall travel distances, as, in line with a constant TTB, the time saved by these online activities on physical travel may be spent on travelling to other destinations.

6.2.4   Travel Time Elasticities, Induced Traffic

As mentioned in the Introduction the responsiveness of people to travel time changes are often expressed in elasticities. In scientific and applied transport research papers and reports, the reader can find many studies on travel time elasticities (e.g., Goodwin, 1996; de Jong and Gunn, 2001; Hensher, 2008; Paulley et al., 2006; Dunkerley et al., 2018; Litman, 2021).

We just give one example. In a large European study de Jong and Gunn (2001) compared modelled car travel time elasticities for commuting between different European regions: the Brussels region (Belgium), Italy and the Netherlands. They found short-term (less than one year) elasticities of -0.31 (Brussels), -0.87 (Italy) and -0.64 (the Netherlands), and long-term elasticities of -0.49 (Brussels), -1.38 (Italy) and -2 (the Netherlands). This example illustrates five important aspects:

1. In interpreting elasticities it is always important to be aware of the specifications. In this case, the travel time elasticity is only related to car commuting travel volumes.
2. It is always important to realize that the difference between the elasticities could be explained because of methodological reasons. It is for the purpose of this book too much detail to discuss methodological issues related to transport elasticities (see Hensher, 2008, for an assessment of systematic sources of variation in public transport elasticities). Here, the main message is that whenever elasticities from other studies are used the user should be aware of the influence of methodological choices on the outcomes.
3. The same elasticity may differ significantly between regions and/or countries, as this example shows, because of different transport circumstances. For example, the regions may differ significantly in public transport quality and availability which makes substitu-tion to public transport when car travel time increases in one region far easier compared to another region. So, this example shows that it is quite risky in policy studies to transfer

uncritically elasticities established for one specific region or country to another. If these elasticities are then used for 'another' region to estimate a policy impact, for example, of a measure to increase public transport travel times, the policy conclusions could be highly wrong.

4. The long-term elasticities are higher compared to the short-term elasticities. This is an often occurring phenomenon related to the fact that in the long term people have more choice options when travel times decrease such as moving or looking for another job compared to the short term.

5. Car commuting is relatively sensitive to travel time changes. The long-term elasticities are often higher than -1 while the average travel time is -1 based on constant travel time budgets (Goodwin, 1996).

From a policy planning perspective, the notion that people are sensitive to travel time changes leads to an important consequence. When governments invest in extra road capacity to relieve present or expected future congestion – as they often do all over the world – new traffic will be generated. Generated traffic refers to all the traffic which would be present if an expansion of road capacity occurred, which would not be there without the expansion (Goodwin and Noland, 2003). These authors also state that the generated traffic hypothesis implies, in essence, that there exists a demand curve for travel – the cheaper the travel, the more will be demanded. So, one effect of making transport 'cheaper' (i.e., faster) by building new roads or extra road lanes is that it results in generated traffic. Generated traffic is also related to the indirect travel time losses; see before. Consequently, congestion relief will be less than anticipated, or shorter in duration, than if there is no such extra traffic. This will influence the cost–benefit appraisal (CBA; see Chapter 15) of the road project, as well as environmental impacts. An elasticity can be estimated that relates the percentage increase in travel demand (vehicle kilometres travelled) to the percentage decrease in travel times due to the added road lanes. Drabicki et al. (2020) summarize the literature on this topic and found that the exact value of elasticities (travel time change due to added road lanes for vehicle kilometres travelled) vary in specific case studies; the literature review part in their paper suggests that the elasticities range usually between -0.3 and-0.6 in the short-term horizon and around -0.5 and -1.1 in the long term. It is important to realize that the generated traffic consists of two kinds of 'new' traffic on the expanded roads, namely diverted traffic and induced traffic, as Drabicki et al. (2020) point out. Diverted traffic is traffic that without the expansion would travel via other roads or by public transport, for example. Induced traffic is really newly generated traffic. In the short and medium term this induced traffic consists of travellers that 'spontaneously' respond to the improved quicker opportunity to travel while in the long run, the improved roads could even induce traffic because people decide to move house or change jobs (or locations of other destinations) or because of other land-use shifts which expand their travel distances (see Figure 2.1 and Chapter 5). This explains the difference between the short- and long-term elasticities for generated traffic, as mentioned before.

6.2.5 Cross Travel Time Elasticities

In many countries policymakers hope to achieve policy goals such as less traffic jams and environmental benefits by investing in public transport. For example, the European Commission aims in their 2011 White Paper that by 2050, the majority of medium–long distance passenger transport (300–800 km) should be by rail, and that by the same year a European high speed rail network should have been completed (Pastori et al., 2018). Despite these ambitions and the expected extension of the high-speed rail network the share of high-speed rail in the modal share for medium–long distance is expected to only increase from 8% in 2020 to 10% in 2050. In this study in 2050 still 70% of all medium–long distance kilometres in Europe will be travelled by car and 13% by plane. This points at low responsiveness of car and aeroplane users to shift to high-speed rail when improvements in high-speed rail are carried out. A manner to express this responsiveness is using cross travel time elasticities. The term 'cross' means that these kinds of elasticities reflect the responsiveness of a percentage change in a characteristic in one mode (e.g., rail travel time changes) to a percentage change in the use of another mode (e.g., car use). Many cross-elasticities from different regions in the world can be found in Litman (2021). To give an example: Paulley et al. (2006) cite UK rail time cross-elasticities for car use of 0.057 and for coach use of 0.20 (based on a study Wardman, 1997). These figures imply that improving rail travel time will have a relatively low impact on car use. The impact on the competing coach market is higher. However, it is important to note that in absolute numbers the car use decrease may still be significant in the UK when train travel time increases by 1%. The reason is that car use expressed in car kilometres travelled has a high market share in the UK, implying that a 0.057% decrease is still a relatively high amount of absolute car kilometres that are substituted to train kilometres. With cross-elasticities it is always important to be aware of the market shares of the modes considered. Transferring a cross-elasticity estimated for a certain region to another region can give highly wrong policy information if the two regions differ significantly in transport mode market shares (Balcombe et al., 2004).

Nevertheless, the rather low car responsiveness is still disappointing for many politicians. One reason for the low responsiveness is that, next to travel time, consumers take other factors into account when deciding to take a certain transport mode. These include monetary costs (see Section 6.3) and effort (see Section 6.4). Also 'inertia' plays a role in the low responsiveness. Inertia relates to habit and refers to the tendency that the outcome of previous choices affect the present choice (La Paix et al., 2022 and Chapter 3 in this volume). The role of habit in decision-making is that people do not tend to consider all the pros and cons of a choice all the time. This practice saves time and energy. Taking the car for commuting could become a kind of a habit and the people with this habit are unaware of or not interested in – perhaps better put: they are less open – information on positive changes in competing transport modes. 'Old habits die hard' describes poignantly people's travel behaviour, as people do not change their travel habits easily (Haggar et al., 2019). Changes in choices often happen only when large new events take place in people's life such as obtaining a new job or when they move (Zarabi et al., 2019). Also large changes in transport mode characteristics could trigger reconsideration of transport mode choice such as the opening of a complete new train line to their village or suburb or 'sudden' large increases in road congestion.

6.3   THE ROLE OF TRAVEL MONETARY COSTS IN PASSENGER TRANSPORT

The second important resistance factor is the money people have to spend for the trip. Like travel time, monetary costs can be split in subcomponents (Table 6.3).

Table 6.3   Possible travel money cost components for four modes of transport

Money – passenger transport			
Car	Public transport	Bike	Walking
Depreciation costs	Fares	Depreciation costs	Depreciation costs (shoes)
Car maintenance costs	Costs for trip to and from station (e.g., taxi)	Maintenance costs	Repair costs (shoes)
Parking costs		Parking costs (in commercial storing facilities)	
Tolls		Insurance costs	
Fuel costs			
Taxes			
Insurance costs			

Monetary costs can be classified in many ways. An often-used classification is fixed costs versus variable costs. Fixed costs are the amount of money to be paid independent of the distance travelled; for example, depreciation costs and yearly annual taxes. In contrast, variable costs are dependent on the distance travelled, such as car fuel costs and public transport fares.

6.3.1   Constant Money Cost Budgets

There seems to be a constant money budget for persons mobility as a percentage of people's income. Schafer (1998) researched worldwide mobility expenditures and confirmed a previous result of Zahavi (1979): on average people per class of income tend to spend a constant share (10–15%) of their income on transportation. Mokhtarian and Chen (2004) comment that at the aggregate level travel expenditures indeed appear to have some stability but they found many empirical studies that gave widely different results related to different times of study and regions. One implication of this 'more or less' constancy at the very aggregate level is that if the resistance factor monetary costs increases travel decreases and vice versa, all other things being equal.

6.3.2   Price and Monetary Costs Elasticities

The responsiveness to monetary changes can be expressed in elasticities, like in the travel time case (Section 6.2). A large amount of transport price, fare and costs elasticities can be found (e.g., Litman, 2021 gives a large overview of all kinds of price and monetary costs which were estimated in studies from all over the world).

To avoid confusion, it is important to realize that in the literature one can find price and fare elasticities and travel costs elasticities. Price elasticities relate to the responsiveness to changes in prices such as fuel price. Travel or transport costs elasticities relate to behavioural changes dependent on actual costs changes. For example, suppose that in a certain region the price of petrol is 2.0 euros per litre. All car users who fill their car tank in that region have to pay this fuel price. However, the actual petrol costs per kilometre driven in that region can be 0.1 euros for a relatively fuel-efficient car user and 0.15 euros for a less fuel-efficient car user.

It seems plausible that fuel price increases will not only result in less car kilometres to avoid the increased travelling costs, but they will probably also result in the purchase of more fuel-efficient cars in order to avoid the costs to increase. In other words, it seems plausible that fuel price elasticities for fuel use are lower compared to fuel cost elasticities for fuel use. To put it differently, fuel price elasticities for car use will probably be lower compared to fuel price elasticities for fuel use; see below when will be shown that this phenomenon is indeed true.

It is impossible to fully summarize the huge amount of scientific research. Very broadly, one could conclude that empiric research worldwide shows that:

1. transport consumers are indeed price and cost sensitive;
2. the extent of their responsiveness is dependent on many factors (culture, income, time and so forth);
3. the responsiveness to price changes is fairly modest in most cases (elasticities are in most cases between 0 and 1).

An overview of fuel price elasticities of fuel demand for many different countries and over different periods of time (from 1970 to roughly 2010) can be found in Hössinger et al. (2017). Another example is the study by Geilenkirchen et al. (2009) who have summarized, as found in numerous studies and reviews, fuel price elasticities for car use and car ownership (Table 6.4a) and fare elasticities for public transport use (Table 6.4b). The numbers presented are applicable – more and less – for Western European countries. However, as in the case of the time travel elasticities (see before), it is important to stress that the specific elasticities for a region can differ considerably from the values presented in Table 6.4a and b dependent on the specific geographic, cultural and technical circumstances. For example, Hössinger et al. (2017) show lower price elasticities for fuel demand in the USA compared to European countries because, amongst others, in the USA average income levels are higher and fuel prices are (far) lower which implies that a percentage change in fuel price in the USA has much less impact on the US consumer compared to a percentage change in fuel price in Europe by the European consumer. The elasticities presented in Tables 6.4a and 6.4b have to be considered indicative.

Table 6.4a Indicative fuel price elasticities

	Short term (1 year)	Long term (5 to 10 years)
Car ownership	−0.05 to −0.2	−0.1 to −0.65
Car use	−0.1 to −0.2	−0.25 to −0.5
Car fuel efficiency	0.1 to 0.15	0.3 to 0.4
Car fuel use	−0.25 to −0.35	−0.6 to −0.8

Source: Geilenkirchen et al. (2009).

Table 6.4b Indicative fare elasticities

	Short term (1 year)	Long term (5 to 10 years)
Bus	−0.2 to −0.5	−0.6 to −1.0
Train	−0.3 to −0.7	−0.6 to −1.1
Metro	−0.1 to −0.3	−0.3 to −0.7

Source: Geilenkirchen et al. (2009).

Tables 6.4a and 6.4b show two interesting aspects. First, regardless the exact values, it is clear that the long-term fuel price elasticity for car use and car fuel usage are higher compared to the short-term elasticities. Hössinger et al. (2017) show exactly this same trend in elasticities for all countries and all periods they included in their study. Also, the price responsiveness for public transport usage is higher in the long term. The explanation is simple: in the short term, it is relatively difficult for people to make changes. In the longer term, this is different. Then, people can choose a different car or change their dwelling or job locations. Secondly, fuel price elasticities for car fuel use are indeed higher compared to the fuel price elasticities for car use, roughly two times (Table 6.4a). Especially in the long run, the elasticities (-0.6 to -0.8) show that as a response to a fuel price increase people do not only use their car somewhat less but, even more, they try to avoid higher fuel costs by purchasing more fuel-efficient cars or, eventually, by driving more fuel-economically.

Dargay and Gately (1997) concluded that consumers show a stronger response to price increases compared to price decreases. This implies that a fuel price increase followed by a price decrease of the same magnitude does not result in restoring the transport and fuel demand which occurred just before the price increase. Dargay (2007) found that an income increase has a greater impact on car ownership compared to an income decrease of the same magnitude. Also, in the relation between air fare changes and demand for aviation, there seems to be asymmetry. Wadud (2015) found for the US a short-run elasticity of demand during an air fare rise of 0.143, and for air fare fall of 0.113. In the long run, these differences are magnified: the long-run demand elasticities for an air fare rise and fall are 0.526 and 0.417, respectively. Wadud suggests that their results tend to agree with the prospect theory of Kahneman and Tvesrky (1979). In this theory, it is assumed that people tend to value losses (e.g., air fare increase) more than gains (e.g., air fare decrease).

6.4   EFFORT RESISTANCE FACTORS

Next to time and money, there are more resistance factors that determine the amount of passenger transport. We summarize these factors in this paragraph as 'effort' factors. 'Effort' may seem to be a relatively unimportant rest factor. However, Chapter 3 shows the existence of a large amount of social and psychological factors which influence travel behaviour.

Effort as a transport resistance factor consists of different aspects (Table 6.5).

Table 6.5   Possible effort aspects for four transport modes that are considered resistance factors

Effort – passenger transport			
Car	Public transport	Bike	Walking
Discomfort/ Physical and mental effort of car driving	Discomfort	Discomfort/ Physical effort[a]	Discomfort/ Physical effort[a]
(Mental) strain, stress	(Mental) strain, stress		
Reliability	Reliability	Accident risk	Accident risk
Accident risk	Physical effort (stairs, walks during transfer, luggage carrying)	Women – feelings of insecurity	Women – feelings of insecurity
Availability of information	Availability of information	Availability of information	Availability of information
	Women – feelings of insecurity		

Note: [a] As mentioned, physical effort due to cycling and walking is perhaps the only resistance factor that is also a kind of attractiveness factor. Some people may assess the physical effort of cycling and walking as just an additional reason to choose these modes, for example, for commuting. These modes give them an 'easy' daily opportunity to be weekly 150 minutes moderately physically active which is beneficial for their health (see Chapter 12)

We will now discuss some effort factors more in detail. We do not pretend to be exhaustive in all effort factors possible but we think we mention the most important ones.

6.4.1   Discomfort, Physical Effort, Status

The resistance factor discomfort contains a large number of different issues. Especially related to public transport discomfort is considered an important resistance factor. In Balcombe et al. (2004) and Paulley et al. (2006) different aspects are mentioned which may influence the comfort of public transport travelling: the waiting environment quality, the vehicle and rolling stock quality, the quality of the front-line staff to customers, crowding, seat-place availability, the quality of on-board facilities, cleanliness and the interchange quality between modes. In an Iranian study on intercity bus users, the viewpoints of bus users on their level of satisfaction were analysed (Ganji et al., 2021). A very diverse group of comfort factors were mentioned:

seat availability, seat cleanness, ticket reservation methods, bus appearance, driver respect for traffic rules and quiet bus with no disturbing engine noise.

For cycling discomfort factors related to the natural environment have a large influence on both the decision to cycle and the frequency (Heinen et al., 2010). These authors found, based on an overview of the literature on commuting by bicycle, that hilliness has a negative effect on cycling and weather has a large influence on the cycling frequency. Commuters are less influenced by temperature than other cyclists, implying that many people only choose to cycle for leisure purposes when the weather is pleasant (Heinen et al., 2010). Kask and Tan (2019) explored key factors influencing school-going children's choice to cycle in Tallinn, Estonia. They found as often mentioned hindering factors: 'there is no good cycle parking facility at school', 'cycling is unsafe because there are no good cycle paths', 'I do not feel comfortable while cycling' and 'my friends/classmates do not cycle to school'. So, also the 'uncoolness' of a particular mode can resist people from using it.

6.4.2   Reliability

A reliable transportation system means that travellers and hauliers can make trips according to their expectations, especially related to expected travel time. The USA Department of Transportation defines travel time reliability as a measure of the consistency, timeliness, predictability and dependability of a trip (FHWA/DoT, 2022). For example, a car commuter who faces every working day the 'same' traffic jam with a 30- to 40- minute delay loses travel time compared to free flow but still has a rather reliable trip. This commuter knows beforehand rather exactly what time (within a 10 minute spread) s/he will be at work or at home and can make arrangements accordingly. However, if the traffic jam in the day-to-day commute is unpredictable – sometimes it is only a few minutes, another day suddenly more than an hour – this commuting trip becomes highly unreliable. The consequence of the unpredictability of travel times means that people will have to adapt their behaviour but because of the unpredictability, they are uncertain about the best course of action. This uncertainty comes with a cost. So, like a VOTT, also a so-called Value of Reliability (VOR) exists which is people's willingness to pay to make their trips more reliable.

Table 6.6   Values of Reliability (VORs) on 2010 euros per hour per person, including VAT

	Car	Train	Bus, tram, metro	All surface modes	Air	Recr. navigation
Commute	3.75	4.75	3.25	4.00		
Business employee	14.50	18.00	12.00	15.50	56.00	
Business employer	15.50	4.75	9.75	12.25		
Business	30.00	22.75	21.75	27.75	56.00	
Other	4.75	4.50	3.75	4.50	30.75	0
All purposes	5.75	5.50	3.75	5.25	33.75	0

Source: Kouwenhoven et al. (2014).

Table 6.6 summarizes the VORs which are estimated to be used in Dutch cost–benefit analysis practices (see Chapter 15 for more on cost–benefit analysis). VORs in the Dutch context give people's willingness to pay for a smaller spread (smaller standard deviation) in their travel times. The table shows, amongst others, that for business purposes and aviation reliability in travel time is valued highest. For air travel, reliability is important because missing a transfer to another flight or arriving too late at the destination (and, for example, missing the arranged bus to the hotel) can be highly stressful and costly for people.

6.4.3   Travelling Information

Another effort resistance factor is *information*, or perhaps better put, the insufficient availability of travelling information or good quality travelling information. There are numerous studies on travel behaviour under limited knowledge (for an overview, see Chorus et al., 2006). These studies have uncovered travellers' dislike of knowledge limitations, and their inclination to reduce these knowledge limitations by acquiring information. Broadly speaking, traveller information relates to route information (en route and beforehand) and mode information (e.g., fares and travel times to be expected, waiting and bicycle storage facilities and so forth). The availability of high-quality traveller information can improve travelling comfort, trip reliability and decrease travel stress. Chorus et al. (2010) used search theory to evaluate the value of travelling information. Their results indicate, amongst others, that travellers prefer information that adds previously unknown alternatives to their choice set over information that provides estimates for uncertain attributes of known alternatives. As to be expected, Chorus et al. (2010) found substantial heterogeneity with respect to travellers' valuation of the costs and benefits of travel information.

Travel information and transport services increasingly become more digitalized. Without apps, PCs, laptops and iPads it becomes increasingly difficult to buy tickets or to find travel information. A potential new transport service – 'Mobility as a Service' (MaaS; see also Chapter 8) – is even completely dependent on digital technology. People can only book a preferred trip at a MaaS provider digitally, e.g., via a MaaS app. For one, digitalization is a good thing because it can lower travel resistance because people can find travel information easily and in real time and they can book transport services quickly and wherever they are. However, there is also a downside: digitization can also increase travel resistance for people who do not have access to digital technologies or who do not have the capabilities to understand digital tools. So, digital technology can for a part of the population lead to higher accessibility but also for a smaller part of the population to lower accessibility, i.e., digitization can lead to digital inequality (Durand and Zijlstra, 2020).

6.4.4   Travellers' Feelings of Insecurity

Travellers' feelings of insecurity is a resistance factor for public transport and the slow modes biking and walking. The factor relates to feelings of uneasiness when people travel, have to wait or transfer on stations or bus stops. Also, using dark or remote roads for biking and walking can be an unattractive endeavour. Heinen et al. (2010) mention darkness as a factor that results in people choosing to cycle less. There is increasing literature on transport and gender (e.g., Ceccato and Loukaitou-Sideris, 2020; Chowdhury and van Wee, 2020; Stark and Meschik, 2018). This literature shows that women experience especially high levels of perceived insecurity – and particularly in relation to sexual harassment and assault – compared to their male counterparts. Women also experience more superficial incidents such as stalking, sexual slur, groping and other events with sexual undertones which can all fuel feelings of anxiety and fear in transit environments. These experiences make women adapt their behaviour in transit and they result in all kinds of mobility constraints for them, such as avoiding certain lines, not travelling at certain times of day, not travelling alone and so forth.

6.4.5   Accident Risk

People might fear that they or their children get involved in traffic accidents when they choose a certain transport mode. This fear might influence their mode choice. US data showed that in 1969 48% of children five to 14 years of age usually walked or cycled to school; in 2009 this decreased to 13% (The National Center for Safe Routes to School, 2011). Next to increased distances, the most important reason for this was 'traffic-related danger'. Also in the Estonian research (see before; Kask and Tan , 2019) worries about unsafe roads with no dedicated cycle paths were often mentioned as a reason not to cycle to school.

6.4.6   Mental Strain, Stress

Stress can be seen as an indicator of the importance of effort resistance factors. Wener and Evans (2011) compared the stress of car and train commuters in Metropolitan New York City. In their paper, they mention several studies that relate travel effort factors to stress such as crowded trains, discomfort from poor design, feelings of no control (a car driver often finds that he or she has more control over a particular trip when driving a car compared to using public transport) and unpredictability. Wener and Evans (2011) found that car commuters showed significantly higher levels of reported stress compared to train commuters. Driving effort and predictability largely accounted for the elevated stress associated with car commuting, according to this study.

6.4.7   Specific Constants

The resistance factors, time and money, are often objectively measurable, however this is far more difficult for most of the effort resistance factors. An often-used method to include effort components in the total resistance factor is using specific weighting factors for the different parts of the trip such as the already mentioned penalties for waiting time or arriving unexpectedly too early at the destination. In transport models often so-called alternative specific constants are used in the resistance functions per transport mode in order to include all kinds of effort components (Chapter 16).

6.5   GOODS TRANSPORT AND RESISTANCE FACTORS

In Sections 6.2 to 6.4, we have focused on passenger transport. Therefore, in this section, we focus specifically on the role of transport resistance factors in freight transport. Broadly speaking, shippers and hauliers take transport resistance factors into account similar to consumers. Monetary costs and transit time are also important factors shippers consider when deciding on a specific transport mode. Additionally, 'transport service quality' (reliability, frequencies and so forth) plays a role in the decision-making process to transport freight and by what mode. Like the 'effort' factor this may seem a vague resistance factor, but increasing empirical evidence shows that it is an important factor.

6.5.1   Transport Time

It seems obvious that in freight transport actors are willing to pay for transport time savings. For example, when due to infrastructural improvements freight transport time is saved carriers can deliver the same amount of goods in less time compared to the situation without the infrastructural improvement, and, by doing so, save personnel and vehicle operating costs. Binsuwadan et al. (2021) performed a large meta-analysis to explain variations in the value of freight travel time savings (VFTTS). Both carriers who transport goods and shippers who supply or own the goods (see also Chapter 4) value transport time savings. Table 6.7 gives for a selection of countries from their study the implied VFTTS. With 'implied' it is meant that their VFTTS values for the different countries are the results of their meta-model.

Three important observations can be made related to Table 6.7. First, like in VOTT for passenger transport, average income (GDP per capita) in a country has an important influence on the willingness to pay for freight travel times savings. Second, the different transport modes have very different VFTTS. Not surprisingly, the faster modes, especially air and to some extent road transport, have relatively high VFTTS. It can be assumed that these modes carry the relatively high value and more time-sensitive commodities (e.g., flowers, non-frozen food), for which it is relatively attractive to trade-off money when that would result in even shorter transport times. For lower value bulk commodities (mainly transported by rail, sea-going and inland shipping) decreasing freight transport times is far less important, and thus less valuable to do. Third, who is the decision-maker explains VFTTS. Carriers consider transport costs while shippers consider cargo costs of which transport costs are just one factor. So, a carrier is more willing to trade-off money against transport time savings because these time savings can, for example, via savings on the wages he has to pay his personnel, directly lower his transport costs and, thus, increase his profits.

Table 6.7   Implied values of travel time in freight transport ($ per-tonne/hour), 2017 incomes and prices for a selection of countries

Country	GDP per capita	Carriers		
		Road	Rail	Air
Netherlands	48,555	11.16	1.90	161.15
Nigeria	1969	0.86	0.15	12.40
Norway	75,704	15.92	2.71	229.91
Pakistan	1467	0.68	0.12	9.80
Philippines	2982	1.20	0.20	17.29
Poland	13,861	4.09	0.70	59.11
Russian Federation	10,751	3.34	0.57	48.24
Saudi Arabia	20,804	5.67	0.96	81.80
Singapore	60,298	13.27	2.26	191.64
South Africa	6127	2.13	0.36	30.77
Spain	28,208	7.23	1.23	104.37
Sweden	53,253	12.02	2.05	173.51
Switzerland	80,333	16.70	2.84	241.09
Thailand	6578	2.26	0.38	32.56
Turkey	10,5	3.28	0.56	47.34
United Arab Emirates	40,325	9.62	1.64	138.90
United Kingdom	39,932	9.54	1.63	137.82
United States	59,928	13.21	2.25	190.70

Source: Binsuwadan et al. (2021).

6.5.2   Monetary Costs

Like in the case of passenger transport, the monetary cost resistance factor for freight transport can be explained using elasticities. For example, Table 6.8 shows the responsiveness of road freight transport in the Netherlands for price increases. The figures are based on international literature but highly indicative as empirical data are relatively scarce. It should be noted that freight demand elasticity studies vary significantly in terms of the demand measure, data type, estimation method, commodity type and so forth (Li et al., 2011). According to Li et al. (2011), this wide variation makes it difficult to compare empirical estimates when the differences may arise partly from the methods and data used.

Table 6.8 Indicative price elasticities for road freight transport demand (in tonne kilometres)

Price elasticity, total[a]	-0.6 to -0.9
Whereof **substitution** (less tonne kilometres road transport, more tonne kilometres rail and/or barge, similar tonnes production and consumption)	-0.4 to -0.5
Whereof **less transport** (less tonne kilometres road transport, similar amount of tonne kilometres rail and/or barge, similar amount of tonnes production and consumption)	-0.2 to -0.4
Whereof **less production and consumption** (less tonne kilometres road transport, similar amount of tonne kilometres rail and/or barge, less tonnes production and consumption)	Low (<-0.1)

Notes: [a] The top row is a summation of the three rows underneath. The elasticities are valid for limited price increases.
Source: Geilenkirchen et al. (2009).

Many people argue that freight transport is non-responsive to price increases as transport costs have a modest share in final product prices. This can be debated. Rodrigue (2020) estimates, for example, that for a product with relatively low added value (stone, clay and glass) the share of transport costs in the product price can be 20% to 25% which is not modest. For higher value products this share is indeed lower and in the range of only a few to 10%. As Table 6.8 illustrates for road transport, even a modest share does not mean that price increases will not affect road transport volumes (in tonne-kilometres) as shippers and carriers have different possible behavioural reactions to deal with a road price increase next to just passing on the price increase to the consumers of goods.

First, transport mode substitution may take place (Table 6.8 second row). Increase of road freight costs by, e.g., new taxes, tolls or oil price rises may entice shippers to switch to other modes such as rail. Secondly, carriers may react by trying to implement increased efficiency in the road freight sector (Table 6.8 third row) in terms of, for example, using larger vehicles (more tonnes per kilometre driven), reducing the number of empty runs (more tonnes per kilometre driven), improved loading (more tonnes per kilometre driven), buying more fuel-efficient trucks (fewer fuel costs per kilometre driven) and concentration in the haulier business (cost reductions because of less overhead). Thirdly (Table 6.8 fourth row), less production and consumption of freight may take place. Shippers may include (a part of the) higher transport costs in the final product price. It is imaginable that for some products the resulting higher prices lead to lower demand and, subsequently, lower production. Nevertheless, this third possible response to a transport price increase is not very strong as shown in Table 6.8. The reason is twofold. First – as remarked before – freight transport costs have only a modest share in final product prices. Secondly, by mode substitution and/or increased transport efficiency (more tonne per kilometre lifted) carriers will absorb some or all of the price increase.

6.5.3   Transport Service and Reliability

Shippers also take transport service quality and reliability into account when deciding to use a particular transport freight mode. For example, Kim et al. (2017) show that for New

Zealand shippers' reliability is an important factor in choosing a particular freight mode. The definition of reliability in this study was the probability of the cargo arriving within a given time. Additionally, also transport service factors, such as more frequent services and less risk for damage, influence their decisions. Kim et al. (2017) identified different classes of shippers, amongst others based on freight distance and specific product markets, and they show that per cluster identified the importance of the service and reliability factors can differ greatly.

6.6   CONCLUSIONS

The most important conclusions of this chapter are next:

1. Important transport resistance factors for passenger transport are travel time, monetary costs and effort. Passengers are responsive to changes in these resistance factors.
2. Important resistance factors for freight transport are transit time, monetary costs and transport services. Shippers and freight forwarders are responsive to changes in these resistance factors.
3. On an aggregated scale (large region or country level) it turns out that people on average tend to keep their travel time budget constant. Thus, on an aggregate level, people tend to exchange lower transport travel times for more kilometres travelled and not to spend the saved travel time on other activities.
4. Travel time and price elasticities for passenger transport, in the long run, are higher compared to short-term elasticities. This phenomenon is related to the fact that in the long term people have more choice options when travel times or prices change compared to the short term such as moving or finding another job.
5. A rise in transportation monetary costs for a certain mode results in less transport and/or mode shifts. However, higher fuel prices do not only result in less road transport and to a small extent to some mode shift but the higher prices also result in the purchase of more fuel-efficient cars. By buying more fuel-efficient cars people can avoid (a part of) the price increase and, thus, can continue to travel by car.

REFERENCES

Balcombe, R., R. Mackett, N. Paulley, J. Preston, J. Shires, H. Titheridge, M. Wardman and P. White (2004), *The Demand for Public Transport: A Practical Guide*, TRL report TRL593, accessed June 2022 at www.demandforpublictransport.co.uk/TRL593.pdf.

Binsuwadan, J., G. De Jong, R. Batley et al. (2021), 'The value of travel time savings in freight transport: a meta-analysis', *Transportation*, 49, 1183–1209, https://doi.org/10.1007/s11116-021-10207-2.

Börjesson, M. and J. Eliasson (2019), 'Should values of time be differentiated?', *Transport Reviews*, 39(3), 357–75, https://doi.org/10.1080/01441647.2018.1480543.

Ceccato, V. and A. Loukaitou-Sideris (eds) (2020), *Transit Crime and Sexual Violence in Cities: International Evidence and Prevention*, New York: Routledge.

Chorus, C.G., E.J.E. Molin and G.P. van Wee (2006), 'Use and effects of advanced traveller information services (ATIS): a review of the literature', *Transport Reviews*, 26(2), 127–49.

Chorus, C.G., J.L. Walker and M.E. Ben-Akiva (2010), 'The value of travel information: a search-theoretic approach', *Journal of Intelligent Transportation Systems*, 14(3), 154–65.

Chowdhury, S. and B. van Wee (2020), 'Examining women's perception of safety during waiting times at public transport terminals', *Transport Policy*, 94, 102–08.

Correia, G., E. Looff, S. van Cranenburgh, M. Snelder and B. van Arem (2019), 'On the impact of vehicle automation on the value of travel time while performing work and leisure activities in a car: theoretical insights and results from a stated preference survey', *Transportation Research Part A*, 119, 359–82.

Dargay, J.M. (2007), 'The effect of prices and income on car travel in the UK', *Transportation Research Part A*, 41, 949–60.

Dargay, J.M. and D. Gately (1997), 'The demand for transportation fuels: imperfect price- reversibility?' *Transportation Research*, 31(1), 71–82.

Drabicki, A., A. Szarata and R. Kucharski (2020), 'Suppressing the effects of induced traffic in urban road systems: impact assessment with macrosimulation tools – results from the city of Krakow (Poland)', *Transportation Research Procedia*, 47, 131–38, https://doi.org/10.1016/j.trpro.2020.03.085.

Dunkerley, F., M. Wardman, C. Rohr and N. Fearnley (2018), *Bus fare and journey time elasticities and diversion factors for all modes*, RR-2367-DfT, RAND Europe and SYSTRA.

Durand, A. and T. Zijlstra, (2020), *The Impact of Digitalisation on the Access to Transport Services: a Literature Review*, The Hague: KIM, https://doi.org/10.13140/RG.2.2.22686.97600.

EC (European Commission) (2011), *White Paper: European Transport Policy for 2010: Time to Decide*, COM (2001)370, Brussels: EC.

Essen, H. van, A. Schroten, D. Sutter, C. Bieler, S. Maffii, M. Brambilla, D. Fiorello, F. Fermi, R. Parolin and K. El Beyrouty (2019), *Handbook on the External Costs of Transport*, Version 2019 – 1.1, Delft: CE Delft.

FHWA/DoT (2022), What is travel time reliability?, https://ops.fhwa.dot.gov/publications/tt_reliability/ttr_report.htm#:~:text=Travel%20time%20reliability%20measures%20the,different%20times%20of%20the%20day.

Ganji, S.S., A.N. Ahangar, A. Awasthi and S. Jamshidi Bandari (2021), 'Psychological analysis of intercity bus passenger satisfaction using Q methodology', *Transportation Research Part A*, 154, 345–63.

Geilenkirchen, G.P., K.T. Geurs, H.P. van Essen, A. Schroten and B. Boon (2009), *Effecten van prijsbeleid in verkeer en vervoer*, Bilthoven, Planbureau voor de Leefomgeving/Delft: CE Delft.

Goodwin, P.B. (1996), 'Empirical evidence on induced traffic: a review and synthesis', *Transportation*, 23, 35–54.

Goodwin, P. and R. Noland (2003), 'Building new roads really does create extra traffic: a response to Prakash et al.', *Applied Economics*, 25(13), 1451–57.

Haggar, P., L. Whitmarsh and S.M. Skippon, S.M. (2019), 'Habit discontinuity and student travel mode choice', *Transportation Research Part F*, 64, 1–13.

Heinen, E., B. van Wee and K. Maat (2010), 'Commuting by bicycle: an overview of the literature', *Transport Reviews*, 30 (1), 59–96.

Hensher, D.A. (2008), 'Assessing systematic sources of variation in public transport elasticities: some comparative warnings', *Transportation Research Part A*, 42, 1031–42.

Hössinger, R., C. Link, A. Sonntag and J. Stark (2017), 'Estimating the price elasticity of fuel demand with stated preferences derived from a situational approach', *Transportation Research Part A*, 103, 154–71.

Inrix (2022), https://inrix.com/scorecard/.

Iseki, H., B.D. Taylor and M. Miller (2006), *The Effects of Out-of-Vehicle Time or Travel Behavior: Implications for Transit Transfers*, Los Angeles: Institute of Transportation Studies, University of California, Los Angeles, accessed at www.its.ucla.edu/research/EPIC/ Appendix%20A.pdf.

Jong, G. de and H. Gunn (2001), 'Recent evidence on car cost and time elasticities of travel demand in Europe', *Journal of Transport Economics and Policy*, 35(2), 137–60.

Kahneman, D. and A. Tvesrky (1979), 'Prospect Theory: an analysis of decision making under risk', *Econometrica*, 47(2), 263–91.

Kask, O. and W.G.Z. Tan (2019), *Cycling to School: Exploring Key Factors Influencing School-Going Children's Mobility Choice to Cycle in Tallinn, Estonia*, AESOP Annual Congress 2019, Italy: Venice, accessed June 2022 at www.aesop2019.eu/wp-content/uploads/2020/02/AESOP_book_of_papers_2 .pdf#page=2646.

KIM (2019). *Mobiliteitsbeeld 2019* [Mobility report], Den Haag: Ministerie van Infrastructuur en Waterstaat (in Dutch).

Kim, H., A. Nicholson and D. Kusumastuti (2017), 'Analysing freight shippers' mode choice preference heterogeneity using latent class modelling', *Transportation Research Procedia*, 25, 1109–25.

Kouwenhoven, M., G.C. de Jong, P. Koster, V.A.C. van den Berg, E.T. Verhoef, J. Bates and P.J.M. Warffemius (2014), 'New values of time and reliability in passenger transport in the Netherlands', *Research in Transportation Economics*, 47(1), 37–49.

Lal, D. (2006), *Reviving the Invisible Hand: The Case for Classical Liberalism in the Twenty-First Century*. Princeton, NJ: Princeton University Press.

La Paix, L., Oakil, A.T., Hofman, F., Geurs, K. (2022), 'The influence of panel effects and inertia on travel cost elasticities for car use and public transport', *Transportation*, 49, 989–1016.

Li, Z., D.A. Hensher and J.M. Rose (2011), 'Identifying sources of systematic variation in direct price elasticities from revealed preference studies of inter-city freight demand', *Transport Policy*, 18(5), 727–34.

Litman, T. (2021), *Understanding Transport Demands and Elasticities How Prices and Other Factors Affect Travel Behavior*, Victoria Transport Policy Institute, at www.vtpi.org/elasticities.pdf.

Lu, H., P. Burge, C. Heywood, R. Sheldon, P. Lee, K. Barber and A. Phillips (2018), 'The impact of real-time information on passengers' value of bus waiting time', *Transportation Research Procedia*, 31, 18–34.

Marchetti, C. (1994), 'Anthropological invariants in travel behavior', *Technological Forecasting and Social Change*, 47, 75–88.

Mokhtarian, P.L. and C. Chen (2004), 'TTB or not TTB, that is the question: a review and analysis of the empirical literature on travel, time (and money) budgets', *Transportation Research Part A*, 38(9/10), 643–75.

Mouratidis, K., S. Peters and B. van Wee (2021), 'Transportation technologies, sharing economy, and teleactivities: Implications for built environment and travel', *Transportation Research Part D*, 92, 1–23.

Pastori, E., M. Brambilla, S. Maffii, R. Vergnani, E. Gualandi and I. Skinner (2018), Research for TRAN Committee – *Modal shift in European transport: a way forward*, European Parliament, Policy Department for Structural and Cohesion Policies, Brussels.

Paulley, N., R. Balcombe, R. Mackett, H. Titheridge, J. Preston, M. Wardman, J. Shires and P. White (2006), 'The demand for public transport: the effects of fares, quality of service, income and car ownership', *Transport Policy*, 12, 295–306.

Pudane, B. and G. Correia (2020), 'On the impact of vehicle automation on the value of travel time while performing work and leisure activities in a car: Theoretical insights and results from a stated preference survey – A comment', *Transportation Research Part A*, 132, 324–28.

Pudane, B., S. van Cranenburgh and C. Chorus (2021), 'A day in the life with an automated vehicle: empirical analysis of data from an interactive stated activity-travel survey', *Journal of Choice Modelling*, 39, 100286.

Rodrigue, J.-P. (2020), *The Geography of Transport Systems*, London: Routledge.

Schafer, A. (1998), 'The global demand for motorized mobility', *Transportation Research A*, 32(6), 455–77.

Schafer, A. (2006), 'Long-term trends in global passenger mobility', *The Bridge*, 36(4), 24–32.

Schafer, A. and D.G. Victor (2000), 'The future mobility of the world population', *Transportation Research A*, 34(3), 171–205.

Stark, J. and M. Meschik (2018), 'Women's everyday mobility: Frightening situations and their impacts on travel behaviour', *Transportation Research Part F*, 54, 311–32.

Stopher, P.R., A. Ahmed and W. Liu (2017), 'Travel time budgets: new evidence from multi-year, multi-day data', *Transportation*, 44, 1069–82.

Szalai, A. (ed.) (1972), *The Use of Time: Daily Activities of Urban and Suburban Populations in Twelve Countries*, The Hague: Mouton.

The National Center for Safe Routes to School (2011), 'How Children Get to School: School Travel Patterns from 1969 to 2009', accessed June 2022 at https://www.healthworkscollective.com/wp-content/uploads/2013/07/NHTS_school_travel_report_2011_0.pdf.

Wadud, Z. (2015), 'Imperfect reversibility of air transport demand: Effects of air fare, fuel prices and price transmission', *Transportation Research Part A: Policy and Practice*, 72, 16–26.

Wardman, M. (1997), 'Inter-urban rail demand, elasticities and competition in Great Britain: Evidence from direct demand models', *Transportation Research Part E*, 33, 1, 15–28.

Wener, R.E. and G.W. Evans (2011), 'Comparing stress of car and train commuters', *Transportation Research Part F*, 14, 111–16.

Zahavi, Y. (1979), *The UMOT Project*, Washington, DC: US Ministry of Transport.

Zarabi, Z., K. Manaugh and S. Lord (2019), 'The impacts of residential relocation on commute habits: A qualitative perspective on households' mobility behaviors and strategies', *Travel Behaviour and Society*, 16, 131–42.

7
Traffic flow theory and modelling

Victor L. Knoop and Serge Hoogendoorn

7.1   INTRODUCTION

When do traffic jams emerge? Can we predict, given certain demand levels, when queuing will occur, how long the queues will be, how they will propagate in space and time, and how long it takes for the congestion to resolve? Why does an overloaded traffic network underperform? This chapter gives a basic introduction in traffic flow theory which can help to answer these kinds of questions.

We start this chapter with explaining how this chapter connects with the other chapters in this book (see Figure 7.1). Top left in the figure the reader recognizes the conceptual model introduced in Chapter 2 in highly simplified form to explain transport and traffic volumes.

One of the results of the interplay between people's and shippers' needs and desires, the locations of activities, and the transport resistance factors (Figure 7.1, top left) is a certain volume of road traffic (Figure 7.1, middle left). Road traffic, and here starts this chapter, can be described using flow variables such as speed and density (Figure 7.1, middle right). The density of traffic is the number of vehicles that is present on a roadway per unit distance. Road traffic flows on certain road stretches during certain time periods can either be free or congested and/or the flows can be unreliable. In the latter two cases, the transport resistance on these road stretches will be relatively high as explained in Chapter 6 using, among others, concepts such as the value of time and value of reliability. Consequently, high transport resistance implies negative repercussions on road traffic volumes (see the arrow from flow variables to transport resistance, Figure 7.1, top).

To be clear, this chapter focuses solely on the road traffic flow variables and the interactions with aspects as driving behaviour, weather, information technology, and so forth (the grey areas in Figure 7.1). Thus, traffic flow operations on a road facility are explained for a given traffic demand profile. Factors such as weather and information technology (e.g., navigation systems) can influence traffic flow characteristics via driving behaviour. Additionally, policies such as road expansions and traffic management measures can also have an impact on traffic flow operations, either directly or indirectly by influencing driving behaviour.

Traffic flow theory entails the knowledge of the fundamental characteristics of traffic flows and the associated analytical methods. Examples of such characteristics are road capacities, the

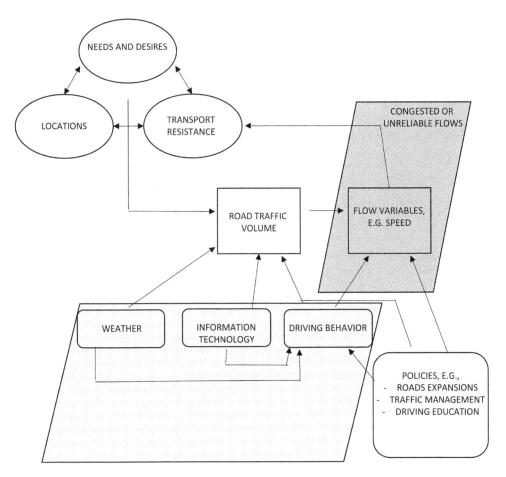

Figure 7.1   The connection of this chapter (grey area) with the simplified conceptual framework (top left) as described in Chapter 2

relation between flow and density, and headway distributions. Examples of analytical methods are shockwave theory and microscopic simulation models.

Using the presented material, the reader will be able to interpret, analyse, and – for simple situations – predict the main characteristics of traffic flows. For the larger part, the chapter considers traffic flow operations on simple infrastructure elements (uninterrupted traffic flow operations, simple discontinuities), although an important side step is made to network dynamics. In doing so, the chapter takes both a *microscopic* and a *macroscopic* perspective. The microscopic perspective reflects the behaviour of individual drivers interacting with surrounding vehicles, while the macroscopic perspective considers the average state of traffic. We discuss empirical facts, and some well known analytical tools, such as shockwave theory, kinematic wave models, and microscopic simulation models. We will also discuss the application of traffic flow theory to bicycle traffic and will consider the impact of the technology of automated vehicles on the traffic stream.

Section 7.2 introduces the basic variables on the microscopic level (the vehicle level), and Section 7.3 the macroscopic variables (i.e. the flow level). Section 7.4 discusses flow characteristics. Section 7.5 looks into the future developments and discusses the effect of autonomous vehicles. Then, in Section 7.6 traffic flow dynamics and the (self-) organization of traffic are discussed. Section 7.7 presents several theories on multi-lane vehicular traffic (i.e., motorways). Section 7.8 discusses microscopic flow models, while Section 7.9 discusses the macroscopic flow models. Section 7.10 adds the dynamics of networks to this. Section 7.11 shows how all theories and methods can be applied to bicycle traffic. Finally, in Section 7.12 the conclusions are presented.

7.2   VEHICLE TRAJECTORIES AND MICROSCOPIC FLOW VARIABLES

The vehicle trajectory (often denoted as $x_i(t)$) of vehicle (i) describes the position of the vehicle over time (t) along the roadway. The trajectory is the core variable in traffic flow theory which allows us to determine all relevant microscopic and macroscopic traffic flow quantities. Note that for the sake of simplicity, the lateral component of the trajectory is not considered here.

To illustrate the versatility of trajectories, Figure 7.2 below shows several vehicle trajectories. From the figure, it is easy to determine the distance headway S_i, and the time headway h_i, over-taking events (crossing trajectories), the speed $v_i = dx_i/dt$, the size of the acceleration (see top left where one vehicle accelerates to overtake another vehicle), the travel time TT_i, and so forth.

However, although the situation is rapidly changing due to so-called floating car data becoming more common, trajectory information is seldom available. Floating car data is information from mobile phones in vehicles that are being driven. In most cases, vehicle trajectory measurements only contain information about average characteristics of the traffic flow, provide only local information, or aggregate information in some other way (e.g., travel times from automatic vehicle identification or licence plate cameras).

Most commonly, traffic is measured by (inductive) loops measuring local (or *time–mean*) traffic flow quantities, such as (local) traffic flow q, and local mean speed u. First, we will discuss the main microscopic traffic flow variables in detail. This type of flow variables reflects the behaviour of individual drivers interacting with surrounding vehicles.

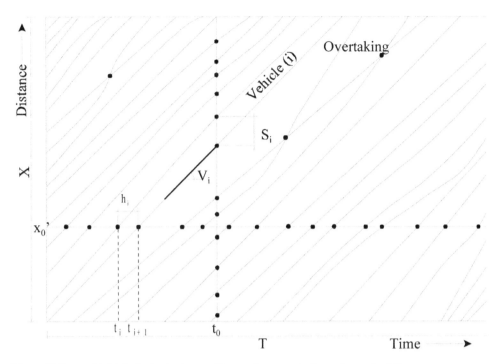

Figure 7.2   Vehicle trajectories and key microscopic flow characteristics

7.2.1   Gross and Net Headways

The (gross) time headway (h) is one of the most important microscopic flow variables. It describes the difference between passage times t_i at a cross-section x of the rear bumpers of two successive vehicles:

$$h_i(x) \;=\; t_i(x) - t_{i-1}(x) \tag{7.1}$$

The time headway, or simply headway, is directly determined by the behaviour of the driver, vehicle characteristics, flow conditions, etc. Its importance stems from the fact that the (minimal) headways directly determine the capacity of a road, a roundabout, and so forth. Typically, these minimal headways are around 1.5 seconds in dry conditions. Time headways, combined with the speeds, leads to the distance headways (see below).

The *net time headway* or *gap* is defined by the difference in passage times between the rear bumper of the lead vehicle and the front bumper of the following vehicle. This value is in particular important for driving behaviour analysis, for instance when analysing and modelling the amount of space drivers need to perform an overtaking manoeuvre (so-called *critical gap analysis*).

7.2.2   Gross and Net Distance Headways

We have seen in the preceding subsection that time headways are *local* microscopic variables: they relate to the behaviour of an individual driver and are measured at a cross-section. On the contrary, distance headways (often denoted with the symbol s) are *instantaneous* (measured at one moment in time) microscopic variables, measuring the distance between the rear bumper of the leader and the rear bumper of the follower at time instant t:

$$s_i(t) \;=\; x_{i-1}(t) - x_i(t) \tag{7.2}$$

In congested conditions, distance headways are determined by the behaviour of drivers, which in turn depends on the traffic conditions, driver abilities, the vehicle characteristics, weather conditions, and so forth. In free flow with no interaction between the drivers, the headways are determined largely by the demand (that is: they are determined by the moments drivers enter the freeway).

Net distance headways are, similar to the net time headways, defined as the distance between the position of the rear bumper of the leader and the front bumper of the follower.

It should be clear that the time headways and the distance headways are strongly correlated. If v_{i-1} denotes the speed of the leading vehicle, it is easy to see that:

$$s_i \;=\; v_{i-1} h_i \tag{7.3}$$

7.3   MACROSCOPIC FLOW VARIABLES

So far, we have mainly looked at microscopic traffic flow variables. Macroscopic flow variables, such as flow, density, speed, and speed variance, reflect the average state of the traffic flow in contrast to the microscopic traffic flow variables which focus on individual drivers. Let us take a closer look at the most important variables.

7.3.1   Traditional Definitions of Flow, Density, and Speed

In general, the flow q (also referred to as intensity, or volume) is traditionally defined by the "average number of vehicles (n) that passes a cross-section during a unit of time (T)". According to this definition, flow is a *local variable* (since it is defined at a cross-section). We have:

$$q \;=\; \frac{n}{T} \;=\; \frac{n}{\sum_{i=1}^{n} h_i} \;=\; \frac{1}{h} \tag{7.4}$$

This expression shows that the flow can be computed easily by taking the number of vehicles n that has passed the measurement location during a period of length T. The expression also shows how the flow q relates to the average headway $\bar{h}$, thereby relating the macroscopic flow variable to average microscopic behaviour (i.e., time headways).

In a similar way, the density k (or *concentration*) is defined by the "number of vehicles per distance unit". Density is, therefore, a so-called *instantaneous variable* (i.e., it is computed at a time instant), defined as follows:

$$k = \frac{m}{X} = \frac{m}{\sum_{i=1}^{m} s_i} = \frac{1}{\bar{s}} \qquad (7.5)$$

This expression shows that the density can be computed by taking a snapshot of a roadway segment of length X and counting the number of vehicles m that occupy the road at that time instant. The expression also shows how density relates to average microscopic behaviour (i.e., distance headways, s). Note that contrary to the flow, which can generally be easily determined in practice using cross-sectional measurement equipment (such as inductive loops), the density is not so easily determined since it requires observations of the entire road at a time instant (e.g., via an aerial photograph).

Similarly to the definitions above, average speeds u can be computed in two ways: at a cross-section (local mean speed or time–mean–speed u_L), or at a time instant (instantaneous mean speed or space–mean-speed u_M). As will be shown in the following paragraph, the difference between these definitions can be very large. Surprisingly, in practice the difference is seldom made. For instance, the Dutch motorway monitoring systems collects time–mean speeds, while for most applications (e.g., average travel time) the space–mean speeds are more suitable.

7.3.2 Continuity Equation

An important relation in traffic flow theory is the continuity equation: $q = ku$ (flow equals density times the speed). This equation is used to relate the instantaneous characteristic density to the local characteristic flow. The derivation of this equation is actually quite straightforward (Figure 7.3).

Consider a road of length X. All vehicles on this road drive at an equal speed u. Let us define the period T by $T = X/u$. Under this assumption, it is easy to see that the number of vehicles that are on the road at time $t = 0$ – which is equal to the density k times the length X of the roadway segment – is equal to the number of vehicles that will pass the exit at $x = X$ during period $[0,T]$ – which is in turn equal to the flow q times the duration of the period T. That is:

$$kX = qT \iff q = k\frac{X}{T} = ku \qquad (7.6)$$

Clearly, the continuity equation holds when the speeds are constant. The question is whether the equation $q = ku$ can also be applied when the speeds are not constant (e.g., u represents an average speed), and if so, which average speed (time–mean or space–mean speed) is to be used. It turns out that $q = ku$ can indeed be applied, but only if $u = u_M$, that is, if we take the space mean speed.

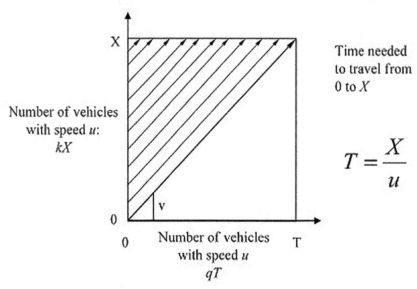

Figure 7.3   Derivation of the continuity equation

Intuitively, one can understand this as follows (a mathematical proof can be found in May, 1990). A detector lies at location x_{det}. Now we reconstruct which vehicles will pass in the time of one aggregation period. For this, the vehicle must be closer to the detector than the distance it travels in the aggregation time t_{agg}:

$$x_{det} - x_j \leq t_{agg} v_i \tag{7.7}$$

In this formula, x is the position on the road. For faster vehicles, this distance is larger. Therefore, if one takes the local arithmetic mean, one overestimates the influence of the faster vehicles. If the influence of the faster vehicles on speeds is overestimated, the average speed u is overestimated (compared to the space mean speed u_m).

The discussion above might be conceived as academic. However, if we look at empirical data, then the differences between the time–mean speeds and space–mean speeds become apparent. Figure 7.4 shows an example where the time–mean speed and space–mean speed have been computed from motorway individual vehicle data collected at the A9 motorway near Amsterdam, the Netherlands. Figure 7.4 clearly shows that the differences between the speeds can be as high as 100%; for more details we refer to Knoop et al. (2009). Also note that the space–mean speeds are always lower than the time–mean speeds. Since in most countries where inductive loops are used to monitor traffic flow operations, *arithmetic–mean speeds* are computed and stored, average speeds are generally overestimated, affecting travel time estimations. Furthermore, since $q = ku$ can only be used for *space–mean speeds*, we cannot determine the density k from the local speed and flow measurements, complicating the use of the collected data from, e.g., traffic information and traffic management purposes.

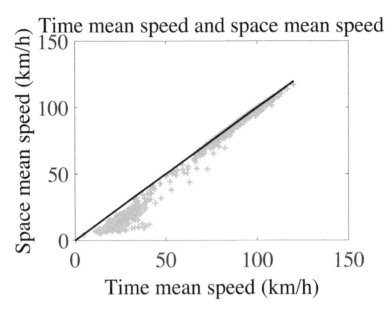

Source: Knoop (2020).

Figure 7.4   Differences between time-mean speed and space-mean speed for the A9 motorway

7.3.3   Generalized Traffic Flow Variables

Alternate measurement methods, such as automatic vehicle identification (AVI), radar, and floating-car measurements, provide new ways to determine the flow variables described above. One of the benefits of these new methods is that they provide information about the temporal and spatial aspects of traffic flow. For instance, using video we can observe the density in a region directly, rather than determine the density from local observations.

For the relation between instantaneous and local variables, the work of Edie (1965) is very relevant. Edie (1965) introduces generalized definitions of flow, density, and speed.

Consider a rectangular region in time and space with dimensions T and X respectively (see Figure 7.5). Let d_i denote the total distance travelled by vehicle i during period T and let r_i denote the total time spent in region X. Let us define the total distance travelled by all vehicles by:

$$P = \sum_i d_i \tag{7.8}$$

Based on this quantity P, which is referred to as the *performance*, Edie defined the generalized flow as follows:

$$q = \frac{P}{XT} \tag{7.9}$$

Note that we can rewrite this equation as follows:

$$q = \frac{\sum_i d_i / X}{T} \tag{7.10}$$

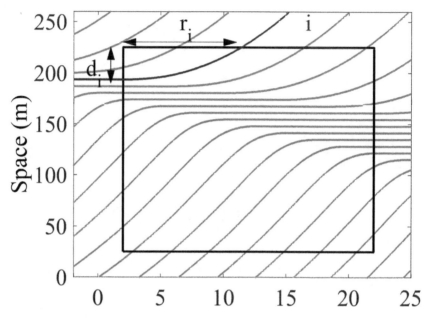

Figure 7.5   Generalization of concepts of flow and density to a generic area in space-time

Let us now define the total travel time R as follows:

$$R = \sum_i r_i \tag{7.11}$$

Edie (1965) defines the generalized density by:

$$k = \frac{R}{XT} = \frac{\sum_i r_i / T}{X} \tag{7.12}$$

For the generalized speed, the following intuitive definition is used:

$$u = \frac{q}{k} = \frac{P}{R} = \frac{\text{total distance travelled}}{\text{total time spent}} \tag{7.13}$$

These definitions can be used for any region in space–time, even non-rectangular ones. These definitions apply to regions in time and space, and will turn out to be increasingly important with the advent of new measurement techniques. This is because traditionally traffic was measured at one location (for instance, by loop detectors). New techniques (apps, connected vehicles) will measure at various locations and times, hence a measurement in space and time is necessary.

Moreover, new techniques (apps on phones) allow tracking for *some individual vehicles*, but do not show all vehicles. This gives completely different challenges to estimating traffic. Estimations of total number of vehicles that pass by still remains useful, as do derivative measures like flow, density, or speed. Van Erp et al. (2019) shows how these data, including findings on overtaking, can be used to get an overall view of the total traffic flow even though not all vehicles are being measured.

7.4 MICROSCOPIC AND MACROSCOPIC FLOW CHARACTERISTICS

The preceding sections introduced the different microscopic and macroscopic variables. This section shows the most common flow characteristics, entailing both relations between the flow variables, typical distribution, etc. These flow characteristics in a sense drive the traffic flow dynamics that will be discussed in this section. Next to providing a short description of the characteristics and their definition, the section will discuss empirical examples as well as key issues in identifying these parameters.

7.4.1 Headway Distributions

If we would collect headways at a specific location x, then we would observe that these headways are not constant but rather follow some probability distribution function. This is also the case when the flow is stationary during the data collection period. The causes are manifold: there are large differences in driving behaviour between different drivers, and differences in the vehicle characteristics, but there is also variation in the behaviour of one driver. A direct and important consequence of this is that the capacity of the road, which is largely determined by the driving behaviour, is not constant either, but a stochastic variable.

The headway distribution can be described by a probability density function (p.d.f.) $f(h)$. In the literature, many different kinds of distribution functions have been proposed, with varying success. It can be shown that if the flows are small – there are few vehicle interactions – the *exponential distribution* will be an adequate model. When the flows become larger, there are more interactions amongst the vehicles, and other distributions are more suitable. A good candidate in many situations is the *log-normal distribution*; we refer to Cowan (1975) for more details. In Hoogendoorn (2005), an overview is given of estimation techniques for the log-normal distributions in specific situations.

The main problem with these relatively simple models is that they are only able to represent available measurements but cannot be extrapolated to other situations. If, for instance, we are interested in a headway distribution for another flow level than the one observed, we need to collect new data and re-estimate the model.

To overcome this, so-called *composite headway models* have been proposed. The main characteristic of these models is that they distinguish between vehicles that are flowing freely and those that are constrained by the vehicle in front. Buckley (1968) was one of the first to propose these models, assuming that the headways of the free driving vehicles are exponentially distributed. He showed that the probability density function $f(h)$ of the observed headways h can be described by the following function:

$$f(h) = \phi g(h) + (1 - \phi)w(h) \tag{7.14}$$

In this equation, g describes the probability density function of the headways of vehicles, which are following (also referred to as the distribution of the *empty zones*), while w denotes the probability density function of those vehicles that are driving freely. For the latter, an exponential distribution is assumed. ϕ denotes the fraction of vehicles that are following.

There are different ways to estimate these probability density functions from available headway observations. Wasielewski (1974), later improved by Hoogendoorn (2005), proposed an approach in which one does not need to choose a prior form of the constrained headway distribution. In illustration, Figure 7.6 shows an example of the application of this estimation method on a two-lane motorway in the Netherlands in the morning (the location is the so-called 'Doenkade').

This example nicely illustrates how the approach can be applied for estimating capacities, even if no capacity observations are available. We find the maximum flow (or capacity flow, C) when all drivers are following. We directly observe from the Buckley model (Buckley, 1968, see above) that the observed headways in that case follow g. The number of vehicles per unit of time is the inverse of time per vehicle. So the maximum flow equals 1 divided by the mean (minimum) headway value, under the condition that all vehicles are following. Accounting for the fact that we measure flows in vehicles per hour, and headways in seconds, we need to include a unit conversion. We then have that the capacity equals 3600 seconds per hour divided by the average headway (H, following distribution g) in seconds (or the expectation value thereof, indicated by E). We therefore get:

$$C = 3600/E(H) \text{ where } H\sim g \tag{7.15}$$

Using this approach, we can find estimates for the capacity even if there are no direct capacity observations available. For the example above, we can compute the mean empty zone value by looking at the p.d.f. $g(h)$, which turns out to be equal to 1.69. Based on this value, we find a capacity estimate of $3600/1.69 = 2134$ vehicles per hour.

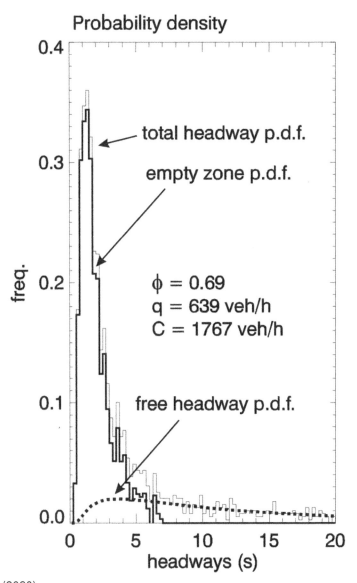

Source: Knoop (2020).
Note: In the figure, W denotes the gross headway, which is composed of the empty zone X and the free headway W-X

Figure 7.6   Composite headway probability density function (p.d.f.) fitted on data of the Doenkade site.

7.4.2   Desired Speed Distributions

Generally, the *free speed or desired speed of a driver–vehicle combination* (simply called vehicle or driver in the ensuing) is defined by the speed driven when other road users do not influence the driver. Knowledge of free speeds on a road under given conditions is relevant for a number of reasons. For instance, the concept of free speed is an important element in many traffic flow models. In illustration, the free speed distribution is an important input for many microscopic simulation models. Insights into free speeds and their distributions are also important from the viewpoint of road design, and for determining suitable traffic rules for a certain facility. For instance, elements of the network should be designed such that drivers using the facility can traverse the road safely and comfortably. It is also of interest to see how desired speed distributions change under varying road, weather and ambient conditions, and how these distributions vary for different types of travellers. That is, speed distribution is an important characteristic of the driver population for design issues.

The free speed will be influenced by the characteristics of the vehicle, the driver, the road, and (road) conditions such as weather and traffic rules (speed limits). Botma (1999) describes how individual drivers choose their free speed, discussing a behavioural model relating the free speed of a driver to a number of counteracting mental stresses a driver is subjected to. A similar model can be found in Jepsen (1998). However, these models have not been successful in their practical application. The problem of determining free speed distributions from available data is not trivial. In Botma (1999), an overview of alternative free speed estimation approaches is presented. Botma (1999) concluded that all methods he reviewed have severe disadvantages, which is the reason why another estimation approach is proposed. This approach is based on the concept of censored observations (Nelson, 1982) using a parametric estimation approach to estimate the parameters of the free speed distribution. Speed observations are marked as either censored (constrained) or uncensored (free flowing) using subjective criteria (headway and relative speed). Hoogendoorn (2005) presents a new approach to estimating the distribution of free speeds based on the method of censored observations.

7.4.3   Gap Acceptance and Critical Gaps

Gap acceptance is a process that occurs in different traffic situations, such as crossing a road, entering a roundabout, or performing an overtaking manoeuvre on a bi-directional road. The minimum gap that a driver will accept is generally called the critical gap. Mathematical representations of the gap acceptance process are an important part of, for instance, traffic simulation models.

In general terms the gap acceptance process can be described as follows: traffic participants that want to make a manoeuvre estimate the space they need and estimate the available space. Based on the comparison between required and available space, they decide to start the manoeuvre or postpone it. The term space is deliberately somewhat vague; it can be expressed either in time or in distance. The required space is dependent on characteristics of the traffic participant, the vehicle, and the road. The available space is dependent on the characteristics of, for instance, the on-coming vehicles and the vehicle to be overtaken (the passive vehicle).

Traffic participants have to perceive all these characteristics, process them, and come to a decision. Humans highly differ in perception capabilities, e.g., the ability to estimate distances can vary substantially between persons, and they differ in the acceptance of risk. The total acceptance process is dependent on many factors of which only a subset is observable. This has led to the introduction of stochastic models.

Many different methods to estimate the distribution of critical gaps, from observations of the gap acceptance process in reality, can be found in the literature (Brilon et al., 1999). Let us consider the problem of estimating the critical gap distribution. Suppose, as an example, a driver successively rejects gaps of 3, 9, 12 and 7 s and accepts a gap of 19 s. The only thing one can conclude from these observations is that this driver has a critical gap between 12 and 19 s. Stated in other words: the critical gap cannot be observed directly. The observations are, thus, censored. Note that it can also be concluded that only the *maximum of the rejected gaps* is informative for the critical gap (assuming that driver behaviour is consistent); the smaller gaps are rejected by definition.

7.4.4   Capacity and Capacity Estimation

Capacity is usually defined as follows: "The maximum hourly rate at which persons or vehicles can reasonably be expected to traverse a point or uniform section of a lane or roadway during a given time period (usually 15 minutes) under prevailing roadway, traffic, and control conditions" (National Academies of Sciences, Engineering, and Medicine, 2022).

Maximum flows (maximum free flows of queue discharge rates) are not constant values and vary under the influence of several factors. Factors influencing the capacity are, among other things, the composition of the vehicle fleet, the composition of traffic with respect to trip purpose, weather-, road-, and ambient conditions, etc. These factors affect the behaviour of driver vehicle combinations and thus the maximum number of vehicles that can pass a cross-section during a given time period. Some of these factors can be observed and their effect can be quantified. Some factors can, however, not be observed directly. Furthermore, differences exist between drivers implying that some drivers will need a larger minimum time headway than other drivers, even if drivers belong to the same class of users. As a result, the minimum headways will not be constant values but follow a distribution function (see discussion on headway distribution modelling). Observed maximum flows thus appear to follow a distribution. The shape of this distribution depends on, among other things, the capacity definition and measurement method or period. In most cases, a normal distribution can be used to describe the capacity.

Several researchers have pointed out the existence of two different maximum flow rates, namely pre-queue and queue discharge respectively (e.g., Cassidy and Bertini, 1999). Each of these has its own maximum flow distribution. We define the *pre-queue maximum flow* as the maximum flow rate observed at the downstream location just before the on-set of congestion (a queue) upstream. These maximum flows are characterized by the absence of queues or congestion upstream of the bottleneck, high speeds, instability leading to congestion on-set within a short period, maximum flows showing a large variance. The *queue discharge flow* is the maximum flow rate observed at the downstream location as long as congestion exists. These maximum flow rates are characterized by the presence of a queue upstream of the bottleneck, lower speeds and densities, a constant outflow with a small variance which can sustain for a long period, however with lower flow rates than in the pre-queue flow state. Both capacities can only be measured downstream of the bottleneck location. The size of the drop depends on the bottleneck type, and particularly on the speed in the queue (Yuan et al., 2015). Average capacity drop changes are in the range of -1% to -15%.

There are many approaches that can be applied to compute the capacity of a specific piece of infrastructure. The suitability of the approach depends on a number of factors, such as:

1. the type of infrastructure (e.g., motorway without off- or on-ramps, on-ramp, roundabout, unsignalized intersection, etc.);
2. type of data (individual vehicle data, aggregate data) and time aggregation;
3. location of data collection (upstream of, in or downstream of the bottleneck);
4. traffic conditions for which data are available (congestion, no congestion).

We refer to Minderhoud et al. (1996) for a critical review of approaches that are available to estimate road capacity.

7.4.5   Fundamental Diagrams

The fundamental diagram describes a statistical relation between the macroscopic traffic flow variables: flow, density and speed. There are different ways to represent this relation, but the most often used is the relation $q = Q(k)$ between the flow and the density. Using the continuity equation, the other relations $u = U(k)$ and $u = U(q)$ can be easily derived.

To understand the origin of the fundamental diagram, we can interpret the relation from a driving behaviour perspective. To this end, recall that the flow and the density relate to the (average) time headway and distance headway according to Equations 7.4 and 7.5 respectively. Based on this, we can clearly see which premise underlies the existence of the fundamental diagram: *under similar traffic conditions, drivers will behave in a similar way*. That is, when traffic operates at a certain speed u, then it is plausible that (on average) drivers will maintain (on average) the same distance headway $s = 1/k$. This behaviour – and therewith the relation between speed and density – is obviously dependent on factors like weather, road characteristics, the composition of traffic, traffic regulations, and so forth.

Figure 7.7 shows typical examples of the relation between flow, density, and speed. The figure shows the most important points in the fundamental diagram, which are the *roadway capacity C*, the *critical density k_c* and the *critical speed u_c* (the density and speed occurring at capacity operations), the *jam density k_{jam}* (density occurring at zero speed), and the *free speed u_0*. In the figure, we clearly see the difference between the free conditions ($k < k_c$) and the congested conditions ($k > k_c$).

It is tempting to infer causality from the fundamental diagram. It is often stated that the relation $u = U(k)$ describes the fact that with increasing density (e.g., reduced spacing between vehicles), the speed is reducing. It is, however, more the other way around. If we take a driving behaviour perspective, then it seems more reasonable to assume that with reduced speed of the leader, drivers need smaller distance headways to drive safely and comfortably.

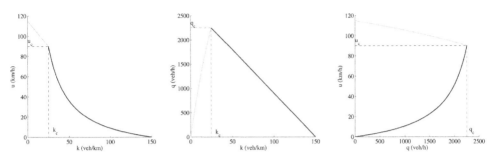

Figure 7.7   Example of fundamental diagram

Fundamental diagrams are often determined from real-life traffic data. This is usually done by assuming that stationary periods can be identified during data measurements. To obtain meaningful fundamental diagrams, the data collection must be performed at the correct location during a selected time period.

7.5   DEVELOPMENTS FOR THE FUTURE: CONNECTED AND AUTOMATED VEHICLES

In the past decade, much effort has been put into the automation of vehicles. The driving tasks of drivers can be handed over to the vehicle. In this section, we will describe the levels of automation, how this will interfere with the traffic operations, and the potential effects.

For traffic automation, various levels of autonomy have been defined. The most commonly used reference is the SAE levels of automation (SAE, 2021). Here, we report their defined levels in a simplified way. For the full description, we refer to (SAE, 2021). There are six levels of autonomy defined, i.e., level 0 to 5.

Level 0 is the automation level where the driver is performing the driving tasks. He is (almost) continuously giving input to the vehicle in terms of steering (lateral driving task) and determining the vehicle's speed (longitudinal driving task).

In level 1, the driver is supported in one driving task, lateral or longitudinal. He either needs to continuously steer or determine the speed. The other dimension is taken over by the system, by means of a system that keeps the vehicle in its lane or determines the acceleration automatically by means of adaptive cruise control (ACC).

In level 2 the car can accelerate and decelerate by means of an ACC and keep itself in lanes. The driver can drive "hand and feet off". Yet, the driver needs to constantly monitor the environment and the system, and the driver should be able to take over control instantaneously without any warning. As of 2022, there are vehicles available that can achieve level 2 automation.

In level 3, the vehicle also monitors the system and warns the driver if he needs to take over ("fallback"). The driver should be able to take over when the system demands so. As of April 2022, no vehicles are on the market that have this level of automation. Some manufacturers claim their vehicles can reach level 3, but at present it has not been legally approved.

From level 4 onwards, this fallback is taken over by the system and the car will – within its predefined bounds, or "operational design domain" – not need driver input. The system is designed to work within a certain operational design domain. What this operational design domain is can be fully determined by the car manufacturer. Examples could be a speed range (e.g., between 20 and 60 km/h), a specific road (e.g., the M1 motorway, between kilometre 12 and 15 in the left lane), or weather conditions (daylight, no precipitation, good sight), or combinations of these. As long as the vehicle remains within this operational domain, in level 4 automation, the driver has no need to interfere with the vehicle and does not need to be the fallback option. This changes if the vehicle comes out of the operational design domain.

For level 5, these operational design domains are removed. Level 5 automated vehicles can drive themselves without human supervision anywhere and anytime.

Note here that the step from level 2 to level 3 implies a different driving experience where a driver (within the operational design domain) does not need to pay constant attention to the road.

An interesting point is that from level 2 onwards, for vehicles that are on the market now, the "operational" driving is done by the vehicle itself. Indeed, the driver needs to constantly monitor and intervene directly and whenever necessary. However, with good systems, this will be rare, and the vehicle decides on its speed and lane itself. The analyses of driving behaviour and how this influences the traffic stream should from this level onwards, therefore, (also) be performed for the vehicle.

In early studies of automated vehicles, it was expected that vehicle automation would strongly increase road capacity. Namely, automated systems have no reaction time, and vehicles can travel closely together at high speed. This will lead to short time headways and hence a high capacity. Rao et al. (1993) predicted flows of up to 6900 veh/h/lane. On a vehicle level, that would mean a time headway of approximately 0.5 seconds. Once the (level 1 and level 2 automation) ACC systems became more commonly available, real-world tests have been performed with vehicles that are on the market. Early ACC systems were studied by Milanés and Shladover (2014). They concluded that the capacity actually decreased because the systems keep a longer time headway than human drivers. This could be in line with reports on lower roadway capacities, which is a change compared to a trend of decades of increasing road capacity for the same road layout (Shiomi et al., 2019; Knoop and Hoogendoorn, 2022).

The large headways found for one brand in the early days have been confirmed for more recent vehicles and a variety of brands (Knoop et al., 2019). The main conclusion of this study is that ACC systems make the traffic stream unstable. That is, if the first vehicle brakes, the (ACC equipped) follower brakes stronger, and the next (ACC equipped) follower even stronger, etc. In such a way, small perturbations will grow to traffic jams and potentially dangerous situations. The market is currently (2022) being flooded with more vehicles with ACC systems, and potentially with updates of current systems. The response of ACC systems to a disturbance is empirically studied, and a database is built where these data are stored and made accessible for researchers; see Ciuffo et al. (2020).

Note that the previous section discussed autonomous vehicles, i.e., vehicles that drive autonomously (i.e., by themselves, without influence from others). This is different from vehicles that exchange messages with each other or a control centre; the latter are called connected vehicles. A common combination for studies of the impact of new technologies is autonomous connected vehicles, which some researchers refer to as automated vehicles. Some of the drawbacks of autonomous vehicles, like the instabilities, can be overcome by sending messages. In the future, communication on anticipated braking manoeuvres between vehicles can potentially solve this stability issue. If a vehicle is certain that it will get a timely message before it needs to brake, it can drive closer to its predecessor and still there would be no need to over-react, or it can form platoons with other vehicles to cross traffic lights.

7.6 TRAFFIC FLOW DYNAMICS AND SELF-ORGANIZATION

So far, we have discussed the main microscopic and macroscopic characteristics of traffic flow. In doing so, we have focused on the static characteristics of traffic flow. However, there are different characteristics, which are dynamic in nature, or rather, have to do with the dynamic properties of traffic flow.

7.6.1 Capacity Drop

The first phenomenon that we discuss is the so-called capacity drop. The capacity drop describes the fact that once congestion has formed, drivers are not maintaining a headway as close as before the speed breakdown. Therefore, the road capacity is lower. This effect is considerable, and values of a reduction up to 30% are quoted (Hall and Agyemang-Duah, 1991; Cassidy and Bertini, 1999; Chung et al., 2007; Yuan et al., 2015). The effect of the capacity drop is illustrated in Figure 7.8. Causes of the capacity drop lie in the individual driving behaviour. The exact cause is unknown and might lie in lane changing (Laval and Daganzo, 2006) or car-following/acceleration behaviour (Yuan et al., 2017).

7.6.2 Traffic Hysteresis

The different microscopic processes that constitute the characteristics of a traffic flow take time: a driver needs time to accelerate when the vehicle in front drives away when the traffic signal turns green. When traffic conditions on a certain location change, for instance when the head of a queue moves upstream, it will generally take time for the flow to adapt to these changing conditions.

Generally, however, we may assume that given that the conditions remain unchanged for a sufficient period of time – say, five minutes – traffic conditions will converge to an average state. This state is often referred to as the equilibrium traffic state. When considering a traffic flow, this equilibrium state is generally expressed in terms of the fundamental diagram. That is, when considering traffic flow under stationary conditions, the flow operations can – on average – be described by some relation between speed, density, and flow. This is why the speed–density relation is often referred to as the equilibrium speed.

From real-life observations of traffic flow, it can be observed that many of the data points collected are not on the fundamental diagram. While some of these points can be explained by

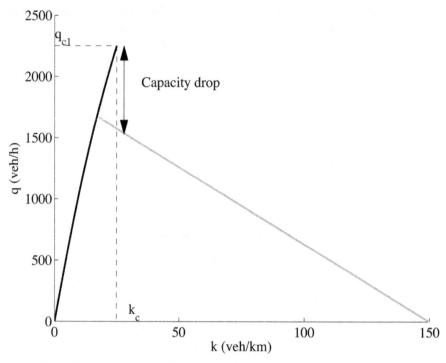

Figure 7.8   The capacity drop in the flow density diagram

stochastic fluctuations (e.g., vehicles have different sizes, drivers have different desired speeds and following distances), a part of it can be structural, and stem from the dynamic properties of traffic flow. That is, they reflect so-called transient states (i.e., changes from congestion to free flow (acceleration phase) or from free flow to congestion (deceleration phase) of traffic flow. It turns out that generally, these changes in the traffic state are not on the fundamental diagram. In other words: if we consider the average behaviour of drivers (assuming stationary traffic conditions), observed mean speeds will generally not equal the "equilibrium" speed. The term "equilibrium" reflects the fact that the observed speeds in time will converge to the equilibrium speed, assuming that the average conditions remain the same. That is, the average speed does not adapt instantaneously to the average or equilibrium speed.

This introduces traffic hysteresis, i.e., at the same time, drivers keep a different headway speed during acceleration then during deceleration. Figure 7.9 shows the first empirical observation thereof by Treiterer and Myers (1974). The figure shows the time it takes for a platoon to pass a point along the roadway. The longer the arrow is, the longer that time is, and hence the lower the flow (vehicles/hour). The arrow is long at the beginning since some drivers are not car-following yet. At the second arrow, all vehicles are car-following and the flow is high (short arrow). In the disturbance, the flow is very low, and we find a long arrow. After the disturbance, the flow increases, but the headways are longer than before the vehicles entered the disturbance. Note that also in exiting the traffic jam, all vehicles will be in car-following mode.

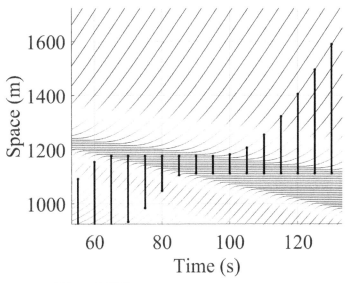

Source: Treiterer and Myers (1974).

Figure 7.9   Vehicle trajectories collected from airborne platform clearly showing
differences in average platoon length before and after disturbance

Decades later, it has been realized that the hysteresis is perhaps not best measured at one time
instance. Whereas hysteresis still occurs, effects might change or have a different magnitude
as shown by Laval (2011).

7.6.3   Three Phase Traffic Flows, Phase Transitions, and Self-Organization

Traffic can have different states or phases. In the early 2000s there was a strong debate on
the number of phases and phase transitions. Kerner (2004) commented that there are three
phases (free flow, synchronized flows, and jams), whereas many others (e.g., Treiber et al.,
2000) argued there are two (free flow and congestion). In traffic patterns, we can identify
congestion with different speeds and different causes. There can be freely flowing traffic at
high speed, a traffic moving at lower speed caused by a restriction of capacity, or completely
stopped traffic. These are identifiable in traffic and are consistent with the states Kerner has
distinguished.

If the vehicles indeed come to a complete stop, arriving vehicles will need to stop upstream.
It will hence grow at the upstream end. At the same time, at the downstream end, vehicles
might start moving again, causing a backward moving front of the queue. As a pattern, this
queue therefore travels in time over space, as is visible in Figure 7.9. This pattern is called
a stop-and-go wave, or (by Kerner) a wide moving jam. The wave speed is approximately 18
km/h opposite the driving direction.

The causes of these jams differ. An example is a jam caused by a bottleneck, such as an on-ramp. In this situation, the simple fact that traffic demand is at some point in time larger than the rest capacity (being the motorway capacity minus the inflow from the on-ramp) causes a jam. Note that these kinds of phase transitions can be described by basic flow theories and models (shockwave theory, kinematic wave models) adequately. As an additional remark, note that these transitions are, although induced, still random events since both the free flow capacity and the supply are random variables.

However, not all phase transitions are induced (directly); some are caused by intrinsic ("spontaneous") properties of traffic flow. An example is the transition from a jam with moving traffic to a stop-and-go wave. (referred to by Kerner as wide moving jams). Due to the unstable nature of specific denser traffic (in the congested state of the fundamental diagram), small disturbances in the congested flow will grow from one vehicle to its leader, and hence also over time. If the gaps between platoons of vehicles are not large enough to absorb a disturbance, it can cause traffic to come to a complete stop (traffic instability; Pueboobpaphan and Van Arem, 2010).

This phenomenon is quite common in day-to-day motorway traffic operations. Figure 7.10 shows an example of the A4 motorway in the Netherlands. Figure 7.10 shows an example of the A4 motorway in the Netherlands. A bottleneck can be identified around km 55. One can find stop-and-go waves propagating backwards at approximately 18 km/h. Note that as wide

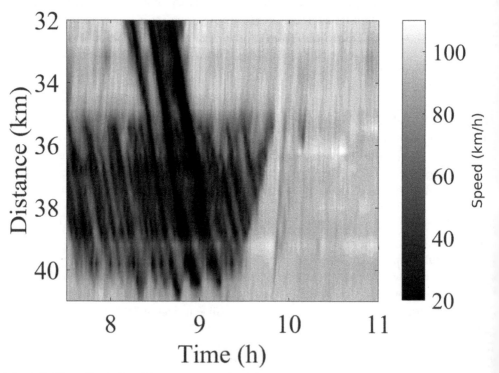

Figure 7.10　Typical traffic patterns on the A4 motorway in the Netherlands

moving jams. Note that as wide moving jams have an outflow rate which is about 30% lower than the free flow capacity, these jams are actually quite undesirable from a traffic efficiency perspective. Furthermore, they imply additional braking and acceleration, yielding increased fuel consumption and emission levels.

7.7   MULTI-LANE TRAFFIC FLOW FACILITIES

Up to now, the chapter has considered each lane of the freeway to be equal. However, there are considerable differences between them. This section only introduces a basic concept. For more insight we refer to the literature mentioned in this paragraph. For the sake of simplicity, we assume here right-hand driving. For countries where a left-hand driving rule applies, like Japan, the United Kingdom, or Australia, the lanes are exactly opposite. Daganzo (2002a, 2002b) poses a theory classifying the drivers as *slugs*, defined by their low desired speed, and *rabbits*, defined by their higher desired flow speed. He states that as soon as the speed in the right lane will go under a threshold, rabbits will move to faster lanes at the left. The theory further states that even if the density in the right lane is lower than in the left lane, the rabbits will not change towards the right lane as long as the speeds in the left lane are higher. This traffic state, with two different speeds, is called a *two pipe regime*, since traffic is flowing as it were in two different, unrelated pipes. In this state, there is no equal density in both lanes. Only once the density in the left lane increases that much that the speed decreases to a value lower than the speed in the right lane, will rabbits move towards the right lane. Then, the rabbits will redistribute themselves in such a way that the traffic in both lanes flows at the same speed. This is called a *one pipe regime*.

Note that the speeds in different lanes at the same densities can be different, due to these effects or basically due to the driver population on that lane. This leads to different fundamental diagrams in the left and right lanes. Usually, the free flow speed in the left lane is higher than in the right lane, due to the higher fraction of rabbits in that lane (see Knoop et al., 2010). Kerner (2004) poses a similar theory on multi-lane traffic flow facilities. This unbalanced lane flows cause inefficiencies in road traffic. By actively influencing lane choice or lane changes, one can try to increase road capacity and hence reduce delays. This has been an active field of research in the past decade (e.g., Roncoli et al., 2017, and Nagalur Subraveti et al., 2020).

7.8   MICROSCOPIC FLOW MODELS

Traffic flow models can be used to simulate the traffic, for instance, to evaluate *ex-ante* the use of a new part of the infrastructure. Traffic flow models may be categorized using various dimensions (deterministic or stochastic, continuous or discrete, analytical or simulation, and so forth). The most common classification is the distinction between microscopic and macroscopic traffic flow modelling approaches. However, this distinction is not unambiguous, due to the existence of hybrid models. This is why here models are categorized based on the following aspects:

1. **Representation** of the traffic flow in terms of flows (macroscopic), groups of drivers (macroscopic), or individual drivers (microscopic).
2. **Underlying behavioural theory**, which can be based on characteristics of the flow (macroscopic), or individual drivers (microscopic behaviour).

The remainder of this section uses this classification to discuss some important flow models. Table 7.1 depicts an overview of these models.

Table 7.1   Overview of traffic flow model classification

Representation	Behavioural rules	
	Microscopic	Macroscopic
Vehicle based	Microscopic flow models	Particle models
Flow based	Gas-kinetic models	Macroscopic models

The observed behaviour of drivers, i.e., headways, driving speeds, driving lane, is influenced by different factors, which can be related to the driver–vehicle combination (vehicle characteristics, driver experience, age, gender, and so forth), the traffic conditions (average speeds, densities), infrastructure conditions (road conditions), and external situational influences (weather, driving regulations). Over the years, different theories have been proposed to (dynamically) relate the observed driving behaviour to the parameters describing these conditions.

In doing so, different driver subtasks are often distinguished. In general, two types of driver tasks are distinguished: longitudinal tasks (acceleration, maintaining speed, distance keeping relative to leading vehicle) and lateral tasks (lane changing, overtaking). In particular the longitudinal and (to a lesser extent) the lateral interaction subtasks have received quite some attention in traffic flow theory research.

A microscopic model provides a description of the movements of individual vehicles that are considered to be a result of the characteristics of drivers and vehicles, the interactions between driver–vehicle elements, the interactions between driver–vehicle elements and the road characteristics, external conditions and the traffic regulations and control. Most microscopic simulation models assume that a driver will only respond to the one vehicle that is driving in the same lane, directly in front of him (the leader).

When the number of driver–vehicle units on the road is very small, the driver can freely choose his speed given his preferences and abilities, the roadway conditions, curvature, prevailing speed limits, and so forth. In any case, there will be little reason for the driver to adapt his speed to the other road users. The target speed of the driver is the so-called free speed. In real life, the free speed will vary from one driver to another, but also the free speed of a single driver will change over time. Most microscopic models assume however that the free speeds have a constant value that is driver-specific. When traffic conditions deteriorate, the driver will no longer be able to choose the speed freely, since he will not always be able to overtake or pass a slower vehicle. The driver will need to adapt his speed to the prevailing traffic conditions, i.e., the driver is following. In the remainder of this section, we will discuss some of these car-following models. Models for the lateral tasks, such as deciding to perform a lane change and gap acceptance, will not be discussed in this section in detail. The Minimizing Overall Braking Induced by Lane Changes (MOBIL) model (Kesting et al., 2007) or Lane Change Model with Relaxation and Synchronization (LMRS) (Schakel et al., 2012) models provide a good basis for realistic lane changing.

7.8.1   Safe-Distance Models

The first car-following models were developed by Pipes (1953) and were based on the assumption that drivers maintain a safe distance. A good rule for following vehicle i-1 at a safe distance s_i is to allow at least the length S_0 of a car between vehicle I and a part which is linear with the speed v_i at which i is travelling:

$$s_i = S(v_i) = S_0 + T_r v_i \tag{7.16}$$

Here, S_0 is the effective length of a stopped vehicle (including additional distance in front), and T_r denotes a parameter (comparable to the reaction time). A similar approach was proposed by Forbes et al. (1958). Both Pipes' and Forbes' theory were compared to field measurements. It was concluded that according to Pipes' theory, the minimum headways are slightly less at low and high velocities than observed in empirical data. However, considering the models' simplicity, agreement with real-life observations was amazing (Pignataro, 1973).

7.8.2   Stimulus-Response Models

However, safe-distance models do not seem to capture many phenomena observed in real-life traffic flows, such as hysteresis, traffic instabilities, etc. Stimulus response models are dynamic models that describe the reaction of drivers as a function of changes in distance, speeds, etc., relative to the vehicle in front, more realistically, e.g. by considering a finite reaction time. These models are applicable to relatively busy traffic flows, where the overtaking possibilities are small, and drivers are obliged to follow the vehicle in front of them. Drivers do not want the gap in front of them to become too large, so that other drivers can enter it. At the same time, the drivers will generally be inclined to keep a safe distance.

Stimulus response models assume that drivers control their acceleration (a). The well-known model of Chandler et al. (1958) is based on the intuitive hypothesis that a driver's acceleration is proportional to the relative speed $v_{i-1} - v_i$:

$$a_i(t) = \frac{d}{dt}v_i(t) = \alpha\left(v_{i-1}(t - T_r) - v_i(t - T_r)\right) \tag{7.17}$$

where T_r again denotes the overall reaction time, and α denotes the sensitivity. Based on field experiments, conducted to quantify the parameter values for the reaction time T_r and the sensitivity α, it was concluded that α depended on the distance between the vehicles: when the vehicles were close together, the sensitivity was high, and vice versa.

Stimulus-response models have been mainly applied to single lane traffic (e.g., tunnels, cf. Newell, 1961) and traffic stability analysis (Herman, 1959; May, 1990). It should be noted that no generally applicable set of parameter estimates has been found so far, i.e., estimates are site-specific. An overview of parameter estimates can be found in Brackstone and McDonald (1999).

7.8.3   Psycho-Spacing Models

The two car-following models discussed so far have a mechanistic character. The only human element is the presence of a finite reaction time T_r. However, in reality a driver is not able to:

1. observe a stimulus lower than a given value (perception threshold);
2. evaluate a situation and determine the required response precisely, for instance due to observation errors resulting from radial motion observation;
3. manipulate the gas and brake pedal precisely.

Furthermore, due to the need to distribute his attention to different tasks, a driver will generally not be permanently occupied with the car-following task. This type of consideration has inspired a different class of car-following models, namely the *psycho-spacing models*. Michaels (1963) provided the bases for the first psycho-spacing based on theories borrowed from perceptual psychology; cf. Leutzbach and Wiedemann (1986).

The so-called action point models (an important psycho-spacing model) form the basis for a large number of contemporary microscopic traffic flow models. An attempt to put these effects into models has been made by Hoogendoorn et al. (2010).

7.9   MACROSCOPIC TRAFFIC FLOW MODELS

In the previous section we have discussed different microscopic traffic flow modelling approaches. In this section, we will discuss the main approaches that have been proposed in literature taking a macroscopic perspective.

7.9.1   Deterministic and Stochastic Queuing Theory

The most straightforward approach to model traffic dynamics is probably the use of queuing theory. In queuing theory, we keep track of the number of vehicles in a queue (n). A queue starts whenever the flow to a bottleneck is larger than the bottleneck capacity, where the cars form a virtual queue. The outflow of the queue is given by the infrastructure (it is the outflow capacity of the bottleneck, given by C), whereas the inflow is the flow towards the bottleneck (q) as given by the traffic model. In an equation, this is written as:

$$dn = q(t)dt - C(t)dt \tag{7.18}$$

The number of vehicles in the queue (n; dn stands for the change in number of vehicles in the queue) will evolve in this way until the queue is completely disappeared. Note that both the inflow and the capacity are time dependent in the description. For the inflow, this is due to the random distribution pattern of the arrivals of the vehicles. Vehicles can arrive in platoons or there can be large gaps in between two vehicles. Also, the capacity is fluctuating. On the one hand, there are vehicle-to-vehicle fluctuations. For instance, some drivers have a shorter reaction time, hence a shorter headway leading to a higher capacity. On the other hand, the capacities will also on a larger scale depend on road or weather conditions (e.g., wet roads, night-time).

Figure 7.11 shows how the number of vehicles in the queue, n, fluctuates with time for a given inflow and outflow curve.

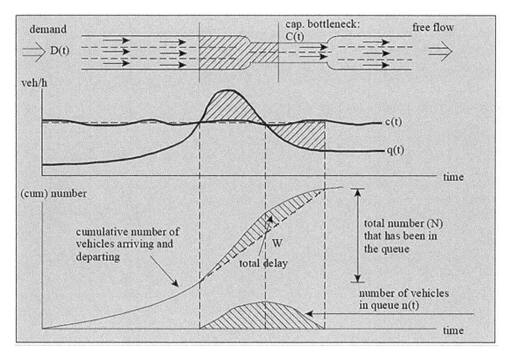

Figure 7.11   Functioning of queuing theory

The disadvantage of the queuing theory is that the queues have no spatial dimension, and they do not have a proper length either (they do not occupy space). Other models, which overcome these problems, are discussed below.

7.9.2   Shockwave Theory

Queuing theory provides some of the simplest models that can be used to model traffic flow conditions. However, in particular the spatial dimension of traffic congestion is not well described, or – in case of vertical queuing models – not described at all. *Shockwave theory* is able to describe the spatio-temporal properties of queues more accurately. This section briefly introduces shockwave theory.

A *shockwave* describes the boundary between two traffic states that are characterized by different densities, speeds, and /or flow rates. Shockwave theory describes the dynamics of shockwaves, in other words: how does the boundary between two traffic states move in time and space.

Suppose that we have two traffic states: state 1 and 2. Let S denote the wave that separates these states. The speed of this shockwave S can be computed by:

$$w_{12} = \frac{q_2 - q_1}{k_2 - k_1}$$

(7.19)

In other words, the speed of the shockwave equals the jump in the flow over the wave divided by the jump in the density. This yields a nice graphical interpretation (Figure 7.12): if we consider the line that connects the two traffic states 1 and 2 in the fundamental diagram, then the slope of this line is exactly the same as the speed of the shock in the time–space plane.

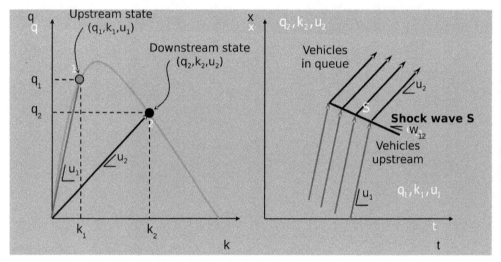

Figure 7.12   Graphical interpretation of shockwave speed

Shockwave theory provides simple means to predict traffic conditions in time and space. These predictions are largely in line with what can be observed in practice, but it has its limitations:

1. Traffic driving away from congestion does not smoothly accelerate towards the free speed but keeps driving at the critical speed.
2. Transition from the one state to the other always occurs jump-wise, not taking into account the bounded acceleration characteristics of real traffic.
3. No consideration of hysteresis.
4. No spontaneous transitions from the one state to the other.
5. Location of congestion occurrence is not in line with reality.

As a result, more advanced approaches have been proposed. To deal with this, continuum traffic models have been developed.

7.9.3   Continuum Traffic Flow Models

Continuum traffic flow deal with traffic flow in terms of aggregate variables, such as flow, densities, and mean speeds. Usually, the models are derived from the analogy between vehicular flow and flow of continuous media (e.g., fluids or gases), complemented by specific relations describing the average macroscopic properties of traffic flow (e.g., the relation between density and speed). Continuum flow models generally have a limited number of equations that are relatively easy to handle.

Most continuum models describe the dynamics of density $k = k(x,t)$, mean instantaneous speed $u = u(x,t)$, and the flow $q = q(x,t)$. The density $k(x,t)$ describes the *expected number of vehicles per unit length* at instant t. The flow $q(x,t)$ equals the *expected number of vehicles* flowing past cross-section x during per time unit. The speed $u(x,t)$ equals the *mean speed of vehicle* defined according to $q=ku$. For an overview of continuum flow models, we refer to Van Wageningen-Kessels et al. (2015).

7.10   NETWORK DYNAMICS

In the preceding sections, we have presented some of the main traffic flow characteristics. Using the microscopic and macroscopic models discussed, flow operations on simple infrastructure elements can be explained and predicted. To predict flow operations in a network is obviously more involved since it requires also predicting the route traffic demand profiles, which in turn means modelling route choice, departure time choice, mode choice, etc.

Interestingly, it turns out the *overall dynamics* of a traffic network can be described using a remarkably simple relation, referred to as the *macroscopic* or *network fundamental diagram (NFD)*. This diagram relates the vehicle accumulation – or average vehicle density – to the network performance. The network performance is defined by the flow, weighted by the number of lanes, and the length of the roadway segment for which the measured flow is representative.

This relation, which will be discussed in the following sections, shows one of the most important properties of network traffic operations, namely that its performance decreases when the number of vehicles becomes larger. In other words, when it is very busy in the network, performance goes down and less vehicles are able to complete their trip per unit of time. As a consequence, problems become even bigger.

7.10.1   Macroscopic Fundamental Diagram

Vehicular traffic network dynamics are atypical. Contrary to many other networks, network production (average rate at which travellers complete their trip) deteriorates once the number of vehicles in the network has surpassed the critical accumulation. Pioneering work of Daganzo and Geroliminis (2008) shows the existence of the NFD, clearly revealing this fundamental property. Figure 7.13 shows an example of the NFD. Knowledge of this fundamental property and its underlying mechanisms is pivotal in the design of effective traffic management.

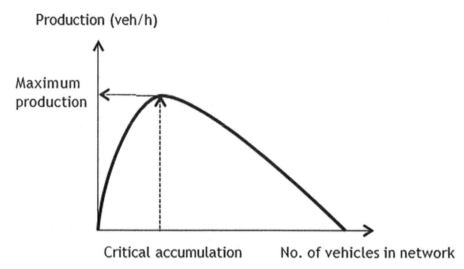

Figure 7.13   Example Network Fundamental Diagram

Developing a macroscopic description of traffic flow is not a new idea. Thomson (1967) found the relationship between average speed and flow using data collected streets in central London. Wardrop (1968) stated that this relation between average speed and flow decreased monotonically and Zahavi (1972) enriched Wardrop's theory by analysing real traffic data collected from various cities in the United Kingdom and the United States. Geroliminis and Daganzo (2008) have proven that NFDs exist in small networks, revealing the relationship between the outflow and accumulation in the network. This has later been confirmed for many other cities (Loder et al., 2019). The accumulation is the number of vehicles in the network. The outflow is also called trip completion rate, reflecting the rate at which trips reach their destinations. Similar to a conventional link fundamental diagram relating the local flow and density, three states are demonstrated on a NFD. When only a few vehicles use the network, the network is in the free flow condition and the outflow is low. With the increase of the number of vehicles, the outflow rises up to the maximum. Like the critical density in a link fundamental diagram, the value of corresponding accumulation when maximum outflow is reached is also an important parameter, called "sweet spot".

As the number of vehicles further increases, travellers will experience delay. If vehicles continue to enter the network, it will result in a congested state where vehicles block each other and the outflow declines (congested conditions). Daganzo et al. (2011) illustrated that once a zone becomes only slightly too full, its performance can quickly deteriorate. In terms of control concepts, Keyvan-Ekbatani et al. (2012) developed rules for limiting the number of vehicles inside a zone in order not to exceed a critical number.

7.10.2   Causes for Network Degeneration

The two main causes for the production deterioration of overloaded networks are spill-back of queues possibly resulting in gridlock effects, and the capacity drop. Spill-back occurs due to the simple fact that queues occupy space: a queue occurring at a bottleneck may propagate so far upstream that it will affect traffic flows that do not have to pass the bottleneck, e.g., when the queue passes a fork or an intersection upstream of the active bottleneck. As a result, congestion will propagate over other links of the network, potentially causing gridlock phenomena. The capacity drop describes the fact that the free flow freeway capacity is considerably larger than the queue discharge rate.

Vehicle automation can partially reduce the effects of network degradation. Traffic light settings can be further optimized to further stretch the network capacity (e.g., Keyvan-Ekbatani et al., 2019). Road capacity can be influenced by the vehicle type, and so can the capacity drop, for instance by pre-notifications (see Section 7.5). Routing might be another way to reduce the network degradation due to spill-back. Once, or even before, queues start to form, vehicles can be rerouted in order to avoid the growth of traffic jams. This means traffic that does not need to pass the bottleneck is not delayed by spill-back queues and can continue. This does come at a cost of inefficiency due to detours. In a fully connected system, these costs can be balanced.

7.11   BICYCLE TRAFFIC

Research into bicycle traffic has increased in the past decade. Whereas there are many studies on the choice of mode, the actual description of the way people cycle operationally has not taken off until recently.

For as long as the modelling assumptions hold, all tools and analyses as described above for vehicles can be used also for cycling. A main difference compared to vehicular traffic is the fact that cyclist traffic is not lane bound, and hence cyclists have freedom to choose a lateral position. Let us in brief revisit the elements in this chapter and indicate how these elements change in cycling traffic. If cyclists move along streams, all tools can be the same as for car traffic. Sometimes, no lanes are indicated, and they mix completely with other traffic, for instance in so-called *shared space.*

Variables can be defined in the same way for cyclists. Microscopically, one has only headways if one can define a leader. Edie's (1965) definitions (equations 7.10, 7.12, and 7.13) can be applied to cyclist traffic, even if it is not lane bound. Note that the distance travelled will be length, and the space–time area can be either a road length times a time, or the road area times a time. Depending on that choice, density is expressed as cyclist per metre, or cyclists per square metre. For pedestrian traffic, a density expression per square metre is most common; for cyclist traffic, both expressions are used depending on whether cyclists can move freely in the lateral direction (i.e., what type of infrastructure is considered: a narrow pathway or a large square).

On the macroscopic level, parts of the properties of bicycle flows along a road have been analysed by Botma and Papendrecht (1991) and Navin (1994). It can be assumed that bicycle traffic should obey some sort of fundamental diagram, but this has not been fully confirmed with empirical (or experimental) data. In fact, congested part of the fundamental diagram is not thoroughly established yet. Zhang et al. (2013) have made a very interesting comparison of fundamental diagrams for cars, cyclists, and pedestrians. They found the fundamental diagrams scale by the size of the traffic participant and the speed; surprisingly and interestingly, also the states in between (combinations of density and speed) scaled similarly. Very recent research (Hogetoorn, 2022) has experimentally established the processes going on for low average speeds: in that case, the speeds do not gradually decrease to zero (cyclists cannot cycle very slowly). What happens is that a higher density leads to a higher fraction of stopped cyclists, but not necessarily a lower speed of the riding cyclists.

Queuing theory and shockwave theory would be applicable. Queuing at intersections is a more studied area of cyclist traffic. Wierbos et al. (2019) studied the capacity of cyclist traffic and how this depends on the width of the road. In short, the capacity increased more or less linearly with the road width. An interesting observation is that the capacity of the traffic leaving a queue at a traffic light is influenced by the density of the queue: the closer the people are together, the higher the flow of traffic once the traffic light turns green. This can also be used in control: if cyclists are put closer together on purpose, the outflow will increase beyond the capacity values obtained in regular traffic (Wierbos et al., 2021).

Modelling of cyclist traffic is done, often by means of the social force model (Helbing and Molnar, 1995), which is adapted for cyclist traffic (e.g., Anvari et al., 2015 for shared space). How cyclists come to a stop when approaching a traffic light is separately modelled (Gavriilidou et al., 2019). Macroscopic models for cyclist traffic are rare. These models can use a form of a fundamental diagram, which is – as mentioned – not universally accepted. A more elaborate framework, including interactions with other modes, is available (e.g., Wierbos et al., 2020), yet requires more experimental validation.

With regard to the operations on the network scale (macroscopic fundamental diagram), cyclists are smaller than cars and can cross intersections next to each other. Hence, a higher fraction of cyclists would increase the maximum flow for a network. Loder et al. (2021) use this and try to model a multi-modal macroscopic fundamental diagram.

7.12   CONCLUSIONS

Traffic flow theory entails the knowledge of the fundamental characteristics of traffic flows. Traffic flow theory and modelling is important, among others, in order to design comfortable and safe roads, to solve road congestion problems and to design adequate traffic management measures.

In traffic flow theory a basic distinction is made between microscopic and macroscopic traffic flow variables. Microscopic traffic flow variables focus on individual drivers. Macroscopic traffic flow variables reflect the average state of the traffic flow.

The fundamental diagram describes a statistical relation between the macroscopic flow variables: flow, density, and speed. The basic premise underlying the fundamental diagram is that under similar traffic conditions drivers will behave in a similar way.

Vehicle automation in its current state, without communication, does not improve road capacity. Future developments with vehicle-to-vehicle communication can do so.

Traffic flow models can be used to simulate the traffic, for instance, to evaluate *ex-ante* the use of a new part of the infrastructure. Models can be categorized based on, firstly, representation of the traffic flow in terms of flows (macroscopic), groups of drivers (macroscopic), or individual drivers (microscopic). Secondly, on underlying behavioural theory which can be based on characteristics of the flow (macroscopic) or individual drivers (microscopic behaviour).

The overall dynamics of a traffic network can be described using a remarkably simple relation, referred to as the macroscopic or network fundamental diagram (NFD). This relation shows one of the most important properties of network traffic operations, namely that its performance decreases when the number of vehicles becomes larger.

Theories and modelling tools (on a microscopic level, on a macroscopic level, and on a network level) developed for car traffic are – to a certain extent – also applicable for other modes.

REFERENCES

Anvari, B., M.G. Bell, A. Sivakumar and W.Y. Ochieng (2015), 'Modelling shared space users via rule-based social force model', *Transportation Research Part C: Emerging Technologies*, 51, 83–103.
Botma, H. (1999), 'The free speed distribution of drivers: Estimation approaches', in P. Bovy (ed.), *Five Years Crossroads of Theory and Practice*, Delft: Delft University Press, 1–22.
Botma, H. and H. Papendrecht (1991), 'Traffic Operation of Bicycle Traffic', *Transportation Research Record: Journal of the Transportation Research Board*, 1320 (1), 65–72.
Brackstone, M. and M. McDonald (1999), 'Car-Following: A Historical Review', *Transportation Research F*, 2, 181–86.
Brilon, W., R. Koenig and R.J. Troutbeck (1999), 'Useful estimation procedures for critical gaps', *Transportation Research Part A: Policy and Practice*, 33 (3–4), 161–86.
Buckley, D. (1968), 'A semi-Poisson model for traffic flow', *Transportation Science*, 2, 107–33.
Cassidy, M.J. and R.L. Bertini (1999), 'Some traffic features at freeway bottlenecks', *Transportation Research Part B: Methodological*, 33 (1), 25–42.
Chandler, R.E., R. Herman and E.W. Montroll (1958), 'Traffic dynamics: studies in car following', *Operations Research*, 6 (2), 165–84.
Chung, K., J. Rudjanakanoknada and M.J. Cassidy (2007), 'Relation between traffic density and capacity drop at three freeway bottlenecks', *Transportation Research Part B: Methodological*, 41 (1), 82–95.
Ciuffo, B., K. Mattas, A. Anesiadou and M. Makridis (2020), 'Open ACC database', accessed 23 May 2023 at http://data.europa.eu/89h/9702c950-c80f-4d2f-982f-44d06ea0009f, technical report. Brussels: European Commission, Joint Research Centre (JRC).
Chung, K., J. Rudjanakanoknada and M.J. Cassidy (2007), 'Relation between traffic density and capacity drop at three freeway bottlenecks', *Transportation Research Part B: Methodological*, 41 (1), 82–95.
Cowan, R. J. (1975), 'Useful headway models', *Transportation Research*, 9 (6), 371–75.
Daganzo, C.F. (2002a), 'A behavioral theory of multi-lane traffic flow. Part I: Long homogeneous freeway sections', *Transportation Research Part B: Methodological*, 36 (2), 131–58.
Daganzo, C.F. (2002b), 'A behavioral theory of multi-lane traffic flow. Part II: Merges and the onset of congestion', *Transportation Research Part B: Methodological*, 36 (2), 159–69.
Daganzo, C.F., V.V. Gayah and E.J. Gonzales (2011), 'Macroscopic relations of urban traffic variables: Bifurcations, multivaluedness and instability', *Transportation Research Part B: Methodological*, 45 (1), 278–88.
Daganzo, C.F. and N. Geroliminis (2008), 'An analytical approximation for the macroscopic fundamental diagram of urban traffic', *Transportation Research Part B: Methodological*, 42 (9), 771–81.
Edie, L. (1965), 'Discussion of traffic stream measurements and definitions', in J. Almond (ed.), *Proceedings of the Second International Symposium on the Theory of Road Traffic Flow*, Paris: OECD, 139–54.
Forbes, T., H. Zagorski, E. Holshouser and W. Deterline (1958), 'Measurement of driver reactions to tunnel conditions', *Highway Research Board Proceedings*, 37, 60–66.

Gavriilidou, A., W. Daamen, Y. Yuan and S.P. Hoogendoorn (2019), 'Modelling cyclist queue formation using a two-layer framework for operational cycling behaviour', *Transportation Research Part C: Emerging Technologies*, 105, 468–84.

Geroliminis, N. and C.F. Daganzo (2008), 'Existence of urban-scale macroscopic fundamental diagrams: Some experimental findings', *Transportation Research Part B: Methodological*, 42 (9), 759–70.

Hall, F.L. and K. Agyemang-Duah (1991), 'Freeway Capacity Drop and the Definition of Capacity', *Transportation Research Record: Journal of the Transportation Research Board*, 1320, 91–98.

Helbing, D. and P. Molnar (1995), 'Social force model for pedestrian dynamics', *Physical review E*, 51 (5), 4282.

Herman, R. (1959), 'Traffic dynamics: Analysis of stability in car-following', *Operation Research*, 7 (1), 86–106.

Hogetoorn, M. (2022), 'Dense cycling conditions: The influence of stopped cyclists on the flow of bicycle traffic'. MSc thesis, Delft University of Technology.

Hoogendoorn, S.P. (2005), 'Unified approach to estimating free speed distributions', *Transportation Research Part B: Methodological*, 39 (8), 709–27.

Hoogendoorn, R., S.P. Hoogendoorn, K. Brookhuis and W. Daamen (2010), 'Mental workload, longitudinal driving behavior, and adequacy of car-following models for incidents in other driving lane', *Transportation Research Record*, 2188 (1), 64–73.

Jepsen, M. (1998), 'On the speed-flow relationships in road traffic: A model of driver behaviour', *Proceedings of the Third International Symposium on Highway Capacity*, Copenhagen, 297–319.

Kerner, B.S. (2004), *The Physics of Traffic: Empirical Freeway Pattern Features, Engineering Applications, and Theory*. Berlin: Springer.

Kesting, A., M. Treiber and D. Helbing (2007), 'General lane-changing model MOBIL for car-following models', *Transportation Research Record*, 1999 (1), 86–94.

Keyvan-Ekbatani, M., X.(S.) Gao, V.V. Gayah and V.L. Knoop (2019), 'Traffic-responsive signals combined with perimeter control: investigating the benefits', *Transportmetrica B: Transport Dynamics*, 7 (1), 1402–25.

Keyvan-Ekbatani, M., A. Kouvelas, I. Papamichail and M. Papageorgiou (2012), 'Exploiting the fundamental diagram of urban networks for feedback-based gating', *Transportation Research Part B: Methodological*, 46 (10), 1393–403.

Knoop, V.L. (2020), *Traffic Flow Theory: An Introduction with Exercises. Third edition*, Delft: TU Delft Open Textbook. DOI: 10.5074/t.2021.002.

Knoop, V.L., A. Duret, C. Buisson and B. Van Arem (2010, September), 'Lane distribution of traffic near merging zones influence of variable speed limits', in *13th International IEEE Conference on Intelligent Transportation Systems*, Madeira: IEEE, 485–90.

Knoop, V.L. and S.P. Hoogendoorn (2022), 'Free Flow Capacity and Queue Discharge Rate: Long Term Changes', *Transportation Research Records*. DOI: 10.1177/03611981221078845.

Knoop, V.L., S.P. Hoogendoorn and H.J. Van Zuylen (2009), 'Empirical Differences between Time Mean Speed and Space Mean Speed', in C. Appert-Rolland, F. Chevoir, P. Gondret, S. Lassarre, J.-P. Lebacque and M. Schreckenberg (ed.), *Proceedings of Traffic and Granular Flow 07*, New York: Springer, 351–56.

Knoop, V.L., M. Wang, I.M. Wilmink, M. Hoedemaeker, M. Maaskant and E.-J. Van der Meer (2019), 'Platoon of SAE level-2 automated vehicles on public roads: setup, traffic interactions, and stability', *Transportation Research Records*, 2673 (9), 311–22.

Laval, J.A. (2011), 'Hysteresis in traffic flow revisited: An improved measurement method', *Transportation Research Part B: Methodological*, 45 (2), 385–91.

Laval, J.A. and C.F. Daganzo (2006), 'Lane-changing in traffic streams', *Transportation Research Part B: Methodological*, 40 (3), 251–64.

Leutzbach, W. and R. Wiedemann (1986), 'Development and applications of traffic simulation models at the Karlsruhe Institut für Verkehrswesen', *Traffic Engineering and Control*, 27, 270–78.

Loder, A., L. Ambühl, M. Menendez and K.W. Axhausen (2019), 'Understanding traffic capacity of urban networks', *Scientific reports*, 9 (1), 1–10.

Loder, A., L. Bressan, M.J. Wierbos, H. Becker, H. Emmonds, M. Obee, V.L. Knoop, M. Menendez and K.W. Axhausen (2021), 'How many cars in the city are too many? Towards finding the optimal modal split for a multi-modal urban road network', *Frontiers in Future Transportation*, 2, 665006.

May, A.D. (1990), *Traffic Flow Fundamentals*, Englewood Cliffs, NJ: Prentice Hall.

Michaels, R. (1963), 'Perceptual factors in car following', , in J. Almond (ed.), *Proceedings of the Second International Symposium on the Theory of Road Traffic Flow*, Paris: OECD, 44–59.

Milanés, V. and S.E. Shladover (2014), 'Modeling cooperative and autonomous adaptive cruise control dynamic responses using experimental data', *Transportation Research Part C: Emerging Technologies*, 48, 285–300.

Minderhoud, M.M., H. Botma and P.H.L. Bovy (1996), 'An Assessment of Roadway Capacity Estimation Methods', Technical Report vk2201.302, Delft University of Technology.

Nagalur Subraveti, H.H.S., V.L. Knoop and B. Van Arem (2020), 'Improving Traffic Flow Efficiency at Motorway Lane Drops by Influencing Lateral Flows', *Transportation Research Records*, 2674 (11) 367–78.

National Academies of Sciences, Engineering, and Medicine (2022), *Highway Capacity Manual 7th Edition: A Guide for Multimodal Mobility Analysis*. Washington, DC: The National Academies Press. https://doi.org/10.17226/26432.

Navin, F.P.D. (1994), 'Bicycle Traffic Flow Characteristics: Experimental Results and Comparisons', *ITE Journal*, 64 (3), 31–37.

Nelson, W. (1982), *Applied Life Time Analysis*, New York: Wiley.

Newell, G.F. (1961), 'A theory of traffic flow in tunnels', in R. Herman (ed.), *Theory of Traffic Flow, Proceedings of the Symposium on the Theory of Traffic flow*, Amsterdam: Elsevier, 193–206.

Pignataro, L. (1973), *Traffic Engineering: Theory and Practice*, Englewood Cliffs, NJ: Prentice Hall.

Pipes, L. (1953), 'Car following models and the fundamental diagram of road traffic', *Transportation Research*, 1, 21–29.

Pueboobpaphan, R. and B. van Arem (2010, January). 'Understanding the relation between driver/vehicle characteristics and platoon/traffic flow stability for the design and assessment of cooperative adaptive cruise control', [paper 10–0994 on DVD], in *89th Transportation Research Board (TRB) Annual Meeting 2010*, Washington, DC: Mira Digital Publishing.

Rao, B., P. Varaiya and F. Eskafi (1993), 'Investigations into achievable capacities and stream stability with coordinated intelligent vehicles', *Transportation Research Record: Journal of the Transportation Research Board*, 1408, 27–35.

Roncoli, C., N. Bekiaris-Liberis and M. Papageorgiou (2017), 'Lane-changing feedback control for efficient lane assignment at motorway bottlenecks', *Transportation Research Record*, 2625 (1), 20–31.

SAE, J3016 (2021), 'Taxonomy and Definitions for Terms Related to On-Road Motor Vehicle Automated Driving Systems'.

Schakel, W.J., V.L. Knoop and B. Van Arem (2012), 'LMRS: Integrated Lane Change Model with Relaxation and Synchronization', *Transportation Research Records: Journal of the Transportation Research Board*, 2316, 47–57.

Shiomi, Y., J. Xing, H. Kai, and T. Katayama (2019), 'Analysis of the Long-Term Variations in Traffic Capacity at Freeway Transportation Research Record Bottleneck', *Transportation Research Record: Journal of the Transportation Research Board*, 2673, 390–401.

Thomson, J.M. (1967), 'Speeds and flows of traffic in Central London: Speed-flow relations', *Traffic Engineering and Control*, 8 (12), 721–25.

Treiber, M., A. Hennecke and D. Helbing (2000), 'Congested traffic states in empirical observations and microscopic simulations', *Physical review E*, 62 (2), 1805.

Treiterer, J. and J.A. Myers (1974), 'The hysteresis phenomenon in traffic flow', in D.J. Buckley (ed.), *Proceedings of the 6th International Symposium on Transportation and Traffic Theory*, New York: Elsevier, 13–38.

Van Erp, P.B., V.L. Knoop and S.P. Hoogendoorn (2019), 'On the value of relative flow data', *Transportation Research Part C: Emerging Technologies*, 113, 74–90.

Van Wageningen-Kessels, F., H. Van Lint, K. Vuik and S. Hoogendoorn (2015), 'Genealogy of traffic flow models', *EURO Journal on Transportation and Logistics*, 4 (4), 445–73.

Wardrop, J.G. (1968), 'Journey speed and flow in central urban areas', *Traffic Engineering and Control*, 9 (11), 528–32.

Wasielewski, P. (1974), 'An integral equation for the semi-Poisson headway distribution', *Transportation Science*, 8, 237–47.

Wierbos, M.J., V.L. Knoop, R.L. Bertini and S.P. Hoogendoorn (2021), 'Influencing the queue configuration to increase bicycle jam density and discharge rate: An experimental study on a single path', *Transportation Research Part C: Emerging Technologies*, 122, 102884.

Wierbos, M.J., V.L. Knoop, F.S. Hänseler and S.P. Hoogendoorn (2019), 'Capacity, capacity drop, and relation of capacity to the path width in bicycle traffic', *Transportation research record*, 2673 (5), 693–702.

Wierbos M.J., V.L. Knoop, F.S. Hänseler and S.P. Hoogendoorn (2020), 'A Macroscopic Flow Model for Mixed Bicycle–Car Traffic', *Transportmetrica A: Transport Science*, 17(3), 9935.

Yuan, K., V.L. Knoop and S.P. Hoogendoorn (2015), 'Capacity drop: a relation between the speed in congestion and the queue discharge rate', in *Transportation Research Record*, 2491, 72–80.

Yuan, K., V.L. Knoop and S.P. Hoogendoorn (2017), 'A microscopic investigation into the capacity drop: impacts of longitudinal behavior on the queue discharge rate', *Transportation Science*, 51 (3), 852–62.

Zahavi, Y. (1972), 'Traffic performance evaluation of road networks by the α-relationship', Parts I and II, *Traffic Engineering and Control*, 14 (5 and 6), 228–31 and 292–93.

Zhang, J., W. Mehner, E. Andresen, S. Holl, M. Boltes, A. Schadschneider and A. Seyfried (2013), 'Comparative Analysis of Pedestrian, Bicycle and Car Traffic Moving in Circuits', *Procedia–Social and Behavioral Sciences*, 104, 1130–38.

8
Transport technology

Jan Anne Annema

8.1   INTRODUCTION

Mobility has changed tremendously over history. About 200 years ago, people walked, rode horses, sat in carriages, and used barges. At the same time, goods and mail were transported on people's backs, in carriages, and by barge and boat. Two centuries later the transport system has revolutionized, as can be illustrated with three examples.

In 2018, around 1.42 billion cars travelled the streets and the roads of the world (rfidtires.com). In 1900 this number was nearly zero. In 1950 containers did not exist. Seventy years later 1.83 billion metric tons of goods are carried by containers (Placek, 2021). The modern container has indeed transformed worldwide trade and economy (Levinson, 2008). According to Levinson, by making shipping so inexpensive the container paved the way for Asia to become the world's workshop, and brought consumers a previously unimaginable variety of low-cost products from around the globe. Finally, one of the first jet airliners (Boeing 707) was introduced in 1959. In 2019, the world's airlines carried around an amazing 4.7 billion passengers on scheduled services (Mazareanu, 2021).

Technological progress in vehicles and infrastructure (see next section) has resulted in more speed – thus, reducing travel times – cheaper transport and more comfort. Related to the themes of Chapter 2 and Chapter 6 of this book, this means that transport technology progress, broadly speaking, often has lowered transport resistance and, thereby, increased transport volumes. At the same time, this increase has resulted in some societal issues such as safety (see Chapter 11 on safety) and environmental damage (see Chapter 10 on environment).

This chapter is mainly about three transport technical innovations which are aimed, amongst others, to reduce these transports drawbacks. The three innovations are alternative powertrains and fuels; Intelligent Transport Systems (ITS) including fully automated vehicles; and vehicle sharing systems. We have chosen these three innovations because at the time of writing this chapter in June 2022, these three, what Fulton et al. (2017) call transportation revolutions, are expected to change the transport system. Vehicle sharing systems such as Mobility as a Service (MaaS) are transport service innovations that require ICT. In the book of van Wee et al. (2022) a larger spectrum of transport innovations is discussed. The goal of this chapter is to explain the potential role of these technological innovations to decrease transport's external effects (see Chapter 13 for an explanation of this concept).

The strong focus on the three innovations selected and external effects is a limited approach. Therefore, this chapter starts with a brief description of the evolution of transport technologies in general (8.2). In Section 8.3 we start by focusing on transport's external effects by explaining why a technologically imperfect transport system has emerged, and what is required from a political-economy perspective to implement new technologies aimed at decreasing the undesirable negative impacts of transport. In Sections 8.4 to 8.6 the three technological innovations are described: alternative powertrains and fuels in 8.4, ITS in 8.5, and vehicle sharing systems in 8.6. In 8.7 some conclusions are drawn.

8.2   THE EVOLUTION OF TRANSPORT TECHNOLOGY

Figure 8.1 shows the development of the average total distance travelled per person per year between 1950 and 2019 in Sweden (in km) (Eliasson, 2022).

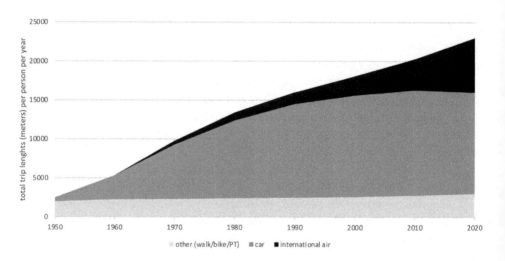

Source: Eliasson (2022).

Figure 8.1   Average total distance travelled by mode in Sweden, km per person per year

From a transport technological perspective, we can observe from Figure 8.1 that the past trend in Sweden is relatively straightforward: they increasingly have used higher-speed technologies. In 1950, the Swedes travelled, on average, 2500km per person per year mainly using the active modes (walk/bicycle) and bus. Seventy years later they travel on average almost ten times more per year mainly by car and international air. The Swedes are no exception. Other and older studies have also shown this trend: e.g., Americans have increased their total mobility by

4.6% each year (kilometres travelled per person per year) since 1870 (Ausubel et al., 1998), and Gruebler (1990) has estimated that the French increased their mobility by about 4% per year since 1800. As already explained in Chapter 6, travel time is an important resistance factor for transport. Thus, humankind apparently has chosen (consciously or unconsciously) to reduce this resistance factor by developing higher-speed transport vehicles and infrastructure. By doing so, people have increased their mobility without violating the 'law' of the constant travel time budget (see Chapter 6).

New transport technology for the future is highly uncertain. Nevertheless, increased demand for (high) speed transport technologies is expected to continue in the next decades. For example, Schäfer (2017) estimated that US travel demand per person could increase by 30–50% by 2100 over the 2010 level, mainly due to an increase in air travel. Perhaps suborbital space travel may grow significantly in the twenty-first century (Cohen and Spector, 2020). Another high-speed technology for the future as discussed in the literature is the vacuum train concept, better known as the hyperloop system (see, for example, Nøland, 2021). In this system, passenger or freight capsules are propelled inside an airless vacuum tube at a very high speed. Currently, no commercial applications of the hyperloop exist.

8.3 IMPLEMENTING NEW TRANSPORTATION TECHNOLOGY TO SOLVE NEGATIVE IMPACTS: A POLICY PERSPECTIVE

From the early 1950s, the car started to dominate the Western world transport system (as shown for Sweden in Figure 8.1) with the US as the frontrunner. Sperling and Gordon (2009) talk about the US baby boom generation which came of age in comfortable car-dependent families already in the late 1950s. However, as these authors point out, the 1960s and 1970s also brought about a rather sudden new attitude and new consciousness. In the 1960s, Ralph Nader campaigned against the reluctance of the car manufacturers to spend money on safety measures (Nader, 1965). Jacobs (1961) observed already in 1961 that 'healthy' cities are ones where the physical environment is organized in a way that strengthens the social networks of streets and communities. Meadows et al. (1972) published their famous book with the telling title *Limit to Growth*. This book, commissioned by the Club of Rome, modelled future population growth and the use of natural resources, showing that oil is a finite resource. Indeed, two worldwide oil crises in 1973 and 1979, and an oil-price peak in 2008, showed the Western world that the supply of cheap oil is less self-evident than perhaps previously thought.

Despite new thinking and a greater awareness of the challenges facing transport and the need for technological change, the system is still not perfect (Table 8.1). Economists explain transport imperfections by pointing toward the existence of external costs (see also Chapter 13).

Evolutionary economics can help to explain how we have ended up with an imperfect transport system as depicted in Table 8.1. The theory can also help to explain why it is so difficult for governments and private parties to change it.

Table 8.1   Examples of external costs of transport which might be (partly) solved by technological innovations

	Current statistics, some examples from all over the world	Historic and expected future trends
Traffic jams	In and around large cities all over the world, a car traveller may lose more than 100 hours in congestion in a year with London, for example, on top with 148 hours lost (INRIX, 2022).	An increasing trend in the past. Without additional policies increase in traffic jams in urbanized areas is to be expected.
Oil dependency	Worldwide transportation is responsible for approximately 60% of oil consumption. The transport sector is the most exposed part of the economy to oil prices. The transport sector accounts for more than two-thirds of the EU's final demand for oil and petroleum products (McGovern et al., 2020).	Technologies such as greater engine efficiency, hybrid cars, electric vehicles, biofuels, and hydrogen (see below) could significantly reduce overall oil demand in transport.
Climate change	In 2019, approximately 15% of total net anthropogenic greenhouse gas (GHG) emissions worldwide came from transport (IPCC, 2022).	According to IPCC (2022), the average annual GHG emissions growth between 2010 and 2019 slowed compared to the previous decade in total but remained roughly constant at about 2% per year in the transport sector. Also here, technologies such as greater engine efficiency, hybrid cars, electric vehicles, biofuels, and hydrogen could significantly reduce GHG emissions.
Acidification and local air pollution (NO_x and PM)	In European cities, the transport sector contributes roughly 40–50% to overall nitrogen oxides emissions (NO_x emissions) and 10–15% to particulate matter (PM) emissions (Hoen et al., 2021).	The end-of-pipe emissions of these road transport air pollutants decreased by roughly 50–60% between 1990 and 2018 mainly due to technical progress (Hoen et al., 2021). A further emission reduction is expected because of the penetration of cleaner fossil fuel-based vehicles and alternative powertrains and fuels in the fleet; see before.
Traffic safety	Worldwide an estimated 1.35 million people are killed on roads each year (WHO, 2018).	The future of traffic safety is uncertain and very diverse among the different regions of the world. It is expected that road fatalities will increase in the near future, especially in low- and middle-income countries. Improved technology such as Intelligent Transport Systems (ITS) can contribute to improved traffic safety.
Noise nuisance	Mapping of EU shows that 25% of the population in Europe are exposed to road traffic noise exceeding the EU guideline limit of 55 dB (L_{DEN}: average over a whole day) (Sorensen et al., 2020).	In OECD countries road noise burdens have remained relatively constant since the 1990s; aircraft noise burdens have increased. In the future, a further increase in transport noise is expected in business-as-usual because of expected road and air volume growth. The reduction potential of technologies (e.g., noise barriers, quieter tyres, quieter planes, low-noise road surfaces) is not expected to be strong enough to beat the volume growth.

8.3.1   Innovation and Selection Towards an Imperfect System[1]

In evolutionary economics, all actors are assumed to have bounded rationality (Simon, 1957). Bounded rationality implies that actors, amongst others, have routines, habits, that they are satisfiers rather than optimizers, and that they have a limited time horizon. Bounded rationality results in heterogeneity in behavioural strategies. Innovation is the result of this diversity. Sovacool (2009) describes how by the end of the nineteenth century a person seeking transport in the United States (and many other corners of the world) could choose between a bewildering array of different options: the horse, bicycles, trains, subways, the new steam-powered horseless 'carriages', gasoline automobiles and electric-powered vehicles.

In evolutionary economics, serendipity plays an important role in explaining the innovation process. This means that a combination of chance, luck, and knowledge results in an invention. Knowledge is important because empirical evidence shows that creative innovations are in most cases the result of a new combination of existing knowledge, techniques, or concepts.

Within the scope of behavioural diversity, 'knowledge' has many faces and it is unavoidable that much knowledge, and therefore money will be wasted. This means that knowledge 'waste' in the form of trial-and-error and cul-de-sacs is needed to get 'fit' technologies (one may even wonder if 'waste' is the right phrase here). In other words, according to evolutionary economics, gasoline and diesel vehicles have emerged as a fit technology in the competition with the train, the steam-powered carriage, and electric-powered vehicles.

Selection processes reduce the innovation diversity. The innovation and selection processes together determine the 'fitness' of a certain new technological alternative. Fitness is a measure of survival and reproduction. In the selection process, the new innovations are put to the test for survival. Selection relates to many different factors: physical possibilities or impossibilities of new technology, technical usage pros and cons, economic factors such as price and the possibilities to produce the technology on a large scale, psychological factors (do people actually like the new invention?), institutional barriers (will governments allow the new invention to enter the market?), and so forth. Sovacool (2009) in his history of early modes of transport in the US argues that all of these factors have played a role in explaining why the gasoline automobile finally became the winner. For example, he shows that even though the electric-powered vehicles initially (1895–1905) had many advantages, they did not break through because they were more expensive than gasoline cars, had slower top speeds, were difficult to charge, were mostly confined to urban areas, and came to be seen, amongst others, as old fashioned.

8.3.2   Path Dependency, Lock-In, and Co-Evolution

The dynamics of evolutionary systems as described here result in three important concepts for this chapter: path dependency, lock-in, and co-evolution. Path dependency means that for a certain technology, as a result of increasing economies of scale, a self-reinforcing feedback loop may emerge which ends up in the dominance of that technology. With economies of scale economists mean that the more one specific technology is used and produced, the lower the average cost will be to produce or use one unit of that technology (e.g., a fossil-fuelled car). For example, all people and shippers using internal combustion engines share the same fuel network and make use of the same maintenance and distribution networks (repair shops and dealers). For car producers, many types of economies of scale exist. One of these is that building cars require large fixed costs such as factories, assembly lines, and so forth. Using such factories to full capacity lowers the average costs of making a car. Thus, economies of scale result in substantially lower costs.

Unfortunately, the consequence of path dependency means that there may be a historically unavoidable path towards the complete dominance of one technology. Disadvantages that did not occur, or were not seen as disadvantages at the early start of its development, can make it difficult to change technologies. A situation of so-called technological 'lock-in' has unintentionally been created. In many ways, the current dominant transport technology (the internal combustion engine fuelled by oil products) can be regarded as such a lock-in situation that has, on the one hand, led to economies of scale and, thus, relatively cheap ways of transportation for many people around the world. However, on the other hand, it has led to many negative externalities (Table 8.1).

Co-evolution is related to the evolutionary notion that innovations are in most cases the consequence of combining already existing ideas or systems. Co-evolution focuses on the ways partial systems (such as, on one hand, cars, vans, and lorries, and on the other hand, the road or the fuel network) develop, work together, and to an increasing extent influence each other's evolution. One may say that co-evolution of different partial technical systems working increasingly together will often result in improved synchronization and extra benefits for the users. However, if the resulting co-evolutionized system has societal disadvantages (Table 8.1), it seems even more difficult to escape the 'lock-in' of the closely intertwined system.

8.3.3   System Innovations (Transitions)

Systems can change via system innovation or transition according to system innovations theory (e.g., Geels, 2005). Central in this theory are so-called socio-technical systems. For example, Figure 8.2 illustrates the socio-technical system for road transport. The picture shows interrelated entities within this socio-technical system and explains the embeddedness of transport technology in society in terms of physical infrastructure, institutions, markets, and culture. The notion of a co-evolutionized closely intertwined system is clearly recognizable in Figure 8.2.

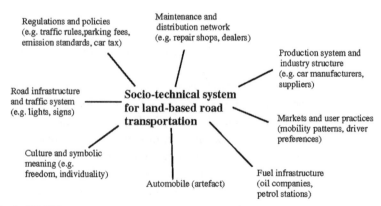

Source: Geels (2005).

Figure 8.2   Socio-technical system for road transport

System innovation is a transition from one socio-technical system to another, potentially characterized by a technological change (e.g., from sailing ships to steamships). Transition is a process that can be explained by using the *multi-level perspective (MLP)* (e.g., Geels, 2002). The multi-level perspective (see Figure 8.3) combines insights from evolutionary economics, innovation studies, and science and technology studies, in order to understand transitions and the dynamics in system innovation.

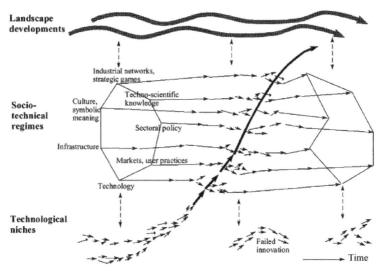

Source: Geels (2002)

Figure 8.3   Multi-level model of system innovations

An existing socio-technical system is depicted as a heptagon somewhere left to the middle of Figure 8.3. The changed socio-technical system is symbolized on the right side (later in time) of Figure 8.3 as a differently shaped heptagon. In the multi-level model of system innovations three levels are distinguished:

1. The middle level is the **socio-technical regimes**, see Figure 8.2 for an example. The crux in the MLP theory is that this level is stable and that innovations will not happen here. As already mentioned, socio-technical systems are locked-in.
2. However, at the lower level, **technological niches** may exist (represented as small arrows) that try to penetrate the middle level of the socio-technical regimes. Some niches succeed and change or become a new socio-technical system, some fail. Niches 'act as incubation rooms for radical innovations nurturing their early development' (Geels, 2002, p. 1261). A niche can be a specific market segment (e.g., car racing where new technologies are tried), R&D projects, pilot programmes, and so forth. The crux is that niches are unstable because they are per definition small with limited user practices, high policy uncertainties (e.g., will electric vehicle subsidy programmes be continued?), and not yet consisting of mature networks between actors.

3. **Landscape developments** are conceptualized as the high level. These are 'a set of deep structural trends external to the regime' (Geels, 2005; p. 78). Landscapes cannot be changed by actors within the socio-technical regime (middle level), in our case transportation. The landscape developments include both tangible (such as the built environment) and non-tangible aspects (such as economic growth, culture, attention for environmental problems, and pandemics). There are slow developments in the landscape (e.g., demographical changes) as well as rapid developments (e.g., oil crises, COVID-19 pandemic). Some landscape developments may help a technical niche to successfully penetrate the socio-technical regime, but other landscape developments may result in failed penetration.

Public authorities often play a role in the technological niche level (for example, 'protect' some early but very promising niches by giving subsidies or by carrying out pilot programmes), but they are also a regime player. This means public authorities can have an accelerating as well as a decelerating role in system innovations.

8.3.4   A Political-Economy Model

A view on transport innovations and the role of public authorities is advanced by Feitelson and Salomon (2004). They have developed a political-economy framework for analysing the adoption of transport innovations (Figure 8.4).

The box 'perception of problems' (see Figure 8.4 top right) is an important factor in the successful adoption of new technology, as will be shown in the subsequent paragraphs on technological innovations aimed at reducing the external costs of transport. The oil crises (in 1973 and 1979), severe smog periods in Los Angeles and London, and a continually increasing amount of traffic casualties in the 1960s have all spurred technical changes in transport. Also, experts such as scientists, advisers, and consultants play a role in their framework (see Figure 8.4 top left). Experts suggest technical innovations and the means to implement these innovations. They research technical issues and societal problems such as congestion, climate change, and air pollution. They also perform formal cost–benefit analysis showing, for example, that certain policies such as implementing nationwide road charging using GPS technology will have a positive benefit-to-cost ratio. Nevertheless, the Feitelson and Salomon framework shows clearly that a favourable benefit-to-cost ratio for a policy does not mean that this policy will be adopted. For politicians the perceived effectiveness and the perceived distribution of benefits and costs (who wins, who loses) of policy also play an important role in their decision-making.

Most important in their framework is that they think that the adoption of innovations is predicated on the economic, social, political, and technical feasibility. Thus, it is insufficient that innovation is technologically superior, that it meets a strict benefit–cost criterion or that there is a majority of voters supporting it. In their view, only a particular combination of these feasibility issues will result in successful innovation.

The Feitelson and Salomon political-economy framework, with its emphasis on the importance of social and political feasibility for explaining the successful adoption of innovations, relates to the notions of the current transport system as a co-evolved lock-in situation or as a socio-technical regime. Both concepts imply that the current situation not only means a strong dependence on one dominant technology but also a strong position for the defenders of the existing socio-technical regime, such as vehicle manufacturers, the oil industry, unions, and billions of consumers worldwide who by using their voice and vote influence the position of non-business interest groups and political parties (Figure 8.4). To illustrate the political power of certain actors: according to the European Automobile Manufacturers' Association (ACEA, 2022) the European automobile industry accounts for 8.5% of total direct EU manufacturing employment. In countries such as Germany (11.1%), Sweden (14.4%), and Slovakia (16%) this share is even higher, representing a workforce amounting to more than the population size of a country such as Belgium. This passage is not meant to blame the defenders of an imperfect system. After all, it is clear that the current dominant transport technology has also many advantages related to economies of scale. So, it seems obvious that industries and people profiting from these advantages are reluctant advocates for a fast and radical change.

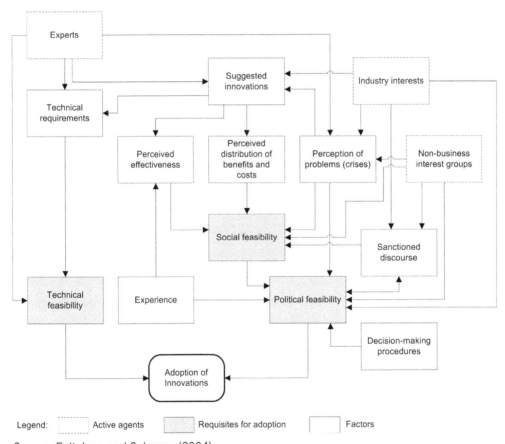

Source: Feitelson and Salomon (2004)

Figure 8.4   A political-economy model for explaining the adoption of innovations

In the next three sections, three technological innovations will be discussed that potentially can change the current socio-technical transport system.

8.4   ALTERNATIVE POWERTRAINS AND FUELS

The 'text box air pollutants' (see below) demonstrates how the policy of vehicle emission standards implemented in the past decades all over the world has spurred the implementation of many technologies in conventional fossil-fuel-based vehicles that reduced emissions. However, it is widely acknowledged that fossil-free technologies are the way forward (IPCC, 2022). Electric cars and vans are considered an important solution for reducing transportation's GHG (carbon dioxide, CO_2) emissions and air pollution (e.g., nitrogen oxides, NO_x and particulate matter, PM). For trucks, lorries, ships, and planes other carbon-free options are also studied (see below in this section).

BOX 8.1   AIR POLLUTANTS REDUCTION WITH CONVENTIONAL TECHNOLOGIES

Air pollutant emissions from conventional fossil-fuel-based vehicles decreased considerably in the past (Table 8.1). All large economies of the world have implemented air pollution emission standards for all kinds of road vehicles (cars, vans, and lorries) since around 1990. A comprehensive overview of these vehicle standards from all over the world can be found on Dieselnet (2022). One of their overviews gives the EU emission standards for passenger cars (see Table 8.2). An important feature of this policy as shown in the table is that the standards are tightened over time.

Table 8.2   EU air pollutant emission standards for passengers cars

Stage*	Date	CO	HC	HC+NO_x	NO_x	PM	PN
		g/km					#/km
Positive Ignition (Gasoline)							
Euro 1†	1992.07	2.72 (3.16)	–	0.97 (1.13)	–	–	–
Euro 2	1996.01	2.2	–	0.5	–	–	–
Euro 3	2000.01	2.30	0.20	–	0.15	–	–
Euro 4	2005.01	1.0	0.10	–	0.08	–	–
Euro 5	2009.09[b]	1.0	0.10[d]	–	0.06	0.005[e,f]	–
Euro 6	2014.09	1.0	0.10[d]	–	0.06	0.005[e,f]	6.0×10^{11} [e,g]
Compression Ignition (Diesel)							
Euro 1†	1992.07	2072 (3.16)	–	0.97 (1.13)	–	0.14 (0.18)	–
Euro 2, IDI	1996.01	1.0	–	0.7	–	0.08	–
Euro 2, DI	1996.01[a]	1.0	–	0.9	–	0.10	–
Euro 3	2000.01	0.64	–	0.56	0.50	0.05	–
Euro 4	2005.01	0.50	–	0.30	0.25	0.025	–

Stage*	Date	CO	HC	HC+NO$_x$	NO$_x$	PM	PN
		g/km					#/km
Euro 5a	2009.09[b]	0.50	–	0.23	0.18	0.005[f]	–
Euro 5b	2011.09[c]	0.50	–	0.23	0.18	0.005[f]	6.0×10^{11}
Euro 6	2014.09	0.50	–	0.17	0.08	0.005[f]	6.0×10^{11}

Notes:
CO = carbon monoxide; HC = hydrocarbons; NO$_x$ = nitrogen oxides; PM = particulate matter (in weight); PN = particulate matter in number of particles
* At the Euro 1–4 stages, passenger vehicles > 2500kg were type approved as Category N$_1$ vehicles
† Values in brackets are conformity of production (COP) limits
a. until 1999.09.30 (after that date DI engines must meet the IDI limits)
b. 2011.01 for all models
c. 2013.01 for all models
d. and NMHC = 0.068 g/km
e. applicable only to vehicles using DI engines
f. 0.0045 g/km using the Particle Measurement Programme (PMP) measurement procedure
g. 6.0×10^{12} 1/km within the first three years from Euro 6 effective dates

With improved motor management and all kinds of end-of-pipe-technologies such as three-way-catalysts, particulate soot filters, exhaust gas recirculation (EGR), and selective catalytic reduction (SCR) technologies, vehicle manufacturers have been able to meet these standards. Kuklinska et al. (2015) give a comprehensive review of air quality policies in the U.S. and the EU, including vehicle emission regulations. Hooftman et al. (2018) have also reviewed the European passenger car regulations including the technologies implemented. Implementing the vehicle emission reduction technologies for air polluting substances such as nitrogen oxides (NO$_x$) and particulate matter (PM$_{10}$) has been a relatively smooth adoption process of new technologies because these technologies can be regarded as purely technological innovations, not as systems innovations. When we refer back to Figure 8.2, the only element in the socio-technical system really affected by implementing these end-of-pipe technologies is the vehicle production system. And although vehicle manufacturers have opposed stricter standards and the speed of implementing the next stricter rule (and some even cheated on meeting the emission standards, Bouzzine and Lueg, 2020), they have always complied in the end.

8.4.1   Cars and Vans

The crux of the electrification of cars is that instead of burning fossil fuel products such as petrol, diesel, LPG in an internal combustion engine (ICE) to produce the propulsion energy for the vehicles, electricity is used in an electromotor. The burning of fossil fuels results in unwanted side products such as CO$_2$ and air pollutants. When using the vehicle's electricity no emissions take place. However, the electricity and electric vehicle components may still produce emissions, and this is discussed below.

Different types of electric vehicles can be distinguished. Battery electric vehicles (EVs) contain a battery that has to be charged using an outside electricity source. In so-called hybrid electric vehicles and plug-in hybrid electric vehicles, the electromotor is combined with an ICE. The difference between these two hybrid vehicles is that plug-in hybrid vehicles' batteries are charged via an outside electricity source (and by using braking energy), while a hybrid vehicle uses its ICE (and also braking energy) to charge the battery. Fuel cell electric vehicles are also considered electric vehicles but their energy source is special. These types of vehicles generate electricity in a fuel cell by using compressed hydrogen and oxygen (from the air). The chemical reaction between hydrogen and oxygen results in electricity and water. So, these vehicles have to be fuelled with hydrogen which has to be produced (see below). Finally, extended-range vehicles are produced to some extent which is quite similar to EVs but they have a (small) ICE that can be used to charge the battery if an extra range is required and no charging options are available.

The sales of EVs have increased rapidly worldwide (Figure 8.5). In Norway, in 2020, more EVs are sold compared to ICEs. It should be noted that these sales are mainly policy driven. When we relate to the political-economy model of Feitelson and Salomon (2004), EVs can be seen as technically feasible and the stimulating policies as being social and politically feasible. Governments across the world support EV sales with all kinds of policies such as tax exemptions, subsidies, and facilitating public charging to contribute to reducing transport externalities. In 2020 governments worldwide spent 14 billion USD to support electric car sales (IEA, 2021). The reason for these policies is that consumers experience barriers in purchasing EVs which are related to their higher purchase costs, range anxiety issues, lack of charging infrastructure, and also more intangible barriers related to emotions (e.g., 'lack of fun', 'no cool noise') (Krishna, 2021). So, without government support, this technology would probably be adopted very slowly, because within the socio-technical regime (Figure 8.2) long-ingrained market preferences and cultural meaning within the old regime (fossil fuel) will have to change due to EV adoption. Thanks to the support EV registration increased globally to almost seven million in 2020 (IPCC, 2022). Due to the resulting economies of scale (see Section 8.3), it seems that some important barriers are slowly disappearing. For example, the total cost of ownership (TCO; includes purchase costs, maintenance costs, and operational costs) of EVs is expected to become lower in 2023–25 for smaller and medium-sized cars and for the bigger cars segment some years later (Element Energy, 2021). Even for the fuel cell electric cars, which in 2020 were far more expensive in TCO terms compared to comparable ICEs, it is expected in this study that around the year 2030 they may break even. The TCO decreases are fuelled by lower battery and fuel cell prices and energy costs. Figure 8.5 shows that the lithium-ion (Li-ion) battery packs unit price has dropped by roughly 90% in the period 2005 to 2020. Also, the range has improved considerably with roughly 40% of the average EVs sold worldwide in the period 2015–20 (IEA, 2021).

Decreasing CO_2 emissions is an important reason for governments worldwide to stimulate EV adoption. As noted before, during the use of EVs no CO_2 emissions will take place but what about producing electricity and hydrogen? In so-called Life Cycle Analysis (LCA) a full comparison between technologies is made. In LCA studies also the CO_2 emissions are taken into account when producing the vehicles and vehicle components (such as the battery), when maintaining the vehicles, and when producing and distributing the fuels. In some LCA studies also the environmental impacts of the end-of-life treatment of vehicles and components (e.g., demolition, recycling) are considered but this stage is not included in the LCA example we give in Figure 8.6 (Bieker, 2021). Figure 8.6 gives the EU the life-cycle GHG emissions in g CO_2-eq[2] per kilometre driven for different car technologies.

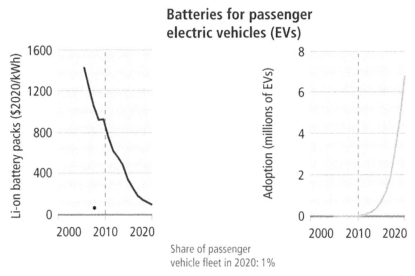

Source: IPCC (2022)

Figure 8.5   Adoption of EVs worldwide and the development of the Li-ion battery unit price

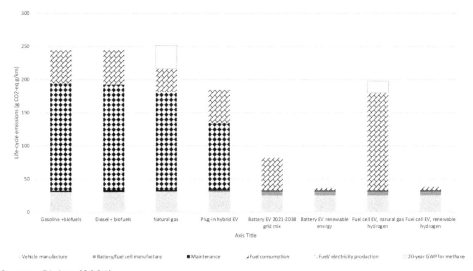

Source: Bieker (2021)

Figure 8.6   Life-cycle GHG emissions of lower medium segment cars (e.g., Ford Focus) with different technologies registered in Europe in 2021

Some observations can be made related to Figure 8.6. The first is that the currently dominant technologies petrol (gasoline) and diesel cars in the EU emit around 250g CO_2-eq/km over the full life cycle. Conventional gasoline and diesel fuels contain some biofuels. The EU has promoted the use of biofuels since the 1990s, amongst others, to save GHG emissions (Puricelli et al., 2021). According to this study around 4.5% of the energy consumption in road transport and non-road mobile machinery is biofuel, mainly ethanol from crops. The idea of biofuels is that plants while growing absorb CO_2. When these plants are converted into liquid fuels and burned, this CO_2 is released and can 'immediately' again be taken up by new plants for biofuel production, and so forth. Puricelli et al. (2021) reviewed many LCA studies on biofuels and conclude that the climate change impacts of biofuels are indeed broadly speaking lower than fossil fuels. However, they also point out that direct and indirect land-use changes due to growing biofuel feedstocks are not always taken into account in these CO_2 emission impact estimations. Additionally, these land-use changes can be harmful, e.g., biodiversity can be lost. It is for these reasons that electrification policies for light-duty vehicles have become more popular, but for heavy vehicles, ships, and aeroplanes biofuels are still seen as a potentially viable option albeit many researchers recommend a shift in producing biofuels towards using non-edible feedstocks, waste, and industrial by-products to avoid the land-use change issues (see below).

The second observation (Figure 8.6) is that natural gas cars do not perform better than conventional petrol and diesel cars. Important reasons are that the obtaining and distribution of natural gas (which is in essence methane) result in methane emissions and also when methane is used in cars some methane will be emitted ('slip'). Methane is a strong GHG, see endnote 2.

The third observation is that plug-in hybrids, EVs, and fuel cell electric cars perform also from an LCA perspective better than the fossil-fuel-based variants (Figure 8.6). The figure shows that the extent of this improvement is highly dependent on the way electricity and hydrogen are produced. Bieker (2021) assumes that in the EU electricity grid mix coal and natural gas (and to a small extent oil) are still used to produce electricity which, compared to a renewable mix, results in a higher CO_2-eq/km value for EVs. Countries that have a higher share of, for example, coal will have higher CO_2-eq per kilometre emission factors compared to the EU, to state the obvious. For fuel cell electric cars natural gas (methane) is seen as a relatively cheap feedstock to produce hydrogen but this choice will result in not much improvement CO_2-eq-wise compared to the conventional fossil fuel cars due to the methane emission problems just mentioned (Figure 8.5). Using renewables such as solar and wind to produce hydrogen from water will result in a far better emission factor.

Next to cars, there is a huge and increasing market for urban transport vehicles (such as vans). The global online retail sales market, for example, quadrupled in the period 2014 to 2020 to around 4200 billion USD (4.2 trillion USD) (Apex Insight, 2021). This implies an enormous growth in the use of delivery vehicles, and, thus, in emissions. For the conventional vans, Castillo et al. (2020) have analysed that full electric battery-powered vehicles seem to be the best-placed solution for reducing these externalities, although they also note that driving range and recharge options are still barriers that need to be solved. Another kind of technology development in the delivery market is the increasing use of 'light electric freight vehicles (LEFV)'. These are bikes, mopeds, or compact vehicles with electric support or drive mechanisms, equipped for the delivery of goods, and goods and people with limited speed (van Duin et al., 2022). Verlinghieri et al. (2021) and van Duin et al. (2022) expect significant growth in LEFVs usage within urban areas all over the world.

8.4.2   Heavy duty vehicles

For heavier vehicles such as trucks and lorries (HDVs), the discussion on alternative power-trains to reduce GHG emissions is still going on (as at 2022). Kluschke et al. (2019) reviewed 19 studies on potential market penetration of alternative fuel powertrains (AFPs) in HDVs, see Figure 8.7. Battery-electric vehicles (BEVs) were mentioned the most but also interesting is to see that many different AFPs are studied and suggested. Ten AFP technologies are considered: six alternative fuels (liquid petroleum gas (LPG), liquid natural gas (LNG), compressed natural gas (CNG), electric methane (eMET), electric Synfuel (eSYN), and biofuels, (BIO)) and four electrified powertrains (catenary (CAT), battery-electric (BEV), hybrid (HYB), and fuel cell electricity (FCEV)). eMET is synthetic methane generated from hydrogen (produced by using electricity) and CO_2. eSYN are any kind of hydrocarbons (e.g., methanol, or more complex products such as diesel or kerosene) also made out of hydrogen (produced by using water and electricity) and CO_2. Which of these technologies or set of technologies will become the AFP or AFPs of the future for HDVs is dependent on many factors, such as their CO_2 performance (see Figure 8.6), costs, energy supply factors, infrastructure development, and user acceptance. Referring to the multi-level model of system innovations, the AFPs HDV can be regarded as niches. Which one (or perhaps two or three) will breakthrough eventually in the socio-technical regime of heavy-duty transport is, at the time of writing this chapter, unknown.

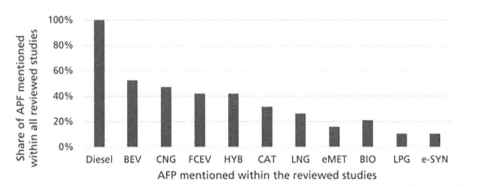

Source: Kluschke et al. (2019)

Figure 8.7   Share of alternative fuel powertrains (AFPs) in HDVs mentioned in reviewed studies

The same kind of uncertainties about the suitability of AFP or AFPs for HDVs in the future also play an important role in other transportation markets such as aviation and inland and sea-going shipping. Dahal et al. (2021) performed a techno-economic review of alternative fuels and propulsion systems for the aviation sector. They assess bio-jet fuels (hydro-processed esters and fatty acids and alcohol-to-jet) as most promising in the near term and electrofuels (eSYN fuels) and hydrogen in the long term. They see the costs of producing these fuels and the design and development of appropriate propulsion systems and aircraft as the major challenge. In relation to the question of whether biofuels are actually sustainable (see before), Dahlah et al. (2021) also see an important issue in the limited supply potential of feedstocks for the bio-jet fuels such as cooking oil, animal fats, vegetable oils, and waste oils. The same kinds of uncertainties about alternative fuels can be found in the literature on the maritime sector. Foretich et al. (2021) map the challenges and opportunities of low-carbon fuels in the maritime sector. Again fuels such as LNG, biodiesel, ammonia (as a source for onboard hydrogen), and various e-synthetic fuels are discussed. Supply issues, costs, safety concerns, spill risks, and actual LCA GHG emission reductions are still important challenges.

Åkerman et al. (2021) present five scenarios for long-distance travel in 2060 which are consistent with a 67% probability of limiting global warming to 1.8 degrees. Foremost is their conclusion is that to meet this global warming goal, (huge) reductions in air travel demand are required but this notion is outside this technology chapter. Additionally, they see also an important role for alternative fuels with biofuels, electrofuels, and liquid hydrogen offering the best options.

8.5   INTELLIGENT TRANSPORT SYSTEMS APPLICATIONS (INCLUDING AUTOMATED DRIVING)

This section covers a wide span of technologies which are summarized in the term 'intelligent transport systems' (ITS). Basically, common to all these technologies is the (sometimes huge amounts of) data generated from the road and public transport users and the infrastructure that are collected, stored, and processed with, increasingly, Artificial Intelligence techniques.[3] Figure 8.8 gives an overview of ITS applications (Shankar Iyer, 2021). Related to this chapter where the role of technologies is discussed to decrease externalities, two notions are important. First, implementing ITS has often a wider goal than solely decreasing externalities. Improving comfort, providing real-time travel information that lowers transport resistance factors (Chapter 6) and making vehicle driving effortless and accessible also to people without driving licences (when full automation is achieved; see below) are examples of these wider goals. Second, it is uncertain if ITS actually decrease externalities which we will illustrate below when we discuss automated vehicles.

One of the pillars in Figure 8.8 is road safety. Advanced driver assistance systems (ADAS) are one category of ITS that promote traffic safety. Applications in this ITS category are lane departure warning systems, automatic and adaptive cruise control systems, monitoring and warning systems for driver vigilance (intervenes when driver drowsiness, fatigue, and inattention occur), or night vision. Also, collision warning and avoidance systems are in use. Collision warning systems use radar and internal-vehicular information to detect any collision

Source: Shankar Iyer (2021)

Figure 8.8   An overview of ITS applications

risk. Intelligent speed assistance (ISA) is another ITS application. In the EU ISA has to be fitted to all new vehicles from May 2022 (EC, 2022). With ISA the vehicle has information on the permitted or recommended maximum speed for the road along which it is travelling. The standard ISA system uses an in-vehicle digital road map onto which speed limits have been coded, combined with a satellite positioning system. If the driver exceeds the permitted or recommended maximum speed a system (which could be the navigation system) intervenes to control the speed of the vehicle. This intervention can have different forms of which actively preventing drivers from exceeding the speed limit is the strongest intervention. The European Commission is proposing a less strict intervention: 'Cascade Auditory Warning System'. This auditory system warns only until the vehicle is well over the speed limit. Carsten (2021) indicates that such information and warning systems have life- and injury-saving potentials of around one-quarter of that of the strongest intervention, what Carsten calls 'true ISA'.

A well-known ITS (in the pillar autonomous driving, Figure 8.8) is adaptive cruise control (ACC) whose use is increasing (Chen et al., 2019). ACC systems detect the position and speed of preceding vehicles on the road through various sensors and automatically adjust the speed according to the control strategy. ACC increases the safety and comfort of driving. The next step is so-called cooperative ACC (CACC) systems in which multi-vehicle information (using the vehicle-to-vehicle information based on advanced wireless communication) is produced and used which can shorten the following gap (see Chapter 7) on the basis of ensuring safety (Chen et al., 2019). CACC systems can potentially have positive impacts on congestion, safety, and energy (however, see below the discussion on autonomous vehicles and their societal impacts). From an energy perspective and, thus, CO_2 perspective, CACC systems seem an important next step as ACC impacts negatively on tractive energy efficiency (He et al., 2020) because unlike human drivers ACC followers lead to string instability.

ITS are also increasingly used in public transport (PT), in cycling, and by road authorities. PIARC (2022) mentions various ITS application terrains in PT such as management information systems (e.g., real-time management data collected from vehicle tracking and locations), en-route information for passengers about delays, disturbances, and changes that seats are available, and PT security information systems. For example, using CCTV PT authorities can monitor 24/7 stations, platforms, parking lots, bus stops, and so forth to gain real-time (manually or automatically) information about risky situations. For cycling examples of ITS are real-time information about parking availability in cycle storage facilities and cycle availability in bike-sharing systems. Road authorities use ITS increasingly to give en-route information about congestion, to instruct road users in real time to lower speed when road intensities approach capacity, to gather information (using sensors) about the quality of road pavements, bridges, viaducts in order to manage their maintenance programmes, and so forth. Also here PIARC (2022) is a very rich source of ITS applications.

One of the technologies that like electrification could potentially transform the transportation socio-technical system is full automated driving (see Figure 8.8). Automation is already extensively used in modern marine vessels and aeroplanes (use of autopilots), although human input is still required but in a more passive role. Unmanned aircraft in the form of drones are already used and 'remotely piloted aircraft' (RPA), whereby a pilot external to the aircraft (ground, ship, another aircraft) controls the plane but people (e.g., for monitoring, searching or inspection tasks) are on board, is foreseeable (ICAO, 2011). In public transport, automation has become more and more common, for example, with the use of communications-based train control (CBTB). The most challenging technology in this respect is automated driving on the road. SAE International distinguishes different levels of driving automation. In levels 0 to 2 people are driving but some of their tasks are automated (such as with an ACC or CACC; see above), in levels 3 to 5 people are not driving when autonomous driving features are engaged. In level 5 these features can drive the vehicle under all conditions. In levels 3 and 4 there are still some limited conditions such as automated driving is only possible on certain roads. Milakis et al. (2017) reviewed the literature to discuss policy and society-related implications of automated driving. They used the ripple model of automated driving (Figure 8.9).

In this model, three sequential impact circles can be distinguished. The first contains the first-order impacts of automated driving on travel resistance (Chapter 6), road capacity, and travel choices. These first-order effects are passed through to the second circle: second-order impacts on vehicle ownership and sharing, locations choices and land use, and transport infrastructure. Finally, in the third-order impacts circle, it is conceptualized what automated driving will have for societal implications. Feedbacks can occur in this ripple model in analogy with the central model in this book in Chapter 2. For example, automation can reduce all kinds of resistance factors (travel time, effort) in the first circle that influence location choices (second circle) which in turn might influence travel choices (first circle). The crux of their review is that it is not known if in the long term automated driving will increase or decrease transport's externalities. The main issue is that automated vehicles are expected to induce road travel demand because of more and longer trips but to what extent is uncertain. They note that potential land use changes may induce additional road travel demand because of automation, but this has not been included in the literature reviewed. Their review shows that automated vehicles can have benefits compared to people-driven vehicles if travel distances remain constant. For example, they can be less risky, leading to less congestion and be more fuel-efficient. However, the unknown induced demand can decrease or even counteract the potential benefits on a system level in the long term. So, in a possible future world of full vehicle automation

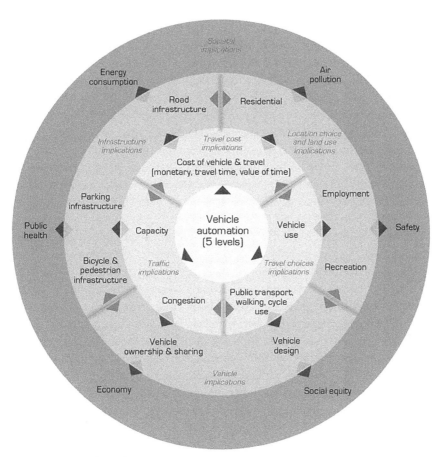

Source: Milakis et al. (2017)

Figure 8.9   The ripple model of automated driving

on the road, transport policies such as pricing still seem required to decrease externalities (Chapter 13).

The ripple model indicates that automated driving, especially the higher levels, might be one of the hardest innovations to realize. The current socio-technical regime (Figure 8.2) will have to change in almost all elements, such as in the culture of being in the driver's seat, in rules and regulations, in infrastructure, in markets and user practices, and so forth.

8.6   SHARING AND NEW MOBILITY SERVICES SUCH AS MAAS

Vehicle sharing has gained popularity in transportation. Sharing can be considered an important change in the current socio-technical regime where private vehicle ownership is the dominant feature. Sharing is a bit of a misleading word because it is actually renting vehicles for a short period of time. There are real sharing schemes, where there is co-ownership of vehicles, but these are relatively uncommon. All over the world, various vehicle sharing systems (VSS) are in use or in development such as car sharing, e-car sharing, bike sharing, cargo-bike sharing, kick scooter sharing, scooter sharing, and so forth (Ataç et al., 2021). Although sharing can be introduced in principle without any advanced technological support, ICT plays an important role in building and maintaining modern VSS. Ticketing and reservations systems require advanced software and apps. Advanced wireless communication technologies are applied in order to open and close vehicles at their docking stations or somewhere on the street when a free-floating sharing system is used. Sometimes geo-fencing is used to make sure that the shared vehicles are parked in a designated area by the users, or to make sure that the use of the shared vehicle is limited to the area over which the vehicle is allowed to be used – a boundary to the scheme.

Like for ITS (previous section), vehicle sharing has wider goals than solely decreasing externalities. Sharing systems can be profitable for entrepreneurs and can be beneficial for users because it increases their accessibility. Still, most governments promote or actively support vehicle sharing systems because of their potential positive social impacts. Nijland and Van Meerkerk (2017) show in a survey amongst 363 car-sharing respondents in the Netherlands that they own 30% fewer cars than prior to car sharing and drive 15% to 20% fewer car kilometres. So, based on this research car sharing indeed has some potential to decrease car use and ownership externalities such as emission and use of public space. In a large review on the impacts of bike sharing, Teixeira et al. (2021) conclude that bike sharing is mostly replacing the sustainable modes PT and walking, with modest car replacing rates. This modest car shift will still have some positive impacts on emissions and noise. New trips generated by bike sharing might have positive health impacts (Chapter 12) due to more physical activity (Teixeira et al., 2021).

Urban planning authorities are looking for ways, such as providing or permitting VSS, that enable people to travel more sustainably (Alyavina et al., 2020). Among these options is MaaS. These are integrated systems that enable travellers to plan, book, and pay for trips through a single online interface. Basically, the idea is that in MaaS people buy their full trip through a single online interface instead of making the trip by using their self-owned vehicle or by having to organize the full trip themselves (e.g., walk to the station, buy a train ticket, rent a bike, buy a tram ticket, and so forth). Like in automated vehicles different levels of MaaS are distinguished in the literature: 0 no integration; 1 integration of information; 2 integration of booking and payment; 3 integration of the service offered, including contracts and responsibilities; 4 integration of societal goals (Sochor et al., 2017). In the highest level 4, people can choose between different mobility offers for a trip by online platforms based on out-of-pocket costs and time but also on information provided to them about the emissions and safety of the particular trip offer. The development of MaaS is still in its early stages, and the exact impact of MaaS on the current transport system is therefore unclear (Araghi et al., 2020). MaaS is expected by some to aid in promoting sustainable transportation modes at the expense of privately owned vehicles (Jittrapirom et al., 2017), potentially reducing the associated externalities of private vehicle ownership, such as climate change, air pollution, and public parking spaces (Butler et al., 2021). However, Casadó et al. (2020) and Alyavina et al.

(2020) also speculate MaaS to potentially be counterproductive by replacing current public or active transport trips (cycling and walking) with vehicle trips (e.g., using taxis or shared cars).

8.7 CONCLUSIONS

The conclusions of this chapter are:

1. It is difficult to change the dominant transportation technology. This can be explained with the concept of 'lock-in' from the theory of evolutionary economics or with the notion of transport as a socio-technical system from the theory of system dynamics. Socio-technical systems theory points at the embeddedness of transport technology in society in terms of physical infrastructure, institutions, markets, and culture.
2. Potential technological innovations that might change the socio-technical systems of transportation radically are alternative powertrains and fuels, automated driving and sharing.
3. It is uncertain for all three innovations paths identified whether they will succeed and what their societal implications will be. The innovations require policies and active governments to be realized and to steer them in such a way that they contribute to meeting sustainability goals.
4. For alternative powertrains and fuels, life cycle analysis gives the full CO_2 impacts.
5. For automated driving on the road, the long-term societal impacts are not known because it is unclear to what extent these vehicles will increase transport volumes.
6. Vehicle sharing systems might have positive societal impacts but can also substitute active modes and public transport.

NOTES

1. The most cited modern book in this area of economic research is by Nelson and Winter (1982). We will now only summarize some important notions (based on Van den Berg et al., 2005).
2. A CO_2-equivalent is a metric used to compare and add the emissions from various GHGs based on the so-called global-warming potential (GWP) of these gases. One ton of CO_2 has a GWP per definition of 1. For example, one ton of methane (CH4) is a stronger GHG with a GWP of 25. This implies that the emission of one ton of CH4 is equivalent to 25 tons of CO_2 emission.
3. Artificial Intelligence (AI) means that a machine is able to perceive, reason, learn, and to solve problems. According to Shankar Iyer (2021), AI methods that support transportation include Artificial Neural Networks (ANN), Genetic algorithms (GA), Simulated Annealing (SA), Fuzzy Logic Model (FLM), and Ant Colony Optimizer (ACO).

REFERENCES

ACEA (2022), *Share of direct automotive employment in the EU, by country*, accessed 15 April 2022 at www.acea.auto/figure/share-of-direct-automotive-employment-in-the-eu-by-country/, European Automobile Manufacturers' Association.

Åkerman, J., A. Kamb, J. Larsson and J. Nässén (2021), 'Low-carbon scenarios for long-distance travel 2060', *Transportation Research Part D: Transport and Environment*, 99, 103010.

Alyavina, E., A. Nikitas and E.T. Njoya (2020), 'Mobility as a service and sustainable travel behaviour: A thematic analysis study', *Transportation Research Part F: Traffic Psychology and Behaviour*, 73, 362–81.

Apex Insight (2021), *Global Parcel Delivery Market Insight Report 2021*, accessed January 2022 at https://apex-insight.com/product/global-parcel-delivery-market/.

Araghi, Y., N. Larco, G. Bouma, C. Doll, D. Vonk Noordegraaf and K. Krausse (2020), *Drivers and Barriers of Mobility-as-a Service in urban areas*. Proceedings of the 8th Transport Research Arena TRA 2020. Helsinki.

Ataç, S., N. Obrenović and M. Bierlaire (2021), 'Vehicle sharing systems: A review and a holistic management framework', *EURO Journal on Transportation and Logistics*, 10, 100033.

Ausubel, J.H., C. Marchetti and P. Meyer (1998), 'Toward green mobility: the evolution of transport', *European Review*, 6(2), 137–56.

Bieker, G. (2021), *A Global Comparison of the Life-Cycle Greenhouse Gas Emissions of Combustion Engine and Electric Passenger Cars*, Berlin: ICCT – International Council on Clean Transportation Europe.

Bouzzine, Y.D. and R. Lueg (2020), 'The contagion effect of environmental violations: The case of dieselgate in Germany', *Business Strategy and the Environment*, 29(8), 3187–202.

Butler, L., T. Yigitcanlar and A. Paz, A. (2021), 'Barriers and risks of Mobility-as-a-Service (MaaS) adoption in cities: A systematic review of the literature', *Cities*, 109, 103036.

Carsten, O. (2021), 'Vehicle safety, technical rules & test procedures for intelligent speed assistance', Feedback from: University of Leeds (europa.eu), accessed January 2022 at https://ec.europa.eu/info/law/better-regulation/have-your-say/initiatives/12222-Vehicle-safety-technical-rules-&-test-procedures-for-intelligent-speed-assistance/F2256609_en.

Casadó, R.G., D. Golightly, K. Laing, R. Palacin and L. Todd (2020), 'Children, young people and mobility as a service: opportunities and barriers for future mobility', *Transportation Research Interdisciplinary Perspectives*, 4, 100107.

Castillo O, R. Álvarez and R. Domingo (2020), 'Opportunities and Barriers of Hydrogen–Electric Hybrid Powertrain Vans: A Systematic Literature Review', *Processes*, 8(10), 1261.

Chen, J., Y. Zhou and H. Liang (2019), 'Effects of ACC and CACC vehicles on traffic', *IET Intell. Transp. Syst.*, 13(9), 1365–1373.

Cohen, E. and S. Spector (2020), 'Space tourism-past to future: A perspective article', *Tourism Review*, 75(1), 136–39.

Dahal, K., S. Brynolf, C. Xisto, J. Hansson, M. Grahn, T. Grönstedt and M. Lehtveer (2021), 'Techno-economic review of alternative fuels and propulsion systems for the aviation sector', *Renewable and Sustainable Energy Reviews*, 151, 111564.

Dieselnet (2022), accessed January 2022 at https://dieselnet.com/standards/.

Duin, P. van der (2006), *Qualitative Futures Research for Innovation*, Delft: Eburon Academic Publishers.

Duin, van, J.H.R., W. Ploos van Amstel and H.J. Quak (2022), 'Explaining the growth in light electric vehicles in city logistics', in van Wee, B., J.A. Annema and J. Kohler (eds), *Innovations in Transport*, Cheltenham, UK and Northampton, MA, USA: Edward Elgar Publishing.

EC (2022), accessed January 2022 at https://ec.europa.eu/info/law/better-regulation/have-your-say/initiatives/12222-Vehicle-safety-technical-rules-&-test-procedures-for-intelligent-speed-assistance_en.

Element Energy (2021), *Electric Cars: Calculating the Total Cost of Ownership for Consumers*, Cambridge: Element Energy Limited

Eliasson, J. (2022), 'Will we travel less after the pandemic?', *Transportation Research Interdisciplinary Perspectives*, 13, 100509.

Feitelson, E. and I. Salomon (2004), 'The political economy of transport innovations', in M. Beuthe, V. Himanen, A. Reggiani and L. Zamparini (eds), *Transport Developments and Innovations in an Evolving World*, Berlin: Springer, 11–26.

Foretich, A., G.G. Zaimes, T.R. Hawkins and E. Newes (2021), 'Challenges and opportunities for alternative fuels in the maritime sector', *Maritime Transport Research*, 2, 100033.

Fulton, L., J. Mason and D. Meroux (2017), *Three Revolutions in Urban Transportation*, UC Davis, ITDP, https://steps.ucdavis.edu/three-revolutions-landing-page/.

Geels, F.W. (2002), 'Technological transitions as evolutionary reconfiguration processes: a multi-level perspective and a case-study', *Research Policy*, 31, 1257–74.

Geels, F. (2005), *Technological Transitions and System Innovations: A Co-Evolutionary and Socio-Technical Analysis*, Cheltenham, UK and Northampton, MA, USA: Edward Elgar.

Gruebler, A. (1990), *The Rise and Fall of Infrastructure: Dynamics of Evolution and Technological Change in Transport*, Heidelberg: Physica.

He, Y., M. Makridis and G. Fontaras (2020), 'The energy impact of adaptive cruise control in real-world highway multiple-car-following scenarios', *European Transport Research Review*, 12(17).

Hoen, A., D. Hilster, J. Király, J. de Vries and S. de Bruyn (2021), *Air Pollution and Transport Policies at City Level Module 2: Policy Perspectives*, Delft: CE Delft.

Hooftman, N., M. Messagie, J. van Nierlo and T. Coosemans (2018), 'A review of the European passenger car regulations – Real driving emissions vs local air quality', *Renewable and Sustainable Energy Reviews*, 86, 1–21.

ICAO (2011), *Unmanned Aircraft Systems (UAS)*, Montreal: International Civil Aviation Organization.

IPCC (2022), *Climate Change 2022. Mitigation of Climate Change, Summary for Policymakers*, United Nations (WMO, UNEP): Intergovernmental Panel on Climate Change.

IEA (2021), *Global EV Outlook 2021*, Paris: International Energy Agency (www.iea.org).

INRIX (2022), *Global Traffic Scorecard*, accessed June 2022 at https://inrix.com/scorecard.

Jacobs, J. (1961), *The Death and Life of Great American Cities*, New York, NY: Random House.

Jittrapirom, P., V. Caiati, A. Feneri, S. Ebrahimigharehbaghi, M. Alonso-González and J. Narayan (2017), 'Mobility as a Service: A Critical Review of Definitions, Assessments of Schemes, and Key Challenges', *Urban Planning*, 2(2), 13–25.

Kluschke, P., T. Gnann, P. Plötz and M. Wietschel (2019), 'Market diffusion of alternative fuels and powertrains in heavy-duty vehicles: A literature review', *Energy Reports*, 5, 1010–24.

Krishna, G. (2021), 'Understanding and identifying barriers to electric vehicle adoption through thematic analysis', *Transportation Research Interdisciplinary Perspectives*, 10, 100364.

Kuklinska, K., L. Wolska and J. Namiesnik (2015), 'Air quality policy in the US and the EU – a review', *Atmospheric Pollution Research*, 6(1), 129–37.

Levinson, M. (2008), *The Box: How the Shipping Container Made the World Smaller and the World Economy Bigger*, Princeton, NJ: Princeton University Press.

Mazareanu (2021), Global air traffic – scheduled passengers 2004–2022, accessed January 2022 at www .statista.com/statistics/564717/airline-industry-passenger-traffic-globally/.

McGovern, M., S. Heald and J. Pirie (2020), *Oil Dependency in the EU*, Cambridge, UK: Cambridge Econometrics.

Meadows, D.H., D.L. Meadows, J. Randers and W.W. Behrens III (1972), *The Limits to Growth*, New York: Universe Books.

Milakis, D., B. van Arem and B. van Wee, B (2017), 'Policy and society related implications of automated driving: A review of literature and directions for future research', *Journal of Intelligent Transportation Systems*, 21(4), 324–48.

Nader, R. (1965), *Unsafe at Any Speed: The Designed-In Dangers of the American Automobile*, New York: Grossman Publishers.

Nelson, R.R. and S.G. Winter (1982), *An Evolutionary Theory of Economic Change*, Cambridge, MA: Belknap Press of Harvard University Press.

Nijland, H. and J. van Meerkerk (2017), 'Mobility and environmental impacts of car sharing in the Netherlands', *Environmental Innovation and Societal Transitions*, 23, 84–91.

Nøland, J.K. (2021), 'Evolving Toward a Scalable Hyperloop Technology: Vacuum transport as a clean alternative to short-haul flights', *IEEE Electrification Magazine*, 9(4), 55–66.

OECD/ITF (2008), 'Oil dependence: is transport running out of affordable fuel?', Discussion Paper no. 2008–5, Organisation for Economic Co-operation and Development/International Transport Forum, accessed at www.internationaltransportforum.org/jtrc/Discussion Papers/DP200805.pdf.

PIARC (2022), *Road network operations and intelligent transport systems*, accessed January 2022 at https://rno-its.piarc.org/en/its-basics.

Placek, M. (2021), *Container shipping – statistics & facts*, accessed January 2022 www.statista.com/topics/1367/container-shipping/.

Puricelli, S., G. Cardellini, S. Casadei, D. Faedo, A.E.M. van den Oever and M. Grosso (2021), 'A review on biofuels for light-duty vehicles in Europe', *Renewable and Sustainable Energy Reviews*, 137, 110398.

rfidtires.com, *How many cars are there in the world today? – Current Status*, accessed July 2022 www.rfidtires.com.

Schäfer, A. (2017), 'Long-term trends in domestic US passenger travel: the past 110 years and the next 90', *Transportation*, 44(2), 293–310. https://doi.org/10.1007/s11116-015-9638-6.

Shankar Iyer, L. (2021), 'AI enabled applications towards intelligent transportation', *Transportation Engineering*, 5, 100083.

Simon, H.A. (1957), *Models of Man*, New York: John Wiley.

Sochor, J., H. Arby, M. Karlsson and S. Sarasini (2017), *A Topological Approach to Mobility as a Service: A Proposed Tool for Understanding Requirements and Effects, and for Aiding the Integration of Societal Goals*, 1st International Conference on Mobility as a Service (ICOMaaS), Tampere, Finland, 28–29 November 2017.

Sørensen, M., T. Münzel, M. Brink, N. Roswall, J.-M. Wunderli, M. Foraster (2020), 'Chapter four – Transport, noise, and health', in M.J. Nieuwenhuijsen and H. Khreis (eds), *Advances in Transportation and Health*, London: Elsevier, 105–31.

Sovacool, B.K. (2009), 'Early Modes of Transport in the United States: Lessons for Modern Energy Policymakers', *Policy & Society*, 27(4), 411–27.

Sperling, D. and D. Gordon (2009), *Two Billion Cars: Driving towards Sustainability*, Oxford: Oxford University Press.

Teixeira, J.P., C. Silva and F. Moura e Sá (2021), 'Empirical evidence on the impacts of bikesharing: a literature review', *Transport Reviews*, 41(3), 329–51.

Van den Bergh, J.C.J.M., A. Faber, A.M. Idenburg and F.H. Oosterhuis (2005), *Survival of the Greenest: Evolutionaire economie als inspiratie voor energie- en transitiebeleid [Survival of the greenest: evolutionary economy as inspiration for energy and transition policy]*, RIVM-rapport 550006002/2005, Bilthoven: Rijksinstituut voor Volksgezondheid en Milieu.

van Wee, B., J.A. Annema and J. Kohler (2022), *Innovations in Transport*, Cheltenham, UK and Northampton, MA, USA: Edward Elgar Publishing.

Verlinghieri, E., I. Itova, N. Collignon and R. Aldred (2021), *The Promise of Low Carbon Freight Benefits of Cargo Bikes in London*, White paper Pedal Me.

WHO (2018), *Global Status Report on Road Safety 2018: A Summary*, Geneva: World Health Organization.

PART II
IMPACTS OF THE TRANSPORT SYSTEM

9

Accessibility: perspectives, measures and applications

Karst Geurs and Bert van Wee

9.1   INTRODUCTION

A principal goal of transport policy is to improve accessibility: the transport system should allow people to travel and participate in activities, and firms to transport goods between locations (from mining, via stages of production, to distribution centres and finally to clients, such as shops or other firms).

The concept of accessibility as a central force in land-use development is traced back by some authors to at least a century ago (e.g. Levine, 2020). Since the first definition of accessibility as the 'potential of opportunities for interaction' (Hansen, 1959: 73) accessibility has taken on a variety of meanings *see* for elaborate reviews of the literature Geurs and van Wee (2004), Levine (2020) and Levinson and Wu (2020). Confusion in understanding of accessibility, according to Wu and Levinson (2020), often arises from the differences in the intellectual heritage in the various disciplines, the different mathematical formulations employed, the different language and words employed to describe related concepts, and the different aims each access measure hopes to achieve. This is problematic because the choice and operationalization of an accessibility measure may strongly affect the conclusions on accessibility.

Furthermore, Handy and Niemeier (1997: 1192) have stated that 'a distinct gap currently exists between the academic literature and the practical application of accessibility measures'. This statement is still valid today. Studies in Europe and North America highlight that although practitioners typically are convinced that comprehensive accessibility measures are useful in the planning practice, many do not use them in their work. A lack of knowledge and data, organizational barriers, and lack of institutionalization of accessibility measures and tools are the main causes of the implementation gap (Silva et al., 2017; Boisjoly and El-Geneidy, 2017).

In this chapter we describe the different perspectives on accessibility (Section 9.2), the different components of accessibility (Section 9.3), the different means by which accessibility can be operationalized (Section 9.4) and the different criteria for choosing accessibility measures (Section 9.5). Section 9.6 describes the impact of ICT on accessibility analysis and measures and Section 9.7 addresses linkages between equity and accessibility. Two examples of accessibility measures are described in Section 9.8, illustrating how the choice and operationalization of accessibility measures can influence the conclusions. Finally, Section 9.9 presents the conclusions.

9.2   DEFINING ACCESSIBILITY

The definition of access, and thus its mathematical formulation, varies between studies and across disciplines (Wu and Levinson, 2020). At its core, as shown in Figure 2.1 in Chapter 2, accessibility can be measured as a product of (1) transport resistance, (2) locations, and (3) travel needs and desires. Following this conceptual framework, we can define accessibility from the perspective of persons (Geurs and van Wee, 2004: 128) and the perspective of locations of activities as:

> The extent to which land-use and transport systems enable (groups of) individuals to reach activities or destinations by means of a (combination of) transport mode(s) at various times of the day (*perspective of persons*), and the extent to which land-use and transport systems enable companies, facilities and other activity places to receive people, goods and information at various times of the day (*perspective of locations of activities*).

The terms 'access' and 'accessibility' in the literature are often used indiscriminately. Here, 'access' is used when talking about a person's perspective: the area that a person can reach from his or her origin location to participate in one or more activities at destination locations at certain times. This is visualized in Figure 9.1. From the perspective of location, 'accessibility' is the catchment area from which people, goods and information from different locations can reach a specific origin location. The size of the area depends, for example, on the time, costs and effort that an individual is willing to accept (the transportation and individual component of accessibility; see Section 9.3). The size of the area varies in time (the temporal component of accessibility; see Section 9.3).

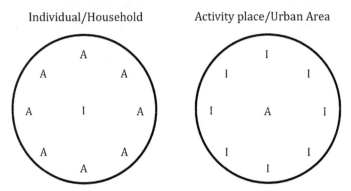

Individual/Household   Activity place/Urban Area

I = individual, A = activity place/urban area

Source: Dijst et al. (2002).

Figure 9.1   Individual and location perspective on accessibility

9.3   COMPONENTS OF ACCESSIBILITY

Four components of accessibility can be distinguished: a land-use, transportation, temporal and individual component (Geurs and van Wee, 2004):

1. **The land-use component** reflects the land-use system, consisting of (1) the amount, quality and spatial distribution opportunities supplied at each destination (jobs, shops, health, social and recreational facilities, etc.), (2) the demand for these opportunities at origin locations (e.g. where inhabitants live), and (3) the confrontation of supply and demand for opportunities, which may result in competition for activities with restricted capacity such as job and school vacancies and hospital beds (see van Wee et al., 2001; see Section 9.8, the Shen (1998) accessibility measure). Find out more about the land-use component in Chapter 5.

2. **The transportation component** describes the transport system, expressed as the disutility for an individual to cover the distance between an origin and a destination using a specific transport mode. As with the transport resistance component (Chapter 6), it includes the amount of time (travel, waiting and parking), costs (fixed and variable) and effort (including reliability, level of comfort, accident risk, etc.). This disutility results from the confrontation between supply and demand. The supply of infrastructure includes its location and characteristics (e.g. maximum travel speed, number of lanes, public transport timetables, travel costs). The demand relates to both passenger and freight travel. Find out more about the transportation component (equivalently, the transport resistance) in Chapter 6.

3. **The temporal component** reflects the temporal constraints, that is, the availability of opportunities at different times of the day and the time available for individuals to participate in certain activities (e.g. work, recreation).

4. **The individual component** reflects the activities in which individuals want to participate and the options they have to fulfil those needs. This directly relates to the Needs-Opportunities-Abilities (NOA) model (Figure 3.1 in Chapter 3). The need to participate in activities depends for example on age, income, educational level and house-

hold situation. Opportunities to travel and participate in activities depend on people's income and travel budget, educational level, having a driving licence, car ownership, etc. People's abilities depend on people's physical and mental capabilities to travel, e.g. being able to drive a car, having digital skills to use a shared bike or car, etc. These characteristics may strongly influence the total aggregate accessibility result. Several studies have shown that, in the case of job accessibility, inclusion of occupational matching strongly affects the resulting accessibility indicators. Pan et al. (2020), for example, show that in automobile-oriented city such as Houston in the United States, job seekers in poverty and relying on public transport have very limited access to blue collar job opportunities.

The four components have a direct influence on accessibility but also an indirect one through interactions between the components. For example, the land-use component (distribution of activities) is an important factor determining travel demand (transport component) and may also introduce time restrictions (temporal component) and influence people's opportunities (individual component). The individual component interacts with all other components: a person's needs and abilities that influence the (valuation of) time, cost and effort of movement, types of relevant activities and the times at which one engages in specific activities.

The four components explained above have been distinguished to measure physical accessibility to spatially distributed activities. Section 9.6 discusses how ICT (e.g. having access to online goods and services) influences the four components of accessibility.

9.4   OPERATIONALIZATION OF ACCESSIBILITY MEASURES

An accessibility measure should ideally take all components and elements within these components into account. In practice, applied accessibility measures focus on one or more components of accessibility, depending on the perspective taken. There are four main types of accessibility measures:

1. **Infrastructure-based accessibility measures** analyze the (observed or simulated) performance or service level of transport infrastructure, such as the length of infrastructure networks, the density of those networks (e.g. kilometre road length per square kilometre), level of congestion and average travel speed on the road network. This type of accessibility measure is typically used in transport planning (for a discussion see Section 9.5). Some of these measures focus only on the supply of infrastructure, while others also use demand factors.
2. **Location-based accessibility measures** analyze accessibility at locations, typically on a macro-level. The measures describe the level of accessibility to spatially distributed activities, such as the number of jobs within 30 minutes' travel time from each origin location. More complex location-based measures explicitly incorporate capacity restrictions of supplied activity characteristics to include competition effects *see* Section 9.8 for two examples.
3. **Person-based accessibility measures** analyze accessibility at the individual level, such as the activities in which an individual can participate at a given time. This type of measure is founded in time geography (Hägerstrand, 1970) that measures limitations on an individual's freedom of action in their environment. This includes the location and duration of

mandatory activities, the time budgets for flexible activities and travel speed allowed by the transport system. For a description of time geography see also Chapter 3, Section 3.6.

4. **Utility-based accessibility measures** analyze the (economic) benefits that people derive from access to the spatially distributed activities. This type of measure has its origin in economic studies, for details see, for example, de Jong et al. (2007). This type of measure is sometimes used in economic appraisals of transport infrastructure investments (Geurs et al., 2010; Beria et al., 2018).

Table 9.1 presents an overview of different types of accessibility measures, applications and examples, with brief comments on the advantages and disadvantages of the measures used. The different accessibility measures focus on different components of accessibility, often ignoring other relevant elements of accessibility.

Table 9.1 Accessibility indicators, applications and examples

Accessibility type	Applications	Examples	Disadvantages and comments
Infrastructure-based accessibility measures:			
Supply-oriented measures – network level	Description and comparison of characteristics of infrastructure supply in a region or country	Length of motorways, density of rail network	Partial measure of accessibility; does not include land-use and individual components of accessibility.
Supply-oriented measures – connectivity of locations to transport networks	Analysis of how well locations are connected to transport networks	Distance to nearest railway station, exit point of a motorway	Partial measure of accessibility; measures are not suited for a comparison of transport modes, taking available opportunities into account.
Supply-oriented measures – network connectivity	Describing network connectivity, expressing how well each node in a network is connected to each adjacent node	Connectivity or centrality of a node relative to the rest of the network	Partial measure of accessibility. It also does not provide plausible results in complex networks with many indirect linkages between nodes.
Demand- and supply-oriented measures	Describing actual quality of performance of infrastructure networks	Actual travel times on the road network	Partial measure of accessibility; does not include land-use and individual components of accessibility.
Location-based accessibility measures:			
Cumulative opportunities	Counts the number of opportunities that can be reached from an original location within a given travel time, distance or cost (fixed costs); or (average or total) time or cost required to access a fixed number of opportunities (fixed opportunities)	Number of jobs within 30 minutes' travel time by car; average travel time or cost to reach 1 million jobs	These measures are relatively undemanding of data and are easy to interpret for researchers and policy makers, as no assumptions are made on a person's perception of transport, land-use and their interaction. The measure is sensitive to travel time changes.

Accessibility type	Applications	Examples	Disadvantages and comments
Potential accessibility measure	Estimates the number of opportunities in destination locations that can be accessed from an original location, weighted by a distance decay function, which describes how more distant opportunities provide diminishing influences	Index of jobs, population or services which can be accessed from an original location	The measure evaluates the combined effect of land-use and transport elements incorporates assumptions on a person's perceptions of transport by using an impedance function. The measure has no meaning in absolute terms (index). The form of the function should be carefully chosen, and the parameters should be estimated using empirical data on travel behaviour in the study area.
Actual accessibility	Estimates total travel distances, times or costs from an original location to all destinations, weighted by the actual number of trips on an original destination location	Analysis of competition between different transport modes	Detailed information of spatial patterns of travel behaviour is needed.
Person-based accessibility measures:			
Space–time approach	The measures analyze accessibility from the viewpoint of individuals, incorporating spatial and temporal constraints	The number of household activity programmes that can be carried out by individuals, given personal and time constraints	Founded in time geography. Measure is theoretically advanced but is very data demanding.
Utility-based accessibility measures:			
Utility of accessibility	The measures estimate the utility or monetary value (when utility is converted into monetary terms)	Logsum accessibility describing the utility of having access to spatially distributed activities	Founded in microeconomic theory. More difficult to communicate to non-experts.

Table 9.2 presents a matrix of the different accessibility measures and components. Infrastructure-based measures do not include a land-use component; that is, they are not sensitive to changes in the spatial distribution of activities if service levels (e.g. travel speed, times or costs) remain constant. The temporal component is explicitly treated in person-based measures and is generally not considered in the other perspectives, or is treated only implicitly, for example by computing peak- and off-peak-hour accessibility levels. Person-based and utility-based measures typically focus on the individual component, analyzing accessibility on an individual level. Location-based measures typically analyze accessibility on a macro-level but focus more on incorporating spatial constraints in the supply of opportunities, usually excluded in the other approaches (see the dark-shaded cells in Table 9.2 – these emphasize the dominant focus of each category of measures).

Table 9.2 Types of accessibility measures and components

Measure	Component			
	Transport	Land-use	Temporal	Individual
Infrastructure-based measures	Travelling speed; vehicle hours lost in congestion		Peak-hour period; 24-hr period	Trip-based stratification, e.g. home-to-work, business
Location-based measures	Travel time and/or costs between locations of activities	Amount and spatial distribution of the demand for and/or supply of opportunities	Travel time and costs may differ, e.g. between hours of the day, between days of the week, or seasons	Stratification of the population (e.g. by income, educational level)
Person-based measures	Travel time between location of activities	Amount and spatial distribution of supplied opportunities	Temporal constraints for activities and time available for activities	Estimated at the individual level
Utility-based measures	Travel costs between locations of activities	Amount and spatial distribution of supplied opportunities	Travel time and costs may differ, e.g. between hours of the day, between days of the week, or seasons	Utility is derived at the individual or homogeneous population group level

Note: Dark grey: primary focus of measures; light grey: non-primary focus.
Source: Geurs and van Wee (2004)

To operationalize accessibility measures, the most suitable type of accessibility measure needs to be chosen (the rows in Table 9.2), and then the various elements within the different components need to be determined (the columns in Table 9.2). A few examples can illustrate this process:

1. In determining travel times between origin and destination locations, one can choose whether or not to weigh the different time components of a trip, such as access and egress times to and from boarding points, in-vehicle travel times, waiting times and so on. Generally speaking, access and egress and waiting time will incur much greater disutility to travellers than in-vehicle time (e.g *see* Schakenbos et al., 2016; see also Chapter 6 of this book). In particular, a comprehensive approach to measuring public transport accessibility introduces a number of complexities, such as access to and from public transport by different modes. For example, Geurs et al. (2016) examined the impacts of bicycle–train integration policies on job accessibility for public transport users, implementing a detailed bicycle network linked to the public transport network, access/egress mode combinations and station specific access and egress penalties by mode and station type derived from a stated choice survey *see* Chapter 6, Section 6.2 for a description of the travel time components in transport impedance.
2. In determining the costs of car trips, one can include only fuel costs, but also total variable costs, including for example parking costs and fixed costs (e.g. depreciation of the car). Several cost elements can also be integrated in a generalized cost function. Koopmans et al. (2013), for example, developed a generalized cost measure for car use to measure

accessibility changes over time in the Netherlands. Their generalized cost measure included fuel costs, travel time, value of travel time and reliability of travel time.

3. Perceived accessibility, as the actual determinant of decisions regarding activity behaviour, may differ from accessibility measurements based on actual spatial data. Perceptions of the land-use, transport and temporal components may for example relate to knowledge of available opportunities, perceived travel times or distances or temporal availability of activities (e.g. opening hours). Objective and perceived factors may differ greatly, e.g. car drivers greatly over-estimate travel time with public transport (e.g *see* van Exel and Rietveld, 2009). Perceptions may also change over time *see* Pot et al. (2021) for a discussion on perceived accessibility.

4. In determining the land-use component, one needs to consider the spatial unit of analysis (e.g. block level, postcode) but also for how many destination opportunities are to be considered, and how these values are to be aggregated. An access measure involving multiple destination types (e.g. jobs, shops, healthcare) can be weighted to produce a single aggregated measure (Levinson and Wu, 2020). Furthermore, one needs to consider if available opportunities have capacity limitations (such as in the case of school locations and healthcare facilities), as a result of which competition exists, and where accessibility measures need to account for differences in the spatial distribution of the demand and supply of these opportunities (see Section 9.8 for a discussion).

9.5   CHOOSING AND USING ACCESSIBILITY MEASURES

In defining and operationalizing accessibility, there is no one best approach because different situations and purposes demand different approaches (Handy and Niemeier, 1997). However, several criteria can be derived to evaluate the usefulness and limitations of accessibility measures for different study purposes *see*, amongst others, Geurs and van Wee (2004). We summarize these criteria here as follows.

9.5.1   Purpose of the Study

This is the starting point of the operationalization process. What is the purpose of the study and, following from that, what is the main reason for analyzing accessibility? All other choices essentially follow on from this. The definition and operationalization would, for example, strongly differ when the study purpose is to evaluate accessibility impacts of a transport project, or to analyze social equity effects, or the economic benefits that people derive from having access to opportunities. This means that the analysis of transport policy can be carried out through more aggregate, location-based accessibility measures, whereas the analysis of social equity effects requires a highly spatially differentiated and disaggregated analysis. The analysis of economic benefits would require choosing a utility-based accessibility measure that is directly linked to microeconomic theory.

In the transport planning practice, there is also a link between the choice of the accessibility measure and policy objectives set in transport policy documents. Since the mid-twentieth century, the fundamental transport policy goal has been to achieve faster vehicle operating speeds. To measure the effectiveness of transport policies to meet that goal, accessibility measures such as delay per capita, vehicle hours or money wasted while waiting in traffic and highway level of service have been used (Levine et al., 2012). These accessibility measures are however not simply after-the-fact assessments, but they are also used proactively to guide policy towards car-based transport investments (Levine et al., 2019). Analysis of over 170 Dutch municipal transport policy documents shows that car-oriented mobility planning and the use of simple infrastructure-based accessibility indicators still dominates Dutch municipal transport planning. Location-based accessibility measures are mostly found in transport policies of a few large cities and highly urban municipalities (Akse et al., 2021).

9.5.2   Scientific Quality

An accessibility measure should ideally take all of the components and elements within these components into account (Section 9.2). Thus an accessibility measure should firstly be sensitive to the changes in the transport and land-use systems and the temporal constraints of opportunities, and it should take individual needs, abilities and opportunities into account. A comprehensive inclusion of all components and their elements implies a level of complexity and detail that can probably never be achieved in practice. However, it is important that the limitations are recognized and described. In the literature, several examples of comparative accessibility studies can be found. Thill and Kim (2010) explored differences between over 70 different location-based accessibility measures and operationalizations. Kwan (1998) and Neutens et al. (2010) explored differences between different location- and person-based accessibility measures. The main conclusion from these studies is that each accessibility measure brings a particular perspective to the measurement of the notion of accessibility that is not fully captured by others. Hence, it is preferable to use multiple accessibility measures and operationalizations in accessibility studies. However, the estimation of multiple accessibility measures requires more effort and it is in conflict with the criterion: operationalization. And it can also be in conflict with the second next criterion, 'Interpretability and communicability', because clients of accessibility research might get confused. The solution may be to estimate multiple accessibility measures, and if the results are highly correlated and not very sensitive to the choices made, to communicate the results of only one measure. If the results differ significantly, this may be communicated as an uncertainty.

9.5.3   Operationalization

The operationalization of accessibility measures is related to the ease with which the measure can be used in practice, for example in ascertaining availability of data, models and techniques, and time and budget. This criterion will usually be in conflict with one or more of the theoretical criteria described above. As noted in Section 9.1, while practitioners typically are convinced that comprehensive accessibility measures are useful in the planning practice, many do not use them in their work. The availability of data, for example, can be an important barrier towards the use of advanced accessibility measures and tools (e.g. software packages) in the planning practice (e.g. Boisjoly and El-Geneidy, 2017). A promising way forward to improve the ease of using accessibility measures is to develop open source, transferable and interactive accessibility tools which have easy-to-use interfaces. The rise of WebGIS-technology allows the development of such tools. Pajares et al. (2021) presents an example of such an attempt, following an iterative software development process in close cooperation with practitioners. The tool was tested and transferred to more than 20 cities in Germany, Colombia and Portugal.

9.5.4   Interpretability and Communicability

Measures of accessibility have evolved with advances in GIS technology and data gathering methods including geocoded spatial data and crowd-sourced, GPS-based travel times (Wu and Levinson, 2020). In academic literature, accessibility studies have developed complex and high resolution accessibility measures, partly in response to the recognition that the aggregate measures lack many important details. However, accessibility measures which are used in the planning practice are typically easy to interpret for researchers and policy makers, such as travel speed on the road network or cumulative opportunity measures, but which have strong methodological disadvantages. It is important that comprehensive approaches to measure accessibility are made practical. Researchers, planners and policy makers should be able to understand and interpret the measure, and communicate results to clients, as otherwise it is not likely to be used in evaluation studies of land-use and/or transport developments or policies and will thus have no impact on the policy making process.

The interpretations of comprehensive accessibility measures can for example be improved by comparing accessibility across place or time, or both place and time, rather than focusing on absolute levels of accessibility. To improve interpretation, accessibility estimations can also be indexed. For example, the base year value or a reference scenario can be indexed at the level of 100. The value of the accessibility indicators could then be indexed and compared to this base level value. Furthermore, location-based accessibility measures by definition capture the combined effects of land-use (distribution of opportunities) and transport impedance (time, cost, etc.) factors. This can make interpretation of accessibility changes difficult. What causes a change in accessibility in an area: a change in travel time or a change in land use? To improve interpretation, the influence of each factor on the overall accessibility change can be shown. An example of such an approach is given by Moya-Gómez and Geurs (2018), who examined the spatial and temporal dynamics in job accessibility by car in the Netherlands during the economic crisis and its aftermath (2009–14) and showed the separate influence of land-use changes and road network investments on the development of (job) accessibility for the Netherlands. Computation of the different components of accessibility facilitates both the explanation of overall accessibility changes and the relative position of regions.

9.6   DIGITAL AND PHYSICAL ACCESSIBILITY

Information and communications technologies (ICTs) are permeating modern lifestyles, shaping and colouring the undertaking of activities and travel (Lyons, 2014). ICTs include personal computer use at fixed locations, mobile devices, such as laptops and smartphones, and infrastructure-related information provision technologies, such as Dynamic Route Information Panels (DRIPS) for roads and public transport travel information. Since the start of the World Wide Web over 30 years ago we have moved into a world where we can search for and engage with almost anything online, whether information, other people, goods or services; and we can do so (if equipped) from (almost) anywhere and anytime – whether at our desks, on the move or in our living rooms (Lyons, 2014). This affects how we travel and access people, goods and services. In contrast to the numerous studies on how various ICTs affect how we travel (e.g *see* for overviews Aguiléra et al., 2012; Lyons, 2014), there are only a few studies on the impacts on accessibility. ICTs can however impact accessibility in various ways. Van Wee et al. (2013) provide a systematic overview of potential impacts of ICT on accessibility, using the four components of accessibility.

ICT can have complex impacts on accessibility as it affects all four of its components:

1. **Transport component**: ICTs can affect travel resistance in many ways. Firstly, a traveller may access (personalized) travel information before and during the trip via individual ICT devices (e.g. PCs, PDAs, smartphone), and as a result reduce access time, and optimize route and mode choice. The development of multi-tasking during journeys (e.g. making phone calls, online working) affects travel resistance. For example, ICTs allow public transport users to use part of their travel time in a useful way and not all travel time should be considered unproductive and 'lost'. Molin et al. (2020) examined the impact of onboard activities on the value of time (VoT) of train users in the Netherlands, and they concluded that VoT due to onboard activities is 30% lower for commuters and almost 50% for leisure travellers. Furthermore, during the COVID-19 pandemic, many governments and companies promoted and facilitated teleworking. In the Netherlands teleworking resulted in significant reductions in car commuting, reducing transport impedance (e.g. lower peak-hour travel times). This might have long-term effects. In the Netherlands, for example, 40% of workers indicated, after one month of teleworking during the lockdown in 2020, that they would like to continue teleworking (one or more days per week) after the pandemic, whereas 23% of workers were teleworking before the pandemic (Olde Kalter et al., 2021).

2. **Land-use component**: ICTs influence which persons carry out which activities at which locations, due to changes in activities or activity locations; e.g. a person deciding to work at home using ICT instead of travelling to work. ICT may directly or indirectly impact the distribution of actors (households, shops, companies, etc.) over the given locations of destinations. An example of a direct impact is that the city of Amsterdam has excellent digital infrastructure and hosts large data-transport hubs which has helped to attract many companies in the information industry. An example of an indirect impact is that the rapid increase in online sales that, particularly during the COVID-19 pandemic, profoundly changes the way consumer goods are bought and sold. Online shopping typically substitutes shopping trips (Le et al., 2021) and changes the spatial distribution of retail businesses. Studies in the UK, for example, show that growth in e-commerce increased the number of vacant shops in particular in (small) town centres and small retail centres. (Dolega and Lord, 2020).

3. **Temporal component**: ICTs affect the availability of opportunities at different times of the day, and the time available for individuals to participate in certain activities (e.g. work, recreation). Thanks to ICT a number of activities can be carried out at non-traditional

times of day (e.g. working at night or on the weekend instead of during office hours). Also, ICTs can allow the traveller to travel more efficiently (e.g. outside rush hours), save time and spend more time on other activities.

4. **Individual component**: ICT can have an impact on the needs (and wants) of people: people might, for example, want to go to a concert they are aware of thanks to ICT. ICT can also have a negative impact on people's abilities to travel. Durand et al. (2021) state that digital technologies are progressively becoming indispensable. In shared mobility such as ride sourcing, car and bike sharing, not only is digital access to services the default option, but it is also nowadays frequently the only option. This can increase transport disadvantage for some groups in society. Durand et al. (2021) conclude in a literature review that vulnerability to digitalization in transport services exists along dimensions of age, income, education, ethnicity, gender and geographical region.

In the literature, some studies developed conceptual frameworks to combine physical and digital accessibility (e.g. Miller, 2005; Lu et al., 2014) but only a few applied these models to real case studies. One example is from Cavallaro and Dianin (2022) who developed a potential job accessibility measure (see also Section 9.8) that combines physical accessibility and teleworking into a single accessibility measure. The study included homeworking costs (such as energy and internet subscriptions) as virtual 'transport' impedance. From an application of the model to a rural and mountainous area in north-western Italy it was concluded that teleworking plays a minor role in the overall job accessibility. This is explained by the partial development of digital infrastructures and low level of teleworking opportunities in that region. In regions or countries with high quality digital infrastructure and high teleworking levels, the impact of teleworking on overall job accessibility can be expected to be much higher.

The overall impact of ICTs on accessibility can be profound. However, there are several gaps in our knowledge on the impacts of ICT on accessibility (see also van Wee et al., 2013). Firstly, it is unknown how the many different interactions between ICT and accessibility components combine overall. For example, research on telecommuting show that telecommuters typically have longer commuting distances due to more remote residential locations (Cerqueira et al., 2020). However, telecommuting can also enable people to achieve a desired but more distant residential location (e.g. bigger home and/or lower housing prices), without a net increase in commute travel. So an interaction exists between residential location, job location and ICT use, but we still poorly understand these interactions. Another example is that the ICT can relax temporal constraints, as consumers no longer depend on the opening times of (physical) shops to buy goods. Thus, an interaction exists between ICT access to shops. However, it is unclear if digital access to shops influences the temporal distribution of activities of persons, and maybe even residential location, and such choices influence the level of accessibility.

Other knowledge gaps relate to, amongst others, the effect of personalized information provision using mobile phone technologies on transport impedances (including comfort of travel) and equity implications of the growing importance of digital accessibility. Over 40% of the EU population still lacks at least basic digital skills and even in the Netherlands, one of the three most digitalized countries in the European Union, about 20% of the working population lack basic digital skills, and these people are generally older, lower educated and more often female (Non et al., 2021). Moreover, digital technologies are progressively becoming indispensable for physical accessibility. Shared mobility services such as ride sourcing, car and bike sharing can often only be used with digital technologies. But we still poorly understand the importance of such developments for accessibility. This relates to the following discussion about the equity of accessibility.

9.7   EQUITY OF ACCESSIBILITY

People, groups of people and regions by definition do not have the same level of access to destinations, such as shops, jobs or medical services. Planners have long been interested in improving the conditions experienced by disadvantaged regions and/or population groups. There is also a large body of research focusing on questions of uneven or inequitable access to places and forms of movement. Early examples use various measures of physical accessibility as a social indicator of the ease with which citizens may reach different employment and services opportunities. Inequalities in accessibility are influenced strongly by the population characteristics of areas as well as by location (Wachs and Kumagai, 1973).

Equity is an important concept but also very difficult to define (van Wee and Mouter, 2021). Transportation equity typically refers to the distribution of transport-related benefits and costs over members of society. Di Ciommo and Shiftan (2017) argue that transportation equity has three key components:

1. the benefits and costs that are being distributed;
2. the population groups over which the benefits and costs are distributed; and
3. the distributive principle that determines whether a particular distribution is 'morally proper' and 'socially acceptable'.

Research on the first two components of transport equity have a long history in transport and urban research. Equity of accessibility is the most assessed aspect in transport policy evaluations (see van Wee and Mouter, 2021, for an overview). There is a large body of literature focusing on questions of uneven or inequitable access to places and forms of movement (e.g. van Wee and Geurs, 2011). Early examples use various measures of physical accessibility as a social indicator of the ease with which citizens can reach different employment and services opportunities (e.g. Wachs and Kumagai, 1973). Equity analysis however is very complex as there are several types of equity (see Thomopoulos et al., 2009, for an overview), various ways to categorize people for equity analysis, numerous impacts to consider and various ways of measuring these impacts (van Wee and Geurs, 2011). In practice, one or more quantitative indicators, such as the Gini index, are often used to express the level of (in)equality of accessibility *see* Chapter 15 for more information on equity measures.

Research on fairness and (distributive) justice (the third component in the list by Di Ciommo and Shiftan, 2017, as presented above) is a fast growing field within transportation research. In particular, recent studies link accessibility approaches to transport justice frameworks based on key theories of justice including Rawls' egalitarianism and the Capability Approaches (CA) (e.g *see* for literature reviews Pereira et al., 2017, and Vecchio and Martens, 2021). Karner et al. (2020) state that transportation justice describes a normative condition in which no person or group is disadvantaged by a lack of access to the opportunities they need to lead a meaningful and dignified life. Several authors have suggested that the Capabilities Approach developed by Amartya Sen and Martha Nussbaum (e.g. Nussbaum and Sen, 1993; Sen, 2009) can provide a conceptual framework to properly appraise the transport system as well as new transport projects. The Capabilities Approach has five key features to understand a person's level of freedom which can be summarized as follows (e.g. Vecchio and Martens, 2021, for more details):

1. Resources: commodities and intangible goods available to a person, which are considered as means to achievement.
2. Capabilities are the freedoms available to a person. Each capability is whatever people are able to do and be in a variety of areas of life.
3. Functionings: what people actually achieve 'to be' or 'to do'. Each person puts into practice (or not) the capabilities available to her. The basic element of an individual's functioning is travelling.
4. Conversion factors: personal, social and environmental conditions that form the individual life experience. The factors determine what possibilities the person has to convert resources into freedoms.
5. Choice refers to the person's decision in favour of a particular 'state' over another, selected from within their capability set.

There is a growing stream of research arguing that accessibility can be understood as a capability within the framework of the Capability Approach. A capability can, as a practical operationalization of this approach, be interpreted as a person's possibility of engaging in a variety of out-of-home activities. Accessibility captures the possibility of each person to actually participate in valued activities. This can involve travel or virtual accessibility (see Section 9.6). This also involves analysis of elements which have not received much attention in the literature so far, such as wellbeing. Vecchio and Martens (2021) argue that the higher a person's accessibility level, the larger the person's freedom to choose to travel to 'the best' opportunities with a substantial positive impact on wellbeing. Even if the person does not always choose that 'best' option, the freedom embodied in a large choice set is in itself likely to enhance wellbeing. It also creates complexity as perceptions of what are minimum levels of access to opportunities differ across people. Furthermore, it has also been argued that transport policy can be seen as a conversion factor to use the Capability Approach in transport policy evaluations (Randal et al., 2020). Transport policy in this perspective can enhance or limit accessibility but also other capabilities such as health and wellbeing. Nahmias-Biran and Shiftan (2019) developed a conceptual framework using a utility-based accessibility measure to translate capabilities into the (monetary) 'Value of Capability Gains' that can be used in cost–benefit analysis. However, the inclusion of capabilities elements in transport policy appraisal tools is quite complex and requires much more exploration.

Furthermore, there is little attention in the literature for the joint analysis of the distribution of advantages and disadvantages of transport (accessibility, air pollution, etc.), their interactions and correlations, and their evolution over time, and resulting equity implications (Geurs et al., 2021). These relationships can be quite complex. For example, da Schio et al. (2019)

found flagrant patterns of inequality in accessibility and air pollution in the Brussels region, but these do not reflect the socio-economic structure of the region.

Finally, some authors argue that to achieve more fair transport planning it is not sufficient to conduct quantitative equity analysis, but also full and fair participation of affected communities in the decision making is needed (Karner and Marcantonio, 2018). To learn more about equity considerations and the newest methods that are used to integrate them in policy appraisal, see Chapter 14.

9.8 APPLICATIONS: TWO EXAMPLES OF ACCESSIBILITY MEASURES

Table 9.1 presented an overview of different types of accessibility measures, applications and examples. In this section we will give two examples of frequently used accessibility measures in the literature: (1) the potential accessibility measure and (2) the Shen accessibility measure. The Shen index takes into account the spatial distribution in the demand for opportunities (competition effects), whereas the potential accessibility measure does not. The application of the two measures illustrates how the choice and operationalization of an accessibility measure may strongly affect the conclusions on accessibility.

9.8.1 Potential Accessibility Measures

Potential accessibility measures (also called gravity-based measures) have been widely used in urban and geographical studies since the late 1940s, including the seminal work of Hansen (1959). The potential accessibility measure estimates the accessibility of opportunities in zone i to all other zones n in which smaller and/or more distant opportunities provide diminishing influences. The measure has the following form, assuming a negative exponential cost function:

$$A_i = \sum_{j=1}^{n} D_j e^{-\beta c_{ij}} \tag{9.1}$$

where Ai is a measure of accessibility in zone i to all opportunities D (e.g. jobs, schools, health facilities) in zone j, c_{ij} the impedance or costs of travel between i and j, and β the cost sensitivity parameter.

The impedance (or distance decay) function makes accessibility decrease if costs increase. The function has a significant influence on the results of the accessibility measure. For plausible results, the form of the function should be carefully chosen, and the parameters of the function should be estimated using recent empirical data of spatial travel behaviour in the study area. Several studies have used different impedance functions, such as negative exponential, power, Gaussian or logistic functions. However, the negative exponential function is the most widely used and the most closely tied to travel behaviour theory.

The standard potential accessibility index calculates the geographic distribution of accessibility between areas or zones of analysis. This does not account for the number of people who potentially access the opportunities. This makes it impossible to compare potential accessibility measures between different case study areas (cities, countries) with different volumes of opportunities. To account for this, potential accessibility can be weighted by the population in each spatial unit or zone @mto estimate person-average accessibility:

$$A_{i\,person} = \frac{A_i}{P_i} \tag{9.2}$$

where $A_{i\,person}$ is the accessibility in zone i per person (by mode); P_i is the population in zone i.

Potential measures have the practical advantage that they can be easily computed using existing land-use and transport data (and/or models), and they have been traditionally employed as an input for estimating infrastructure-based measures. A potential measure is however not so easy to interpret, as it combines land-use and transport elements and weighs opportunities according to the impedance function. Moreover, in practice potential accessibility measures (and other location-based measures) are typically measured for a particular place, mode, purpose and time in a particular year. Levinson and Wu (2020) argue that more generalized measures of (potential) accessibility are needed that ideally would be measured for all places, all modes, all purposes, at all times. In case the measure is used in transport project evaluation, it ideally is also measured over the lifecycle of a project.

9.8.2   Shen Accessibility Measure

Standard potential accessibility measures ignore the spatial distribution in the demand for opportunities, i.e. the so-called competition effects. For example, the workers compete for jobs; firms compete for workers in the labour force. Ignoring such effects could lead to misleading conclusions. This is illustrated in Figure 9.2. A potential accessibility indicator would estimate (left side) that jobs in location j_4 are the most accessible (closest by). However, accounting for

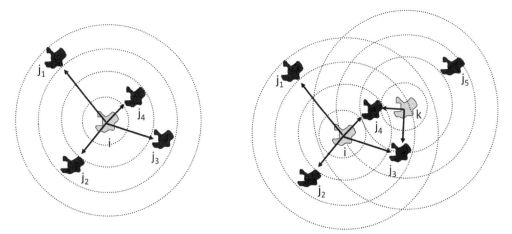

Figure 9.2   Visualization of potential accessibility (left) and Shen measure (right)

competition with persons in location k means jobs in location j_2 are more accessible, as opportunities in locations j_3 and j_4 are within reach of competitors in location k.

To incorporate competition effects, several authors have adapted potential accessibility measures. A relatively simple approach has been to measure accessibility to certain opportunities (jobs) and to individuals (workers) from a given location and then divide one measure by the other (Levinson, 1998; van Wee et al., 2001). This approach is useful if the travel distance between origins and destinations is relatively small, such as for elementary schools. A more advanced approach developed by Shen (1998) involves incorporating the demand potential (job seekers) to the calculation by dividing the supply (jobs) located in destination zone j by the demand potential within reach of that zone j. This approach is also called the two-step floating catchment area method which is frequently used in studies examining (spatial inequalities in) accessibility of healthcare services (see for an overview see Chen and Jia, 2019). Figure 9.2 visualizes the difference between a standard potential accessibility measure and the Shen index. The Shen index (S_i) has the following functional form:

$$S_i = \sum_j \frac{O_j \cdot f(t_{ij})}{D_j} , \quad D_j = \sum_k P_k \cdot f(t_{kj}) \qquad (9.3)$$

where S_i is the accessibility in zone i (by mode) while considering competition from other zones k by users (of a specific mode); P_k is the population in location k; $f(t_{kj})$ is the impedance as a function of the travel time t_{kj} between k and j using a specific mode. Figure 9.2 illustrates the effect of competition. The Shen index (Equation 9.3) accounts for the competition using only the selected mode of travel, e.g. for car only competition between car commuters are included. This is a simplification. Pritchard et al. (2019) developed a multi-modal Shen index (Equation 9.4). The denominator, which accounts for population, uses the fastest travel time alternative t_{kj}^m between each origin–destination (O–D) pair (i.e. the greatest possible competition from each zone k to any zone j). This means that if the travel time by car is faster than, for example, public transport from zone k to j then the travel time by car is selected for this O–D pair. This is a good indicator because like potential accessibility it focuses on the supply side of accessibility and does not assess the modal choice of individual residents; the greatest potential competition from any area k is considered.

$$S_i^{m_x} = \sum_j \frac{O_j \cdot f(t_{ij}^{m_x})}{D_j^{fastest}} , \quad D_j^{fastest} = \sum_k P_k \cdot f(t_{kj}^{m_j}) \qquad (9.4)$$

where: $S_{i\,MM}^{m_x}$ is the accessibility in zone i by mode x with competition from any mode; $f(t_{kj}^{m_j})$ is the impedance as a function of the fastest travel time by any mode between k and j.

In the literature, more advanced approaches are used to include competition effects. The Shen index simplifies competition effects, which can be illustrated using Figure 9.2. The Shen index does not include job opportunities in location j_5 within reach of workers in location k but outside reach of workers living in location i. To allow for these effects, iterative procedures are needed, incorporating the competition on supplied opportunities and the competition on demand (e.g. Geurs and Ritsema van Eck, 2003; El-Geneidy and Levinson, 2011).

   An application of the potential accessibility and Shen accessibility measures is presented by Pritchard et al. (2019). They conducted a comparative accessibility study, and estimated job accessibility for car and public transport in Greater London, São Paulo and the Dutch Randstad region, the most populated area in the west of the Netherlands. Pritchard et al. (2019) estimated two types of potential accessibility measures (zonal and person based; Table 9.3) and two types of Shen measures (intra-modal and multi-modal; Table 9.3). The results can be found in Table 9.3. The car provides, on average, higher zonal potential accessibility to the residents of all three city-regions. The standard potential accessibility measure indicates that residents in São Paulo are the best off, having the highest average accessibility by car and transit, and Londoners having the lowest. However, the city-regions have different total volumes of opportunities and working-age population, with São Paulo having the most jobs but also workers (4.7 and 7.8 million, respectively) and the Randstad area having the least jobs and also the smallest working-age population (3.6 and 5.3 million, respectively). This changes the ranking of cities; the car provides access to more jobs per resident in London than São Paulo and the Randstad area. Incorporating job competition has a stronger effect on the conclusion. The mode-specific Shen index shows that workers in the Randstad area are the best off – they have access to 0.8 jobs per worker – whereas in São Paulo this is about 0.6. However, the position of public transport users changes radically if competition with car drivers is included as competitors. Dutch public transport users are worse off – the accessible number of jobs per worker drops from 0.8 to 0.1 jobs per worker. Thus, the choice and operationalization of accessibility measures affect the results and conclusions of accessibility studies.

Table 9.3 Job accessibility in the Randstad area, Greater London and São Paulo based on different operationalizations of potential and Shen accessibility measures (Pritchard et al., 2019)

			Car	Public transport
São Paulo	Potential Accessibility	Standard	2,166,153	638,993
		Person-Averaged	409	144
	Shen Accessibility	Mode-Specific	0.62	0.58
		Best-Alternative	0.62	0.18
London	Potential Accessibility	Standard	786,490	179,334
		Person-Averaged	477	116
	Shen Accessibility	Mode-Specific	0.70	0.71
		Best-Alternative	0.70	0.15
Randstad	Potential Accessibility	Standard	1,585,952	202,858
		Person-Averaged	355	37
	Shen Accessibility	Mode-Specific	0.81	0.76
		Best-Alternative	0.81	0.09

9.9   CONCLUSIONS

This chapter has provided an overview of different perspectives, components and operationalizations of accessibility, together with applications of accessibility measures. Furthermore, new research areas related to the impact of ICTs on accessibility and measurement of equity in accessibility are described. The main conclusions are as follows.

It is very important to make careful decisions on the definition and operationalization of accessibility, as the output is dependent on the definition and the choice of accessibility measure. The four criteria on which decisions can be based are (1) purpose of the study, (2) scientific quality, (3) operationalization (cost, effort) and (4) interpretation and communication.

In practice, the accessibility measures used are often those that are easy to operationalize and interpret, rather than those that satisfy more stringent theoretical criteria. Applying a full set of scientific quality criteria would imply a level of complexity and detail that is difficult to achieve in practice. This means that different situations and study purposes demand different approaches. However, it is important to recognize the implications of ignoring one or more of these criteria.

Location- and utility-based accessibility measures can be considered effective measures of accessibility, which can also be used as input for social and economic evaluations. These measures overcome the most important shortcomings of infrastructure-based measures and can be computed with state-of-the-practice land-use and transport data and models.

Equity analysis of accessibility is increasingly becoming important in transport planning. Equity analysis is however not straightforward. There are several types of equity, various ways to categorize people for equity analysis, numerous impacts to consider and various ways of measuring these impacts. Dealing with fairness and justice in transportation requires a more complete understanding of accessibility than traditional approaches have been able to deliver to date.

ICTs affect how we travel and access people, goods and services. The COVID-19 pandemic has amplified this affect. ICTs affect all four components of accessibility, and their interactions. There is relatively little research combining physical and digital accessibility in accessibility measures. Moreover, there are many gaps in our knowledge on the possible impacts of ICT on the different components of accessibility, and the equity implications of the growing importance of digital accessibility for physical accessibility. Shared mobility services for example can often only be accessed using digital technologies.

REFERENCES

Aguiléra, A., C. Guillot and A. Rallet (2012), 'Mobile ICTs and physical mobility: Review and research agenda', *Transportation Research Part A: Policy and Practice*, 46, 664–72.

Akse, R., T. Thomas and K. Geurs (2021), 'Mobility and accessibility paradigms in Dutch policies: An empirical analysis', *Journal of Transport and Land Use*, 14(1), 1317–40.

Beria, P., A. Bertolin and R. Grimaldi (2018), 'Integration between Transport Models and Cost-Benefit Analysis to Support Decision-Making Practices: Two Applications in Northern Italy', *Advances in Operations Research*, 2018, 1–16.

Boisjoly, G. and A.M. El-Geneidy (2017), 'The insider: A planners' perspective on accessibility', *Journal of Transport Geography*, 64, 33–43.

Cavallaro, F. and A. Dianin (2022), 'Combining transport and digital accessibilities in the evaluation of regional work opportunities', *Journal of Transport Geography*, 98, 1–12.

Cerqueira, E.D.V., B. Motte-Baumvol, L.B. Chevallier and O. Bonin (2020), 'Does working from home reduce CO_2 emissions? An analysis of travel patterns as dictated by workplaces', *Transportation Research Part D: Transport and Environment*, 83, 1–12.

Chen, X. and O. Jia (2019), 'A comparative analysis of accessibility measures by the two-step floating catchment area (2SFCA) method', *International Journal of Geographical Information Science*, 33(9), 1739–58.

da Schio, N., K. Boussauw and J. Sansen (2019), 'Accessibility versus air pollution: A geography of externalities in the Brussels agglomeration', *Cities*, 84, 178–89.

de Jong, G., A. Daly, M. Pieters and T. van der Hoorn (2007), 'The logsum as an evaluation measure: review of the literature and new results', *Transportation Research Part A: Policy and Practice*, 41, 874–89.

Di Ciommo, F. and Y. Shiftan (2017), 'Transport equity analysis', *Transport Reviews*, 37(2), 139–51.

Dijst, M., H. Jayet and I. Thomas (2002), 'Transportation and urban performance: accessibility, daily mobility and location of households and facilities', in M. Dijst, W. Schenkel and I. Thomas (eds), *Governing Cities on the Move: Functional and Management Perspectives on Transformations of Urban Infrastructures in European Agglomerations*, 19–41, Aldershot: Ashgate.

Dolega, L. and A. Lord (2020), 'Exploring the geography of retail success and decline: A case study of the Liverpool City Region', *Cities* 96, 1–11.

Durand, A., T. Zijlstra, N. van Oort, S. Hoogendoorn-Lanser and S. Hoogendoorn (2021), 'Access denied? Digital inequality in transport services', *Transport Reviews*, 2021, 1–25.

El-Geneidy, A. and D. Levinson (2011), 'Place Rank: Valuing Spatial Interactions', *Networks and Spatial Economics*, 2011(11), 643–59.

Geurs, K.T., La Paix, L. and van Weperen, S. (2016), 'A multi-modal network approach to model public transport accessibility impacts of bicycle-train integration policies'. *European Transport Research Review*, 8, 1–15.

Geurs, K.T., D. Niemeier and M. Giannotti (2021), 'The uneven geography of the accessibility and environmental quality in the global north and south: Introduction to the special issue', *Journal of Transport Geography*, 97, 1–6.

Geurs, K.T. and J.R. Ritsema van Eck (2003), 'Accessibility evaluation of land-use scenarios: the impact of job competition, land-use and infrastructure developments for the Netherlands', *Environment and Planning B: Planning and Design*, 30, 69–87.

Geurs, K.T. and B. van Wee (2004), 'Accessibility evaluation of land-use and transport strategies: review and research directions', *Journal of Transport Geography*, 12, 127–40.

Geurs, K., B. Zondag, G. de Jong and M. de Bok (2010), 'Accessibility appraisal of integrated land-use/ transport policy strategies: more than just adding up travel time savings', *Transportation Research Part D*, 15, 382–93.

Hägerstrand, T. (1970), 'What about people in regional science?', *Papers of the Regional Science Association*, 24, 7–21.

Handy, S.L. and D.A. Niemeier (1997), 'Measuring accessibility: an exploration of issues and alternatives', *Environment and Planning A*, 29, 1175–94.

Hansen, W.G. (1959), 'How accessibility shapes land use', *Journal of the American Institute of Planners*, 25, 73–76.

Karner, A., J. London, D. Rowangould and K. Manaugh (2020), 'From Transportation Equity to Transportation Justice: Within, Through, and Beyond the State', *Journal of Planning Literature*, 35(4), 440 59.

Karner, A. and R.A. Marcantonio (2018), 'Achieving Transportation Equity: Meaningful Public Involvement to Meet the Needs of Underserved Communities'. *Public Works Management and Policy*, 23(2), 105–26.

Koopmans, C., W. Groot, P. Warffemius, J.A. Annema and S. Hoogendoorn-Lanser (2013), 'Measuring generalised transport costs as an indicator of accessibility changes over time', *Transport Policy*, 29, 154–59.

Kwan, M.-P. (1998), 'Space-time and Integral Measures of Individual Accessibility: A Comparative Analysis Using a Point-based Framework', *Geographical Analysis*, 30, 191–216.

Le, H.T.K., A.L. Carrel and H. Shah (2021), 'Impacts of online shopping on travel demand: a systematic review', *Transport Reviews*, 1–23.

Levine, J. (2020), 'A century of evolution of the accessibility concept'. *Transportation Research Part D: Transport and Environment*, 83, 1–5.

Levine, J., J. Grengs and L.A. Merlin (2019), *From Mobility to Accessibility: Transforming Transportation and Land-Use Planning*, Ithaca/London: Cornell University Press.

Levine, J., J. Grengs, Q. Shen and Q. Shen (2012), 'Does accessibility require density or speed?', *Journal of the American Planning Association*, 78, 157–72.

Levinson, D.M. (1998), 'Accessibility and the journey to work', *Journal of Transport Geography*, 6(1), 1–21.

Levinson, D.M. and H. Wu (2020), 'Towards a general theory of access', *Journal of Transport and Land Use*, 13, 129–58.

Lu, R., C.G. Chorus and B. van Wee (2014), 'The effects of different forms of ICT on accessibility – a behavioural model and numerical examples', *Transportmetrica A: Transport Science*, 10(3), 233–54.

Lyons, G. (2014), 'Transport's Digital Age Transition', *Journal of Transport and Land Use*, 8(2), 1–19.

Miller, H.J. (2005), 'Necessary space–time conditions for human interaction'. *Environment and Planning B: Planning and Design*, 32(3), 381–401.

Molin, E., K. Adjenughwure, M. de Bruyn, O. Cats and P. Warffemius (2020), 'Does conducting activities while traveling reduce the value of time? Evidence from a within-subjects choice experiment', *Transportation Research Part A: Policy and Practice*, 132, 18–29.

Moya-Gómez, B. and K.T. Geurs (2018), 'The spatial–temporal dynamics in job accessibility by car in the Netherlands during the crisis', *Regional Studies*, 2018, 1–12.

Nahmias-Biran, B. and Y. Shiftan (2019), 'Using activity-based models and the capability approach to evaluate equity considerations in transportation projects', *Transportation*, 47(5), 2287–305.

Neutens, T., T. Schwanen, F. Witlox and P. de Maeyer (2010), 'Equity of urban service delivery: A comparison of different accessibility measures', *Environment and Planning A*, 42(7), 1613–35.

Non, M., M. Dinkova and B. Dahmen (2021), 'Skill up or get left behind? Digital skills and labor market outcomes in the Netherlands'. CPB Discussion Paper 419. CPB Netherlands Bureau for Economic Policy Analysis, The Hague.

Nussbaum, M. C. and A. K. Sen (1993), *The Quality of Life*. Oxford: Clarendon.

Olde Kalter, MJ, K.T. Geurs, L. Wismans (2021), 'Post COVID-19 teleworking and car use intentions. Evidence from large scale GPS-tracking and survey data in the Netherlands', *Transportation Research Interdisciplinary Perspectives*, 12, 1–11.

Pajares, E., B. Büttner, U. Jehle, A. Nichols and G. Wulfhorst, G (2021), 'Accessibility by proximity: Addressing the lack of interactive accessibility instruments for active mobility', *Journal of Transport Geography*, 93, 1–16.

Pan, Q., Z. Jin and X. Liu (2020), 'Measuring the effects of job competition and matching on employment accessibility', *Transportation Research Part D: Transport and Environment*, 87, 1–16.

Pereira, R.H.M., T. Schwanen and D. Banister (2017), 'Distributive justice and equity in transportation', *Transport Reviews*, 37, 170–91.

Pot, F.J., B. van Wee and T. Tillema (2021), 'Perceived accessibility: What it is and why it differs from calculated accessibility measures based on spatial data', *Journal of Transport Geography*, 94, 2021, 1–11.

Pritchard, J.P., D. Tomasiello, M. Giannotti and K.T. Geurs (2019), 'An international comparison of temporal and spatial inequalities in job accessibility – London, São Paulo and the Netherlands Randstad Area', *Transport Findings*, 2019, 1–12.

Randal, E., C. Shaw, A. Woodward, P. Howden-Chapman, A. Macmillan, J. Hosking, R. Chapman, A.M. Waa and M. Keall (2020), 'Fairness in Transport Policy: A New Approach to Applying Distributive Justice Theories', *Sustainability*, 12(23), 10102.

Schakenbos, R., L. La Paix, S. Nijenstein and K.T. Geurs (2016), 'Valuation of a transfer in a multimodal public transport trip', *Transport Policy*, 46, 72–81.

Sen, A. (2009), *The Idea of Justice*. London: Allen Lane.

Shen, Q. (1998), 'Location characteristics of inner-city neighborhoods and employment accessibility of low-wage workers', *Environment and Planning B: Planning and Design*, 25, 345–65.

Silva, C., L. Bertolini, M. te Brömmelstroet, D. Milakis and E. Papa (2017), 'Accessibility instruments in planning practice: Bridging the implementation gap', *Transport Policy*, 53, 135–45.

Thill, J.C. and M. Kim (2005), 'Trip making, induced travel demand, and accessibility', *Journal of Geographical Systems*, 2005(7), 229–48.

Thomopoulos, N., S. Grant-Muller and M.R. Tight (2009), 'Incorporating equity considerations in transport infrastructure evaluation: Current practice and a proposed methodology', *Evaluation and Program Planning*, 32(4), 351–59.

Van Exel, N.J.A. and P. Rietveld (2009), 'Could you also have made this trip by another mode? An investigation of perceived travel possibilities of car and train travellers on the main travel corridors to the city of Amsterdam, The Netherlands', *Transportation Research Part A: Policy and Practice*, 43, 374–85.

van Wee, B., C. Chorus and K. Geurs (2013), 'Information, communication, travel behaviour and accessibility', *Journal of Transport and Land Use*, 6, 1–16.

van Wee, B. and K.T. Geurs (2011), 'Discussing equity and social exclusion in accessibility evaluations', *European Journal of Transport and Infrastructure Research*, 11(4), 350–67.

van Wee, G.P., M. Hagoort and J.A. Annema (2001), 'Accessibility measures with competition', *Journal of Transport Geography*, 9, 199–208.

van Wee, B., and N. Mouter (2021), 'Evaluating transport equity', in N. Mouter (ed.), *New Methods, Reflections and Application Domains in Transport Appraisal*. Elsevier Series Advances in Transport Policy and Planning, Volume 7, 103–126. London: Elsevier.

Vecchio, G. and K. Martens (2021), 'Accessibility and the Capabilities Approach: a review of the literature and proposal for conceptual advancements', *Transport Reviews*, 41, 833–54.

Wachs, M. and T.G. Kumagai (1973), 'Physical accessibility as a social indicator', *Socio-Economic Planning Science*, 6, 357–79.

Wu, H. and D. Levinson (2020), 'Unifying access', *Transportation Research Part D: Transport and Environment*, 83. https://doi.org/10.1016/j.trd.2020.102355.

10
Transport and the environment

Natalia Barbour

10.1.   INTRODUCTION

Transport has diverse environmental impacts. These negative impacts have been found harmful to biodiversity, air quality, and public health. Table 10.1 gives an overview of the dominant environmental impacts per transport mode. It is nearly impossible to discuss all these harmful environmental effects of the transport system in one chapter, therefore, the focus will primarily fall on the road-related climate change impacts, measures, and mitigation strategies with also some attention on air pollution and noise. The reason to assess transport in the context of climate change is because of the huge role it plays in the overall emissions. The ongoing challenges, coupled with the Paris Agreement[1] goals that legally bound carbon dioxide (CO_2) emission reduction, provide an underlying framework needed to evaluate the environmental opportunities available for the transport sector.

Table 10.1 Dominant environmental impacts per transport mode

	Road	Rail	Air	Water
Climate change (carbon dioxide emissions)	*	*	*	*
Energy use (oil depleting)	*	*	*	*
Use of raw materials and waste production	*	*	*	*
Air pollution: NO_x (nitrogen oxides), particulate matter (PM) and others	*	*	*	*
Soil and water pollution	*			*
Odor pollution	*		*	
Noise pollution	*	*	*	

Improvements in the road transportation system and technologies have delivered countless benefits to society and made travel easier and, in many cases, less expensive. Some of the positive effects of transportation such as economic growth, job creation, or technological progress cause negative externalities in other domains. Economic growth and employment opportunities are very beneficial to communities, however accessing these economic opportunities often leads to long and auto-dependent commutes and consequently brings negative environmental impacts. Much of this growth and harmful impacts have been a consequence of inexpensive and abundant oil that is used for powering the vehicles that emit a variety of pollutants and gasses. While the transportation sector is responsible for non-CO_2 pollutants including methane, volatile organic compounds (VOCs), nitrogen oxides (NO_x), sulfur dioxide (SO_2), carbon monoxide (CO), F-gasses, black carbon, and non-absorbing aerosols (Sims et al., 2014), lately – as noted before – much attention goes to CO_2 emissions. CO_2 is the most important gas that contributes to raising global temperatures. CO_2 emissions have steeply increased since 1900, with this becoming exponential since around the 1950s. The steady growth after the 1950s can be mainly attributed to the increased reliance on fossil fuel-driven transportation and industry. Although the annual CO_2 emissions from burning fossil fuels have been increasing globally, not all countries contribute to this equally. Figure 10.1 shows how much different countries contributed to the overall emissions between 1970 to 2020 in the total number of tons of CO_2 (not per capita).

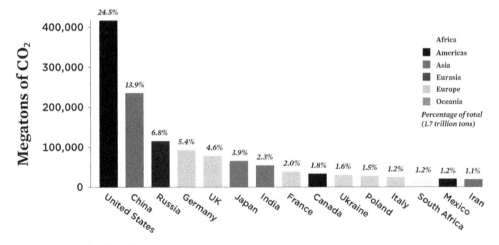

Source: UCSUSA (2022).

Figure 10.1   Top CO_2 emitting countries from 1975 to 2020

Although there are multiple key sectors that contribute to the overall emissions, the transportation sector plays a significant role by producing 24% of direct CO_2 emissions from fuel combustion (International Energy Agency, 2020). In developed economies these contributions are driven by road transportation and become even more significant, reaching around 30% of their national total (Sims et al., 2014). In general, electricity (29%) and transportation (27%)

have been the main contributors to greenhouse gas emissions in the United States (EPA, 2017; Van Fan et al., 2018).

The history of environmental concerns in transport will be discussed in a broader context in Section 10.2. In 10.3 the trends in transport related CO_2 emissions will be examined and in 10.4 the relationship between transport and air and noise pollution will be presented. In 10.5 this chapter returns to transport's CO_2 emissions and introduces some innovations to mitigate them. The environmental performance of different transport modes is treated in 10.6, using CO_2 emissions as criterion for comparison. In 10.7 some key environmental policy instruments for transport are discussed and Section 10.8 gives some ideas how to evaluate these policies and is followed by conclusions in the final Section 10.9.

10.2   THE HISTORY OF ENVIRONMENTAL CONCERNS IN TRANSPORT IN A BROAD CONTEXT

Concern over environmental problems increased rapidly in the late 1960s, mainly because of the rapid growth in population, industrialization, incomes, and consumption levels. In 1972 the Club of Rome produced an influential report titled *The Limits to Growth* (Meadows et al., 1972; see Meadows et al., 2005, for an update) that discussed ecological footprints for humanity in the context of the capacity of the Earth and the concept of limits to growth. After decades of gas, oil, coal exploitation these resources were found shrinking. Within the fossil fuel economy and high levels of exhaust emissions, the transportation sector was also shown to contribute to high levels of noise pollution as well as non-exhaust emissions coming primarily from tire and brake wear.

The growth in emissions can be generally linked to increased travel. Figure 10.2 shows growth in vehicle miles travelled (VMT) in the United States from 1920. Today, the United States is one of the most motorized nations, at 816 vehicles per 1,000 people in 2019 (Federal Highway Administration, 2017). Over the last century, other developed countries have been following similar trends and increasing their auto-dependence. In 2019, Luxembourg had the highest number of passenger cars per inhabitant in the EU, with 681 cars per thousand inhabitants (Eurostat, 2021).

In *The Limits to Growth* it is argued that the environment should be protected for future worldwide growth of the population and the economy. The unequal distribution of welfare could be a source of conflicts and ecological destruction, which could lead to stagnation in social, economic, and technological development. Because of its environmental and societal impacts, the transportation sector has been in the center of these discussions.

Air pollution and greenhouse gas emissions resulting from burning gasoline or diesel fuels for transportation (primary environmental effects) steal the headlines. The so-called secondary environmental effects of oil extraction are also not trivial and are related to drilling, fracking, and mining operations that generate enormous volumes of wastewater, which can be contaminated with heavy metals, radioactive materials, and other pollutants. Industries store this waste in open-air pits or underground wells that can leak or overflow into waterways and contaminate aquifers with pollutants linked to cancer, birth defects, neurological damage, and

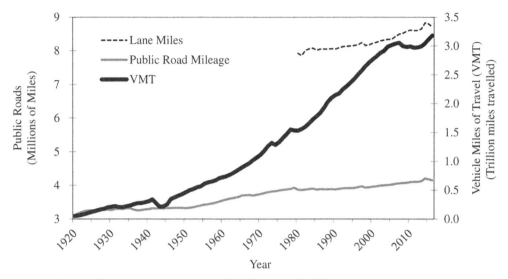

Source: Federal Highway Administration (2017); Frey (2018).

Figure 10.2   Growth in vehicle miles travelled (VMT), public road mileage, and public road lane miles in the United States 1920–2016

much more. Land and wildlife degradation are also some of the undesired and irreversible consequences of fossil fuel extraction. Although the number of oil spills has been decreasing since 1970 (Figure 10.3), the spilled oil has already created a permanent damage to the ecosystem.

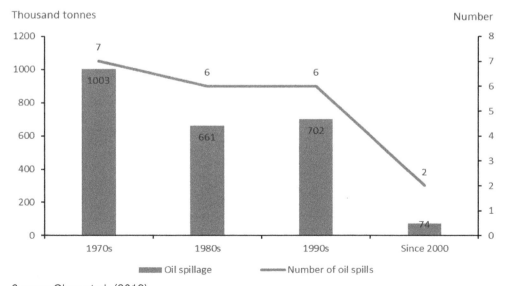

Source: Chen et al. (2019).

Figure 10.3   Oil spillage by major oil spill accidents 1970–2017

Furthermore, fossil fuels are non-renewable meaning that there is a certain amount of them left, and once depleted, they cannot be easily produced. Depletion of cheap and easily accessible fossil fuels, more specifically oil, raises major concerns.

Inexpensive oil that contributed to high reliance on automobiles has also brought many unintended consequences relating to livability. Past research has concluded that the quality of the urban environment is positively associated with individual well-being (Dong and Qin, 2017). Although there is still no unified definition and measurement of urban livability in the literature due to its complex and multi-dimensional nature (Zhan et al., 2018), car-centric designs, traffic, or exposure to pollution have been found to negatively impact livability and well-being (Park and Kwan, 2017). Natural environment, followed by transportation convenience and environmental health are some of the key factors affecting overall satisfaction with urban livability (Zhan et al., 2018). Lastly, neighborhood level of livability is particularly important in the context of space allocation and creating car-free and car-lite spaces where citizens of all ages and abilities can participate in urban mobility. Past studies argued that a livable city accommodates a healthy life and increases the chance for easy mobility (Hahlweg, 1997).

Given the wide scope of the environmental concerns, there are various ways to address them. Policy instruments to reduce the environmental impacts of transport will be discussed in Section 10.7. Other chapters in this book also address transport technology (Chapter 8), land-use and infrastructure (Chapter 5), and driving behavior (Chapter 8). Legislative measures often aim to increase transport resistance for motorized vehicles (Chapter 6), which

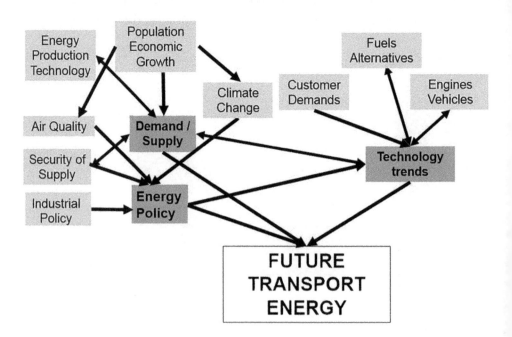

Source: Kalghatgi (2018).

Figure 10.4   Factors in future transport energy

reduces environmental impact via lower transport volumes or modal shares of motorized vehicles.

Lastly, the technical solutions for the environmental impact of transport are also related to the future energy system. The future energy system for transport is dependent on many factors. Kalghatgi (2018) identified these factors and their relationships in Figure 10.4. Energy production, security of supply, policy, available fuel alternatives among others, will ultimately impact the direction of innovation and fossil-free energy transition in the transport sector.

10.3   TRENDS IN CO_2 EMISSIONS FROM TRANSPORT

It was relatively recently when CO_2 became the center of conversations around transportation and its impact on the environment. Although the Swedish scientist Arrhenius had first speculated about the greenhouse gas effect over 100 years ago, climate change has not been globally addressed until a few decades ago. Since the 1990s climate change has been prominent on the international agenda of researchers and policy makers, and the reports of the Intergovernmental Panel on Climate Change (IPCC) provide the best-known and most influential overviews about state-of-the-art scientific knowledge. The IPCC (151; 2014) concluded that 'Human influence on climate change is clear and recent anthropogenic emissions of greenhouse gasses are the highest in the history. Recent climate changes have had widespread impacts on human and natural systems.'

Global trends in the transportation sector greenhouse gas emissions have been dominated by the road transport, international shipping, and aviation. With regard to regional differences, Northern America and Europe have been the largest emitters since 1900.

Although in Europe, historical greenhouse gas emissions have been increasing, given the current policies, the projections accounting for existing and future measures have downward trends (Figure 10.5). The European Environment Agency (EEA, 2021) predicts a significant decrease in emissions from transport by mid-century.

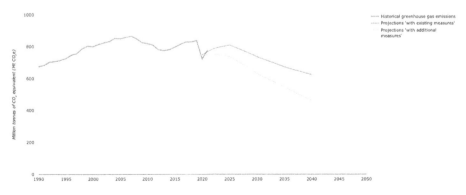

Source: European Environment Agency (2021).

Figure 10.5   Greenhouse gas emissions from transport in Europe

Transport emits CO_2 because of the high use of fossil fuels. In the internal combustion engines of cars, vans, lorries, ships, and planes the fossil fuels are burned, resulting in the desired energy for propulsion and in the undesired waste product CO_2. The popularity of oil as a transport fuel can be explained technically because of its high energy content. This means that, with a relatively low fuel volume on board, vehicles can cover many kilometers. Furthermore, inexpensive fuel has led to its wide adoption, particularly in passenger cars and vans, and therefore resulted in high emissions from these vehicles.

Even though there have been concerns over the price and availability of oil since the 1970s, it is only recently that more fundamental questions have been raised over its future. Transport has been almost totally dependent on oil, and the world price of oil has fluctuated between an average annual price of $27 and $110 a barrel between 2000 and 2020 (with even wider daily fluctuations). It is uncertain how that might change in the short or longer term. The oil price has historically had an impact on travel demand and on the adoption of alternative technologies and will likely remain one of the key players in the energy transition. In addition, there is the question of the availability of oil, which again influences the price of travel.

In essence, the trends in CO_2 emissions and fuel use in road transport are a function of the number of vehicles on the road (affected by affordability and consumer incomes and preference, see Chapter 3, and fuel price), distances driven (affected by infrastructure characteristics, see Chapter 5), prices such as fuel price and tax policies such as car taxation, tolls or congestion charge (see also Chapter 6), land-use (see Chapter 5), and the level of fuel economy of the cars (amount of motor fuel consumed per kilometer driven per year; see also Chapter 8) *see* Chapter 2 of this book for a general overview of links between the determinants. The personal vehicle has impeded the decarbonization of world transport activity because of, among other things, the increase in vehicle size (which requires more energy input; see Chapter 8 of this book for more details).

10.4   OTHER TYPES OF POLLUTION AND THEIR CAUSES

As already noted in Section 10.1 of this Chapter, CO_2 emissions have gained the most attention in conversations around creating more environmentally friendly transportation systems. Nevertheless, limiting emissions of CO_2 is not the only problem the sector is currently facing. Other pollutants include, but are not limited to, particulate matter (often noted as PM), nitrogen oxide (NO_x), carbon monoxide (CO), as well as noise.

The exhaust air pollution has been the focus of policy makers leaving the other types of air pollution (non-exhaust) often unregulated. Non-exhaust air pollution is a result of particles (PM) coming from breaking and tire wear. Noise pollution is a consequence of engines (dominant at slower speeds) and tires making contact with the road surface at high speeds (dominant at speeds higher than roughly 50 km/h), see below.

Traffic is one of the main reasons why PM levels are high as well as being the primary source of PM emissions in urban areas (Charron et al., 2007; Kousoulidou et al., 2008; Pant and Harrison, 2013). Vehicles emit PM through their exhaust and non-exhaust sources, such as tire wear, brake wear, road surface wear, and resuspension of road dust (Thorpe et al., 2007;

Shi et al., 2017). The numbers next to PM in $PM_{2.5}$ and PM_{10} stand for different PM fractions. 'Particulate matter' is a term for very small particles floating in the air, which humans can deeply inhale. The suffix 2.5 points at the fraction of particles that are smaller than 2.5 mm (micrometers); the suffix 10 means smaller than 10 mm.

It has been speculated that vehicle weight largely determines the rate of non-exhaust emissions per vehicle, however, there is very little research that directly links non-exhaust PM emissions to the vehicle weight (Timmers and Achten, 2016). Because electric vehicles (EVs) are 24% heavier than their conventional counterparts, Timmers and Achten (2016) concluded that the increased popularity of EVs will likely not have a beneficial effect on the non-exhaust PM levels. The same authors also stated that the non-exhaust emissions already account for over 90% of PM_{10} and 85% of $PM_{2.5}$ emissions from road traffic and cautioned that these proportions will continue to increase as exhaust standards improve and average vehicle weight increases. Figure 10.6 shows the relationship between PM non-exhaust emissions and car size.

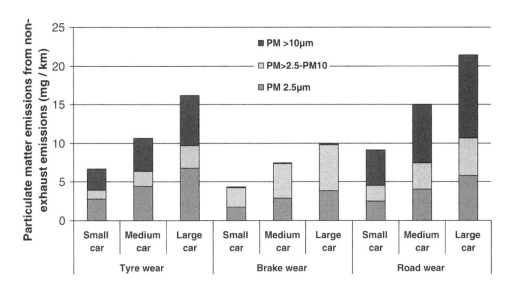

Source: Simons (2013); Ntziachristos and Boulter (2009).

Figure 10.6   Non-exhaust particulate matter emissions by source and car size

According to the European Environmental Agency (EEA), PM is one of Europe's most problematic pollutants in terms of harm to human health (European Environment Agency, 2021). Deep inhalation of PM has been linked to severe health impacts (respiratory problems and even premature deaths) (Wu et al., 2018). Exposure to both $PM_{2.5}$ and PM_{10}, especially, affects people's health (Pope and Dockery, 2006; Grahame and Schlesinger, 2010). Epidemiologic studies have provided strong evidence for associations of PM inhalation with inflammatory lung and cardiovascular diseases. In general, there is sufficient evidence of the adverse effects related to short-term exposure, whereas fewer studies have addressed the longer-term health effects (Simoni et al., 2015). Although the generally coherent link between the ambient PM and pulmonary disease is perhaps not surprising, it is remarkable that the association between PM and inflammation-related cardiovascular diseases, such as heart disease, cardiac dysrhythmias, congestive heart failure, and stroke, has been also consistently found in medical literature (Langrish et al., 2012).

Despite the transportation sector being not the only sector emitting PM to the atmosphere, transport's share in negative effects is high, as (on average) the distance between road traffic and the people exposed is much shorter than from other emission sources of pollution, such as power plants. Traffic emissions, therefore, have a greater health impact per kilogram than average emissions, as people live close to the sources of pollution and are exposed to continuous levels, particularly along busy roads (Eyre et al., 1997).

Due to the chemical differences between non-exhaust and exhaust emissions, many of the non-exhaust emissions include different secondary PM. Secondary PM is formed in the atmosphere through chemical reactions, rather than being directly emitted by a source. The volatile organic compounds in the exhaust gasses react with sunlight in the atmosphere to form secondary organic aerosols, whereas non-exhaust emissions are mainly inorganic and therefore form secondary inorganic aerosols, which ultimately lead to increased difficulty in modeling secondary organic aerosols and secondary inorganic aerosols emissions regardless of the location (Hoogerbrugge et al., 2015; Timmers and Achten, 2016).

In addition to CO_2 and PM emissions, other polluting substances such as NO_x (nitrogen oxide), CO (carbon monoxide), SO_2 (sulfur dioxide), O_3 (ozone), as well as other non-methane gasses are included in the transportation sector emission inventory. On a global scale, these emissions are often unregulated, and the allowed amounts of pollutants can vary by region. Figure 10.7 shows the differences in emission regulations for key pollutants between the USA and the European Union.

Vehicle emission pollutants	USA	European Union
Nitrogen oxide (NO_x)	0.04 g/mi	0.06/0.08* g/mi
Carbon monoxide (CO)	2.61 g/mi	1.0/0.5* g/mi
Carbon dioxide (CO_2)	155 g/mi	130 g/mi
Particulate matter (PM)	0.003 g/m	0.008 g/mi
Non-methane organic gases	0.06 g/mi	0.07/na* g/mi

Source: Gruzieva et al. (2013); Hime et al. (2018); Glanzer and Khreis (2019).
Note: *Petrol/diesel fuels

Figure 10.7   Comparison of the vehicle emission regulations per pollutant between the USA and the EU for light duty vehicles set to last until 2025

Given that only the exhaust pollutants are regulated, it is essential that policies should focus on setting clear global standards for both exhaust and non-exhaust emissions. Some researchers suggest that encouraging weight reduction of all vehicles has the potential to significantly reduce emissions from traffic, particularly in the context of PM emissions (Timmers and Achten, 2016).

Transport-related emissions are a function of the number of vehicles on the roads. Even if all vehicles become electric, the non-exhaust pollution will remain problematic. Similar concerns apply to noise pollution that cannot be mitigated by electrifying the fleet (Figure 10.8). The figure shows that drive-line noise (motor) – the black line – is the dominant source of noise below 45 km/h speeds. From this speed level, tire-road surface contact noise becomes dominant which also grows for EVs. The 'bumps' in the black line signify the moment that gears are shifted.

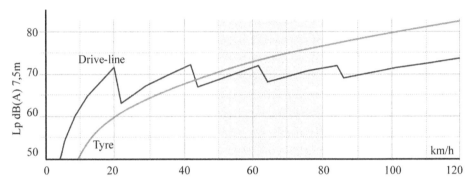

Source: den Boer and Schroten (2007); Jacyna et al. (2017).

Figure 10.8   Correlation between velocity and noise emitted by car

Studies from the US have shown a fairly consistent relationship between individuals or communities of lower socioeconomic position and increased exposure to noise pollution (Hajat et al., 2015). Evidence on noise pollution exposure from Europe has been mixed (Temam et al., 2017) and shown to have potential to affect all socio-demographic groups. Individuals with high socioeconomic positions living in city centers can also disproportionally experience high exposures to noise pollution (Goodman et al., 2011; Havard et al., 2011). Nevertheless, transport-related air and noise pollution has been consistently linked to adverse health outcomes and found to often vary within cities, potentially resulting in exposure inequalities *see* Chapter 12 for more information on the relationships between transport and health. Relatively little is known regarding inequalities in personal exposure to air pollution or transport-related noise pollution (Tonne et al., 2018).

10.5 CO_2-DRIVEN INNOVATIONS IN THE TRANSPORT SECTOR

To address the increasing CO_2 emissions and to activate behavioral changes that would pave the way to decarbonizing the transport sector, there have been many innovations. They can be divided into different categories. In this chapter, two distinctive categories which may play a huge role in CO_2 emission reduction will be discussed. The first category includes all the technical innovations that relate to electrification, battery capacities and durability, charging infrastructure, the use of hydrogen, to name a few (Section 10.5.1). The other category, while it is enabled by technological progress, aims to target the behavioral component (lowering kilometers travelled) in transportation such as applications allowing easy access to carsharing, Mobility-as-a-Service (MaaS), ridesharing, etc. (Section 10.5.2). Both have the same goal of lowering the emissions, however, they approach achieving this goal from different angles.

10.5.1   Towards Electrification

Electrification as a mitigation strategy to combat climate change has been stealing the headlines. There are different battery technologies currently available and depending on their composition, they will have a unique set of operational characteristics, limitations, and applications. One of the most common types is a lithium-ion battery (LIB) but there are also others like lithium-sulphur batteries, lithium-air batteries, or pre-LIB batteries. Although the wide application of batteries in the automotive sector does provide a substantial reduction in emissions as they do not require burning fossil fuels for vehicle operations, they come with their own set of constraints.

One is the weight of the battery, which has implications on the weight of the vehicle and thus non-exhaust emissions (discussed in Section 10.4), and the other one is sourcing of the raw materials needed for battery production. As outlined in the newest IPCC report (Jaramillo et al., 2022), for EVs sold in 2018, 11 kilotons (kt) of lithium, 15 kt of cobalt, 33 kt of manganese, and 34 kt of nickel were used (International Energy Agency, 2019). International Energy Agency projections for 2030 show that the demand for these materials would increase by 30 times for lithium and around 25 times for cobalt. There are efforts to move away from expensive materials such as cobalt (International Energy Agency, 2019). The dependence on lithium will remain, which causes concerns relating to its high demand and mining practices (You and Manthiram, 2018; Olivetti et al., 2017).

To maintain the efforts of decarbonization of the transport sector, battery technologies must be supported by charging infrastructure. Studies in this space found that without proper and widely available charging infrastructure, the adoption of electric mobility will be challenging, and consumers will be less likely to purchase an EV (Nicholas et al., 2017). Ongoing research tries to also capture and address user preferences and key attributes regarding charging preferences and vehicle purchases. Past research found that for light vehicles, the majority of charging (75–90%) has been reported to be done near homes (Figenbaum, 2017; Webb et al., 2019; Wenig et al., 2019). A reliable and comprehensive network of public charging infrastructure is essential to support the transition to an EV fleet (Gnann et al., 2018). Public charging infrastructure and EV registrations per million of the population by metropolitan area are shown in Figure 10.9.

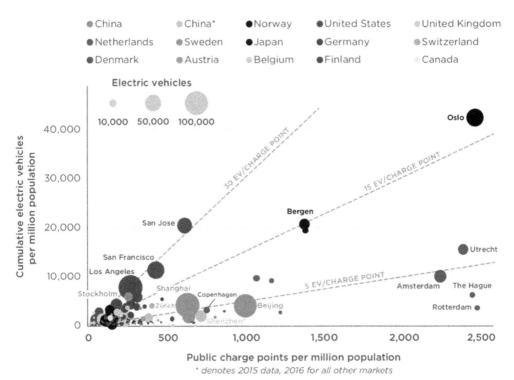

Source: Hall and Lutsey (2020).

Figure 10.9   Public charging infrastructure and electric vehicle registration per million population by metropolitan areas, with size of circles indicating total number of electric vehicles

Much attention has also been paid to studying the potential of hydrogen fuel cell vehicles particularly to support heavy and long-haul freight or marine shipping. So far this has been only emerging technology and its direction and success have not yet been determined, partly because it is very much dependent on the advancements in the energy sector. Hydrogen is expected to play an important role as an energy carrier for supporting the decarbonization of the heavy vehicle sector (Tokimatsu et al., 2016). There are, however, a few main barriers that the sector needs to overcome. Producing hydrogen from renewable resources and using it in vehicles has been found less efficient than directly charging electric batteries. Substantial losses happen on the pathway from the 'well to tank' and 'tank to wheel' and therefore this fueling method has not been found as efficient as direct electrification (although charging times are in favor of hydrogen fuel cell vehicles compared to EVs). The main challenges of hydrogen fuel cell mobility are similar to the ones that are faced by the standard EV sector and include charging infrastructure, price, and maturity of the technology (Transport and Environment, 2020).

Biofuels are another fuel technology that has been seen to play a role in the transportation sector and particularly in freight, marine, and aviation domains. Biofuels are considered to complement measures aimed at constraining the sector's energy needs and the enhanced role of electrification in urban and other shorter-haul transport applications (Jaramillo et al., 2022). While some biofuels such as ethanol from fermentation of sugars and biodiesel from oil crops have already achieved commercial scale in many countries, this sector has been facing many challenges in adoption on a global scale and rather limited technology development to produce biofuels derived from lignocellulosic feedstocks (agricultural crop residues, forest residues, and grass materials that are relatively inexpensive and highly abundant in nature), which are still struggling to achieve full commercial scale.

Achieving low-carbon transport implies a strong link between the transport and energy sector. First, regardless of which non-carbon energy carrier is used for rail, urban transport, and medium-distance transport (electricity or hydrogen), it has to be produced with low carbon emissions. Without a low-carbon energy sector, low-carbon transport is not feasible. Second, failure to decrease CO_2 emissions from transport will most likely need to be compensated in the energy sector. Third, electrification has been the most promising thus far, however the key will be to assure that the electricity for transportation is derived from renewable sources.

The use of non-renewable raw materials that are essential for battery production has recently received increasing attention. Emerging technologies needed for electric mobility often need 'rare' materials that are expensive, scarce, and can only be found in a few places worldwide. Given the increased production of rechargeable batteries, there have been discussions on the continued availability of materials like cobalt. Furthermore, there are a lot of concerns regarding extraction of these materials and unethical labor laws in countries where they occur. On the other hand, it is always a possibility that scarce materials may in the future be substituted by other materials that are currently being developed, researched, and tested.

10.5.2   Behavioral and Shared Mobility Innovations Enabled by Technology

Aside from innovation in technology, reducing emissions can be also achieved through large scale behavioral changes that are promoted by incentives, campaigns, and designs for new ways of transporting. In addition to the vehicle related innovations, MaaS (Mobility-as-a-Service) has been gaining popularity and reshaping urban mobility. (MaaS is a concept that bundles personal mobility services from multiple mobility providers into a combined interface through which the services can be searched, booked, and purchased.) There have also been innovations in public transport (e.g., related to travel information–showing the expected train occupancy on selected routes and real-time arrivals and delays), advances in micromobility (e-scooters, bikesharing), or other behavioral changes related to the infrastructure (real-time parking availability and reservation or smart infrastructure).

Many innovations around personal mobility aim to reduce car ownership and car travel. Given that a significant part of total emissions from the transport sector has been linked to car and road travel, policy makers and city officials have targeted car travel the most. Some of the strategies include reducing car travel through schemes like congestion pricing, reducing car ownership through taxes, reducing available parking, and increasing the prices of the existing one, as well as incentivizing sharing of the already existing vehicles. Sharing economy and in particular shared mobility have experienced a steady growth over the last years.

Although sharing is not a behavioral innovation, it depends on the technological progress. In particular, the mobile applications allow vehicle owners to connect to people outside of their immediate communities. Sharing can be simultaneous like sharing a ride when two people sit in the same vehicle going to the same destination, or sequential when the same vehicle is used by different customers one after another. Over the last decade, ridesourcing companies together with bike- and e-scooter sharing companies have revolutionized how mobility works and how it is perceived. The growth in mobility solutions was once again stimulated by advancements in technology, a decrease in prices of mobile devices, and the availability of internet connections.

Ultimately, any new mobility adoption (regardless of whether it is shared or not) is linked to household income as well as other socio-demographic and residential location characteristics. Often, differences in behavior may also depend on the differences in gender, age, norms, values, and social status. Simićević et al. (2013) concluded that women were more sensitive to parking prices than men, which then can be translated in their other mobility preferences. The price of the emerging services has also a very strong relationship to their adoption, which is often captured in the elasticity value (more on elasticity can be found in Chapter 3). Shared mobility modes are already a part of the mobility paradigm in many parts of the world; however, their maturity and adoption rates still vary by regions. The largest number of car-sharing memberships is in Asia and is responsible for 58% of worldwide memberships (Dhar et al., 2019), followed by Europe, which accounts for 29% of worldwide members (Shaheen et al., 2018).

Over the last decade the disruptions in technology and usage have been seen in ridesourcing, carsharing, and micromobility spaces. Cuevas et al. (2016) concluded that carsharing could provide the same level of service as taxis, however the taxis could be three times more expensive. The shared mobility sector that includes bikesharing, carsharing, and on-demand mobility services has been rapidly growing over the last decade (Greenblatt and Shaheen, 2015). The use of micromobility services depends on various factors such as age, gender, social and economic inequalities, time of day, or weather conditions. It has been shown that men and women do not follow the same usage patterns. In the e-scooter sector, it was found that the users were predominantly young men while low-income neighborhoods were underrepresented in the existing studies and trials (Latinopoulos et al., 2021; Bai and Jiao, 2020). Similarly, researchers have been studying the adoption of shared mobility and micromobility services (Barbour et al., 2019; Barbour et al., 2020). Because the needs of the users are not homogeneous, the adoption will likely take place in phases and different users will adopt using these services and technologies in different moments of time. Recent studies also point towards the intended adoption patterns of automated and shared automated vehicles varying by gender, age, presence of children, education, or residential location (Menon et al., 2017; Barbour et al., 2019).

Although they offer a great potential, shared mobility solutions are not without their legislative issues that include regulations and policies not being able to keep up with the fast pace of technological innovations. Shared mobility research is expanding but the literature has not yet been consistent on how much this sector will contribute to decarbonization or how much it will impact the ridership from transit or active modes like walking.

10.6   A COMPARISON OF THE ENVIRONMENTAL PERFORMANCE OF TRANSPORT MODES

From a policy perspective, it is interesting to know the environmental performance of different transport modes. The focus in Sections 10.2, 10.3, and 10.4 was on their environmental impacts, but electric mobility also uses the energy and produces emissions, and all direct and indirect impacts of a mode should be evaluated for a proper analysis.

Walking, bicycle, or train are the most efficient and the least pollution intensive modes. Department for Business, Energy & Industrial Strategy (2020) concluded that substituting a car for a bike for short trips would reduce travel emissions to negligible amounts of CO_2. Taking a train instead of a car for medium-length distances has a potential to cut emissions by ~80% and travelling by train instead of a taking a domestic flight would reduce emissions by ~84%.

Despite many studies delivering promising results, comparing the emissions performance of transport modes is not straightforward because of the differences in methods applied to perform the analysis (Figure 10.10), as can be demonstrated through the following range of questions (based on van Wee et al., 2005):

1. Which emissions are selected for the comparison?
2. Which emissions are compared: only direct emissions in the use stage, or also indirect emissions, such as those arising from the production of vehicles, even infrastructure, breaking or tires?
3. In the case of direct emissions, are emissions of electricity production and of refineries included?
4. For which year(s) are emissions compared?
5. Are average emissions compared, or emissions for sub-segments (such as for short- or long-distance travel only, or for containers only)?
6. Are average emissions compared or marginal emissions (extra emissions due to extra travel – Rietveld, 2002)?
7. Are average emissions compared, or for specific time periods (e.g., rush hour versus off-peak hours)? Note that, in the case of public transport, the choice for peak versus off-peak interacts with marginal versus average values: marginal peak hour emissions are relatively high, whereas average peak hour emissions are relatively low. The difference is linked to the level of ridership, meaning the more passengers on a bus, the lower the average emissions. For off-peak hours the opposite is true.
8. For the operational use of vehicles (e.g., driving circumstances of road vehicles), are real-world circumstances assumed, or test circumstances?
9. Which load factors or occupancy rates are assumed (real-world averages versus assumed factors)?

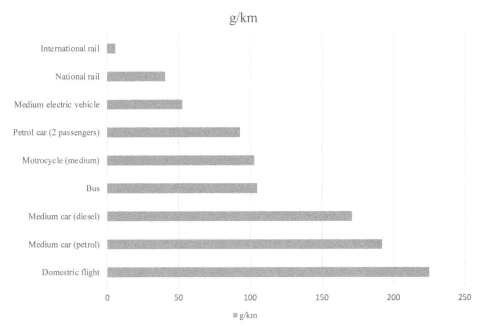

Source: Department for Business, Energy & Industrial Strategy (2020).

Figure 10.10   Carbon footprint of travel per kilometer in 2018

An alternative evaluation to emissions per kilometer (or passenger kilometer of travel), like in the Figure 10.10 above (based on the United Kingdom's values), is to use life cycle assessment (LCA) methods, which were developed in the 1960s and have been used in transport since the late 1990s. They take account of the non-negligible impacts of transport activity through vehicle production and scrapping, energy (fuel) extraction, and production and the full environmental impacts associated with infrastructure such as land take, materials use, and the construction itself (Chester and Horvath, 2009). LCA has demonstrated the full range of transport activities associated with the entire supply chain of products (Browne et al., 2005). Even if these life cycle factors are included in the costs of transport (internalized), they have little effect on transport volumes (Maibach et al., 2007), as the demand elasticities for travel are low and rising income levels reduce the effectiveness of higher prices (Goodwin et al., 2004; Graham and Glaister, 2004; see also Chapter 6).

10.7   POLICY INSTRUMENTS TO REDUCE THE ENVIRONMENTAL IMPACT OF TRANSPORT

This section focuses on the different types of policy measures – regulations, pricing, land-use planning, infrastructure policies, marketing, information, and communication. These types of policy measures have been implemented all over the world, albeit every country or region differs in the specific policies chosen. More information on transport policy can be found in Chapter 13.

Regulations with respect to the access of motorized vehicles to central urban areas have been successful in improving the attractiveness of these areas by changing at least the modal shift, and probably also the total transport volumes (owing to the increased travel times and costs of traveling by car). The distribution over time and space of transport volumes has also been influenced by regulations (e.g., limitations for access of trucks and vans, and loading and unloading times for these vehicles). In other words, the regulations can sometimes directly impact mobility behavior, transport, and traffic flows, depicted in Figure 2.1 (Chapter 2).

Although one policy measure often addresses cross-sectional domains (Santos et al., 2010), policies could be also classified into three types: physical, soft, and knowledge policies. Physical policies are related to building and maintaining infrastructure for public transport, walking and cycling, and freight transport. Soft policies include more non-tangible measures aiming to bring about behavioral change by informing actors about the consequences of their transport choices and potentially persuading them to change their behavior and they include e.g., incentives, pricing, regulations. These measures often try to boost more efficient use of vehicles and incentivize behaviors like carsharing and carpooling, teleworking and teleshopping, eco-driving, as well as provide general information and advertising campaigns. And lastly, knowledge policies emphasize the important role of investment in research and development for a sustainable model of mobility for the future. In the next sections, some of the most common environmental policy instruments will be introduced.

10.7.1   Regulations

It is clear (at least in Organization for Economic Co-operation and Development (OECD) countries) that emission regulations for road vehicles have been successful in reducing transport emissions of pollutants. Emissions of CO, VOC (volatile organic compounds) and NO_x per car and truck kilometer have all decreased by a factor of between 5 and 10 or even more between 1980 and 2020s (see Chapter 8). Lead emissions from petrol cars have decreased to almost zero because of regulations in the 1970s and 1980s to ban lead in petrol. Regulations have also included speed regulations and therefore indirectly impacted emissions.

However, not all interventions have been this successful. Vehicle regulations for noise emissions have been much less effective. Although the emission standards have been tightened and vehicles should have become much quieter, the reality is different, the car fleets have not become quieter (1980–96), and the noise from fleets of trucks has only reduced by 3 dB(A) (van der Toorn et al., 1997).

Limiting speed reduces noise, especially between 50 and 80 km/h. Speed limits do not require investment and have a direct effect on noise pollution but the costs associated with travel time losses may be significant (Jacyna et al., 2017). Because the elements of the transport system are often closely related to each other (like in this case speed and noise), the environmental policies in transport can address multiple layers of concerns if phrased and implemented properly. Going back to the conceptual model from Chapter 2, reducing speed limits would not only help in reducing noise pollution but lower speeds could also consequently impact safety – both frequency and severity of vehicle crashes.

10.7.2   Pricing

Pricing is one of the most powerful policy tools. Pricing policies include subsidies for public transport, taxes on vehicles and fuels, prices for parking, and road pricing. Subsidies on public transport (PT) have reduced the fares for public transit, decreased transport resistance (Chapter 6), and increased public transit usage. The stated political reasons for subsidies have often included environmental improvement (by changing modal choice from car to public transit), reduced congestion (also because of the change in modal choice), or improved access for people not having a car available (reduced social exclusion). The effectiveness discussion then becomes more complicated. For the impact of public transit subsidies on the environment, the substitution effects (from car to public transit) are important, as are the potential generation effects of additional travel ('induced demand' – see Chapter 6, and Goodwin, 1996). Because of the limited overlap in markets between public transit and cars (Bovy et al., 1991), overall decreases in public transit pricing could have a negative impact on the environment, as the positive effect of mode change is more than compensated for by the negative effect of the generation of additional travel, at least for energy use and CO_2 emissions (van Wee et al., 2005).

Taxes on fuels can change the share between different fuel types and address, to some extent, environmental concerns. As there are differences between countries in types of taxes, the share of diesel cars is much lower in some countries, such as the UK or the Netherlands, as compared with others, such as Belgium and France. A higher share of diesel reduces CO_2 emissions (at least on a per-kilometer basis) and increases emissions of PM and NO_x. Secondly, such taxes increase transport resistance (see Chapter 6) and have an impact on the overall level of car use and on modal split.

Looking in the past, long-term fuel price elasticity for car use was in the magnitude of −0.25 (see Graham and Glaister, 2004, for a review of elasticities), which means that a 1% increase in fuel prices reduces car use in the longer term by approximately 0.25%. Note that most of the studies reviewed used data from the 1980s and 1990s, under conditions of lower incomes. Because people with higher incomes are less sensitive to price increases, the impact of fuel price increases now and in the future could be lower. Nevertheless, these values indicate that prices do matter. Dargay et al. (2007) estimated the car price elasticity of ownership to be −0.12. For energy use and CO_2 emissions, elasticity values are higher than the fuel price elasticities because, in addition to the effect on car use, people buy more fuel-efficient cars and tend to drive a little bit more efficiently if prices are higher (see Graham and Glaister, 2004), leading to an elasticity of approximately −0.77. Higher prices are a stimulus for higher load factors for transport.

In 2021, Goetzke and Vance compared the fuel price elasticity values on miles driven in the United States. In 2017, the fuel price elasticity was estimated to be equal to −0.29. The same authors also found that those who drive the most are the least responsive to fuel prices. More information on fuel price elasticities and their values relating to the car use or car ownership can be found in Section 6.3.

To address environmental concerns, negative externalities of driving, and to improve air quality several cities and towns introduced parking charges in the 1960s and 1970s, often in combination with a reduction in the number of parking places in central urban areas. If parking is expensive, this increases transport resistance, leading to less car use and an increase in the use of alternatives.

Road pricing is probably the most controversial of all the categories of pricing policies. The controversy is not so much related to its effects but more to the difficulties in implementation (Nikitas et al., 2018). Nevertheless, several examples of real-world implementation of road pricing schemes can be found, including Singapore, some Norwegian cities, London, and Stockholm. Once road pricing is introduced, it may change transport resistance and how people move around.

Singapore was the first city to implement congestion pricing. It successfully reduced congestion by lowering peak hour traffic by 65%. About a decade later Electronic Road Pricing was implemented in 1998, which reduced traffic volume in the restricted zone by an additional 15% (Wilson, 1988; Phang and Toh, 1997; Santos and Fraser, 2006).

London implemented its road pricing scheme in 2003. It was an area licensing system with a fixed fee for all vehicles entering the congestion zone. This was one of the differences between the London initial scheme and Singapore's, as the charges in Singapore were imposed per trip, while in London a payment lasted for the entire day, allowing vehicles to enter and exit the zone multiple times. After the implementation of this scheme, traffic volume entering the zone when congestion pricing was in operation reduced by 18%. Travel time decreased by 30% during the first year of the implementation while bus riders increased by 18% (Santos et al., 2010). To further address air pollution, the pricing scheme in London was restructured, the area expanded, and consequently more improvements in the air quality were observed. The pricing scheme contributed to the number of Londoners living in areas with high levels of NO_x falling by 94% between 2016 and 2020 (Greater London Authority, 2020).

Stockholm adopted a slightly different approach and did not charge per trip or day but was using 18 entry and exit points. Congestion charges differed according to the time of day. Vehicle distance driven in the congestion zone decreased by 16%, while traffic volume also decreased by 5% outside the city center, and traffic emissions reduced by 10% to 15% between 2005 and 2006, which was the year of the launch of the congestion pricing scheme. The decrease in vehicle distance and traffic volume in the congestion zone and beyond could be due to the 24% of work trips by car that switched to transit, which would affect both traffic entering and surrounding the area (Santos et al., 2010; Eliasson, 2008). The road pricing has had an impact on other transportation-related areas such as parking or alternative travel modes and therefore impacted travel resistance or desires and needs.

Appropriate pricing schemes and incentive programs are not limited to only decrease auto usage but also stimulate uptake of cycling/e-cycling. In the case of the Netherlands, cycling is a very popular mode of travel, accounting for 26% of all national trips (KiM, 2015). Of all trips shorter than 7.5km, which is 70% of all trips, 35% are made by bicycle. Despite this high share of cycling trips, there is still considerable potential for an increase in cycling. De Kruijf et al. (2018) evaluated an incentive program to stimulate the shift from car commuting to e-cycling in the Netherlands and found that half of e-bike trips substitute car trips, while the other half substituted conventional bicycle trips. They also found that e-bike use by former car commuters in an e-cycling incentive program amounted to 73% after half a year of participation.

Another pricing strategy aiming to reduce emissions, kilometers driven, and improve air quality is carbon pricing. A price placed on carbon encourages travelers to use vehicle fuel types that pollute and cost less per mile or kilometer of travel. The idea behind carbon tax can be easily explained with an example of EVs.

To better understand the mechanisms of carbon pricing, let's consider a standard Toyota Camry and Model 3 Tesla with the following annual fuel costs: $950 for Toyota Camry and $500 for Tesla (Figure 10.11).

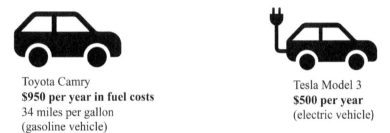

Toyota Camry
$950 per year in fuel costs
34 miles per gallon
(gasoline vehicle)

Tesla Model 3
$500 per year
(electric vehicle)

Figure 10.11   Fuel standards and annual fuel costs for Toyota Camry (gasoline vehicle) and Tesla Model 3 (electric vehicle)

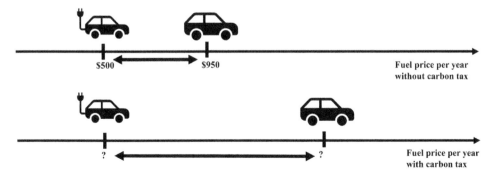

$500

$950

Fuel price per year
without carbon tax

?

?

Fuel price per year
with carbon tax

Figure 10.12   The change in fuel price per year with additional carbon tax

If additionally, the more carbon-intensive option is taxed, the price gap between refueling these two different models will widen. Many countries are considering this approach, however, the most important question that remains to be answered relates to the appropriate and stable price for carbon.

The added fuel cost resulting from the carbon price would increase this price gap (Figure 10.12) and encourage consumers to consider EVs, although the effect would likely be small if the carbon price was equal to, say, \$50 per metric ton of CO_2.

The price of CO_2 per ton in emission trading systems has varied over the years. The price has also varied over time and regions but continues to remain relatively low. Historically, it varied between a few euros per ton to around 30 euros per ton. In November 2021, the price hit a record of more than 71 euros per ton (Buli, 2021).

As of now, many factors are playing a role in determining the price of carbon, and the carbon market is seen to be impacted by the geopolitical situation, climate policies, and technology development. The value of carbon price will then impact which vehicles people choose to travel by, where they live, and how much they travel (consider the conceptual model in Figure 2.1, Chapter 2).

10.7.3　Land-Use Planning

Land-use planning can have an impact on travel volumes and modal split (Chapter 5). Building at high densities can reduce travel distances and locating offices and residential neighborhoods close to railway stations can increase the share of public transit. Attractive neighborhood design can increase the share of slow modes, and mixed land-use (e.g., mixing housing, shops, schools, and services) can reduce transport distances and increase the share of slow modes. In addition, because land-use planning can change the distribution of vehicle kilometers of road types and related driving behaviors, it can have an impact on emissions and safety levels, and on distances between the source of emissions (noise, pollutants) and the recipients. There is still debate on the impacts of land-use planning on travel behaviors (see Chapter 5), and this is partly explained by the fact that the actual impacts on travel behaviors seem to be less than expected. This conclusion may be due to the problems of measurement and the long-term effects that land-use has on travel, but as with a lot of analysis it is the behavioral factors that are important, and current understanding of these responses is not sufficient.

10.7.4　Transport Infrastructure Policy

In almost all countries infrastructure provision is a public matter. Even in the case of toll roads, such as in France and Portugal, the government decides which motorways will be built and where they will be located, and the government sets the institutional context including regulations, tendering, and so on. It is beyond any doubt that the quality and quantity of road and rail networks have a major impact on transport volumes and modal split (see Chapters 3 and 6). In addition, these networks strongly influence the distribution of traffic across the networks, certainly in the case of roads, and therefore driving behaviors (Chapter 8), route choice (see Chapter 7), safety and emission levels, and distances between the source of emissions and receivers.

Furthermore, investments in infrastructure supporting alternative modes that include cycling, bikesharing, e-cycling, and walking are also a prominent and viable approach to reducing emissions. To support cycling, public agencies often invest in bicycle infrastructure networks to increase network connectivity and accessibility. These infrastructure investments include bike lanes, pavement maintenance, etc. In the past few years, bike-friendly initiatives have increased around the world and many improvements for cycling were made. Research has found that the installation of one additional mile of bike lanes in NYC led to an average increase of 102 bikesharing daily trips (Xu and Chow, 2020).

10.7.5   Public Transport Policies

Excluding policies involving public transport in one of the other categories (such as pricing or subsidizing and infrastructure policies), there are ways to make public transport more attractive. For example, routing and frequency of buses may be adjusted and facilities at railway stations may be improved. Investing in TODs (transit-oriented developments) could also make public transit more attractive and convenient.

10.7.6   Policies to Stimulate Work-from-Home

Particularly during the COVID-19 pandemic, the world has experienced a sudden change in commute patterns and consequently work-from-home was adopted virtually overnight. Most cities have seen a decrease in pollution and traffic. Since the transport sector emissions, and particularly CO_2 emissions, have grown steadily for the last three decades (International Transport Forum, 2021), it is essential to explore work-from-home as a viable alternative to auto commute. Many researchers have used the disruptions to transport systems caused by the COVID-19 pandemic to gain more insights into work-from-home adoption and study its relevance in relation to decreasing transportation-related environmental impacts (Barbour et al., 2021). It remains to be seen how the work-from-home paradigm will lead to stimulating work-from-home policies that may impact the environment, traffic patterns, and air quality in the long term and how cities decide to leverage the disruption in mobility caused by the pandemic. Flexible work hours or attractive tax deductions relating to the maintenance of home office or even new legislations to support telehealth and other fields where consumer privacy is an issue could further stimulate the uptake of work-from-home.

10.8   CRITERIA TO EVALUATE CANDIDATE ENVIRONMENTAL POLICY OPTIONS

Policy evaluation can take place before a policy is implemented (*ex-ante* evaluation) or after the policy has been in place for some time (*ex-post* evaluation). *Ex-ante* evaluation generally requires two separate actions; to estimate what will happen if the policy is not introduced and to estimate what will happen if it is introduced. *Ex-post* evaluation estimates what has happened with the introduction of the policy instrument. Additionally, an estimate still needs to be made of what would have happened if the policy instruments had not been introduced (Blok and Nieuwlaar, 2021).

To meet ambitious emissions reductions in the transport sector, multiple policies must be implemented, and their effectiveness continuously evaluated. As policies may be difficult to implement and may have various side-effects, an important question is which criteria should be used to evaluate the available options. Typically, the criteria include expectations with respect to all of the following, both individually and in combination:

1. CO_2 emission reductions;
2. Costs;
3. Other environmental impacts (such as emissions of other pollutants besides CO_2, noise);
4. Risks, or at least risk perceptions (these could be relevant in the case of hydrogen mobility adoption, available infrastructure, usage safety, and CO_2 capture and storage);
5. Land-use and spatial impacts (especially in the case of biofuels – the production of biofuels competes with food production and impacts nature and biodiversity);
6. Psychological factors (e.g., will the car driver accept hydrogen or EVs);
7. Legal, institutional, and political factors (important barriers might exist, e.g., legal barriers, the position of interest groups, political acceptability);
8. The position of important stakeholders, such as car producers, oil companies, and the agricultural sector (e.g., in the case of biofuels);
9. The question of whether transitions can take place evolutionarily starting with the current system, or if radical changes are needed, resulting in a 'difficult' transition phase (van Wee et al., 2013).

10.9   CONCLUSIONS

The most important conclusions of this chapter are:

1. Road transportation (including passenger transport and freight) that is a result of increased auto-dependency is one the biggest contributors to transport-related emissions.
2. The most problematic pollutants currently in transport are CO_2 and PM.
3. There are many policy instruments available to reduce the environmental impact of transport, including regulations, pricing, land-use planning, infrastructure policies, public transport policies, marketing, and information and communication. These instruments can influence the environmental pressure of transport by reducing transport volumes, changing modal split, and influencing the technologies used, the efficiency of vehicle use, and the way vehicles are used.
4. In many ways the options to decarbonize transport are clear, but the problem is the effective implementation of the measures so that desired environmental outcomes can be achieved.
5. In the future, the dominant environmental problems related to transport will probably continue to be the energy use, climate change, health, the use of raw materials, and noise nuisance. Raw material availability as well as harmful labor laws are particularly important for battery production.

6. The most challenging problems for the coming decades are mitigating CO_2 emissions and oil dependency as well as the largely unregulated non-exhaust emissions (like PM).
7. Pricing is a very powerful tool to change behavior. Examining how carbon tax schemes unfold in the coming years are especially important to mitigating climate change.
8. Improvements in technology need to be supported by its smart adoption and usage as well as timely regulated.

NOTE

1. The Paris Agreement is a legally binding international treaty on climate change (https://unfccc.int/process -and-meetings/the-paris-agreement/the-paris-agreement, accessed February 2022). Its goal is to limit global warming to well below 2, preferably to 1.5 degrees Celsius, compared to pre-industrial levels.

REFERENCES

Bai, S., and J. Jiao (2020), 'Dockless E-scooter usage patterns and urban built Environments: A comparison study of Austin, TX, and Minneapolis, MN', *Travel Behaviour and Society*, 20, 264–72.

Barbour, N., N. Menon and F. Mannering (2021), 'A statistical assessment of work-from-home participation during different stages of the COVID-19 pandemic', *Transportation Research Interdisciplinary Perspectives*, 11, 100441.

Barbour, N., Y. Zhang and F. Mannering (2019), 'A statistical analysis of bikesharing use and its potential as an auto-trip substitute', *Journal of Transport and Health*, 12, 253–62.

Barbour, N., Y. Zhang and F. Mannering (2020), 'Individuals' willingness to rent their personal vehicle to others: An exploratory assessment', *Transportation Research Interdisciplinary Perspectives*, 5, 100138, 1–7.

Blok, K. and E. Nieuwlaar (2021), *Introduction to Energy Analysis*. Third edition. Routledge, Taylor and Francis Group: Abingdon, Oxon.

Bovy, P., J. van der Waard and A. Baanders (1991), 'Substitution of travel demand between car and public transport: a discussion of possibilities', paper presented at the PTRC Summer Annual Meeting.

Browne, M., S. Rizet, J. Anderson, J. Allen and B. Keita (2005), 'Life cycle assessment in the supply chain: a review and case study', *Transport Reviews*, 25(6), 761–82.

Buli, N. (2021), *EU carbon price hits record above 71 euros*. Reuters. Retrieved from www.reuters .com/business/sustainable-business/benchmark-eu-carbon-price-breaches-70-eurtonne-first-time -2021-11-22/.

Charron, A., R. Harrison and P. Quincey (2007), 'What are the sources and conditions responsible for exceedences of the 24h PM10 limit value at a heavily trafficked London site?', *Atmospheric Environment*, 41(9), 1960–75.

Chen, J., W. Zhang, Z. Wan, S. Li, T. Huang and Y. Fei (2019), 'Oil spills from global tankers: Status review and future governance', *Journal of Cleaner Production*, 227, 20–32.

Chester, M. and A. Horvath (2009), 'Environmental assessment of passenger transportation should include infrastructure and supply chains', *Environmental Research Letters*, 4, 024008.

Cuevas, V., M. Estrada and J. Salanova (2016), 'Management of on-demand transport services in urban contexts. Barcelona case study', *Transportation Research Procedia*, 13, 155–65.

Dargay, J., D. Gately and M. Sommer (2007), 'Vehicle ownership and income growth, worldwide: 1960–2030', *The Energy Journal*, 28(4), 143–70.

de Kruijf, J., D. Ettema, C. Kamphuis and M. Dijst (2018), 'Evaluation of an incentive program to stimulate the shift from car commuting to e-cycling in the Netherlands', *Journal of Transport & Health*, 10, 74–83.

Den Boer, L. and A. Schroten (2007), *Traffic Noise Reduction in Europe CE Report*. CE Delft: the Netherlands.

Department for Business, Energy & Industrial Strategy (2020), *Government greenhouse gas conversion factors for company reporting: Methodology paper for Conversion factors*. Final Report. London, UK.

Dhar, S., T. Munshi, P. Newman and Y. Gao (2019), 'Mobility in cities in emerging economies: Trends and drivers', in B. Jørgensen, K. Andersen and O. Nielsen, *DTU International Energy Report 2019: Transforming Urban Mobility*. Copenhagen: Technical University of Denmark.

Dong, H. and B. Qin (2017), 'Exploring the link between neighborhood environment and mental wellbeing: A case study in Beijing, China', *Landscape and Urban Planning*, 164, 71–80.

EEA, European Environment Agency (2021), *Greenhouse gas emissions from transport in Europe*. Retrieved from www.eea.europa.eu/ims/greenhouse-gas-emissions-from-transport.

Eliasson, J. (2008), 'Lessons from Stockholm congestion charging trial', *Transport Policy*, 15(6), 395–404.

EPA, United States Environmental Protection Agency (2017), *Sources of greenhouse gas emission*. Retrieved from www.epa.gov/ghgemissions/sources-greenhouse-gas-emissions.

Eurostat (2021), *Passenger cars in the EU*. Retrieved from https://ec.europa.eu/eurostat/statistics-explained/index.php?title=Passenger_cars_in_the_EU.

Eyre, N., E. Ozdemiroglu, D. Pearce and P. Steele (1997), 'Fuel and location effects on the damage costs of transport emissions', *Journal of Transport Economics and Policy*, 31(1), 5–24.

Federal Highway Administration (2017), *Highway statistics – 2016*, U.S. Department of Transportation: Washington, DC.

Figenbaum, E. (2017), 'Perspectives on Norway's supercharged electric vehicle policy', *Environmental Innovation and Societal Transitions*, 25, 14–34.

Frey, H. (2018), 'Trends in onroad transportation energy and emissions', *Journal of the Air & Waste Management Association*, 68(6), 514–63.

Glanzer, A. and H. Khreis (2019), 'Transforming our cities: Best practices towards clean air and active transportation', *Current Environmental Health Reports*, 6(1), 22–37.

Gnann, T., S. Funke, N. Jakobsson, P. Plötz, F. Sprei and A. Bennehag (2018), 'Fast charging infrastructure for electric vehicles: Today's situation and future needs', *Transportation Research Part D*, 62, 314–29.

Goetzke, F. and C. Vance (2021), 'An increasing gasoline price elasticity in the United States?' *Energy Economics*, 95, 104982.

Goodman, A., P. Wilkinson, M. Stafford and C. Tonne (2011), 'Characterising socio-economic inequalities in exposure to air pollution: a comparison of socio-economic markers and scales of measurement', *Health Place*, 17(3), 767–74.

Goodwin, P. (1996), 'Empirical evidence on induced traffic: a review and synthesis', *Transportation*, 23, 35–54.

Goodwin, P., J. Dargay and M. Hanly (2004), 'Elasticities of road traffic and fuel consumption with respect to price and income: a review', *Transport Reviews*, 24(3), 275–92.

Graham, D. and S. Glaister (2004), 'Road traffic demand elasticity estimates: a review', *Transport Reviews*, 24(3), 261–74.

Grahame, T. and R. Schlesinger (2010), 'Cardiovascular health and particulate vehicular emissions: a critical evaluation of the evidence', *Air Quality, Atmosphere, and Health*, 3(1), 3–27.

Greater London Authority (2020), *Air quality in London 2016-2020, London environment strategy: Air quality impact evaluation*, London, UK.

Greenblatt, J. and S. Shaheen (2015), 'Automated vehicles, on-demand mobility, and environmental impacts', *Current Sustainable/Renewable Energy Reports*, 2(3), 74–81.

Gruzieva, O., A. Bergström, O. Hulchiy, I. Kull, T. Lind, E. Melén, V. Moskalenko, G. Pershagen and T. Bellander (2013), 'Exposure to air pollution from traffic and childhood asthma until 12 years of age', *Epidemiology*, 24(1), 54–61.

Hahlweg, D. (1997), *The City as a Family. Making Cities Livable*. International Making Cities Livable Conferences. California, USA: Gondolier Press.

Hajat, A., C. Hsia and M. O'Neill (2015), 'Socioeconomic disparities and air pollution exposure: a global review', *Current Environmental Health Reports*, 2(4), 440–50.

Hall, D. and N. Lutsey (2020), *Electric vehicle charging guide for cities. International Council on Clean Transportation, Consulting Report*. https://theicct.org/publications/city-EV-charging-guide.

Havard, S., B. Reich, K. Bean and B. Chaix (2011), 'Social inequalities in residential exposure to road traffic noise: an environmental justice analysis based on the RECORD cohort study', *Occupational and Environmental Medicine*, 68(5), 366–74.

Hime, N., G. Marks and C. Cowie (2018), 'A comparison of the health effects of ambient particulate matter air pollution from five emission sources', *International Journal of Environmental Research and Public Health*, 15(6), 1206.

Hoogerbrugge, R., H. Denier van der Gon, M. van Zanten and J. Matthijsen (2015), *Trends in Particulate Matter*. Netherlands Research Program on Particulate Matter, Bilthoven. www.researchgate.net/ publication/ 264408355_Trends_in_Particulate_Matter.

IEA, International Energy Agency (2019*), Global EV Outlook 2019: Scaling-up the transition to electric mobility*. Paris, France.

IEA, International Energy Agency (2020), *Tracking transport 2020*. Paris, France. Retrieved from www .iea.org/reports/tracking-transport-2020.

International Transport Forum (2021), *ITF Transport Outlook 2021*. Organisation for Economic Cooperation and Development (OECD) Publishing: Paris, France.

IPCC (2014), *Climate Change 2014: Synthesis Report. Contribution of Working Groups I, II and III to the Fifth Assessment Report of the Intergovernmental Panel on Climate Change* [Core Writing Team, R.K. Pachauri and L.A. Meyer (eds)]. IPCC: Geneva, Switzerland.

Jacyna, M., M. Wasiak, K. Lewczuk and G. Karon (2017), 'Noise and environmental pollution from transport: decisive problems in developing ecologically efficient transport systems', *Journal of Vibroengineering*, 19(7), 5639–55.

Jaramillo, P., S. Kahn Ribeiro, P. Newman, S. Dhar, O. Diemuodeke, T. Kajino, D. Lee, S. Nugroho, X. Ou, A. Hammer Strømman and J. Whitehead (2022), Transport. In IPCC, *Climate change 2022: Mitigation of climate change. Contribution of Working Group III to the Sixth Assessment Report of the Intergovernmental Panel on Climate Change* [P.R. Shukla, J. Skea, R. Slade, A. Al Khourdajie, R. van Diemen, D. McCollum, M. Pathak, S. Some, P. Vyas, R. Fradera, M. Belkacemi, A. Hasija, G. Lisboa, S. Luz, J. Malley, (eds)]. Cambridge University Press: Cambridge, UK and New York, NY, USA. doi: 10.1017/9781009157926.012.

Kalghatgi, G. (2018), 'Is it really the end of internal combustion engines and petroleum in transport?' *Applied Energy*, 225(C), 965–74.

KiM (2015), *Mobiliteitsbeeld2015*, Kennisinstituut voor Mobiliteitsbeleid: Den Haag.

Kousoulidou, M., L. Ntziachristos, G. Mellios and Z. Samaras (2008), 'Road-transport emission projections to 2020 in European urban environments', *Atmospheric Environment*, 42(32), 7465–75.

Langrish, J., J. Bosson, J. Unosson, A. Muala, D. Newby, N. Mills, A. Blomberg and T. Sandstrom (2012), 'Cardiovascular effects of particulate air pollution exposure: time course and underlying mechanisms', *Journal of Internal Medicine*, 272(3), 224–39.

Latinopoulos, C., A. Patrier and A. Sivakumar (2021), 'Planning for e-scooter use in metropolitan cities: A case study for Paris', *Transportation Research Part D*, 100, 103037.

Maibach, M., C. Schreyer, D. Sutter, H. van Essen, B. Boon, R. Smokers, A. Schroten, C. Doll, B. Pawlowska and M. Bak (2007), *Handbook on estimation of external cost in the transport sector: Internalisation measures and policies for all external costs of transport (IMPACT)*. Delft: CE Delft.

Meadows, D.H, D.L., Meadows, J. Randers and W. Behrens III (1972), *The Limits to Growth*, New York: Universe Books.

Meadows, D.H, D.L., Meadows, J. Randers and W. Behrens III (2005), *The Limits to Growth: The 30-Year Update*. New York: Universe Books.

Menon, N., N. Barbour, Y. Zhang, A. Pinjari and F. Mannering (2017), 'Shared autonomous vehicles and their potential impacts on household vehicle ownership: An empirical assessment', *International Journal of Sustainable Transportation*, 13(2), 111–22.

Nicholas, M., G. Tal and T. Turrentine (2017), *Advanced plug-in electric vehicle travel and charging behavior interim report*. Institute of Transportation Studies: University of California, Davis, CA.

Nikitas, A., E. Avineri and G. Parkhurst (2018), 'Understanding the public acceptability of road pricing and the roles of older age, social norms, pro-social values and trust for urban policy-making: The case of Bristol', *Cities*, 79, 78–91.

Ntziachristos, L. and P. Boulter (2009), *EMEP/EEA Air pollutant emissions inventory guidebook 2009: Road vehicle tyre and brake wear; road surface wear*. European Environment Agency: Copenhagen.

Olivetti, E., G. Ceder, G. Gaustad and X. Fu (2017), 'Lithium-ion battery supply chain considerations: Analysis of potential bottlenecks in critical metals', *Joule*, 1(2), 229–43.

Pant, P. and R. Harrison, R. (2013), 'Estimation of the contribution of road traffic emissions to particulate matter concentrations from field measurements: a review', *Atmospheric Environment*, 77, 78–97.

Park, Y. and M. Kwan (2017), 'Individual exposure estimates may be erroneous when spatiotemporal variability of air pollution and human mobility are ignored', *Health & Place*, 43, 85–94.

Phang, S. and R. Toh (1997), 'Road congestion pricing in Singapore: 1975–2003', Transportation Journal, 43(2), 16–25.

Pope, C. III, and D. Dockery (2006), 'Health effects of fine particulate air pollution: lines that connect', *Journal of the Air and Waste Management Association*, 56(6), 709–42.

Rietveld, P. (2002), 'Why railway passengers are more polluting in the peak than in the off-peak: environmental effects of capacity management by railway companies under conditions of fluctuating demand', *Transportation Research Part D*, 7(5), 347–56.

Santos, G., H. Behrendt and A. Teytelboym (2010), 'Part II: policy instruments for sustainable road transport', *Research in* Transportation Economics, 28(1), 46–91.

Santos, G. and G. Fraser (2006), 'Road pricing: Lessons from London', Economic Policy, 21(46), 264–310.

Shaheen, S., A. Cohen and M. Jaffee (2018), *Innovative mobility: Carsharing outlook*. Retrieved from https://doi.org/https://doi.org/10.7922/G2CC0XVW.

Shi, Z., J. Li, L. Huang, P. Wang, L. Wu, Q. Ying, H. Zhang, L. Lu, X, Liu, H. Liao and J. Hu (2017), 'Source apportionment of fine particulate matter in China in 2013 using a source-oriented chemical transport model', *Science of the Total Environment*, 601–02, 1476–87.

Simićević, J., S. Vukanovic and N. Milosavljevic (2013), 'The effect of parking charges and time limit to car usage and parking behaviour', *Transport Policy*, 30, 125–32.

Simoni, M., S. Baldacci, S. Maio, S. Cerrai, G. Sarno and G. Viegi (2015), 'Adverse effects of outdoor pollution in the elderly', *Journal of Thoracic Disease*, 7(1), 34–45.

Simons, A. (2013), 'Road transport: new life cycle inventories for fossil-fueled passenger cars and non-exhaust emissions in ecoinvent v3', *International Journal of Life Cycle Assessment*, 21, 1299–313.

Sims, R., R. Schaeffer, F. Creutzig, X. Cruz-Núñez, M. D'Agosto, D. Dimitriu, M. Meza, L. Fulton, S. Kobayashi, O. Lah, A. McKinnon, P. Newman, M. Ouyang, J. Schauer, D. Sperling and G. Tiwari (2014), 'Transport', in *Climate change 2014: Mitigation of climate change. Contribution of Working Group III to the Fifth Assessment Report of the Intergovernmental Panel on Climate Change* [O., Edenhofer, R. Pichs-Madruga, Y. Sokona, E. Farahani, S. Kadner, K. Seyboth, A. Adler, I. Baum, S. Brunner, P. Eickemeier, B. Kriemann, J. Savolainen, S. Schlömer, C. von Stechow, T. Zwickel and J.C. Minx (eds)]. Cambridge University Press: Cambridge, United Kingdom and New York, NY, USA.

Temam, S., E. Burte, M. Adam, J. Antó X. Basagaña, J. Bousquet, A. Carsin, B. Galobardes, D. Keidel, N. Künzli, N. Le Moual, M. Sanchez, J. Sunyer, R. Bono, B. Brunekreef, J. Heinrich, K. de Hoogh, D. Jarvis, A. Marcon, L. Modig, R. Nadif, M. Nieuwenhuijsen, I. Pin, V. Siroux, M. Stempfelet, M. Tsai, N. Probst-Hensch and B Jacquemin (2017), 'Socioeconomic position and outdoor nitrogen dioxide (NO_2) exposure in Western Europe: a multi-city analysis', *Environment International*, 101, 117–24.

Thorpe, A., R. Harrison, P. Boulter and I. McCrae (2007), 'Estimation of particle resuspension source strength on a major London road', *Atmospheric Environment*, 41(37), 8007–20.

Timmers, V. and P. Achten (2016), 'Non-exhaust PM emissions from electric vehicles', *Atmospheric Environment*, 134, 10–17.

Tokimatsu, K., S. Konishi, K. Ishihara, T. Tezuka, R. Yasuoka and M. Nishio (2016), 'Role of innovative technologies under the global zero emissions scenarios', *Applied Energy*, 162(C), 1483–93.

Tonne, C., C. Milà, D. Fecht, M. Alvarez, J. Gulliver, J. Smith, S. Beevers, R. Anderson and F. Kelly (2018), 'Socioeconomic and ethnic inequalities in exposure to air and noise pollution in London', *Environment International*, 115, 170–79.

Transport and Environment (2020), *Electrofuels? Yes, we can ... if we're efficient*. Retrieved from www.transportenvironment.org/wp-content/uploads/2020/12/2020_12_Briefing_feasibility_study_renewables_decarbonisation.pdf.

UCSUSA (2022), *Each country's share of CO_2 emissions*. Retrieved from www.ucsusa.org/resources/each-countrys-share-co2-emissions.

van der Toorn, J., T. Dool and F. de Roo (1997), *Geluidemissie door motorvoertuigen: klassieke metingen met de Syntakan* [Noise emissions from motor vehicles: classic measurements using Syntaken], report TPD-HAG-RPT-950033, Delft: TNO-TPD.

Van Fan, Y., S. Perry, J. Klemeš and C. Tin Lee (2018), 'A review on air emissions assessment: Transportation', *Journal of Cleaner Production*, 194, 673–84.

van Wee, J. Annema and D. Banister (2013), *The Transport System and Transport Policy*. Edward Elgar Publishing: Cheltenham, UK and Northampton, MA, USA.

van Wee, B., P. Janse and R. van den Brink (2005), 'Comparing environmental performance of land transport modes', *Transport Reviews*, 25(1), 3–24.

Webb, J., J. Whitehead and C. Wilson (2019), *Who will fuel your electric vehicle in the future? You or your utility? Consumer, Prosumer, Prosumager, How Service Innovations will Disrupt the Utility Business Model*. Elsevier: London.

Wenig, J., M. Sodenkamp and T. Staake (2019), Battery versus infrastructure: Tradeoffs between battery capacity and charging infrastructure for plug-in hybrid electric vehicles, *Applied Energy*, 255(C), 113787.

Wilson, P. (1988), 'Welfare Effects of Congestion Pricing in Singapore', *Transportation*, 15, 191–210.

Wu., W., Y. Jin and C. Carlsten (2018), 'Inflammatory health effects of indoor and outdoor particulate matter', *Clinical Reviews in Allergy and Immunology*, 141(3), 833–44.

Xu, S. and J. Chow (2020), 'A longitudinal study of bike infrastructure impact on bikesharing system performance in New York City', *International Journal of Sustainable Transportation*, 14(11), 886–902.

You, Y. and A. Manthiram (2018), 'Progress in high-voltage cathode materials for rechargeable sodium-ion batteries', *Advanced Energy Materials*, 8(2), 1701785.

Zhan, D., M. Kwan, W. Zhang, J. Fan, J. Yu and Y. Dang (2018), 'Assessment and determinants of satisfaction with urban livability in China', *Cities*, 79, 92–101.

11
Traffic safety

Fred Wegman and Paul Schepers

11.1   INTRODUCTION

The number of road crashes, fatalities and injuries is considered unacceptably high in many countries. This is illustrated, for example, by the fact that the European Parliament in its resolution of 6 October 2021 welcomed the European Union reaffirming in its 2021–30 EU road safety policy framework (EC, 2019), the long-term strategic goal to get close to zero deaths and zero serious injuries on EU roads by 2050. In many highly developed and highly motorized countries the number of fatalities has been decreasing over the last few decades, although in recent years the speed of reduction has slowed down in most countries (OECD/ITF, 2020). The sharp drop in 2020 is related to the COVID-19 pandemic (Wegman and Katrakazas, 2021). However, so far this favourable development cannot be observed in low- and middle-income countries (WHO, 2018). The WHO report states: 'The number of road traffic deaths continues to climb, reaching 1.35 million in 2016' (WHO 2018, 16). It would not be surprising if these worldwide numbers were higher today.

Risks in road traffic are considerably higher than in other transport modes, and the number of injuries in road traffic is far higher than the numbers in train, plane or ferry transport (ETSC, 2003; Savage, 2013). Unfortunately, more recent figures are not available, but this conclusion seems to be still valid. Although crashes in these other modes attract a lot of public and media attention, road crashes kill far more people, but in a 'diluted' way, resulting in only limited media coverage and relatively limited attention from the public and politicians (Van der Meer et al., 2021). At the same time, serious road crashes are tragedies at a personal level. Road crashes can happen to everybody, anytime, anywhere, and they are unexpected. Often the lives of young people and their families are suddenly changed. Road traffic injury is now the leading cause of death for children and young adults aged 5 to 29 years (WHO, 2018).

This chapter aims to give a concise introduction to road safety. Using this chapter the reader will be able to explain basic concepts of road safety, get an insight into some recent traffic safety developments and be able to talk about a new policy vision and options for how to reduce the number of crashes and (serious) injuries. The relevance of various technologies has been discussed in Chapter 8.

Risk factors in traffic are discussed in Section 11.2. Section 11.3 deals with the subject of identifying the causes of crashes. Section 11.4 provides an explanation of three important components of road traffic when it comes to risks: transport mode, age of road users and road types. In Section 11.5 the difficulties of measuring road safety are discussed. Some developments in road safety are presented in Section 11.6. Section 11.7 explains the development in dominant thoughts about traffic safety. This section shows that the amount of knowledge on causes of road crashes and on how to implement successful policies has increased dramatically over the years. Still, the next steps for further improvements can be made. Scientific information to support this statement and one possible next step, the Safe System approach, are presented in Section 11.8. Section 11.9 focuses on vulnerable road users and Section 11.10 discusses promising options to further improve road safety. The chapter's main findings are presented in Section 11.11.

11.2   RISK FACTORS IN TRAFFIC

Taking part in traffic is a dangerous act in itself. This is due to some fundamental risk factors in traffic (sometimes also denoted as basic factors): the vulnerability of the body of road users in combination with speed levels in traffic as well as the presence of objects with large mass and/or stiffness with which one can collide. In addition, there are factors that affect driving behaviour and increase the crash risk, such as alcohol use, fatigue or distraction.

Figure 2.1 (in Chapter 2) identifies three major sources for risks to traffic safety. First are the characteristics of the transport flows – i.e., the volume, modal split and composition of traffic (including the mix between passenger and goods vehicles), division over time (including traffic jams) and distribution over space (including the use of different road types). Second is the driving behaviour, which includes speed, the acceleration and breaking behaviour, and reaction time. The third factor is technology, including especially vehicle technology (such as the adaptive cruise control) and vehicle designs that improve the safety of their occupants and other (especially vulnerable) road users. In addition, use of other technology (especially mobile devices) during travel is a risk to traffic safety. The following sections describe risk factors originating from these three sources, in order of their importance.

11.2.1   Fundamental Risk Factors

Fundamental risks are inherent to road traffic and are the basis of the lack of safety in current road traffic. These are a combination of factors such as speed and mass (and the kinetic energy in a crash) and the vulnerability of the human body.

- **Speed.** Speed is related to the risk of being involved in a crash and its severity (for an overview, see Aarts and van Schagen, 2006). Higher absolute speeds of individual vehicles are related to an exponential increase in risk, illustrating a strong link between the driving behaviour and safety (see Figure 2.1). A meta-analysis by Elvik et al. (2019) shows that both an Exponential model (basically change equals $Exp(\beta(speed_{after} - speed_{before}))$ in which β is to be determined) and a Power model (change equals $speed_{after}/speed_{before}^{power}$

in which the power parameter is to be determined) accurately describe by how much risk increases with increased driving speed, assuming other conditions remain the same. The models apply both to an individual operator and at the aggregate level for average speed on a road. The change in risk according to a Power model with exponent x can be calculated as (final speed / initial speed)^x – 1 (Elvik, 2013). The meta-analyses by Elvik et al. (2019) yields estimates of the exponent of the Power model of 5.5 for fatalities and 3.9 for injury accidents. For instance, an increase of driving speed by 1%, such as from 100 to 101 km/h, increases the number of fatalities by 5.6% and the number of injury accidents by 3.9%: $(101/100)^{5.5}$ – 1 respectively $(101/100)^{3.9}$ – 1. This is due to the kinetic energy (of which speed is an important component), which is converted into other energy forms and/or bodily damage during a crash. Injury risk (the chance of being injured in a crash) is also determined by (impact) speed level, the relative directions of crash partners, their mass differences and the protection level. Pedestrians and cyclists are about five times more likely to sustain fatal injuries in collisions with motor vehicles at a 50 km/h impact speed as compared to at 30 km/h (Nie et al., 2015). To reduce the probability of severe injuries in such crashes to approximately 10%, impact speeds need to be reduced further to around 20 km/h (Jurewicz et al., 2016).

- **Speed variance.** Speed differences at the level of road sections are also linked to increased crash risk (Aarts and van Schagen, 2006). Driving at a different speed than other traffic participants increases the risk inherently. However, the importance of speed variance also relates to the disproportionately high risk of speeding drivers as risk increases exponentially as speed increases. If two roads A and B have the same mean driving speed while road B has a greater speed variance, road B will have more fast drivers. Due to the exponential or power increase in risk as a function of speed (see above), their risk increase is much greater than the risk decrease of slow drivers who also contribute to speed variance.

- **Mass differences.** Mass differences are also fundamental risk factors. In a crash between two incompatible parties, the lighter party (smaller cars, cyclists, pedestrians) is at a disadvantage, because this party absorbs more kinetic energy and a smaller vehicle generally offers less protection to its occupants than a heavier vehicle. Mass ratio between colliding objects can be as high as 300 (a pedestrian weighing 60 kg versus a heavy goods vehicle weighing 20,000 kg). Furthermore, in view of their stiffness and structure, heavier vehicle types generally offer better protection to their occupants in the event of a crash. For occupants of vehicles with a high mass, injury risk is much lower than that of occupants of the lighter crash party. If we assume the injury risk for a crash party of an 850 kg passenger car as 1, then the injury risk for an average crash partner is 1.4 if the car weighs 1000 kg, and 1.8 if the vehicle weighs more than 1500 kg (Elvik and Vaa, 2004). Increases in vehicle masses (SUVs) will result in growing mass differences between vehicles and this might impact road safety negatively.

- **Vulnerability.** Finally, vulnerability is to be considered a fundamental risk factor. Several methods can be used to protect the human body in a crash, foremost by improving the crashworthiness of a vehicle (i.e., improving the vehicle technology; see Figure 2.1 and Chapter 8). Over the years great progress has been made to improve vehicle design to protect car occupants. The most famous example is the use of seat belts in combination with airbags. Mbarga et al. (2018) found in their meta-analysis that seat belts reduce the risk of any major injury by 53%. Glassbrenner and Starnes (2009) estimate that seat belts reduce fatality and injury risks by more than 40%, and in combination with airbags by more than 50%. However, vulnerable road users such as pedestrians and cyclists have almost no possibilities to protect themselves from injury risk in a crash. Only a crash helmet for (motorized) two-wheelers can be considered, and some developments of airbags for motorcyclists can be seen in practice. Furthermore, modern car designers try to incorporate safety features when designing a car front, with the aim to make them safer for pedestrians and cyclists in the case of a crash.

11.2.2   Risk-Increasing Factors

In addition to these fundamental risk factors, road traffic has to contend with risk-increasing factors caused by road users (see also the link from driving behaviour in Figure 2.1):

- **Lack of driving experience.** Lack of driving experience results in higher risks. The effect of (lack of) driving experience on crash risk is strongly linked to age effects. Since driving experience is strongly correlated with age and as both factors are associated with specific characteristics which increase risk, it is difficult to separate the effects of age and experience. For Dutch road traffic, it is estimated that about 60% of the (relatively high) crash risk for novice drivers (broadly speaking, people who have driven less than 100,000 kilometres) can be explained by lack of driving experience, and the other 40% is age related (see Wegman and Aarts, 2006). Male novice drivers especially run an additional risk (a factor of 10) compared to more experienced drivers (male and female) and compared to female novice drivers (a factor of 2.5). The increased crash risk for novice drivers decreases rapidly within the first year after passing a driving test (Vlakveld, 2005; Curry et al., 2017).
- **Psycho-active substances: alcohol and drugs.** Alcohol consumption by road users is one of the most important factors that increase crash risk in traffic. This increases exponentially with increased blood alcohol content (BAC). Compared to sober drivers, the crash risk is a factor of 1.3 with a BAC between 0.5 and 0.8 per mille, a factor of 6 with a BAC between 0.8 and 1.5 per mille and a factor of 18 above 1.5 per mille (Blomberg et al., 2005). A BAC of 0.5 per mille means 0.5 gram of alcohol per litre blood. The crash risk of road users under the influence of psycho-active substances (Walsh et al., 2004) can be about 25 times higher. This risk can even increase up to a factor of 200 with the combined use of alcohol and drugs, relative to sober road users, also depending on the quantity of alcohol consumed (Schulze et al., 2012). Drugs in traffic is not a very mature area of research and policy-making; it has, however, received quite a lot of (political) attention recently with the trend in most nations toward enforcement of zero-tolerance laws (Jones et al., 2019). Roadside surveys show a reduction of drunk driving over time in countries having longitudinal data, while use of non-alcohol drugs increases (Christophersen et al., 2016).

- **Fatigue.** Fatigue is probably a much more important risk factor than data from police reports shows. Participating in traffic whilst fatigued is dangerous because, in addition to the risk of actually falling asleep behind the steering wheel, fatigue reduces the general ability to drive (e.g., keeping course), reaction time and motivation to comply with traffic rules. Research shows that people suffering from a sleep disorder or an acute lack of sleep have a three to eight times higher risk of injury crash involvement (Connor et al., 2002). A review by Moradi et al. (2019) shows the odds of a crash is 1.3 times higher in fatigued drivers than in other drivers.
- **Distraction.** Like fatigue, distraction is probably a much more frequent crash cause than reported police data shows (Regan et al., 2009). Currently, common sources of distraction are talking and texting on the mobile phone while driving or cycling (De Waard et al., 2015; Lipovac et al., 2017). Dingus et al. (2019) studied the impact of secondary tasks by a Naturalistic Driving study in which drivers were monitored using in-vehicle cameras, GPS, accelerometers, etc. Overall, they found a small but significant increase in crash risk due to cognitive secondary tasks. Tasks that require the eyes to be directed away from the road such as manipulating a cell phone to browse or dial increase the risk the most, i.e., roughly 2 to 3.5 times compared to model driving.

11.3   CAUSE: 'UNINTENTIONAL ERRORS' OR 'INTENTIONAL VIOLATIONS'?

In identifying the cause of crashes in whatever system, 'man' is always quoted as the most important cause of crashes in any system. People make errors, no matter how hard they try. At the same time, people do not always (consciously or otherwise) obey rules and regulations designed to reduce risks. The question arises: how serious are intentional violations or offences for road safety and with what frequency do they cause traffic crashes? This section will show that no clear picture emerges from the research of the relative contribution to crashes by intentional violations and unintentional errors.

A Canadian study looked into the relationship between violations and crashes as evidenced by driver behaviour (Redelmeier et al., 2003). The research team tracked car drivers who were convicted of causing a fatal crash and recorded the crash involvement of these offenders in the period following the conviction. The first month after the penalty, the chance of being involved in a fatal crash was 35% lower than could be expected on the basis of coincidence. The authors attributed this effect to the fact that there were fewer traffic violations immediately after the period in which the drivers were fined. However, this benefit lessened substantially over time and disappeared after three to four months. Out of the above research, a strong relationship emerges, particularly between violations and crash involvement. It must be emphasized, however, that this type of research does not prove the causality between the two phenomena.

Thus, both errors and violations (and related extreme behaviour) play a role in the cause of crashes and therefore deserve a place in road safety policies. How large the share of (unintentional) error and (intentional) violation is exactly cannot be stated, based on current knowledge. The role of (unintentional) error seems to be the more important one. Unfortunately, the information that can be extracted from police registration forms about crash causes cannot be used to identify the underlying causes of crashes. This is not surprising given that the data is gathered primarily with the objective of being able to identify the guilty party, rather than identifying precisely the underlying causes of a crash. In addition, crashes are nearly always the result of a combination of factors.

On the one hand, it is logical that unintentional errors form the lion's share of crash causes, given that intentional offending in itself hardly leads directly to a crash. Violations certainly can increase the risk of error and the serious consequences of these errors. On the other hand, there is no evidence to support the widely held opinion that anti-social road hogs are the major perpetrators of crashes. Without doubt they cause part of the road safety problem, if only because other road users cannot always react appropriately to them. However, many crashes are the result of unintentional errors that everybody can make in an unguarded moment, as illustrated by Dingus et al. (2006) and Khattak et al. (2021).

Dingus et al. (2006) concluded that, in nearly 80% of the recorded crashes driver inattention was involved just prior to the onset of the conflict. The most common human errors observed by Khattak et al. (2021) were recognition and decision errors, which occurred in 39% and 34% of crashes. In these studies drivers were followed by observation systems installed in their cars: a black box and small cameras. The idea was to observe everyday driving behaviour and to learn about the role of driver inattention and errors, which are rarely found on police registration forms. After all, who would tell the police that a cigarette fell to the floor just prior to the crash and that in a state of some panic the driver was trying to retrieve it? Therefore, it is time to rethink the widespread belief (held also by road safety professionals and decision-makers) that crashes are caused exclusively or even primarily by the traffic offences that are frequently found on police registration forms.

Two recent studies (Shinar, 2019; Hauer, 2020) doubt whether the current three primary methods for crash causation analysis – (1) post-crash clinical analysis using subjective evaluations by experts, (2) naturalistic driving studies and (3) epidemiological studies – are appropriate methods to identify crash causes. Furthermore, both studies recommend the linking of causes and countermeasures, as is being applied in the medical model of finding a cure for a disease. The framing of '90%-plus of the crashes are due to human errors or failures' is a direct consequence of how causes have been defined in the past and this approach is no longer considered to be adequate. Both authors propose to put human errors, failures and violations in the context of the environment of these behaviours and trying to change behaviour in a safe direction by adapting the environment. This insight is one of the reasons to think about a paradigm shift in road safety, as presented in Section 11.7.

11.4   RISKS FOR TRANSPORT MODES, AGE GROUPS AND ROAD TYPES

Transport modes and road types relate to the fundamental risk factors (Section 11.2): speed, mass and vulnerability, in combination with protection. Users of motorized two-wheelers, for example, have the highest fatality and injury risk in road traffic (Table 11.1), which can largely

Table 11.1 Road fatalities per one billion vehicle kilometres (2019) for a selected number of countries that made data available to the IRTAD-database from International Transport Forum

	All modes	Motorized two-wheelers	Mopeds	Motorcycles	Passenger cars	Heavy goods vehicles
Australia	4.5	87.6			3.0	2.7
Austria	4.9	50.6	22.9	59.8	2.9	0.4
Denmark	3.6			558	2.1	0.9
France	5.3	66			3.4	1.0
Germany	4	43.8	16.2	54.7	2.1	
Great Britain	3.1	70.2			1.6	0.7
Hungary	13	148			8.3	2.4
Ireland	3	140.4			2.3	
Israel	5.6	64.8			2.5	
Poland	7			68.9	6.5	1.1
Slovenia	4.5	142.9			2.5	1.9
Sweden	2.6			50.6	1.5	0.6
Switzerland	2.7	18.9	32	17.5	1.1	0.9
United States	6.9	159.2			5.6	

Note: Motorized two-wheelers encompass moped + motorcycles

be explained by a combination of high speed with the relatively low mass of the vehicle in conflict with other motorized traffic, as well as poor crash protection. On top of these factors, two-wheelers (especially mopeds) are popular among young people. Besides, youngsters have a relatively high risk in traffic because of age-specific characteristics and needs, and the lack of driving experience (Table 11.2 and Figure 11.1).

On the one hand, the car is a fast and weighty collision partner in conflicts with two-wheelers and pedestrians, who also include especially vulnerable road users such as children and the elderly. On the other hand, cars are more severely damaged in crashes with heavy goods vehicles.

Young people are an especially high-risk group of those involved in serious crashes because of their lack of driving or riding experience and age-specific characteristics. Elderly road users (of 75 years old or more; see Figure 11.1) are the next most important risk group because of their physical frailty. In many low- and middle-income countries the majority of the casualties are vulnerable road users such as pedestrians and cyclists, most of the time young people.

Differences of risks for different road types can also, to a large extent, be explained by a combination of the fundamental risk factors introduced earlier. For example, serious crashes outside urban areas, and particularly on rural roads, are dominated by single-vehicle crashes along sections of road, often running off the road. These are usually the result of inappropriate speeds, possibly in combination with other factors which increase risk such as alcohol

Table 11.2 Road user fatalities per 100,000 population by age group (2019) for a selected number of countries that made data available to the IRTAD-database from International Transport Forum

	All	0–14	15–17	18–20	21–24	25–64	65+
Australia	4.7	0.7	3.2	9.2	7.8	4.9	6.8
Austria	4.7	1.3	5.1	6.1	6.5	4.4	7.6
Belgium	5.6	0.6	2.9	8.8	9.8	5.9	7.7
Canada	4.7	0.7	4.6	6.0	7.1	4.8	6.7
Czech Republic	5.8	1.1	3.2	12.2	11.6	6.0	7.4
Denmark	3.4	0.5	3.0	4.7	4.1	3.4	5.5
Finland	3.8	0.6	5.7	8.9	5.8	3.9	4.5
France	5.0	0.6	3.7	10.3	10.7	5.2	6.5
Germany	3.7	0.5	2.9	7.3	4.7	3.4	5.8
Greece	6.4	0.8	4.3	9.1	10.4	6.8	7.7
Hungary	6.2	1.1	3.1	5.4	7.2	6.9	8.2
Iceland	1.7	0.0	7.8	0.0	0.0	2.1	2.0
Ireland	2.9	0.4	1.0	3.7	6.8	2.9	5.1
Israel	3.9	1.3	2.7	8.0	6.8	4.3	6.2
Italy	5.3	0.4	3.9	8.2	8.1	5.2	7.2
Japan	3.1	0.4	1.4	3.7	2.5	2.0	6.3
Korea	6.5	0.5	2.1	3.9	3.7	5.0	19.8
Luxemburg	3.6	0.0	0.0	4.8	16.1	3.9	2.3
Netherlands*	3.5	0.4		4.7		2.8	7.7
New Zealand	7.1	2.8	6.4	8.7	10.6	7.7	8.8
Norway	2.0	0.0	0.5	4.5	3.3	2.1	3.3
Poland	7.7	1.2	4.7	14.7	12.6	8.0	9.9
Portugal	6.0	0.9	1.9	6.2	11.0	5.7	9.8
Slovenia	4.9	0.3	3.6	8.7	3.6	5.4	6.8
Spain	3.7	0.5	2.4	4.4	4.2	4.0	5.4
Sweden	2.2	0.2	1.5	2.1	2.5	2.3	3.7
Switzerland	2.2	0.3	1.2	2.2	2.0	1.9	4.8
United Kingdom	2.7	0.3	1.8	4.2	4.1	2.7	4.5
USA	11.1	1.8	7.1	15.4	17.2	12.9	13.4

Note: Netherlands*: age group 15-25

consumption, distraction and/or fatigue. The fact that many roadsides are not 'forgiving' also results in severe outcomes. On urban roads, transverse conflicts (side impacts) dominate. It is on these streets and roads where most people are killed, and where mass differentials and the vulnerability of road users are the most important factors, combined with comparatively high speeds and the vulnerability of vehicles in transverse conflicts. Motorways are the safest

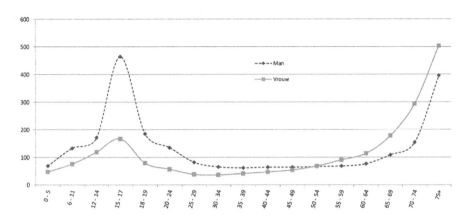

Figure 11.1   Number of severely injured people in traffic per 1 billion kilometres travelled of age group and gender for the Netherlands in the period 1999 to 2009

roads when it comes to crash risk. This is due to a combination of high-quality road design and slow-moving traffic not being allowed on these roads. For high driving speed conditions, as is the case on motorways, good design is extremely important, both physically (separation of driving direction, grade-separated intersections) and psychologically (predictable design). Only then high speeds can be managed safely. In situations where vulnerable road users and motorized traffic share the same physical space, a low risk can only be achieved when travelling speeds are low (see also Section 11.8).

11.5   MEASURING SAFETY AND DANGER

All countries in the world seem to have the ambition to improve road safety, or at least no country is known to be making public statements that the road toll of today is acceptable. However, measuring road safety is not as simple as measuring a temperature. Researchers or policy-makers cannot read a simple measuring instrument. A simple definition of road safety is complicated and we don't have a simple 'thermometer' to read. Moreover, people can have a discussion on what to include in a definition. The most common measure used to define road safety is the number of road crashes and/or the number of casualties and the associated negative consequences resulting from such crashes. Sometimes subjective feelings related to fears of being involved in a crash are included in the measure as well. In those cases, people's perceptions about (lack of) road safety are taken into account in the measure.

The widely accepted definition of a road traffic crash is a collision or incident on a public road (or private road to which the public has right of access) that results in damage to objects and/or injury to people and that involves at least one vehicle in motion. This means, for example, that a single bicycle crash is included, but not a pedestrian fall. The international definition of a road death, taken from the UNECE Glossary of Transport Statistics 2019, is someone who dies immediately or dies within 30 days as a result of a road crash, excluding suicides. For countries that do not apply the threshold of 30 days, conversion coefficients are estimated for international comparison purposes. The Maximum Abbreviated Injury Scale (MAIS) is a medical classification of the severity of injuries using the coding system created by the Association for the Advancement of Automotive Medicine. MAIS 1–2 are regarded as slight injuries and 3–6 as serious injuries. This system is presently being used in road safety. The European Union and its member states, for example, indicated an ambition not only to reduce the number of road fatalities, but also the number of serious injuries. For that purpose, the EU decided to use MAIS3+ to define serious injuries. Several methods can be applied to arrive at a good estimate of the number of serious injuries: by applying a correction on police data, by using hospital data and by using linked police and hospital data (e.g. Deliverable 7.2 of the SafetyCube project (Weijermars et al., 2016).

Crashes can result in more serious or less serious outcomes: fatal injuries, other injuries or damage only to vehicles involved in a crash. Sometimes, damage-only crashes are not considered serious enough to be included in official crash statistics. Data collection is needed to learn how many crashes occurred in a certain time period and in a certain geographical area. The longer the time period or the larger the area, the more crashes. For that reason, it is a good habit to normalize the number of crashes for time and space, expressing the road safety level. This normalizing can be done in different ways serving different purposes. If we relate the number of fatalities or injuries to the number of inhabitants (the first ratio) we have the mortality rate (fatalities per 100,000 inhabitants; see also Table 11.2, where mortality rates are presented for different countries) or morbidity rate (injuries per 100,000 inhabitants). These rates are public health indicators, allowing us to compare road injuries with other threats or diseases. (See also the link between safety and health in Figure 2.1.) Mortality rates are often used in international comparisons. An important reason is that fatal road crashes have a common definition (dead within 30 days) and are well recorded in many countries, as is the case with the number of inhabitants. This is not the case for injuries.

A second ratio is the so-called fatality rate or injury rate. In this case we relate the number of fatalities or injuries to the degree to which people are exposed to traffic or, more precisely, to risks in traffic. Often, the number of kilometres travelled is used to estimate this 'exposure' or, even more often, the number of motorized kilometres (see Table 11.1). We can also use time in traffic as a measure of exposure.

Unfortunately, the measuring of road crashes, and their consequences, and the measuring of exposure suffer from problems related to the use of different definitions, data quality, data completeness and data availability. In most countries the crash registration is carried out by the police. However, crash statistics are always incomplete as a result of underreporting. Furthermore, data collections suffer from certain biases: crashes involving motorized vehicles are better registered than crashes involving non-motorized transport, such as pedestrians and cyclists (Derriks and Mak, 2007; Shinar et al., 2018). Alcohol-related crashes are also underreported (Vissers et al., 2017). Another bias in data collection is that less severe injuries are more underreported.

An important measure for road crashes is their associated costs. There are two good reasons to estimate road crash costs. Firstly, it allows policy-makers to compare the economic consequences of road crashes with other impacts of traffic and transport, such as environmental impacts and congestion. A second reason is that it allows policy-makers to compare these costs with the costs of other public health issues. For that purpose, public health indicators denoted as 'DALY' (disability adjusted life years) or 'QALY' (quality adjusted life years) are also sometimes used (Wijnen, 2008). These are measures for loss of life years and/or quality of life.

In many countries, a growing interest in estimating the costs of road crashes can be observed. The cost estimation methods have improved considerably. Although an internationally accepted 'standard' method does not exist at the time of writing this chapter (in 2023) and methods differ in including or excluding certain cost categories (Elvik, 1995), there is some convergence on the most important cost categories (Alfaro et al., 1994):

1. medical costs;
2. production loss;
3. human costs;
4. property damage;
5. settlement costs.

Sometimes costs related to congestion as a consequence of a crash are added and/or costs related to replacement of transport (in a sixth category). For the cost categories 1, 4 and 5, a method is used called 'restitution cost method' and for 2 the 'human capital method' (Wijnen and Stipdonk, 2016). Categories 1, 2, 4 and 5 estimate the direct financial costs related to crash injuries, for example, the amount of money hospitals have to spend on injury treatment, vehicle repair costs, lost production hours (e.g. lost wages) and so forth.

Estimating human costs (cost category 3) is based on people's willingness to pay for lower risks (or willingness to accept a reward for higher risks). Human costs for casualties and their relatives and friends are costs in the form of suffering, pain, sorrow and loss of quality of life and joy of life. Cost estimates result in the so-called 'value of a statistical life' (VOSL; e.g. De Blaeij, 2003). A VOSL does not reflect the monetized value of an individual life, which is, naturally, priceless. Instead, the VOSL is based on the relation between changes in risks and willingness to pay for these changes. For example, if someone drives on a road with a risk of 2.5/1,000,000 of death, but is willing to pay 6 minutes by taking a detour to drive on a road with a lower risk of 2/1,000,000, this driver is valuing his or her 'statistical life' at 2 million euros. The reason is that the VOSL is (assuming a value of time of 10 euros/hour, which equals 1 euro/6 minutes; see Chapter 15):

$$\frac{d(travel\ time)}{d(risk)} = \frac{1\ Euro}{\left(\frac{0.5}{1,000,000}\right)} = 2,000,000\ Euro \tag{11.1}$$

In the VALOR project (Schoeters et al., 2021) estimates have been made for four European countries (Belgium, France, Germany and the Netherlands) of the VOSL and the Value of a Statistical Serious Injury (VSSI). The average VOSL was estimated at 6.2 million euros and the VSSI at 950,000 euros. Accordingly, the ratio of values between fatalities and serious injuries is estimated at around 7 to 1. These estimates turned out to be higher than formerly assumed in, for example, the Netherlands.

11.6   DEVELOPMENTS IN IMPROVING ROAD SAFETY

Globally, each year more than 1.35 million road users are killed in a road crash, and 20 to 50 million suffer non-fatal injuries worldwide (WHO, 2018). By far the majority of all crashes, deaths and injuries occur in low- and middle-income countries: 93% of road traffic deaths. Moreover, mortality rates are relatively high in these countries (see Table 11.3 for road injury mortality rates per income class worldwide). The majority of these deaths and injuries are vulnerable road users. The social economic costs of road crashes in high-income countries range from 0.5% to 6.0% of the GDP with an average cost of 3.3% of GDP. For low- and middle-income countries the range is from 1.1% to 2.9% (Wijnen and Stipdonk, 2016).

Table 11.3 Road traffic injury mortality rates (per 100,000 population) by WHO regions for 2019

WHO region	Low- and middle-income	High-income
African Region	27.2	12.2
Region of the Americas	17.4	12.1
South-East Asia Region	15.8	-
European Region	10.4	5.1
Eastern Mediterranean Region	17.2	25.4
Western Pacific Region	17.9	5

Source: www.who.int/data/gho/data/indicators/indicator-details/GHO (July 2023)

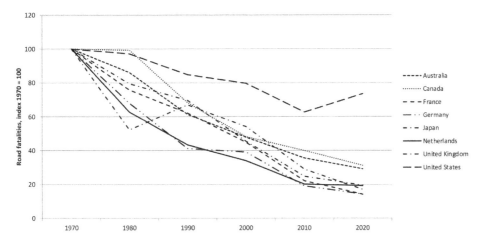

Figure 11.2   Long-term trends in road fatalities 1970–2020 (index 1970 = 100) for a selected number of countries that made data available to the IRTAD-database from International Transport Forum

Since 1970, many high-income countries have made remarkable progress in reducing the number of road fatalities (see Figure 11.2). However, this progress has slowed down during the last decade, with the exception of 2020, due to the COVID-19 pandemic (Wegman and Katrakazas, 2021).

11.6.1   An Example: The Netherlands

To give more detail on the description and explanations for the relatively high rate of improvement in some countries, the Netherlands has been chosen as an example. Details for more countries can be found in *Safety Science*, 'Scientific Research on Road Safety Management' (Wegman and Hagenzieker, 2010). A 50% reduction in the mortality rate occurred in the period 1995–2007 in the Netherlands, whereas Great Britain and Sweden reached a little bit more than 20%. This is partly due to a 'learning society' or an 'investing society', which has adapted itself to motorized, fast-moving traffic and making substantial safety investments at the same time. Infrastructural adaptation has taken place (such as the construction of relatively safe motorways), safety in vehicles has been improved and there is more safety legislation and enforcement which takes account of factors that increase risk and reduce injury (such as alcohol consumption in traffic and mandatory crash helmet and seat belt use, respectively). These measures have all contributed to reductions in the number of traffic fatalities and injuries, despite increased mobility (Koornstra et al., 2002; Elvik and Vaa, 2004). But, as yet, researchers do not have a totally conclusive explanation for the observed trends in road fatalities and to which extent improvements in the road transport system contributed.

Figure 11.3   The development of the number of traffic deaths in the Netherlands 1950–2020

Between 2010 and 2020 just over 600 traffic deaths were recorded each year in the Netherlands. This amounts to one fifth of the 3264 traffic deaths in the disastrous year 1972.

SWOV (2007) describes the major changes that occurred during the period 1950–2005 in a report with the striking title 'The summit conquered'. To begin with, there is a rise in the number of traffic fatalities, which is followed by a decline. This report illustrates that, for an understanding of why the annual number of fatalities has decreased, one should not look at the total number of traffic deaths; it is preferable to consider separate components (transport modes, age, road type, etc.), because these components develop differently than the totals (as elaborated by Stipdonk, 2013). It becomes clear, for instance, that passenger car mobility in terms of vehicle ownership and vehicle use has been increasing steadily during this period. The sales and use of motorized two-wheelers, however, show a less steady picture: they fluctuate strongly and are sometimes popular, sometimes much less popular. This is clearly reflected in the road safety developments. The number of road deaths among cyclists does not seem to have decreased for years. In recent years more cyclists than car occupants were killed in traffic and about one third of the cyclists killed rode an e-bike.

Stipdonk (2020) argues that the bell-clock shape of the number of annual road deaths in many highly motorized countries, with a peak value in the early 1970s, cannot only be seen as the result of 'exposure' (distance travelled by a population) times risk (fatalities per unit of exposure). From this perspective, reduction in the number of road deaths is the result of a higher reduction in the fatality rate (by risk reducing interventions) than the observed increase in exposure. Stipdonk suggests that the average driving experience is an essential factor to understand trends in car crashes.

The quality of roads and vehicles with regard to safety has shown considerable improvement in the past few decades. The structure of the road network in the Netherlands has undergone considerable adaptations to meet the increased mobility. This can be illustrated by the fact that approximately half of all motorized vehicle kilometres are made on relatively safe motorways. The separation of different traffic modes, mainly by the construction of safe bicycle facilities, has taken a considerable step forward. Primary and secondary vehicle safety has been improved considerably. While primary safety systems focus on providing assistance to the driver to prevent crashes (e.g. electronic stability control, anti-lock braking, daytime running lights), secondary safety aims to mitigate the consequences of the crash (e.g. crumple zones, safety belts, airbags and child restraint systems). Today's conception of vehicle safety has blurred the boundary between primary and secondary safety.

Three important aspects of safety related human behaviour have also improved: drinking and driving has decreased, the safety belt is worn much more frequently and the helmet for motorized two-wheelers is also worn much more often. More specifically, these three unsafe practices are kept by 'only' a hard core of offenders. In the Netherlands, the speeds driven have gone down because the speed limits have been lowered on a substantial part of the road network. For driving speeds, it may be observed that, although road users have reduced their speed somewhat, a considerable proportion of road users exceed the limit.

11.7   SHIFTS IN ROAD SAFETY PARADIGMS

Different countries in the world are at a completely different stage of development of road safety and the maturity of policies to reduce crash and injury risks on the roads. At the same time, we see a positive development in many highly motorized and highly developed countries (Figure 11.2). How can these improvements be explained, and which road safety problems still remain? This section focuses on highly motorized countries.

Over the years, there have been very many different ways of tracing crash causes and how they can best be avoided. Table 11.4 presents, by means of a few words, what the dominant thoughts in the OECD countries were in the past century (see also OECD, 1997).

Table 11.4 Road safety 'paradigms' as seen in time

Period	Characteristic
1900–20	Crashes as chance phenomenon
1920–50	Crashes caused by the crash-prone
1940–60	Crashes are mono-causal
1950–80	A combination of crash causes fitting within a 'system approach'
1980–2000	The person is the weak link: more behavioural influence
2000–	Better implementation of existing policies Safe System Approach, e.g., Sustainably Safety (NL) and Vision Zero (S)

Source: Inspired by OECD (1997).

In short, one can notice an increase in sophistication in thinking about road safety. The 'crash-prone theory' (1920–50) dates primarily from the phase in which the legal guilt question was the main one: which road user had broken which law and was, thus, both guilty and liable? This question was answered by the police on the registration form of a crash, finally decided inside or outside the court room, and used by insurance companies to determine how to compensate damages. From 1940 to 1960 the idea shifted to the notion that crashes could be explained using a mono-causal model. In-depth studies showed, however, that there are few mono- or single-cause crashes; accidents are usually caused by, and the result of, a combination of circumstances, which led to the so-called 'multi-causal approach' (1950–80).

This approach, sometimes also called the system approach, was strongly influenced by the so-called Haddon matrix. Haddon (1972) designed a matrix using two axes: on the one hand he distinguishes three phases in the crash process: before a crash, during a crash and after a crash. The other axis is filled with the three components of our traffic system: the road user, the road and the vehicle. Consequently, this 3×3 matrix comprises nine cells. The Haddon matrix was used to classify crash factors and to indicate that more action could be taken than just 'pre-crash – road user related interventions', as was a tradition at the time. As Haddon tried to structure road safety (in nine cells of a matrix), other attempts were made.

One came from Sweden (Rumar, 1999) in which the size of the traffic safety problem is explained as the product of three dimensions:

1. exposure (E);
2. accident risk (A/E: number of accidents per exposure);
3. injury risk (I/A: number of people killed or injured per accident).

The additional 'dimension' given by Rumar (and also by Nilsson, 2004) was the inclusion of exposure as a variable or dimension to be used to improve road safety and to reduce the number of fatalities and injuries.

Since around 2000, two new main lines (paradigms) in road safety have appeared. The first one is especially aimed at evidence-based policies implemented in an efficient way. A lot of information has become available about several road safety interventions (see, for example, Elvik et al., 2009), and the idea here is not to develop new policy interventions but to improve the quality of implementing existing ones using evidence-based or research-based information on effects and costs of interventions. An example is to make police enforcement more effective and efficient or to improve roadsides alongside rural roads and motorways in a systematic way. Greater effectiveness is considered to be a matter of scale and quality. Improving road safety in such a way that the number of casualties substantially decreases generally requires a considerable effort, given the relatively low frequency of crashes, their low densities in space and the modest effects of most safety interventions. There has been growing attention given to what is called 'safety culture' and 'cultural change' in the field of decision-making on road safety (Johnston, 2010). In this analysis, road safety progress results from an increased emphasis on strategic planning – comprising the data-driven selection of the major problems to address, the setting of realistic and ambitious targets and a focus on effective implementation of programmes and measures through institutional cooperation and coordination: 'evidence-based policies' are the key words. However, despite overwhelming scientific evidence about certain themes, such as reducing speed limits to reduce speed and risks, both politicians and the public are not always convinced about introducing certain measures, even though the evidence supports this.

The second new line of thinking in traffic safety discipline since 2000 is the Safe System Approach (OECD/ITF, 2008 and 2016; see also Section 11.8). The Safe System approach recognizes that, prevention efforts notwithstanding, road users will remain fallible and crashes will occur. The approach also stresses that those involved in the design of the road transport system need to accept and share responsibility for the safety of the system and those that use the system need to accept responsibility for complying with the rules and constraints of the system. Furthermore, the Safe System Approach aligns safety management decisions with broader transport and planning decisions that meet wider economic, human and environmental goals (Academic Expert Group, 2019), and the approach shapes interventions to meet a long-term goal, rather than relying on 'traditional' interventions to set the limits of any long-term targets. An example is setting a maximum speed limit of 30 km/h in urban areas, unless strong evidence exists that high speeds are safe (for example, by separating vulnerable road users from high speed motorized traffic).

The Safe System Approach paradigm shift is based on two assumptions: (1) the current traffic system is inherently dangerous, and (2) intensifying current efforts could lead to fewer casualties, but not to substantially safer traffic, and the investments are less efficient than in the past and will be even more so in the future. To understand this position, it is useful to analyze the 'remaining' road safety problems in high-income countries.

In very broad terms, two types of problems can be identified in analyzing road safety (Wegman, 2010): generic problems and specific problems. Specific problems are those safety problems that are concentrated on specific locations, specific road user groups, specific behaviour or specific vehicles (they relate, among other things, to the risk-increasing factors, as explained in Section 11.2). Generic problems are caused by the fact that road traffic is inherently unsafe: ordinary people are killed in crashes under normal circumstances. This means that anybody can be involved in a crash at any time and that many people will be involved in a crash at some time in their lifetime because road traffic has not been designed with safety as an important requirement for design and operations.

In road safety policies in many highly motorized countries, for a long time the idea was to identify risk-increasing factors and reduce these specific risks. In public health too, this is a well-known and widely supported approach: cure those who are ill and identify and treat high-risk groups or circumstances *see*, for example, vaccination strategies to protect 'high-risk groups' from viruses, such as the COVID-19 virus. As a matter of fact, much of past road safety policy was based on high risks, high numbers and frequent causes, and on well-identified crash patterns. Crash and casualty rates, for example, were determined and divided into age groups, which showed that the young and the elderly had increased risks. The answer that policy-makers have come up with is the effort to reduce these high risks: smoothing the peaks in distributions. Analysis of road safety was aimed at the detection of peaks, explaining them and finding measures to overcome them.

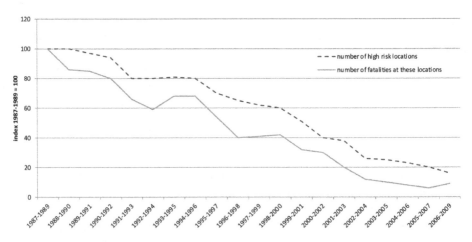

Source: SWOV (2010).

Figure 11.4   Number of high-risk locations and the number of fatalities at these locations in the Netherlands (1987–2008)

The specific high-risk approach has resulted in successful policies, which can be illustrated by an example from the Netherlands (Figure 11.4). Whereas, in the period 1987–89, 10% of the serious traffic injured were associated with 'high-risk locations', this decreased to 1.8% in the period 2004–06.

Therefore, the least safe locations have successfully been dealt with. However, it is hardly possible for such an approach to have further positive effect in the future. One could say that the approach has come to the end if its life cycle and it will barely make a further contribution to the reduction of the number of road crash casualties in countries with a relatively long history of transport safety policies, such as the Netherlands.

The same case can be used when dealing with crash-prone drivers and for eliminating near wrecks, although the evidence is weaker. In many countries 'peaks in distributions' (e.g. hazardous locations, dangerous road users and defective vehicles) still exist and can still be eliminated. However, this approach will increasingly pose practical problems for high-income countries, such as *how* to identify and eliminate these 'relatively small peaks'.

11.8 SUSTAINABLE SAFETY: THE DUTCH VERSION OF A SAFE SYSTEM APPROACH

The Sustainable Safety vision was developed in the Netherlands because the traditional policies were becoming less effective and less efficient and because the idea was that the Netherlands had not yet found out the core characteristics of its road safety problems (Koornstra et al., 1992). Although, at first glance, the vision seems to be a one-country approach, in this case for the Netherlands, Sustainable Safety is in fact considered to be an appropriate and general vision for the future and not just for highly motorized and relatively safe countries like the Netherlands. Sustainable Safety is one of the examples of a Safe System approach. This has been illustrated in several reports: OECD/ITF (2016), European Commission (2019), Academic Expert Group (2019) and the World Health Organization (2021).

The main lines of this vision will be explained below. For more detailed information about Sustainable Safety, we refer to Koornstra et al. (1992), Wegman and Aarts (2006), SWOV (2018) and Wegman et al. (2023). These publications describe in more detail the three versions of Sustainable Safety. The vision aims for 'inherently safe' traffic (a concept used in rail and air traffic and also in energy production, for example). The Sustainable Safety approach starts with the idea that the present traffic system is inherently hazardous (that serious crashes can happen anywhere and at any time) and that all possible solutions are considered in an integral and rational manner. There is no a priori preference for improving roads or vehicles or changing behaviour. Furthermore, the rationale should not be restricted to road safety only, but wider deliberations are preferable (congestion, environment, scenery, economic development, health care and so on).

The following key aspects of the Sustainable Safety vision were identified:

1. Ethics:
   a. It is unfair to hand over a traffic system to the next generation with the current casualty levels.

    b. A proactive approach instead of a reactive approach.
2. An integral approach which:
    a. integrates road user, vehicle and road into one safe system.
    b. covers the whole network, all vehicles and all road users.
    c. integrates with other policy areas.
3. Man is the measure of all things:
    a. Human capacities and limitations are the guiding factors.
4. Reduction of latent errors (system gaps) in the system:
    a. In preventing a crash it is better not to be fully dependent on whether or not a road user makes a mistake or error.
5. Use criterion of preventable injuries:
    a. Which interventions are most effective and cost-effective?

As indicated in Section 11.3, intentional or unintentional human errors play a role in nearly every crash. Intentional errors are committed by the 'unwilling' road user; unintentional errors are committed by the 'incapable' road user. No matter how well trained and motivated people are, they commit errors and do not always abide by the rules. Errors originate in many cases from the interaction between the road user and the complex road traffic environment. For avoiding crashes and injuries in crashes, road users now are almost completely dependent on the extent to which they are capable of correcting (and sometimes willing to correct) their own errors. The basic idea of the Safe System approach starts with the insight that human error should no longer be seen as the primary cause of crashes (OECD/ITF, 2016). But, present-day road traffic has not been designed with safety in mind to reduce or even eliminate human errors or to mitigate the consequences when errors are being made. And errors are also made in doing this. Both intentional errors and unintentional errors are made.

Additionally, a crash is rarely caused by one single unsafe action; it is usually preceded by a whole chain of poorly attuned occurrences. This means that it is not only one or a series of unsafe road user actions that cause a crash; hiatuses or weaknesses in the traffic system also contribute to the fact that unsafe road user actions can in certain situations result in a crash. These hiatuses are also called latent errors (Reason, 1990) (Figure 11.5). Road crashes occur when latent errors in the traffic system and unsafe actions during traffic participation coincide in a sequence of time and place.

As unsafe actions can never entirely be prevented, the Sustainable Safety vision aims at banishing the latent errors from traffic. The road traffic system must be forgiving with respect to unsafe actions by road users, so that these unsafe actions cannot result in crashes. The sustainable character of measures mainly lies in the fact that actions during traffic participation are made less dependent on momentary and individual choices. Such choices may be less than optimal and can therefore be risk-increasing.

Adjusting the environment to the abilities and limitations of the human being is derived from cognitive ergonomics, which made its entry in the early 1980s, coming from aviation and the processing industry. In all types of transport other than road traffic, this approach has already resulted in a widespread safety culture. Further incorporation of the Sustainable Safety vision should eventually lead to road traffic that can be considered 'inherently safe' as the result of such an approach.

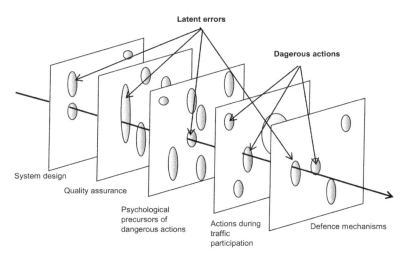

Source: Wegman and Aarts (2006), adapted from Reason (1990).

Figure 11.5   The development of a crash (bold arrow) as a result of latent errors and dangerous road user actions, also known as the Swiss Cheese model

To make traffic inherently safer is to adjust the environment to the human measure in such a way that people commit fewer errors. Here, environment not only means the physical environment (road and vehicle) but also includes the required 'software' like legislation and the traffic education that is made available. Adjustments can be made along three lines. In the first place, road designers can make potentially dangerous situations less frequent so that road users need to make fewer decisions and therefore can commit fewer errors. An example of this is physical direction separation on secondary roads, which prevents head-on collisions. The second possibility is to design the road user environment in such a way that fewer errors are committed, and it is easier to make correct and safe decisions; this can, for instance, be done by the construction of a roundabout which makes high speeds at an intersection impossible. Thirdly, a traffic environment may be designed in such a way that *if* errors are still being committed, they will not have very serious consequences for the road user. To achieve this, the road user must be presented with an environment which is forgiving of errors that are committed. For example, when a car driver, for whatever reason, is starting to leave the road, road markings (rumble strips) could alert the driver in order to correct and the roadside itself should be (made) safe. In a Safe System approach this should be done in a proactive way because this approach moves beyond a reactive, crash history-based approach.

Five principles are identified as crucial for a sustainably safe traffic system in the second version (see Table 11.5). These are: functionality, homogeneity, forgivingness, predictability and state awareness.

Reduction percentages in traffic deaths in the Netherlands of more than 30% and 40% from 1998 through 2007 compared to business-as-usual levels have been estimated for policy interventions coming from or inspired by the Sustainable Safety vision (Weijermars and van Schagen, 2009; Weijermars and Wegman, 2011). Setting the societal cost of the investments

Table 11.5 The five Sustainable Safety principles

Sustainable Safety Principle	Description
Functionality of roads	Mono functionality of roads as either through roads, distributor roads, or access roads in a hierarchical road network
Homogeneity of mass and/or speed and direction	Equality in speed, direction and mass at moderate and high speeds
Forgivingness of the environment and of road users	Injury limitation through a forgiving road environment and anticipation of road user behaviour
Predictability of road course and road user behaviour by a recognizable road design	Road environment and road user behaviour that support road user expectations through consistency and continuity in road design
State awareness by the road user	Ability to assess one's task capability to handle the driving task

Source: Wegman and Aarts (2006).

alongside the societal benefits of the fatalities, injured and crashes saved shows that these interventions are socially cost-effective. The benefit–cost ratio is highly positive, around 4:1 (Weijermars and van Schagen, 2009).

The moment of the introduction of the third version of this approach (SWOV, 2018) coincided with an increase of the number of road casualties. It tried to respond to developments regarding demography, urbanization and technology and national as well as international discussions on the organization of and responsibility for societal benefits such as road safety. The third edition gave room to these developments by adding organizational principles like 'effective allocation of responsibilities', and the renewal principle of 'learning and innovating' (SWOV, 2018 and Wegman et al., 2021).

As long as individual road users make decisions in traffic and the context of these decisions will be shaped by the many stakeholders involved, the Safe System approach will remain a valid and effective approach. Strong leadership and institutional management remain needed (Wegman et al., 2021). The current paradigm in road safety – the Safe System approach – has a solid basis in scientific knowledge and recognizes that the responsibilities to make road traffic truly safe (without serious injuries) is shared between individuals and a wide range of stakeholders. Integration with other policy goals and expanding stakeholders is introduced in Section 11.10.

Several countries have based their road safety policies on the Safe System approach, including Sweden, Norway, Finland, Canada and Australia, often under the Swedish term Vision Zero. More and more large cities have been following as well. In 2019, the Norwegian capital Oslo became a benchmark for road safety with zero traffic deaths among pedestrians, cyclists and motorcyclists for an entire year. Norway started to implement Vision Zero nationwide in 2002 with national regulations on vehicle safety, speed limits and highway design. In addition, Oslo invested in road infrastructure improvements, bike lanes and public transport funded by tolls from the city's toll roads. The latter and increased car parking charges in the city centre led to a decrease of car traffic. Traffic safety improvements are standard practice in every road project and the city regularly revises speed limits and implements traffic-calming measures (Belin et al., 2022). Finland's capital Helsinki followed a similar road safety strategy and recorded no traffic deaths in 2019. The city has reduced speed limits to 30 km/h on most residential streets and the city centre with speed humps to enforce. Driving lanes were narrowed to provide more space for pedestrians and cyclists and less for car traffic. The city of Helsinki has built dozens of roundabouts since the 1990s (Murray, 2020).

11.9   VULNERABLE ROAD USERS

Pedestrians, cyclists, moped riders, motorcyclists and users of light electric vehicles (LEVs) such as standing e-scooters (e-steps) are vulnerable. A helmet is effective to protect their heads (Olivier and Creighton, 2017), but even wearing a helmet they are less protected than car occupants. These vulnerable road users (VRUs) constitute 54% of all road deaths worldwide (WHO, 2018). Children, youngsters and the elderly are particularly likely to be involved in fatal VRU accidents (Varhelyi et al., 2018). In the remainder of this section, we mainly focus on pedestrians and cyclists as governments encourage these transport modes because of their benefits for society, such as less air pollution and reduced mortality and morbidity due to physical activity (Kelly et al., 2014) – see also the discussion in the chapter on environment (Chapter 10) and health (Chapter 12).

While most fatal VRU crashes are collisions with motor vehicles, most serious injury crashes are single vehicle incidents, such as falls and collisions with obstacles such as kerbs and bollards. An international review of studies based on hospital data showed that between 60% and 95% of cyclists admitted to hospitals or treated at emergency departments are victims of single-bicycle crashes (Schepers et al., 2015). International definitions include single-vehicle crashes on public roads with cyclists, motorized two-wheelers, while pedestrian falls without a vehicle being involved are excluded.

As explained in Section 11.2, pedestrians and cyclists are about five times more likely to sustain fatal injuries in collisions at a 50 km/h impact speed as compared to at 30 km/h. Many measures to promote the safety of vulnerable road users therefore focus on speed management. Area-wide urban traffic-calming schemes in residential areas, sometimes called 'Zone 30', reduce the total number of injury crashes, in particular among cyclists and pedestrians (Elvik et al., 2009; Inada et al., 2020). Road safety may therefore be improved by decisions to reduce the general speed limit to 30 km/h in cities (Academic Expert Group, 2019). Road design and roadside environment are important to achieve compliance with the reduced speed limit (Yao et al., 2020). An effective strategy fitting excellently in the Safe System approach along roads with higher driving speeds is separation of VRUs by cycle tracks and sidewalks (Thomas and DeRobertis, 2013; Van Petegem et al., 2021). While a 50 km/h road is safer with cycle tracks than with marked cycle lanes or mixed traffic, Schepers et al. (2013) point out collisions are still much more likely than in traffic calmed areas. At intersections of roads with high-speed limits, cyclists and pedestrians are still exposed to the high-speed motor vehicles and are frequently involved in collisions. Schepers et al. (2013) found that more cycling along low speed access roads corresponds to a higher level of road safety for cyclists. The authors describe this strategy as unbundling vehicular and cycle traffic.

Advanced Driver Support Systems (ADAS) may also play a role in speed management. By 2024 every new car sold in the EU will need to be fitted with systems such as Autonomous Emergency Braking (AEB) and Intelligent Speed Assistance (ISA). AEB intervenes autonomously when (after several warnings) the driver does not apply the brakes. ISA aids the driver in maintaining the appropriate speed. ISA is mandatory on all new vehicles in the EU from 2024 onwards, but drivers are allowed to switch it off.

The majority of non-fatal crashes with classic bicycles and e-bikes are single-bicycle crashes (Hertach et al., 2018; Schepers et al., 2015). A fall is hard to prevent when the front wheel skids or is locked or after hitting an obstacle such as a curb. Infrastructure is an important factor and under winter conditions it is of particular importance to prevent skidding. Other factors in bicycle crashes are a bicycle track being insufficiently wide, the course of the bicycle track or obstacles being insufficiently visible and road surface irregularities such as tram tracks and potholes. To summarize, a forgiving environment is needed. Options that are less related to infrastructure are for instance braking mistakes or sudden braking to avoid another vehicle/cyclist.

In Europe, where e-bikes offer pedal assistance up to 25 km/h, e-bikes on average travel only a few km/h faster than conventional bicycles. This may explain why most studies suggest that crashes with both bicycle types are equally likely and severe (Fyhri et al., 2019; Schepers et al., 2020). Few studies have focused on LEVs (light electric vehicles) such as standing e-scooters as their use has only recently started to grow. The studies that have been conducted show that similar to bicycle crashes, most standing e-scooter crashes are single vehicle crashes. More research is needed to compare risks to other travel modes such as walking and cycling (International Transport Forum, 2020).

11.10   SOME PROMISING OPTIONS FOR FURTHER IMPROVING ROAD SAFETY

Road safety has improved considerably in many (highly motorized) countries, although the absolute numbers of fatalities and serious injuries across the globe are still growing. Improvements are mainly due to risk reducing interventions, improvements in the safety quality of roads and vehicles and better post-crash management. It is reasonable to expect that many of these improvements will bear more fruit in the future: lower travelling speeds in urban areas, more separation of vulnerable road users and motorized traffic, etc. We conclude with presenting two more promising options for further improvements: automation in driving and the contributions by businesses and enterprises.

A promising option for further improvement is the further development and use of Advanced Driver Assistance Systems (ADAS) and in the longer term autonomous driving. While passive safety equipment such as seat belts and air bags greatly reduced crash severity over the past decades, active safety systems are introduced in new cars with the potential to prevent crashes. The development of ADAS began with Anti-lock Braking System (ABS) in the late 1970s for improved braking and expanded to Electronic Stability Control (ESC) to prevent skidding while steering. Other examples of ADAS to improve road safety are Lane

Departure Warning (LDW), Blind Spot Detection (BSD), and the ISA and AEB mentioned in the previous section (Ziebinski et al., 2017). Driver assistance systems are paving the way for autonomous driving. The Society of Automotive Engineers (SAE) defined six different levels of driving automation. While the driver lacks ADAS in level 0, ADAS assist speed and steering in levels 1 and 2 in which the driver still monitors the driving environment. ADAS monitors the driving environment in higher-level (levels 3 to 5) vehicles (Kukkala et al., 2018).

As most crashes result from human errors and violations, it has been claimed that autonomous driving reduces traffic deaths by over 90% (Shinar 2019). These claims are untested. In addition to its great advantages, autonomous driving can also introduce new risks that we must learn to manage. Automated vehicles will be able to respond faster to critical events happening on the road and will not be affected by fatigue, for example. An example of a new challenge in conditional automation in SAE level 3 is that the human driver should be able to intervene in a timely manner if the system requires so, even when the drivers were not paying attention or performing non-driving related tasks (Inagaki and Sheridan, 2019). Furthermore, more complex systems to allow for further automation may rely on vehicle-to-vehicle communication introducing new cybersecurity challenges (Katrakazas et al., 2020). It is not yet possible to predict how much and how quickly road safety can be improved by the introduction of autonomous driving (International Transport Forum, 2018).

We have a better understanding of why crashes occur, and we have gained a lot of knowledge on the effectiveness and sometimes on the efficiency of road safety interventions. The vast majority of these improvements were an initiative from governments, at a federal, national, regional or local level, sometimes as a result of activities by non-governmental organizations (NGOs – organizations representing road crash victims, for example) or from the public. It could be considered to explore how an important, and still rather absent, stakeholder in our society, the private sector, can make a contribution to further improve road safety without being invited (or even forced) by governments.

It is considered to be a responsibility of businesses and enterprises to contribute to the achievement of the Sustainable Development Goals (SDGs) from the United Nations (2015) and to the Agenda 2030 for Sustainable Development more specifically. Improving traffic safety is included in this Agenda. Businesses recognize the opportunities that the SDGs offer them to engage in the Agenda 2030. These go far beyond the corporate social responsibility of businesses, as they deal with the total corporate value chain: inbound logistics, operations, outbound logistics, marketing, sales and service (Porter, 1998). It is from this perspective that it has been proposed to make the private sector an important stakeholder and actor to improve road safety (Academic Expert Group, 2019). Two (of the nine) recommendations of this Group deal with the private sector. One deals with the procurement of fleet vehicles and transport services. This concerns, for example, the specification of vehicle safety levels, training of drivers and scheduling and planning of driving operations. The first recommendation for businesses and enterprises (page 28) says:

require the highest level of road safety according to Safe System principles in their internal practices, in policies concerning the health and safety of their employees, and in the process and policies of the full range of suppliers, distributors and partners throughout their value chain or production and distribution system.

For instance, time pressure due to delivery deadlines and payment per delivery in commercial transportation contribute to stress, fatigue and more risky driving or riding (Delhomme and Gheorghiu, 2021) and should be prevented. Workplace road safety risk management and a positive road safety culture help to control these risks (Warmerdam et al., 2017).

Looking back at the history of road safety and how to reduce risks and the number of road casualties, we may conclude that these attempts took place inside the 'road safety silo', that is to say they were attempts with the only or main goal to improve road safety. We can observe developments to include road safety in a more integral approach for improving the human condition and the condition of the planet, as for example being recommended in the report of the Academic Expert Group (2019) and in the policy proposals for the European Union (EC, 2019) and by the World Health Organization in their Action Plan (WHO, 2021). Improving road safety is part of improving health, climate, equity and prosperity. Active transport modes such as walking and cycling are good for health, reduce air and noise pollution, as well as energy use and greenhouse gas emissions (see also Chapters 10 and 12 of this book), but from a road safety perspective this could only be supported if walking and cycling is safe.

11.11   CONCLUSIONS

The most important conclusions from this chapter are:

1. Speed, speed and mass differences, and vulnerability are fundamental risk factors for road crashes and injuries. These fundamental risk factors explain the fact that pedestrians and cyclists are vulnerable road users in collisions with (high-speed) motorized vehicles.
2. Risk-increasing factors from the road users' side are impaired driving (alcohol and drugs), fatigue and distraction.
3. Both human errors and (intentional) violations (and related extreme behaviour) are important contributory factors for road crashes.
4. Measuring road safety is not without its problems, because of non-harmonized definitions, poor data quality, data incompleteness and lack of data availability.
5. Positive development in many highly motorized and highly developed countries can be noted. These highly motorized countries haves made considerable progress by implementing behaviour-, vehicle- and infrastructure-related measures in the last decades.
6. However, the effectiveness of many 'traditional' policies will reduce. The next step is to move from policies targeted at decreasing specific risks to policies aimed at lowering generic or inherent risks: in other words, to a Safe System approach.
7. A Safe System approach starts by using the idea that the present traffic system is inherently hazardous (that serious crashes can happen anywhere and at any time) and that all possible solutions should be considered in an integral and rational manner. Cost–benefit analyses show that such an approach can have positive benefit-to-cost ratios.
8. Vulnerable road users (pedestrians, cyclists, powered two-wheelers) are disproportionally impacted by road crashes and this group accounts for more than 50% of road deaths world-

wide. Risks for this group will be lowered by separating them from high-speed motorized traffic and by speed reduction at locations where they interact with motorized traffic, for example by installing 30 km/h zones. A forgiving environment is needed to prevent severe injuries due to falls.

9. Automated and autonomous driving are very promising for improving road safety, however it is not yet possible to predict how much and how quickly road safety improvements will reduce the number of road fatalities and injuries.

10. Road safety shall be further improved by expanding and intensifying the engagement of stakeholders in the public sector and by engaging new partners especially in the private sector. Improving traffic safety is part of the Sustainable Development Agenda which connects improving road safety with other goals on good health and well-being, green mobility, gender equality, sustainable cities and communities, etc.

REFERENCES

Aarts, L. and I. van Schagen (2006), 'Driving speeds and the risk of road crashes: a review', *Accident Analysis and Prevention*, 38 (2), 215–24.

Academic Expert Group (2019*), Saving lives beyond 2020: The next steps,* Recommendations of the Academic Expert Group for the 3rd Global Ministerial Conference on Road Safety 2020. TRV 2019:209. Borlänge: Swedish Transportation Administration.

Alfaro, J.-L., M. Chapuis and F. Fabre (1994), *Socioeconomic Cost of Road Accidents*, Transport Research COST 313, Brussels and Luxembourg: Commission of the European Communities.

Belin, M.Å., A. Hartmann, M. Svolsbru, B. Turner and M.S. Griffith (2022), 'Applying a Safe System Approach Across the Globe', *Public Roads*, 85 (4), 36–42.

Blomberg, R.D., R.C. Peck, H. Moskowitz, M. Burns and D. Fiorentino (2005), *Crash Risk of Alcohol Involved Driving: A Case-Control Study*, Stamford, CT: Dunlap and Associates.

Christophersen A. S., J. Mørland, K. Steward and H. Gjerde (2016), 'International trends in alcohol and drug use among motor vehicle drivers', *Forensic Science Review*, 28–37.

Connor, J., R. Norton, S. Ameratunga, E. Robinson, I. Civil, R. Dunn, J. Bailey and R. Jackson (2002), 'Driver sleepiness and risk of serious injury to car occupants: population based case control study', *British Medical Journal*, 324 (7346), 1125–29.

Curry, A. E., K.B. Metzger, A.F. Williams, and B.C. Tefft (2017), 'Comparison of older and younger novice driver crash rates: informing the need for extended Graduated Driver Licensing restrictions', *Accident Analysis and Prevention*, 108, 66–73.

De Blaeij, A.T. (2003), *The Value of a Statistical Life in Road Safety: Stated Preference Methodologies and Empirical Estimates for the Netherlands*, Research Series, Amsterdam: Vrije Universiteit.

De Waard, F. Westerhuis and B. Lewis-Evans (2015), 'More screen operation than calling: the results of observing cyclists' behaviour while using mobile phones', *Accident Analysis and Prevention*, 76, 42–48.

Delhomme, P. and A. Gheorghiu (2021), 'Perceived stress, mental health, organizational factors, and self-reported risky driving behaviors among truck drivers circulating in France', *Journal of Safety Research*, 79, 341–351.

Derriks, H. and P. Mak (2007), *Underreporting of Road Traffic Casualties*, Paris: Organisation for Economic Co-operation and Development (OECD)/IRTAD.

Dingus, T.A., S.G. Klauer, V.L. Neale, A. Petersen, S.E. Lee, J. Sudweeks, M.A. Perez, J. Hankey, D. Ramsey, S. Gupta, C. Bucher, Z.R. Doerzaph, J. Jermeland and R.R. Knipling (2006), 'The 100-Car Naturalistic Driving Study, Phase II: Results of the 100-Car Field Experiment', Washington, DC: National Highway Traffic Safety Administration, USDOT.

Dingus, T.A., J.M. Owens, F. Guo, Y. Fang, M. Perez, J. McClafferty, M. Buchanan-King and G.M. Fitch (2019), 'The prevalence of and crash risk associated with primarily cognitive secondary tasks', *Safety Science*, 119, 98–105.

EC (European Commission) (2019), *EU road safety policy framework 2021–2030 – Next steps towards 'Vision Zero'*. Commission Staff Working Document SWD(2019) 283 final. Brussels: European Commission.

Elvik, R. (1995), 'An analysis of official economic evaluations of traffic accident fatalities in 20 countries', *Accident Analysis and Prevention*, 27 (2), 237–47.

Elvik, R. (2013), 'A re-parameterisation of the Power Model of the relationship between the speed of traffic and the number of accidents and accident victims', *Accident Analysis and Prevention*, 50, 854–60.

Elvik, R. and T. Vaa (2004), *The Handbook of Road Safety Measures*, Amsterdam: Pergamon Press.

Elvik, R., T. Vaa, A. Hoye, A. Erke and M. Sorenson (2009), *The Handbook of Road Safety Measures*, 2nd revised edition, Bingley: Emerald Group Publishing.

Elvik, R., A. Vadeby, T.Hels and I. van Schagen (2019), 'Updated estimates of the relationship between speed and road safety at the aggregate and individual levels', *Accident Analysis and Prevention*, 123, 114–22.

European Transport Safety Council (2003), *Transport Safety Performance in the EU – A Statistical Overview*, Brussels: ETSC.

Fyhri, A., O. Johansson and T. Bjørnskau (2019), 'Gender differences in accident risk with e-bikes-Survey data from Norway', *Accident Analysis and Prevention*, 132, 105248.

Glassbrenner, D. and M. Starnes (2009), *Lives Saved Calculations for Seat Belts and Frontal Airbags*, Washington, DC: National Highway Traffic Safety Administration.

Haddon, W. (1972), 'A logical framework for categorizing highway safety phenomena and activity', *Journal of Trauma*, 12 (3), 193–207.

Hauer, E. (2020), 'Crash causation and prevention', *Accident Analysis and Prevention*, 143, 105528.

Hertach, P., A. Uhr, S. Niemann and M. Cavegn (2018), 'Characteristics of single-vehicle crashes with e-bikes in Switzerland', *Accident Analysis and Prevention*, 117, 232–38.

Inada, H., J. Tomio, S. Nakahara and M. Ichikawa (2020), 'Area-wide traffic-calming Zone 30 policy of Japan and incidence of road traffic injuries among cyclists and pedestrians', *American Journal of Public Health*, 110 (2), 237–43.

Inagaki, T. and T. Sheridan (2019). 'A critique of the SAE conditional driving automation definition, and analyses of options for improvement', *Cognition, Technology & Work*, 21 (4), 569–78.

International Transport Forum (2018), *Safer Roads with Automated Vehicles?* Paris: ITF.

International Transport Forum (2020), *Safe Micromobility*, Paris: ITF.

Johnston, I. (2010), 'Beyond "best practice" road safety thinking and systems management: a case for culture change research', *Safety Science*, 48 (9), 1175–81.

Jones, A.W., J.G. Mørland and R.H. Liu (2019), 'Driving under the influence of psychoactive substances-a historical review', *Forensic Science Review*, 31 (2), 103–40.

Jurewicz, C., A. Sobhani, J. Woolley, J. Dutschke and B. Corben (2016), 'Exploration of vehicle impact speed–injury severity relationships for application in safer road design', *Transportation Research Procedia*, 14, 4247–56.

Katrakazas, C., A. Theofilatos, G. Papastefanatos, J. Härri and C. Antoniou (2020), 'Cyber security and its impact on CAV safety: Overview, policy needs and challenges', in D. Milakis, N. Thomopoulos and B. van Wee (eds), *Policy Implications of Autonomous Vehicles. Advances in Transport Policy and Planning Volume 5*, 1st Edn, Cambridge/San Diego/Oxford/London: Elsevier, 73–94.

Kelly, P., S. Kahlmeier, T. Götschi, N. Orsini, J. Richards, N. Roberts, P. Scarborough and C. Foster (2014), 'Systematic review and meta-analysis of reduction in all-cause mortality from walking and cycling and shape of dose response relationship', *International Journal of Behavioral Nutrition and Physical Activity*, 11 (132), 1–15.

Khattak, A.J., N. Ahmad, B. Wali and E. Dumbaugh (2021), 'A taxonomy of driving errors and violations: Evidence from the naturalistic driving study', *Accident Analysis and Prevention*, 151, 105873.

Koornstra, M.J., D. Lynam, G. Nilsson, P.C. Noordzij, H.-E. Petterson, F.C.M. Wegman and P.I.J. Wouters (2002), *SUNflower: A Comparative Study of the Development of Road Safety in Sweden, the United Kingdom, and the Netherlands*, Leidschendam, Crowthorne and Linköping: Stichting Wetenschappelijk Onderzoek Verkeersveiligheid (SWOV)/TRL/VTI.

Koornstra, M.J., M.P.M. Mathijssen, J.A.G. Mulder, R. Roszbach and F.C.M. Wegman (eds) (1992), *Naar een duurzaam veilig wegverkeer: nationale verkeersveiligheidsverkenning voor de jaren 1990/2010*

[*Towards sustainably safe road traffic: national road safety survey for 1990/2010*], Leidschendam: SWOV.

Kukkala, V.K., J. Tunnell, S. Pasricha and T. Bradley (2018), 'Advanced driver-assistance systems: A path toward autonomous vehicles', *IEEE Consumer Electronics Magazine*, 7 (5), 18–25.

Lipovac, K., M. Đerić, M. Tešić, Z. Andrić and B. Marić (2017), 'Mobile phone use while driving-literary review', *Transportation Research Part F*, 47, 132–42.

Mbarga, N.F., A.-R. Abubakari, L.N. Aminde and A.R. Morgan (2018), 'Seatbelt use and risk of major injuries sustained by vehicle occupants during motor-vehicle crashes: a systematic review and meta-analysis of cohort studies', *BMC Public Health*, 18 (1), 1–11.

Moradi, A., S.S.H. Nazari and K. Rahmani (2019), 'Sleepiness and the risk of road traffic accidents: A systematic review and meta-analysis of previous studies', *Transportation Research Part F: Traffic Psychology and Behaviour*, 65, 620–629.

Murray, J. (2020), 'How Helsinki and Oslo cut pedestrian deaths to zero', *The Guardian*.

Nie, J., G. Li and J. Yang. (2015), 'A Study of Fatality Risk and Head Dynamic Response of Cyclist and Pedestrian Based on Passenger Car Accident Data Analysis and Simulations', *Traffic Injury Prevention*, 16 (1), 76–83.

Nilsson, G. (2004), *Traffic Safety Dimensions and the Power Model to Describe the Effect of Speed on Safety*, Lund Bulletin 221, Lund: Traffic Engineering, Lund Institute for Technology and Society.

OECD (Organisation for Economic Co-operation and Development) (1997), *Road Safety Principles and Models: Review of Descriptive, Predictive, Risk and Accident Consequence Models*, Paris: OECD.

OECD/ITF (International Transport Forum) (2008), *Towards Zero: Ambitious Road Safety Targets and the Safe System Approach*, Paris: OECD/ITF.

OECD/ITF (International Transport Forum) (2016), *Zero Road Deaths and Serious Injuries: Leading a Paradigm Shift to a Safe System*, Paris: OECD/ITF.

OECD/ITF (International Transport Forum) (2020), *IRTAD Road Safety Annual Report 2020*, Paris: OECD/ITF.

Olivier, J. and P. Creighton (2017), 'Bicycle injuries and helmet use: a systematic review and meta-analysis', *International Journal of Epidemiology*, 46 (1), 278–92.

Porter, M.E. (1998), *Competitive Advantage: Creating and Sustaining Superior Performance*, New York: The Free Press.

Reason, J. (1990), *Human Error*, Cambridge: Cambridge University Press.

Redelmeier, D.A., R.J. Tibshirani and L. Evans (2003), 'Traffic-law enforcement and risk of death from motor-vehicle crashes: case-crossover study', *The Lancet*, 361 (9376), 2177–82.

Regan, M.A., J.D. Lee and K.L. Young (eds) (2009), *Driver Distraction: Theory, Effects and Mitigation*, Boca Raton, FL: Taylor & Francis.

Rumar, K. (1999), *Transport Safety Visions, Targets and Strategies: Beyond 2000*, Brussels: European Transport Safety Council.

Savage, I. (2013), 'Comparing the fatality risks in United States transportation across modes and over time', *Research in Transportation Economics*, 43 (1), 9–22.

Schepers, P., N. Agerholm, E. Amoros, R. Benington, T. Bjørnskau, S. Dhondt, B. de Geus,C. Hagemeister, B.P.Y. Loo and A. Niska (2015), 'An international review of the frequency of single-bicycle crashes (SBCs) and their relation to bicycle modal share', *Injury Prevention*, 21 (1), 138–143

Schepers, P., E. Heinen, R. Methorst and F. Wegman (2013), 'Road safety and bicycle usage impacts of unbundling vehicular and cycle traffic in Dutch urban networks', *European Journal of Transport and Infrastructure Research*, 13 (3), 221–38.

Schepers, P., K.K. Wolt, M. Helbich and E. Fishman (2020), 'Safety of e-bikes compared to conventional bicycles: What role does cyclists' health condition play?' *Journal of Transport and Health*, 19, 100961.

Schoeters, A., M. Large, M. Koning, L. Carnis, S. Daniels, D. Mignot, R. Urmeew, W. Wijnen, F. Bijleveld and M. van der Horst (2021), *Monetary valuation of the prevention of road fatalities and serious road injuries. Results of the VALOR project*, Brussels: VIAS Institute.

Schulze, H., M. Schumacher, R. Urmeew and K. Auerbach (2012), *DRUID Final Report: Work performed, main results and recommendations*, Deliverable (0.1.8) at www.druid-project.eu.

Shinar, D. (2019), 'Crash causes, countermeasures, and safety policy implications', *Accident Analysis and Prevention*, 125, 224–31.

Shinar, D., P. Valero-Mora, M. van Strijp-Houtenbos, N. Haworth, et al. (2018), 'Under-reporting bicycle accidents to police in the COST TU1101 international survey: Cross-country comparisons and associated factors', *Accident Analysis and Prevention*, 110, 177–86.

Stipdonk, H. (2013), *Road Safety in Bits and Pieces. For a Better Understanding of the Development of the Number of Road Fatalities*, Leidschendam: SWOV.

Stipdonk, H. (2020), 'A car road deaths model to explain the annual road death peak near 1970 in high income countries, using driver experience and travel', *Safety Science*, 129, 104635.

SWOV (2007), *De top bedwongen: balans van de verkeersonveiligheid in Nederland 1950–2005 [The summit conquered: assessment of road safety in the Netherlands 1950–2005]*, Leidschendam: SWOV.

SWOV (2010), 'The high risk location approach', fact sheet, SWOV, Leidschendam.

SWOV (2018). *Sustainable Safety, 3rd edition – The advanced vision for 2018–2030: Principles for design and organization of a casualty-free road traffic system*, The Hague: SWOV.

Thomas, B. and M. DeRobertis (2013), 'The safety of urban cycle tracks: A review of the literature', *Accident Analysis and Prevention*, 52, 219–27.

UNECE (2019), *Illustrated Glossary for Transport Statistics*, 4th edition, accessed at http://epp.eurostat.ec .europa.eu/cache/ITY_OFFPUB/KS-RA-10-028/EN/KS-RA-10-028-EN.PDF.

United Nations (2015), *Transforming our world: The 2030 agenda for sustainable development A/ RES/70/1*. New York: UN.

Van der Meer, T.G.L.A., A.C. Kroon and R. Vliegenthart (2021), 'Do News Media Kill? How a Biased News Reality can Overshadow Real Societal Risks, The Case of Aviation and Road Traffic Accidents', *Social Forces*, 114, 1–25.

Van Petegem, J.W.H., J.P. Schepers and G.J. Wijlhuizen (2021), 'The safety of physically separated cycle tracks compared to marked cycle lanes and mixed traffic conditions in Amsterdam', *European Journal of Transport and Infrastructure Research*, 21 (3), 19–37.

Varhelyi, A., A. Laureshyn, C. Johnsson, N. Saunier, R. van der Horst, M. de Goede and T. Kidholm Osmann Madsen (2018), 'Surrogate measures of safety and traffic conflict observations', in E. Polders, and T. Brijs (eds), *How to Analyse Accident Causation? A Handbook with FocusoOn Vulnerable Road Users*, Hasselt: University, Diepenbeek, 93–126.

Vissers, L., S. Houwing and F. Wegman (2017), *Alcohol-related road casualties in official statistics*. IRTAD Research report. Paris: OECD/ITF.

Vlakveld, W. (2005), *Jonge beginnende automobilisten, hun ongevalsrisico en maatregelen om dit terug te dringen [Young novice drivers, their risk of accident and measures to reduce this]*, R-2005–3, Leidschendam: SWOV.

Walsh, J.M., J.J. de Gier, A.S. Christophersen and A.G. Verstrate (2004), 'Drugs and driving', *Traffic Injury Prevention*, 5, 241–53.

Warmerdam, A., S. Newnam, D. Sheppard, M. Griffin and M. Stevenson (2017), 'Workplace road safety risk management: An investigation into Australian practices', *Accident Analysis and Prevention*, 98, 64–73.

Wegman, F.C.M. (2010), 'De prijs van water bij de wijn' ['The price of making a compromise'], inaugural lecture, January, Delft University of Technology, TU Delft.

Wegman, F.C.M. and L.T. Aarts (eds) (2006), *Advancing Sustainable Safety: National Road Safety Outlook for 2005–2020*, Leidschendam: SWOV.

Wegman, F., L. Aarts and P. van der Knaap (2023), 'Sustainable Safety: a short history of a Safe System approach in the Netherlands', in K.E. Björnberg, S.O. Hansson, M-A Belin, C. Tingvall (eds), *The Vision Zero Handbook: Theory, Technology and Management for a Zero Causality Policy*. Cham: Springer International Publishing, 307–336.

Wegman, F. and M. Hagenzieker (2010), 'Scientific Research on Road Safety Management', *Safety Science*, 48 (9), 1081–224.

Wegman, F. and C. Katrakazas (2021), 'Did the COVID-19 pandemic influence traffic fatalities in 2020? A presentation of first findings', *IATSS Research*, 45 (4), 469–84.

Weijermars, W., J.-C. Meunier, N. Bos, C. Perez, M. Hours, H. Johannsen, J. Barnes et al. (2016), *Physical and psychological consequences of serious road traffic injuries*, Deliverable 7.2 of the H2020 project SafetyCube.

Weijermars, W.A.M. and I.N.L.G. van Schagen (eds) (2009), *Tien jaar duurzaam veilig: verkeers-veiligheidsbalans 1998–2007 [Ten years of sustainable safety: road safety assessment 1998– 2007]*, R-2009–14, Leidschendam: SWOV.

Weijermars, W.A.M. and F.C.M. Wegman (2011), 'Ten years of sustainable safety in the Netherlands: an assessment'. *Transportation Research Record*, 2213 (1), 1–8.

Wijnen, W. (2008), *Bruikbaarheid van QALY's en DALY's voor de verkeersveiligheid* [*Usefulness of QALYs and DALYs for road safety*], R-2007–13, Leidschendam: SWOV.

Wijnen, W. and H. Stipdonk (2016), 'Social costs of road crashes: An international analysis, Accident Analysis and Prevention', 94, 97–106.

World Health Organization (2018), *Global Status Report on Road Safety 2018*, Geneva: WHO.

World Health Organization (2021), *Global Plan for the Decade of Action for Road Safety 2021–2030*, Geneva: WHO.

Yao, Y., O. Carsten and D. Hibberd (2020), 'A close examination of speed limit credibility and compliance on UK roads', *IATSS Research*, 44 (1), 17–29.

Ziebinski, A., R. Cupek, D. Grzechca and L. Chruszczyk (2017), *Review of advanced driver assistance systems (ADAS)*, in AIP Conference Proceedings, 1906, p. 120002. AIP Publishing LLC.

12
Travel behaviour and health

Bert van Wee and Dick Ettema[1]

12.1   INTRODUCTION

The health impacts of the transport system are a topic of growing importance in both research and policy making. These impacts first of all apply to people in their role of travellers, but in addition the health of non-travellers is influenced by the travel behaviour of other people, an important reason being the exposure to pollutants and noise. The growing interest in the links between travel behaviour and health are partly the result of the increasing focus on cycling (and also walking) in research and policy. This interest is due to the simple reason that cycling (and walking) are forms of exercise, and they are thus healthy. Several cities worldwide have implemented cycling policies, examples being New York, Portland, London, and Paris. In addition, the increased interest in the relationship between travel and health is due to the growing concerns about the effects of urban air pollution on public health.

This chapter aims to give an overview of the health impacts of the transport system. We start by discussing the links between travel behaviour and health of travellers (Section 12.2), followed by the links between travel behaviour and health of non-travellers (Section 12.3). Section 12.4 summarizes the most important conclusions. Because some of the health effects depend on environmental pressure and safety, we refer to Chapters 10 (environment) and 11 (safety) for factors influencing environmental pressure and safety levels, and in this chapter, we only pay limited attention to these factors. Because health and well-being effects are strongly related, as we will explain below, we also discuss the dominant well-being effects of the transport system.

12.2   A CONCEPTUAL MODEL FOR THE LINKS
BETWEEN TRAVEL BEHAVIOUR AND HEALTH

The WHO defines health as 'a state of complete physical, mental and social well-being and not merely the absence of disease or infirmity' (WHO, 2020). We adopt this definition but apply a demarcation: we exclude the social dimension, the reason being that the social dimension is only indirectly related to the links between travel behaviour and health. Next, we distinguish between a mental and physical component of health. Both are interrelated, but distinguishing both allows us to better conceptualize the links between travel behaviour and well-being on the one hand, and physical health on the other hand. In line with generally used terminology, we use the term 'health' to denote physical health, and 'subjective well-being' to denote mental well-being. Subjective well-being and mental health are related. However, whereas mental health studies focus on symptoms of mental illness, such as anxiety or depression, well-being studies focus on a wider spectrum of mental states, which also differentiate between people without symptoms of mental illness.

We conceptualize that the following travel-related components impact the health of travellers:

1. Level of physical activity
2. Air pollution intake
3. Casualties/injuries
4. Subjective well-being

These factors are interrelated; for instance, walking and cycling may result in increased subjective well-being (Olsson et al., 2013), but may also lead to crashes/falls. Incident risks could be a reason for people to reduce or eliminate their walk or cycle trips (see Lee et al., 2015). In addition, high concentrations of pollutants may deter people from cycling or walking.

Figure 12.1 presents a conceptual model for the dominant links between travel behaviour and health of the traveller. It relates to the conceptual model explaining the structure for a large part of this book, Figure 2.1 ('A conceptual framework for the book: How the transport system shapes travel behaviour and impacts accessibility, the environment, safety, health, and well-being'), but contrary to that figure, Figure 12.1 is a figure at the individual level. 'Travel behaviour' is the individualized factor of the 'volume' factor in the core of Figure 2.1. 'Residential choice' is a subcategory of the 'locations' factor, and 'personal characteristics' are major drivers for the 'needs and desires' of people. Figure 12.1 shows that the health effects of travel result from physical activity (component A in Figure 12.1), exposure to and intake of air pollutants (B), and involvement in casualties/collisions/falls (C). These health effects are well documented, see for example, Handy (2014) or Cohen et al. (2014). In addition, we assume that health and subjective well-being (D) are related, but the causality is debatable. Subjective well-being is commonly defined as a combination of a person's assessment of his/her quality of life and satisfaction with life, and his/her affective state, as the net effect of positive and negative emotions (Ettema et al., 2010). Studies of subjective well-being show health to be the most important determinant of life satisfaction (e.g., Walasek et al., 2019). On the other hand, we argue that a sufficient level of satisfaction with life and a good mood are beneficial to one's physical health. Diener and Chan (2011) and Diener et al. (2017) extensively review empirical longitudinal studies in this area, concluding that an individual's current affective state influences physiological health indicators measured afterwards such as blood pressure, inflammatory activity or immune functioning. In addition, they report many long-term longitudinal studies showing the impact of subjective well-being on longevity and developing diseases several years to decades later.

The conceptual model includes the dominant, but not all, relationships between factors important for the relationships between travel behaviour and health. Three examples highlight other factors that are excluded from the conceptual model. First, health also depends on genetics and other behaviours, like smoking and drinking. Second, high levels of accessibility may positively influence well-being, whereas social exclusion (the fact that people cannot adequately participate in society because of too low levels of access to destinations) could negatively influence well-being. For the links between health, transport, and social exclusion we refer to Mackett and Thoreau (2015). Third, the final impact of casualties and the health impacts of exposure to pollutants also depends on access to (Bauer et al., 2020) and the quality of the health care system. Because of the scope of this chapter and to reduce complexity such factors are not included in our conceptual model, nor discussed further in this chapter.

The conceptual model includes numbered lines for the direct relationships between (factors influencing) travel behaviour and health. In addition, dashed lines represent relationships relevant for the understanding of causalities, but these lines do not represent direct relationships between travel behaviour and health – we do not further discuss these in this chapter. It is good to realize that the conceptual model we present is not the only conceptual model available in this area. For another model see, for example, Glazener et al. (2021).

12.2.1   Dominant First Order Relationship

We next discuss the dominant direct relationships between travel behaviour and health (bold lines in Figure 12.1), in other words:

1. From travel behaviour to physical activity (arrow 1)
2. From travel behaviour to pollution intake (arrow 2)
3. From travel behaviour to casualties (arrow 3)
4. From travel behaviour to subjective well-being (arrow 4)

These relationships are 'first order' relationships because travel behaviour influences health via these routes. We call all other relationships in Figure 12.1 'second order' relationships. There is much more research on first order effects than on the second order effects.

Travel behaviour and physical activity (arrow 1)

For health reasons, adults should be moderately physically active (MPA) for 150 minutes or vigorously physically active (VPA) for 75 minutes every week. They can also combine the two pro rata (US Department of Health and Human Services, 2019; UK Department of Health and Social Care, 2019). Walking and cycling can contribute to meeting these requirements (Handy, 2014), especially when it is part of people's daily routines. The time and intensity of walking and cycling depends on the chosen destinations (distances) and routes and the frequency of walking and cycling trips.

Travel behaviour and air pollution intake (arrow 2)

The exposure to air pollution applies to all categories of travellers, ranging from drivers and passengers of cars and other motorized vehicles, people cycling and walking, and people

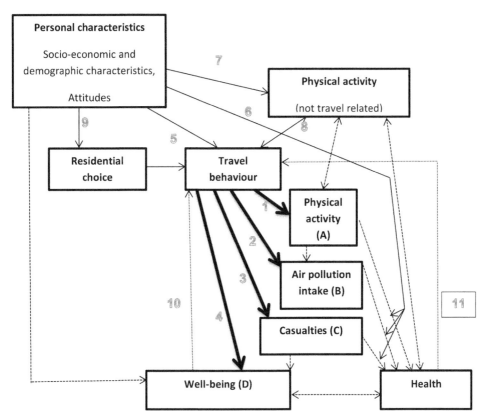

Note: bold lines represent dominant impacts of travel behaviour on health aspects. Numbered lines represent the direct relationships between (factors influencing) travel behaviour and health. Dashed lines represent other relationships between boxes in the model.

Source: adapted from van Wee and Ettema (2016)

Figure 12.1   Conceptual model for the relationships between travel behaviour and health

travelling by underground. Concentrations of pollutants are highest on the roads, and they decrease as distance from the road increases (Janssen et al., 2002), so drivers and passengers of motorized vehicles are exposed to relatively high concentrations. Based on an overview of literature, van Wee (2007) concluded that concentrations of pollutants in vehicles are between 1.5 and over 10 times higher than in the ambient air. Concentrations of pollutants depend on the density of traffic and technical characteristics of vehicles (strongly related to year of manufacturing vehicles and engine/fuel type) and the distance between the recipient and these sources. For the importance of this distance for cyclists we refer to Schepers et al. (2015). In addition, ambient factors such as the morphology of the built environment, trees, and weather (temperature, wind speed) influence the dispersion of pollutants and consequently concentrations and exposure. Although cyclists are exposed to lower concentrations than drivers, because of the larger distance between cyclists and polluting vehicles (Mitsakou et al., 2021), cyclists inhale more air than car drivers, because they are physical active (van Wee, 2007). In Figure 12.1 this effect is conceptualized via the arrow from 'physical activity' to 'air pollution intake'. In addition, the exposure to pollutants of cyclists and pedestrians depends on travel speed. The higher the speed, the higher the breathing rates, and the higher the pollution inhaled per unit of time (Nyhan et al., 2014). However, for a given trip higher speeds also imply shorter travel times, and thus a shorter duration of exposure. The latter effect generally prevails, leading to less exposure when cycling or walking faster (McNabola et al., 2007).

People travelling by underground are often exposed to high concentrations of PM originating from mechanical friction process (wheel on rail, brakes); see Şahin et al. (2012) for a study on particles containing Fe (iron) and Cu (copper) in six subway stations in Istanbul, and Cheng and Yan (2011) for a study on particulate matter (PM) concentrations in underground environments in Tampei.

Negative health effects due to the exposure of pollutants include cardiovascular diseases, eye and throat irritation, respiratory health problems (asthma, lung damage), high blood pressure, neurological disorders and cancer, and brain and kidney damage, amongst others *see* Handy (2014) for a detailed overview of health effects of pollution. The extent to which these effects occur depends not only on the duration and accumulation of exposure, but also on personal characteristics. For instance, infants, the elderly, and pregnant women are more sensitive to certain pollutants (Lee et al., 2021). In addition, one's health status, resulting from certain behaviours such as smoking, obesity, and diabetes has an impact on the health effects resulting from exposure.

Travel behaviour and casualties (arrow 3)

Travelling goes together with incident risk. Risks relate to fatalities and injuries. No mode is 100% risk free. Risk factors are mode-specific and for road-related modes they vary between road types (see Chapter 11 of this book). It is important to realize that risk factors are highly context specific, and probably even more so for cycling than for driving, because cycling is very common in some countries (such as Denmark and the Netherlands) but not in others (such as the USA), resulting in large differences in cycling infrastructure, experience of cyclists, and the behaviour of drivers of motorized vehicles. In addition, it is not at all straightforward to estimate the risks and incident rates of *additional* cycling (and probably also walking), for several reasons. Firstly, higher cycling levels result in lower risk factors (the so-called 'safety in numbers' effect – see Elvik and Goel (2019) for a meta-analysis of many quantitative studies exploring this phenomenon). Secondly, for decisions on policy options competing trips should be compared. In other words, comparisons should not be based on aggregate average risk factors. People do not substitute a long interurban car trip of, for example, 75 kilometres for a cycling trip. But they might be inclined to substitute a 3-kilometre urban trip. In that latter case the comparison should be based on risk factors for urban roads only. Thirdly, in many countries there is a lack of data on cycling behaviour (Handy et al., 2014). Fourthly, cycling is poorly included in mainstream transport models, even in countries with a strong cycling tradition like Denmark and the Netherlands, limiting the usability of models for *ex ante* evaluations of candidate policy options. Finally, the mode specific risk factors are influenced by different risk-taking behaviours dependent on gender and age, and the different gender and age characteristics of users of different travel modes (Mindell et al., 2012).

Travel behaviour and subjective well-being (arrow 4)

The effect of travel on subjective well-being may materialize in different ways. Firstly, the experience of travel itself and the interaction with the physical and social environment during travel may influence one's mood and well-being. Secondly, access to travel facilitates participation in meaningful activities that foster subjective well-being (Ettema et al., 2010; Churchill and Smyth, 2019). Both effects will be discussed here.

The travel environment to which one is exposed has an impact on one's mood, as a result of direct emotional responses. In case of repeated trips (such as commuting) the aggregation of these responses has an impact on one's overall subjective well-being (e.g., Stutzer and Frey, 2008). These effects have been shown first and foremost in relation to different travel modes (e.g., Olsson et al., 2013; Abenoza et al., 2017; Friman et al., 2017). A consistent finding across different geographies is that active travel modes (walking, cycling) are associated with higher levels of satisfaction and well-being than car and public transport, and that public transport is associated with the lowest level of well-being (Ye and Titheridge, 2017; Olsson et al., 2013; St-Louis et al., 2014). The effect of different public transport modes is not consistent, and it appears to depend on the context and the quality of local public transport. For instance, Lunke (2020) found in Oslo that subway users had the highest travel satisfaction, followed by tram, then train and bus scored lowest. Abenoza et al. (2017) found for Stockholm that bus users had the highest satisfaction, followed by train, metro, and tram. Potential explanations for the positive effect of using active modes on well-being include the involved physical activity (Ekkekakis et al., 2008), the higher level of interaction with the environment (Gatersleben and Uzzell, 2007), the experience of autonomy and mastery (Ettema and Smajic, 2015; Ziegler and Schwanen, 2011), and the options active modes offer for social interactions in one's neighbourhood (Ziegler and Schwanen, 2011).

The effect of car driving on well-being via one's mood depends on driving circumstances. Longer duration (e.g., long commutes) and congestion lead to more stress and lower levels of subjective well-being (Novaco et al., 1990). In addition, road characteristics have an impact on the well-being effects of driving (Ettema et al., 2013). The use of public transport is consistently associated with lower satisfaction and lower subjective well-being across geographies (Olsson et al., 2013; St-Louis et al., 2014). Factors that lead to lower satisfaction and well-being while using public transport include critical incidents, such as delays or unpleasant interaction with co-travellers or staff (Friman and Gärling, 2001). More general factors that influence travel satisfaction and well-being across modes include longer trip durations, crowding and congestion.

Travel may also influence well-being in an indirect way, by facilitating participation in meaningful or pleasant activities that contribute to life goals (Pychyl and Little, 1998; Oishi et al., 1999). Levels of access to important destinations for a person and the potential to travel ('motility') therefore influence well-being (not conceptualized in Figure 12.1, but explicitly conceptualized in Figure 2.1) (Mokhtarian, 2019). Lack of transport options may lead to reduced participation in activities and access to relevant activities (Lucas, 2012). Various studies indicate that insufficient transport options are associated with less involvement in social, cultural, and economic activities and lower subjective well-being (Lucas, 2012; Delbosc and Currie, 2011). Well-being also depends on characteristics of the environment, as explained above (arrow 4) and as conceptualized and explained in Chapter 2, for example, because of the attractiveness of the environment, or noise levels.

12.2.2   Second Order Relationships

In addition to these first order relationships between travel behaviour and health, Figure 12.1 show that several second order relationships exist:

1. Socio-economic and demographic characteristics and travel behaviour (arrows 5, 6, 7)
2. Physical activity: walking and cycling versus physical activity that is not related to travel (arrow 8)
3. Subjective well-being and the use of active modes (arrow 10)
4. Health and travel behaviour (arrow 11)
5. Self-selection effects (arrows 5 and 9)

Socio-economic and demographic variables (arrows 5, 6, 7)

The importance of socio-economic and demographic variables for travel behaviour (arrow 5) is generally recognized, examples being age, education level, gender, and household characteristics (see Chapter 16). In addition, as conceptualized via arrow 6, demographic variables can also influence the impact of physical activity, crashes/falls and pollution on health. In other words, health impacts may be moderated by personal characteristics, and these effects are studied much less than the direct health effects of travel behaviour. For example, a fall from a bicycle may have more impact on someone who is 85 years old than on a 14-year old. As another example, individuals who are overweight or have diabetes profit more from being physically active than other groups (Bauman, 2004).

The effects of socio-demographic characteristics on travel-related health outcomes may be contradictory, depending on the four mechanisms as conceptualized by arrows 1–4. For instance, whereas the elderly may benefit the most from physical activities such as walking and cycling, they are also more vulnerable to crashes/falls (and will be more seriously injured) and more sensitive to pollution. Note that personal characteristics such as age and gender can also influence non-travel related physical activity (arrow 7) and its impact on health, as well as the impact of well-being on health.

Interaction of travel-related physical activity and other physical activity (arrow 8)

Walking and cycling are not the only two forms of physical activity (Figure 12.1), and therefore people may substitute other physical activities, such as going to the gym, with walking or cycling. This will reduce the additional health benefits of walking and cycling. On the other hand, it is also possible that because people who walk or cycle may feel fitter, they engage more in other forms of physical activity. We hypothesize that both effects occur, probably for different (groups of) people. The scarce studies in this area differ with respect to their results. Forsyth et al. (2008) and Troped et al. (2010) conclude that differences in spatial setting influence the amount of transport and leisure walking, but overall physical activity is not affected. Brown et al. (2015) found that the introduction of a light rail system in Salt Lake City resulted in an increase of physical activity in access and egress travel, and that also the total level of physical activity (PA) increased. Saelens et al. (2014: 854) found that 'transit users had more daily overall physical activity and more total walking than did non-transit users but did not differ on either non-transit-related walking or non-walking physical activity'. Clearly, more research is needed to better understand the relationships between travel related and other forms of physical activity. From a policy point of view, it is very important to know to what extent transport policies that result in more walking and cycling have *additional* health benefits.

Causality of subjective well-being and the use of active modes (arrow 10)

While the use of active travel is mostly assumed to lead to higher travel satisfaction and higher subjective well-being, it can also be argued that people with a higher subjective well-being are more likely to use active modes (arrow 10). While this has, to the authors' knowledge, not been investigated in the context of travel, some studies have addressed the relationship between subjective well-being and physical activity in general. Although most studies focus on the effect of physical activity on mood and mental health (e.g., Wood et al., 2013; Paluska and Schwenk 2000), only a few have investigated the reversed causality. Baruth et al. (2011) investigated the impact of subjective well-being on the effect of a physical activity intervention programme, and found that those with higher subjective well-being were more likely to increase their levels of physical activity. Other studies (e.g., Standage et al., 2012) suggest that the causality might work both ways. The effect of active travel on subjective well-being should therefore be treated carefully, since ignoring the bi-directional causality would lead to an overestimation of the well-being effects of active travel.

Health and travel behaviour (arrow 11)

Travel behaviour not only influences health via the multiple routes conceptualized in Figure 12.1, but health also influences travel behaviour. For example, people with a lower health level might walk and cycle more to improve their health, but it is also possible that their lower health level results in lower levels of walking and cycling. De Haas et al. (2021) found that the latter effect dominates, at least for cycling: people with a higher body mass index (BMI) cycle less than average.

Self-selection effects (arrows 5 and 9)

Related to the causality discussion above, we next address self-selection effects (which are also covered in Chapter 5). People often self-select in several respects. We limit ourselves to self-selection that is related to attitudes, and therefore first generally discuss the importance of attitudes in travel behaviour modelling. Above we already discussed that socio-economic and demographic variables influence travel behaviour (arrow 5). In addition, people's attitudes influence their travel behaviour. Regardless of age, gender, income etc., some people have a preference to travel by car, public transport or bike, or they prefer to walk. From the perspective of health, it is important to realize that attitudes not only influence mode choice (e.g., Lyu and Forsyth, 2021), but also the way people make use of modes, an example being the question if people use information and communication (ICT) devices while driving (increasing risk factors) (Buhler et al., 2021).

We now limit ourselves to the role of attitudes for self-selection. Arrow 9 conceptualizes that people may self-select with respect to residential location, a phenomenon called 'residential self-selection' (RSS) – see Chapter 5. For example, people who like travelling by active modes (because of a pro-environmental attitude, or for health reasons), may self-select residential areas that support the use of these modes. Ettema and Nieuwenhuis (2015) conclude that differences in the cycling frequency of people living in different neighbourhoods were partly explained by cycling preferences of people, and these cycling preferences influenced RSS. On the other hand, Van Dyck et al. (2011) conclude that walking behaviour of people living in different neighbourhoods in Ghent was primarily the result of neighbourhood walkability, not so much of walking preferences related RSS. Finally, Handy et al. (2006) found that walking related RSS only limitedly explains differences in walking frequency across neighbourhoods in Northern California. They also noted a substantial independent effect of the built environment on walking frequency. For a review of the literature on the effect of the built environment on walking, cycling and physical activity, we refer to Smith et al. (2017).

It could also be that (perceived) health of people influences their residential choice (this is not explicitly conceptualized in Figure 12.1). For instance, a person with lung disease may choose a residential location so that they are not exposed to high concentrations of pollutants of traffic (or other sources) (Anselin and Le Gallo, 2006). Or people who are sensitive to noise might select a dwelling in a quiet area. Research in this area is scarce and inconclusive (see, for example, Wardman and Bristow, 2004; Van Praag and Baarsma, 2001; Nijland et al., 2007).

To conclude, it is important to realize that self-selection effects should be better understood for assessing the relationships between travel behaviour and health.

12.3   TRAVEL BEHAVIOUR AND THE HEALTH OF NON-TRAVELLERS

We now broaden our scope to address the health of non-travellers. Travel behaviour of people does not only influence the health of the traveller, but also others, both other travellers and non-travellers. These are called 'external effects' or 'externalities' in economic literature (see Chapter 13). Because we discussed the relationships of all travellers in Section 12.2, we here limit ourselves to the non-traveller. Figure 12.2 conceptualizes health impacts of non-travellers.

Figure 12.2 shows that travel behaviour of people has an impact on the health of others first of all via nearby or 'local' effects (noise, air pollution, risks, and 'barrier effects' (e.g., crossing ability) are the dominant effects) (arrow 1). Risks of non-travellers, such as the risks of being affected by a crashed aeroplane or exploding lorry carrying fuels, are relatively rare events. People living or having daily activities (office, school) near trafficked roads are exposed to noise and pollution, as well as experience the consequences of lower levels of liveability (see also Figure 2.1). Traffic also contributes to larger scale air pollution in the form of smog (not explicitly included in Figure 12.2, to keep it simple), but in Organisation for Economic

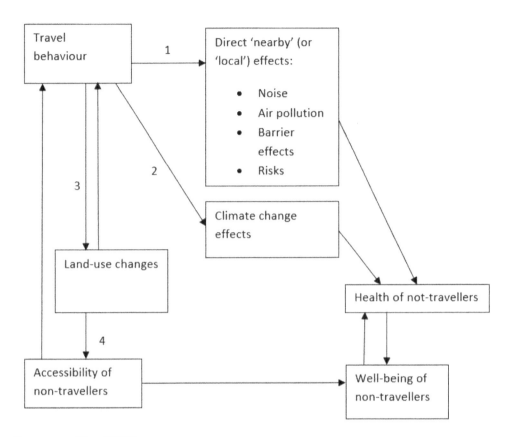

Source: van Wee (2018).

Figure 12.2 A conceptual model for the dominant relationships between travel behaviour and health of others than the non-travellers

Co-operation and Development (OECD) countries smog is less of a problem than a few decades ago. In addition, people travelling and infrastructure in general result in barrier effects: the more traffic, the more difficult it is to cross streets. And major infrastructures like motorways, other main roads, or railways have limited options to cross at all. Secondly transport contributes to climate change, mainly due to CO_2 emissions (see Chapter 10) and climate change will have a range of health-related effects (e.g., Patz et al., 2005), such as extremely hot temperatures, exposure to flood risks, and the spread of diseases (arrow 2). Next, the transport system and travel behaviour of people in the long run induces land-use changes – see the literature on land-use and transport interaction (e.g., Wegener and Fürst, 1999, and Chapter 5 of this book). For example, if more people travel by car (as opposed to other modes), then shops, companies, and services value car accessibility higher and next might prefer to be placed at locations that are accessible by car (arrow 3). For example, a shift of activities (employment, schools, shops, etc.) to locations accessible by car might result in social exclusion of those not having access to a car, decreasing the well-being of those people, and their health. Land use changes also influence the proximity of green space and reduce the potential health benefits from being close to green space (arrow 4).

To conclude, travel behaviour influences health of non-travellers via many complex mechanisms. Although the conceptual model is not as complex as the model for health of travellers, it is difficult to include all mechanisms in empirical research, possibly resulting in biased results.

12.4   CONCLUSIONS

The main conclusions from this chapter are:

1. Health is a topic of growing importance in transport research and in policy making.
2. Superficially, the impact of travel behaviour on health of travellers seems straightforward, and the argument is related to the level of physical activity (walking and cycling), air pollution intake, casualties, and subjective well-being. However, the relationships between travel behaviour and health are complex. Travel behaviour influences health via multiple direct and indirect routes, and feedbacks and self-selection effects are all evident. In addition, travel behaviour not only influences the health of the traveller, but also of non-travellers, such as people exposed to pollution and noise. The complex nature of the links between travel behaviour and health suggest that researchers should consider advanced research methods.

The second conclusion raises three further recommendations for future research:

3. Because of these complex relationships it is difficult to assess the quantitative impacts of travel behaviour on health. It is not impossible to include all mechanisms included in our conceptual models, and therefore research can easily draw 'wrong' conclusions. Research into the area of health and travel should preferably make the conceptual structure of variables (not) included explicit, and it should also discuss the importance of not including important relationships.
4. Because it is difficult to quantify the effects of travel behaviour on health, it is problematic to include health effects in *ex ante* assessments of candidate policies, such as cost–benefit analyses (CBAs) and multi-criteria analyses (MCAs), especially if quantitative effects are needed, such as in case of CBA (see Chapter 15).
5. Several relationships between travel behaviour and health are still poorly understood, and consequently much additional research is needed before health effects can be included in *ex ante* evaluations of candidate transport policy options. Important topics include the interactions between travel behaviour and other physical activity, the complex relationship between cycling and health, and self-selection effects.

NOTE

1.   This chapter is partly based on van Wee and Ettema (2016) and van Wee (2018).

REFERENCES

Abenoza, R. F., O. Cats and Y.O. Susilo (2017), 'Travel satisfaction with public transport: Determinants, user classes, regional disparities and their evolution', *Transportation Research Part A: Policy and Practice*, 95, 64–84.

Abenoza, R.F., D. Ettema and Y.O. Susilo (2018), 'Do accessibility, vulnerability, opportunity, and travel characteristics have uniform impacts on traveler experience?', *Transportation Research Part A: Policy and Practice*, 114, 38–51.

Anselin, L. and J. Le Gallo (2006), 'Interpolation of air quality measures in hedonic house price models: Spatial aspects' ['Interpolation des mesures de la qualité de l'air dans les modèles hédoniste de l'estimation immobilière: Aspects spatiaux'], *Spatial Economic Analysis*, 1(1), 31–52.

Baruth, M., D. Lee, X. Sui, T.S. Church, B.H. Marcus, S. Wilcox and S.N. Blair (2011), 'Emotional outlook on life predicts increases in physical activity among initially inactive men', *Health Education and Behavior*, 38(2), 150–58.

Bauer, J., D. Klingelhöfer, W. Maier, L. Schwettmann and D.A. Groneberg (2020), 'Prediction of hospital visits for the general inpatient care using floating catchment area methods: A reconceptualization of spatial accessibility', *International Journal of Health Geographics*, 19(1), Article 29.

Bauman, A.E. (2004), 'Updating the evidence that physical activity is good for health: an epidemiological review 2000–2003', *Journal of Science and Medicine in Sport*, 7(1), 6–19.

Brown, B.B., C.M. Werner, C.P. Tribby, H.J. Miller and K.R. Smith (2015), 'Transit Use, Physical Activity, and Body Mass Index Changes: Objective Measures Associated With Complete Street Light-Rail Construction', *American Journal of Public Health*, 105(7), 1468–74.

Buhler, T., E. Comby, L. Vaudor, L. and T. von Pape (2021), 'Beyond "good" and "bad" cyclists. On compensation effects between risk taking, safety equipment and secondary tasks', *Journal of Transport and Health*, 22, 101131.

Cheng, Y.-H. and J.-W. Yan (2011), 'Comparisons of particulate matter, CO, and CO_2 levels in underground and ground-level stations in the Taipei mass rapid transit system', *Atmospheric Environment*, 45(28), 4882–91.

Churchill, S.A. and R. Smyth (2019), 'Transport poverty and subjective wellbeing', *Transportation Research Part A: Policy and Practice*, 124, 40–54.

Cohen, J.M., S. Boniface and S. Watkins (2014), 'Health implications of transport planning, development and operations', *Journal of Transport and Health*, 1(1), 63–72.

De Haas, M., M. Kroesen, C. Chorus, S. Hoogendoorn-Lanser and S. Hoogendoorn (2021), 'Causal relations between body-mass index, self-rated health and active travel: An empirical study based on longitudinal data', *Journal of Transport and Health*, 22, 101113.

Delbosc, A. and G. Currie (2011), 'Exploring the relative influences of transport disadvantage and social exclusion on well-being', *Transport Policy*, 18(4), 555–62.

Diener, E. and M.Y. Chan (2011), 'Happy people live longer: Subjective well-being contributes to health and longevity', *Applied Psychology: Health and Well-being*, 3(1), 1–43.

Diener, E., S.D. Pressman, J. Hunter and D. Delgadillo-Chase (2017), 'If, why, and when subjective well-being influences health, and future needed research', *Applied Psychology: Health and Well-Being*, 9(2), 133–67.

Ekkekakis, P., E.E. Hall and S.J. Petruzzello (2008), 'The relationship between exercise intensity and affective responses demystified: To crack the 40-year-old nut, replace the 40-year-old nutcracker!' *Annals of Behavioral Medicine*, 35(2), 136–49.

Elvik, R. and R. Goel (2019), 'Safety-in-numbers: An updated meta-analysis of estimates', *Accident Analysis and Prevention*, 129, 136–47.

Ettema, D., T. Gärling, L.E. Olsson and M. Friman (2010), 'Out-of-home activities, daily travel, and subjective well-being', *Transportation Research Part A*, 44(9), 723–32.

Ettema, D., T. Gärling, L.E. Olsson, M. Friman and S. Moerdijk (2013), 'The road to happiness: Measuring Dutch car drivers' satisfaction with travel', *Transport Policy*, 27, 171–78.

Ettema, D. and R. Nieuwenhuis (2015), 'Residential self-selection effects and TOD development: How does relocation motivation influence the effect of built environment?', Paper presented at 2015 TRB Annual Meeting.

Ettema, D. and I. Smajic (2015), 'Walking, places and wellbeing', *Geographical Journal*, 181(2), 102–09.

Forsyth, A., M. Hearst, J. Oakes and K.H. Schmitz (2008), 'Design and destinations: Factors influencing walking and total physical activity', *Urban Studies*, 45(9), 1973–96.

Friman, M. and T. Gärling (2001), 'Frequency of negative critical incidents and satisfaction with public transport services. II', *Journal of Retailing and Consumer Services*, 8(2), 105–114.

Friman, M., T. Gärling, D. Ettema and L.E. Olsson (2017), 'How does travel affect emotional well-being and life satisfaction?', *Transportation Research Part A: Policy and Practice*, 106, 170–80.

Gatersleben, B. and D. Uzzell (2007), 'Affective appraisals of the daily commute: comparing perceptions of drivers, cyclists, walkers and users of public transport', *Environment and Behavior*, 39(3), 416–31.

Glazener, A., K. Sanchez, T. Ramani, J. Zietsma, M.J. Nieuwenhuijsen, J.S. Mindell, M. Fox and H. Khreis (2021), 'Fourteen pathways between urban transportation and health: A conceptual model and literature review', *Journal of Transport and Health*, 21, 101070.

Handy, S. (2014). 'Health and travel', in T. Gärling, D. Ettema and M. Friman (eds), *Handbook of Sustainable Travel*, Dordrecht/Heidelberg/New York/London: Springer, 199–214.

Handy, S., X. Cao and P.L. Mokhtarian (2006), 'Self-selection in the relationship between the built environment and walking: Empirical evidence from Northern California', *Journal of the American Planning Association*, 72(1), 55–74.

Handy, S., B. van Wee and M. Kroesen (2014), 'Promoting Cycling for Transport: Research Needs and Challenges', *Transport Reviews*, 34(1), 4–24.

Janssen, N.A.H., B. Brunekreef, G. Hoek and P. Keuken (2002), *Traffic-related air pollution and health*. Utrecht/Apeldoorn: Utrecht University, Institute for Risk Assessment Sciences, Environmental and Occupational Health Division / TNO Milieu, Energie en Procesinnovatie.

Lee, A.E., S. Underwood and S. Handy (2015), 'Crashes and other safety-related incidents in the formation of attitudes toward bicycling', *Transportation Research Part F*, 28, 14–24.

Lee, J.-E., H.J. Lim and Y.-Y. Kim (2021), 'Publication trends in research on particulate matter and health impact over a 10-year period: 2009–2018', *Environmental Health and Toxicology*, 36(1), e2021005.

Lucas, K. (2012), 'Transport and social exclusion: Where are we now?', *Transport Policy*, 20, 115–13.

Lunke, E.B. (2020). 'Commuters' satisfaction with public transport', *Journal of Transport & Health*, 16, 100842.

Lyu, Y. and A. Forsyth (2021), 'Attitudes, perceptions, and walking behavior in a Chinese city', *Journal of Transport and Health*, 21, 101047.

Mackett, R.L. and Thoreau, R. (2015). 'Transport, social exclusion and health', *Journal of Transport and Health*, 2(4), 610–17.

McNabola, A., B. Broderick and L.W. Gill (2007), 'Optimal cycling and walking speed for minimum absorption of traffic emissions in the lungs', *Journal of Environmental Science and Health - Part A Toxic/Hazardous Substances and Environmental Engineering*, 42(13), 1999–2007.

Mindell, J.S., D. Leslie and M. Wardlaw (2012), 'Exposure-Based, 'Like-for-Like' Assessment of Road Safety by Travel Mode Using Routine Health Data', *Plos One*, 4 December.

Mitsakou, C., J.P. Adamson, A. Doutsi, H. Brunt, S.J. Jones, A.M. Gowers and K.S. Exley (2021), 'Assessing the exposure to air pollution during transport in urban areas – Evidence review', *Journal of Transport and Health*, 21, 101064.

Mokhtarian, P.L. (2019), 'Subjective well-being and travel: retrospect and prospect', *Transportation*, 46, 493–513.

Nijland, H.A., S. Hartemink, I. Van Kamp and B. Van Wee (2007), 'The influence of sensitivity for road traffic noise on residential location: Does it trigger a process of spatial selection?', *Journal of the Acoustical Society of America*, 122(3), 1595–601.

Novaco, R.W., D. Stokols and L. Milanesi (1990), 'Objective and subjective dimensions of travel impedance as determinants of commuting stress', *American Journal of Community Psychology*, 18(2), 231–57.

Nyhan, M., A. McNabola and B Misstear (2014), 'Evaluating artificial neural networks for predicting minute ventilation and lung deposited dose in commuting cyclists', *Journal of Transport and Health*, 1(4), 305–15.

Oishi, S., E.F. Diener, R.E. Lucas and E.M. Suh (1999), 'Cross-cultural variations in predictors of life satisfaction: Perspectives from needs and values', *Personality and Social Psychology Bulletin*, 25(8), 980–90.

Olsson, L.E., T. Gärling, D. Ettema, M. Friman and S. Fujii (2013), 'Happiness and satisfaction with work commute', *Social Indicators Research*, 111(1), 255–63.

Paluska, S.A. and T.L. Schwenk (2000), 'Physical activity and mental health: Current concepts', *Sports Medicine*, 29(3), 167–80.

Patz, J.A., Campbell-Lendrum, D., Holloway, T. and Foley, J. A. (2005), Impact of regional climate change on human health. Nature, 438, 310–317.

Pychyl, T.A., and B.R. Little (1998), 'Dimensional specificity in the prediction of subjective well-being: Personal projects in pursuit of the PhD', *Social Indicators Research*, 45(1–3), 423–73.

Saelens, B.E., A. Vernez Moudon, B. Kang, P.M. Hurvitz and C. Zhou (2014), 'Relation between higher physical activity and public transit use', *American Journal of Public Health* 104(5), 854–59.

Şahin, Ü.A., B. Onat, B. Stakeeva, T. Ceran and P. Karim (2012), 'PM10 concentrations and the size distribution of Cu and Fe-containing particles in Istanbul's subway system', *Transportation Research Part D*, 17(1), 48–53.

Schepers, P., E. Fishman, R. Beelen, E. Heinen, W. Wijnen and J. Parkin (2015), 'The mortality impact of bicycle paths and lanes related to physical activity, air pollution exposure and road safety', *Journal of Transport and Health*, 2(4), 460–73.

Smith, M., J. Hosking, A. Woodward, K. Witten, A. MacMillan, A. Field, P. Baas and H. Mackie (2017), 'Systematic literature review of built environment effects on physical activity and active transport – an update and new findings on health equity', *International Journal of Behavioral Nutrition and Physical Activity*, 14(1), Paper 158.

Standage, M., F.B. Gillison, N. Ntoumanis and D.C. Treasure (2012), 'Predicting students' physical activity and health-related well-being: A prospective cross-domain investigation of motivation across school physical education and exercise settings', *Journal of Sport and Exercise Psychology*, 34(1), 37–60.

St-Louis, E., K. Manaugh, D. Van Lierop and A. El-Geneidy (2014), 'The happy commuter: A comparison of commuter satisfaction across modes', *Transportation Research Part F*, 26, 160–70.

Stutzer, A. and S.B.S. Frey (2008). 'Stress That Doesn't Pay: The Commuting Paradox', *The Scandinavian Journal of Economics*, 110(2), 339–66.

Troped, P.J., J.S. Wilson, C.E. Matthews, E.K. Cromley and S.J. Melly (2010), 'The built environment and location-based physical activity', *American Journal of Preventive Medicine*, 38(4), 429–38.

UK Department of Health and Social Care (2019), 'Physical activity for adults and older adults'. https://assets.publishing.service.gov.uk/government/uploads/system/uploads/attachment_data/file/1054541/physical-activity-for-adults-and-older-adults.pdf (Accessed 23/05/2023)

US Department of Health and Human Services (2019), 'Physical Activity Guidelines for Americans, 2nd edn'. https://health.gov/sites/default/files/2019–09/Physical_Activity_Guidelines_2nd_edition.pdf. (Accessed 23/05/2023)

Van Dyck, D., G. Cardon, B. Deforche, N. Owen and I. De Bourdeaudhuij (2011), 'Relationships between neighborhood walkability and adults' physical activity: How important is residential self-selection?' *Health & Place*, 17(4), 1011–14.

Van Praag, B.M.S. and B.E. Baarsma (2001), 'The Shadow Price of Aircraft Noise Nuisance', Tinbergen Institute Discussion Paper, No. 01–010/3.

van Wee, B. (2007), 'Environmental effects of urban traffic', in T. Garling and L. Steg (eds), *Threats from Car Traffic to the Quality of Urban Life. Problems, Causes, and Solutions*, Amsterdam: Elsevier, 9-32.

van Wee, B. (2018), 'Land use policy, travel behavior and health', in M. Nieuwenhuijsen and H. Khreis (eds), *Integrating Human Health into Urban and Transport Planning*, Dordrecht/Heidelberg/New York/London: Springer, 253–269.

van Wee, B. and D. Ettema (2016), 'Travel behaviour and health: A conceptual model and research agenda', *Journal of Transport and Health*, 3(3), 240–48.

Wardman, M. and A.L. Bristow (2004), 'Traffic related noise and air quality valuations: Evidence from stated preference residential choice models', *Transportation Research Part D*, 9(1), 1–27.

Walasek, L., G.D. Brown and G.D. Ovens (2019), 'Subjective well-being and valuation of future health states: Discrepancies between anticipated and experienced life satisfaction', *Journal of Applied Social Psychology*, 49(12), 746–54.

Wegener, M. and Fürst, F. (1999), Land-Use Transport Interaction: State of the Art. Transland. Integration of Transport and Land Use Planning. Work Package 2, Deliverable D2a. Institute of Spatial Planning, University of Dortmund, Dortmund.

WHO (2020) (World Health Organization), 'Basis documents, forty-ninth edition. https://apps.who.int/gb/bd/pdf_files/BD_49th-en.pdf, assessed 22-5-2023, page 1. (Accessed 23/05/2023)

Wood, C., C. Angus, J. Pretty, G. Sandercock and J. Barton (2013), 'A randomised control trial of physical activity in a perceived environment on self-esteem and mood in UK adolescents', *International Journal of Environmental Health Research*, 23(4), 311–20.

Ye, R. and H. Titheridge (2017), 'Satisfaction with the commute: The role of travel mode choice, built environment and attitudes', *Transportation Research Part D: Transport and Environment*, 52, 535–47.

Ziegler, F. and T. Schwanen (2011), '"I like to go out to be energised by different people": An exploratory analysis of mobility and wellbeing in later life', *Ageing and Society*, 31(5), 758–81.

PART III
TRANSPORT POLICY AND RESEARCH

13
Transport policy

Jan Anne Annema

13.1   INTRODUCTION

In Chapters 3 to 6 the different factors are discussed which explain mobility. Broadly speaking, people and companies base the decision to travel or to transport freight by weighing the private benefits and costs of the trip. A trip to a certain location is beneficial to them if it fulfils their needs. The private costs of a trip consist of monetary costs, travel time, and effort. This chapter shifts the range of view from the private to the government perspective. Governments also weigh the costs and benefits of mobility, but they also take a societal perspective. If a government concludes that the transport market from a societal perspective results in undesired outcomes (e.g., congestion, air pollution, traffic casualties) they often intervene with transport policy.

The aim of this chapter is twofold. The first aim is to explain the main reasons why governments intervene in the transport market. Secondly, a concise overview is given of the dominant transport policies. Transport policy covers many topics, much more than can be discussed in this chapter. For more detail and a far more in-depth analysis of transport planning issues, we refer the reader to Banister (2002). Guy Peters (2018) discusses in his book policy problems and policy design issues which we will only touch upon in this chapter. Although Guy Peters' book is not specifically aimed at transport policies, valuable lessons can be learned from his book for transport policy-making.

Transport is still one of the most regulated sectors in any economy as already noted by Button and Gillingwater (1986). Governments provide and own transport infrastructure, tax car owners, subsidize public transport, decide by implementing traffic rules who has right of way, implement emission standards to make vehicles cleaner and safer, and so forth. There are many reasons why governments intervene with these policies in the transport market. Different political parties and different political systems all over the world will have different considerations. However, generally speaking, all over the world three main reasons can be found for government interference in the transport market:

1. Market failure;
2. Equity reasons;
3. To generate revenues.

Market failure is an economic concept meaning that the market itself will not result in optimal outcomes from a societal perspective. In economic jargon: the market does not result in efficient allocation of resources. The 'transport market' stands for the interaction between, on the one hand, suppliers of transport services such as the infrastructure providers (in most cases governments), public transport companies, and vehicle manufacturers, and, on the other hand, people and shippers who demand transport services. Resources are any scarce goods that are needed to satisfy people's needs or wants. Transport-related examples of scarce goods are road capacity, cars, aircraft seating capacity, clean air, quiet living areas, land for transport facilities, and so forth. If a market does not result in an efficient allocation of resources, economists mean that the market cannot sustain 'desirable' outcomes or stop 'undesirable' outcomes. In Section 13.3 we will discuss efficient allocation of resources (or Pareto optimal) more in detail. For now, it is important to realize that when people decide to make a car trip (desirable outcome for them) they do not take into account, for example, the fact that they pollute the air (a scarce good) for people living close to the road when driving, so the result of their choice is poorer air quality for others (an undesirable result). This is a classic example of a transport market failure related to the existence of so-called transport external effects. In Section 13.2 we will explain the concept of external effects more in detail. An important policy aim for many governments is to maximize efficiency in the transport market (Section 13.3).

Equity reasons also explain why governments intervene in the transport market. The equity policy objectives can vary but are related to the distribution of the costs and benefits of transport in a fair way, or to give all people at least a sufficient ('fair') amount of mobility and accessibility. For example, many governments subsidize public transport because they think it is desirable that all people in a country have nearby public transport at their disposal; even in very low population density areas where running a profitable public transport service is impossible. Section 13.4 focuses on 'equity issues' related to transport policy-making.

Finally, governments may tax the transport market as a source of general *revenue*. For example, the total car tax revenue in the Netherlands was around 17 billion euros in 2018 consisting of vehicle purchase tax, fixed annual car tax, fuel levies, and the addition of the private use of company cars in the payroll and income tax (Algemene Rekenkamer, 2019). In the Dutch tax law it is motivated that these car taxes are partly meant to be supportive to improve the transport system but it is specifically mentioned in the law that this money is also meant to be an important and stable revenue stream for the government which can be spent for any purpose politicians choose to.

Section 13.5 explains that next to improving efficiency and equity also politicians' self-interest is a reason for implementing transport policies. Section 13.6 discusses criteria that can be used to define healthy transport policies. Section 13.7 gives some examples of transport policy-making. Conclusions can be found in Section 13.8.

13.2   EXTERNAL EFFECTS OF TRANSPORT

An important reason for government intervention is transport market failure in the form of external effects. External effects of transport are mostly costs (rarely benefits, see below) which people and shippers do not take into account when deciding to make a trip or to transport freight. What they do take into account are the costs (the resistance factors, Chapter 6) for themselves (internal costs) such as their travel time, fuel costs, and effort. However, when deciding to make a trip they also produce costs – unintentionally – to third parties which are outside the decision of the trip makers because the trip makers do not have to compensate for those costs. External effects can be both negative (costs) as well as positive (benefits) but almost all debates and research in transport is on negative external costs and how to decrease these. External costs (or external benefits) accrue per definition to a third party. A third party can be a non-traffic participant such as people living close to a road who are exposed to poor air quality (see example above). Also, other traffic participants can be a third party such as cyclists who may be at risk of an accident because a car driver has decided to drive on the same road. Most external costs are related to the environment, safety, and accessibility. Chapters 9–12 have introduced the reader to these areas and Chapter 8 has discussed the importance of technologies for these areas. This chapter introduces the reader to the area of external costs from a policy perspective.

13.2.1   External Costs

Negative external effects are called external costs. Verhoef (1996) distinguishes three kinds of external transport costs:

1. costs due to the use of transport means such as road vehicles, ships, or aeroplanes;
2. costs due to vehicle ownership and availability;
3. costs due to infrastructure.

We will now discuss these three kinds of external costs more in detail.

Costs due to the use of transport means such as road vehicles, ships, or aeroplanes

The use of cars, lorries, trains, aeroplanes, and ships result in external costs. Figure 13.1 shows the share of external cost categories for transportation within the EU28 for 2016 (the UK was part of the EU at that time) (Van Essen et al., 2019). The figure also shows the share of the different transport modes. In order to estimate these shares, all the different cost categories are expressed in money units so that they have the same unit. As external costs are per definition not included in market transactions, it may be a surprise that the external costs can be expressed in money units at all. However, there are different methods developed to estimate people's willingness to pay (WTP) to avoid external costs (or people's willingness to accept (WTA) a monetary reward to compensate for external costs). For more details on this issue, see Chapter 14. These WTPs and WTAs are used in Figure 13.1 to estimate the external costs per category and mode. Delucchi and McCubbin (2010) give an overview of external costs for transport in the US; Van Essen et al., (2019) provide an extensive 'Handbook on the external costs of transport' for the EU with, amongst others, all kinds of detailed information on WTPs and WTAs. Below we will briefly explain that estimating these WTPs and WTAs is difficult and sometimes severely criticized.

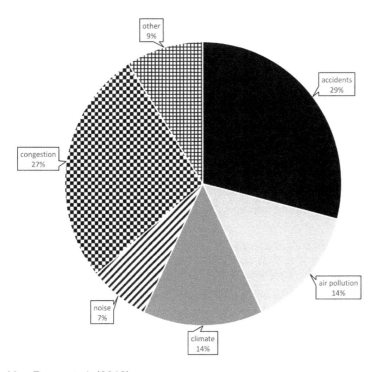

Source: Van Essen et al. (2019).

Figure 13.1   Share of the different cost categories on total external costs within the
EU28 for 2016

Accidents are shown to be an important external cost category (Figure 13.1). For example, cars in Europe had an external accident cost of more than 200 billion euros in 2016 according to Van Essen et al. (2019). Cars pose a relatively large risk for other road users to be involved in an accident with sometimes huge implications ('costs') such as deaths and severe injuries (see Chapter 11 on safety). The WTP to avoid these risks is high. Also, congestion is an important external cost category according to the data presented. When a car driver decides to use the road during peak hours s/he causes unintendedly time delays for other road users which s/he does not have to compensate. The valuation of congestion costs are depicted in Figure 13.1 using 'Value of Travel Times' (see Chapter 6).

Figure 13.1 includes for accidents and congestion the direct external costs. However, as also explained in Chapter 6, the risks of having an accident or losing time in a traffic jam can motivate people not to travel. These travelling avoidance costs are also part of external costs. Not including these avoidance costs could be an important omission. For example, Adams (1999) showed that in 1971 around 80% of British children went to school by themselves. In 2014 this share has decreased to 12% for seven to ten year-olds and 69% for 11 to 13 years-old (UK National Travel Survey, 2014). The most important reason for the seven to ten year-olds is that parents are afraid of their children being involved in traffic accidents. The external costs of preventing children from cycling or walking to school relate to freedom loss for children to partially develop themselves in a space without parental supervision and, probably, to children losing the opportunity to have some 'easy' daily physical exercise.

Costs due to vehicle ownership and availability

The second external costs category distinguished by Verhoef is related to the non-use phase of vehicles. For example, vehicles sometimes use space for parking in the public domain for which the vehicle owner does not have to pay or the payment is not sufficient to cover all costs. Also, environmental effects related to producing and scrapping vehicles, aircraft, or ships are part of this external cost category. Here, a relation can be made with the concept of Life Cycle Analysis (LCA; see Chapters 8 and 9). LCA takes the environmental impacts into account over the whole life cycle of a product such as a car. So, in those kinds of analyses, the external costs can be found related to the non-use phase of products.

Costs due to infrastructure

Finally, external costs arise according to Verhoef because of the construction and existence of transport infrastructure. In a review, Geurs et al. (2009) point out that the mere presence of transport infrastructures (roads, railway lines, waterways, etc.) may affect the quality of the physical environment. This applies to, for example, noise, visual quality, light pollution and people's perception of the environment or neighbourhood, aesthetics, and quality of life. Furthermore, Geurs et al. (2009) cite research that showed that new or existing transport schemes, such as roads or railways, can have detrimental social impacts on communities (severance). Transport infrastructure can also act as both physical and biological barriers to many wildlife species, as Kreling et al. (2019) show related to Interstate-280 in California, USA. Roads can affect the quality and quantity of available wildlife habitat, most notably through fragmentation. Furthermore, producing asphalt, making or scrapping roads and/or road maintenance can result in environmental impacts or direct negative health impacts to the construction workers which are not sufficiently reflected in their wages. These environmental and health-related impacts are also negative external costs of infrastructure; see LCA in the previous paragraph.

13.2.2   External Benefits

External benefits are the positive external effects of mobility. The existence of external benefits can be a reason for governments to intervene as in the case of external costs. These benefits work per definition outside the 'normal' market: people or shippers who participate in a transport activity do not take these positive impacts into account when they decide to make a trip. This could, as opposed to negative external effects, result in an amount of transport which is too low from a societal perspective. External benefits have been discussed for a long time. In most cases, there was confusion in these discussions about the concept. For example, some people claim that freight transport results in 'external' impacts such as lower production costs, low consumer prices, and a broad product variety. However, these benefits are all monetized impacts in the freight transport market. Producers and shippers take all of these impacts into account when deciding to transport freight. Others sometimes claim that mobility leads to external benefits such as enhanced family relations or to a smaller world as thanks to cheap aviation people can get acquainted in a relatively easy way with far-away cultures. However, these benefits are not external because they are intended. Thus, external benefits of transport are limited to the well-known classic examples such as aeroplane or train spotting. In the remainder of this chapter external transport benefits are not discussed.

13.3   MAXIMIZING WELFARE

As stated in Section 13.1 maximizing welfare (improving efficiency) is an important transport policy aim. The aim is based on the so-called economic welfare theory (a relatively easy introduction to welfare economics can be found in Johansson, 1991). The economic welfare theory states that we should strive in policy-making for Pareto optimal welfare, or Pareto efficiency. The Italian economist Vilfredo Pareto is one of the founders of the welfare theory. According to many standard economic textbooks Pareto efficiency is said to exist when no other improvements can be made in the allocation of resources to one individual without it causing a loss to others. It is important to realize that Pareto efficiency does not mean that resources are distributed fairly (see Section 13.4). A way of explaining Pareto efficiency in the transport market is to think of a policy (e.g., lowering existing fuel levies) that would result in more transport. Assume that noise nuisance is the only transport externality. The people who can make more car kilometres due to this policy are better off. However, the extra car kilometres will result in an increase in the road noise load. Perhaps lowering the fuel levy to a small extent would only result in some small traffic increase and, thus, only some small amount of extra noise load very close to the road where nobody is affected by it. By increasingly lowering the fuel levy more traffic arises and at a certain point, the first persons living close to the road will hear the increased noise load and will be perhaps bothered by it. If this is the case, these people are worse off at that point. Thus, lowering fuel levies is a Pareto efficient policy just before the point that the first people are worse off due to this policy.

The Pareto optimum is a strict criterion. Later in history, a more applicable criterion was formulated by Nicholas Kaldor and John Hicks (Hicks, 1939; Kaldor, 1993). They have stated the now so-called Kaldor-Hicks efficiency criterion (also called compensation criterion), which means that an outcome of a policy is efficient if those that are made better off could in theory compensate those that are made worse off. The compensation criterion is the most used criterion in cost–benefit analysis (CBA) (Chapter 15 and below). Related to the previous example, the Kaldor-Hicks optimum of the fuel levy decrease policy is not reached as long as the benefits to the people who can drive more than outweigh the costs of the people who suffer from the extra noise load. It is important to note that in Kaldor–Hicks it is not required that the compensation is actually being paid, merely that the possibility for compensation exists. Thus, using the Kaldor–Hicks criterion in practice, a more efficient outcome in case of the fuel levy decrease policy can in fact leave some people worse off, namely, the people who will suffer from the increased noise load and who are only in theory compensated. In contrast, using Pareto efficiency in practice nobody can become worse off.

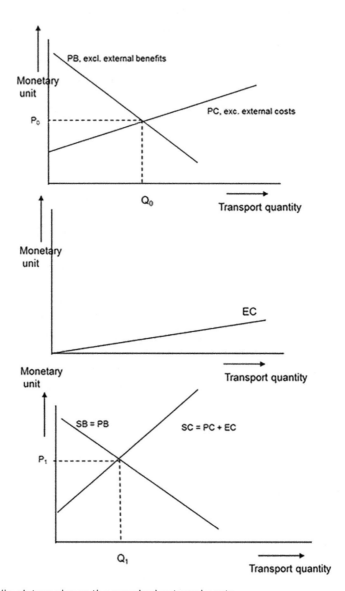

Note: The middle picture shows the marginal external costs.

Figure 13.2   Transport prices and quantities in two equilibrium situations: without external benefits and costs (top) and with external benefits and costs

Welfare theory can also be explained using Figure 13.2 (based on Schmidtchen et al., 2009 but in economic textbooks many more examples can be found). The figure shows so-called marginal costs and benefits. 'Marginal' means per extra unit of transport such as one extra passenger kilometre or one extra ton freight kilometre. The top figure (13.2a) reflects the situation on the transport market where external costs (EC, see middle picture) are not taken into account. In the top figure marginal private benefits (PB) of transport are sorted in such a way that they decrease according to the amount of transport. The explanation is that people value the kilometres they travel differently. There are highly beneficial trips for them, for example, the trips to their work where they can earn money. For these trips, they are willing to pay relatively much money, travel time, and/or effort. They make also less important trips for which they are not willing to pay much money, travel time, and/or effort. It seems obvious that people prioritize their kilometres from the most beneficial ones to the lesser beneficial ones. In Figure 13.2a the trips are sorted from higher to lower beneficial ones. For the marginal private costs (PC) it is the other way around (Figure 13.2a): it is assumed in the figure that the marginal private costs increase according to transport quantity. To be clear, the figure is schematic. In reality, it is highly probable that the private cost line will stay constant for a long while: the marginal private costs for the first kilometres are more or less the same as for the 20,000th kilometre travelled. However, for sake of clarity, an increasing marginal private cost line is assumed, because now it can be shown more clearly to the reader that there is an equilibrium at quantity Q0 with price P0. Of course, there would also be an equilibrium at the intersection assuming a constant private marginal cost line but the picture would be messier. No matter how, at Q0 with price P0 the private optimum is reached. At the equilibrium, the marginal private cost (PC) of the last kilometre travelled equals exactly the marginal private benefit (PB) of that kilometre. Adding one more kilometre would still result in marginal private benefits but, at the same time, the marginal private costs of that one more kilometre is higher. Thus, it is from a private perspective not rational to drive that extra kilometre.

As follows from the definition, private parties do not take external costs into account when deciding to make a trip. In the Figure 13.2c bottom it is depicted what would happen if marginal external costs are taken into account in the transport price. This 'taking into account' is also called internalization of external costs. The marginal social cost line will become steeper when external costs are internalized compared to the marginal private cost line (SC = PC + EC). The reason is that increasing quantities of transport often result in higher marginal external costs (see middle picture). For example, the first car or lorry kilometres hardly result in traffic jams. However, above a certain point traffic jams grow more or less exponentially in proportion as traffic quantities increase without adding new road capacity. Thus, as a result of the steeper SC line, a new equilibrium arises at price P1 and transport quantity Q1 (Figure 13.2c bottom): the so-called social optimum. Figure 13.2 shows how to internalize from a theoretical point of view: governments should increase the private transport price (P0) with a charge equal to P1 minus P0. By doing so, the social optimum in the transport market will arise resulting in less transport (Q1) compared to the situation where external costs are not internalized (Q0). In other words, in a world without internalizing external costs, there is too much traffic (Q0) from a societal point of view.

On the basis of the welfare theory governments carry out transport pricing policies. For example, one of the focus points in the 'European Strategy for Low-Emission Mobility' is a fair and efficient pricing in transport which should better reflect negative externalities of transport (DG MOVE, 2019, p. 3). Another global example, based on the notion of external costs, is urban charging schemes that are implemented or studied. Congestion charging schemes have different motivations but one of them is to internalize the external costs of road traffic. Cities such as Singapore in 1975, Oslo in 1990, Trondheim in 1991, Durham in 2002, London in 2003, Valletta and Stockholm in 2007, Milan in 2012, and Gothenburg in 2013 have implemented a kind of road or area pricing system (Ortúzar et al., 2021).

As already mentioned, societal CBA is based on the welfare theory. CBA is applied to evaluate many transport policies. For example, Bouscasse et al. (2022) applied CBA for policies aiming at decreasing transport air pollutants (fine particulate matter, $PM_{2.5}$, see Chapter10). CBA is, however, mostly used as an appraisal tool for new transport infrastructure in Western countries (Koopmans and Mouter, 2020). A CBA aims to quantify all marginal impacts of new infrastructure as much as possible and puts a monetary value to these impacts. Impacts are, for example, construction costs, decreased travel times, lower air quality, and so forth. In most cases, travel time gains are the most important marginal benefit and construction costs the most important marginal costs. The idea is that if the marginal benefits of new infrastructure outweigh the marginal costs, politicians could decide to build the new infrastructure as, by doing so, they increase total welfare in a country or region. For more details on CBA, see Chapter 15.

13.3.1   The Practice

The welfare theory may seem elegant and rather straightforward. However, implementing the theory in practice is not particularly easy. One important reason is that it is complicated to monetize external costs. To determine the charge level (P1 minus P0) or to carry out a proper CBA researchers need to know the price people or shippers are willing to pay to avoid one unit of traffic jam, noise nuisance, traffic accident, air pollution, and so forth. The problem here is that these impacts are external, thus, per definition, outside a market of supply and demand where prices are determined. Still, based on different kinds of valuation techniques scientists are capable to monetize external effects (see before). Contingent valuation methods (CVM) are prominent in trying to find people's WTPs or WTAs for goods that are not traded at markets, which external effects per definition are not. CVM are survey-based methods where people can state their preferences or where via choice experiments people's valuations for non-tradable goods can be estimated. The valuation results are uncertain and sometimes highly debated (see, for example, Aldred, 2002 and 2006). Especially, the valuation of one tonne extra or less carbon dioxide (CO_2) emissions or the valuation of damage to nature or landscapes due to new infrastructure is often highly controversial (see Niemeyer and Spash, 2001, for a critique on nature valuation). Koopmans and Mouter (2020) give in their chapter on CBA an overview of the pros and cons of CVM to find people's valuations for travel time savings and all kinds of external effects.

13.4   EQUITY

Next to policies aimed at improving efficiency, governments all over the world implement or may implement transport policies because they consider them as being fair. Equity has received growing attention in the scientific literature. In this section, only some main lines will be sketched. Banister (2018), Martens (2017), and van Wee (2011) are some examples of books by scholars that address in far more detail issues and solutions related to fair transport policies.

Equity in transport literature is often referred to as a 'fair' or 'just' distribution of transport benefits and costs (Camporeale et al., 2019). The difficulty lies in the words 'fair' and 'just'. Within a country, the better-off can travel faster and further, leaving the poor in the slow lane closer to home, as Banister (2018) notes. To judge if this is unfair or unjust and to decide if policies are required to make the distribution of faster transport more equal among income groups depends on a moral judgement. Pereira et al. (2017) point out that philosophers who think about morality have no single overarching definition of justice. In their paper, they give an overview of ethical theories of justice in political philosophy.

Relatively often mentioned ethical theories in the transport literature are utilitarianism, egalitarianism, and sufficientarianism. Utilitarianism is strongly related to CBA and holds that if the consequences of a policy imply a net welfare gain for the greater number of people, this policy is just. Egalitarianism is concerned with inequalities in society. The theory is more complicated than described here but broadly speaking an egalitarian finds a transport policy just if it maximizes the minimum level of primary goods (such as accessibility to primary schools) of the people in the worst-off position (taken from Pereira et al., 2017). People in the worst-off position could be people with low incomes in suburbs relatively far away from areas where there are many primary schools to choose from. A just egalitarian policy would, especially for these 'worst-off' people, improve school accessibility in terms of lowering travel time or 'out-of-pocket' costs to this school area for them. Sufficientarianism argues that policies are just if they result in an improvement so that everybody is sufficiently well-off ('has an adequate amount of that good'). Egalitarianian policies strive to decrease the differences between worst-off and better-off groups or areas, whilst under sufficientarianistic policies there is a threshold expressing what is 'sufficient' for all (van Wee and Geurs, 2011). This threshold should be aimed for by politicians according to sufficientarianism and could be something such as every household should at least have access to destinations with many primary schools within y minutes travelling or z euros "out-of-pocket" costs.

Transport-related social exclusion is a notion that is often mentioned in the transport equity literature (Lucas, 2018). Transport-related social exclusion means that if people lack mobility options (e.g., no car availability, not enough money to pay regularly for public transport), their level of access to jobs, goods, medical services, education, and so forth can be low, which can contribute significantly to social exclusion for these people and to feelings of social isolation for them. Lucas (2018) cites an older study which also found that these transport inequalities are highly correlated with social disadvantage which means that some parts of the population are more at risk than others for transport-related social exclusion.

In the practice of transport policy, ethical theories of egalitarianism and sufficientarianism are applied to some extent to government provided public transport and public transport subsidies. There are various motivations for such a policy (Button, 1993; van Goeverden et al., 2006) but one of them is the so-called 'social function' of public transport, meaning that vulnerable groups such as low-income households, persons without a driver licence, elderly, and persons with a disability, need public transport to avoid problems of social exclusion (e.g., Lucas, 2018). However, despite good intentions a redistribution is not always actually reached with public investments in rail and transport fare reduction subsidies. Banister (2018) found, for example, that in the UK each household on average receives a transport subsidy of £151, but that the richest 10% receive more than twice as much as the poorest 10%. Börjesson et al. (2020) analysed that the average transit subsidy rate in Stockholm, Sweden, is 44%. They indeed found that these subsidies are mildly progressive because of discounts for students and retired and because top-income citizens make fewer transit trips per person. However, they also conclude that the progressivity of the subsidy scheme is weak and that the current way of subsidizing Stockholm transit is not an effective policy from an equity point of view.

Governments can find it fair that certain transport mode users (e.g., all car users) pay for their total social costs even if this means that in this way of pricing, the marginal social costs outweigh the marginal social benefits. To explain the notion of total social costs we have made a balance of total costs and benefits of a transport mode (see Table 13.1 with car driving as an example). We can assume in this balance that total internal benefits are equal to total internal costs. Thus, the total social balance is reached when on the one hand the external costs caused by car driving and government expenditures for roads and policies are equal to the tax revenues paid by the car drivers. So, car drivers pay for their total costs when the government revenue from fixed and variable car taxes equals the external car costs and government expenditures on car driving.

Table 13.1 Balance of costs and benefits of car driving – an example

Car driving benefits	Car driving costs
Internal benefits: the car driver has benefits because he or she can reach the desired destination; some car drivers will have benefits because he or she can satisfy certain social-psychological needs (e.g., car driving results in pure joy or status enhancement)	Internal costs: travel time, effort, money costs related to fuel, car purchase, taxes (see Chapter 6)
External benefits: negligible[a]	External costs: accident risks, environmental damage, traffic jams, and so forth
Benefits for the government: fixed and variable tax revenues	Costs for the government: road construction and maintenance, traffic police, and so forth

Note: [a] With the exception that people may enjoy watching ships, trains, aircraft, or a beautiful modern or historic car that is owned by another person (see external benefits before).

Governments have the choice to charge transport modes their marginal or total social costs dependent on their policy goal. They can aim for an efficient or fair transportation system. In scientific literature, the tension in this policy choice is sometimes denoted as efficiency versus equity (see, for example, Verhoef, 1994). To explain this tension a bit more we give an example of rail infrastructure construction. The social costs in this example are construction costs and external costs such as damage to landscapes and nature. The construction and damage costs to landscapes and nature are not directly related to use. If it be 25,000 or 50,000 train movements per year between locations 'A' or 'B', the whole track between 'A' and 'B' has to be built because it makes no sense to only build half of the track. When governments aim at equity they will charge the rail track users with a price based on covering total social costs. Thus, a price per kilometre has to be paid that includes the construction and landscape/nature costs which are not directly related to the amount of use. However, with this charge a price level per kilometre travelled may arise which is higher compared to the price where marginal social costs equal marginal social benefits: point P1 in Figure 13.2c. Consequently, too few rail kilometres will be travelled from a social optimum point of view. In conclusion, the tension is that it may seem fair to confront road or rail users with their total social costs, but this may result in an inefficient transport system. On the contrary, if these users are only charged according to their marginal social costs, governments cannot cover all their social costs.

As mentioned above, CBA is a much-used appraisal method for transport policies. However, the CBA is often criticized for ignoring equity issues such as distribution effects (see also Chapter 15). Other equity-related criticisms are, first, that rich people matter more than poor people in CBA because, for example, rich people are – *ceteris paribus* – willing to pay more for travel time gains and environmental benefits compared to poor people. Second, when using discounting, current generations matter more than future generations. It is important to realize that CBA does not exclude reporting distribution effects, e.g., over income classes or regions, or the use of a discount rate of zero or even a negative discount rate. So, these critics mainly relate to the use of CBA in practice. However, there is also more fundamental criticism on CBA (perhaps on the broader idea of utilitarianism) related to justice. Some point out that it would not be sensible to use highest total utility as the only yardstick in decision-making. In their view it is not wise to disregard the presence of tragic choices in politics (Nussbaum, 2000), as when CBA leads to a choice of course A (many winners) over course B (hardly any winner), but course A leads to uncompensated losers (a potentially small group whose members may suffer from, for example, losing their homes, serious illnesses, and even death which are, of course, tragic impacts of course A). For more discussion on the limitations of CBA from an ethical perspective see van Wee (2011). To overcome problems of tragic choices in CBA, appraisal methods such as multi criteria analysis (MCA), environmental impact assessment and social impact assessment are used. Sometimes these evaluation studies are additional to CBA outcomes, sometimes only these appraisal methods are applied *see* Chapter 15 for more information on MCA.

13.5   PUBLIC CHOICE THEORY

Sections 13.3 and 13.4 describe rational considerations or aims which politicians can apply when deciding to implement a new transport policy or not. But there are other reasons – perhaps more irrational – which explain the actual behaviour of politicians and bureaucrats in the practice of transport policy-making. Here, the core idea is that psychological reasons and politicians' self-interest explain the choice of transport policies. The idea of self-interest is rooted in 'public choice theory' (Buchanan and Tullock, 1962). In this economic theory it is assumed that people acting in the political marketplace act in the same way as in other markets: they are mainly concerned for themselves (and their nearest relatives).

When building new transport infrastructure there is a substantial body of scientific literature that points at psychology and 'self-interest' as explanations for the question of why new infrastructure is sometimes built that does not meet the expected efficiency and/or equity considerations. Also for the worldwide CBA practice, Flyvbjerg and Bester (2021) found based on a large dataset that cost and benefit estimates of public investments are often inaccurate and biased. Flyvbjerg et al. (2003a) have built a database of 258 transport infrastructure projects all over the world. Of these projects 86% showed cost overruns, with an average overrun of 28% of the estimated costs. 'Cost overruns' means that the costs of building the new infrastructure is higher compared to the cost estimation used for making the political decision. Later in time, Cantarelli et al. (2012) found for the Netherlands average cost overrun of 10.6% for rail, 18.6% for roads, and 21.7% for fixed links. Flyvbjerg et al. (2003b, 2006, Flyvbjerg 2007) also investigated 210 projects on demand shortfalls, comparing transport demand the first year after introduction of the new infrastructure with the *ex ante* estimate. Mainly for rail projects, they found large inaccuracies. For the occurrence of these problems, the literature distinguishes four different types of explanations: technical, psychological, economic, and political explanations (Flyvbjerg, 2005; Cantarelli et al., 2010). Technical explanations explain failure in terms of honest mistakes, related to difficulties in predicting the future (Flyvbjerg, 2005). Nevertheless, if only technical reasons explain the mistakes, it seems improbable that mainly cost underestimations and benefit overestimations (for rail) would occur. Therefore, two additional reasons are proposed. First, it seems probable that politicians and bureaucrats are unintentionally too optimistic about their projects. Psychological explanations state that humans tend to overemphasize their own abilities and to be overly optimistic about the future, rather than rationally weighing gains, losses, and probabilities (Lovallo and Kahneman, 2003). Second, and here self-interest comes into play, it is probable that decision-makers deliberately present wrong numbers (Flyvbjerg et al., 2003a; Flyvbjerg, 2005; Cantarelli et al., 2010). Project funds are scarce, and projects that look good on paper can more easily be financed than projects that do not. Politicians, planners, and forecasters are said to deliberately underestimate costs while overestimating benefits in order to gain approval and funding for their 'own' (sometimes much loved) project.

Flyvbjerg and Bester (2021) argue also for the worldwide CBA practice that the root causes of inaccuracies in CBA outcomes are not technical as often is mentioned by the planners of the projects. Flyvbjerg and Bester agree that scope changes, unexpected technical drawbacks, and changes in the economy are very difficult to predict and can explain the inaccuracy. Their point is, however, that again and again in CBAs for public projects these well-known phenomena are underestimated. Overwhelmingly the CBA analysts are far too optimistic in their assumptions due to aspects such as 'overconfidence bias, the planning fallacy, and strategic misrepresentation' (Flyvbjerg and Bester, 2021, p. 405). Here, the important point is that there does not seem to have been any improvement in estimation methods over time – there is no feedback loop and a learning process in place.

13.6 'HEALTHY' TRANSPORT POLICIES

An important question is: how to achieve a 'healthy' transport policy? (Van Wee, 2009). Much transport research and analysis is aimed at helping decision-makers to answer this question. Researchers and consultants help by developing and improving tools such as CBA and MCA

(Chapter 15) and by carrying out future studies (Chapter 14) and all kinds of effectiveness studies. Van Wee (2009) distinguishes six general criteria for policy interventions that should be taken into account in the decision-making process in order to achieve healthy policies: (1) effectiveness, (2) efficiency, (3) equity, (4) ease of implementation, (5) flexibility, and (6) long-term robustness:

1. Effectiveness relates to the question: does the policy do what it is supposed to do? For example, if free public transport is implemented because of environmental reasons, the question is: will it lead to less environmental pressure? Van Wee (2009) notes that it is not only the question of whether the policy is effective at all, but also the level of effects.

2. Efficiency can be expressed in terms of cost-effectiveness or cost-to-benefit ratio. Cost-effectiveness is generally a relatively easy indicator in the case of 'simple' policy options, having one dominant effect, and only monetary costs. It can, for example, be applied to helping the political choice between subsidizing technology A or B which only differ in technical costs and carbon dioxide (CO_2) emission reduction potential. Of course, it is 'healthy' to subsidize the technology which has the lowest costs in achieving one kg of emission reduction. It is less simple to use cost-effectiveness as an efficiency indicator if a policy option has (1) multiple effects, or (2) monetary as well as non-monetary costs. An example of multiple effects: improvements in public transport may contribute to accessibility, safety, and the environment. An example of non-monetary effects: reduction in speeds on motorways could result in lower emissions. In addition, they result in reduced fuel use and costs, which can be expressed in monetary terms, but they also increase travel times and might reduce the fun of driving for some, both being non-monetary costs. For such less simple policy options a (simple) CBA is to be preferred to estimate efficiency.

3. As explained earlier, equity relates to questions about the distribution of benefits and costs of the policy. Policies may be aimed to solve equity issues. In that case, it is important that the aim is formulated very clearly, for example, from a more egalitarian or sufficientarian principle. Which group is to be helped with improved accessibility precisely? And what is meant precisely with improved accessibility for that group? As shown in the previous example with the transit fare subsidies, with only good intentions equity aims do not have to be met. So, healthy equity policies must be defined very precisely so that effectiveness (see item 1) can be analysed. On the other hand, policies can have non-equity aims but can have equity implications. It seems obvious that policy instruments with hardly any equity issues are relatively much easier to implement compared to instruments with many equity issues.

4. It is an advantage if a policy option is easy to implement. But van Wee (2009) stresses that this criterion is not included to suggest that only easy-to-implement policy options are 'healthy'. A policy option should be considered as an important candidate option particularly if it could have major effects and is cost-effective. For example, some road pricing designs could belong to this category. However, it is worth trying to understand the major barriers for implementation and to learn from successful implementations elsewhere. For example, the equity barrier (see above) can be reduced or even solved by carefully selecting options for revenue use. It could be an option to reduce income tax for low-income people, or to reduce tax on fuel efficient cars which tend to be owned by low-income people.

5. Flexibility relates to the ease to adapt the policy, because of the ease or difficulty to foresee changes. For example, once introduced, levies on fuels and cars, and emissions regulations

can be changed relatively easy. The importance of the flexibility criterion will be discussed more in detail in Chapter 14 (exploring the future).

6. Long-term robustness, the final criterion, relates to the question of whether a policy is 'no regret' under uncertain long-term developments that could have a major impact on society. This criterion is strongly related to flexibility (see further Chapter 14). Here, the term 'flexibility' is used for any foreseen or unforeseen changes, also short-term changes and changes with relatively low impacts. Long-term robustness relates to major changes. A check on robustness is recommended by van Wee (2009) at least in cases of expensive land-use or transport infrastructure policies. Are these policies no-regret in case of major changes?

13.7   CURRENT TRANSPORT POLICY

The previous chapters contained many topics for which government policies are developed. Some transport policies aim at decreasing transport resistance factors, other policies try to influence the needs and location of activities or try to improve the environmental performance of vehicles and so forth. It is impossible to give a complete overview of all policies at all levels. Therefore, this section will only outline some main policies. When using keywords such as 'transportation policy' or 'transport policy' in a search engine such as 'Scopus' easily almost 40,000 documents pop up.

There are different ways to classify transport policies:

1. According to policy goal. For example, policies to improve accessibility or to improve transport safety.
2. According to kind of instrument. For example, pricing policies or policies providing new infrastructure.
3. According to the policy body responsible for implementing the policy. These bodies are: national governments, regional governments (federal states or provinces), city councils, supranational bodies (such as the International Civil Aviation Organization (ICAO) and the International Maritime Organization (IMO) of the United Nations), and international economic and political blocks (e.g., the European Union, EU).

In Table 13.2 we have chosen to give a transport policy overview according to goal and dominant instruments. In the column remarks, we give some examples of bodies responsible for the policy. Note that this table is not complete.

Table 13.2 Much used transport policy instruments

Goal	Important instruments	Remarks
Improving accessibility	Providing and maintaining road, port, and rail infrastructure; Subsidizing public transport fares; Road pricing; Providing traffic management; Implementing land-use policies	These policies are mostly implemented by national governments. Road pricing is the exception as almost all current road pricing schemes are implemented in specific cities.
Improving the environment, liveability, and health	Setting vehicle emission and noise standards; Setting fuel standards; Providing noise barriers along (rail) roads, providing eco-tunnels and tunnels in urban areas; Promoting the use of active modes (e.g., improving the cycling and walking infrastructure, providing and maintaining public cycle parking facilities)	National governments implement standards in most cases. In Europe the EU sets standards which are transferred to national laws accordingly. For aviation and shipping the ICAO and IMO sign international agreements to make, amongst others, aircraft less noisy and aircraft and ships less polluting and more fuel-efficient. Adapting infrastructure is national and/or local/regional policy.
Improving transport safety	Setting safety standards for vehicles; Implementing rules such as making wearing seat belts and crash helmets mandatory; Adapting infrastructure to make traffic situations safer (e.g., constructing roundabouts in place of junctions)	National governments implement standards in most cases. Adapting infrastructure is national and/or regional local/policy.
Improving equity	Subsidizing public transport fares; Providing railroads, ports, and roads in poor and/or low densely populated areas	National, regional, and local governments subsidize public transport fares. National governments but also international economic blocks (such as the EU) sometimes decide to subsidize new infrastructure being built in poorer or slow developing regions or countries (the aim is often also improving accessibility next to social inclusion). Additionally, the World Bank[a] offers low-interest loans to poorer countries, for example, in order to make it possible for them to build new transport infrastructure. One of the aims of the World Bank is to fight poverty.
Generate government revenues	Implementing taxes on vehicles and fuels	Mostly national and regional governments tax transport vehicles and fuels.

Note: [a]The World Bank is like a cooperative, where its 187 member countries are shareholders (for more information, see http://web.worldbank.org).

13.8 CONCLUSIONS

The main conclusions are:

1. Governments implement transport policies from a societal perspective. They weigh all social costs and benefits of transport, including so-called external effects.

2. External effects of transport are 'real' effects which people and shippers do not take into account when deciding to make a trip or to transport freight. External effects can be both negative (costs) as well as positive (benefits). Nearly all policies aimed at external effects relate to decreasing external costs such as congestion delays, air pollution, climate change, and accident risks.

3. Governments implement policies because they aim to improve efficiency: with this aim they want to increase total welfare. Another main reason for transport policies is because governments consider them as being fair: with this aim, they want to distribute welfare more fairly.

4. Also psychological reasons and politicians' self-interest can explain the implementation of policy.

5. The policy goal to improve accessibility is mainly reached by providing new infrastructure. The improvement of equity is mainly fulfilled by providing new infrastructure also and by subsidizing public transport fares. For policy goals such as improving environment and liveability and transport safety, dominant policy instruments are vehicle and fuel standards and regulations which try to improve the technical characteristics of vehicles and fuels.

REFERENCES

Adams, J. (1999), 'The social implications of hypermobility: speculations about the social consequences of the OECD scenarios for environmentally sustainable transport and business-as-usual trend projections', in Project on Environmentally Sustainable Transport (EST), *The Economic Implications of Sustainable Transportation*, Ottawa Workshop, 20–21 October 1998, Paris: OECD.

Aldred, J. (2002), 'Cost–benefit analysis, incommensurability and rough equality', *Environmental Values*, 11 (1), 27–47.

Aldred, J. (2006), 'Incommensurability and monetary valuation', *Land Economics*, 82 (2), 141–61.

Algemene Rekenkamer (2019), *Autobelastingen als beleidsinstrument [Car taxation as a policy instrument]*, The Hague: Algemene Rekenkamer (www.rekenkamer.nl) (in Dutch).

Banister, D. (2002), *Transport Planning* (2nd edn), London and New York: Spon Press.

Banister, D. (2018), *Inequality in Transport*, Oxford: Alexandrine Press.

Börjesson, M., J. Eliasson and I. Rubensson (2020), 'Distributional effects of public transport subsidies', *Journal of Transport Geography*, 84, 102674.

Bouscasse, H., S. Gabet, G. Kerneis, A. Provent, C. Rieux, N. Ben Salem and R. Slama (2022), 'Designing local air pollution policies focusing on mobility and heating to avoid a targeted number of pollution-related deaths: Forward and backward approaches combining air pollution modeling, health impact assessment and cost-benefit analysis', *Environment International*, 159, 107030.

Buchanan, J. M. and G. Tullock (1962), *The Calculus of Consent*, Ann Arbor: University of Michigan Press.

Button, K.J. (1993), *Transport Economics* (2nd edn), Aldershot, UK and Brookfield, VT, USA: Edward Elgar.

Button, K.J. and D. Gillingwater (1986), *Future Transport Policy*, London: Routledge.

Camporeale, R., L. Caggiani, M. Ottomanelli (2019), 'Modeling horizontal and vertical equity in the public transport design problem: a case study', *Transportation Research Part A: Policy and Practice*, 125, p. 184-206.

Cantarelli, C.C., B. Flyvbjerg, E.J.E. Molin and B. van Wee (2010), 'Cost overruns in large-scale transportation infrastructure projects: explanations and their theoretical embeddedness', *European Journal of Transport Infrastructure Research*, 10 (1), 5–18.

Cantarelli, C.C., B. van Wee, E.J.E. Molin and B. Fluvbjerg (2012), 'Different cost performance: different determinants?: The case of cost overruns in Dutch transport infrastructure projects', *Transport Policy*, 22, 88–95.

Delucchi, M.A. and D.R. McCubbin (2010), *External Costs of Transport in the U.S.*, Davis, CA: Institute of Transportation Studies, UC Davis, at http://escholarship. org/uc/item/13n8v8gq.

DG MOVE (2019), *Transport in the European Union Current Trends and Issues*, Brussels, European Commission, Directorate-General Mobility and Transport.

Essen, H. L. van, Wijngaarden L. van, A. Schroten, D. Sutter, C. Bieler, M. Silvia Maffii, M. Brambilla, D. Fiorello, F. Fermi, R. Parolin and K. El Beyrouty (2019), *Handbook on the External Costs of Transport Version 2019 – 1.1*, Luxembourg: Publications Office of the European Union, 2020.

Flyvbjerg, B. (2005), 'Policy and planning for large infrastructure projects: problems, causes, cures', Policy Research Working Paper, World Bank: Washington, DC.

Flyvbjerg, B. (2007), 'Megaproject policy and planning: problems, causes, cures', Ph.D. thesis, Aalborg University.

Flyvbjerg, B. and D.W. Bester (2021), 'The cost-benefit fallacy: Why cost-benefit analysis is broken and how to fix it', *Journal of Benefit-Cost Analysis*, 12 (3), 395–419.

Flyvbjerg, B., N. Bruzelius and W. Rothengatter (2003a), *Megaprojects and Risk: An Anatomy of Ambition*, Cambridge: Cambridge University Press.

Flyvbjerg, B., M.K. Skamris Holm and S.L. Buhl (2003b), 'How common and how large are cost overruns in transport infrastructure projects?' *Transport Reviews*, 23 (1), 71–88.

Flyvbjerg, B., M.K. Skamris Holm and S.L. Buhl (2006), 'Inaccuracy in traffic forecasts', *Transport Reviews*, 26 (1), 1–24.

Geurs, K.T., W. Boon and B. van Wee (2009), 'Social impacts of transport: literature review and the state of the practice of transport appraisal in the Netherlands and the United Kingdom', *Transport Reviews*, 29 (1), 69–90.

Goeverden, C. van, P. Rietveld, J. Koelemeijer and P. Peeters (2006), 'Subsidies in public transport', *European Transport [Trasporti Europei]*, 32, 5–25.

Guy Peters, B. (2018), *Policy Problems and Policy Design*, Cheltenham, UK and Northampton, MA, USA: Edward Elgar.

Hicks, J.R (1939), 'The foundations of welfare economics', *Economic Journal*, 49 (196), 696–712.

Johansson, P.-O. (1991), *An Introduction to Modern Welfare Economics*, Cambridge: Cambridge University Press.

Kaldor, N. (1993), 'Welfare propositions of economics and interpersonal comparisons of utility', *Economic Journal*, 49 (195), 549–52.

Koopmans, C. and N. Mouter (2020), 'Cost-benefit analysis', in N. Mouter (ed.), *Advances in Transport Policy and Planning. Standard Transport Appraisal Methods*, 225-254. London: Elsevier.

Kreling, S.E.S., K.M. Gaynor and C.A.C. Coon (2019), 'Roadkill distribution at the wildland-urban interface', *Journal of Wildlife Management*, 83 (6), 1427–36.

Lovallo, D. and D. Kahneman (2003), 'Delusions of success: how optimism undermines executives' decisions', *Harvard Business Review*, 81 (7), 56–63.

Lucas, K. (2018) 'A new evolution for transport-related social exclusion research?' *Journal of Transport Geography*, 81, 102529 https://doi.org/10.1016/j.jtrangeo.2019.102529.

Martens, K. (2017), *Transport Justice. Designing Fair Transportation Systems*, New York: Routledge.

Naess, P., (2020), 'Project appraisal methods: Tools for optimizing or for informed political debate?' in N. Mouter (ed.), *Advances in Transport Policy and Planning. Standard Transport Appraisal Methods*, 266-289. London: Elsevier.

Niemeyer, S. and C.L. Spash (2001), 'Environmental valuation analysis, public deliberation, and their pragmatic syntheses: a critical appraisal', *Environment and Planning C: Government and Policy*, 19, 567–85.

Nussbaum, M.C. (2000), 'The costs of tragedy: some moral limits of cost–benefit analysis', *Journal of Legal Studies*, XXIX (June), 1005–36.

Ortúzar, J.D., R. Bascuñán, L.I. Rizzi and A. Salata (2021), 'Assessing the potential acceptability of road pricing in Santiago', *Transportation Research Part A: Policy and Practice*, 144, 153–69.

Pereira, R.H., T. Schwanen and B. David Banister (2017), 'Distributive justice and equity in transportation', *Transport Reviews*, 37 (2), 170–91.

Rietveld, P., J. Rouwendal and A.J. van der Vlist (2007), 'Equity issues in the evaluation of transport policies and transport infrastructure projects', in M. van Geenhuizen, A. Reggiani and P. Rietveld (eds), *Policy Analysis of Transport Networks*, Aldershot: Ashgate, pp. 19–36.

Schmidtchen, D., C. Koboldt, J. Helstroffer, B. Will, G. Haas and S. Witte (2009), *Transport, Welfare and Externalities*, Cheltenham, UK and Northampton, MA, USA: Edward Elgar.

Thomopoulos, N., S. Grant-Muller and M.R. Tight (2009), 'Incorporating equity considerations in transport infrastructure evaluation: current practice and a proposed methodology', *Evaluation and Program Planning*, 32 (4), 351–59.

UK National Travel Survey (2014), accessed April 2022 at https://assets.publishing.service.gov.uk/government/uploads/system/uploads/attachment_data/file/476635/travel-to-school.pdf.

van Wee, B. (2009), *Transport Policy: What Can It and What Can't It Do?* European Transport Conference 2009, http://etcproceedings.org/paper/ transport-policy-what-it-can-and-what-it-can-t-do.

van Wee, B. (2011), *Transport and Ethics. Ethics and the Evaluation of Transport Projects and Policies*, Cheltenham, UK and Northampton, MA, USA: Edgard Elgar.

van Wee, B. and K. Geurs (2011), 'Discussing Equity and Social Exclusion in Accessibility Evaluations', *European Journal of Transport and Infrastructure Research*, 11 (4), 350–67.

Verhoef, E.T. (1994), 'Efficiency and equity in externalities: a partial equilibrium analysis', *Environment and Planning*, 26A, 361–82.

Verhoef, E.T. (1996), *Economic Efficiency and Social Feasibility in the Regulation of Road Transport Externalities*, Tinbergen Research Series 108, Amsterdam: Thesis Publishers.

14
Transport futures research

Vincent Marchau, Warren Walker and Jan Anne Annema

14.1 INTRODUCTION

It has often been said that 'to govern means to foresee'. This adage is also valid for transport policymaking. For example, an increasing transport demand in the future could lead to politically unacceptable future levels of congestion, air pollution, and traffic casualties if no additional policies are taken. Thus, it is important for governments to know about possible future transport expectations in their region in order to be able to implement new policies in time. For several decades, governments have been developing policies to reduce the negative impacts of transport (see Chapters 9–13). Chapter 13 discusses criteria for 'sound' policies. But how to explore the future impacts of candidate transport policy options? To do this we enter the area of transport futures research – this area is the scope of this chapter. Chapter 15 will then discuss how to evaluate ex ante all impacts via a cost–benefit analysis or multi-criteria analysis. Chapter 16 discusses the use of transport (impact) models.

Research can map *possible* futures and transport policymaking strategies. Here, it is very important to note the term 'possible'. In fact, the future is unknown and is largely determined by non-predictable developments (Taleb, 2007). This implies that future outcomes are surrounded by a lot of uncertainty. In our view, in proper transport futures research this uncertainty should be adequately taken into account and clearly communicated to the decision-makers. In poor transport futures research, the opposite is true. The analysts in poor quality transport futures research often seem to think that they are able to predict the future, which is, of course, impossible. An example of sometimes huge inaccuracies in future studies is given by Cruz and Sarmento (2020). Based on an extensive international review study on the accuracy of traffic demand forecasts for road and rail projects over the past decades, it is shown that there can be (huge) inaccuracy in traffic/ridership forecasting with a tendency to be over-optimistic in futures studies. In particular, a (weighted) average deviation of -23.6% (meaning that the real traffic was lower than forecast) was found for railways and -9.3% for roads. The authors also found that over the last couple of decades the accuracy in the futures studies they reviewed had not improved.

This chapter is written from the perspective of transport policy analysis. The aim is to specify research approaches to the study of transport futures, and to explain the role of futures research related to transport policy analysis. Generally speaking, futures research in transport policy analysis is carried out for two reasons: (1) to identify the types and magnitudes of future transport problems (and/or opportunities), and (2) to identify ways to reduce these transport problems (and/or take advantage of these opportunities).

With respect to future transport problems, an increase in future transport could result in societally unacceptable levels of air pollution, congestion, and traffic casualties, for example (see Chapters 9–11). Here, transport futures research supports estimating the future levels of these problems. By doing so, policymakers may decide to implement new policies, for example. On the other hand, futures research on economic and demographic developments, for example, might show that transport demand will decrease. As such, problems could be solved, or at least reduced, without intervention.

Next, if future transport problems are identified, policymakers often desire to know the policy options that could help solve the problems, their effects, and their costs and benefits (see Chapter 15). The specification and analysis of current and future options is not trivial. For instance, some options might currently be under development (e.g. new vehicle technologies) or even unknown. In addition, most transport policy options have a long-term character. For instance, building new infrastructure often takes a long time (including the period from the initial discussions to the final decision, the time needed to start building after a decision has been taken, and the time the building itself takes). Furthermore, the benefits from new infrastructure will be realized over decades from when it is opened. Finally, it takes years before the full impacts of pricing and technical measures for new vehicles are reached. Transport futures research can help to specify current and future options, and to estimate their long-term impacts.

In Section 14.2, futures research in relation to the transport policy domain is explained and a framework for futures uncertainty is discussed. This framework distinguishes different levels of uncertainty, including Level 3 (or scenario) uncertainty and Level 4 (or deep) uncertainty. In Section 14.3, scenario planning approaches are explained to handle Level 3 uncertainty. Next, in Section 14.4, flexible and adaptive approaches are presented to handle Level 4 uncertainty. Finally, Section 14.5 contains the conclusions.

14.2   FUTURES RESEARCH AND TRANSPORT POLICY ANALYSIS

Futures research to help public decision-making starts with an understanding of the policy domain. As detailed by Walker (2000a), a common approach to a rational-style policy analysis is to create a model of the system of interest (in this book: the transport system) that defines the boundaries of the system and describes its structure and operations – i.e. the elements, and the links, flows, and relationships among these elements (see Figure 14.1).

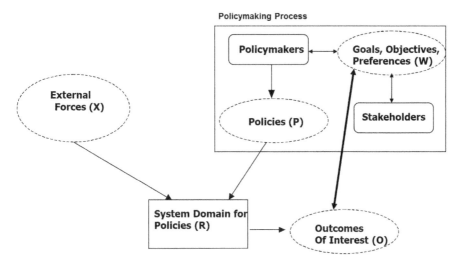

Policymaking Process

Policymakers

Goals, Objectives, Preferences (W)

External Forces (X)

Policies (P)

Stakeholders

System Domain for Policies (R)

Outcomes Of Interest (O)

Source: Walker (2000a).

Figure 14.1   A framework for policy analysis

In Figure 14.1, different elements and links can be distinguished:

1. **External forces** (X) are forces that work from outside the transport system, i.e. are not under the control of the problem owner. These forces have influence on the demand for transport and the supply of transport (e.g. technical developments for vehicles and infrastructure, oil price, cultural changes, etc.).
2. The **transport system** box (R) represents the elements of the transport system (e.g. drivers, operators, vehicles, infrastructure) and their interactions. These elements and their interactions are affected by the external forces and future policies (see below), and result in intermediate transport system outputs (such as the amount of transport in passenger-kilometres and/or ton-kilometres per transport mode in a future year).
3. The **outcomes of interest** (O) box represents policy relevant outcomes from the transport system – output such as traffic congestion, air pollution, and traffic casualties. In a future estimation, these amounts are the transport system output levels as estimated by the transportation model (see Chapter 16 on transport modelling).
4. The estimated outcomes of interest for the future may not be in accordance with policy goals or preferences. This produces a need for new future transport **policies** (P), such as new infrastructure, road or fuel pricing, stricter vehicle emission standards, etc., which can be fed into a new estimation of outcomes via the link from policies to the transport system.
5. The **valuation of outcomes or weights** (W) involves the relative, subjective importance given to the outcomes of interest by crucial stakeholders. It involves how stakeholders value the results of the changes in the transport system, such as improved traffic efficiency, fewer fatalities, reduced emissions, etc. (see Chapter 15 on evaluation methods).

To be most useful (and to increase the chances of the results of a policy analysis actually being used) a policy analysis study should be carried out as a partnership between the policymakers and the researchers. The four main steps in performing a policy analysis are summarized below. Note that this will generally not be a linear process, and there will often be feedback between the steps, particularly from Step 3 to Step 1.

1. Formulate the transport problem: Problem definition, setting goals, specifying options (often done in close partnership between the researchers and the problem owners/policymakers).
2. Estimate the future impacts (outcomes of interest (O) of the various policy options for different futures using transport system models and scenarios, for example (done mainly by the researchers).
3. Compare options (done mainly by the problem owners/policymakers, but often supported by the researchers through quantitative, analytical tools (e.g. cost–benefit analysis, multi-criteria analysis)).
4. Choose and implement the chosen option (done mainly by the problem owners/policymakers).

This chapter focuses on methodological approaches to estimate the future impacts of policies and external forces (using e.g. scenarios) on the transport system. An essential criterion for choosing an approach is how uncertain the future is assumed to be, i.e. the level of future uncertainty assumed. In general, uncertainty can be defined as limited knowledge about future, past, or current events. Formally, as defined by Walker et al. (2003), we consider uncertainty in this chapter to be 'any departure from the (unachievable) ideal of complete determinism' (p. 8). Or, in mathematical terms:

Let Y be some event. If Probability (Y) $\neq$ 0 or 1, then the event Y is uncertain.

This abstract formula can be illustrated with an example of a future transport outcome of interest. Suppose Y is the estimate produced by a model of the carbon dioxide (CO_2) emitted by road transport in 2030 in some country. The model estimates that Y = 25 billion kilograms. The probability of this event actually happening in 2030 is not 0 or 1. In fact the probability is unknown. Thus, the estimate of 25 billion kilograms of CO_2 emitted by road transport in 2030 is uncertain.

Based on the policy analysis framework (Figure 14.1), a classification of uncertainties with respect to policymaking can be made. Such a classification was developed by Walker et al. (2003). For the purposes of this chapter, we do not need to elaborate on the issue of uncertainty (for this, we refer the reader to Marchau et al., 2019; Lyons and Marsden, 2019). Here, the most important notion is to realize that transport policy analysis problems can be characterized by different levels of uncertainty about the external forces (X), the transport system and transport system models (R), the outcomes of interest (O), and valuations of the outcomes (W).

A way of representing different levels of uncertainty is shown in Figure 14.2 (Marchau et al., 2019). Level 1 uncertainty is often treated through a simple sensitivity analysis of transport model parameters, where the impacts of small perturbations of model input parameters on the outcomes of a model are assessed. Level 2 uncertainty is any uncertainty that can be described adequately in statistical terms. In the case of uncertainty about the future, Level 2 uncertainty is often captured in the form of either a (single) forecast (usually trend based) with a confidence interval, or multiple forecasts ('scenarios') with associated probabilities.

Many (quantitative) analytical approaches for transport policy analysis deal with future uncertainties as being Level 1 and Level 2 uncertainties, which is highly questionable because the future is in almost all cases 'not clear enough' (as is assumed by Level 1) or it is hardly possible to attach probabilities to different possible futures (as is assumed by Level 2). As an example of a Level 1 mistaken attribution, Figure 14.3 gives figures for forecasted investment costs of High Speed 2 (HS2)[1] in the UK that had initially been given.

Uncertainty Level Location	1	2	3	4
Context (X)	A clear enough future	Alternate futures (with probabilities)	A few plausible futures	Unknown Futures
System (R)	A single (deterministic) system model	A single (stochastic) system model	A few alternative system models	Unknown System Models
Outcomes (O)	A point estimate for each outcome	A confidence interval for each outcome	A limited range of outcomes	Unknown Outcomes
Weights (W)	A single set of weights	Several sets of weights, with a probability per set	A limited range weights	Unknown Weights

Source: Marchau et al. (2019).

Figure 14.2   The progressive transition of levels of uncertainty

Even for forecasting future 'investment costs', which may seem at first glance an 'easy' item to forecast, the uncertainties are huge, as Figure 14.3 shows. In the earlier studies to support decision-making on HS2 (2011–17), the analysts had clearly informed decision-makers incorrectly about their assumptions about the future. Their cost estimates were far too low compared to recent insights, and their future cost estimates were just presented as point estimates, as if there was no uncertainty. The 2019 cost estimate is a 'stunning' factor two to three times higher compared to the earlier estimates and presented in a range (in 2020 prices).

In the view of the authors of this chapter, all long-term transport policy analysis problems are characterized by higher levels of uncertainty (i.e. Levels 3 and 4; see Figure 14.2). Only relatively short time 'predictions' (for example, forecasts for one day or one week ahead of congestion levels on certain road stretches) can be characterized as Level 1 and Level 2 uncertainties.

Note that with respect to Level 4 uncertainty a distinction can be made between situations in which we are still able (or assume we are still able) to bound the future around many plausible futures and situations in which we only know that we do not know. This vacuum can be due to a lack of knowledge or data about the mechanism or functional relationships being studied (bounding is possible), but this can also stem from the potential for unpredictable, surprising events (we only know we do not know).

The long-term related Level 3 and Level 4 uncertainties cannot be dealt with through the use of probabilities and cannot be reduced by gathering more information, but they are basically unknowable and unpredictable at the present time. These higher levels of uncertainty can involve uncertainties about all aspects of a transport policy analysis problem – external or internal developments, the appropriate (future) system model, the parameterization of the model, the model outcomes, and the valuation of the outcomes by (future) stakeholders. Many of the negative consequences from policy decisions in the past were due to the use of approaches that did not take into account the fact that they were facing conditions of Level 3 and 4 uncertainty (e.g. Cruz and Sarmento, 2020; Flyvbjerg et al., 2003, 2006).

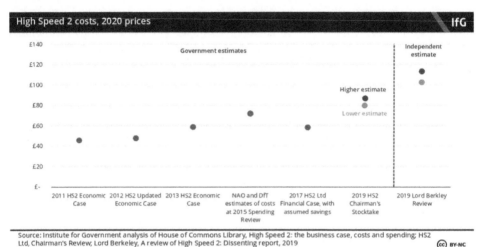

Source: Institute for Government (2021).

Figure 14.3   Development in HS2 cost estimates, in billion pounds Sterling, in 2020 prices

14.3   LEVEL 3 APPROACHES: FORWARD-LOOKING SCENARIOS AND BACKCASTING

14.3.1   Forward-Looking Scenarios

When faced with Level 3 uncertainties, transport policy analysts will generally use scenarios. The core of this approach is the assumption that the future can be specified well enough to identify policies that will produce favourable outcomes in one or more specific plausible future worlds. The future worlds are called scenarios. Börjeson et al. (2006) call these 'explorative scenarios' to differentiate them from 'predictive scenarios', which some analysts think they can use to deal with Level 1 and Level 2 uncertainties (which is not the case for long-term transport planning, in our view), and 'normative scenarios', which use backcasting (see, for example, Quist (2007)) to determine how a specific desired target can be reached.

Scenarios are 'stories' of possible futures, based upon logical, consistent sets of assumptions, and fleshed out in sufficient detail to provide a useful context for engaging planners and stakeholders. A forward-looking scenario includes assumptions about developments within the system being studied and developments outside the system that affect the system, but they exclude the policy options to be examined (see also Figure 14.1). Because the only sure thing about a future scenario is that it will not be exactly what happens, different scenarios, spanning a range of developments, are constructed to span a range of futures of interest. No probabilities are attached to the futures represented by each of the scenarios. They have a qualitative function, not a quantitative function. Scenarios do not tell us what will happen in the future; rather they tell us what can (plausibly) happen. They are used to prepare for the future: to identify possible future problems, and to identify robust (static) policies for dealing with the problems.

In transport policy analysis, best-estimate models are often used (based on the most up-to-date scientific knowledge; see Chapter 16) to examine the consequences that would follow from the implementation of each of several possible policies. They do this 'impact assessment' for each of the scenarios. The 'best' policy is the one that produces the most favourable outcomes across the scenarios. Such a policy is called a robust (static) policy.

There is no general theory that allows us to assess scenario adequacy or quality. There are, however, a number of criteria that are often mentioned in literature as being important. Schwarz (1988) gives a brief summary of them. The most important of these are consistency, plausibility, credibility, and relevance.

1. **Consistency**: the assumptions made are not self-contradictory; a sequence of events could be constructed, leading from the present world to the future world.
2. **Plausibility**: the posited chain of events can happen.
3. **Credibility**: each change in the chain can be explained (causality).
4. **Relevance**: changes in the values of each of the scenario variables are likely to have a large effect on at least one outcome of interest.

A structured process for developing forward-looking scenarios, consisting of a number of explicit steps, has been used in several policy analysis studies. The steps, summarized by Thissen (1999), and based on the more detailed specifications of RAND Europe (1997), Schwartz (1996), and Van der Heijden, et al. (2002), are (see also Figure 14.1):

1. **Specify the system, its outcomes of interest, and the relevant time horizon.** A system diagram can be used to identify what is considered inside and outside the system, the system elements that affect or influence the outcomes of interest, and their interrelationships.
2. **Identify external forces (X) driving changes in the system (and thereby producing changes in the outcomes of interest (O)).** Whether or not a particular external force is potentially relevant depends on the magnitude of the change in the system and its implications for the outcomes of interest. There are many judgements involved in defining the system under consideration, the relationships among the subsystems, and the definition of what is relevant. Thus, the determination of relevant forces and changes is necessarily subjective. Potentially relevant forces and changes are often best identified by conducting a series of interactive brainstorming or focus group sessions involving experts and/or stakeholders.
3. **Categorize forces and resulting system changes as fairly certain or uncertain.** The forces/system changes from Step 2 are placed into one of two categories – fairly certain or uncertain (see Table 14.1). Those forces/system changes about which the researcher is fairly certain are placed into this category. The remaining forces/changes are placed into the uncertain category. The forces/system changes in the fairly certain category are

included in all the scenarios. The uncertain forces/system changes are used to identify the most important and relevant uncertainties that have to be taken into account.

4. **Assess the relevance of the uncertain forces/system changes.** The analyses should focus on the uncertain forces/system changes that have the largest effects on the outcomes of interest. To identify them, the impact of each uncertain force/system change is considered with respect to each of the outcomes of interest. Based on the estimated impact that the resulting system change has on the outcomes of interest, the force/system change is placed in either a high or low impact category (see Table 14.1). The uncertain forces and system changes in the low impact category are dropped from further consideration (or can be left in for 'colour'). The uncertain forces and system changes in the high impact category (those that have a high impact on at least one of the outcomes of interest), along with the fairly certain elements, form the basis for the scenarios.

5. **Design several future scenarios based on combinations of different developments in the driving forces.** These should provide strikingly different images of the future that span the space of what is plausible. A brief but imaginative description of the essential characteristics of the future depicted by each of the scenarios should then be provided. Once the specific scenarios are identified, the assumptions underlying them are converted into inputs that can be used by the system models. This forms the basis for the subsequent assessment of policy options.

Table 14.1 Selecting relevant forces for system changes for forward-looking scenarios

	Change would lead to a low impact (for all outcomes of interest)	Change would lead to a high impact (on at least one outcome of interest)
Force or change is uncertain	These forces/changes can be included (for 'colour') or left out of the scenarios	These forces/changes are candidates for scenarios
Force and change are fairly certain	These forces/changes can be included (for 'colour') or left out of the scenarios	These forces/changes are included in all the scenarios as 'autonomous developments'

After constructing scenarios using Steps 1 to 5, these are first used to specify the (magnitude of the) future problem if no additional action is undertaken. For example, these 'reference scenarios' might imply high congestion levels, a high increase in CO_2 emissions, and so forth. In other words, related to Figure 14.1, the scenario outcomes of interest may not be in accordance with the goals. The idea is that these reference scenarios assume that only the already existing and/or agreed upon policies will be implemented. As such, the need for additional policies can be identified. In practice, these reference scenarios are sometimes given other names – e.g. business-as-usual scenarios, baseline scenarios, or background scenarios.

Figure 14.4 summarizes the model-based evaluation process of policy options. In the 'validation case', the current system is used in the model to make sure that the outcomes are reasonably close to the real world outcomes. More on model validation can be found in Chapter 16. In evaluating the impacts of policy options, the researcher should always include the reference case (see Figure 14.4; see also Chapter 15), i.e. the future transport system with no policy changes. If a transportation model (see Chapter 15) was used to estimate the reference scenario outcomes, the same model should be used again with exactly the same input, except for the input parameter changes or model changes due to the policy option (or options) under study. This then results in the 'policy case', i.e. specification of the future transport system with policy changes. To be clear, the impact assessment shows the differences between the validation case (O_1 and O_2), the reference outcomes of interest (O'_1 and O'_2), and the outcomes of interest due to the policy measure (O''_1 and O''_2). These differences – the final pros and cons of the policy option – can be evaluated by the policymakers using different methods. For example, they can ask for a multi-criteria analysis (MCA), a cost-effectiveness study, or a cost–benefit analysis (see Chapter 15).

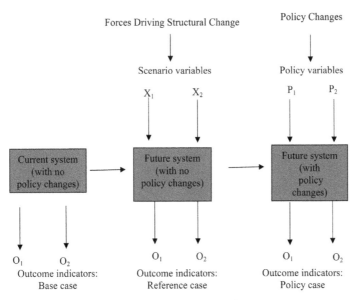

Figure 14.4   Evaluating policy options using scenarios

The policy option or options to be studied and the relevant outcomes of interest are dependent on the policy question. Impacts of new roads compared to the reference scenarios can be studied, or extra investments in public transport, or new vehicle emission standards, or kilometre charging, etc. It is also possible to evaluate the impacts of policy packages (combinations of policies) or technology packages (see also Chapter 13). Figure 14.5 gives an example of an evaluation of the impact of a future technology package (which requires strict policies to be adopted by the market) on worldwide greenhouse gas emissions (CO_2 emissions) for aviation, shipping, and heavy-duty trucking in the long term (2070) (IEA, 2021). The figure shows that, compared to the STEPS (Stated Policies Scenario) in the SDS (Sustainable Development Scenario), huge CO_2 emission reductions in 2070 are deemed possible, from almost 6 gigatons in STEPS to 1 gigaton in SDS. STEPS represents a business-as-usual scenario in which only the stated policies at the time of developing the scenarios are taken into account. In SDS, alternative fuel technologies such as electricity, hydrogen, biofuels, and synthetic aviation fuels are assumed to have been adopted on a large scale in aviation, shipping, and heavy-duty trucking, showing the huge decarbonizing potential of these technologies to politicians and the market. In Chapter 8 these technologies will be explained in more detail.

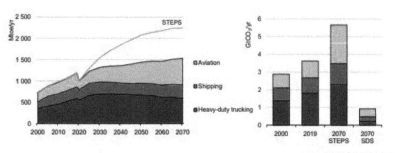

Note: STEPS = Stated Policies Scenario; SDS = Sustainable Development Scenario.

Note: The left graph is energy with STEPS presented in a bandwidth: between 2300 and 1500 Mtoe in 2070; the right graph is the CO_2 emissions with STEPS (the high range) near 6Gt and SDS about 1 Gt in 2070.
Source: IEA (2021).

Figure 14.5   Global energy consumption (Mtoe/yr) and CO_2 emissions (Gtons/yr) in aviation, shipping, and heavy-duty trucking by sub-sector in two scenarios: the Sustainable Development (SDS) and Stated Policies (STEPS) Scenarios

14.3.2   Pros and Cons of the Forward-Looking Scenario Approach

The benefits from using scenarios in policy analysis are threefold. First, scenarios help analysts and policymakers deal with situations in which there are many sources of uncertainty. Second, scenarios allow analysts to examine the 'what ifs' related to external uncertainties. They suggest ways in which the system could change in the future, and facilitate the examination of the implications of these changes. Finally, scenarios provide a way to explore the implications of Level 3 uncertainties for policymaking (prepare for the future) by identifying possible future problems and identifying (static) robust policies for dealing with the problems. These advantages have also been recognized by transport policymakers, and scenarios are becoming more and more used in strategic transport planning (Lyons et al., 2021).

However, from an analytic perspective the scenario approach has some problems. The first problem is deciding which assumptions about future external developments to include in the scenarios. Typically, these assumptions are decided upon by experts (collectively and individually). However, in the face of uncertainty, none is in a position to make this judgment. A second problem is that the researcher has little idea about whether the range of futures provided by the scenarios covers all, 95%, or some other percentage of the possible futures. A third problem with the scenario approach has to do with the large number of performance estimates generated by the scenarios. If the range is large, policymakers often tend to fall back on a single, 'most likely' scenario (implicitly assuming Level 2 uncertainty) or the do-nothing approach, arguing that 'we do not have sufficient information to make a decision at this time'. The latter is probably the worst possible outcome – when the level of uncertainty is high and the potential consequences are large, it would probably be better if policymakers acted rather than waited.

14.3.3 Backcasting Approach

Backcasting is quite different from the forward-looking scenario approach described above. Here, a normative target in the future – a desired outcome – is chosen as the starting point of the future analysis; then appropriate paths towards this desired outcome are searched for. In general, in backcasting, first an image is found that might be a future solution for the societal problem at hand. If such an image can be made explicit, the next step is to identify and assess a path between today and that future image. If no path can be found, the image will be redeveloped and adjusted (Hojer, 1998).

Within transport, several studies on sustainable development, or specifically on reducing CO_2 emissions in future transport, have used the backcasting approach – e.g. the OECD project 'Environmentally Sustainable Transport', the EU project POSSUM, and the UK project VIBAT (Geurs and van Wee, 2000; Banister et al., 2000; Hickman and Banister, 2014). Soria-Lara and Banister (2018) have developed and applied a more collaborative backcasting approach using a desired transport future for Andalusia, Spain.

Four different steps in the backcasting process related to policymaking can be distinguished:

1. **The definition of a future target or targets**, which can (for example) be zero CO_2 emissions in year 2050 for international aviation.
2. **The construction of a reference (forward-looking) scenario.** By comparing this reference case to the defined target(s) the required scale of change is specified. For example, STEPS is an example of reference scenarios (see Figure 14.5) that shows that without additional technologies and policies, CO_2 emissions in the long-distance transportation sector in Europe will increase instead of decreasing to zero in 2050. The reference scenario points to a huge gap that has to be bridged by implementing additional policies.
3. **The design of 'images of the future'.** Images are descriptions of the future that (from today's point of view) seem to meet the targets. Banister et al. (2008) have suggested criteria for future images. Schippl and Leisner (2009) summarize these: (1) the images should meet the targets; (2) each image should be plausible, but can be relatively extreme; (3) the images should be clearly different from each other, in order to give an idea of the huge variety of possible futures; and (4) the images should cover a sufficiently wide range of possibilities. However, to keep the research manageable, a small number of images should be selected. Soria-Lara and Banister (2018) also experiment with involving policymakers or other stakeholders in creating images.
4. **The specification of potential policies.** Policies that might help meet the images are specified. They are then analyzed and assessed by identifying the trajectories leading from the future images back to the present state and vice versa. Note that in some backcasting studies, the trajectories proposed are also called scenarios, which can be confusing.

Related to the uncertainty framework used in this chapter (Figure 14.2), we can identify two potential weak points in state-of-the-art backcasting methods. First, it seems highly risky to assume the future to be as forecast by the reference scenario (Step 2), as in STEPS (EIA, 2021), for example. By doing so, the future is treated as a Level 1 uncertainty, which is, of course, untrue. Here, the risk is that the policymakers are given a false feeling about the predictability of future development without additional policies, which may result in wrong policy actions (too many or too few changes to the system; or changes made too early or too late). Second, in Step 4 it is (implicitly) assumed that the specified policies will actually lead to the desired future, which is an incorrect assumption.

14.4   LEVEL 4 APPROACHES: FLEXIBLE AND ADAPTIVE APPROACHES

The previous sections focused on approaches to handle Level 3 uncertainties. However, transport policy problems increasingly emerge in which the uncertainty can be characterized as Level 4. In this case, what is known is only that the researcher does not know the future situation (or only knows the boundaries). Level 4 uncertainty is also called 'deep uncertainty'; it is defined as a condition in which analysts do not know (and/or the parties to a decision cannot agree upon) (1) the appropriate models to describe interactions among a system's variables; (2) the probability distributions to represent uncertainty about key parameters in the models; and/or (3) how to value the desirability of alternative outcomes (Lempert et al., 2003).

In most policy analysis studies involving lower levels of uncertainty, the study ends with the researcher presenting the impacts of alternative policies, leaving the choice and implementation of a preferred policy to the policymaker(s) (although the analyst and policymaker(s) should be working closely during the course of the study, as stated in Section 14.2). In the case of deep uncertainty, the implementation step of a policy analysis is explicitly addressed by the researcher. This 'implementation research' focuses on how the chosen policy could fail, and ways to protect it from failing.

In general, the literature offers three (overlapping, not mutually exclusive) ways for dealing with deep uncertainty in making policies, although there are differences in definitions, and ambiguities in terminology (see, for example, Leusink and Zanting, 2009):

1. **Resistance**: plan for the worst conceivable case or future situation (e.g. over dimensioning of infrastructure).
2. **Resilience**: whatever happens in the future, make sure to have a policy that will result in the system recovering quickly (e.g. floating roads, traffic incident management).
3. **Adaptive robustness**: prepare a policy that is flexible and adaptable, which will perform well across the full range of plausible futures (including surprises).

The first way is likely to be very costly and might not produce a policy that works well, because of Black Swans. The Black Swans metaphor is used by Taleb (2007) to explain that many events in the world are a surprise (to the observer) and can have major unforeseen impacts on world development. The second way accepts short-term pain (negative system performance) but focuses on recovery. The third way appears to be the most robust and efficacious way of dealing with deep uncertainties (Kwakkel et al., 2010b).

A variety of analytical approaches and tools have been developed to design robust and adaptive policies. Their underlying paradigm is the need for actions to reduce the vulnerability of a policy or strategy to uncertain future developments. Dewar et al. (1993) called this 'Assumption-Based Planning' (ABP). Within this paradigm, analysts use 'Exploratory Modeling' (EM) and 'Scenario Discovery' (SD). EM is a tool to explore a wide variety of scenarios, alternative model structures, and alternative value systems based on computational experiments (Bankes, 1993). A computational experiment is a single run with a given model structure and a given parameterization of that structure. It reveals how the real world would behave if the various hypotheses presented by the structure and the parameterization were correct. By exploring a large number of these hypotheses, one can get insights into how the system would behave under a large variety of assumptions (Bankes et al., 2013). SD is a tool to identify futures in which proposed strategies meet or miss their goals. It begins with a large database of model runs (e.g. from EM) in which each model run represents the performance of a strategy in one future. The SD algorithms identify those combinations of future conditions that best distinguish the cases in which the policy or strategy does or does not meet its goals.

A potential problem in EM is that, since the number of uncertainties is large, the number of model runs will be large. The set of resulting scorecards will, therefore, comprise a very large database. It is very difficult for anyone to scan this large database and interpret the results in order to identify a preferred policy for each of the plausible scenarios. Therefore, software that offers graphical tools to summarize the results of an exploratory analysis is required. Given complete sets of external forces, policies, system models, outcomes, and their weights, software is now available that is able to determine the values of the (uncertain) parameters that would lead to preferences for the different policy options (i.e. it is able to map the decision space). Agusdinata (2008), Kwakkel et al. (2010b), Van der Pas et al. (2010), and Milkovits et al. (2019) supply examples of how EM can be applied to transport policy analysis problems involving Level 4 uncertainty.

ABP was a first step towards an evolving set of analytical approaches for supporting Decision Making under Deep Uncertainty (DMDU). Four of the most commonly used approaches are:

1. **Robust Decision Making (RDM)**: RDM begins with one or more alternatives under consideration (often a current or best-estimate plan) and uses EM to make many runs of a system model to identify the futures most relevant to the plan's success. RDM uses Scenario Discovery (SD) to analyze data across the model runs to help decision-makers address such questions as: what are the key characteristics that differentiate those futures in which a plan succeeds from those in which it fails?; and what steps can be taken to help the plan to succeed over a wider range of futures? (Lempert, 2019).

2. **Dynamic Adaptive Policymaking (DAP)**: DAP focuses on implementation of an initial policy prior to the resolution of all major uncertainties, with the policy being adapted over time based on new knowledge. DAP specifies the development of a monitoring programme and responses when specific trigger values are reached. Hence, DAP makes adaptation over time explicit at the outset of plan formulation. DAP occurs in two phases: (1) the design phase, in which the basic policy, monitoring programme, and various pre- and post-implementation actions are designed; and (2) the implementation phase, in which the basic policy and the monitoring programmes are implemented, and contingent actions are taken, if necessary (Walker et al., 2019).

3. **Dynamic Adaptive Policy Pathways (DAPP)**: DAPP considers the timing of actions explicitly in its approach. It produces an overview of alternative routes into the future. The alternative routes are based on Adaptation Tipping Points (ATP). An Adaptation Tipping Point focuses on 'under what conditions will a given plan fail', which is analogous to the question that is asked in ABP or in SD (Haasnoot et al., 2019).
4. **Engineering Options Analysis (EOA)**: EOA refers to the process of assigning economic value to technical flexibility. It consists of a set of procedures for calculating the value of an option (i.e. the value of having a right (not an obligation) to take some action (e.g. expand a road because you have the space) at some cost (e.g. for road construction) over some time period), and is based on Real Options Analysis (de Neufville and Smet, 2019).

With respect to the transport domain, several DAP studies have been undertaken (a first example of DAP is presented by Hadjidemetriou et al. (2022)). As such, we will elaborate below on DAP. The basic concept of a dynamic adaptive policy is easy to explain (Walker, 2000b). It is analogous to the approach used in guiding a ship through a long ocean voyage. The goal – the end point – is set at the beginning of the journey. But, along the way, unpredictable storms and other traffic may interfere with the original trajectory. So, the policy – the specific route – is changed along the way. It is understood before the ship leaves port that some changes are likely to take place – and contingency plans may have already been formulated for some of the unpredictable events. The important thing is that the ultimate goal remains unchanged, and the policy actions implemented over time remain directed toward that goal. If the goal is changed, an entirely new plan must be developed. However, this does not mean completely starting over, as the knowledge of outcomes, objectives, measures, etc. learned during the initial DAP process would accelerate and simplify the new planning process.

An adaptive policy would include a systematic method for monitoring the environment, gathering information, implementing pieces of the policy over time, and adjusting and re-adjusting to new circumstances. The policies themselves would be designed to be incremental, adaptive, and conditional.

We now illustrate the steps to operationalize DAP using an example. The example concerns strategic planning for a large airport close to a built-up area (Kwakkel et al., 2010c). The design of the adaptive policy consists of four steps (from Marchau et al., 2010).

- **Step 1   Specification of problem, objectives, the definition of success, and constraints**
  In the past decennia, the rate of growth in air traffic was twice as large as the growth of the world economy. It is expected that, due to the increase of the world population, economic growth, and globalization, air traffic will continue to grow. Hence, an objective of an airport operator might be to improve the airport's capacity to handle increased demand. The related definition of success is that future capacity will meet future demand. Success means having a good match between supply and demand – not too much capacity, which would mean a lot of unused capacity, but not too little capacity, which would lead to delays in take-offs and landings. The constraints on policy options include costs, safety, life quality, spatial restrictions, and public acceptance.

- **Step 2   Specification of a basic policy and its conditions for success**

A basic policy might be to expand the physical capacity of the airport (add a runway). Conditions for success of this basic policy include that demand continues to grow and that the extra aircraft noise generated does not bring strong protests. Traditional policy analysis tools are available for identifying a basic policy (Findeisen and Quade, 1985).

- **Step 3   Identifying the vulnerabilities of the basic policy and anticipatory actions to protect it**

In Step 3 of the DAP process, the actions to be taken immediately to enhance the chances of success of the basic policy are specified. This step is based on identifying, in advance, the vulnerabilities associated with the basic policy, and specifying actions to be taken in anticipation. *Vulnerabilities* are external developments that could degrade the performance of the policy so that it is no longer successful. In short, the question is asked 'how can the basic policy fail?', and then actions are designed to prevent it from failing.

Scenarios are used in this step and in Step 4; but they are used in a different way from the way they are used in dealing with Level 3 uncertainty. They are used to identify the ways in which the basic policy could go wrong (i.e. not lead to success), using EM (i.e. exploring a wide variety of scenarios, models, and value systems) and SD (i.e. identifying futures in which proposed strategies meet or miss their goals). In DAP, since the researcher is looking for changes in the world that can make the basic policy fail, the scenarios should differ from the present in major ways. For example, there should be some very negative scenarios. People tend to view very negative scenarios as implausible and reject them out of hand. Nevertheless, they are crucial to an adaptive policy; having thought about a situation (no matter how implausible) in advance allows contingency plans to be formulated so that they are ready to be implemented in the (however unlikely) event they are needed. So, as many Black Swans as possible should be identified in order to 'be prepared' in case one of them actually occurs. In the airport case, demand for air transport is one of the key scenario variables. There could be a sharp decrease in demand, for example due to a financial crisis. This would make the policy fail. But, there could be a sharp increase in demand, which could lead to unacceptable delays in take-offs and landings, which would also make the policy fail. We deal with this vulnerability in Step 4.

Another vulnerability of the basic policy is resistance from people living around the airport because of the noise from the anticipated additional flights. This vulnerability is fairly certain. So, at the same time as the new runway is agreed upon, it would be wise to offer financial compensation to residents in the high noise zone to enhance the chances of success of the basic policy.

- **Step 4   Setting up a monitoring system and preparing to adapt the policy**

After the basic policy and anticipatory actions are implemented, there is still a need to monitor changes in the world and the performance of the policy, and to take actions, if needed, to guarantee the policy's progress and success. Similar to the approach in Step 3, scenarios (or even EM and SD) can be used to identify what to monitor and when to trigger responsive actions, and the specific actions to take. In this step, actions that might be taken to guarantee the basic policy's progress and success are prepared. Also, *signposts* are identified that specify information that should be tracked, and critical values of signpost variables (called *triggers*) are specified beyond which actions to change the policy should be implemented to ensure that the resulting policy keeps moving the system in the right direction and at a proper speed. The starting point for the identification of signposts is the set of vulnerabilities specified in Step 3.

In the airport case, it is possible that the increases in demand are much greater than expected. This would lead to unacceptable delays, and airlines might decide to shift flights (or even their hubs) to other airports, which would lead to failure of the plan. In preparation, plans could be made to shift specific types of flights to surrounding airports (e.g. all-cargo flights or flights by low-cost carriers). Making these plans would not be expensive and they may never be needed. But, if the conditions warranted them, the plans would be there and could be implemented quickly at the appropriate time (specified by the trigger), thus saving the basic policy.

Although they are promising, adaptive policies have not yet become commonplace in public policymaking. More research is required before this will happen. First, their validity and efficacy needs to be established. Evidence is being gathered through a variety of methods, including gaming and computational experiments. Also, the costs and benefits of dynamic adaptation measures compared to traditional policymaking approaches need to be studied. Finally, the implementation of dynamic adaptation will require significant institutional and governance changes, since some aspects of these policies are currently not supported by laws and regulations (e.g. the implementation of a policy triggered by an external event).

14.5 CONCLUSIONS

The most important conclusions of this chapter are:

1. Futures research often plays an important role in transport policymaking. However, it is very important to note that the future is unknown, which makes future research outcomes (highly) uncertain, by definition. Uncertainty in this chapter is defined as being any departure from the (unachievable) ideal of complete determinism.
2. That uncertainties exist in practically all long-term transport policymaking situations is generally understood by most policymakers, as well as by most policy analysts. But there is little appreciation for the fact that there are many different dimensions of uncertainty, and there is a lack of understanding about their different characteristics, their relative magnitudes, and the available approaches and tools for dealing with them.
3. A much used approach in transport policy planning is the scenario approach. An important advantage of using scenarios in futures research is that scenarios provide a way to explore the implications of deep uncertainty for policymaking (prepare for the future) by identifying possible future problems and identifying potential policies for dealing with the problems.
4. An important disadvantage of the use of scenarios is that the scenario results are often used as 'certain' predictions, while they should be interpreted as 'what if' estimates for some plausible futures, and it is unknown (and unknowable) whether the actual future is covered by them.

5. In the backcasting method, a normative target in the future – a desired outcome – is chosen as a starting point for the futures analysis. Images of the future have to be designed that meet the specified targets. They should be clearly different from each other, in order to give an idea of the huge variety of possible futures, all of which meet the specified targets. Also in the backcasting method (1) it is important to avoid using forecasted futures as certainties, and (2) it is incorrect to assume that specified policies will actually lead to the desired future.
6. Some scientists are now thinking about policies that take uncertainty into account. The key idea is not to specify an 'optimal' policy for a single best estimate future, but rather to design a policy that is flexible and adaptable.

NOTE

1. High Speed 2 (HS2) was a British proposal to build a high-speed rail line in two parts – 'Phase 1' between London and Birmingham, and then 'Phase 2' between Birmingham and Crewe, and Birmingham and Manchester and Leeds (High Speed 2 costs | The Institute for Government, accessed December 2021). In November 2021, the UK government cancelled part of HS2 from East Midlands Parkway to Sheffield and Leeds – it is now only the route to Manchester that is going to be built. This has implications for future studies (political uncertainty) and the construction costs, etc. (www.theguardian.com/uk-news/2021/nov/18/hs2 -rail-leg-to-leeds-scrapped-grant-shapps-confirms).

REFERENCES

Agusdinata, D.B. (2008), *Exploratory Modeling and Analysis: A Promising Method to Deal with Deep Uncertainty,* Delft: Next Generation Infrastructures Foundation.
Banister, D., D. Stead and R. Hickman (2008), 'Looking over the horizon: visioning and back casting', in A. Perrels, V. Himanen and M. Lee-Gosselin (eds), *Building Blocks for Sustainable Transport: Obstacles, Trends, Solutions,* Helsinki: VATT and Emerald, 25–54.
Banister, D., D. Stead, P. Steen, J. Åkerman, K. Dreborg, P. Nijkamp and R. Schleicher-Tappeser (2000), *European Transport Policy and Sustainable Mobility,* London and New York: Spon Press.
Bankes, S. (1993), 'Exploratory modeling for policy analysis', *Operations Research*, 43 (3), 435–44.
Bankes S.C., W.E. Walker, and J.H. Kwakkel (2013), 'Exploratory modeling and analysis', in S. Gass and M.C. Fu (eds), *Encyclopedia of Operations Research and Management Science,* 3rd edn, Berlin: Springer.
Börjeson, L., M. Höjera, K.-H. Dreborg, T. Ekvall and G. Finnvedena (2006), 'Scenario types and techniques: Towards a user's guide', *Futures*, 38 (7), 723–39.
Cruz, C.O. and J. M. Sarmento (2020), 'Traffic forecast inaccuracy in transportation: a literature review of roads and railways projects; *Transportation*, 47 (4), 1571–606, DOI: 10.1007/s11116–019–09972-y
de Neufville, R. and K. Smet (2019), 'Engineering options analysis', in V.A.W.J. Marchau, W.E. Walker, P.J. Bloemen and S.W. Popper (eds), *Decision Making Under Deep Uncertainty: From Theory to Practice.* New York: Springer.
Dewar, J.A., C.H. Builder, W.M. Hix and M. Levin (1993), *Assumption-Based Planning: A Planning Tool for Very Uncertain Times,* MR114-A, Santa Monica, CA: RAND.
Findeisen, W. and E.S. Quade (1985), 'The methodology of systems analysis: an introduction and overview', in H.J. Miser and E.S. Quade (eds), *Handbook of Systems Analysis: Overview of Uses, Procedures, Applications, and Practice,* New York: Elsevier Science, 117–49.
Flyvbjerg, B., N. Bruzelius and W. Rothengatter (2003), *Megaprojects and Risk: An Anatomy of Ambition,* Cambridge: Cambridge University Press.

Flyvbjerg, B., M.K. Skamris Holm and S.L. Buhl (2006), 'Inaccuracy in Traffic Forecasts', *Transport Reviews*, 26 (1), 1–24.

Geurs, K.T. and G.P. van Wee (2000), *Environmentally Sustainable Transport: Implementation and Impacts for the Netherlands for 2030. Phase 3 Report of the OECD Project 'Environmentally Sustainable Transport'*, RIVM report 773002013, Bilthoven: Rijksinstituut voor Volksgezondheid en Milieu.

Haasnoot, M., A. Warren, and J.H. Kwakkel, (2019) 'Dynamic Adaptive Policy Pathways (DAPP)', in V.A.W.J. Marchau, W.E. Walker, P.J.T.M. Bloemen and S.W. Popper (eds), *Decision Making Under Deep Uncertainty: From Theory to Practice*. New York: Springer.

Hadjidemetriou, G. M., J. Teal, L. Kapetas and A.K. Parlikad (2022), 'Flexible planning for intercity multimodal transport infrastructure', *Journal of Infrastructure Systems*, 28 (1), doi:10.1061/(ASCE) IS.1943–555X.0000664

Hickman, R. and D. Banister (2014), *Transport, Climate Change and the City*, London: Routledge.

Hojer, M. (1998), 'Transport telematics in urban systems: a backcasting Delphi study', *Transportation Research D*, 3 (6), 445–63.

International Energy Agency (2021), *Energy Technology Perspectives 2020*, Paris: IEA, www.iea.org.

International Energy Agency (2021), *World Energy Outlook 2021*, revised version, December 2021, Paris: IEA, www.iea.org.

Institute for Government (2021), *High Speed 2 costs*, accessed December 2021 at www.institutefor government.org.uk/explainers/high-speed-2-costs.

Kwakkel, J.H., W.E. Walker and V.A.W.J. Marchau (2010a), 'Classifying and communicating uncertainties in model-based policy analysis', *International Journal of Technology, Policy and Management*, 10 (4), 299–315.

Kwakkel, J.H., W.E. Walker and V.A.W.J. Marchau (2010b), 'Assessing the efficacy of adaptive airport strategic planning: results from computational experiments', *Environment and Planning B: Planning and Design*, 39, 533–50.

Kwakkel, J.H., W.E. Walker and V.A.W.J. Marchau (2010c), 'Adaptive Airport Strategic Planning', *European Journal of Transport and Infrastructure Research*, 10 (3), 249–73.

Lempert, R.J. (2019), 'Robust Decision Making (RDM)', in V.A.W.J. Marchau, W.E. Walker, P.J.T.M. Bloemen and S.W. Popper (eds), *Decision Making Under Deep Uncertainty: From Theory to Practice*, New York: Springer.

Lempert, R.J., S.W. Popper and S.C. Bankes (2003), *Shaping the Next One Hundred Years: New Methods for Quantitative, Long-Term Policy Analysis*, MR-1626-RPC, Santa Monica, CA: RAND.

Leusink, A. and H.A. Zanting (2009), *Naar een afwegingskader voor een klimaatbestendig Nederland, met ervaringen uit 4 case studies: samenvatting voor bestuurders [Towards a trade-off framework for climate-proofing the Netherlands, with experiences from 4 case studies: executive summary]*, accessed August 2011 at http://edepot.wur.nl/15219.

Lyons, G. and G. Marsden (2019), 'Opening out and closing down: the treatment of uncertainty in transport planning's forecasting paradigm', *Transportation*, 48, 595–616, https://doi.org/10.1007/s11116-019-10067-x.

Lyons, G., C. Rohr, A. Smith, A. Rothnie and A. Curry (2021), 'Scenario planning for transport practitioners', *Transportation Research Interdisciplinary Perspectives*, vol. 11, https://doi.org/10.1016/j.trip.2021.100438.

Marchau, V.A.W.J., W.E. Walker, P.J.T.M. Bloemen and S.W. Popper (eds) (2019), *Decision Making Under Deep Uncertainty: From Theory to Practice*, New York: Springer.

Marchau, V.A.W.J., W.E. Walker and G.P. van Wee (2010), 'Dynamic adaptive transport policies for handling deep uncertainty', *Technological Forecasting and Social Change*, 77 (6), 940–50.

Milkovits, M., R. Copperman, J. Newman, J. Lemp, T. Rossi and S. Sun (2019), 'Exploratory Modeling and Analysis for Transportation: An Approach and Support Tool - TMIP-EMAT', *Transportation Research Record*, 2673 (9), 407–18. https://doi.org/10.1177/0361198119844463.

Quist, J. (2007), *Backcasting for a Sustainable Future: The Impact after 10 Years*, Delft: Eburon Academic Publishers.

RAND Europe (1997), *Scenarios for Examining Civil Aviation Infrastructure Options in the Netherlands*, DRU-1513-VW/VROM/EZ, Santa Monica, CA: RAND.

Schippl, J. and I. Leisner (2009), 'Backcasting in transport scenarios for the future of European long-distance transport', *Technikfolgenabschätzung: Theorie und Praxis*, 2 (18), 63–69.

Schwarz, B. (1988), 'Forecasting and scenarios', in H.J. Miser and E.S. Quade (eds), *Handbook of Systems Analysis: Craft Issues and Procedural Choices*, New York: Elsevier Science, 327–67.

Schwartz, P. (1996), *The Art of the Long View: Paths to Strategic Insight for Yourself and Your Company*, New York: Currency Doubleday.

Soria-Lara, J. and D. Banister (2018), 'Evaluating the impacts of transport backcasting scenarios with multi-criteria analysis', *Transportation Research Part A: Policy and Practice*, 110, 26–37. https://doi .org/10.1016/j.tra.2018.02.004.

Taleb, N.N. (2007), *The Black Swan: The Impact of the Highly Improbable*, New York: Random House.

Thissen, W.A.H. (1999), 'A Scenario Approach for Identification of Research Topics', in M.P.C. Weijnen and E.F. ten Heuvelhof (eds), *The Infrastructure Playing Field in 2030: Design and Management of Infrastructures*, Delft: Delft University Press, 5–10.

Van der Heijden, K., R. Bradfield, G. Burt and G. Cairns (2002), *The Sixth Sense: Accelerating Organisational Learning with Scenarios*, Chichester: John Wiley & Sons, Ltd.

Van der Pas, J.W.G.M., W.E. Walker, V.A.W.J. Marchau, G.P. van Wee and D.B. Agusdinata (2010), 'Exploratory MCDA for handling deep uncertainties: the case of intelligent speed adaptation implementation', *Journal of Multi-Criteria Decision Analysis*, 17, 1–23.

Van Wee, B. (2009), *Transport policy: what can it and what can't it do?*, European Transport Conference 2009, accessed February 2011 at http://etcproceedings.org/paper/transport-policy-what-it-can-and -what-it-can-t-do.

Walker, W.E. (2000a), 'Policy Analysis: A Systematic Approach to Supporting Policymaking in the Public Sector', *Journal of Multicriteria Decision Analysis*, 9 (1–3), 11–27.

Walker, W.E. (2000b), *Uncertainty: The Challenge for Policy Analysis in the 21st Century*, P-8051, Santa Monica, CA: RAND.

Walker, W.E., J. Cave and S.A. Rahman (2001), 'Adaptive Policies, Policy Analysis, and Policymaking', *European Journal of Operational Research*, 128 (2), 282–89.

Walker, W.E., P. Harremoës, J. Rotmans, J.P. van der Sluijs, M.B.A. van Asselt, P. Janssen and M.P. Krayer von Krauss (2003), 'Defining uncertainty: a conceptual basis for uncertainty management in model-based decision support', *Integrated Assessment*, 4 (1), 5–17.

Walker, W.E., V.A.W.J. Marchau, and J.H. Kwakkel (2019), 'Dynamic Adaptive Planning (DAP)' in V.A.W.J. Marchau, W.E. Walker, P.J.T.M. Bloemen and S.W. Popper (eds) (2019), *Decision Making Under Deep Uncertainty: From Theory to Practice*. New York: Springer.

15
Appraisal methods for transport policy

Niek Mouter and Piet Rietveld

15.1   INTRODUCTION

Transportation networks provide an array of benefits in the forms of goods delivery, access to services and personal mobility. However, transport can also result in several adverse effects such as damage to the environment (nature reserves, CO_2 emissions and noise pollution (see Chapter 10) and crashes (see Chapter 11)). Governments are in many ways involved in transport policy and planning (see Chapter 13). For instance, they determine regulations such as speed limits and they can decide to invest public budget in the extension and/or maintenance of transport infrastructure. In many cases, policy makers want to make decisions informed by the expected positive and negative impacts of a transport policy option. Various ex-ante evaluation methods are available which can be used to provide such information.

This chapter surveys five evaluation methods that are used to inform policy makers about transport impacts: Social Cost–Benefit Analysis (SCBA), Participatory Value Evaluation (PVE), Multi-Criteria Analysis (MCA), Environmental Impact Assessment (EIA) and the Social Impact Assessment (SIA). The five methods will be introduced, and differences will be described. Knowledge about the differences, virtues and limitations of each of the methods can be used by policy makers to select the most appropriate ex-ante evaluation method for the assessment of a specific transport policy decision. Section 15.2 will discuss SCBA which is the most frequently used and hotly debated appraisal method in transport decision-making. Subsequently, Sections 15.3–15.6 will discuss the other four methods. Section 15.7 compares the methods. Finally, Section 15.8 summarizes the main conclusions of this chapter.

15.2   SOCIAL COST–BENEFIT ANALYSIS

In virtually all western countries Social Cost–Benefit Analysis (SCBA) is mandatory when national funding is asked for large transport projects (Mackie et al., 2014). Basically, a SCBA is an overview of all the positive effects (benefits) and negative effects (costs) of a project or policy option (e.g. van Wee, 2012). These costs and benefits are quantified as far as possible and expressed in monetary terms. Finally, government projects are typically intertemporal in nature, so the benefits and costs occur over a number of periods. To deal with this, they are presented as so-called present values, implying that – even after a correction for inflation – it is better to have one euro or dollar now than in ten years' time, for example (van Wee, 2012). The discount rate is used to express this valuation (Mouter, 2018). Often, present values are aggregated to yield an indicator of the project's net impact on social welfare.

Hence, the aim of SCBA is to derive a summary indicator of the costs and benefits for *all* the actors affected. The term 'social' is used to indicate that the interests of *all* groups are incorporated. This is one of the main differences from the notion of a 'business case', which exclusively focuses on the interests of one particular actor. A SCBA measures the social desirability of a transport policy option in a systematic way based on economic theory. SCBA quantifies the project's positive and negative effects and translates these quantified effects in monetary terms.

15.2.1   General Description

Welfare economics provides the theoretical underpinnings of SCBA (Boadway and Bruce, 1984). One of the key concepts in welfare economics is the Pareto criterion which states that the social welfare effect of a project is positive if it makes someone better off without making anyone worse off (Nyborg, 2014). The problem here is that government policies will hardly ever be able to pass this criterion. For instance, when considering new transport infrastructure, taxpayers will pay the costs, and quite probably there will be negative external effects, e.g. noise or CO_2 emissions. A more practical concept is the Kaldor–Hicks efficiency criterion (Hicks, 1939; Kaldor, 1939), which relaxes the Pareto conditions by adding the possibility of (potential) compensation. The Kaldor–Hicks efficiency criterion asserts that a policy (or other change) can be considered as welfare-increasing if those who benefit can compensate those who suffer from it, creating a Pareto improvement after compensation. According to the Kaldor–Hicks efficiency criterion, the compensation does not actually have to take place: it is enough that it is theoretically possible. This implies that there is only a potential Pareto improvement, and not necessarily an actual Pareto improvement. Standard SCBAs are generally based on the Kaldor–Hicks efficiency criterion. SCBA assesses whether a transport project passes the Kaldor–Hicks efficiency test by expressing all the positive and negative effects of a policy in monetary terms and adding them up. If the sum is positive the project is considered to be welfare enhancing as those who benefit can theoretically compensate those who suffer.

Welfare economics provides strict procedures for the objects that have standing in the SCBA analysis, for the impacts that are considered in the analysis and for the way different impacts are valued. In principle, welfare economics prescribes two principles when conducting a SCBA being individualism and non-paternalism. Individualism implies that the preferences of individual citizens form the basis of a SCBA (Sen, 1979) and non-paternalism assumes that individuals are the best judges of their own welfare. In combination these postulates imply that the citizens and firms that are affected by the policy are the sole objects who have standing in a SCBA study, and their preferences are respected. In principle, preferences of experts, stakeholders and policy makers related to the impacts of the transport project do not play any role in the analysis as these actors are only consulted to provide methodologies for deriving the preferences of citizens. Welfare economics also provides SCBA researchers with a clear frame of reference when selecting the impacts of transport policy options that should (not) be included in a SCBA because only impacts that affect the welfare of individuals should be included. For instance, citizens' preferences for the way that the benefits and burdens of a transport policy option are distributed across society are not part of the total net benefits in a SCBA (Mouter et al., 2017b). Another consequence that is excluded from a SCBA is public support for a transport policy option (Mouter, 2017).

Welfare economics also provides clear guidance for the weighting procedure that is used in SCBA to evaluate the impacts of a transport policy option. SCBA measures a project's societal value by quantifying the project's societal impacts in monetary terms using the notion of the amount of money individuals are willing to pay (WTP) from their private income. For a positive effect, the WTP is the maximum amount which a person is willing to pay for it. For negative effects, the WTP is negative (then often called willingness-to-accept).

One example of an approach to derive the amount of money that individuals are willing to pay for reductions in travel time and accident risk concerns using (hypothetical) route choice experiments. Participants in these choice experiments are asked to make a series of private choices between routes which differ in terms of travel time, accident risk and travel costs (e.g. Batley et al., 2019; Bahamonde-Birke et al., 2015; Börjesson and Eliasson, 2014; Hensher et al., 2009).

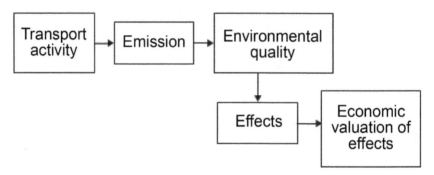

Figure 15.1   Illustration of the consumer surplus (CS) concept

With the choice of consumer preferences as the starting point for SCBA, the consumers' willingness to pay is an important element of the valuation of costs and benefits (Small and Verhoef, 2007). The consumers' preferences can be described by means of a demand function (see Figure 15.1). A demand function describes how much a group of consumers is prepared to pay for a certain product or service. For example, in Figure 15.1, when P0 is the price, N0 consumers will use the service provided. When the price decreases to p1 the number of consumers increases to N1. In the context of transport, the 'transport service' may mean: making a bus trip from A to B, or making use of the road to drive from C to D. Consider now the group of N0 consumers who make use of a certain transport service who are prepared to pay the price P0 for this service. Note that their willingness to pay is at least P0: most of these consumers are prepared to pay more than just P0. The difference between what a consumer actually pays and what he would be prepared to pay is called the 'consumer surplus'. In Figure 15.2 the consumer surplus of all users of the service when the price P0 is represented by the triangle CS.

The term consumer surplus can be useful in discussions on 'the economic importance of transport'. The total amount of money actually paid by consumers (N0×P0) provides an underestimate of what these consumers are willing to pay for this service. Note that in Figure 15.2 when the price is P0 the consumer surplus is considerably smaller than the actual expenditure for this transport service, but for lower prices, this no longer applies.

Consider now an improvement of a certain connection so that the costs of using it decrease from P0 to P1. For the present users of the transport service the consumer surplus changes from N0×P0 to N0×P1, which implies an increase of N0×(P0−P1). Another consequence of the price decrease is that it generates new users N1−N0. The change in consumer surplus of this group is represented by the triangle DCS1 in Figure 15.2. This change is equal to the increase in the number of users N1−N0 multiplied by half of the price decrease P0−P1: DCS1=0.5×(N1−N0)×(P0−P1). This is the so-called 'rule of half'. It means that the benefits of a price decrease for new consumers are 50% of the benefits of incumbent consumers. That the result is 50% can be made intuitively clear by first considering a new consumer with a willingness to pay very close to P0. This consumer benefits almost fully from the price decrease. But a consumer with a willingness to pay close to P1 hardly benefits from the price decrease. Then the average new consumer's benefit will be 50% of the benefit of incumbent consumers. The rule of half is exact when the demand function is linear, but in real world cases the demand function might not be linear.[1] In such a case, the rule of half is only an approximation.

The notion of consumer surplus can of course also be used in the case of price increases. The analysis is entirely symmetric. Note that in this case the disadvantage of a price decrease is largest for the consumers who continue to use the service and smaller for the consumers who stop using the service because they apparently have another alternative (another transport mode, another destination, staying at home) which is sufficiently attractive for them to decide to change their behaviour. Thus, the economic approach implies that people who do not change their behaviour as a consequence of a price increase are hit harder than people who do change their behaviour. It is worth noting that this result may be rather different from a political economy perspective, where consumers who do change their behaviour are considered to be the ones hurt most by a price increase. These consumers cannot afford to pay the high price and hence should be considered as the greatest victims. This may well lead to a gap between cost–benefit analysis where consumers who change their behaviour get a low weighting and political debates where these consumers get a high weighting.[2] This is an illustration of the difficulties that may emerge when SCBA is applied in situations where equity concerns are high. We will address this subject later in this chapter.

To be able to assess the benefits of a change in transport services leading to a decrease in the price, information is needed on the price in the reference situation and the new situation (see Chapter 14) and the number of consumers in both cases. The reference situation may be the current situation, but in many practical applications of SCBA the alternatives refer to infrastructure projects that may take a long time before they are completed. Hence, predictions are needed of prices and numbers of users in the future, with and without the policy alternative.

Table 15.1 Example of an SCBA table for a road upgrade involving separation of motorized and non-motorized transport

	Valuation
Benefits:	
Decrease of travel time for present road users	200
Welfare improvement of new road users	60
Improvement in traffic safety	20
Costs:	
Environmental costs (higher emissions because of higher speeds and greater traffic volumes)	15
Extra noise nuisance	20
Construction costs	160
Additional maintenance costs	10
Deterioration of landscape PM (pro memory) Benefits – costs	75 – PM

Note: Figures in net present values in million euros.

For this purpose, one needs projections on how the economy and the transport system will look in the future and how transport demand will be affected by a price change. These changes in demand can be estimated using transport models (see Chapter 16) or price elasticities, as mentioned in Chapters 3 and 6.

The final step of SCBA is that an overall assessment of alternatives is carried out by comparing the alternatives with a reference alternative as mentioned above. The changes in costs and benefits for all actors are determined for each alternative (compared with the reference alternative) and then the net balance in the change in costs and benefits can be computed. The alternative with the highest positive net balance is the best candidate to be implemented according to SCBA. Since the results of SCBA depend on many uncertain inputs, sensitivity analysis is recommended. For an example of the results of SCBA, see Table 15.1.[3] Government projects are typically intertemporal in nature, so the benefits and costs occur over a number of periods (e.g. Boadway, 2006). To deal with this, they are presented as so-called present values, implying that – even after a correction for inflation – it is better to have one euro or dollar now than in ten years' time, for example (van Wee, 2012). The discount rate is used to express this valuation. A discount rate is expressed as a percentage per year. If the discount rate is d, then the present value someone puts on a benefit gained from a euro in a year's time is equal to $1/(1+d)$; a euro in two years' time is now worth $1/(1+d)2$ etc. This is called discounting. The resulting value today of a future euro is called the present value. Finally, in a SCBA, present values are aggregated into a final indicator such as the net present value (NPV) - which implies subtracting the present values of all costs from the present values of all benefits – or the Benefit–Cost Ratio (BCR) – benefits divided by the costs.

15.2.2   Valuation Methods

As said, one crucial step in a SCBA is to obtain monetary values for all non-priced impacts. For instance, a Value of Travel Time Savings is obtained to value travel time savings (see Chapter 6) and various valuation metrics are obtained to monetize safety impacts (see Chapter 11). The valuation of environmental impacts of a transport project is relatively challenging as it addresses the final results of a whole chain of effects from transport via emissions to impacts on environmental quality (see Figure 15.2). This chain will vary according to type of environmental effect (see also Chapter 10). In the case of noise, the effect on environmental quality will be restricted to the local environment. The effects concerned are, among others, annoyance, disturbance of sleep, stress and heart diseases for those living or working close by. In the case of CO_2 emissions the spread is much broader, and the effects will be in terms of damage to health and ecosystems, among other things.

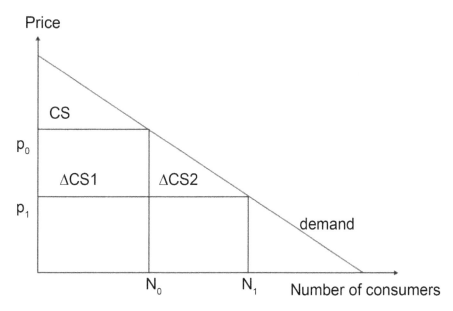

Figure 15.2   Chain from transport to economic valuation of emissions

There are various methods for arriving at monetary values for the environmental effects of transport. For a discussion of various methods, we refer to Johansson (1991) and Perman et al. (2003). Two different classes of valuation approaches can be distinguished. The first class focuses on the valuation of environmental effects via observed behaviour in markets. The second approach focuses on the valuation of environmental effects via stated preferences techniques such as a discrete choice experiment (Train, 2009). Below, we will discuss examples of both approaches in some detail.

    An example of the valuation of environmental effects via observed behaviour in markets is that houses in noisy areas will most probably have a lower value. Via a so-called hedonic price approach one can isolate the effect of noise from the effects of many other factors that have an impact on the value of dwellings. The outcome of a hedonic price analysis is the percentage change in the value of a house due to exposure to a certain noise level when all other features of a house are kept constant. This econometric approach is often applied to the valuation of noise near airports (see, for example, Schipper, 2001; Dekkers and van der Straaten, 2009). Impacts of transport policy options on landscape, nature and the proximity of highways and light rail transit are evaluated through analysing the private decisions of individuals in the real estate market (e.g. Allen et al., 2015; Seo et al., 2014; Tijm et al., 2019). Note that consumers will be heterogeneous with respect to the noise annoyance: people who strongly prefer a quiet environment will usually not live in very noisy places, since people who give less priority to a quiet place will bid higher prices. Thus, the phenomenon of self-selection will reduce the burden of noise (Nijland et al., 2003). A sudden increase in noise levels due to the opening of a new runway, for example, will then affect people with a strong dislike of noise. In the long run a new equilibrium will emerge via spatial sorting of households. A basic assumption behind hedonic price analyses is that the housing market is in equilibrium. Thus, this may lead to an underestimate of the effects in the short run when a sudden unanticipated increase in noise levels occurs.

A related method that is close to actual market-oriented behaviour concerns the costs that people incur to visit nature areas. These costs appear from the travel costs they incur and the entrance fee, if there is one, among others. This so-called travel cost method (see Perman et al., 2003) can be used to determine the use value of nature areas. This method also has its limitations, since it is not so clear how to value the travel time of these leisure trips. In addition, the travel cost method does not address so-called non-use values of a nature area. An implication is that, when there are two identical nature areas, one in a region with high population density and the other one in a sparsely populated area, the former one will attract more visitors who express their willingness to pay via their travel cost than the latter. So, the use value of the former will be larger than that of the latter.

The second approach in the field of valuations is to base them on the subjective valuations of consumers elicited via surveys. These stated preference methods come in different shapes. The Contingent Valuation Method (CVM) uses surveys to ask people directly, in open-ended questions, what money value they attach to effects they (may) experience. For instance, participants are asked how much they are willing to pay to reduce the numbers of animals killed by transport in a certain area. Another stated preference method uses stated choice experiments (Carson and Czajkowski, 2014). Using this method, the respondents in a survey choose between different options, including financial changes. From their choices, the average value they attach to an effect can be derived.

A third method to determine prices when there is no market is the so-called 'prevention cost method'. This method indicates how much it would cost to prevent a certain target being exceeded. For example, how much would it cost to reduce CO_2 emissions such that they comply with international agreements? This method is rather different from the methods discussed above because it is formulated in terms of prevention costs, so that the damage cost is not estimated. The prevention cost method can be used in cases where no damage cost estimates are available, in particular when a clear target has been formulated in the policy

Table 15.2 Assessment of evaluation methods for environmental damage

Method	Scientific basis	Information needed	Reliability	Applicable to
Travel cost method	Good	Observed choice behaviour	Good	Use value of nature and landscape
Hedonic price method	Good	Outcomes of market processes	Good	Noise nuisance, local emissions, safety
Stated preference	Reasonable	Hypothetical choices	Reasonable	Broad range of applications; also for global effects
Contingent valuation	Reasonable	Hypothetical choices	Difficult to verify	Broad range of applications; also for global effects
Shadow price method	Dubious	Prevention costs	Good	Broad range of applications; also for global effects

domain.[4] It is worth noting that the principle of individualism is breached here because it is not the preferences of individuals who form the bases of valuing reduction of CO_2 emissions, but the preferences of politicians who set the targets of reduction of CO_2 emissions. A concise comparison of the methods discussed here can be found in Table 15.2.

15.2.3 Issues in SCBA

The use of SCBA as a decision support tool for the public sector is not without problems. One of the first issues is that the distribution of costs and benefits may be very uneven so a dichotomy of winners and losers may emerge (see also Chapter 12). For example, users of the road presented in Table 15.1 experience safer and faster traffic, but residents around the road may not like the noise. The final outcome of SCBA is the net result of winners and losers so that the distribution is not directly visible. As said, the main idea behind SCBA is that the gains should be high enough so that the winners can compensate the losers (this is the so-called Hicks–Kaldor principle) and still be better off in the end. In that case everybody would be better off (this is known as the Pareto principle). However, the above only involves a hypothetical possibility to compensate, and there is no guarantee at all that an actual compensation will take place. Hence, almost every policy alternative will lead to the situation that there is a group of losers who may see a reason to protest against the proposed plan.

Thus, the strict use of the hypothetical compensation notion in SCBA may lead to the situation that alternatives are selected with a very unequal distribution of costs and benefits. Suppose now that there is another alternative with a somewhat lower net outcome but with a more balanced distribution of costs and benefits. Taking distributional considerations into account, policy makers might prefer the second alternative above the one with the higher benefit–cost result. The issue of transport equity is much discussed in the literature (Aparicio, 2018; Bills and Walker, 2017; Lucas and Jones, 2012; Nahmias-Biran et al., 2017; Pereira et al., 2017). A fair distribution of impacts (benefits and costs) is by far the most discussed type of equity. Van Wee (2012) observes that equity not only refers to a fair distribution of burdens and benefits, but that it can also refer to other ethical principles such as procedural justice. Equity concerns are cited as the most neglected (and difficult to measure) in transport policy (Berechman, 2018). For instance, SCBA has been criticised for placing too much value on increasing mobility overall, rather than ensuring equitable access to transport services for different age groups, genders or ethnic groups at risk of social exclusion (Ferreira et al., 2012). Transport-related inequalities that tend to be neglected in the literature relate to affordability, proximity to services, inclusivity (e.g. for the disabled), agency, freedom of choice and transport accessibility levels (Pereira et al., 2017).

A second critique on SCBA concerns how SCBA does not distinguish between private and public preferences. SCBA's monetization of the impacts of government projects is based on how much affected individuals are willing to pay from their private income (Persky, 2001), but SCBA fails to consider that private choices may not fully reflect citizens' preferences about public goods and means (Mouter et al., 2021a). As said, transport SCBA use monetary metrics that are either directly derived from individuals' market behaviour or from hypothetical consumer choices. This 'private willingness-to-pay approach' has been criticized by scholars who assert that the way that individuals balance their own after-tax incomes against the attributes of government projects when making private choices may be a poor proxy for showing what individuals believe how their government should trade-off public budgets and impacts of public projects (Mouter et al., 2018). Many of these limitations of SCBA arise due to individuals' perception that the government should allocate public resources in a different way than they allocate their own private income.

The literature discusses various problems with using individual private willingness-to-pay to infer the welfare of a government policy in the context of public choices. A first reason is that private choices may be distorted through collective action problems (e.g. Lusk and Norwood, 2011; Sen, 1995). For instance, people may not be willing to contribute individually to a public good (e.g. air pollution) because the impact of their individual contribution is negligible, but people may be willing to contribute when the whole community is forced to contribute through a new law or a tax increase because the impact of this coordinated contribution can be substantial (Lusk and Norwood, 2011; Sen, 1995). A second reason for a distinction between private preferences and public preferences concerns how individuals value the same impact differently in a private sphere (the real estate market) and the public sphere (ballot box), as distributional considerations might be more relevant in the latter context (e.g. Mouter et al., 2019; Sagoff, 1988). A third reason why scholars criticize the private willingness to pay paradigm in SCBA is that they think that this is an inappropriate way to value impacts of government projects that are not possible to measure with private income (Aldred, 2006). For instance, Sunstein (1993) asserts that values which are not traded in a real-life market setting, such as biodiversity and landscape, might be valued incorrectly when they are expressed in private income.

As well as many theoretical arguments about why individuals entertain different preferences in a private and public setting, the literature also includes empirical insights showing that individuals value impacts of transport projects such as travel time savings and accident risk differently when they trade these impacts against their own budget or the public budget (Mouter et al., 2017a, 2018).

15.3 PARTICIPATORY VALUE EVALUATION

Scholars developed the Participatory Value Evaluation (PVE) to alleviate some of the issues addressed above (e.g. Mouter et al., 2021a). In a PVE, participants are offered several possible public projects, information about the impacts of these projects and a constrained public budget in an (online) experiment (Mouter et al., 2021a). Participants are asked to choose the public projects they like to see implemented while respecting the public budget constraint. The trade-offs made in selecting their preferred portfolio can be used to establish individuals' preferences for (the impacts of) the public projects and to rank these projects in terms of their desirability (Dekker et al., 2020; Mouter et al., 2021b). The PVE approach thus aspires to infer welfare effects of (impacts of) government projects from individuals' preferences regarding the expenditure of public budget. The innovations of the PVE appraisal method are described in various papers (Dekker et al., 2020; Mouter et al., 2021a and b). Mouter et al. (2021b) explain that PVE cannot only be considered as a valuation method which provides input for a SCBA, but that the outcomes of a PVE can also be directly used for establishing the social welfare effects of government policy options. In that case, PVE can be considered as a full-fledged alternative to SCBA. Dekker et al. (2020) present the technical details of such a welfare analysis.

The most important benefit of the PVE approach is that individuals who believe that government budgets should be spent on different purposes than their own money can express these preferences (Mouter et al., 2021a). A second advantage of PVE is that it bypasses the concern that WTP-based valuation might be an inappropriate way to value impacts of government projects that are relatively difficult to translate into private income. As said, examples here include landscape and nature. PVE does not require translation of government project impacts into private income. Instead, an impact of a government project is valued through the extent to which individuals are willing to sacrifice other impacts of government projects (Mouter et al., 2021a). For instance, in a PVE experiment, individuals are asked to trade-off noise pollution against other impacts of governmental policy (e.g. reduction of mortality risk) which contrasts the WTP valuation approach in which individuals are asked to trade-off environmental impacts against private income. Moreover, the other issues with the private WTP paradigm addressed in the previous paragraph ('people may be willing to contribute collectively, but may not be willing to contribute individually' and 'people may place a value on the way collective decisions are made') are addressed in a PVE setting because impacts of transport projects are valued in a collective setting in which overall burdens and benefits of proposed transport projects are considered together in the context of a government decision (Mouter et al., 2019).

At the time of writing this chapter (mid 2022), four large scale PVEs have been conducted for the evaluation of transport projects. In one PVE, 2,498 inhabitants from the Transport Authority Amsterdam were presented with 16 transport projects and related societal impacts (Mouter et al., 2021a). The total cost of the 16 projects was 386.5 million euros but with only 100 million euros to spend. Hence, it was not possible for the respondents to include all projects in their portfolio. The portfolio selections of the respondents were used to establish individuals' preferences for (the impacts of) the public projects and to rank these projects in terms of their desirability (Mouter et al., 2021a). In the study SCBAs made about the 16 projects under scrutiny. It turned out that projects which focus on improving traffic safety and cycling facilities perform relatively good in the PVE, whereas car projects perform relatively good in the SCBA analysis. Finally, this study revealed that participants in the PVE considered the spatial distribution of projects across the region of the Transport Authority Amsterdam in their portfolio selection.

15.4   MULTI-CRITERIA ANALYSIS

The multi-criteria analysis (MCA), also known as multiple-criteria decision-making (MCDM) or multiple-criteria decision analysis (MCDA), typically encompass the following stages:

1. identification of criteria against which to test transport policy options;
2. weighting and/or scoring the different criteria to arrive at a ranking of options.

Many different MCA methods have been developed (Dean, 2018). A certain class of MCA approaches can be defined by the set of rules establishing the nature of options, objectives, criteria, scores and weights as well as the way in which objectives/criteria, scores and weights are used to assess, compare, screen in/out or rank options.

A distinction can be made between 'sophisticated MCA methods' and 'simple MCA methods'. Sophisticated methods use advanced mathematical principles and procedures to weigh criteria and rank options. One example of such a method is the analytic hierarchical process (AHP) (Saaty, 1990). AHP begins by arranging the elements of the analysis in three main hierarchical levels: the overall goal of the decision-making problem at the top (e.g. satisfaction with a transport policy option); a set of decision criteria in the middle layers (e.g. factors that influence the satisfaction of transport policy options); and a group of competing options at the bottom (e.g. transport policy options). Next, the relative importance of each criterion with respect to the goal of the analysis is determined through a series of pairwise comparisons of criteria. The subjective judgements of experts or policy makers regarding the relevance of the different criteria are translated into a quantitative score and subsequently the most desirable option can be determined. Another example of a sophisticated MCA technique is the best-worst method (BWM) developed by Rezaei (2015). Similar to AHP, the BWM method starts with determining a set of decision criteria. A key difference with AHP is that in the second stage decision-makers participating in a BWM are asked to select the best and the worst criteria after which they should determine the preference of the best criterion over all the other criteria and the preference of all the other criteria over the worst criterion. Based on these choices both the direction and the strength of the preferences of one criterion over the other are computed which provides the basis of selecting the best alternative.

Simple MCA methods use relatively rough procedures to score options or even abstain from scoring and ranking the options. One example is the UK Appraisal Summary Table which does not aim to provide a final ranking of the options. Simplified MCA techniques are very popular, mainly because they are easy to use and understand (Dean, 2018). MCA studies can be undertaken either in non-participatory (i.e. expert-led) or participatory manner. In non-participatory assessments, the analysis is carried out autonomously by one or more experts, according to a typical technocratic approach. A key argument in favour of this approach is that a group of scientists and trained experts is better suited to make complex decisions than the average citizen. By contrast, participatory techniques adopt a more collaborative decision-making style, with the direct involvement of the different interested and affected parties (i.e. problem stakeholders) in the analysis (Macharis and Bernardini, 2015). Although participatory MCA techniques have been championed by transport scholars in the literature it is not totally clear whether techniques have enjoyed real-world applications or constitute mere academic proposals (Dean, 2018).

15.5 ENVIRONMENTAL IMPACT ASSESSMENT

An Environmental Impact Assessment (EIA) is a comprehensive evaluation of the likely effects of a transport project that significantly affects the environment. An EAI aims to contribute to environmental awareness and environmental protection by providing decision-makers with ex-ante information of environmental impacts of public and private initiatives (Jay et al., 2007). Since the 1970s EIA has become increasingly more important in planning practice and has been introduced in national legislation worldwide (Cornero, 2010). The National Environmental Policy Act of 1969 (NEPA) implemented EIA for federal agency actions in the United States. In the European Union (EU), the EIA Directive 85/337/EEC, which called 'on the assessment of the effects of certain public and private projects on the environment', has been in force since 1985. The goal of the Directive is to ensure that environmental values are fully considered in decision-making. Since 1985, EIA has been incorporated into the legislation of European member states; see Soria-Lara et al. (2020).

The usual information contained in an EIA report is:

1. a description of project alternatives and a baseline description of the environment where the project is located;
2. a prediction of significant effects of the project on the environment;
3. measures envisaged to avoid, prevent or reduce the effects on the environment;
4. description of alternatives and the main reasons for the alternative chosen;
5. a non-technical summary.

One crucial step in EIA is how to measure the environmental impacts originated by transport projects, an issue that has been frequently addressed in the academic literature (Soria-Lara et al., 2020). This is done using the concept of significance (Briggs and Hudson, 2013), which depends on both the magnitude (degree of environmental change caused) and the scale of the environmental impact. The magnitude is measured in terms of the corresponding indicator of altered environmental quality (Joumard and Gundmunson, 2010). These indicators may be quantitative (e.g. soil surface affected, number of people affected by a specific noise level) or qualitative (e.g. alteration of landscape quality).

Initiators of transport projects, which are either governmental agencies or private companies, are responsible for conducting an EIA. The competent authority decides on how to use the EIA outcomes and has to justify its decision, giving consent to the activity. Proponents may adjust their initiatives voluntarily (Arts et al., 2012).

Due to the legal requirements for EIA implementation, there are now strict guidelines for the EIA process for different countries and regions (Cornero 2010). However, because there was much freedom to adapt EIA to the specific needs of the different member states, there are considerable differences between EIA systems throughout the EU regarding various elements (Arts et al., 2012). For instance, when comparing the Dutch and UK EIA practice, Arts et al. (2012) establish that in the UK, there is no formal requirement to assess alternatives, in contrast to the Netherlands. Moreover, quality reviews of EIAs are better institutionalized in the Netherlands than in the UK. The Netherlands is one of the few countries that have established an independent expert commission charged with quality review. Notwithstanding the differences between the Dutch and the UK practice, Arts et al. (2012) identify that overall the EIA is about equally effective in both countries with regard to the incorporation of environmental concerns in decision-making.

Next to EIA in many countries Strategic Environmental Assessment (SEA) is applied also. In EIA concrete and specific projects are assessed (e.g. building a new highway between two specific cities). SEA is aimed at assessing policies, plans and programmes at a strategic level. The idea behind SEA can be explained with the highway building example just given. Before deciding on such a specific project, in many countries in the world a strategic planning phase takes place in which many more options to improve the accessibility in the region where the highway might be built are considered, compared and discussed. Examples of other options could be building or expanding railways, implementing road pricing, not building a new highway but improving the existing highway network, and so forth. So, assessing such a strategic plan on its environmental impacts gives decision-makers a broad insight in environmental effects of a range of options to improve accessibility discussed on the strategic level. Another key characteristic of SEA compared to EIA is that on a strategic level often combinations of specific plans become clear, e.g. next to building the new highway between the two cities potential plans are also presented to expand the cities with new residential and/or industrial areas. In SEA the cumulative environmental effects of the projects combined can be assessed. If only EIAs were carried out for specific projects, consequently only insights would be given to policy makers on environmental impacts of those specific projects and on mitigations options to make those specific projects more environmentally friendly. This would 'narrow' policy makers' decision-making information. Faith-Ell and Fischer (2021) provide an overview of SEA usage in transport planning.

15.6   SOCIAL IMPACT ASSESSMENT

Social Impact Assessment (SIA) was introduced in the late 1970s in the United States due to the perception of EIA being an assessment method with a strong biophysical bias (Morgan, 2012). The primary purpose of a SIA is to bring about a more sustainable and equitable biophysical and human environment (Vanclay, 2003). SIAs utilize participatory processes to analyze the concerns of interested and affected parties. It heavily involves stakeholders in the assessment of social impacts, the analysis of alternatives and monitoring of the planned intervention. A typical SIA consists of various steps, such as the identification of interested/affected people, selecting alternatives, assessing the social impacts, developing mitigation measures, developing strategies for dealing with residual or non-mitigatable impacts and proactively developing better outcomes (e.g. Mottee and Howitt, 2018; Vanclay, 2003). Hence, the focus of concern of SIA is a proactive stance to development and developing better outcomes, not just the identification or amelioration of negative or unintended outcomes.

Vanclay (2003) describes the core values of the SIA community and a set of principles to guide SIA practice. The role of SIA goes far beyond the ex-ante (in advance) prediction of adverse impacts and the determination of who wins and who loses (Vanclay, 2003). Esteves and Vanclay (2012) argue that SIA practitioners also believe that there should be an emphasis on enhancing the lives of vulnerable and disadvantaged people, and in particular, that there should be a specific focus on improving the lives of the worst-off members of society. Hence, the normative postulations of SIA are more in line with Rawlsian ethics which differs from the utilitarian philosophy which undergirds SCBA.

Mottee (2022) observes that despite the availability of authoritative international guidelines such as Vanclay et al. (2015), SIA is neither consistently mandated in legislation nor applied in the processes and procedures for infrastructure planning, even across established democracies. SIA in this context, if required at all, is often limited to an EIA 'add-on' technical study as part of a statutory planning process, which diminishes its potential to improve social outcomes (Mottee, 2022). Mottee (2022) observes in focus groups that a key limitation is that current SIA practice in many jurisdictions falls short of the good practice methodologies and theory as proposed in the academic and professional literature. Moreover, she claims that SIA should be deployed more in the strategic stages of integrated urban and transport planning to increase the potential to achieve more sustainable and equitable outcomes from urban planning processes.

15.7   COMPARING THE FIVE APPRAISAL METHODS

SCBA, PVE and MCA are quite similar in several respects. The three appraisal methods all aim to provide policy makers with information to assess the desirability of a transport policy option and the methods all rely on transportation model results. The most important difference between SCBA and PVE on the one hand and MCA on the other hand is that welfare economics provides the theoretical framework underlying SCBA and PVE, whereas MCA methods are not built on welfare economics. Welfare economics provides strict procedures for the objects which have standing in the SCBA/PVE analysis, for the criteria/impacts that are considered in the analysis and for the way different impacts are valued. MCA analysts, on the other hand, have a larger degree of freedom when selecting criteria and developing procedures to determine the weights (e.g. Macharis and Bernardini, 2015). For instance, a MCA analyst can decide to include distributional aspects and public support for a transport policy option as separate criteria which affect the final outcome of a MCA. Both impacts cannot affect the final indicators of a SCBA that is grounded in the Kaldor–Hicks efficiency criterion. PVE assumes that individuals define the attractiveness of a transport policy option based on standard impacts of a transport project such as reductions in travel time and accident risk (which are reflected in taste parameters) as well as other criteria that might not be on the radar of policy makers and experts (which are reflected in project specific parameters). Hence, PVE includes distributional impacts such as spatial equity (Mouter et al., 2021a) and there is no fundamental difference between PVE and MCA when it comes to the inclusion of transport impacts in the evaluation.

Moreover, the weighting procedure that is used in SCBA to evaluate the impacts of a transport policy option is very clear in the sense that the only criterion that defines the weight that should be assigned to an impact concerns the amount of money individuals are willing to pay from their private income. The same holds for PVE in the sense that transport policy options are valued based on the willingness of individuals to allocate public budget to (the impacts of) the transport policy option. The weighting of impacts/criteria in MCA can be partly based on translating impacts/criteria into monetary units, but the aggregation is also based on at least one other weighting method (e.g. scoring, ranking or weighting of a wide range of qualitative impact categories and criteria).

In sum, the three methods differ in terms of degrees of freedom for the analyst to select impacts and criteria that are relevant for the evaluation as well as weighting procedures. An SCBA analyst has to follow strict procedures of welfare economics when selecting impacts, and weighting procedures and as a result the degrees of freedom are limited; a PVE analyst has more liberty when selecting impacts although participants in the PVE (and not the analysts) eventually determine the relevance of a criterion for the evaluation. As stated above, a PVE analyst has no degrees of freedom when selecting a weighting procedure. Finally, an MCA analyst has large degrees of freedom in terms of selecting impacts and weighting procedures. The relatively large degree of freedom can be seen as a strength of MCA when benchmarked against SCBA and PVE. For instance, Gühnemann et al. (2012) asserts that MCA seems to be better in measuring intangibles and soft impacts than SCBA as these effects do not have to be converted into private income. For this reason, MCA has been used in many countries as complementary to SCBA to capture impacts not properly accounted for by the latter method (e.g. Mackie et al., 2014).

Although the flexibility of MCA can be seen as a strength, this characteristic of the evaluation method has been criticized for the arbitrariness in the selection of the weights applicable to different criteria and risks of double counting impacts (Annema et al., 2015). Qualitative assessment and the imputation of value-laden weightings to different criteria may lead to subjective biasing.

The most important differences between EIA and the three methods that were previously discussed (SCBA, PVE and MCA) is that the EIA puts emphasis on a specific set of (environmental) effects. A second difference is that an EIA also includes recommendations regarding the mitigation and management of negative environmental impacts. The purpose of the other methods that were discussed is not to provide such recommendations.

SIA is an anthropomorphic methodology in the sense that analysts consider all issues that affect people. The main difference with SCBA (and PVE) is that all social impacts are considered in an SIA and not only to the extent that humans are willing to pay (or willing to allocate public budget) for the impacts of the transport project. As a result, the degrees of freedom for the analyst to include impacts is relatively large likewise the MCA.

15.8 CONCLUSIONS

This chapter surveyed five evaluation methods that are used to inform policy makers about transport impacts: Social Cost–Benefit Analysis (SCBA), Participatory Value Evaluation (PVE), Multi-Criteria Analysis (MCA), Environmental Impact Assessment (EIA) and the Social Impact Assessment (SIA). These are the most important conclusions of this chapter:

1. SCBA is the most frequently used method for the ex-ante evaluation of transport projects. A SCBA measures the social desirability of a transport policy option in a systematic way based on economic theory. SCBA measures a project's societal value by quantifying the project's societal impacts in monetary terms using the notion of the amount of money individuals are willing to pay (WTP) from their private income.
2. In the literature, SCBA is criticized for various reasons. Firstly, citizens' preferences for the way that the benefits and burdens of a transport policy option are distributed across society are not part of the total net benefits in a SCBA. A second critique is that SCBA fails to consider that private choices may not fully reflect citizens' preferences about public goods and means.
3. PVE establishes the desirability of government projects based on an experiment in which individuals select their preferred portfolio of government projects given a constrained public budget. The main difference between the SCBA and PVE is that PVE establishes the desirability of government projects based on people's advice regarding the allocation of the public budget toward (impacts of) government projects, whereas SCBA establishes the desirability of government projects through analysing people's trade-offs between their private income and impacts of government projects.
4. MCA comprises various classes of methods, techniques and tools (with different degrees of complexity) which explicitly consider multiple objectives and criteria (or attributes) in decision-making problems.
5. The most important difference between SCBA and PVE on the one hand and MCA on the other hand is that SCBA and PVE are both based on welfare economics which provides strict procedures for the criteria/impacts that are considered in the analysis and for the way different impacts are weighted, whereas MCA analysts have a larger degree of freedom when selecting criteria and developing procedures to determine the weights. The relatively large degree of freedom can be seen as a strength of MCA as the methods seem to be better in measuring intangibles. Although the flexibility of MCA can be seen as a strength, this characteristic of the evaluation method has been criticized for the arbitrariness in the selection of the weights applicable to different criteria.
6. EIA is a comprehensive evaluation of the likely effects of a transport project that significantly affects the environment. Due to the legal requirements for EIA implementation, there are now strict guidelines for the EIA process for different countries and regions.
7. SIA aims to bring about a more sustainable and equitable biophysical and human environment. A SIA includes the processes of analysing, monitoring and managing the intended and unintended social consequences of planned transport interventions.

8. The most important difference between EIA and SIA and the other three methods is that EIA and SIA put emphasis on a specific set of effects (environmental or improving the lives of the worst-off members of society). A second difference is that an EIA and SIA also include recommendations regarding the mitigation and management of environmental and/or social impacts.
9. The five methods surveyed in this chapter all have their merits and limitations. It is important for practitioners to first define their appraisal need(s) and then select the appraisal method that best fits these needs. Practitioners should also realize that the five methods are not substitutable and therefore a smart combination of methods might be desirable in many cases.

ACKNOWLEDGEMENTS

The chapter is an update of a previous version composed by Professor Piet Rietveld. Professor Rietveld was an eminent and inspiring Dutch professor in Transport Economics who sadly passed away in 2013.

NOTES

1. Note that in our discussion of the demand curve we did not go into the issues of asymmetric responses with respect to changes in prices.
2. Of course, the range of effects will usually be broader, since price policies may also lead to changes in congestion and hence to travel times, but the essence of the gap between cost–benefit analysis and policy weights remains.
3. The meaning of the PM outcome will be discussed in more detail in Section 15.3.
4. The shadow price method and the conjoint analysis method clearly share the property that a price is obtained that cannot directly be observed in a market. The distinguishing feature of the shadow price method is that it follows from the costs to be made to satisfy a policy constraint, and as a consequence the price is based on prevention costs instead of damage costs.

REFERENCES

Aldred, J. (2006), 'Incommensurability and monetary valuation', *Land Economics*, 82(2), 141–61.
Allen, M.T., G.W. Austin and M. Swaleheen (2015), 'Measuring highway impacts on house prices using spatial regression', *Journal of Sustainable Real Estate*, 7(1), 83–98.
Annema, J.A., N. Mouter and J. Rezaei (2015), 'Cost-Benefit Analysis (CBA), or Multi-Criteria Decision-Making (MCDM) or Both: Politicians Perspective in Transport Policy Appraisal', *Transportation Research Procedia*, 10, 788–97.
Aparicio, Á. (2018), 'Equity Challenges in Major Transport Plans', *Transportation Research Procedia*, 31, 121–35. https://doi.org/10.1016/j.trpro.2018.09.054
Arts, J., H.A.C. Runhaar., T.B. Fischer, U. Jhathakur, F. van Laerhoven, P.P.J. Driessen and V. Onyango (2012), 'The effectiveness of EIA as an instrument for environmental governance: reflecting on 25 years of EIA practice in the Netherlands and the UK', *Journal of Environmental Assessment Policy and Management*, 14(4), 1250025.

Bahamonde-Birke, F.J., U. Kunert and H. Link (2015), 'The Value of a Statistical Life in a Road Safety Context – A Review of the Current Literature', *Transport Reviews*, 35(4), 488–511.

Batley, R., J. Bates, M. Bliemer, M. Börjesson, J. Bourdon, M.O. Cabral, P.K. Chintakayala, C. Choudhury, A. Daly, T. Dekker, E. Drivyla, T. Fowker, S. Hess, C. Heywood, D. Johnson, J. Laird, P. Mackie, J. Parkin, S. Sanders, R. Sheldon, M. Wardman and T. Worsley (2019), 'New appraisal values of travel time savings and reliability in Great Britain', *Transportation*, 46(3), 583–621.

Berechman, J. (2018), *The Infrastructure We Ride On: Decision Making in Transportation Investment*, Basingstoke: Palgrave Macmillan. https://doi.org/https://doi-org.tudelft.idm.oclc.org/10.1007/978-3-319-74606-7

Bills, T.S. and J.L. Walker (2017), 'Looking beyond the mean for equity analysis: Examining distributional impacts of transportation improvements', *Transport Policy*, 54, 61–69. https://doi.org/10.1016/j.tranpol.2016.08.003

Boadway, R. (2006), 'Principles of Cost-Benefit Analysis', *Public Policy Review*, 2(1), 1–44.

Boadway, R.W. and N. Bruce (1984), *Welfare Economics*, New York: B. Blackwell.

Börjesson, M. and J. Eliasson (2014), 'Experiences from the Swedish value of time study', *Transportation Research Part A: Policy and Practice*, 59, 144–58.

Briggs, S. and M.D. Hudson (2013), 'Determination of significance in ecological impact assessment: past change, current practice and future improvements', *Environmental Impact Assessment Review*, 38, 16–25.

Carson, R.T. and M. Czajkowski (2014), 'The discrete choice experiment approach to environmental contingent valuation', in S. Hess and A. Daly (eds), *Handbook of Choice Modelling*, Cheltenham, UK and Northampton, MA, USA: Edward Elgar Publishing.

Cornero, A. (2010), *Improving the Implementation of Environmental Impact Assessment. Report*, European Environmental Agency.

Dean, M. (2018), 'Assessing the Applicability of Participatory Multi-Criteria Analysis Methodologies to the Appraisal of Mega Transport Infrastructure', Ph.D. dissertation, The Bartlett School of Planning, University College London, UK.

Dekker, T., P.R. Koster and N. Mouter (2020), 'The economics of participatory value evaluation experiments', Working Paper, Tinbergen Institute.

Dekkers, J. and J.W. van der Straaten (2009), 'Monetary valuation of aircraft noise: a hedonic analysis around Schiphol airport', *Ecological Economics*, 68(11), 2850–58.

Esteves, A. Maria, Franks, D. and Vanclay, F. (2012), 'Social impact assessment: the state of the art', *Impact Assessment and Project Appraisal* 30(1), 34–42.

Faith-Ell, C. and T.B. Fischer (2021), 'Strategic environmental assessment in transport planning', in T.B. Fischer and A. González (eds), *Handbook on Strategic Environmental Assessment*, Cheltenham: Elgaronline, https://doi.org/10.4337/9781789909937, 164–81.

Ferreira, A., E. Beukers and M. Te Brömmelstroet (2012), 'Accessibility is gold, mobility is not: a proposal for the improvement of Dutch transport-related cost–benefit analysis', *Environment and Planning B*, 39, 683–97.

Gühnemann, A., J.J. Laird and A.D. Pearman (2012), 'Combining cost-benefit and multi-criteria analysis to prioritise a national road infrastructure programme', *Transport Policy*, 23, 15–24.

Hensher, D. A., J.M. Rose, J. de D. Ortúzar and L.L. Rizzi (2009), 'Estimating the willingness to pay and value of risk reduction for car occupants in the road environment', *Transportation Research Part A*, 43(7), 692–707.

Hicks, J. (1939), 'The Foundations of Welfare Economics', *Economic Journal*, 49(196), 696–712.

Jay, S., C. Jones, P. Slinn and C. Wood (2007), 'Environmental impact assessment: Retrospect and prospect', *Environmental impact assessment review*, 27(4), 287–300.

Johansson, P.O. (1991), *The Economic Theory and Measurement of Environmental Benefits*, Cambridge: Cambridge University Press.

Joumard, R. and H. Gudmundsson (2010), 'Indicators of environmental sustainability in transport: An interdisciplinary approach to methods', Lyngby: European Commission, Recherches.

Kaldor, N. (1939), 'Welfare propositions of economics and interpersonal comparisons of utility', *Economic Journal*, 49(195), 549–52.

Lucas, K. and P. Jones (2012) 'Social impacts and equity issues in transport: An introduction', *Journal of Transport Geography*, 21, 1–3. https://doi.org/10.1016/j.jtrangeo.2012.01.032

Lusk, J.L. and F.B. Norwood (2011), 'Animal Welfare Economics', *Applied Economic Perspectives and Policy*, 33(4), 463–83.

Macharis, C. and A. Bernardini (2015), 'Reviewing the use of Multi-Criteria Decision Analysis for the evaluation of transport projects: Time for a multi-actor approach', *Transport Policy*, 37, 177–86. https://doi.org/10.1016/J.TRANPOL.2014.11.002

Mackie, P., T. Worsley and J. Eliasson (2014), 'Transport appraisal revisited', *Research in Transportation Economics*, 47, 3–18.

Morgan, R.K. (2012), 'Environmental impact assessment: the state of the art', *Impact Assess Project Appraisal*, 30(1), 5–15.

Mottee, L.K. (2022), 'Advancing beyond project-scale Social Impact Assessment of transport infrastructure: insights into contextual constraints on practice', *Impact Assessment and Project Appraisal*, 40(1), 60–74.

Mottee, L.K. and R. Howitt (2018), 'Follow-up and social impact assessment (SIA) in urban transport-infrastructure projects: insights from the parramatta rail link', *Australian Planner*, 55(1), 46–56. https://doi.org/10.1080/07293682.2018.1506496

Mouter, N. (2017), 'Dutch politicians use of cost-benefit analysis', *Transportation*, 44(5), 1127–45.

Mouter, N. (2018), 'A critical assessment of discounting policies for transport Cost-Benefit Analysis in five European practices', *European Journal of Transport and Infrastructure Research*, 18(4), 389–412.

Mouter, N., S. van Cranenburgh and G.P. van Wee (2017a), 'Do individuals have different preferences as consumer and citizen? The trade-off between travel time and safety', *Transportation Research Part A*, 106, 333–49.

Mouter, N., S. van Cranenburgh and G.P. van Wee (2017b), 'An empirical assessment of Dutch citizens' preferences for spatial equality in the context of a national transport investment plan', *Journal of Transport Geography*, 60, 217–30.

Mouter, N., S. van Cranenburgh and G.P. van Wee (2018), 'The consumer-citizen duality: ten reasons why citizens prefer safety and drivers desire speed', *Accident Analysis and Prevention*, 121, 53–63.

Mouter, N., P. Koster and T. Dekker (2021a), 'Contrasting the recommendations of participatory value evaluation and cost-benefit analysis in the context of urban mobility in-vestments', *Transportation Research Part A: Policy and Practice*, 144, 54–73.

Mouter N., P.R. Koster and T. Dekker (2021b), 'Participatory Value Evaluation for the evaluation of flood protection schemes', *Water Resources and Economics*, 36, 100188.

Mouter, N., M. Ojeda Cabral, T. Dekker and S. van Cranenburgh (2019), 'The value of travel time, noise pollution, recreation and biodiversity: a social choice valuation perspective', *Research in Transportation Economics*, 76, 100733.

Nahmias-Biran, B.H., K. Martens and Y. Shiftan (2017), 'Integrating equity in transportation project assessment: a philosophical exploration and its practical implications', *Transport Reviews*, 37(2), 192–210. https://doi.org/10.1080/01441647.2017.1276604

Nijland, H.A., E.E.M.M. van Kempen, G.P. van Wee and J. Jabben (2003), 'Costs and benefits of noise abatement measures', *Transport Policy*, 10, 131–40.

Nyborg, K. (2014), 'Project evaluation with democratic decision-making: what does cost–benefit analysis really measure?', *Ecological Economics*, 105, 124–31.

Pereira, R.H.M., T. Schwanen and D. Banister (2017), 'Distributive justice and equity in transportation', *Transport Reviews*, 37(2), 170–91. https://doi.org/10.1080/01441647.2016.1257660

Perman, R., Y. Ma, J. McGilvray and M. Common (2003), *Natural Resource and Environmental Economics*, Harlow: Pearson Education.

Persky, J. (2001), 'Cost-benefit analysis and the classical creed', *Journal of Economic Perspectives*, 15(4), 199–208.

Rezaei, J. (2015), 'Best-Worst Multi-Criteria Decision-Making Method', *Omega*, 53, 49–57.

Saaty, T.L. (1990), 'How to make a decision: The Analytic Hierarchy Process', *European Journal of Operational Research*, 48, 9–26.

Sagoff, M. (1988), *The Economy of the Earth: Philosophy, Law, and the Environment*, Cambridge: Cambridge University Press.

Schipper, Y. (2001), *Environmental Costs and Liberalization in European Air Transport: A Welfare Economic Analysis*, Cheltenham, UK and Northampton, MA, USA: Edward Elgar.

Sen, A. (1979), 'Utilitarianism and Welfarism', *Journal of Philosophy*, 76, 463–89.

Sen, A. (1995), 'Environment Evaluation and Social Choice: Contingent Valuation and the Market Analogy', *The Japanese Economic Review*, 46 (1), 23–37.

Seo, K., A. Golub and M. Kuby (2014), 'Combined Impacts of Highways and Light Rail Transit on Residential Property Values: A Spatial Hedonic Price Model for Phoenix, Arizona', *Journal of Transport Geography*, 41, 53–62.

Small, K.A. and E.T. Verhoef (2007), *The Economics of Urban Transportation*, London: Routledge.

Soria-Lara, J.A., R.M. Arce-Ruiz, A. Arranz-López and A. Ariza-Álvarez (2020), 'Environmental impact assessment for transport projects: a review of technical and process-related issues', in N. Mouter (ed.), *Standard Appraisal Methods, Advances in Transport Policy and Planning*, vol. 6, Amsterdam: Elsevier.

Sunstein, C.R. (1993), 'Incommensurability and Valuation in Law', *Michigan Law Review*, 92, 779.

Tijm, J., T.O. Michielsen, R. van Maarseveen and P. Zwaneveld (2019), 'How large are the non-travel time effects of urban highway tunneling? Evidence from Maastricht, the Netherlands', *Transportation Research Part A: Policy and Practice*, 130, 570–92.

Train, K. (2009), *Discrete Choice Methods with Simulation*, 2nd edition, New York: Cambridge University Press.

Vanclay, F. (2003), 'International principles for social impact assessment', *Impact Assessment and Project Appraisal*, 21(1), 5–12. https://doi.org/10.3152/147154603781766491

Vanclay, F., A.M. Esteves, C.I. Group, I. Aucamp, C. Services and D.M. Franks (2015), *Social Impact Assessment: Guidance for Assessing and Managing the Social Impacts of Projects*, Groningen: International Association for Impact Assessment.

Van Wee, B. (2012), 'How suitable is CBA for the ex-ante evaluation of transport projects and policies? A discussion from the perspective of ethics', *Transport Policy*, 19(1), 1–7.

16
Transportation models and their applications

Gonçalo Homem de Almeida Correia and Bert van Wee

16.1   INTRODUCTION

Transport models have been defined in many ways and there are various kinds of models. In this chapter, a model is defined as a simplified representation of part of reality. The main goal of transport models is to estimate the behaviour of the real system in different scenarios (see Chapter 14) in a specific forecasting year. Possible outputs of these models may be, for example, the number of passenger kilometres in a country, region or city, in a certain year or, often combining transport models and impact models, societally relevant outcomes in the area of accessibility, safety or the environment, and increasingly health. Models are often used to get an insight into the behaviour of the system in a do-nothing scenario and/or to gain an insight into the effects of proposed measures/policies on transport and other system-related components such as land use. Usually, not one but several futures are predicted whereby the effects of transport are computed for several scenarios concerning the socio-economic development and policy variants (see Chapters 14 and 15).

This chapter provides readers with an introduction to how transport models work and shows what they can be used for. This knowledge should enable the reader to form an opinion as to whether a specific model can be used to answer certain questions. This chapter is focused on what are often called 'strategic models'. These are models that aggregate volumes of travellers for a faster representation of mobility patterns in a city, region or country. In contrast, models for reproducing traffic flows on highways, intended for real-time traffic management, require modelling each vehicle. They are presented in Chapter 7 and are not dealt with in this chapter. At specific places in the text, we may refer to other modelling levels for the sake of distinction and clarification. For further insights into transport modelling, the authors recommend the book by Ortúzar and Willumsen (2011).

Section 16.2 provides an overview of strategic models. Section 16.3 introduces the concept of elasticity which is used in many strategic models. Section 16.4 discusses the traditional strategic aggregated models, while disaggregated models are discussed in Section 16.5. Section 16.6 deals with model validation. Section 16.7 presents some examples of models currently used in The Netherlands. Section 16.8 addresses the question of what can and cannot be done using transport models. The main conclusions of the chapter are presented in Section 16.9.

16.2 TYPES OF TRANSPORT MODELS

Models can be classified in various ways. Some of these classifications are presented in this section, but we do not claim to have covered them all. Before discussing the model categories, it is useful to remember what all models have in common, as indicated in the introduction: they are a simplified representation of part of reality.

A transport model describes human behaviour based on a theory of how humans behave in their daily mobility choices. This theory describes the connections between the variables in the model. Exogenous (independent) variables are variables that are determined externally, outside of the model. From these, we can distinguish variables the modeller will not change, for example, the GDP growth estimations coming from economics experts, and the experimental factors which will be changed to form scenarios such as the capacity of several road links or the public transport price. Endogenous variables are variables whose value depends on the model behaviour over time. For example, in a model where one wants to determine car ownership as a function of (among other things) economic growth, economic growth is exogenous and car ownership is endogenous. For a causal relationship at least three main criteria should be met: (1) empirical association, (2) temporal priority of the independent variable, (3) non-spuriousness, and preferably two more: (4) identifying a causal mechanism, and (5) specifying the context in which the effect occurs (Chambliss and Schutt, 2019).

The mathematical formulas in a model often contain so-called coefficients, which quantitatively indicate how the value of an exogenous variable affects the value of an endogenous one. A fictional example of a model based on elasticities (see Section 16.3, and Chapters 3 and 6) is a 1% increase in the income level leading to a 0.4% increase in car ownership. The value of 0.4 is the coefficient here. Determining the coefficients in a model is known as the model estimation. The aim is to make the model results as similar as possible to the collected empirical data that is kept for validation purposes. It is often the case that part of the data is used for the estimation of coefficients (calibration) and the other part for validation purposes. Statistical methods are often used to achieve this in a so-called statistical estimation method. Maximum likelihood estimation is an example of such methods, a method whereby one aims at maximizing the probability that the empirical data can be obtained by the mathematical structure that has been chosen to explain the phenomenon. Statistical estimation packages such as SPSS, Statistica or the R language allow you to apply this and other statistical methods.

16.2.1 Descriptive Versus Explanatory Models

Descriptive models represent the correlations between variables without explicitly considering causality, whereas explanatory models will map out causes as well as consequences.

In general, statistical data and their analyses provide only limited indications as to what the theory should be like. It is possible to develop a perfect statistical (descriptive) model about the relationship between the number of storks and the number of births (most storks are to be found in developing countries, where the number of births is high). But the statistical correlation between variables does not provide an insight into the causality and its direction. In other words, that model is not an explanatory model. An explanatory model could reveal, for example, if the presence of an airport in a region causes extra economic growth or if airports are typically situated in regions with a strongly developing economy.

Although models should ideally be based on an explicit theory of cause and effect, descriptive models can nonetheless often be useful. For example, by using data mining techniques a file containing many variables can be searched systematically for the existence of correlations which are a good start to building explanatory models. A concrete example in traffic safety is relating accident frequencies to road characteristics, regional characteristics, time of day and period, and so on (Wang et al., 2013). Afterwards, it can be studied whether the relationships that have been found can be explained in any useful way. In other words, are the relationships theoretically underpinned? In general, in any research project, it is advisable to start with descriptive analysis (e.g. by frequency and cross-tabulations) before developing models. The current trend in modelling based on machine learning and artificial intelligence ('big data') often departs from descriptive models, that, in later stages, can be further developed into explanatory models.

16.2.2 Spatial Versus Non-Spatial Models

Models can be divided into spatial and non-spatial models. In the latter, physical space does not play a role whilst in the former, the location of activities in space is an explicit component in the model.

An example of a non-spatial model is a model to explain car use in a country, estimated based on a time series using as explanatory variables (exogenous) the population age groups, the gross domestic product (GDP), fuel prices, road capacity and the price per kilometre for road transport.

In the case of spatial models, the research area is often divided into zones/regions/areas. Furthermore, there are networks for cars and other transport modes, often with many thousands of nodes and links (intersections and road segments). Each zone has its centroid, which is connected to the networks for cars and public transport through so-called connector links. One of the objectives of such spatial models is to estimate the origin-destination (OD) matrices, which indicate for each transport mode the number of trips between every pair of zones in the study area. But they can be used just for the statistical analysis of the relation between car usage and public transport accessibility using statistical regression.

Between the spatial and non-spatial models, one can have spatial statistical explanatory models. These are models that aim to explain a certain dependent variable that is expressed at the level of a zoning system but recognize the influence that zones have on each other. For example, the usage of metro in a city does not only affect the zone in which a metro station exists but also the zones around. This is known as spatial autocorrelation (Ibraeva et al., 2021).

16.2.3 Aggregated Versus Disaggregated Models

In the traditional aggregated models such as the 4-step model (see Section 16.4), the zone is the unit of generation and attraction of trips, and the trips are aggregated per time interval. In disaggregated models (see Section 16.5) travellers are modelled individually often with very specific descriptions for their origin and destination locations.

The aggregated models date back to the 1950s in the USA. They have been developed at a period where the 'predict-and-provide' approach was the mainstream transport planning policy, especially in the USA. Owing to prosperity, car ownership and car use strongly increased, which required extra road infrastructure. Forecasts were being produced for car usage in the next decade(s) ('predict') and, based on those forecasts, the roads and/or the extra number of lanes to be built were being determined ('provide'). During the 1970s in many Organisation for Economic Cooperation and Development (OECD) cities and regions, this line of thought shifted in favour of the idea that it would be impossible to meet the demand for car mobility indefinitely and therefore it was decided to opt for a different approach: a combination of containing measures, regulations, promoting alternatives for the car, optimal use of existing infrastructure and limited building of new infrastructure. Such a combination of measures, which can generally be called "transport demand management", arguably requires a different type of models, models that are disaggregated.

Owing to the progress achieved in statistical estimation techniques from the 1970s onwards, disaggregated models can nowadays be estimated much more efficiently by focusing on individual mobility rather than zone averages. Note though that the models thus developed need to be aggregated to make them workable for forecasting. After all, it is not the mobility of one specific individual that transport policy-makers are interested in, their interest is in the aggregated passenger flows on the roads and in public transport.

16.2.4 Static Versus Dynamic Models

In dynamic models, as opposed to static models, time plays a crucial role in the status of the variables that measure the state of the system. Changes in behaviour are assumed not to occur instantly but over a certain period. More importantly, the area (often: region) of interest is assumed never to reach a final equilibrium, there are always factors (exogenous or endogenous) that lead to change in the system over time.

One example is a model for the effect of the price of fuel on car use. If the fuel price per litre were to rise from €1.35 to €2.70 tomorrow, the short-term effect would be limited. Many commuters go to work by car and would have to do so tomorrow as well, for lack of alternatives. Any effects would only become visible in the medium to the long run (see also Chapter 6). These effects may be choosing a different mode of transport, different destinations closer by (e.g. for shopping), fewer frequent trips, finding a job closer to home, moving to a place closer to work, keeping the currently owned car for a longer time (to keep down depreciation costs), switching to a more fuel-efficient car, cut back on expenditures other than those linked to the car, and so on. In this case, the effect of the variable (e.g. the fuel price) on other variables (e.g. the commuting distance) is 'lagged' with unexpected consequences in the long term that are difficult to predict with a static model, for example on the land use. For the reader's reference, System Dynamics is a good modelling approach for such systems that exhibit delays and multiple feedback loops. However, they do have the disadvantage of only rarely being used for studying spatial interactions given their very aggregated nature (Legêne et al., 2020).

In transport studies, static models are usually estimated based on what are called cross-section data. These data constitute a snapshot taken at one moment in time. Dynamic models require time-series data. Preferably, these data capture a constant group of individuals over time, the so-called panel data. An advantage of such data is that the development of the exogenous as well as the endogenous variables over time is known for each individual.

16.2.5　Models Based on Revealed Preference Versus Stated Preference Data

When collecting data on individual choice behaviour, regarding transport mode choice or house buying location, for example, two options are open: that of revealed preference (RP) and that of stated preference (SP). In the case of RP, the actual choices made by the individual are observed in a real situation whilst in the case of SP, the researcher confronts the individual with hypothetical selection situations.

In the case of RP, people are asked, for example, to keep a travel diary indicating data like origin, destination, travel mode, time of day and travel purpose for every trip. Or data are collected automatically by making use of information and communications technologies (ICT) ('big data'), for example via cellphones (Demissie et al., 2015). In the case of SP, respondents, for example, are shown five to ten choice sets each with two trip alternatives, from which they are currently asked to choose their preferred one. This kind of data has two major advantages. Firstly, it is often less expensive. Secondly, it can be used for making predictions regarding non-existent alternatives, like the demand for an automated vehicle for accessing a train station as first-mile transport (Yap et al., 2016). Of course, there are also drawbacks, the most important of which is that the models have to be adjusted for respondents' bias as many times social norms dictate an answer that is not what the respondent would opt for in reality. So-called social-desirability bias can be quite critical in evaluating new technologies such as electric vehicle adoption (Smith et al., 2017).

It's also possible to combine RP and SP data, and often advisable. RP data provides a scale of realistic preferences between the existing alternatives whilst SP is used to compare such alternatives with the new ones to be introduced, like in the example of introducing new vehicles to the market. A vehicle is still a vehicle with some common attributes like size and power, but new fuel/energy (electricity, hydrogen) can change some of the characteristics of the vehicle as well as of its usage (Brownstone et al., 2000).

16.2.6　Trip-Based Versus Activity-Based Models

Early transport models, and still most of the currently used models, consider travel behaviour in isolation, studying trip OD matrices as being generated in space by the land use of a region but with very little connection between the demand over different time periods. Later, so-called activity-based models made travel dependent on the activity patterns of the individuals and their households.

In the early models, the interactions between successive trips of an individual or household were not considered; in fact, individuals and their families were not the units of analysis, as explained, the zone was. However, it is known that individual characteristics such as income and time-budget restrictions greatly affect travel behaviour. There are all kinds of constraints that are connected to the life-cycle stage in which the individual and the household find themselves that influence the trips that are taken during a day, a week, a month or a year. Synchronization of different activities within the family (for example meals or shopping activities) as recognized in time geography, (see Chapter 3) put extra time restrictions on the choice of behaviour concerning the activities and the travelling between those. These constraints ultimately determine the set of feasible alternatives (see Chapter 3). The advantages of these 'activity-based models' are (1) that they provide a better description of behaviour and, in connection with this, (2) that they produce better estimations of aggregate behaviour under a wider range of policies and measures. The major drawback is that this type of model rapidly gets very complex and it needs a larger number of resources to estimate and use.

16.2.7 Models That Consider Versus Do Not Consider Land-Use Changes

Traditional models describe transportation as a derivative of spatial planning. In practice, however, transport and land use mutually interact. The presence or absence of transport infrastructure affects the pattern of spatial activities, and land-use patterns influence the development of transport networks (see also Chapter 2 and Figure 2.1). The models that take the interaction between land use and transport into account are the so-called Land Use and Transportation Interaction (LUTI) models.

The spatial effects of the transport infrastructure can be considerable, especially in the long run (think of cities that came into being near natural harbours or river crossings). The building of a new road or railway, for example, may well lead to businesses settling in their vicinity, or businesses may leave an area because this is now under heavy congestion.

The first example of an operational LUTI static model is the Lowry model (Lowry, 1964), which became quite famous. Using road accessibility to explain where people live and work in a city, Lowry produces a static equilibrium between the different areas of an urban region in terms of population and jobs mediated by transport accessibility. This is what came to be called a spatial interaction type of model (Iacono et al., 2008).

A drawback of the use of these spatial interaction models is, however, that in reality the land-use effects only appear after a long time and need not be solely due to infrastructure changes. Therefore the possibility of validating these models remains difficult. In particular, the validation relies on data about the development of several system variables over time, such as population dynamics and house market supply and demand. This data may be difficult to access.

An example of a more modern and complete dynamic LUTI model is the Integrated Land Use, Transportation, Environment (ILUTE) model developed for the region of

Toronto-Hamilton by the University of Toronto (Farooq and Miller, 2012). This model will be explained in Section 15.7. More information about LUTI models can be found in Geurs and Ritsema van Eck, 2004, Iacono et al., 2008 and Lopes et al., 2019. The TIGRIS XL model should also be mentioned; this is a LUTI model that is used in The Netherlands by government agencies to assess long-term mobility and transport policies (Zondag et al., 2015).

16.2.8   Passenger Transport Versus Freight Transport Models

The majority of the transport modelling studies deal with passenger transport, not addressing, the freight component. In fact, on most roads, the share of freight transport is limited. Yet models for freight transport have gained importance in recent years (Tavasszy and de Jong, 2014). Freight transport has been growing and is expected to continue to grow more than passenger transport. Trucks are an increasingly important part of road transport modelling studies because the CO_2 emissions per passenger car have been decreasing more rapidly than that of trucks. Besides, heavy trucks damage the road surface, and slow, heavy trucks can induce traffic jams.

One of the problems in developing freight transport models is the availability of data. Aggregated economic statistics often use a too coarse classification of economic sectors. Disaggregated data are hard to collect, because their collection is dependent on the voluntary cooperation of businesses and because one company encompasses many different actors (management, administration, production departments, logistics department, transportation department) (Thoen et al., 2020).

16.2.9   Agent-Based Models

The last generation of transport models is the so-called agent-based models (ABMs) (Iacono et al., 2008). This is a methodology for modelling any kind of complex system and it has been used in the transport domain for the past two decades. The agent-based principle is one of 'emergence of behaviour', a bottom-up approach that is grounded on modelling the system agents in their relationships with each other and also with the relevant environment. For example, a vehicle driver in traffic can be considered an agent that has to interact with other vehicles and make decisions on braking, steering and accelerating as well as more strategic decisions such as which route to choose based on traffic congestion (Wang et al., 2019). ABMs, therefore, are highly disaggregated, dynamic, spatial transport models that can incorporate a lot of the knowledge that has been built over the years in the previous modelling methodologies.

In advanced transport models, especially those that have a LUTI component, the main agents are typically citizens in a region who choose between which activities to perform, what modes of transport to take and what paths to take to reach their daily destinations. The agents are representative of the real population, and it is possible today, with modern computers, to model one synthetic agent for each real citizen. There is a natural relationship between the ABM approach and the activity-based models explained before. A computer agent representing a citizen will require the generation of an activity plan for him/her and possibly for the household that it belongs to.

The level of detail of these models can vary considerably with the objectives of the model. Typically the modeller decides which agents are relevant for the problem, the level of detail of the agents' behaviour and the level of detail of the environment. The ILUTE model that was mentioned above is also an ABM that integrates an activity-based module; it considers what its agents need to do daily. Furthermore, it goes beyond the transport sector by aiming at forecasting how land use will evolve in a region (Farooq and Miller, 2012). Nevertheless, it lacks the details of how humans behave in the transport system itself, meaning, for example, how they drive and behave when they face traffic congestion. A popular ABM (and activity-based model) of the traffic component of a city is MATSim (Axhausen, 2016) which has been recently used for several purposes such as modelling the impacts of automated vehicles (Fagnant et al., 2016).

16.3   ELASTICITIES

Many models contain what are called 'elasticities'. This has already been briefly discussed in Chapters 3 and 6. In this section, the notion is further elaborated on.

Elasticities enable us to quickly get an insight into the following question: to what extent is a change in one variable associated with changes in other variables? An example is the elasticity of car use (in kilometres) as a function of the fuel price. If this elasticity is −0.4, car use will reduce by 4% if the fuel price rises by 10%. In general, elasticity E of a variable y because of a change in a variable x is defined as:

$$x - elasticity\ of\ y{:}E\ =\ \frac{\partial y/y}{\partial x/y} \tag{16.1}$$

Two kinds of elasticities are distinguished: direct elasticities and cross elasticities. The previous example is about direct elasticities: the effect of an attribute of cars on the car usage itself. If we look at the effect of fuel price changes on, for example, public transport, we are dealing with cross elasticity. If one focuses on price elasticities, direct elasticities are negative (an increase in price leads to lower demand) whereas cross elasticities are usually positive (the competing mode gets transferred demand). Cross elasticity of the use of public transport as a function of the car's fuel price might be, for example, 0.1. In that case, the use of public transport would increase by 1% if the fuel price rose by 10%. In this example, therefore, the cross elasticity is quite small or inelastic: this corresponds to the fact that substitution between the car and public transport is very limited (Cullinane and Cullinane, 2003; Lunke et al., 2021; Steg, 2003). If fully independent goods or services are at stake, the cross elasticity is 0.

Elasticities are especially popular because they are simple and understandable. However, the risk of misuse is considerable. Elasticities are usually not constant: a rise in fuel prices from €1.35 to €2.70 (double the cost) may have a different effect than what a fuel price rise from €2 to €4 would (also double). Therefore elasticities are point specific and direction-specific (increase or decrease). For mode choice instead of making simple approximations with elasticities, one may have to consider the demand curve as a function of price. To obtain such a demand curve, one would have to estimate a statistical model. Based on such a model, it is possible to calculate the elasticity at any point as another indicator of the behaviour of the curve. Nevertheless using elasticities as a single method is a too simplistic approach, even if derived from a statistical model that explains demand as a function of price, and that is because the transport system is a complex system with multiple feedbacks connecting different components. Take the example of induced demand in an urban road network, once the fuel prices increase there will be a reduction of demand, however with that reduction of demand there is a reduction in the travel time which in the medium and long run will continue to attract people to use the car (perhaps different people). Demand is therefore not just the result of one variable and is affected by several dynamic feedback loops that many times need to be modelled to get a realistic estimation of the impact of a policy or measure.

16.4   THE 4-STEP MODEL: A TRADITIONAL AGGREGATE MODELLING APPROACH

As was mentioned above, in the case of spatially aggregated models a study area is divided into zones. Furthermore, the main transport modes (car, public transport and active modes) have pre-defined networks, which may have thousands of nodes and links. Each zone has its own centroid node, which is connected to the transport networks through connector links.

The 4-step modelling procedure that was applied for the first time in the USA in the 1950s (Ortúzar and Willumsen, 2011) is the following:

1st Step: Generation (production) and attraction – answering the question as to how many trips depart from a zone and how many arrive at each zone.
2nd Step: Distribution – from the trips that depart from each zone what are their destination zones?
3rd Step: Modal split – from the trips that start and end at different zones how many are done using each mode or combination of modes of transport?
4th Step: Assignment – which route is taken to get from an origin to the destination zone in the existing networks?

Trip generation models compute the total number of trips O_i departing from zone i in a certain period of time. That number is based on the characteristics of the zone concerned, like population size, retail area and employment. These characteristics are known as land-use variables. The popular Trip Generation handbook in the United States is a good source for relating trip generation factors and the number of trips for many common functions (Hooper and Institute of Transportation Engineers, 2017). Trip-attraction models compute the total number of trips D_j in the OD matrix that have their destination at a certain zone j.

The most classic distribution model has been derived from the gravity theory (Newton's laws about attraction between celestial bodies). In accessibility, though, a distribution model usually looks like the following expression where the constants that Newton estimated are replaced by parameters to be estimated for each application region:

$$T_{ij} = A_i \ O_i \ B_j \ D_j f(c_{ij}) \tag{16.2}$$

where T_{ij} is the number of trips between zones i and j, and O_i and D_j are the generation from zone i and the attraction from zone j, respectively, as derived from the generation and attraction model.

The balancing factors A_i and B_j for the zone of origin i and the zone of destination j ensure that the trip-distribution results are consistent with the results from the trip-generation and trip-attraction models. This results in what is called a 'doubly constrained model' since both O_i and D_j are respected. Single-constrained or unconstrained models are used as well but they are not discussed here.

In the impedance function $f(c_{ij})$, c_{ij} represents the generalized travel costs between zone i and zone j. For example, c_{ij} = $\alpha \times$ *travel distance* + $\beta \times$ *travel time* + $\gamma \times$ *toll charge* (where a, β and γ are weighting factors). In the generalized travel costs, times and other factors such as the number of transfers in public transport are all translated into costs. The translation takes place through the so-called value of time, which is the number of monetary units a traveller is willing to spend to decrease a unit of his/her travel time (see Chapter 15).

Modal split models divide the number of trips T_{ij} in trips per mode T_{ij}^m where m is the index of the modes of transport available between the OD pair $< i,j >$. Most often, discrete choice models are used for this (for a general introduction to the logit model, the most classical one, see Section 16.5 on disaggregated models). At the end of this step, there are as many trip matrices as there are modes in the region of study (or combinations of modes in multimodal transport).

Usually, the last step in this 4-step aggregated modelling approach is the allocation of trips to the network (trips assignment). Various methodologies are available for this. The first and most simple methodology is that of all-or-nothing. In this case, it is assumed that everyone takes the same, shortest route between i and j. Shortest is defined here in terms of travel time or generalized costs of travelling (as defined above). Such shortest paths are computed by using an algorithm, for example, the Dijkstra algorithm (Dijkstra, 1959). The second methodology is that of stochastic allocation, also called multiple routing. In this case, differences in the perception and taste of individuals are included in the model, therefore, distributing the travellers along the several possible competitive paths for each OD pair according to their perceived utility. The assignment can be done using a logit model, explained in the next section on human behaviour modelling, whereby the travellers are assigned to paths according to their probability of choosing each path of the choice set. The third and most used methodology, user equilibrium (UE) traffic assignment, is especially meant to be used for car networks as it takes traffic congestion into account. Congestion causes changes in the travel times on the road network. The relationship between the traffic intensity on a stretch of road, on the one hand, and its capacity, on the other hand, is described by a speed-flow curve (see Chapter 7). Because of delays due to congestion, the original free-flow shortest route between zone i and j will become less attractive. Finding all the routes and their number of travellers for each OD pair in an equilibrium situation is obtained by following the so-called first Wardrop principle: in stable conditions, all routes used between i and j have identical travel times so that no driver can improve his/her travel time by opting for a different route. If in this situation of congestion, the methodology of stochastic allocation is used as well, meaning that there is uncertainty on the perception of travel times, a fourth methodology emerges: the stochastic user equilibrium assignment. Under this approach, no driver can improve his or her perceived travel time by unilaterally changing routes. Models that take into account the departure time of the drivers are relatively more recent and belong to the dynamic traffic assignment methods. For further details, see for example Ortúzar and Willumsen (2011) or Sheffi, (1986).

The way the four steps have been presented makes it seem like the sequence from the first to the last step makes perfect sense, just like a traveller would first decide if he/she will travel or not (1st step), then where he/she would travel to (2nd step), finally deciding which mode to take (3rd step) and which path to follow (4th step). However, this may be deceiving: some of these decisions are highly interconnected. As an example, consider the effect of traffic congestion on the mode choice. If everyone would like to use their private car that would be physically impossible, since the network does not carry so many vehicles under an acceptable travel time. That is why in several 4-step model applications there is feedback from the trip assignment step to the mode choice step, especially in highly congested urban areas. And mode and destination choice are often made simultaneously *see* in the next section on disaggregated models how the destination choice (equivalent to the distribution step) can also be connected to mode choice.

Even today, the aggregated 4-step model is still widely used. Most large cities in the developed but also developing world run some type of 4-step method to help plan their transport system. The method is usually implemented in software such as PTV-VISUM, Omnitrans or Cube, to name a few.

Disaggregated models make better use of individual data compared to aggregated models. And nowadays, as explained above, big data is being collected about people's behaviour everywhere including cellphone usage data, which is a good proxy for location data (Demissie et al., 2013; Wang et al., 2018). Nevertheless, in many cases, those individual data have to be specifically collected for the study at hand. In addition, a disaggregated model has to be aggregated before it is ready for forecasting. Data for aggregated models at a zone level are often easier to estimate from routinely collected statistical data.

16.5   HUMAN BEHAVIOUR MODELLING

The disaggregated approach (Ben-Akiva and Lerman, 1985; Ortúzar and Willumsen, 2011) uses the individual or the household as the basic unit for the analysis. When participating in traffic and transport, an individual needs to choose between alternatives. His or her travel behaviour can be unravelled into many decisions, such as for instance:

1. To make a certain trip, or not to make it (generation).
2. The choice of the destination (distribution).
3. The choice of the means of transport (travel mode selection).
4. The choice of the route to be taken (route selection).
5. The choice of the time of day for the trip (time-of-day selection).

Except for the last one the other decisions can be associated with the classic 4-step model that has been explained in the previous section. The time of day decision can be seen as an improvement on the assignment of trips to the network, recognizing that some travellers may avoid travelling at their desired departure time due to traffic congestion.

For explaining these decisions there is the need for a model to indicate the alternative that the individual will select from the set of alternatives offered. A rational individual will prefer the alternative that will yield the highest utility. Utility is a construct in economics that reflects the satisfaction or benefit that individuals gain from choosing a certain choice alternative. This utility cannot be measured or observed directly. Instead, the planners or analysts infer what is the utility of each alternative by observing how frequently the individuals choose it. Furthermore, the planner assumes that total utility consists of the sum of a deterministic component and a stochastic component. The deterministic component is a function of all variables that the analyst/planner can collect about the choice and the decision-maker such as the characteristics of transport mode i that are relevant for the individual (like speed, costs and comfort) and the individual's socio-economic characteristics (like gender, age, education and income). The stochastic component describes what cannot be observed by the planner meaning that, by knowing all variables in the deterministic part of utility, the analyst still cannot explain and predict an individual's choice exactly. However, he/she can assign a probability that each alternative is chosen. From here, a Random Utility Maximization principle arises to explain human choices. From the assumptions made regarding the stochastic component different choice modelling structures are generated.

The most used choice model is the multinomial logit model:

$$P_i = \frac{e^{V_i}}{\sum_{j \in M} e^{V_j}} \tag{16.3}$$

where P_i is the probability that the individual will select alternative i, V_i is the deterministic or systematic part of the utility of alternative i and M is the set of all the alternatives.

In the case of applying choice models for explaining transport mode choice, all the variables defined above can be plugged into the systematic component of the utility function. The utility functions determining the probabilities will then look like this example of a choice between public transport and car:

$$V_{PT} = \beta_0 + \beta_1 TT_{PT} + \beta_2 TC_{PT} + \beta_3 WT_{PT} + \beta_4 TrT_{PT} + \beta_5 CO \tag{16.4}$$

$$V_{Car} = \beta_6 TT_{Car} + \beta_7 TC_{Car} + \beta_8 PrC_{Car} \tag{16.5}$$

where TT_{PT} is the travel time of PT, TC_{PT} is the travel cost of PT, WT_{PT} is the waiting time for PT, TrT_{PT} is the transfer time of PT, CO is a dummy variable that takes the value 1 if the person has a private car and 0 if not, TT_{Car} is the travel time of car, TC_{Car} is the travel cost of car, and PrC_{Car} is the parking cost.

The β coefficients in the utility functions indicate how the various variables affect the utility of each specific transport mode. The larger a coefficient is in relation to the others, the more it affects the utility an individual derives from the travel mode concerned. Negative coeffi-cients indicate that the corresponding variable decreases the utility of the transport mode, for example, all the coefficients of cost and time are expected to be negative. The coefficient for the dummy variable CO should be negative as well since having a car should lead people to use less public transport. β_0 is the so-called alternative specific coefficient (ASC) which measures the average unexplained part of the utility, that is, the mean of the error term. A positive or negative value of this coefficient gives clues to aspects that are not being expressed in the exist-ing utility functions, like for example a positive or negative attitude toward a particular mode.

The values of the beta coefficients are determined by using statistical estimation techniques. Most estimation is done by maximum likelihood. The basis for this is a random sample of trips actually made (called 'revealed preference' data) or trips that respondents say they would make in hypothetical choice situations (called 'stated preference' data).

It can be demonstrated that the natural logarithm of the denominator of the multinomial logit expression (16.3) $ln\left(\sum_{j\in M}e^{V_j}\right)$, also called the 'logsum term', is the maximum expected utility that can be obtained from the choice of those modes for a particular trip for the average decision-maker (Ben-Akiva and Lerman, 1985). It can also be demonstrated that this is the expected consumer surplus in economic theory for choosing to consume a certain product, here a mode of transport (de Jong et al., 2005).

A trip distribution model can also be a logit model. In such a model the choices are not the modes, but the destinations. Here, also, characteristics can be identified that affect the likelihood of the individual selecting destination d from a collection of possible destinations D. On the one hand, the effort required from the individual to reach a certain destination plays a part, and on the other hand, there is the attractiveness of a destination. Interestingly it can be demonstrated that if an exponential impedance function $f\left(c_{ij}\right)$ is used in the trip distribution gravitational method (explained in the previous section) this becomes a multinomial logit destination choice model (Anas, 1983).

In a model where a multinomial logit structure is used to explain the destination choices, the logsum term, which as explained above is the maximum expected utility from the choice situation, becomes a measure of accessibility in the region since it weights the different desti-nations according to their reachability and desirability to the average citizen (Geurs and van Wee, 2004). As mentioned, variables that describe the travel to the destination as well as the characteristics of the destination should be used.

Since the choice of the transport modes is most often also a multimodal logit model, loca-tion and mode choices can be joined in a so-called nested model. Because there are several alternatives to travel to the same destination, the transport effort required to get to d can be expressed as a weighted sum of the effort using each travel mode to get to d. Here once again one can use the so-called logsum (or "inclusive value" as referred to by other researchers) var-iable which is determined from the underlying modal split model, thus forming a nested logit model of the joint choice of location and mode of transport (Ben-Akiva and Lerman, 1985). To evaluate if such a choice structure compared to a simpler one makes sense, the typical validation procedures of a nested logit model can be used (Train, 2003).

The way in which destinations and modes of transport are chosen can vary with the trip motive. Regarding commuter trips, most likely, an individual will first choose a destination (workplace) and next a travel mode. In this case, the two steps can be kept separate with travel impedance playing a lesser role in explaining the destination choice. However regarding shopping trips, for example, the choices of destination and travel mode may be simultaneous, comparing options like travelling by car to a suburban shopping mall or by tram to the city centre.

When modelling an individual's trip frequencies in a disaggregated trip-generation model, various explanatory variables can be distinguished. Socio-economic characteristics like income, profession and age have been demonstrated to be important determinants. Furthermore, characteristics of the household that the individual is a part of, like the number of members of the household and whether or not there are children, are important. Besides, factors like the accessibility of destinations from the individual's residence and the attractiveness of making a trip from the residence (sometimes) play a part.

A disaggregated model for time-of-day selection usually uses the current time of departure and several periods (e.g. per quarter of an hour) before and after as alternatives. The utility of each alternative period is a function of the travel time and the travel costs in that period. If there is a lot of congestion, the travel time will be high. Travel costs can get high if a peak charge is introduced, for example. High travel time or costs diminish the utility of such a period and with it the likelihood that that particular period will be selected for a trip.

Various other disaggregated models exist besides the logit model. In the logit model, it is assumed that the stochastic component of the utility follows an extreme value distribution (a family of continuous probability distributions) (Hensher et al., 2005). One alternative is the 'probit' model, in which the stochastic component follows a normal distribution. Furthermore, over the last few years, the mixed logit model has become very popular, especially among researchers. In this model, the β coefficients do not have a fixed value; instead, they are individual-specific, following a certain statistical distribution over the population with a mean and a standard deviation (Hensher et al., 2005; Ortúzar and Willumsen, 2011). Because of its complexity, the mixed logit model is better suited for describing behaviour than for predicting future behaviour. Other models that are not within the family of logit models or are not based on the principle of random utility maximization have also been proposed such as random regret minimization (Chorus, 2012).

As already indicated in Section 16.4, the results of disaggregated models need to be aggregated before they can be used for forecasting. A description of an aggregation procedure is beyond the scope of this chapter (see Ben-Akiva and Lerman, 1985; Ortúzar and Willumsen, 2011). After aggregated OD matrices have been obtained through that process these can be used for the traffic assignment, in the same way as described above for aggregated models.

16.6   VALIDATION OF MODELS

Validation is defined as the assessment of whether or not the model describes reality correctly. The question is phrased simply, but the answer is usually complicated (Cambridge Systematics, 2010). For validation purposes, designers use independent data not used during the construction of the model. They want to know the reliability of the model for a wide range of situations.

Aspects that have to be taken care of during validation of a transport model may be:

1. Application scope. For example, when using a peak model designed for working days, model users cannot expect the model to perform well for peak travel during holidays.
2. Qualitative criteria. For example, for which policy measures should the model be suitable in general?
3. The level of validation. On which road links should the model be able to calculate delays due to congestion? All roads or just a few important roads under scrutiny? The model designers must also define their levels of confidence in the forecasts that they judge to be acceptable.

The analysis of the non-conformities of the model with the requirements in terms of model validation will ideally give clues about needed improvements:

1. At the lowest level, additional model parameters could be added.
2. At the level of computation, the accuracy could be increased, for example by calculating with more digits or taking smaller time steps (in dynamic models).
3. In iterative model-solving algorithms, the step size could be reduced or the number of iterations could be increased.
4. The mathematical model might not sufficiently adhere to the conceptual model and hence might need to be enhanced.
5. Finally, at the highest level, the conceptual model might need some modifications because the dependencies are not correctly modelled or because the theory needs amendment.

16.7   SOME EXAMPLES OF MODELS

In this section, we present three models. We first describe the LMS, the national Dutch model system, being an example of a state-of-the-art mainstream strategic transport model. This is followed by ILUTE, a state-of-the-art agent-based LUTI model. Finally we present DYNAMO, an example of an impact model, in this case a model for car ownership, energy use and emissions.

16.7.1   The Dutch National Model System

The Dutch National Model System (in Dutch: Landelijk Model Systeem – LMS) is an internationally renowned, unique instrument for designing transportation policies. Rijkswaterstaat, the public works department of the Dutch Ministry of Infrastructure and the Environment, has been using it since 1986. Besides the LMS there are four regional models, together covering the whole of The Netherlands and fully consistent with the LMS (Rijkswaterstaat, 2017).

The LMS is a disaggregated model system (modelling individual decisions) that can estimate future traffic flows, both on the trunk-road network and in public transport. The LMS is a spatial model, which means that The Netherlands and small parts of bordering countries have been compartmented into about 1500 zones, each with its characteristics (e.g. employment, number of students, income, size of the working population in the base year). These characteristics were mainly derived from statistics prepared by the CBS (the Dutch Central Statistical Office). For the forecasting year, these data were derived from scenarios designed by the Dutch planning agencies PBL (environment) and CPB (economy), partly based on other models.

When using the model, the following steps can be distinguished:

- Step 1: Choice behaviour for each type of household

   The model starts with the choice behaviour of individuals or households. Households decide on car ownership. An individual makes a comparative assessment of travel costs versus travel time for the different modes of transport. For example, using the car in the morning peak hours will take more time than making the same trip at a later point in time. These choices are based on behaviour actually observed (RP data; see Section 16.2), as found either in the trip diaries from the annual OVIN, the Dutch national travel survey (CBS, 2021), or derived from the responses from a study in which individuals were asked to state what their behaviour might be in reaction to a change (SP data; see Section 16.2). The latter applies to the planned introduction of a per kilometre tax (road pricing), for example.

- Step 2: Type of travellers in the base year

   Using the choices made by individuals and households, the LMS establishes what are called traveller types. What are the characteristics of the people making the choices? The following characteristics may be distinguished, among others, by: age (grouped into 18 classes), gender (2 classes), car availability (5 classes), participation in society (working, retired, etc., 5 classes), income (10 classes), education level (4 classes) and owner of a student OV-chipcard (a public transport smart card) or not (2 classes). For households, there is a similar classification. This is done for every zone, in both the base year and the forecasting year, and is necessary for being able to estimate future traffic flows. For example, if the number of people over 50 years of age in 2030 is twice as large, *ceteris paribus* the model takes into account an increase in the number of trips made especially by people in that age group.

- Step 3: Applying the choice models

   In step 2 the traveller types and their choice behaviour have been generated. In this step, the choice models are computed. The following choices are taken into account:
   1. the choice to obtain a driving licence and to own a car;
   2. the decision as to whether or not to make a trip;
   3. the selection of the travel destination, the travel mode, the time of day, station choice and access/egress mode choice;
   4. for car drivers the selection of the route to take. For people travelling by train, bus or tram/metro the assignment to lines is done using a commercially available software package.

   In addition, for car drivers and train passengers, time of day choices are included. The LMS thus mainly consists of four choice models which are directly related to the choices listed above. To determine the transport demand, the first three choice models, in particular, are important. The LMS brings the transport supply from the network data. Using the driving licence and car ownership model, the LMS determines car ownership per household and zone but uses the DYNAMO forecast (see 'DYNAMO' below in 16.7.3) for the whole of The Netherlands as a constraint. The car ownership model, therefore, works as a distribution model for a given external national total. The LMS determines the choice of destination, travel mode, station choice and access and egress mode choice and time of day based on the tour generation and accessibility. Except for the choice of the route, all LMS choice models are disaggregated logit models.

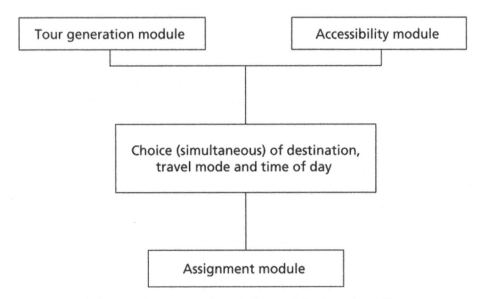

Figure 16.1   Coherence between various choice modules from the LMS

Figure 16.1 shows the coherence between various choice modules from the LMS. Note that the figure includes the dominant modules, but not all. In addition, the LMS has a time-of-day module, models for secondary destinations and non-home-based trips, a model for border crossing car traffic and a model for destinations (or origins) of air travellers including the mode choice for getting to the airport or the destination within The Netherlands.

For the assignment of the car trips, QBLOK is used (Significance, 2021). The essential difference between QBLOK and other equilibrium assignments (see Section 16.4) is the calculation of the link travel times. During the calculation of the travel time on a link, QBLOK takes into account the inflow from the preceding links. The inflow on the link is constrained when there is congestion on the preceding links. It is also investigated whether blockades occur. These limit the maximum outflow from a link, owing to the distribution of congestion over the network. A blockade occurs when traffic on a link is halted by a bottleneck elsewhere, but will not pass that particular bottleneck itself.

- Step 4: Types of travellers in the forecasting year

  After the choice models have all been run the model can compute the situation in a future year. The model now determines the size and composition of the future traveller population for each location in The Netherlands, thereby using all input on demographic and socio-economic data as well as spatial developments. The model thus computes the types of travellers in 2030, for example.

- Step 5: Changed circumstances

  In this step, the planned policy options that may affect the choice behaviour are taken into account. An example of such a policy option is increasing the frequency of railway connections between Amsterdam and Rotterdam. This may mean that more people may opt for public transport. A second example is making parking in Rotterdam more expensive, in which case people would use the tram more often and leave their car at home. A further example is widening a stretch of the A4 motorway (connecting Amsterdam and Rotterdam via The Hague), in which case the trip to work would take less time (at least in the short run), so car owners would rather travel by car on this route.

- Step 6: Forecast: new travelling behaviour

  The model computes both the short and the long-term changes in the choice behaviour. A heavier load of traffic on a stretch of the road means, in the short run, that people opt for a different route, whereas in the long run, they will opt for a different time of departure, while in the even longer run they will opt for a different travel mode and ultimately maybe even for a different destination. The model forecasts the number of travellers for each transport mode as well as the number of kilometres they travel. It also computes the transport flows within and between zones. Finally, the model allocates these trips to the trunk-road network and public transport.

  In order to be able to run the LMS, input is required. As could be deduced from the outline presented above, this input consists of:

  1. road networks, including, for example, toll charges;
  2. public transport networks;
  3. parking costs;
  4. socio-economic and employment data for each zone, both in the base year and in the forecast year;
  5. driving licence and car ownership data;
  6. a description of passenger mobility and freight transport in the base year including OD matrices for the modes car driver, train, bus and tram/metro.

  The LMS distinguishes various transport modes: car driver, car passenger, train, bus, tram/metro, bicycle, walk, and finally bus/tram/metro as access transport for the train.

There are 11 travel purposes distinguished in the LMS, covering commuting, business, school and private travel. Some travel purposes are non-home-based. There are nine times of day distinguished, covering peak, off-peak, evening and night. The number of day periods is this large because the peaks widen more and more. To be ahead of traffic jams motorists leave earlier or later. For the benefit of a correct prediction of the travel time losses due to traffic jams, it is essential to predict the distribution across times of day as precisely as possible.

The output of the LMS consists of:

1. Forecasts about passenger mobility in The Netherlands in the forecast year. For the transport modes and travel purposes listed, as well as for the time of day, the LMS distinguishes: morning peak, evening peak and the remainder of the day.
2. Forecasts of the load on the trunk-road network in the forecast year. In the assignment, the LMS distinguishes commute, business, other and freight, and as vehicle types car, short delivery van, long delivery van, lorries with medium length and long lorries. Synthetic results concerning tours, kilometres travelled, travel times, etc. are available for combinations of mode and travel purpose. A simple example is presented in Figure 16.2 where traffic intensity is represented in vehicles per day for 2021.

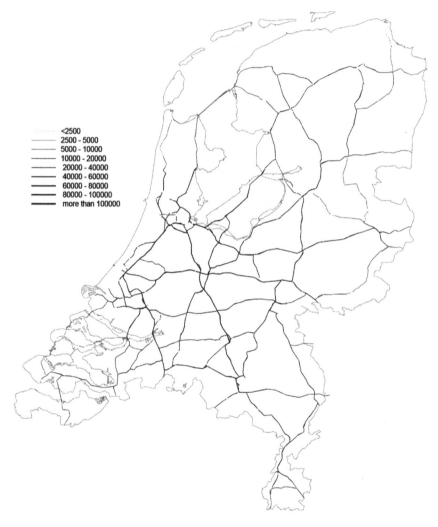

Figure 16.2   Example of an intensity forecast in vehicles per day for 2021, in The Netherlands

In what regards to the quality of the model, ten years after the completion of the LMS, in 1996, this was tested by way of an audit (Bates et al., 1996), followed by another audit in 2012 (Tavasszy et al., 2012). Bates et al. (1996) concluded that the LMS had been prepared using the latest academic insights. Tavasszy et al. (2012) concluded that the model is fit-for-purpose, although they spotted some weaknesses with respect to public transport modelling and some limitations concerning the ability to answer complex policy questions. On various occasions, further quality checks were conducted by comparing the forecasts to the actual developments (de Jong et al., 2008; Gunn and van der Hoorn, 1998). In this way, the 1986 forecasts for 1996 were compared with the 1996 reality. Except for the fact that the model underestimated the growth of the recreational traffic, the quality of the forecasts proved to be reasonable. Backcasting has been performed successfully on the scope of the TIGRIS-XL model development which uses the LMS as a backbone.[1]

Since then, the development of household incomes has been incorporated into the model. In 2010 a comparison was made for the total mobility growth which was well predicted. Car driver kilometres were overestimated; those of car passengers and walking/cycling were underestimated. A large part of the less good forecasts was caused by unexpected developments in society outside of the realm of transportation. In particular, both the population and the workforce (particularly women) grew more than expected. Incomes per household increased less than expected. The anticipated pricing measures (road pricing, kilometre charge) did not materialize. Public transport increased strongly through the introduction of a free public transport pass for students. The biggest matter of concern was the underestimation of the growth of road congestion. Therefore the periods of the day have been refined in the later LMS. The assignment method QBLOK has been improved as well. Transport models are in constant evolution taking advantage of the progress in scientific research as well as practice with these tools *see* also Chapter 14 for uncertainties about future developments.

16.7.2   ILUTE: An Agent-Based LUTI Model

A state-of-the-art example of an ABM that is also a LUTI model (see Section 16.2) is the ILUTE model (Salvini and Miller, 2005). The ILUTE model is an agent-based LUTI model of the whole region of Toronto-Hamilton in Canada where the system state is evolved from an initial base case to some future end state in discrete time steps. The system state is defined in terms of the individual persons, households, housing units, firms, etc. (so-called agents) that collectively define the urban region state. The project led by Eric Miller of Toronto University has been developing for the past three decades with many contributions from different researchers on several of its modules.

The model has the following main modules (Figure 16.3):

1. a demographics module whose objective is to model how the population and households evolve over time including births, deaths and migration as well as marriages and divorces, among other life events (Chingcuanco and Miller, 2018);
2. a housing market component that explains endogenously the supply of housing by type and location with their corresponding prices (Farooq and Miller, 2012);

3. household automobile ownership which is dynamically updated using models of household vehicle transactions (Mohammadian and Miller, 2003);
4. an activity generator for the agents called Travel Activity Scheduler for Household Agents (TASHA) that runs the activities of the synthetic population in the regions (Roorda et al., 2008);
5. a method to assign the trips resulting from the agents' movements to modes of transport (public transport and car) as well as to the paths in the networks. This process can be executed using traditional aggregated traffic assignment methods as explained above or even be fed into an agent-based dynamic traffic simulation model like MATSim (see Section 16.2).

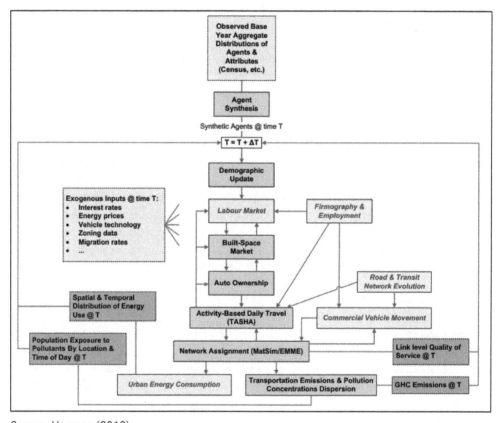

Source: Harmon (2013).

Figure 16.3   The ILUTE model structure

Preliminary models have been tested for adding a labour market into the model (Harmon and Miller, 2020) and there is also the intention to implement some form of firms' characteristics recognizing the importance of the location of companies in explaining the dynamics of the population in terms of mobility, but also in terms of choosing places to live. At the time of writing this chapter (Autumn 2022) this has not yet been accomplished (Chingcuanco and Miller, 2018).

Several of these modules use the principle of random utility maximization for simulating choices coupled with specific procedures to enhance the realism of those choices. For example, regarding house choice, it is well known that a decision-maker does not consider at the same time all the available houses on the market. Often a home seeker will first consider specific areas on which s/he is willing to move as well as house characteristics that are compatible with his/her lifestyle before checking specific houses. Therefore the choice set is much more limited than the whole number of houses on the market.

Because of its disaggregated dynamic and spatial nature, ILUTE allows following each agent across time as it evolves regarding his/her workplace, household composition, modes of transport, chosen paths, etc. This provides a unique opportunity to study how policies may affect different populations in different ways. For example, ILUTE has been used to model the population exposure to pollution in the region of Toronto by coupling the traffic network with a model for pollutant emissions and dispersion. Since the agents can be traced it's possible to know the total amount of pollution they have been exposed to in all their daily activities (Hatzopoulou et al., 2007).

16.7.3 DYNAMO

DYNAMO (Meurs and Haaijer, 2006) is a model to forecast the size, composition and use of the Dutch passenger car fleet for the period 2003–40, together with the resulting emissions. It is a dynamic model, which means that the effects in one year affect results in the next. The heart of the model is an equilibrium module where the prices for second-hand cars emerge in such a way that demand and supply are in equilibrium each year, both for the fleet as a whole and for individual household types. Size, use and composition of the car fleet are functions of the household and car characteristics (like the fixed and variable car expenses, among other things).

The model needs the following input

1. the number of cars per household;
2. the type of fuel;
3. the weight category;
4. car age;
5. fuel consumption;
6. type of owner (private, lease or company cars);
7. car use (the number of kilometres driven);
8. types of households (relative to the types of cars), which are defined by four characteristics: the size of the household, number of working people, age of the oldest individual in the household and real disposable household income;
9. income effects on car use and car choice for each group of households;
10. effects of the fleet composition and corresponding usage on government income (raised through taxes).

Figure 16.4 represents the DYNAMO model's structure.

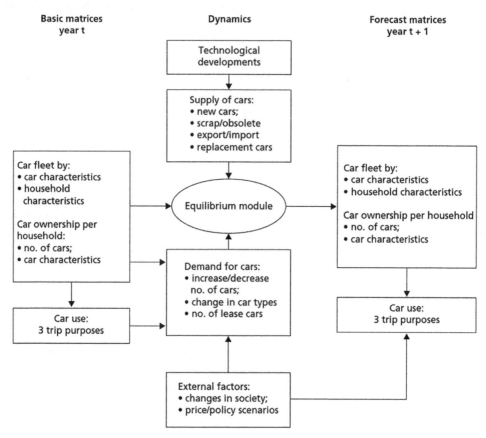

Figure 16.4   Structure of the DYNAMO model

16.8   WHAT CAN AND WHAT CAN'T A TRANSPORT MODEL BE USED FOR?

The main reason for using transport models is that they provide an insight into the magnitude of effects of developments or policy measures on transportation and on indicators that convey something about the quality characteristics or the effects of transportation. Examples of quality characteristics and effects are pollutant emissions, the level of congestion or long-term suburbanization. This may involve the effects of demographic, economic, spatial or infrastructural developments *see* also Figure 2.1 in Chapter 2 about how travel behaviour leads to various societal impacts (on environment, safety, accessibility, health and well-being).

Whether or not it is advisable to answer a research question or solve a policy issue using a model cannot be answered in a general way. In some situations, it may be sufficient to use the results of earlier empirical research or simulations carried out previously. In other cases, new model simulations may be required. Much depends on the amount of time available for answering the question, and on whether any (and if so how much) money is available for new studies and what the outcomes will be used for. The greater the potential effect of system changes, the higher the expenditures (in time and money) that will be made available, and the sooner model simulations will come into the picture. In general, it is important to weigh possible extra costs against the enhanced quality of the answer to be produced in a study. For some questions, a rough estimation of the magnitude of effects may suffice, whereas for other questions a higher quality, more precise output is required.

Furthermore, it is important to set up a structure of a model corresponding to the real world. The structure of a model should be compared to a schematic conceptual representation of that particular part of reality that is relevant for answering the questions. An example elucidates this. Suppose policy-makers want to know the effect of the acquisition of more fuel-efficient types of cars on pollutant emissions. The effect of more fuel-efficient cars is, on the one hand, a decrease per kilometre in the average fuel use and some emissions and, on the other hand, an increase in the number of kilometres, as the fuel costs of more fuel-efficient cars are, on average, lower. A model that first models car ownership and car use ignoring fuel efficiency in the costs of travelling will overestimate the effect of a more fuel-efficient car fleet on the reduction in fuel use and emissions (see also Chapters 2 and 6 for such relationships). In another example, suppose that policy-makers want to know the effect of ABS on traffic safety. Presumably, ABS will lead to different driving behaviour. A model that does not take this into account overestimates the positive effect of ABS on traffic safety. Put differently, researchers who aim to support policy-making first need to get an idea of what will change in practice and how these changes will affect human behaviour, and next need to establish whether these changes can adequately be modelled by the model they would like to use. This is an important advantage of the use of models, or rather, of considering the use of models: it stimulates thinking about how to conceptualize the complexity of the system that needs to be modelled. Just that activity alone is a long way to understanding potential problems and avoiding undesired impacts on society.

Besides, it should be realized that most models are better able to study the effect of relatively small changes than to study the effect of major changes. The effect of an increase in fuel prices of half a euro can be estimated reasonably well by using the current models, whereas that would not hold for an increase by five euros. Greater changes are outside the boundaries of the usual behaviour of the agents in the transport system which may lead to bigger adaptations not yet seen in the system itself before. A good example would be the oil crisis of 1973 during which the Western world had to resort to ways of organizing transportation that were not being used systematically before, like car sharing (Correia and Viegas, 2011).

An important advantage of using models is that they enable us to make the research or policy questions more explicit. The researcher who poses the question needs to make a general question concrete. A question like 'What happens if fuel prices increase?' is very vague. A model forces the researcher to make the question explicit, otherwise simulations are impossible. Therefore the researcher needs to answer questions like: Which kinds of fuel are becoming more expensive? And to what extent? When will the price increase become effective? For which year, or for which years? Which effects does one want to measure? Only the effect on car use? Or also the effect on car ownership, the use of other means of transport, mobility behaviour, emissions of pollutant emissions, or noise pollution? Of course, a research question always has to be concretized, but the use of model simulations can be very helpful in doing so.

A further advantage of using models is that, usually, a model can be used quickly to compute the effects on variants for socio-economic developments and policy variants. Because expressly only a few variables are changed and the other factors are kept constant, comparability of those variants is warranted, and the right conclusions can be drawn as to the effects of the supposed changes.

Another advantage is that the comparability of the results from individual studies can be enhanced by using models. Various studies on the same issue often (seemingly) arrive at different results. For example, many studies have been carried out on the effects of increases in fuel prices. The effects are rather diverse: when expressed in the fuel price elasticity of car use, the range goes from -0.1 to -1.0. Models that can be used to compute the effects of increasing fuel prices teach us that the effects will be larger for people with lower incomes when compared to people with higher incomes. A study carried out in Portugal in 1980 would, therefore, in principle, show a higher price sensitivity than would a study carried out in the US in 2000. Furthermore, models show that the effect of an increase in (solely) the price of petrol will be less if other, cheaper kinds of fuel are available. So the effect of an increase in the price of petrol will be larger if no LPG is available and if the price difference, when compared to diesel oil, is limited. If we look at the effect of fuel price increases on the demand for fuel, model simulations teach us that, in the short run, the only effect is a decrease in car usage. In the long run, however, a further effect will be that people acquire more fuel-efficient cars if fuel prices increase. In some cases, this phenomenon also explains part of the seeming differences in the study results. In the even longer run, a further effect may be that people will select a different place to work or to live, which will increase the effect on car use (a LUTI model is required for this). On the other hand, in most countries, incomes are gradually increasing, which partly counterbalances the effects of price increases. Therefore model simulations can mean that researchers get a better insight into the causes of differences between empirical studies.

A drawback of model use is that their usage can be overestimated. A model is nothing more than a tool, and one should refrain from attaching too much absolute value to its results. Especially if the result of simulations is that certain government objectives are, or are not, achieved by a small margin only, these simulations have a great impact on the policy-makers' way of thinking. It is hardly relevant whether a certain package of policy measures, according to the model and in a certain context, will only just, or will only just not, lead to achieving a goal in 2040. For example, consider the objective of reducing NO_x emissions. The message then is first and foremost that, in that context, the package will lead to NO_x emissions in the magnitude of the set aim. And, in the case of air pollution, some people often assume the results to have a great degree of certainty, even though these results are relatively uncertain.

Researchers may sometimes attach too much weight to a model's results. They often hide behind the model and then make statements like 'Well, that is what the model has come up with.' Once again, a model is no more than a tool. The researcher answers a research question and in doing so he/she is responsible for whether or not to use a model and, if so, in which way, and how to use and interpret the results.

16.9 CONCLUSIONS

The major conclusions to be drawn in this chapter are the following.

1. A model is a simplified representation of a part of a real system.
2. Transportation models are first and foremost a means to gain insights into the effects of various developments (like policy developments) on transportation.
3. There are many kinds of models. They can be classified, among other things, by the transport mode they focus on (e.g. passenger cars, public transport), the period of time they focus on, the technical characteristics (e.g. dynamic versus static models), or the question as to whether or not they contain spatially varying data.
4. Aggregated models such as the 4-step method have been used extensively for the past decades to support transport policy decisions in urban areas. With the need to study more complex measures and their interaction effects in a dynamic context disaggregated models started to be used supported by the advances in computational speed.
5. Whether or not it is advisable to answer a certain research or policy question by using a model cannot easily be established. It requires adequately weighing the available alternatives as well as the pros and cons of model simulations and the relevant alternatives.

ACKNOWLEDGEMENT

We thank Dr Frank Hofman, Rijkswaterstaat (Duch road authority) for his input on the text on the National Model System. We would also like to thank Prof. Eric Miller for his support in the section about the ILUTE model.

NOTE

1. Historische forecast TIGRIS-XL (https://significance.nl).

REFERENCES

Anas, A. (1983), 'Discrete choice theory, information theory and the multinomial logit and gravity models', *Transportation Research Part B: Methodological*, 17, 13–23. https://doi.org/10.1016/0191–2615(83)90023–1

Axhausen, K.W. (2016), *The Multi-Agent Transport Simulation MATSim*, Switzerland: Ubiquity Press. https://doi.org/10.5334/baw

Bates, J., M. Dasgupta, N. Daha, G.R.M. Jansen and M.J.M. van der Vlist (1996), *Audit of the Dutch National Model: Final Report*, Report INRO-VVG 1996–29, Delft: TNO INRO.

Ben-Akiva, M. and S. Lerman (1985), *Discrete Choice Analysis: Theory and Application to Travel Demand*, MIT Press series in transportation studies, 9, Cambridge, MA: MIT Press.

Brownstone, D., D.S. Bunch and K. Train (2000), 'Joint mixed logit models of stated and revealed preferences for alternative-fuel vehicles', *Transportation Research Part B: Methodological*, 34, 315–38. https://doi.org/10.1016/S0191–2615(99)00031–4

Cambridge Systematics, Inc. (2010), *Travel Model Validation and Reasonability Checking Manual Second Edition*. Federal Highway Administration.

CBS (2021), *Dutch National Travel Survey*. CBS. www.cbs.nl/en-gb/onze-diensten/methods/surveys/korte-onderzoeksbeschrijvingen/dutch-national-travel-survey (accessed 28 December 2021).

Chambliss F. and R. Schutt (2019), 'Causation and experimental design', in Daniel F. Chambliss, Russel K. Schutt (Eds.), *Making Sense of the Social World: Methods of Investigation*, London: SAGE, 130–61.

Chingcuanco, F. and E.J. Miller (2018), 'The ILUTE Demographic Microsimulation Model for the Greater Toronto-Hamilton Area: Current Operational Status and Historical Validation', *GeoComputational Analysis and Modelling of Regional Systems*, Cham: Springer, 167–87. https://link.springer.com/chapter/10.1007/978-3-319-59511-5_10

Chorus, C. (2012), 'Random Regret Minimization: An Overview of Model Properties and Empirical Evidence', *Transport Reviews*, 32(1), 75–92. https://doi.org/10.1080/01441647.2011.609947

Correia, G. and J.M. Viegas (2011), 'Carpooling and carpool clubs: Clarifying concepts and assessing value enhancement possibilities through a Stated Preference web survey in Lisbon, Portugal', *Transportation Research Part A: Policy and Practice*, 45(2), 81–90. https://doi.org/10.1016/j.tra.2010.11.001

Cullinane, S. and K. Cullinane (2003), 'Car dependence in a public transport dominated city: evidence from Hong Kong', *Transportation Research Part D: Transport and Environment*, 8(2), 129–38. https://doi.org/10.1016/S1361-9209(02)00037-8

de Jong, G., M. Pieters, A. Daly, I. Graafland-Essers, E. Kroes and C. Koopmans (2005), *Using the Logsum as an Evaluation Measure*. Leiden: RAND.

de Jong, G., J.G. Tuinenga and M. Kouwenhoven (2008), 'Prognoses van het Landelijk Model Systeem: komen ze uit?', *Colloquium Vervoersplanologisch Speurwerk*, 1–14.

Demissie, M.G., G.H. de A. Correia and C. Bento (2013), 'Exploring cellular network handover information for urban mobility analysis', *Journal of Transport Geography*, 31, 164–70. https://doi.org/10.1016/j.jtrangeo.2013.06.016

Demissie, M.G., G.H. de A. Correia and C. Bento (2015), 'Analysis of the pattern and intensity of urban activities through aggregate cellphone usage', *Transportmetrica A: Transport Science*, 11(6), 502–24. https://doi.org/10.1080/23249935.2015.1019591

Dijkstra, E.W. (1959), 'A note on two problems in connexion with graphs', *Numerische Mathematik*, 1, 269–71. https://doi.org/10.1007/BF01386390

Fagnant, D.J., K.M. Kockelman and P. Bansal (2016), 'Operations of a shared autonomous vehicle fleet for the Austin, Texas Market', *Transportation Research Record: Journal of the Transportation Research Board*, (1) 98–106. https://doi.org/10.3141/2536-12

Farooq, B. and E.J. Miller (2012), 'Towards integrated land use and transportation: A dynamic disequilibrium based microsimulation framework for built space markets', *Transportation Research Part A: Policy and Practice*, 46(7), 1030–53. https://doi.org/10.1016/j.tra.2012.04.005

Geurs, K. and J. Ritsema van Eck (2004), 'Editorial: Special issue: Land Use Transport Interaction Modelling', *European Journal of Transport and Infrastructure Research*, 4. https://doi.org/10.18757/ejtir.2004.4.3.4267

Geurs, K.T. and B. van Wee (2004), 'Accessibility evaluation of land-use and transport strategies: Review and research directions', *Journal of Transport Geography*, 12, 127–40. https://doi.org/10.1016/j.jtrangeo.2003.10.005

Gunn, H. and A. van der Hoorn (1998), 'The predictive power of operational demand models', *Proceedings of the Seminar Transportation Planning Methods. European Transport Conference*, Loughborough University, 249–64.

Harmon, A. (2013), *A Microsimulated Industrial and Occupation-Based Labour Market Model for Use in the Integrated Land Use, Transportation, Environment (ILUTE) Modelling System*, Master's Thesis, University of Toronto.

Harmon, A. and E.J. Miller (2020), 'Microsimulating labour market job-worker matching', *Journal of Ambient Intelligence and Humanized Computing*, 11, 993–1006. https://doi.org/10.1007/s12652-019-01206-4

Hatzopoulou, M., E.J. Miller and B. Santos (2007), 'Integrating Vehicle Emission Modeling with Activity-Based Travel Demand Modeling', *Transportation Research Record: Journal of the Transportation Research Board*, 2011, (1) 29–39. https://doi.org/10.3141/2011-04

Hensher, D.A., J.M. Rose and W.H. Green (2005), *Applied Choice Analysis - A Primer*, Cambridge: Cambridge University Press.

Hooper, K.G. and Institute of Transportation Engineers (2017), *Trip Generation Handbook*, Washington, DC: Institute of Transportation Engineers.

Iacono, M., D. Levinson and A. El-Geneidy (2008), 'Models of Transportation and Land Use Change: A Guide to the Territory', *Journal of Planning Literature*, 22, 323–40. https://doi.org/10.1177/0885412207314010

Ibraeva, A., B. van Wee, G.H. de A. Correia and A. Pais Antunes (2021), 'Longitudinal macro-analysis of car-use changes resulting from a TOD-type project: The case of Metro do Porto (Portugal)', *Journal of Transport Geography*, 92, 103036. https://doi.org/10.1016/j.jtrangeo.2021.103036

Legêne, M.F., W.L. Auping, G.H. de A. Correia and B. van Arem (2020), 'Spatial impact of automated driving in urban areas', *Journal of Simulation*, 14, 295–303. https://doi.org/10.1080/17477778.2020.1806747

Lopes, A.S., C.F.G. Loureiro and B. van Wee (2019), 'LUTI operational models review based on the proposition of an a priori ALUTI conceptual model', *Transport Reviews*, 39, 204–25. https://doi.org/10.1080/01441647.2018.1442890

Lowry, I.S. (1964), *A Model of Metropolis*, RM-4035-RC. Abingdon: Routledge.

Lunke, E.B., N. Fearnley and J. Aarhaug (2021), 'Public transport competitiveness vs. the car: Impact of relative journey time and service attributes', *Research in Transportation Economics*, 90, 101098. https://doi.org/10.1016/j.retrec.2021.101098

Meurs, H. and R. Haaijer (2006), 'DYNAMO: a new dynamic model for the Dutch passenger car market', *Colloquium Vervoersplanologisch Speurwerk,* Amsterdam.

Mohammadian, A. and E.J. Miller (2003), 'Dynamic Modeling of Household Automobile Transactions', *Transportation Research Record: Journal of the Transportation Research Board*, 1831, 98–105. https://doi.org/10.3141/1831-11

Ortúzar, J. de D. and L.G. Willumsen (2011), *Modelling Transport*, Chichester: Wiley. https://doi.org/10.1002/9781119993308

Rijkswaterstaat (2017), *Traffic and Transport: National Model System (LMS)*. Ministerie van Infrastructuur en Waterstaat. https://puc.overheid.nl/rijkswaterstaat/doc/PUC_156019_31/ (accessed 28 December 2021).

Roorda, M.J., E.J. Miller and K.M.N. Habib (2008), 'Validation of TASHA: A 24-h activity scheduling microsimulation model', *Transportation Research Part A: Policy and Practice*, 42, 360–75. https://doi.org/10.1016/j.tra.2007.10.004

Salvini, P. and E.J. Miller (2005), 'ILUTE: An Operational Prototype of a Comprehensive Microsimulation Model of Urban Systems', *Networks and Spatial Economics*, 5, 217–34. https://doi.org/10.1007/s11067-005-2630-5

Sheffi, Y. (1986), 'Urban transportation networks: Equilibrium analysis with mathematical programming methods', *Transportation Research Part A: General*, 20, 76–77. https://doi.org/10.1016/0191-2607(86)90023-3

Significance (2021), *Documentatie van GM4 Deel D7–6*, Programma QBLOK4 (versie 4.21).

Smith, B., D. Olaru, J. Jabeen and S. Greaves (2017), 'Electric vehicles adoption: Environmental enthusiast bias in discrete choice models', *Transportation Research Part D: Transport and Environment*, 51, 290–303. https://doi.org/10.1016/j.trd.2017.01.008

Steg, L. (2003), 'Can public transport compete with the private car?', *IATSS Research*, 27, 27–35. https://doi.org/10.1016/S0386-1112(14)60141-2

Tavasszy, L.A., M. Snelder, M. Duijnisveld, R. Haaijer, H. Meurs, R. van Nes, E. Verroen, C. Schie, J. Bates and B. Jansen (2012), *Audit LMS en NRM syntheserapport*. Delft: TNO. https://research.tudelft.nl/en/publications/audit-lms-en-nrm-syntheserapport

Tavasszy, L.A. and G. de Jong (2014), *Modelling Freight Transport*, London and Waltham: Elsevier.

Thoen, S., L. Tavasszy, M. de Bok, G.H. de A. Correia and R. van Duin (2020), 'Descriptive modeling of freight tour formation: A shipment-based approach', *Transportation Research Part E: Logistics and Transportation Review*, 140, 101989. https://doi.org/10.1016/j.tre.2020.101989

Train, K.E. (2003), *Discrete Choice Methods with Simulation, Discrete Choice Methods with Simulation*, Cambridge: Cambridge University Press. https://doi.org/10.1017/CBO9780511753930

Wang, C., M.A. Quddus and S.G. Ison (2013), 'The effect of traffic and road characteristics on road safety: A review and future research direction', *Safety Science*, 57, 264–75. https://doi.org/10.1016/j.ssci.2013.02.012

Wang, S., G.H. de A. Correia, and H.X. Lin (2019), 'Exploring the Performance of Different On-Demand Transit Services Provided by a Fleet of Shared Automated Vehicles: An Agent-Based Model', *Journal of Advanced Transportation*, 2019, 1–16. https://doi.org/10.1155/2019/7878042

Wang, Y., G.H. de A. Correia, E. de Romph and B.F. Santos (2018), 'Road Network Design in a Developing Country Using Mobile Phone Data: An Application to Senegal', *IEEE Intelligent Transportation Systems Magazine*, 31, 1–1. https://doi.org/10.1109/MITS.2018.2879168

Yap, M.D.M.D., G.H. de A. Correia and B. van Arem (2016), 'Preferences of travellers for using automated vehicles as last mile public transport of multimodal train trips', *Transportation Research Part A: Policy and Practice*, 94, 1–16. https://doi.org/10.1016/j.tra.2016.09.003

Zondag, B., M. de Bok, K.T. Geurs and E. Molenwijk (2015), 'Accessibility modeling and evaluation: The TIGRIS XL land-use and transport interaction model for the Netherlands', *Computers, Environment and Urban Systems*, 49, 115–25. https://doi.org/10.1016/J.COMPENVURBSYS.2014.06.001

INDEX